Substance Use among Children and Adolescents

Its Nature, Extent, and Effects from Conception to Adulthood

Ann Marie Pagliaro and Louis A. Pagliaro
University of Alberta

JOHN WILEY & SONS, INC.

New York • Chichester • Brisbane • Toronto • Singapore

To the countless infants, children, and adolescents who suffer from the physiological, psychological, and sociological harm associated with their exposure to and use of the various substances of abuse and to those who work in many different capacities to reduce this suffering.

Library of Congress Cataloging-in-Publication Data:

Pagliaro, Ann Marie
    Substance use among children and adolescents / by Ann Marie Pagliaro and Louis A. Pagliaro.
        p. cm.
    Includes bibliographical references and indexes.
    ISBN 0-471-58042-2 (alk. paper)
    1. Children—Drug use—United States. 2. Teenagers—Drug use—United States. 3. Drug abuse—Treatment—United States. 4. Drug abuse—United States—Prevention. I. Pagliaro, Louis A. II. Title.
HV5824.C45P34 1996
362.29'12'083—dc20   95-25496
                                                                           CIP

Printed in the United States of America

10 9 8 7 6 5 4 3 2 1

Not to deride, not to grieve, not to detest, but to understand.

Spinoza, *Tractatus Politicus*

Acknowledgments

We wish to acknowledge and thank the following individuals for their assistance with the completion of this text: Lynn Szoo for typing all of the many manuscript drafts and revisions; Dianne Henderson for seemingly endless hours of library and computer work in retrieving needed references; and John Driedger for preparing all of the figures, which he revised tirelessly as we continued to develop our ideas.

In addition, we would like to express sincere appreciation and respect for our many patients and research subjects over the years, some of whose experiences have been shared in this text. We have learned much, and continue to learn, from our interactions with them and have come to a keen appreciation of the unique ability of the human heart and soul to overcome seemingly overwhelming adversity if provided with genuine respect, kindness, and hope.

Preface

An increasing number of clinical psychologists, counselors, psychiatrists, pediatricians, pediatric nurse practitioners, social workers, teachers, and other health and social care workers are concerned about substance use among children and adolescents and its impact on their mental health and physical functioning. This book is written for these professionals and for students, interns, and residents who are assimilating knowledge in the area of child and adolescent mental health and for health and social policymakers.

The purpose of this book is to present an integrated compilation and synthesis of the theoretical, empirical, and clinical knowledge concerning substance exposure and use among infants, children, and adolescents, with attention to their impact on mental and physical health. Accordingly, each chapter deals with a major issue or area of importance in relation to substance exposure and use among infants, children, and adolescents. The current relevant literature emphasizing contemporary theoretical and research directions and their application to clinical practice are also presented. Although reference citations within the text predominantly focus upon recent original human studies, citations for general review articles and significant texts have been included to complement these studies and to encourage further study by interested readers.

Chapter 1, "Introduction and Overview," introduces the reader to the current nature and extent of substance exposure and use among infants, children, and adolescents in North America. Chapter 2, "Explaining Substance Use among Children and Adolescents," explores, from a pluralistic perspective, the major current theories of substance use. Emphasis is placed on theoretical developments that have focused on or addressed substance use among children and adolescents and the relationship of these theories to research and practice. Chapter 3, "Prenatal Exposure to Substances of Abuse," provides detailed information regarding maternal ingestion of substances of abuse during pregnancy and the resultant effects on the developing fetus and neonate. Chapter 4, "Exposure to and Use of Substances of Abuse during

Infancy and Childhood," details the various ways in which young children are exposed, both deliberately and inadvertently, to substances of abuse. Chapter 5, "Adolescent Substance Use," identifies and discusses the major antecedents of substance use in this age group. Chapter 6, "Dual Diagnosis among Adolescents," examines the concurrence of other mental disorders in adolescents with substance use disorders. The role of these concurrent disorders as either antecedents or consequences of substance use is discussed. Chapter 7, "Effects of Substance Use on Learning and Memory among Children and Adolescents," discusses the behavioral and cognitive effects of substance use in relation to effects on learning and memory. Chapter 8, "Substance-Related Accidents and Violence: Children and Adolescents as Victims," discusses substance-related morbidity (e.g., physical and sexual abuse) and mortality (e.g., homicide and suicide), which have become widespread among North American children and adolescents. Chapter 9, "Substance-Related Crime: Children and Adolescents as Perpetrators," discusses the relationship between substance use and "youth crime," including the nature and types of crimes committed and the relationship to gang involvement. Chapter 10, "Preventing and Treating Substance Use among Children and Adolescents," describes and explains, from a pluralistic perspective, the various methods and techniques used to prevent or treat problematic patterns of substance use among children and adolescents. The efficacy, prognosis, recidivism, and other associated strengths and weaknesses of these various approaches are described and discussed.

Substance use, as documented in the chapters of this book, has the propensity to murder the soul and kill the heart. It is hoped that, by applying the information presented in this book to the assessment and treatment of infants, children, and adolescents, child and family care professionals from a variety of concerned disciplines will be better able to prevent or minimize the harmful effects associated with exposure to and use of substances of abuse. In this way, we can work together to make a significant contribution to improved mental and physical health during childhood and adolescence, from conception to adulthood.

A. M. P. / L. A. P.
1996

Contents

CHAPTER 1

Introduction and Overview

Substance use (Table 1.1 and Fig. 1.1) can and does affect all North American children and adolescents directly or indirectly, regardless of age, gender, culture, ethnic background, education, race, or socioeconomic status (R. S. Hoffman & Goldfrank, 1990; E. M. Johnson, 1990; L. A. Pagliaro & Pagliaro, 1993; Spiegler & Harford, 1987). Even children and adolescents in rural America, once thought to be protected from the scourge of substance use, find themselves affected in a variety of ways (Kelleher, Rickert, Hardin, Pope, & Farmer, 1992; Sarvela, Pape, Odulana, & Bajracharya, 1990) and demonstrate use and availability patterns similar to those observed in any urban setting (Chaiken, 1995). For example, one major study found that the percentages of rural high school students using alcohol, cannabis, and tobacco in a 30-day period were 54.4, 12.6, and 30.4 percent, respectively. These are rates similar to those cited for urban and suburban high school seniors (Morra, 1992).

Substance use is a phenomenon experienced by children and adolescents worldwide (Garvey, 1991; Ruegg, 1991; Senay, Kozel, & Gonzalez, 1991; R. G. Smart & Murray, 1985; Soueif, Darweesh, & Taha, 1985; Spencer, 1985; Wray & Young, 1992; J. D. Wright & Pearl, 1995; Zarkovic, 1982); it has been prevalent throughout recorded history and is expected to continue in the future (A. M. Pagliaro, 1991; L. A. Pagliaro, 1988a). Substance use appears to be beginning at progressively younger ages (G. W. Bailey, 1992; Famularo, Stone, & Popper, 1985; Norwood, 1985; Senay et al., 1991; Westermeyer, 1992; see Chap. 4). Although some reports seem to indicate that use is decreasing and that children and adolescents tend to "mature out" of their substance use (Miller-Tutzauer, Leonard, & Windle, 1991), these data may be misleading and require careful interpretation. In fact, careful scrutiny reveals that although single episodes of marijuana and cocaine use are reportedly decreasing, the concurrent or concomitant use of more than one substance of abuse is pervasive and appears to be increasing (Clayton, 1986; Senay et al., 1991; L. S. Wright, 1985a). The frequency of more serious patterns of use, such as abuse and compulsive use (Fig. 1.2), and their associated morbidity and mortality also are increasing (Adger, 1991). As noted by Lloyd Johnston, principal investigator for the National Institute on Drug Abuse

TABLE 1.1   Major Substances of Abuse[a]

Central Nervous System Depressants
Opiates (e.g., codeine, heroin, meperidine, methadone, morphine, pentazocine)
Sedative-hypnotics (e.g., alcohol [beer, wine, distilled spirits], barbiturates, benzodiazepines)
Volatile solvents and inhalants (e.g., gasoline, glue)
Central Nervous System Stimulants
Amphetamines (e.g., dextroamphetamine)
Caffeine (e.g., caffeinated soft drinks, coffee, tea)
Cocaine (e.g., cocaine hydrochloride, crack cocaine)
Nicotine (e.g., tobacco cigarettes, tobacco cigars)
Psychedelics (partial list)
Lysergic acid diethylamide (LSD)
Mescaline (peyote)
Phencyclidine (PCP)
Psilocybin (hallucinogenic mushrooms)
Tetrahydrocannabinol (THC; e.g., hashish, hashish oil, marijuana)

[a]Classification scheme from A. M. Pagliaro (1990a, 1991).

(NIDA) 1994 "Monitoring the Future" survey: "Following a 12- to 13-year period of decline in adolescent drug use—a decline which brought use down to considerably lower levels than existed in the seventies—we are seeing the problem start to grow again. The arduously woven fabric of attitudes, beliefs, and peer norms which brought about that decline, is beginning to unravel" ("Survey Finds," 1995). This increase in substance use by children and adolescents is taxing the ability of established social services to meet greatly increasing demands (Crites, Fischer, McNeish-Stengel, & Siegel, 1992; Curtis & McCullough, 1993).

Morbidity related to substance use in North America is significant (Senay et al., 1991). Substance use is involved in most cases of child abuse ("Child Abuse," 1991; Pribor & Dinwiddie, 1992; Rose, Peabody, & Stratigeas, 1991b) and in physical trauma involving children and adolescents (Lindenbaum, Carroll, Daskal, & Kapusnick, 1989; Sloan et al., 1989; U.S. Department of Justice, 1994a; see Chap. 8). It is also a significant factor in urban and rural crime (Abram, 1989; Dembo, Williams, Schmeidler, et al., 1991; DeWitt, O'Neil, & Baldau, 1991; see Chap. 9).

The chronic abuse of alcohol by adolescent girls and increasing rates of teenage pregnancy have increased the potential for fetal alcohol syndrome, the most common preventable cause of mental retardation in North America (Pietrantoni & Knuppel, 1991; Streissguth et al., 1991). Cocaine use also has increased over the past decade, and attention is only now being focused on the learning deficits and other developmental problems observed among toddlers, preschoolers, and young school-aged children possibly related to in utero cocaine exposure (as crack babies; Adler, 1992; see Chap. 3 for addi-

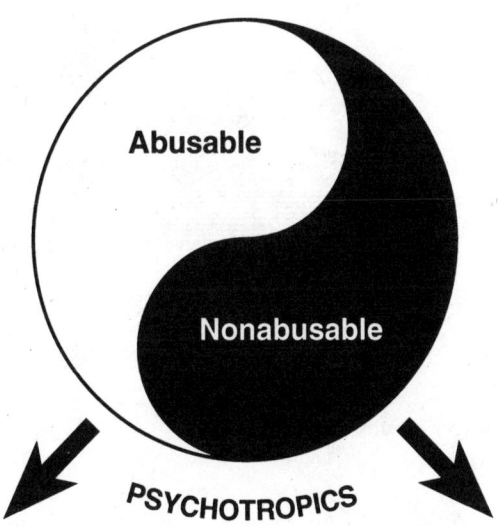

FIGURE 1.1   Abusable and nonabusable psychotropics

Note: The term *psychotropics* refers to all exogenous substances (chemicals, drugs, medications, substances, and xenobiotics) that elicit a direct effect on the central nervous system resulting in changes in cognition, learning, memory, behavior, perception, or affect. The psychotropics can be further conveniently classified as either "abusable" or "nonabusable" (L. A. Pagliaro & Pagliaro, 1993). The nonabusable psychotropics have not been consistently associated with addiction or habituation phenomena and thus are not considered in this book (see L. A. Pagliaro & Pagliaro, 1995, for a discussion of antidepressants). This classification has been found to be both accurate and parsimonious. However, because "abusable psychotropics" may be a new and awkward term for many readers, we consistently use the term "substances of abuse."

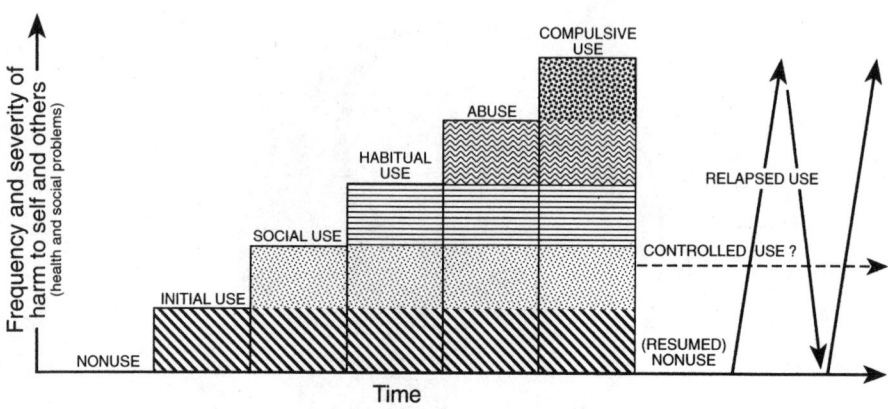

FIGURE 1.2   Patterns of substance use

tional details). Increased substance use by adolescents of both genders is also associated with increased incidence of sexually transmitted diseases (STDs), such as syphilis and AIDS (J. M. Cox, D'Angelo, & Silber, 1992; Hibbs & Gunn, 1991; Nwanyanwu, Chu, Green, Buehler, & Berkelman, 1993).

Mortality associated with child and adolescent substance use is also significant ("Tobacco, Alcohol," 1992). For example, the majority of fatal motor vehicle crashes involving adolescents are the result of alcohol and cannabis intoxication ("Alcohol-Related," 1991; "Consensus Report," 1985; R. E. Ward, Flynn, Miller, & Blaisdell, 1982). Of equally serious concern is the relationship between substance use and suicide, which is now the second leading cause of death reported for adolescents 15–19 years of age in the United States (Felts, Chenier, & Barnes, 1991; Fowler, Rich, & Young, 1986; Hoberman & Garfinkel, 1988; see Chap. 5). The number of murders related to substance use has also grown dramatically, particularly among inner city youth, and accounts for a significant percentage of the annual deaths reported for the 15–19 age group (E. M. Johnson, 1990; see Chap. 8).

MEGA INTERACTIVE MODEL OF SUBSTANCE EXPOSURE AND USE AMONG INFANTS, CHILDREN, AND ADOLESCENTS

The Mega Interactive Model of Substance Exposure and Use among Infants, Children, and Adolescents (MIMSEUICA), extended from a model originally proposed by L. A. Pagliaro and Pagliaro (1993), has been developed to help clinical psychologists, counselors, and other health and social care professionals concerned about substance exposure and use during infancy, childhood, and adolescence understand and deal with this complex phenomenon

(Fig. 1.3). MIMSEUICA can be used for assessing, developing, delivering, and evaluating individualized prevention and treatment programs aimed at infants, children, and adolescents who present with actual or potential problems related to substance exposure and use.

The model consists of four interacting variable dimensions: 1. infant/child/ adolescent dimension, 2. societal dimension, 3. substance dimension, and 4. time dimension. The substance use milieu is represented in Figure 1.3 as comprising a number of interacting subsets of the four identified variable

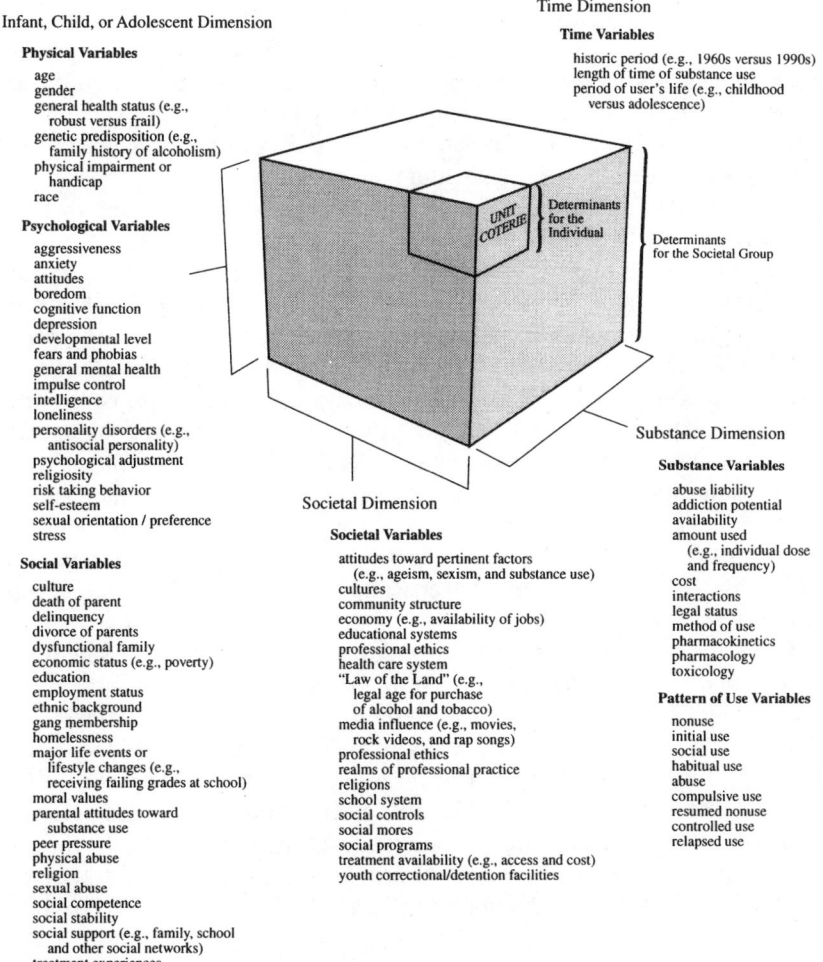

Infant, Child, or Adolescent Dimension

Physical Variables

age
gender
general health status (e.g.,
   robust versus frail)
genetic predisposition (e.g.,
   family history of alcoholism)
physical impairment or
   handicap
race

Psychological Variables

aggressiveness
anxiety
attitudes
boredom
cognitive function
depression
developmental level
fears and phobias
general mental health
impulse control
intelligence
loneliness
personality disorders (e.g.,
   antisocial personality)
psychological adjustment
religiosity
risk taking behavior
self-esteem
sexual orientation / preference
stress

Social Variables

culture
death of parent
delinquency
divorce of parents
dysfunctional family
economic status (e.g., poverty)
education
employment status
ethnic background
gang membership
homelessness
major life events or
   lifestyle changes (e.g.,
   receiving failing grades at school)
moral values
parental attitudes toward
   substance use
peer pressure
physical abuse
religion
sexual abuse
social competence
social stability
social support (e.g., family, school
   and other social networks)
treatment experiences

Time Dimension

Time Variables

historic period (e.g., 1960s versus 1990s)
length of time of substance use
period of user's life (e.g., childhood
   versus adolescence)

UNIT COTERIE

Determinants
for the
Individual

Determinants
for the Societal Group

Substance Dimension

Substance Variables

abuse liability
addiction potential
availability
amount used
   (e.g., individual dose
   and frequency)
cost
interactions
legal status
method of use
pharmacokinetics
pharmacology
toxicology

Pattern of Use Variables

nonuse
initial use
social use
habitual use
abuse
compulsive use
resumed nonuse
controlled use
relapsed use

Societal Dimension

Societal Variables

attitudes toward pertinent factors
   (e.g., ageism, sexism, and substance use)
cultures
community structure
economy (e.g., availability of jobs)
educational systems
professional ethics
health care system
"Law of the Land" (e.g.,
   legal age for purchase
   of alcohol and tobacco)
media influence (e.g., movies,
   rock videos, and rap songs)
professional ethics
realms of professional practice
religions
school system
social controls
social mores
social programs
treatment availability (e.g., access and cost)
youth correctional/detention facilities

FIGURE 1.3   Mega Interactive Model of Substance Exposure and Use among Infants, Children, and Adolescents (MIMSEUICA)

dimensions that are referred to collectively as *unit coteries*. Each unit coterie represents the phenomenon of substance exposure or use as displayed by a single infant, child, or adolescent. A collection of unit coteries represents the larger social group or community to which the individual belongs (e.g., preschool day care facility, particular gang, junior high school class, 10th-grade girls, or high school basketball team). Thus, the model is useful for both individual and group assessment and intervention.

MIMSEUICA accounts for the multidimensional etiology of substance exposure and use without the imposition of a singular, restrictive theoretical focus (e.g., illness/disease or psychoanalytic) or classification system (e.g., *Diagnostic and Statistical Manual of Mental Disorders*), which has been found to be inadequate by many clinicians and researchers.[1] This approach is important in providing comprehensive psychological and other services. MIMSEUICA can be used as a generic theoretical framework by mental health professionals from a variety of theoretical orientations when diagnosing problematic patterns of substance exposure or use and planning, implementing, and evaluating the pluralistic and multimodal therapy that is often required and that can be delivered only by using a transdisciplinary approach.

The complexity of MIMSEUICA reflects the nature of substance exposure and use during infancy, childhood, and adolescence, which always has been and always will be a complex phenomenon (see Chap. 2). The multifactorial etiology of substance exposure and use and the myriad possible interacting and confounding variables that mental health professionals must consider to individualize prevention and treatment programs and optimize therapeutic results are incorporated into MIMSEUICA. As illustrated in the following example using MIMSEUICA, mental health professionals should abandon stereotypic and unidimensional thinking in relation to the etiology and treatment of substance exposure and use and develop broad perspectives in regard to the possibilities open for a more diverse and varied approach to dealing with this complex problem.

J.B., a 17-year-old boy, reportedly consumes alcoholic beverages in excess on a regular basis. When encountered in a clinical context, he would generally be simply labeled an "alcoholic" and referred to a generic treatment program for alcoholics. Alternatively, J.B.'s alcohol-consuming behavior could be characterized in the context of the four dimensions using MIMSEUICA. The mental health professional would identify relevant variables to address when developing and implementing an individualized treatment plan. In this example, J.B. had developed an alcohol problem as a preadolescent after the death of his father from alcohol-related cardiopathology. J.B. received be-

---

[1] E.g., Newcomb and Bentler (1989) noted: "We feel that it is critical to draw a distinction between use and abuse of drugs and to do so from a multidimensional perspective that includes aspects of the stimulus (drug), organism (individual), response, and consequences" (p. 242).

reavement counseling and had abstained from alcohol use until 6 months ago when his girlfriend broke up with him. Attention to the previously successful treatment, which involved resolution of grief, development and strengthening of coping abilities, and provision of alternative support systems, may do much to alleviate the current problem (see Chap. 10 for further discussion of various treatment approaches).

MIMSEUICA serves as a heuristic device to help in the identification of the variables associated with exposure to and use of substances of abuse among infants, children, and adolescents. It also encourages a better understanding of the complexity of the phenomenon. MIMSEUICA offers insight into important considerations involving the infant/child/adolescent, societal, substance of abuse, and time dimensions. Although the primary focus of this chapter will be on the substance dimension, a brief overview of the other three dimensions first will be presented so that the substance dimension may be considered in the proper context.

Infant/Child/Adolescent Dimension

Over a decade ago A. Weil (1983) noted: "It's a real problem when you classify drugs as good and bad. . . . Drugs are drugs [i.e., inanimate objects without any inherent goodness or badness]. The only point that good and bad comes in is in the individual use of drugs." Thus, the use of morphine to relieve severe cancer pain in a terminally ill adolescent is considered "good." However, the use of morphine on a dare from a peer that results in overdose and death is considered "bad." The MIMSEUICA perspective encourages a scientific (rational and logical) approach to substance exposure and use that goes beyond the substance of abuse dimension to include the physical, psychological, and social characteristics and their interactions.

The influence of the physical, psychological, and social variables of the infant/child/adolescent dimension is significant (e.g., see Chap. 2). These variables must be fully addressed when assessing infants, children, and adolescents and when planning and implementing prevention and treatment programs. For example, the effective approach and treatment plan for a young "alcoholic" will differ greatly for: 1. a 12-year-old, middle-class, Native American boy who previously performed well academically in school and is living in a stable, supportive family unit, but who has a family history of alcoholism in both maternal and paternal grandfathers and a paternal uncle; 2. a 9-year-old Caucasian girl who is clinically depressed and living in a foster home where she is being sexually abused; 3. a 16-year-old black girl who is a sex-trade worker and is currently pregnant and living on her own in a youth emergency shelter; 4. a 17-year-old Hispanic boy who is a gang member living in the inner city and who is the principal source of financial support for his girlfriend and her baby as well as for his mother, grandmother, and four siblings; 5. a 14-year-old Chinese boy, with above-average intelligence, who recently immigrated to the United States, does not speak English well, and is not happy in his new home country; and 6. a 17-year-old Haitian boy who is an illegal immigrant without any family or social support, works as a male prostitute, and is positive for the human immunodeficiency virus (HIV). Clearly, all children and adolescents are *not* alike. Consideration of the variables associated with the infant/child/adolescent dimension can assist in differentiating the unique aspects of their clinical or educational situations. This differentiation and appropriate intervention encourage individualized assessment and treatment and optimize therapeutic outcomes.

Societal Dimension

The societal dimension is sometimes given less attention than the other dimensions. This dimension reflects the law of the land (legal restrictions), professional ethics, realms of professional practice, attitudes toward substance use, and myriad other variables. The societal dimension has a significant impact on the prevention and treatment programs that are available for and provided to infants, children, and adolescents. For example, the availability of prenatal and postnatal treatment programs for mothers who use crack cocaine in terms of access and cost—Is the program available only to the affluent, who have the necessary finances or insurance?—needs to be considered when planning or recommending intervention at the local, state or provincial, and national levels. Other societal variables, such as the dominant culture of a community, can also have a significant effect on treatment outcomes. Children and adolescents are more likely to seek, enter, and complete treatment if the treatment program is consonant with their cultural and social needs (Peele, 1989). Although the variables in the societal dimension of MIMSEUICA are generally not amenable to immediate change, they significantly affect the availability and comprehensiveness of treatment. Therefore, they must be realistically and appropriately addressed at the local and national levels, as necessary.

Time Dimension

The time dimension also often receives insufficient attention. The time dimension includes variables such as the historical period during which a particular substance of abuse is available for use, the length of time during which it is used in relation to its pattern of use, and the specific period of the user's life. The time dimension plays a significant role in terms of the historical context of substance use in relation to each of the other dimensions. It also affects the consequences associated with the use of a particular substance of abuse (P. M. O'Malley, Bachman, & Johnston, 1988). For example, the consequences of cannabis use in North America 100 years ago were significantly different than they are today because the use of cannabis was legal during the late 1800s. Although cocaine was available in various forms for nasal insufflation and injection and could be found in popular "invigorating" beverages (e.g., Vin Mariani and, later, Coca Cola) during the late 19th and early 20th centuries, the crack form of cocaine, now widely used by adolescents in North America, was not used previously by this age group because of the simple fact that it had not yet been formulated. Similarly, new substances of abuse (e.g., various new "designer" drugs) and new methods for using currently available substances of abuse (e.g., smoking pure heroin) can be expected in the future.

SUBSTANCE DIMENSION

The substance dimension comprises two major types of variables: 1. substance variables and 2. pattern of use variables. This dimension has obvious relevance. The pharmacology, pharmacokinetics, toxicology, abuse liability, addiction potential, and related parameters of a particular substance of abuse are critical factors that continue to receive a great deal of attention in relation to the prevention and treatment of substance use.

Substance Variables

North American infants, children, and adolescents are exposed to and use a variety of substances of abuse, including alcohol, cannabis, cocaine, lysergic acid diethylamide (LSD), nicotine, and volatile solvents and inhalants (Senay et al., 1991). This discussion addresses the common use patterns and the social trends associated with substance exposure and use by this population.

The description of substances of abuse in this chapter, and the statistics presented concerning their use, reflects generally the behavior of children and adolescents in North America. However, there are regional differences with annual fluctuations (DeWitt, 1991). In addition, the use of various substances by certain subpopulations (e.g., incarcerated adolescents, inner city youth, Native American children, and homeless youth) is significantly higher than what is reported in this chapter for the general population (Beauvais, 1992b; Beauvais, Oetting, Wolf, & Edwards, 1989; E. M. Johnson, 1990; Moncher, Holden, & Trimble, 1990; Rhoades, Mason, Eddy, Smith, & Burns, 1988; Sherman, 1992; Swartz, 1991a). For example, a study of street youth in Toronto indicated that more than 90 percent used both alcohol and illicit drugs (R. G. Smart & Adlaf, 1991). Although studies have suggested, sometimes seemingly for political reasons, that substance use by particular groups of youth or within particular geographic regions in North America has decreased (Hauschildt, 1992), reports of serious substance use patterns (i.e., use patterns associated with high frequency and severity of harm to self and others; "Coke Emergencies," 1992) and admissions to alcohol and drug treatment centers ("Adolescents and Substance," 1991) are currently at an all-time high.

Central Nervous System Depressants

Alcohol. The use of alcohol is a common part of adult socializing and is often seen by North American children and adolescents as a sign of maturity or adulthood. For this reason, it appears to be particularly attractive to youth. Perhaps then, it is not surprising that "the average age for first-time experience with alcohol is 11 years old for boys and 11 and a half years old for girls" (Leite & Parrish, 1994). As noted by Harrison and Luxenberg (1995), "Alcohol was the primary substance of abuse among students, regardless of age or level of substance involvement" (p. 137). Adolescents who develop alcohol problems generally begin drinking alcoholic beverages in the form of beer, wine, or distilled spirits during their early or midteen years. By their senior year of high school, more than 75 percent of adolescents report having used alcohol (Fournet, Estes, & Martin, 1990) and over 50 percent report having had at least one alcoholic drink during the previous month (Swan, 1995a). The major factors contributing to this alcohol use are thought to include: 1. a desire to be more "adultlike," 2. peer pressure, 3. risk-taking behavior, 4. desire for sexual activity (alcohol decreases social inhibitions as a direct pharmacopsychological effect), 5. availability, and 6. societal attitudes that encourage its use (e.g., media advertisements; L. A. Pagliaro, 1993a). It should not be surprising then that "alcohol remains the 'drug of choice' among American adolescents" (Huizinga, Loeber, & Thornberry, 1993, p. 93).

Inappropriate alcohol use by children and adolescents is responsible for more physiological, psychological, and sociological harm than all other substance use combined. In addition to the adverse effects noted earlier in this chapter (fetal alcohol syndrome and fatal motor vehicle crashes), inappropriate alcohol use has reportedly been associated with up to 70 percent of criminal assaults, armed robberies, drownings, and murders and up to 50 percent of cases of child abuse, rape, and suicide (Berlin, 1986; Hoberman & Garfinkel, 1988; Milgram, 1993; *Prevention Plus II,* 1989; *Youth and Alcohol,* 1992). The net effects are staggering not only in terms of economic costs (e.g., lost productivity and direct health care costs) but also in terms of emotional costs. In the New Mexico county with the second highest rate of alcohol-related problems in the United States, "at least one person was killed every day in an alcohol-related traffic accident" and no one "was untouched by drunk driving deaths" (U.S. General Accounting Office, 1992; see Chaps. 8 and 9).

The concept of *alcoholism* is rooted in the classic disease theory and may be defined as the sporadic or continuous inappropriate use of alcohol that harms or interferes with a person's physical or mental health, work, family, and/or social life. Alcoholism is characterized as: 1. *progressive* (the condition slowly becomes more serious over time), 2. *chronic* (whether use of alcohol is sporadic or continuous, the pattern of inappropriate use occurs over long periods and, in some cases, over a lifetime), and 3. *insidious* (even though most friends, relatives, or teachers may be aware of a drinking problem, alcoholics themselves are usually unable to recognize, without external assistance, that they are alcoholics; Seixas, 1982b).

The classic signs and symptoms of alcoholism include: 1. starting the day with a drink, 2. drinking alone, 3. gulping down drinks (e.g., as commonly done with "shooters"), 4. increased tolerance to alcohol, 5. blackouts, and 6. personality changes (R. Segal & Sisson, 1985; Seixas, 1982a). Once identified as an adult disease, these signs and symptoms are observed among children and adolescents in increasing numbers (Dunne & Schipperheijn, 1989). Although 20 years of age has been generally considered the age at which problems associated with inappropriate alcohol use become clearly recognizable (Swartz, 1991b), problems are now documented in late childhood and early adolescence (Famularo et al., 1985; A. M. Pagliaro & L. A. Pagliaro, clinical patient file notes).

As with adults, there are two major types of young alcoholics: 1. "bender" or "binge" drinkers, who drink heavily for short periods, such as on weekends or after a major school sporting event,[2] and 2. daily or chronic drinkers, who drink heavily every day or whenever alcohol is available (J. Wallace, 1982). Significant problems can be associated with inappropriate alcohol use among all age groups. However, among adolescents, accidents and violence-related injuries are more frequently encountered than cirrhosis or alcoholism because of the shorter duration of adolescents' alcohol use and the nature of this use, which tends to be more episodic (Shanks, 1990). Arrests for impaired driving; aggressive or violent behavior, often involving peers or family members (Pelletier & Coutu, 1992); expulsion from school; and job firings are common. The major adverse effects related to acute alcohol intoxication among children and adolescents are listed in Table 1.2 (Harper & Kril, 1990; Korsten & Lieber, 1985; Lindberg & Oyler, 1990; Van Natta, Malin, Bertolucci, & Kaelber, 1985).[3] Some data suggest that severe alcohol intoxication may result in coma at a lower blood level in children than in adults (Lamminpaa, Vilska, Korri, & Riihimaki, 1993).

Opiates. The opiates comprise a group of natural (e.g., morphine) and synthetic (e.g., heroin, or diacetylmorphine) derivatives of opium (i.e., the resin

[2] This pattern of alcohol use has also been referred to in the literature as "episodic."
[3] Alcohol is a demonstrated risk factor for additional serious adverse effects such as cancer of the gastrointestinal tract (Cullen, 1982) and heart disease. However, these effects are not listed in Table 1.2 because their associated pathology takes many years to develop and is, therefore, generally only noticeable in adults.

TABLE 1.2   Adverse Effects Commonly Associated with Alcohol Use

Accidents, general (e.g., drowning)
Abusive and aggressive behavior, physical and psychological
Cognitive dysfunction
Coma
Delinquency and criminal behavior
Depression
Memory dysfunction
Motor vehicle crashes
Psychomotor impairment
Psychosis
Respiratory depression
Self-neglect
Social problems (e.g., arguments with family members and truancy)
Suicide
Violent behavior, including assault and rape

derived from the unripe seed pod of the plant *Papaver somniferum*—"poppy that causes sleep"). When intravenous drug users are asked to name the first drug they injected and their age at the time they first injected, they generally report that they first injected cocaine or heroin when they were about 16 or 17 years of age (A. M. Pagliaro, Pagliaro, Thauberger, Hewitt, & Reddon, 1993). Over the past two decades the use of heroin within the previous year by high school seniors has remained fairly stable (~0.5 percent; U.S. Department of Justice, 1994a). However, this figure is expected to rise during the next decade as more adolescents begin to "chase the dragon." "Chasing the dragon" refers to heating high-purity heroin (alone or in combination with crack cocaine) and inhaling the trail of smoke through a tube. The increased purity of heroin now available at the street level (an increase from ~7 to ~30 percent purity during the last two decades) and decreased cost have contributed to a renewed interest in heroin and this noninjection method of heroin use (Gettman, 1994).

The short-term physiological effects of opiates are listed in Table 1.3. The signs and symptoms of acute opiate overdose are presented in Table 1.4, and the sequence of events related to acute overdose are presented in Figure 1.4. Acute overdoses are treated with the opiate antagonist naloxone (Narcan) along with appropriate supportive care (Dupuis, Smith, & Kowalcyzk, 1995).

Volatile solvents and inhalants.   Children and adolescents use many different volatile solvents and inhalants (Table 1.5) in order to produce a desired state of intoxication similar to that produced by alcohol. As with other substances

TABLE 1.3   Short-Term Physiological Effects of Opiates

Central nervous system depression[a]
Constriction of the pupil of the eye
Decreased gastrointestinal activity[a]
Depression of the cough reflex[a]
Dilation of superficial blood vessels and a warming of the skin ("rush")
Increased perspiration
Nausea
Reduced breathing rate
Reduced cardiovascular activity

[a]These effects are used for their therapeutic properties. The *other* physiological effects can be considered adverse drug reactions.

of abuse, the physiological and psychological effects of the volatile solvents and inhalants vary depending on such factors as the solvent or inhalant used, the amount and method of use, and the circumstances associated with use. Typically, volatile solvents and inhalants produce an initial sensation of excitation followed by varying degrees of central nervous system (CNS) depression. Although the desired effects of most volatile solvents and inhalants occur readily with rapid recovery within minutes, their use is commonly accompanied by headaches, dizziness, and nausea.

Whereas the use of volatile solvents and inhalants for their psychotropic effects can be traced back to antiquity (Pickens, 1985), their current use among children and adolescents has been consistently documented only since the middle of the 20th century (R. G. Smart, 1986; Watson, 1980). Although volatile solvent and inhalant use has been noted among adults (Hershey & Miller, 1982), it remains predominantly a youthful practice with the majority of users being between 8 and 12 years of age (Beauvais & Oetting, 1988; Gay, Meller, & Stanley, 1982; Watson, 1982). "In 1994, one in five eighth graders . . . had used inhalants" (U.S. Department of Justice, 1994a).

TABLE 1.4   Signs and Symptoms of Acute Opiate Overdose

Pupils: generally *constricted* (pinpoint pupils); *however,* with meperidine, or extreme hypoxia, may be dilated
Blood pressure: decreased (shock)
Body temperature: subnormal
Respirations: decreased, or absent with cyanosis
Reflexes: diminished or absent
Central nervous system status: stupor or coma; however, with meperidine, propoxyphene, or anoxia, may cause convulsions
Miscellaneous: constipation, pulmonary edema

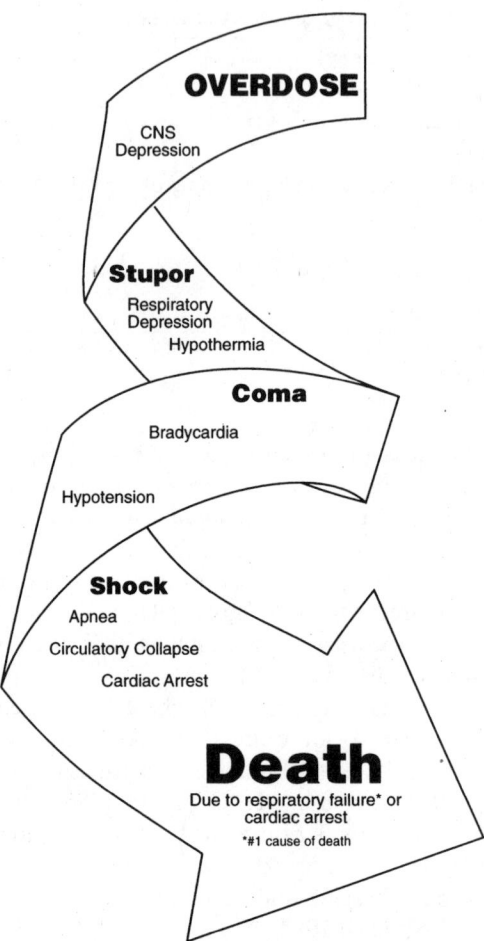

FIGURE 1.4   Sequence of events in opiate overdose

However, use by children as young as 4 years of age has been documented ("It's an Important," 1986).

The prevalence of volatile solvent and inhalant use among children and adolescents varies with time, geographical region, culture, ethnicity, and socioeconomic status. Thus, although approximately 15 percent of all North American youth report having used volatile solvents and inhalants, use is reported to be approximately 50 percent in lower socioeconomic groups—for example, 47 percent in a sample of Mexican American youth (DeBarona & Simpson, 1984) and 50 percent in a sample of Native American youth (G. E. Barnes, 1979). A gender effect has also been reported, with a consistent two-

TABLE 1.5   Commonly Used Volatile Solvents and Inhalants

Volatile Solvent or Inhalant	Major Chemical Ingredients (partial list)
Aerosols	Difluorodichloromethane
	Isobutane
	Methylene chloride
	Nitrous oxide
	Propane
	Trichlorofluoromethane
Butane	Butane
Dry cleaning fluid	Trichloroethane
Fingernail polish remover	Acetone
	Amyl acetate
Fire extinguishers	Bromochlorodifluoromethane
	Dibromotetrafluoroethane
	Trifluorobromomethane
Gasoline	Benzene
	Heptane
	Hexane
	Hydrocarbons
	Naphthalene
	Tetraethyl lead
	Toluene
	Xylene
Glue	Acetone
	Benzene
	Ethyl acetate
	Heptane
	Hexane
	Isopropyl acetate
	Methyl ethyl ketone
	Methylene chloride
	Naphtha
	Toluene
	Trichloroethane
	Xylene
Kerosene	Hydrocarbons
Nitrous oxide	Nitrous oxide
Paint thinner	Ethyl acetate
	Isopropanol
	Methanol
	Methylene chloride
	Toluene
	Trichloroethylene
Shoe polish	Chlorinated hydrocarbons
	Toluene
Typists' correction fluid	Amyl acetate
	Trichloroethane

to threefold higher incidence of volatile solvent and inhalant use by boys when compared to girls (Johnston, Bachman, & O'Malley, 1983; Swerhun & LeBreton, 1983; Watson, 1980).

For the most part, volatile solvents and inhalants are nonaddictive and their use is self-limited. There has been no documented permanent brain or organ damage directly related to the chronic use of volatile solvents and inhalants. However, additives, such as lead in gasoline, can cause significant physical morbidity and mortality in chronic users. In addition, acute toxicity, such as cardiac dysrhythmias associated with fluorinated hydrocarbon propellant use, can also result in significant morbidity or death. Death caused by asphyxiation among children and adolescents who lost consciousness while sniffing glue from a plastic bag that was held over their noses and mouths ("bagging") has been reported all too commonly. Accidental injury associated with flammable products has also been a serious consequence of volatile solvent and inhalant use (A. M. Pagliaro & Pagliaro, 1995). The most commonly used volatile solvents and inhalants are gasoline and glue (Caputo, 1993; Johns, 1991).

Gasoline is virtually universally available. It comprises a mixture of aliphatic and aromatic hydrocarbons and also generally contains several additives, including benzene and lead, to improve engine performance or as a result of the petrochemical refining process. Children and adolescents inhale the fumes from an open container (e.g., a metal can or plastic bag) filled with gasoline. Some children and adolescents inhale the fumes from a gasoline-soaked rag held over their noses and mouths ("huffing"; G. E. Barnes, 1979; A. M. Pagliaro & Pagliaro, 1995; Sarathi, Sharan, & Saxena, 1992; Watson, 1982). The latter method has also been used by some parents to quiet their crying infants (Hickl-Szabo, 1987).

The inhalation of gasoline fumes causes CNS depression (Banner & Walson, 1983) and produces effects similar to those associated with the ingestion of alcohol. However, because of the efficiency of the respiratory system, the inhalation of gasoline fumes can result in high levels of exposure and, consequently, dizziness, coma, and death (Andrews & Snyder, 1991). The additives commonly found in gasoline, particularly lead, are a major source of toxicity for children and adolescents who chronically inhale gasoline fumes—for example, chronic lead poisoning with resultant neuropathy.

Composed of several volatile organic constituents (Table 1.5), *glue* is the most widely used of the volatile solvents among children and adolescents (Pickens, 1985). The fumes from glue are inhaled by holding the glue container adjacent to the nostrils or by putting some glue in a small plastic bag and placing the opening of the bag tightly over the nose and mouth (Watson, 1980). In order to increase the volatility of the glue, the glue container or plastic bag is often warmed in the hands or held close to a car or apartment radiator. The inhaled glue fumes produce euphoric effects and toxicities that generally resemble those associated with inhaling gasoline fumes or ingesting alcohol (Watson, 1982; see Chap. 4 for additional details).

Central Nervous System Stimulants

Amphetamines.   The amphetamines (e.g., amphetamine [Benzedrine], dextroamphetamine [Dexedrine], and methamphetamine [Desoxyn]), their derivatives (e.g., chlorphentermine [Pre-Sate], fenfluramine [Pondimin], and phentermine [Fastin]), and closely related compounds (e.g., methylphenidate [Ritalin]) are CNS stimulants that elicit their pharmacological action presumably by increasing the release of norepinephrine and by directly stimulating the postsynaptic norepinephrine receptors. Amphetamines and their related derivatives are commonly used for the treatment of attention deficit hyperactivity disorder (ADHD) (L. A. Pagliaro, 1992b). It has been estimated that 20–40 percent of children diagnosed with ADHD develop problematic patterns of substance use (Wilens, Biederman, Spencer, & Frances, 1994). Few children and adolescents use amphetamines, unless they are prescribed. Once popular among adolescent girls, the use of amphetamines has been largely replaced in North America over the past three decades with the CNS stimulant cocaine (see below).

Those adolescents who use amphetamines (~10 percent within the past year; U.S. Department of Justice, 1994a) generally do so in order to increase physical performance (e.g., to stay awake at night to study for a high school examination) or to assist with weight reduction (appetite control). In regard to the latter group of users, these adolescents have reportedly been more likely to be white girls who also smoke cigarettes (Gritz & Crane, 1991).

In the late 1980s a new form of amphetamine called "ice" or "crystal meth" (the street names for the rocklike crystal form of methamphetamine also known as speed or crank) was introduced. Ice is available on the street in virtually pure form (92–98 percent) and can be injected or smoked in virtually the same manner as crack cocaine because of its high purity. Smoking ice gives the user a high that is reportedly similar in effect to that obtained from crack, except that the high typically lasts for hours instead of minutes. Ice has the real potential to become the "drug of the next decade" (Davis, 1995; L. A. Pagliaro, 1988c) because of its prolonged action and the fact that it can be produced domestically at low cost. However, thus far its use is not widespread, most likely because of the ready availability and decreased cost of cocaine. The physical and psychological effects of amphetamines in relation to dosage are listed in Figure 1.5.

Cocaine.   Cocaine has been used by approximately 15 percent of North American children and adolescents (Kandel & Davies, 1991; Tarr & Macklin, 1987). However, this percentage is expected to increase significantly as this century comes to an end, primarily because of the continually increasing

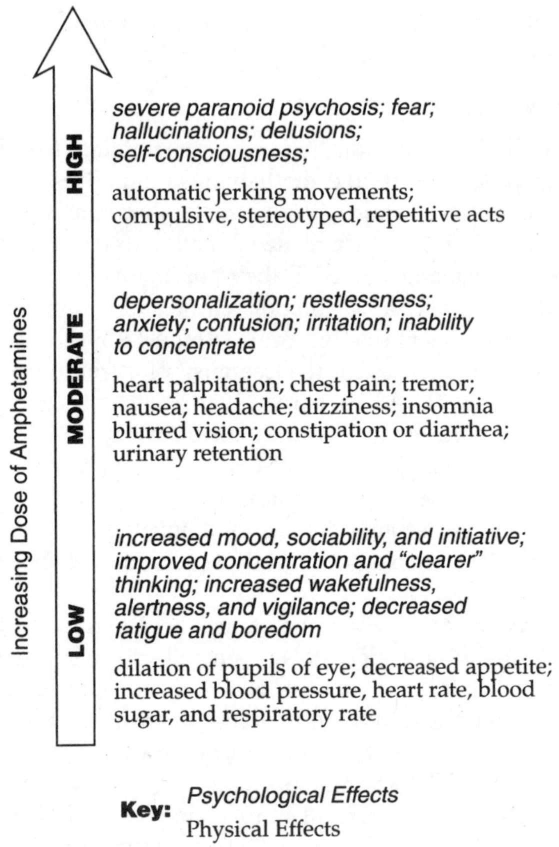

Key: *Psychological Effects*
Physical Effects

FIGURE 1.5 Physical and psychological effects of the amphetamines

availability of the smokable form, crack (L. A. Pagliaro, 1992c; "Survey Finds," 1995; Swan, 1995a). Currently, approximately 15 percent of high school seniors, 21 percent of college students, and 30 percent of young adults in the United States have reported a lifetime prevalence of cocaine use (P. M. O'Malley, Johnston, & Bachman, 1991). Other data indicate that the use of cocaine by children and adolescents is significantly related to the incidence of actual and attempted suicides among these age groups (Marzuk et al., 1992).

The adverse effects of cocaine are listed in Table 1.6. The intravenous use of cocaine and its association with high-risk behaviors for infection with HIV (e.g., sharing used needles and unprotected sex with multiple partners) is a growing and alarming trend (A. M. Pagliaro et al., 1993). This trend comes at a time when the transmission of HIV is increasing among intravenous drug

TABLE 1.6   Adverse Effects Associated with Cocaine Use

General (independent of method of use)
    Cardiac dysrhythmias
    Compulsive use
    Convulsions
    Habituation (psychological dependence)
    Hyperpyrexia
    Pseudohallucinations (e.g., "cocaine bugs" and "snow lights")
    Psychosis, including hypervigilance and paranoia
    Respiratory depression
Crack Cocaine Inhalation
    Respiratory irritation
Cocaine Hydrochloride Injection
    Abscess formation
    Embolism
    Infection (e.g., septicemia, hepatitis, and HIV)
    Phlebitis
Cocaine Hydrochloride Insufflation
    Erosion of nasal septum
    Nasal congestion

users in North America and poses one of the greatest risks for the transmission of infection among heterosexuals. In addition, the relationship between cocaine use and other substance use (e.g., alcohol use) and increase in sexual experimentation has important public health implications with respect to the current AIDS pandemic (R. G. Carlson & Siegal, 1991; Gibb, 1987; M. F. Goldsmith, 1988; Kandel & Davies, 1991) and the spread of other STDs (e.g., genital ulcers and syphilis; Balshem, Oxman, van Rooyen, & Girod, 1992; Chirgwin, DeHovitz, Dillon, & McCormack, 1991; Farley, Hadler, & Gunn, 1990; Hibbs & Gunn, 1991).

Cocaine use by adult women appears to be increasing at a faster rate than cocaine use by men, and sexual favors are commonly exchanged for cocaine (Ratner, 1993; Rolfs, Goldberg, & Sharrar, 1990; Schwarcz et al., 1992). Cocaine use by adolescents has also been associated with prostitution and the exchange of sexual favors (sex-for-drug exchanges). Sex-for-drug exchange to support cocaine, particularly crack cocaine, use usually involves girls but may also involve boys, who are known as "strawberries" and "raspberries," respectively (A. M. Pagliaro, Pagliaro, Thauberger, Hewitt, & Reddon, 1992; A. M. Pagliaro et al., 1993; Ratner, 1993). The phenomenon of "popcorn pimps" is also becoming increasingly recognized; older adolescent boys and girls pimp for younger children and adolescents to support their own cocaine use (A. M. Pagliaro & L. A. Pagliaro, clinical patient file notes; see also Chap. 9).

Nicotine (tobacco smoke).   Nicotine, an autonomic ganglionic stimulant, is one of more than 4,000 chemicals inhaled with tobacco smoke (Dawson & Vestal, 1982; D. Hoffman & Wynder, 1986). It is also absorbed buccally as a constituent of chewing tobacco, nicotine chewing gum, and cigars[4] (Benowitz, 1988; Gori, Benowitz, & Lynch, 1986). In addition, nicotine has been formulated for transdermal absorption by various therapeutic transdermal delivery systems (e.g., Habitrol and Nicoderm) which are a part of selected smoking cessation programs (Generali, 1992; "Nicotine Patches," 1992). Nicotine is used regularly in the form of cigarettes and chewing tobacco by approximately 3 million North American children and adolescents ("Accessibility of Cigarettes," 1992). In fact, 60 percent of current cigarette smokers began smoking tobacco before the age of 14 years, and each day more than 3,000 additional children and adolescents in the United States begin to use tobacco (Epps & Manley, 1991). This use is generally in response to peer pressure and social role models (Hunter, Vizelberg, & Berenson, 1991; Iannotti & Bush, 1992; Tuakli, Smith, & Heaton, 1990; see Chap. 5). Many of these children and adolescents will become physically addicted to nicotine by the end of their adolescence (Epps & Manley, 1991).

Tobacco smoking is the largest single preventable cause of illness in North America and is responsible for approximately 15 percent of all deaths. A large proportion of deaths from coronary heart disease (25 percent) and cancer (30 percent of all cancer deaths and 87 percent of lung cancer deaths) are attributed to tobacco smoking (Collishaw & Leahy, 1991; "Selected Tobacco-Use Behaviors," 1992; "Smoking-Attributable Mortality," 1991; "Smoking Control," 1983). Although smoking-related deaths do not generally occur during childhood or adolescence, the pathology (e.g., atherosclerosis) begins at this time (Watkins & Strong, 1984), and prevention effects should also begin here (Pentz et al., 1989; see Chap. 10). Children and adolescents exposed to passive or secondhand smoke are also at risk for the adverse effects of smoking, including alterations in lipid profiles, atherosclerosis, and lung cancer (J. Feldman et al., 1991; Lesmes & Donofrio, 1992). Impaired respiratory function, respiratory infections, and bronchitis occur significantly more often among children and adolescents whose parents smoke than among those children and adolescents whose parents never smoked (Masi, Hanley, Ernst, & Becklaki, 1988; Stone, 1992; Ugnat, Mao, Miller, & Wigle, 1990; Weitzman, Gortmaker, Walker, & Sobol, 1990). The majority of the adverse effects associated with tobacco smoking (e.g., respiratory tract irritation and lung cancer) are related to the other constituents found in tobacco smoke, and not to nicotine (see Table 1.7).

---

[4]Cigar and pipe tobacco, having generally been air-cured, have an alkaline pH that enhances buccal absorption.

TABLE 1.7   Adverse Effects Associated with Nicotine Use

Addiction (physical dependence)
Blood pressure, increase
Heart rate, increase
Nausea
Tremor
Vomiting

Psychedelics

Cannabis.   *Cannabis sativa* in its plant form (marijuana), resin form (hashish), or extracted oil form (hashish oil) has been used by approximately 25 percent of North Americans. In fact, marijuana is the illicit drug that is most frequently used by teenagers, and more than half of high school seniors report that they have used marijuana at least once (American Academy of Pediatrics, 1991; Macdonald, 1989). The use of cannabis by children and adolescents is significantly higher than use by the general adult population. Although use statistics vary by state, province, city, and study, it is generally estimated that approximately 30 percent of North American teenagers have used marijuana within the previous year and 15 percent have used it within the previous month (B. Segal, 1990; "Survey Finds," 1995). Since 1992, the percentage of 8th, 10th, and 12th graders who have used marijuana during the previous year has steadily increased (Chaiken, 1995; Swan, 1995a).

The adverse effects associated with cannabis use are listed in Table 1.8. Contrary to popular beliefs about cannabis, its use does *not* cause permanent brain injury or damage as portrayed, for example, in the cult movie *Reefer Madness* (Dewey, 1986; Meade, Hirliman, & Gasnier, 1937). However, several

TABLE 1.8   Adverse Effects Associated with Cannabis Use

Acute
  Paranoia
  Panic reaction
  Psychomotor impairment and related motor vehicle
    crashes
  Tachycardia
  Toxic delirium
Chronic
  Amotivation syndrome
  Habituation (psychological dependence)
  Learning disabilities (e.g., disruption of short-term
    memory)
  Respiratory irritation and disease (e.g., asthma and
    bronchitis)

well-defined toxicities related to cannabis use have been identified that are particularly significant for children and adolescents. These toxicities include adverse effects on the respiratory system, including irritant effects, and on the CNS, particularly amotivational syndrome, impaired ability to operate a motor vehicle, and learning impairment (L. A. Pagliaro, 1983, 1995c). Other CNS toxicities include habituation (psychological dependence), panic attacks, and paranoia (Hollister, 1988). These CNS toxicities have been clearly associated with cannabis use, but appear to depend also on genetic and psychological predisposition.

Among *respiratory toxicities*, a number of studies have documented the direct irritant effects (e.g., coughing, dry mouth, and sore throat) of cannabis smoke on the respiratory tract and its associated negative effects on pulmonary function, including chronic obstructive pulmonary diseases such as asthma and bronchitis (Fligiel, Venkat, Gong, & Tashkin, 1988; Kalant, Fehr, Arras, & Anglin, 1983; "Negative Pulmonary Effects," 1987). The severity of these respiratory toxicities appears to be clearly related to the smoking techniques used by cannabis smokers (e.g., inhaling deeply and holding the smoke in the respiratory tract for several seconds to obtain optimal psychotropic effects; Agurell et al., 1986). Many researchers have reported an increased risk of lung cancer in cannabis users and have also noted that in terms of respiratory toxicity, smoking one marijuana joint is roughly equivalent to smoking a package of 20 tobacco cigarettes (L. A. Pagliaro, 1988b).

Among CNS *toxicities*, the use of even moderate amounts of cannabis produces an acute state of intoxication and a dose-related impairment in the ability to drive a motor vehicle or to operate other complex and hazardous machinery (L. A. Pagliaro, 1983; R. H. Schwartz, 1987). This impairment is related primarily to the following effects of tetrahydrocannabinol (THC), the principle active psychotropic ingredient in cannabis: 1. time-space distortion, 2. impaired visual accommodation, 3. decreased muscular coordination, and 4. impaired short-term memory (Gettman, 1995). These effects impair perceptual-motor skills and performance on decision-making tasks and, hence, the ability to operate a motor vehicle or other hazardous machinery. These adverse effects are significantly exacerbated by the concurrent ingestion of alcohol, a commonly observed phenomenon among children and adolescents who are cannabis smokers (V. Johnson & White, 1989; Poklis, Maginn, & Barr, 1987; Smiley, Moskowitz, & Ziedman, 1985).

Amotivational syndrome was originally associated in the 1950s with chronic barbiturate use. However, since the 1970s, this syndrome has been predominantly associated with chronic cannabis use, particularly by children and adolescents (ages 11–14 years; Baumrind & Moselle, 1985; Tunving, 1987). Typically, these youth lack the motivation and drive observed among others of the same age and background who do not smoke cannabis. They generally spend an inordinate amount of time alone "stoned," listening to music or watching music videos on television, and are often referred to by their peers as being "burned" or "burned out." A major psychological problem faced by these children and adolescents is that they increasingly use cannabis as a means for handling the various problems that they encounter in their daily lives. This pattern of use does not encourage the development of the skills necessary to progress psychologically from childhood to adulthood and leaves these children and adolescents ill prepared to function adequately in the adult world (S. Cohen, 1981; Hollister, 1986).

Cannabis use by children and adolescents can cause *learning impairment* in several ways. It alters perception, decreases attention, and impairs short-term memory, and hence retention of what is presented by teachers in the classroom (L. A. Pagliaro, 1992a, 1993). In addition, the amotivational syndrome associated with chronic, high-dose use of cannabis is a significant impediment to learning because children and adolescents who display this pattern of use are frequently absent from school and do not appear to be able to adequately address learning tasks when they are in the classroom (L. A. Pagliaro, 1992b; see Chap. 7).

LSD.   Reportedly, 10 percent of North American children and adolescents have used LSD, a psychedelic popularized during the 1960s and 1970s by the writings of Harvard professors Timothy Leary and Richard Alpert and by the music of the Beatles, Jimi Hendrix, Jefferson Airplane, and other performers during the height of the "acid rock" years (R. T. Brown & Braden, 1987). The use of LSD waned during the 1980s, but it has now been rediscovered by the grandchildren of the hippie generation who use LSD on Bart Simpson window panes (i.e., doses adsorbed to small pieces of gelatin for insertion into the conjunctival sac of the eye), often as they gather in groups of hundreds to "rave" ("Survey Finds," 1995). Another psychedelic drug, "ecstasy" (3,4-methylenedioxymethamphetamine, or MDMA), also is used in this social context, particularly in the United Kingdom (Randall, 1992a, 1992b).

Although various types of physical toxicities have been purportedly associated with the use of LSD, virtually all of these have been refuted. It is now recognized that LSD is not a human teratogen (see Chap. 3; L. A. Pagliaro, 1991b) and is not addictive. However, the use of LSD can result in "bad trips" and other psychological sequelae, including psychosis (Table 1.9), particularly among children and adolescents who have a history of mental disorders or a genetic predisposition in this regard, as demonstrated by a positive fam-

TABLE 1.9   Adverse Effects Associated with LSD Use

"Bad trips" (i.e., panic reactions)
"Flashbacks"
Psychosis

ily history, for example (S. Cohen, 1985; Hurlbut, 1991; Leikin, Krantz, Zell-Kanter, Barkin, & Hryhorczuk, 1989).

Polysubstance Use

During the 1980s, the trend of using several different substances of abuse concurrently or concomitantly, or *polysubstance use,* became firmly established among children and adolescents (Chatlos, 1989; Cornwall, 1990). This trend has continued into the 1990s (W. Feigelman, Hyman, Amann, & Feigelman, 1990). Polysubstance use is characterized by: 1. concurrent use of more than one substance of abuse and 2. concomitant use of different substances of abuse at different times predicated primarily on availability and cost (Beauvais et al., 1989; Carroll, Malloy, Hannigan, Santo, & Kenrick, 1977; Speck & Santo, 1981).

Polysubstance use is also associated with producing various synergistic and interactive effects among the different substances of abuse. For example, use of alcohol, cannabis, and nicotine are highly correlated with each other and with the use of other substances of abuse. Many specific patterns of polysubstance use have been identified. Alcohol is commonly used with cocaine not only in social contexts but also to "come down" and "get straight" from a cocaine high. Alcohol is also commonly used with LSD as part of a new ritual of use, as a vehicle to facilitate the oral ingestion of LSD "blotter" dosage forms (i.e., doses adsorbed to paper for oral ingestion), and as a way to "mellow out LSD's head trip." "It is clear that alcohol abuse by adolescents rarely exists today without the concurrent use of other drugs" (C. S. Martin, Arria, Mezzich, & Bukstein, 1993, p. 511). Other examples of common patterns of polysubstance use include putting hashish oil on a tobacco cigarette, mixing marijuana or hashish with tobacco and rolling the mixture into a cigarette or placing it in a pipe, and mixing cocaine in tobacco or marijuana before rolling it into a cigarette (A. M. Pagliaro & Pagliaro, 1995). Polysubstance use by children and adolescents appears to be significantly influenced by peer pressure and behavioral group norms (Clayton & Ritter, 1985; Fournet et al., 1990).

The importance of the substance dimension and variables cannot be denied. However, quantitative, as well as qualitative, descriptions of substance use behavior are required to better reflect varying degrees of use and associated consequences (Shedler & Block, 1990). The pattern of use variables are particularly useful in this regard (A. M. Pagliaro & Pagliaro, 1995; L. A. Pagliaro & Pagliaro, 1993).

Pattern of Use Variables

Over the past decade, children and adolescents have experimented increasingly with and have come to widely use such substances of abuse as alcohol,

cannabis, and cocaine. Today's youth are perhaps not unlike previous generations who used these and other substances of abuse, including phencyclidine,
or "PeaCe Pills" (PCP), and LSD. However, current use patterns have been
increasingly associated with serious, harmful effects (Boyle & Offord, 1991;
L. A. Pagliaro, 1986, 1990a, 1991a, 1993a; see Chaps. 3 and 8). This situation
is expected to worsen as the decade comes to an end and substance use continues to increase annually.

There are five well-defined patterns of use that represent a continuum
of increasingly more compulsive and harmful substance use: 1. initial use,
2. social use, 3. habitual use, 4. abuse, and 5. compulsive use (Fig. 1.2). Obviously, initial and social use do not always progress to abuse and compulsive
use. However, this conceptualization offers a means for identifying the nature
and severity of actual or potential problems associated with substance use
that may require different treatment approaches. The focus of this approach
is on the overall pattern of substance use instead of only the characteristics
of a specific substance of abuse.

Initial Use

The first-time use of a particular substance of abuse generally involves some
degree of curiosity and experimentation, and it does not usually develop into
a pattern of abuse or compulsive use. However, as many emergency room
staff know, admission to a hospital or morgue can result from the initial
use of a particular substance of abuse by a particular child or adolescent.
Fortunately, this occurrence is not commonly encountered. Most children
and adolescents are curious about the effects of a particular substance of
abuse and use it only once as an experiment when the opportunity presents
itself and suffer no long-term adverse effects. For example, a sixth-grader
may try a cigarette or take a puff of crack cocaine with the encouragement
of an older sibling. Younger children, including toddlers and preschoolers,
may be given a sip of beer or a toke of a marijuana joint by older siblings
and their friends "just to see their reaction." Initial use may also be prompted
by a parent, an adult relative, or a family friend (see Chap. 8).

Social Use

The second pattern of use is social use. Although the substance of abuse
typically is actively sought, use is limited, and there are no major adverse
effects associated with its use. An example of this pattern of use is drinking
an alcoholic beverage "for fun" at a friend's house when the parents are away
or drinking spiked punch at a school dance. In these situations, the child or
adolescent did not go to the friend's house or school dance primarily for the
alcohol, but once there, sought it and used it.

Habitual Use

Habitual use involves the establishment of a definite pattern of substance use (e.g., smoking marijuana every day after school or "drinking with the guys" every Friday and Saturday night). The characteristics of this pattern of use include the absence of *addiction* (physical dependence) and the infrequent occurrence of major adverse effects. However, *habituation* (psychological dependence) is an integral feature of this pattern of substance use.

Abuse

In the abuse pattern, the substance of abuse is actively sought and continues to be used despite well-recognized harmful effects. Examples of this pattern of substance use include an adolescent who has been charged with driving under the influence of alcohol but who continues to drink alcohol and drive, an adolescent with asthma controlled by bronchodilators who continues to smoke cigarettes, and a pregnant teenager who continues to use crack cocaine even though she has been warned about the dangers to her unborn baby. In this pattern of use, the negative consequences associated with the use of a particular substance are generally recognized, but it continues to be actively sought and used.

Compulsive Use

The most serious pattern of substance use is compulsive use. This pattern is characterized by a complete lack of control over the use of the substance of abuse. For example, alcohol may be taken to school in a thermos so that it will be available between classes. Children and adolescents who display this pattern of use generally indicate that they simply cannot help themselves. The substance of abuse, whether it is alcohol, cocaine, nicotine, or gasoline, becomes the major focus of concern. Compulsive users spend most of their time thinking about, obtaining, and using the substance of abuse. These children and adolescents feel a lack of control over its use and continue use despite expected and predictable harmful effects (e.g., fetal alcohol syndrome).

Resumed Nonuse, Controlled Use, and Relapsed Use

Once the pattern of compulsive use is reached, a return to previous and less severe patterns of use (e.g., social use) has been thought to be virtually impossible. Complete abstinence has been the accepted therapeutic approach for the treatment of children and adolescents who compulsively use a substance of abuse. This traditional approach has been challenged and continues to be debated by experts (M. Levy, 1992; Littrell, 1991; Sobell & Sobell, 1972). However, until further research produces clear evidence to the contrary, complete abstinence is probably the best way to maintain resumed nonuse and prevent relapsed use or the return to compulsive use. This therapeutic caveat appears to apply to the use of all substances of abuse and all children and adolescents.

The eight patterns of substance use depict steps in the progressive development of addiction and habituation. A better understanding of these patterns of substance use will help to encourage better assessment of children and adolescents for potential and actual problems related to their substance use. It will also help to guide the development of prevention strategies and treatment programs that are tailored to meet the needs of children and adolescents who have not yet begun to use substances of abuse or who are developing patterns of abuse or compulsive use. Attention to the eight patterns of use also encourages attention to the development of abstinence and relapse prevention programs specifically formulated for this age group, for which extremely high recidivism rates are usually encountered (e.g., in excess of 70 percent over 12 months after treatment; see Chap. 10).

TREATMENT

Pharmacological advances in the prevention and treatment of substance use have been significant and include methadone maintenance programs (Dole, 1971; Dole & Nyswander, 1980; L. A. Pagliaro, 1985b) and the use of naltrexone (Crabtree, 1984; Greenstein, Arndt, McLellan, O'Brien, & Evans, 1984) for the treatment of opiate addiction,[5] clonidine-aided opiate detoxification (M. S. Gold & Dackis, 1984; Washton, Gold, & Pottash, 1985), naloxone for the treatment of opiate overdose (Handal, Schauben, & Salamone, 1983), flumazenil for the treatment of benzodiazepine overdose ("Flumazenil," 1992; Karavokiros & Tsipis, 1990), and disulfiram (Antabuse) for the treatment of alcoholism (Chick et al., 1992).

Pharmaceutical advances also include the development of dosage forms that can prevent or help reduce the illicit intravenous use of various substances of abuse such as pentazocine, the use of which has now been all but eliminated in the United States by the development of combination pentazocine/naloxone tablets (Talwin-Nx; Poklik, 1984). Transdermal nicotine delivery systems have become important adjuncts to smoking cessation programs (Tonnesen, Norregaard, Simonsen, & Sawe, 1991). Attention has also been given to pharmacological management of the withdrawal phenomenon associated with the use of several substances of abuse—for example, bromocriptine-aided cocaine withdrawal (Herridge & Gold, 1988) and buspirone-aided nicotine withdrawal (Hilleman, Mohiuddin, Del Core, & Sketch, 1992). A number of promising pharmacological interventions are on

[5] Naltrexone (ReVia) has more recently (e.g., Volpicelli, Watson, King, Sherman, & O'Brien, 1995) been used as an adjunct in the treatment of alcoholism among adults.

the horizon, including several aimed at the pharmacological prevention and treatment of cocaine addiction (Lacombe, Stanislav, & Marken, 1991).

Although researchers have been successful in developing knowledge regarding the pharmacology, toxicology, abuse potential, and addiction liability of substances of abuse for adults, increased attention must be directed toward the prevention and treatment of substance use by children and adolescents. Thus, it must be recognized that:

1. Certain substances of abuse are particularly attractive to children and adolescents and are used preferentially for a variety of reasons (e.g., major psychotropic effect, availability, and social norms);

2. Children and adolescents are at particular risk for personal and social problems associated with their substance use (e.g., overdose death; morbidity and mortality related to automobile crashes; learning disorders; incarceration for drug-related offenses, such as possession of illicit substances, breaking and entering, and prostitution; family violence and incest; teenage pregnancy; suicide; and infection with STDs, including gonorrhea, syphilis, and HIV; and

3. Because of its heterogeneity, this age group requires individualized and diverse prevention and treatment approaches (e.g., what works for a crack-habituated 14-year-old pregnant Hispanic girl who is from a poor, single-parent family living in a large inner city and is a gang member probably will not work for an alcohol-addicted 16-year-old boy who is of Japanese ancestry from an upper-middle-class, two-parent family living in the suburbs).

Although it is generally agreed that multimodal prevention and treatment approaches have the greatest potential for success, further research is required in order to deter or curtail substance use by children and adolescents.

Obviously, the best treatment for problematic patterns of substance use is prevention, and considerable effort has been made in this regard (Durell & Bukoski, 1984; E. M. Johnson, Davis, & Denniston, 1991; Schinke & Gilchrist, 1985; Sullivan, 1986). To achieve maximum success in the treatment of young substance users, approaches must be tailored to meet their individual needs (G. R. Ross, 1994). Efforts must be made to more widely disseminate available knowledge of substance use by children and adolescents and to apply it in clinical practice. Attempts at preventing substance use among children and adolescents fail more often than they succeed, but such failures are rarely reported in the literature (Oetting & Beauvais, 1991). Thus, development of efficacious prevention and treatment strategies must address methods that have failed in the past as well as those that have been successful with particular groups. MIMSEUICA can facilitate this endeavor.

MIMSEUICA can help in the planning of treatment by identifying the variables in each dimension that are amenable to change. For example, if in the substance dimension, the substance of abuse is identified as particularly harmful, a less harmful substance from the same pharmacological classification might be substituted (e.g., methadone for heroin).[6] If the method of use is identified as particularly dangerous, a less-dangerous method might be used (e.g., substituting heroin cigarettes for heroin injection)[7] as part of a treatment plan.

Similarly, if specific stresses and maladaptive coping mechanisms are identified among the psychological variables in the infant/child/adolescent dimension, techniques for stress reduction and the development of better coping abilities would be an integral component of the treatment plan. If lack of family support is identified as a major contributing factor in regard to substance use among the social variables in the infant/child/adolescent dimension, intervention might include attempts to increase family or other support (e.g., family therapy might be considered). If lack of adequate health care resources (e.g., youth programs with appropriately trained staff) is identified as a major factor contributing to substance use in the societal dimension, intervention may include attempts to increase social assistance (e.g., specific social programs for children and adolescents might be developed) and the training of counselors and social workers.

Evaluation of treatment is a crucial, yet perhaps the most frequently overlooked, step in the treatment process. It is useless to prescribe treatment, or for a child or adolescent to follow a plan of treatment, if the treatment is ineffective. Evaluation can be readily performed using MIMSEUICA by comparing the variables before treatment (*baseline evaluation*), during treatment (*formative evaluation*), and at a predetermined interval(s) after treatment is completed (*summative evaluation*).

For example, if unemployment is a social variable in the infant/child/adolescent dimension that is identified as a major contributory factor to the history of substance use and if sufficient attention is not given to appropriate job training and employment strategies, the prognosis is bleak in spite of treatment interventions. Although program evaluators and researchers are often particularly interested in the summative evaluation in terms of program success and recidivism rates, others may be most interested in the formative evaluation because an ineffective treatment plan can be modified "midstream" to optimize therapy.

MIMSEUICA is also useful because it can reveal factors that may for a particular child or adolescent contribute to relapse if not addressed. Such factors include substance use related to inadequate coping when the young person is faced with significant stressors such as the death of a loved one, a diagnosis of cancer, or an arrest. In addition, MIMSEUICA can be useful as a framework for helping children and adolescents understand the factors affecting their substance use and, thus, enable them to become better participants in their treatment planning and implementation (see Chap. 10 for a more comprehensive discussion).

SUMMARY

The use of various substances of abuse is a significant problem among North American children and adolescents and is expected to worsen over the final years of the 20th century as polysubstance use increases. The major substances used by children and adolescents include alcohol, amphetamines, cannabis, cocaine, LSD, nicotine, and volatile solvents and inhalants. The Mega Interactive Model of Substance Exposure and Use among Infants, Children, and Adolescents (MIMSEUICA) is a heuristic device that can encourage the analysis of the myriad variables associated with substance use. MIMSEUICA can be used to improve understanding of the complex phenomenon of substance use and encourage the provision of more effective prevention and treatment strategies.

CHAPTER 2

Explaining Substance Use among Children and Adolescents

Substance use among children and adolescents in North America, often viewed as part of the rite of passage from childhood to adulthood (at least for boys), is invariably accompanied by significant concern on the part of parents, teachers, researchers, and policymakers. Public concern about substance use among adolescents is not new, and several patterns of concern regarding the use of various substances of abuse over the modern period have been noted.[1] For example, marijuana use during the 1920s (Prohibition Era) was cause for alarm in many states and provinces, as was heroin use during the 1950s in New York City and other North American cities. The use of psychedelics by the flower children in the Haight-Ashbury district of San Francisco, and elsewhere, during the 1960s and 1970s occasioned much public outcry, as did alcohol, nicotine, and cocaine use among children and adolescents during the 1980s. The 1990s have been characterized by worries about crack cocaine and polysubstance use among girls and boys from all socioeconomic groups living in rural and urban regions of North America (see Chap. 1). More recently, attention has been directed at the relationship between substance use and the apparent rising incidence of violent crime. In fact, homicide has become the leading cause of death for young black males and suicide for young white males (see Chap. 8).

In response to these concerns, parents, teachers, and professionals involved with various aspects of childhood and adolescent health have sought to understand why adolescents use the various substances of abuse, so that their use might be prevented or at least controlled or minimized. Several hundred theories purporting to explain substance use by both youth and adults have been published during the last decades of the twentieth century as North Americans acknowledge that they are losing the "war on drugs" (A. M. Pagliaro, 1995). Unfortunately, few of the explanations advanced to

---

[1] The modern period is roughly that period of history from 1840 to the present. The late modern period, the focus of this chapter, encompasses more specifically the last decades of the twentieth century, 1960–95.

date in an effort to explain these patterns of use have been adequately tested and developed, and children and adolescents continue to use the various substances of abuse, increasingly in the context of problematic patterns of use (i.e., abuse and compulsive use; see Chap. 1). The purpose of this chapter is to put into context the various late modern explanations regarding childhood and adolescent substance use in an effort to: 1. provide readers with a better understanding of the varied explanations that have been advanced; 2. encourage increased formal choice, testing, and use of these published theories; and 3. put into perspective the work that has been done, with a view to the need for future work aimed at the prevention and treatment of substance use among children and adolescents. It is hoped that this chapter will help to stimulate novel explanations that will contribute significantly to more effective substance use prevention and treatment approaches for children and adolescents.

In order to prepare this chapter, a computerized search was completed of all relevant databases for theories purporting to explain substance use among children and adolescents. Hand searches were performed for those years not accessible on computer databases (generally from 1900 to 1960). Approximately 100 theories were identified that purported to explain why children and adolescents used, or did not use, the various substances of abuse. These data were further analyzed in regard to the specific population addressed, including age (child or adolescent years), gender (female or male), race (e.g., American Indian and black), and substance of abuse (e.g., alcohol, cocaine, heroin, and marijuana). The theoretical reviews published by D. B. Kandel (1980b, 1986), Lettieri, Sayers, and Wallenstein Pearson (1980), Chassin (1984), Long and Scherl (1984), C. L. Jones and Battjes (1985), Lettieri (1985), Zinberg and Shaffer (1985), Labouvie (1986a, 1986b), Zucker and Lisansky Gomberg (1986), Blane and Leonard (1987), Sadava (1987), Chaudron and Wilkinson (1988), Glantz and Pickens (1992), Glynn and Haenlein (1988), and others were also used in the preparation of this chapter. Although a comprehensive review of these data are beyond the scope of this chapter, the theories and themes discussed range from one of the first identified theories, the general theory of suicide (Menninger, 1938), to one of the most recently advanced theories, the cognitive-behavioral theory of adolescent chemical dependency (G. R. Ross, 1994).[2]

MID-MODERN PERIOD (1901–60)

Menninger (1938), extending Freudian psychoanalytic theory, proposed a general theory of suicide in an effort to explain substance use, particularly

---

[2] For a comprehensive overview of the several hundred modern theories advanced in an effort to explain human substance use among both youth and adults, readers are referred to A. M. Pagliaro (1995).

alcohol use, among adolescent boys and men identified as chronic alcoholics. However, serious attention was not given specifically to youth until the 1950s and 1960s when Glueck and Glueck (1950, 1968) proposed their classic juvenile delinquency theory.[3] The argument that personality was the major factor in predicting substance use among adolescents influenced another theoretical direction taken at this time, developed by Ausubel (1958, 1961) in work extending psychoanalytic and developmental theory that also addressed adults.

By the 1960s, increasing attention was given to explaining alcohol use among adolescents. In this regard, such work as McCord and McCord's (1960) model of alcoholism received much attention. These theorists explored the role of ethnicity as a possible factor explaining substance use. In their longitudinal study of male alcoholism between 1935 and 1945, 255 male subjects and their families were repeatedly observed by a variety of physicians, psychiatrists, and social workers for approximately 5 years of their childhood. An additional 255 subjects were interviewed and observed less extensively. The subjects averaged 9 years of age at the time when initial contact was made. All of the subjects were cases in the Cambridge-Somerville project and had been selected for reasons other than their potential for becoming alcoholic (about half were selected as potential delinquents and half were selected because of their "normal" behavior). Although the subjects differed from a random American sample—all were male, came from urban areas, and overrepresented "social deviants" and lower socioeconomic, immigrant, and Roman Catholic groups—their distinguishing characteristics were identified as having certain advantages for the study of alcoholism (McCord & McCord, 1960, p. 20).

The social, familial, psychological, and physiological background of all the subjects were categorized, and information regarding their physical status and intelligence was obtained using a series of interviews and assessments conducted by physicians, psychologists, and psychiatrists. In this manner, data regarding familial background, childhood personality, and social milieu were collected over an average of 5 years by the staff of the Cambridge-Somerville project. "These observations were detailed, extensive, and considered to be relatively free from preconceived biases" by McCord and McCord (1960) because they were recorded in "raw" form by a number of different observers representing a variety of theoretical traditions (pp. 20–21). In addition, they had no knowledge of the adult lives of the boys and no knowledge as to the research questions.

McCord and McCord (1960) noted:

These raw observations were then rated into discrete, largely behaviorally defined categories. *The raters had no knowledge about which of their subjects were alcoholic and which were nonalcoholic.* Rigid definitions of the categories and

[3] This study of Boston delinquents and schoolboys, for which the latter was a control group, was later extended into a 40-year longitudinal study by Vaillant (1983a, 1995).

repeated tests of inter-rater agreement resulted in a relatively high degree of reliability and, presumably, the elimination of "the halo effect" in rating. (p. 21)

In order to make sense of their data, McCord and McCord completed an extensive review of the literature on current theories of alcoholism, finding diverse physiological, psychoanalytical, and sociological theories. From this work they compiled in 1957 a set of hypotheses concerning the genesis of alcoholism.

As summarized by the theorists, three types of external pressures—family background, cultural pressure, and the adult situation—interact with personality structure to cause alcoholism in adulthood: 1. intense parental conflict; 2. neural disorder, especially in combination with intense family conflict; 3. being reared in a family characterized by incest or illegitimacy; and 4. having a weakly Catholic mother. As explained by McCord and McCord (1960), "by creating anxiety or by offering outlets for anxiety, these influences tended to promote alcoholism or retard it" (p. 53). Thus, as a child the potential alcoholic is likely to have had a variety of frustrating experiences (e.g., neurological disorder or a family disrupted by a high degree of conflict and disagreement and characterized by incest and illegitimacy) that created a high level of stress and insecurity during childhood. This stress and insecurity in turn led to a basic unsureness about his expected role in life. (This stress could be expressed in ways other than alcoholism, such as criminal behavior.) In addition to these sources of high general stress and insecurity, he had erratic satisfaction of dependency needs (e.g., was raised in an environment in which his desire to be loved was satisfied and then frustrated in an erratic fashion—mother alternated between loving indulgence and overt rejection, saw herself as a martyr whose own interests were sacrificed for those of her family, reacted to crises in an escapist manner, participated in deviant behavior, or was held in low esteem by father) that led him to express his anxiety in alcoholism.

In addition, the extreme dependency conflict had two major effects on the child's personality: intensified need for love and anxiety about the satisfaction of this heightened need. Inadequate specification of the male role was also identified as important. In regard to this family background factor, the potential alcoholic was not offered a clear, specific image of manhood (e.g., father tended to be antagonistic and tried to escape from the pressure of critical situations and the responsibility of the male role was neither exemplified nor enforced). In addition to the father's behavior, which generally contradicted the usual stereotype of the American male's role in society, teachers and media messages (e.g., radio and newspapers) portrayed the typical male as responsible, courageous, law abiding, and loving, traits usually the opposite of those displayed by the alcoholic's father. These experiences resulted in confusion in self-image.

In response, the child seeks to resolve his conflicts behind a "supermasculine" facade (aggressive, outwardly self-confident, and highly independent) that can satisfy his dependency conflict, end his confusion about his self-image, ensure his societal approval, and achieve a temporary resolution of his disturbing conflicts. Underneath his facade, however, he continues to feel anxious, suffers conflict, and is desirous of dependent relationships. Consequently, he attempts to satisfy these forbidden urges in various vicarious ways (e.g., finds a wife to serve as a "pseudomother" or chooses an occupation where he is under the care of comforting figures). As an adult, the typical prealcoholic involves himself in a quest to satisfy his dual desires to be independent and dependent. However, because of his particular background or social class (i.e., middle class), certain outlets for expression of dependency are closed to him (e.g., reliance on church or seeking a career in professional prizefighting with the manager taking over the maternal role).

To such a person, alcohol provides an available outlet having several functions. When intoxicated, feelings of warmth, comfort, and omnipotence are achieved and strong desires to be dependent are satisfied while an image of independence and self-reliance is maintained. As noted by the theorists, in American society the hard drinker is pictured as "tough, extroverted, and manly—exactly the masculine virtues the alcoholic strives to incorporate into his own self-image." His basic psychological makeup and social pressures, the absence of alternative resolutions, and the lack of strong social proscriptions against alcohol use increase his likelihood of succumbing to alcohol. However, the severe effects of alcoholism do not become apparent until middle age. Social drinking at parties, then habitual weekend binges, and then daily use to abuse throughout the day are noted. Blacking out after heavy drinking sessions, sneaking drinks, and orienting his life around securing his daily supply characterize his progression to compulsive use patterns or alcoholism, with its associated sequelae (e.g., loss of job, family, and image of self; McCord & McCord, 1960, pp. 150–155). Regardless, the confirmed alcoholic increases his alcohol use because intoxication satisfies his dependency urges and "obliterates reminders of his own inadequacies." Because it is assumed that "his character is organized around a quest for dependency, in alcohol he finds a permanent, easily available, and, at first, nonthreatening method of satisfaction." In addition, unless he "finds some resolution of his conflicts (e.g., membership in Alcoholics Anonymous [AA]), his repressed traits of dependency, inferiority, and passivity become openly manifested; his attempt to maintain a façade of independent manliness collapses" (McCord & McCord, 1960, p. 156).

An eclectic orientation was used in the development of the role theory (sociobiological theory of the genesis of drug dependence) advanced by Winick (1957, 1959–60) that was further developed during the 1960s and early 1970s (e.g., see Winick, 1961a, 1961b, 1962a, 1962b, 1964, 1968, 1973, 1974a,

1974b, 1974c). This theory addressed adolescents, as well as men and women employed in various occupations (e.g., musicians, nurses, and physicians). As an eclectic theory, it implicated social psychological and sociological factors, particularly normative roles, as being central to the development of drug dependence.

LATE MODERN PERIOD (1961–95)

The 1960s

Using an epidemiological and psychoanalytic orientation, Chein and colleagues (Chein, Gerard, Lee, & Rosenfeld, 1964) advanced the now-classic disruptive environment theory. This theory examined the *Road to H* as traveled by adolescent girls and boys and young adult men and women (16–20 years of age) living in the urban areas of New York City (the Bronx, Brooklyn, and Manhattan): "'H' is for heaven; 'H' is for hell; 'H' is for heroin. In the life of the addict, these three meanings of 'H' seem inextricably intertwined" (p. 3). Two major hypotheses were put forward by Chein et al. (1964) at the beginning of their study of adolescent opiate addiction in order to "help to put the manifold characteristics of the addict in clear perspective": 1. opiate addiction was an extension of, or a development out of, long-lasting severe personality disturbance and maladjustment; and 2. opiate addiction was adaptive, functional, and dynamic (Chein et al., 1964, p. 194). Although opiate addiction for the adolescents studied appeared to be associated with a long history of maladjustment and for which structural aspects of the personality were significant, neither maladjustment nor personality structure were sufficient to account for their addiction. Thus, a third hypothesis was formulated: 3. "assuming that other conditions are favorable, *the probability of addiction is greater if the adolescent experiences changes in his situation in connection with his use of opiates, a change that can be described as adaptive, functional, or ego-syntonic* and which he describes in terms which tell us that he regards the use of opiates as worthwhile despite, or perhaps especially because of, the inconveniences and difficulties of being an addict in our society" (Chein et al., 1964, pp. 227–228). These functional or adaptive changes were conceptualized as forces operating at four levels within the adolescent: 1. level of conscious experience, 2. level of certain defenses, 3. level of unconscious process, and 4. level of psychophysiological reaction (Chein et al., 1964, p. 228).

At the *conscious level,* certain common adaptive aspects of opiate use are known to users: symptom relief, social facilitation, and the experienced high. Symptom relief was considered the most striking. Overt symptoms of anxiety, obsessive thinking, and early delusional formations are modified or eliminated. Many users reported feeling tense and restless before their initiation of opiate use, the result of which made them feel comfortable, relaxed, and peaceful. The symptom relief phenomenon was also previously reported by Lindesmith (1947) and Wikler (1953).

Another important consciously experienced phenomenon is the intoxication experience itself, the high. This experience is appreciated and enjoyed by addicts and by regular users, but only by a minority of experimental "normal" subjects. According to the theorists, the high is not, however, in any true sense a euphoria—a feeling of stimulation, happiness, or excitement (Chein et al., 1964, p. 229). Rather, it is an enjoyment of "negatives." Awareness of tension and distress is markedly reduced. Contact with reality diminishes. Ideational and fantasy activity are decreased, often blotting out a disquieting and disturbing fantasy life that is characteristic of the unintoxicated state.

At the *level of defenses,* opiate addiction is integrated into the psychological defenses of the adolescent addict. The general function of a psychic defense is to avoid anxiety. This may be accomplished by a subtle reordering of experience or by an alteration in the perception or in the manifestations of inner impulses or outer events (e.g., denial, projection, and reaction formation). Whereas level-one phenomena are to a large extent expressions of the capacity of opiates to inhibit or blunt the perception of inner anxiety and outer strain, at level two, the opiate itself is a diffuse pharmacological defense. The general structure of this integration is a mixture of projection, rationalization, and denial: "Not I, but the drug in me does these things. I am not responsible; it is the monkey on my back" (Chein et al., 1964, p. 234).

The wishes and impulses expressed through this auxiliary ego are highly individualized. In the course of the addiction, the unspeakable is spoken and that which should never be done, is done. This does not occur in diffuse, patternless, or random misbehavior, but with remarkable precision of aim and aptness to the life situations and the relationships with important people in the lives of the addicts. They do not, of course, recognize the intentions of their behavior, however obvious these intentions may be to us. It requires months of work before a patient can accept the integration of his behavior with ideas or feelings he fears to perceive or communicate. Although there is no limit to the variety of such integrations, there are a few general classes which occur frequently.

In the course of addiction, the addict may begin to express hostility toward parental figures—whom he regards as emasculating or controlling—through theft from the parental home, overt anger (becoming evil and nasty), or through the spiteful, wasteful, or destructive use of parental furnishings, money, decorations, or clothing. Even his general delinquency and the use of narcotics may contain a strong component vector aimed at his parents. By becoming an addict, he can disappoint or frustrate those parents whose hopes or ambitions for their son were of the highest. Similarly, he may use his addiction for the expression of passive-dependent wishes, e.g., by giving up or avoiding employment; begging for money and gifts; soliciting loans without attempt to repay them; and withdrawing from activities, interests, and relationships out-side his parental home. (Chein et al., 1964, pp. 234–235).

At the *level of unconsciousness*, the role of unconscious symbolism in ad-diction requires clarification. As described by the theorists:

> Dreams, neurotic symptoms, wit, and the psychopathology of everyday life are enriched or burdened by their unconscious meanings. Similarly, many aspects of the addiction experience and process are linked with and emotionally col-ored by wishes, drives, and bodily experiences pertinent to the addict's early development and relationships. With exceptions, these tend to be communi-cated or expressed symbolically in the dreams and in the art work of the pa-tients and in their responses to projective test material. . . . Dreams have the manifest content of a needle, fat, long, sticking into my body; being snowed under a mound of heroin; drinking heroin or being attacked by a monster with a huge syringe. . . . Exceptions . . . are patients who tell quite directly that the syringe and needle . . . are like a breast; when he is high, he feels that he is together with his mother, long ago, warm, comfortable, happy, at peace; when he injects the opiate solution, he mixes the solution with his blood [in the sy-ringe] and bounces the blood-opiate mixture back and forth from syringe to vein, and, as he does this, he has fantasies about intercourse. (Chein et al., 1964, pp. 235–236; see also A. M. Pagliaro et al., 1993)

According to the theorists, it is these adolescents who directly associate their addiction experiences with oral concepts and who have the most clinically evident ego disturbances; "they suffer from anxiety verging on panic or are overtly psychotic. They are least able to repress or otherwise defend them-selves against the perception of such ideas and images, and they are thus able to directly verbalize what may only be inferred from the symbolic communi-cations of the others" (Chein et al., 1964, p. 236).

However, male adolescents do not become opiate addicts simply because they have unconscious oral fantasies and cravings for breasts, sustenance, or warmth. Rather, as they become addicts, "the techniques and circumstances of drug use lend themselves as vehicles of expression for these facets of their unconscious mental processes." Although these unconscious symbolizations are less likely to be the major motivations for becoming an addict—being secondary to "the forces of conscious experience, especially the high, or the forces of the integration of the addiction in the psychic defenses" (p. 236)—they contribute importantly to the appetite for opiate use "in the same sense that spices, with their volatile oils and esters, may contribute to the appetite for otherwise prosaic foods. However, as the addiction progresses and the addict becomes increasingly involved with his addiction and correspondingly less involved in any attempt to deal with the world and current relationships, ever-larger portions of his psychic life are given over to this primitive level of gratification" (Chein et al., 1964, p. 236).

The *level of psychophysiological reaction* addresses such concepts as craving, dependence, and tolerance as developed by the theorists in relation to male adolescent opiate addiction. *Craving* is identified as a pathological phenomenon that entails recurrent states of liking, wanting, and seeking an entity but that differs from "normal" wanting, liking, and seeking in several ways. Craving implies: 1. an abnormal intensity of desire; 2. an abnormal intensification of the reaction to the failure to fulfil the desire (e.g., instead of legitimate means to satisfy the desire, there are intense emotional reactions of anger, rage, sulking, withdrawal, sullen resentment, or action aimed at getting that which is desired without regard to the consequence); and 3. an abnormal limitation in the "modifiability" of the desire (e.g., giving it up or accepting a substitute) as a result of experiences that emphasize the costs or the consequences of the satisfaction sought (Chein et al., 1964, p. 237).

Dependence, the need for opiates for the maintenance of normal physiological functioning that occurs variably with regular use, is not seen by the theorists as a conscious process. However, the *acute abstinence syndrome* is. Accordingly, when opiates are used regularly, they become essential elements of the psychological processes (enzyme systems) of the central nervous system. "Dependence is *not* associated with psychological needs or motives," but is identified as a biological process entailing the maintenance of a certain level of opiates to continue apparently normal bodily function. In this way, "the biological dependence on the opiates can be a force in the addiction process; without the opiate, the person becomes physically ill" (Chein et al., 1964, p. 247). By contrast, the *abstinence syndrome,* unlike dependence, is much influenced and modified by psychosocial factors. In the novice addict, the intensity of this self-limiting illness is far from unbearable, hardly justifying the illicit use of opiates for the relief of symptoms, particularly because each evasion of the acute abstinence syndrome intensifies the ultimate experience of the abstinence syndrome. To adolescent addicts and adolescents in the process of becoming addicts, "even this relatively minor distress is intolerable"; their "inability to act in terms of long-range goals precludes consideration of the inevitable consequences of permitting the degree of dependence to build up" (Chein et al., 1964, p. 247). For experienced addicts who depend on four or more injections of heroin a day to prevent the abstinence syndrome, "abrupt withdrawal is an unquestionably severe physiological disturbance," the intensity of which is affected by the setting in which the distress is experienced (alone or in the care of hospital staff).

Tolerance involves the body's adaptation to the effects of the opiate. According to the theorists, "tolerance is developed to the subtle emotional effects of the opiate which the addict craves. . . . He can 'keep normal' but 'can't get high.' . . . He is 'tranquilized' so long as he can avoid withdrawal symptoms, but gets 'no kicks,' and cannot 'go on the nod'" (Chein et al., 1964, p. 249). If his "life situation is particularly difficult at this point in his addiction, he will not be satisfied with keeping normal; he will strive to get high again by increasing his dosage either in frequency or in quantity." He has reached a point in a cycle of addiction at which "he cannot do more than keep normal either for economic reasons . . . or because he has become negatively adapted to the subtle emotional effects of the drugs." This type of substance user usually undergoes a few weeks of detoxification in an effort to "recapture the most valued experience of being high at a far lower level of dosage" (see Radó, 1933). "Such patterns (postponement of drug taking to enhance the effects, seeking a 'free period,' and discontent with dosage levels sufficient to merely ward off the abstinence syndrome) . . . may well provide diagnostic criteria of craving" (Chein et al., 1964, pp. 249–250).

As summarized by the theorists:

> Insofar as psychophysiological factors play a role in addiction, the primary force in initiating and intensifying a cycle of addiction is craving. Dependence is a sustaining force, both physiologically and psychologically—relevant, but clearly secondary. Tolerance is a psychophysiological phenomenon which forces either increasing dosage or a free period, i.e., a period of abstinence to recapture certain of the satisfactions of opiate intoxication. Dependence is, of course, also relevant in the noncraving types of addiction, but is again secondary in importance to the underlying motivations in the development of addiction. It may, however, play a major role in affecting the likelihood of getting into trouble. The development of tolerance is relatively unimportant in the involvement-without-craving type of addiction; in the noncraving, noninvolvement type, it plays a role in those searching for "kicks." (Chein et al., 1964, p. 250)

H. S. Becker (1967) proposed a theory of drug-induced experiences, which addressed LSD use among adolescents and adults. LSD was also the subject of S. Cohen's (1967) disinhibitory theory of LSD use. In general, these theories attempted to explain various patterns of alcohol, marijuana, LSD, and heroin use among inner city youth and would pave the way for later attention to delinquency and problem behavior.

Zuckerman proposed the *sensation-seeking scale* (designed to quantify the construct *optimal stimulation level*) with Kolin, Price, and Zoob (Zuckerman, Kolin, Price, & Zoob, 1964; see also Zuckerman & Link, 1968; Zuckerman, Persky, & Link, 1967; Zuckerman, Schultz, & Hopkins, 1967). Use of this scale assumed that: 1. individuals differ in a reliable fashion in their optimal levels of stimulation or arousal and 2. individual differences in optimal levels of stimulation or arousal are basic personality dimensions not adequately measured by then-existing tests.

The study of the trait "sensation seeking" grew out of studies on sensory deprivation (Zubek, 1969) and the attempt to define personality traits that might predict reactions to this experimental situation of reduced and restricted stimulation. As the trait was originally construed, it represented an attempt to operationalize and quantify the constructs of optimal levels of stimulation and arousal (Zuckerman, 1969) in the form of a personality questionnaire (Zuckerman et al., 1964; see also the discussion of eclectic theories of the 1980s).

The 1970s

The 1970s witnessed a proliferation in theoretical development reflecting the major disciplinary orientations of biology, psychology, and sociology. Over 30 theories were proposed during this period in an effort to explain adolescent substance use. These theories are described in relation to their major disciplinary orientations.

Biological Theories

While the biological theories developed during this period focused on neurochemical (e.g., Brecher, 1972), genetic (e.g., K. Blum, 1977; Schuckit, Goodwin, & Winokur, 1972), and other factors explaining substance use among adults, none of these theories focused specifically on children and adolescents. However, several eclectic theories were advanced that emphasized biological factors in addition to psychological and sociological factors (see the discussion of eclectic theories below).

Psychological Theories

Drive theories such as Bejerot's (1972) addiction-to-pleasure theory, B. D. Johnson's (1973) theory of drug subculture, Hochhauser's (1978a, 1978b, 1980) chronobiological control theory, and other psychological theories such as B. Segal's (1974, 1978, 1983, 1985–86) sensation-seeking motive of drug use, Mercer's (Mercer, Hundleby, & Carpenter, 1978; Mercer & Kohn, 1980; Mercer & Smart, 1974) model of adolescent drug use, and Hertzman and Bendit's (1975) depression equivalence/theory of self-destructive behavior were advanced. Existential theories (e.g., Greaves, 1974) were also proposed, along with developmental stages theories (e.g., Kandel & Faust, 1975; Kandel, Treiman, Faust, & Single, 1976). Attention was also given to developmental theories by Norem-Hebeisen and Lucas (1977), Huba and Bentler (1979, 1980; Huba, Wingard, & Bentler, 1979a, 1979b, 1980a, 1980b, 1980c), and Robins and her colleagues, who argued for a natural history of drug use (Robins, Helzer, & Davis, 1975) with attention to black youth and young men (Robins & Murphy, 1967), Vietnam veterans (Robins, 1973, 1974, 1977, 1978a, 1978b; Robins, Davis, & Wish, 1977), and nonveterans (Robins, Hesselbrock, Wish, & Helzer, 1978).[4]

Personality theories. The addiction-to-pleasure theory (Bejerot, 1972) incorporated psychoanalytic and social learning theories in explaining general

---

[4] This theory was later modified by Sadava (1984), as the generalized tendency toward psychoactive drug use.

adolescent substance use. Hendin (1973a, 1973b, 1974a, 1974b, 1974c, 1975, 1980; Hendin, Pollinger, Ulman, & Carr, 1981; Hendin & Haas, 1985) proposed his psychosocial theory of drug abuse, which addressed adolescents, as well as college students, who displayed problematic patterns of substance use, followed by the adaptational theory, both of which were rooted in psychoanalytic theory. Mercer and Smart (1974) proposed a personality and social psychology model of adolescent drug use. G. M. Smith and Fogg (G. M. Smith, 1977, 1980; G. M. Smith & Fogg, 1977, 1978, 1979) advanced a perceived effects theory focusing on general personality factors in explaining substance use among preadolescents as well as adults.

The more general personality theory proposed by Smith and Fogg addressed the use of opiates, sedative-hypnotics, amphetamines, caffeine, cocaine, nicotine, and psychedelics. Attention was given to patterns of initial through compulsive use as well as resumed nonuse and relapse ("continuation of use, escalation, cessation, and relapse") among preadolescent boys and girls, as well as adult men and women. The theorists hypothesized that: 1. whatever its amount, frequency, and pattern of use, substance use will continue until the user perceives the disadvantages of use as outweighing its benefits; and 2. influence varies directly with the clarity and certitude of the perception of each effect and with the significance attributed to it by the user.

The theory is referred to as "general" because it attempts to identify common processes and mechanisms involved in the use of a variety of "substances" by children, adolescents, and adults. Specifically, focus is on the effects of substance use as perceived by the user, whether or not those perceptions are in accord with other evidence. The theorists propose the following several stages of use and describe selected factors associated with their development: initiation (perceived benefits); well-regulated, noncompulsive use; continuation of use; cessation of use; compulsive substance use (addiction or readdiction); withdrawal; and self-perpetuation of use.

Recognizing that the satisfying and self-enhancing nature of substance use is essential to understanding the processes of initiation, continuation of use, escalation, cessation, and relapse, the theorists attempt to answer the following two questions: 1. When and how is substance use satisfying and/or self-enhancing? 2. What mechanisms enable use to continue and escalate even after its disadvantages have become substantially greater than its advantages? Question 1 is difficult to answer. In relation to question 2, the user's perceptions of the costs and benefits of his or her substance use are critically important to the determination of continuation or cessation of use. However erroneous those perceptions might be, it is believed that substance use will continue as long as the perceived aggregate benefits are valued more highly by the user than the perceived aggregate costs, a cost-benefit relationship that depends on many variables (e.g., the substance used and its strength and the frequency of its use). Other factors include the immediacy and intensity of its perceived effects, the needs that the substance is seen to satisfy or frustrate, the intensity of those needs and their centrality in the user's life, and the effects substance use has on the user's concepts of self and ideal self. Although the theory was initially developed from surveys of adolescents in the United States during the 1970s (see G. M. Smith, 1977, 1980; G. M. Smith & Fogg, 1977, 1978, 1979), no further formal theoretical development or testing has been noted (see also discussion below).

Learning theories.   Among others, the work of Bandura (1969) did much to stimulate attention to the role of social learning theory (neobehaviorism) in regard to explaining adolescent substance use.[5] Cognitive theorists in the 1970s included: S. R. Gold and Coghlan (1976), who proposed the cognitive-affective-pharmacogenic (CAP) control theory of heroin use, which addressed adolescent boys and girls accessing opiate and other treatment services in the New York City area; G. E. Barnes (1979), who proposed the theoretical causal model of adolescent solvent abuse (neobehaviorism); Frederick (1972, 1973), who proposed the learned behavior theory (drug and substance abuse as self-destructive behavior), which used concepts of Skinnerian behaviorism to address heroin and cocaine use among young adults (see also Frederick & Resnik, 1971; Frederick, Resnik, & Wittlin, 1973); G. M. Smith and Fogg (G. M. Smith, 1977, 1980; G. M. Smith & Fogg, 1977, 1978, 1979), who advanced the perceived effects theory; and Dembo and his colleagues (Dembo, Farrow, Schmeidler, & Burgos, 1979; Dembo, Pilaro, Burgos, Des Jarlais, & Schmeidler, 1979), who proposed the environmental theory of drug involvement, which addressed preadolescent boys and girls.

As developed and tested by S. R. Gold and his colleagues (S. R. Gold, 1980; S. R. Gold & Coghlan, 1975–76; Coghlan, Gold, Dohrenwend, & Zimmerman, 1973), the CAP theory emphasizes the interaction of cognitive style and the affective experience of substance use with the substance's "pharmacogenic" effects. Cognitive style is seen as the pivotal factor in a person's moving from initial use ("experimentation") to compulsive use patterns ("drug abuse"). As described by S. R. Gold (1980), substance use begins with conflict as a predisposing factor. People who have difficulty meeting the demands or expectations placed on them by themselves or others find themselves in conflict, which they experience as anxiety. The anxiety they experience, however, is not the main reason why they begin to use substances of abuse. They begin to use substances of abuse because of their interpretation of the anxiety and their perceived inability to reduce it.

According to the theory, which was developed primarily on the basis of experiences gained working with adolescent "drug abusers," adolescents who

[5]Subsequently developed as cognitive social learning theory (Bandura, 1986), this theoretical direction stimulated much later theorizing.

use substances of abuse believe that they cannot alter or control a particular situation in order to eliminate a source of anxiety. "The belief that they are powerless to cope with stress is the major cognitive distortion of drug abusers" and results in "the intense feeling of low self-esteem. . . . Feelings of self-depreciation, which form the belief that one is powerless, represent the affective component of the CAP theory" (S. R. Gold, 1980, p. 9). Because they believe they are powerless, they resort to substance use, such as heroin use, for its antianxiety and euphorogenic effects; this is the *pharmacogenic* dimension of the CAP theory. Although they find that the substances of abuse can do for them what they could not do for themselves (i.e., rid them of anxiety; provide a good feeling about themselves; and enable them to believe that they are competent, in control, and able to master their environments), the effects are temporary and users find that they must increase their use of the substance of abuse; otherwise, their previous feelings of anxiety and lack of control will not only return but will be stronger and will be accompanied by feelings of being less capable of coping on their own.

In addition to making users less tolerant of anxiety, substance use prevents them from learning more adaptive methods of coping. Thus, substance use continues with increased frequency of use and with application to an increasing number of different situations.

> For example, arguments with parents may be a primary source of conflict and anxiety for the adolescent drug abuser. Drug taking will frequently follow such an argument. An adolescent experiencing school-related stress, having learned that drug taking is an effective means of anxiety reduction, may turn to additional drug taking to compensate for academic failures. The reliance on drugs to cope with stress therefore creates a vicious cycle; the more drugs are used, the more the individual believes they are necessary. Each drug experience serves to confirm for users the belief that they are powerless to function on their own. (S. R. Gold, 1980, p. 9)

The CAP theory is seen as being consistent with cognitive models that emphasize the role of internal thoughts and beliefs in the development of maladaptive behavior. Successful treatment of substance users requires a multimodal approach aimed at altering faulty thinking, teaching new interpersonal skills, helping users cope more adaptively with anxiety, and encouraging the development of a positive self-image (S. R. Gold, 1980).

Robins's (1975) natural history of drug use, an eclectic psychological and sociological theory reflective of a decade of work (e.g., Robins, 1966, 1973, 1974, 1977, 1978a, 1978b; Robins et al., 1975, 1977, 1978), considered use of opiates, sedative-hypnotics, amphetamines, cocaine, and psychedelics. Attention was given to compulsive use patterns (opiate addiction) and polysubstance use among black youth (Robins & Murphy, 1967) and Vietnam veterans (Robins et al., 1977). The theory came about as an attempt to fashion a natural history of substance use by summarizing what was known about the circumstances of substance use (its initiation, which groups were most vulnerable, motivations for use, methods of use, and to what extent dosages tend to increase). The theorists recognized the limitations of their studies in regard to their task of attempting to construct a natural history of substance use, noting that their focus would describe only a particular historical phase of the "drug epidemics" and in this regard would be relative to time and culture.

The researchers' attention was focused on the extent to which "the natural history of drug abuse suggests that it is a disorder for which those with antisocial personalities are particularly at risk" (Robins, 1980, p. 216). As described by Robins (1980):

> The behavior of drug abusers prior to the onset of drugs resembles that of mild delinquents. They tend to be sexually active at a very young age; they tend to have committed a number of minor socially disapproved acts, such as getting into fights, truancy, getting drunk at a young age, and smoking early. Few have held full-time jobs at the time they take up drug abuse. If they delay drug use until they enter college, those in the humanities or social sciences seem more vulnerable than those in the hard sciences and mathematics. The belief system of those vulnerable to drug use has clearly been nonconformist. They are generally areligious [sic], not greatly attached to home, and generally tolerant of deviance in others. They do not, for instance, voice strong disapproval of shoplifting or truancy.
>
> The characteristics we have described not only tell us which children who have not yet used drugs are particularly liable to become drug users, but they also predict the timing of use—those with these characteristics tend to use at a younger age than those without them—and the frequency of use—those who have these characteristics tend to use more heavily than children without these characteristics even when both use drugs. . . . The present picture is a confusing one. . . . The most reasonable position at the present time seems to be that drug abuse can be part of antisocial personality, but that most drug abusers probably do not have that syndrome, since the typical drug abuser is so different in terms of IQ, social class, history of elementary school problems, and very early termination. . . . It is exposure to drugs itself that may be harmful, in addition to any underlying effects of the predisposition of the drug user. . . . I am afraid that the implications of these findings are that we must continue to rely on supply control as a chief preventive measure, until we can provide some other explanation for the adverse outcomes of those who become frequent users of illicit drugs. (pp. 219, 224)

Existential theories.   Greaves (1974, 1980), in his existential theory of drug dependence, addressed substance use among adolescents (as well as adults). He assumed A. T. Weil's (1972) assertion that the desire to alter consciousness periodically is an innate, normal drive analogous to hunger or the sexual drive. Accordingly, he hypothesized that: 1. alternative states serve an adaptive purpose to the organism; 2. it is natural to pursue such states; 3. children, because of their relative lack of rational enculturation, more readily enter some of these states; 4. people use substances of abuse to restore themselves to a state of being from which they are able to access both usual and alternate states); 5. substances of abuse, as a form of "automedication," are used in an attempt to rectify an abnormal state of personality that forms the cornerstone of all "drug dependency"; and 6. if people could access altered states to a more normal degree (in the ways people with normal personalities do) they might use substances of abuse, but they would not "abuse" them or become "dependent" on them (Greaves, 1980, p. 26). As summarized by Greaves (1980):

> Persons who become drug dependent are those who are markedly lacking in pleasurable sensory awareness, who have lost the child-like ability to create natural euphoria through active play, including recreational sex, and who, upon experimentation with drugs, tend to employ these agents in large quantities as a passive means of euphoria, or at least as a means of removing some of the pain and anxiety attending a humorless, dysphoric life style. (p. 27)

An outspoken critic of treatment programs based on "asceticism, privation, and harsh behavioral treatment," Greaves (1980) argues for programs more commensurate with his theory and its underpinnings:

> Instead of conceiving of drugs as the enemy and seeing drug abstinence as a great struggle against the enemy, to be hopefully brought about through great striving and strictly regimented behavior, we need to adopt a human growth and need-fulfillment model. We need to help persons to become the agents of their pleasure, not the passive recipients. We need to provide body-sensory awareness programs, meditation, expressive art therapy, psychotherapy. We need to turn our clients on to music, dancing, fishing, camping, boating, photography, and sex. . . . We need to help clients to realize that not only is it all right to pursue actively a wide range of pleasurable experiences, but how to. (p. 28)

Sociological Theories

By the 1970s, attention was focused increasingly on the role of the family in childhood and adolescent substance use. Several theorists turned their attention to explaining alcohol use, including Steinglass (Steinglass, Weiner, & Mendelson, 1971a, 1971b), who advanced the family systems model of alcoholism, which was later extended as the interactional model of alcoholism in families (Steinglass, Davis, & Berenson, 1977) and the simulated drinking gang experimental model for the study of a systems approach to alcoholism (Steinglass, 1975; see also Steinglass, 1979, 1980; Steinglass, Bennett, Wolin, & Reiss, 1987). Other family theorists included Stanton and his colleagues (M. D. Stanton, 1977, 1978a, 1978b, 1978c. M. D. Stanton et al., 1978), who addressed heroin use in their theory of addiction as a family phenomenon. Later work with Coleman (M. D. Stanton, 1979a, 1979b, 1979c, 1980a, 1980b, 1981, 1985, 1988; M. D. Stanton & Coleman, 1980; M. D. Stanton & Todd, 1982a, 1982b) continued the family focus with the familial interpersonal system model of addict suicide (addict as savoir model), which, also reflecting Menninger's (1938) concepts, addressed families that included "heroin addicts" and approaches to treatment. Coleman and her colleagues (Coleman, 1978, 1979a, 1979b, 1980, 1985; Coleman & Davis, 1978; Coleman & Stanton, 1978a, 1978b) advanced the incomplete mourning theory that addressed the relationship among adolescents who used substances of abuse and their family members. These theories emphasized the notion that adolescent substance use serves a "family function"— as a system, families encourage adolescent substance use because it serves a role in maintaining "balance" in the family. As explained by Stanton and Coleman (1980):

> Addiction, then, can be seen as part of a *death-related continuum*. Different self-destructive behaviors rest at various points along it according to their severity. From this viewpoint, the distinction between ISDB [indirect self-destructive behavior] and more direct actions may be more apparent than real. These two facets may differ more in a quantitative than a qualitative sense. In fact, such a dichotomy may even be misleading if taken too literally. Addiction is a way of travelling along the continuum without necessarily reaching the end point, i.e., of responding to the wishes of significant others without total surrender. It can serve as a means for at least partially fulfilling the family "death wish" while avoiding complete demise. . . .
>
> . . . [The homeostatic model] is based on a linear model in which a causal chain of events occurs, e.g., premature loss by parent of grandparent leads to the fear of separation by parent(s), thence to dependence on offspring, then to fear of loss of offspring, consequent disallowance of autonomy, emergent drug use by offspring, etc. It does not take into account the complex set of feedback mechanisms involved in the drug-taking process and the repetitive cycles that evolve. It tends to "blame" parents or even the whole family rather than recognizing that all are involved in a sequence of behaviors. . . . The sequence, not just the drug-taking, serves some kind of change-resistant, or homeostatic, function. Moreover, this kind of sequence does not represent causality in the usual sense but is a cycle. Each person's behavior is influenced by the behavior of the other person, and influences their behaviors in turn. . . . [What is needed is a] sort of nonlinear model . . . [that conceptualizes] what is happening within the interpersonal system at the present time. (pp. 197–198)

Other sociological theories included: that advanced by Lukoff (1972, 1974, 1977; see also Lukoff, 1980); the cross-cultural theory proposed by Zinberg and Harding (1979), social control theory; and deviance theories such as H. B. Kaplan's (1975a, 1975b, 1980a, 1980b) general theory of deviant behavior, Akers's (1977; Akers, Krohn, Lanza-Kaduce, & Radosevich, 1979) social learning theory of deviant behavior, and Gorsuch and Butler's (1976a, 1976b) multiple models theory.

Lukoff (1980), building on his earlier work (Lukoff, 1972, 1974, 1977) and on the work of others (e.g., Jessor & Jessor, 1977) argued "that the key social structural feature associated with drug use is found in the one unambiguous association, that of illicit substance use with young people"—that is, with age, rather than with social class or ethnic group. He also held the view that "it is less useful to speak of drug use alone, because those who are heavily invested in drug use are also part of more integrated lifestyles, different in the ghettos than on the campuses, but at variance with many aspects of conventional adult culture" (Lukoff, 1980, p. 211). He suggests that for those youth who begin marijuana use when they are young and use it with reasonable frequency, the evidence is consistent with the theme that illicit substance use is not an isolated phenomenon but must be understood in a larger context. According to Lukoff, a process of disengagement from conventional values and norms precedes initiation, suggesting that "sources of the rapid escalation" of substance use "are located in the forces that influence the declining legitimacy of conventional norms and values and agents of social control, on the one hand, and in the structural forces that increase the opportunity for younger people to operate with greater freedom outside the confines of the usual [social] control mechanism," on the other. As such, substance use and the "attendant cultural prescriptions represent a process of social change" (Lukoff, 1980, p. 211).

B. D. Johnson (1973) advanced the theory of drug subculture (in which the "youthful society classification" consists of parent culture, peer culture, and drug subculture), focusing on a sociological orientation in an effort to explain alcohol, amphetamine, and marijuana use by adolescents and young adults (11–25 years of age). Focusing specifically on "illicit drug use," the theory emerges from middle-range theories in criminology and deviant behavior, with attention to fundamental sociological concepts (e.g., values, norms, and roles). The theory is "distinctly sociological" and does not attempt to incorporate biological or psychological orientations and insights about substance use, although overlaps with these disciplinary orientations are suggested (B. D. Johnson, 1980, p. 111).

Eclectic Theories

Winick (1973, 1974a, 1974b, 1974c) advanced the role theory (a sociological theory of the genesis of drug dependence). Based on a psychological (social psychology) and sociological orientation, the theory addressed opiate, sedative-hypnotic, amphetamine, and psychedelic use (nonuse to compulsive use, resumed nonuse, and relapsed use) among adolescents, as well as adults (musicians, nurses, and physicians).

Winick hypothesized that: 1. all points of taking on new roles or all points of being tested for adequacy in a role are likely to be related to role strain and thus to a greater incidence of drug dependence in a group; 2. incompatible demands within one role, such as between two roles in the same role set, are likely to lead to a greater incidence of drug dependence; and 3. the amount of role strain is a function of various factors, so that the larger the volume of properties of a role set, the greater the potential for strain. A *role* is a set of expectations and behaviors associated with a specific position in a social system. A *role strain* is a felt difficulty in meeting the obligations of a role. *Role deprivation* is the reaction to the termination of a significant role relationship (Winick, 1980, p. 226).

The theory suggests that drug dependence will tend to cease among a population or subgroup when: 1. access to the substances declines; 2. negative attitudes to their use become salient; and 3. role strain and/or deprivation are less prevalent. If all three of these trends are operative, rather than only one or two trends, the rate of drug dependence will decline more rapidly (Winick, 1980). The theory views relapse as reflecting the person's inability to sustain the role nonuser. Each period of abstinence may represent a person's trying out of the role of nonuser.[6]

In order to test directly the predictive ability of the theory, Winick (1974a) developed a role inventory for adolescents, which was administered to 1,311 high school juniors in New York City. As Winick (1980) noted, "There is good reason to expect that the adolescent years will be heavily complicated because of the ambiguity of the status of adolescents in our society, who have lost the role of children but are not yet able to assume an adult role" (p. 227). In a large-scale study of the life cycle of addiction (Winick, 1964), it was concluded that "its genesis was concentrated during the years of late adolescence and early adulthood because of the role strain stemming from decisions about sex, adult responsibility, social relationships, family situations, school, and work, as well as from role deprivation resulting from the loss of familiar patterns of behavior" (Winick, 1980, p. 228).[7] Reflecting the later

---

[6] An earlier formulation of the theory argued that drug-dependent people mature out of substance use when there is a lessening of the role pressures that had led to the beginning of regular substance use (Winick, 1962a). The process of maturing out is slow and typically involves a stop-start pattern of substance use until the person feels comfortable with the role of nonuser. This way of ceasing substance use was the most frequent and probably remains the most prevalent form of termination of regular substance use. In the original study that led to the formulation of the maturing out theory, based on a national sample, the mean age of maturing out was 35 years (Winick, 1962a). The narrow clustering of age (around 35 years of age) at maturing out in different samples at different times suggests, according to the theorist, that there are underlying regularities in the process.

[7] According to Winick (1980), many other existing theories of drug dependence among young people can be constructively interpreted in terms of the theory of role strain/deprivation, access, and attitudes, including Cloward and Ohlin (1960; delinquents), Finestone (1957; Chicago heroin addicts), Jessor and Jessor (1973, 1978; Colorado marijuana users), and Chein et al. (1964; New York City addicts). The theory can also explain the high incidence of drug dependence in a variety of groups: Native Americans (see Spindler, 1952), soldiers in Vietnam (see Robins, 1973), college students (see Groves, 1974; Marra, 1967; McKenzie, 1969; Suchman, 1968; Winick, 1973), jazz musicians (see Winick, 1959–60, 1961b, 1962b), physicians (see Winick, 1961a), and nurses (see Winick, 1974a). The theory has been successfully used to clarify the reasons for

emphasis of Zoja (1989) on the importance of initiation and ritual, Winick (1980), citing his earlier work (Winick, 1968), explained:

> Americans have increasingly been deprived of significant role-related ritual experiences that help in the achievement of an emotional state that could bridge the gap between old and new. The role-related ritual helped to give meaning to the conclusion of one phase of the life cycle and the commencement of another, providing a sense of community and publicly affirming the subject's social and personal identity and the move from one age and status group to another. As modern American rites of passage have become more subdued, people have had a lesser role identity and less opportunity to develop a sense of self. Insufficiently graded sequences of role positions through which people move may be dysfunctional and could be related to the onset of drug dependence. (p. 229)

Zinberg and Harding (1979) argued for the social control theory, which addressed "illicit" substance use among adolescents and adults, with a focus on controlled use. The "decision to use an intoxicant, the effects it has on the user, and the ongoing psychological and social implications of that use depend not only on the pharmaceutical properties of the intoxicant [the drug] and the attitudes and personality of the user [the set], but also on the physical and social setting in which such use takes place" (Zinberg, 1980, p. 236). Attention is given to the precise ways in which the setting influences both use itself and the effects of use, acting either in a positive way to help to control use or in a negative way to weaken control. The focus of the theory is on the mechanisms of control ("natural" processes of social learning) developed within the social setting and the internalization of social sanctions (informal and formal norms defining whether and how a particular substance should be used, such as "Don't drink and drive") and rituals (stylized, prescribed behavior patterns surrounding the use of a substance, such as "Let's have a drink") and how these mechanisms become active in controlling use.

> Centuries of experience with intoxicants point clearly to social control, not prohibition, as the only humane and reasonably successful means of managing their use. Social control means that a society permits the use of intoxicants under various legal restraints and develops various customs, rituals, and social sanctions which define *acceptable use*. The elements which comprise social control are often unarticulated and nonspecific, thus allowing for regional, ethnic, and class diversity. From early childhood individuals learn both consciously and unconsciously about the acceptable use of intoxicants. Support for use and

---

the increase in drug dependence in the three countries that experienced the most thoroughly documented post–World War II epidemics: Japan (amphetamines; see Brill & Hirose, 1969), Switzerland (analgesic compounds containing phenacetin, caffeine, and a hypnotic drug), and Sweden (amphetamines; see Goldberg, 1968).

reinforcement against abuse continue throughout adult life, as use is normalized with other life activities. . . . Despite the lack of larger cultural support for controlled illicit drug use and other obstacles, users are able to develop and maintain moderate, long-term, nonabusive, i.e., controlled, drug using patterns . . . primarily supported by the development of social drug-using situations in which sanctions and rituals permit use while condemning abuse. (Zinberg, Jacobson, & Harding, 1975, pp. 165–166)

The argument of social control theory was developed during the 1970s (see Harding, Zinberg, Stelmack, & Barry, 1980; Zinberg, 1971, 1972a, 1972b, 1974a, 1974b, 1975, 1979; Zinberg & DeLong, 1974; Zinberg & Fraser, 1979; Zinberg & Harding, 1979; Zinberg, Harding, Stelmack, & Marblestone, 1978; Zinberg, Harding, & Winkeller, 1977; Zinberg & Jacobson, 1976; Zinberg, Jacobson, & Harding, 1975; Zinberg & Robertson, 1972) against the backdrop of the counterculture movement (Zinberg, 1980; see also Barr, Langs, Holt, Goldberger, & Klein, 1972; H. S. Becker, 1967; Huxley, 1960; Robbins, Frosch, & Stern, 1967; Robbins, Robbins, Frosch, & Stern, 1967; A. T. Weil, 1972) and the Vietnam War (see Robins, 1973, 1974, 1977, 1978b). The evidence presented supports the recommendation that theories attempting to explain substance use must address drug, set, and setting and that research attention must be given to understanding "how the specific characteristics of the drug and the personality of the user interact and are modified by the social setting and its controls" (Zinberg, 1980, p. 244).

The interactive models of nonmedical drug use, or multiple model theory, proposed by Gorsuch and Butler (1976a, 1976b; see also Butler, 1980) emphasize multiple pathways to substance use with a particular focus on multiple stages of drug involvement (initial use, continual use, and addiction). The theory assumes that initial substance use and the development of more problematic patterns of use probably have different causes. Three independent models—1. nonsocialized drug users model, 2. prodrug socialization model, and 3. iatrogenic model—are described. For example, the prodrug socialization model assumes that there are prodrug socializing agents in the child's or adolescent's immediate environment that provide easy access to substances of abuse and opportunity and models for their use. In contrast, the iatrogenic model explains the primary motivation for initial substance use as physical pain or mental anguish which leads the child or adolescent to self-prescribe the substance of abuse. In the former, the substance is used when life is going well; in the latter, when it is going poorly.

In the late 1970s, Huba and Bentler proposed the developmental theory of drug use (domain theory) addressing genetic, personality, and learning factors as important in adolescent drinking and other behaviors (e.g., gambling and overeating). Later, Huba, Wingard, and Bentler (1979a, 1979b, 1980a, 1980b, 1980c) proposed the interactive theory of drug use to explain adolescent alcohol, cocaine, PCP, and marijuana use.[8] Other classic work during this period included Jessor and Jessor's (1977b) problem behavior theory, which considered substance use patterns among Anglo, Hispanic, and Ute Indian adolescents in Colorado from personality (interactionism), neobehaviorism, and anomie perspectives. Akers (1977; Akers et al., 1979) addressed the general use of substances of abuse by adolescent boys and girls living in the midwestern United States in his social learning theory of deviant behavior.

Hochhauser (1978a, 1978b, 1978c, 1980) considered heroin, alcohol, and other sedative-hypnotic use among adolescents, as well as adults and the elderly, in his chronobiological control theory, which integrated biological (metabolic and neurochemical) and psychological theories. Hochhauser (1978b) argued:

> The adolescent differs in many ways from the older drug user. . . . The period of adolescence is characterized by significant internal changes: hormonal changes, brain maturation, cognitive development, etc. As a potential consequence of these changes, it may be that the adolescent responds uniquely to drugs consumed during these critical periods. . . . Such internal changes will significantly affect the adolescent's response to the environment, both in terms of behavioral events (the development of helpless behaviors) and chemical events (the use of drugs as agents of control). (pp. 67–68)

Assuming that substances of abuse may be used as agents of control:

1. Drug use may represent an initial attempt to achieve some degree of internal control over perceptions of helplessness . . . [and] may be a relatively quick and effective means of obtaining such control, especially when other control measures are unavailable;
2. If a drug is used for control and is found effective, then its use will probably escalate, as the individual may develop a relatively predictable and controllable method of coping;
3. Dependency may develop if there are no other effective coping mechanisms available;
4. Depending upon the addictive liability of the drug, addiction may occur with continued use, as the physiological consequences of the drug (e.g., withdrawal symptoms) may eventually establish control over the user. . . . Addicts may seek treatment, since they are no longer using the drug for control; rather, they are being controlled by the drug. (Hochhauser, 1980, p. 267)

Hochhauser (1978c), developing his theory further, argues:

> Chronobiology may affect the development and maintenance of alcohol and drug abuse problems, insofar as an individual's response to a particular chemi-

---

[8] This work was followed by Huba, Wingard, and Bentler's (1981a) latent variable causal model of adolescent drug use, which focused on alcohol, amphetamine, cocaine, hallucinogen, heroin, marijuana, and "tranquilizer" use among adolescents.

cal substance will be a function of several chronobiological variables: time of day, light-dark cycles, sleep-wake patterns, and other intrinsic biochemical rhythms.

Consequently, an accurate analysis of alcohol and drug abuse problems requires not only an understanding of the psychopharmacological properties of the particular drugs involved, but a corresponding awareness of the drug user's unique responsivity to that drug, insofar as such responses may be rhythmically determined. Such an analysis is necessary to account for individual variations in the acquisition and continuation of alcohol and drug problems, since not only will the biological rhythm determine, in part, the effect of a given drug, but a drug may well affect the biological rhythm itself. (p. 855)

Numerous experiments have shown that both animal and human behavior vary as a function of such rhythms and that the effects of a substance of abuse may be particularly sensitive to changes in chronobiological rhythms. If substance use is viewed as a possible form of self-medication (i.e., an agent of control or "regulating device"), then it is conceivable that some substance use represents an attempt on the part of the user to induce artificially certain rhythmic patterns where none have existed before or perhaps to reestablish such patterns when they have been lost.

Rather than studying only retrospective patterns of substance use (e.g., what substance of abuse was used and how often it had been used in the past), the research focus is on *when* a given substance was used and on its long-term chronobiological patterns of use. (E.g., heroin users may use heroin in an attempt to maintain some rhythm in their physiological and psychological functioning. Death from a barbiturate or heroin overdose, according to this theory, might be due in part to when the substance was used; if it was used at a time of maximal susceptibility within the chronobiological rhythm, the effect may have been quite different than if it had been used during a time of minimal susceptibility—the individual might have survived.) As such, substances of abuse may be used as agents of control that permit users to exert some degree of internal control over their perceptions of helplessness. As summarized by Hochhauser (1980):

Significant psychological and physiological changes occur during adolescence, and the effect of drugs upon such developmental changes is largely unknown. Studies of adolescent drug abuse suggest, however, that depression is often a characteristic variable associated with drug abuse and that the inability to cope with stressful experiences may play a significant role in the development of drug dependence. The interrelationship between changing chronobiological rhythms, perceptions of internal control, and drug abuse must be more clearly defined. (p. 267)

The Iowa theory of substance abuse among hyperactive adolescents proposed by Loney and his colleagues in 1978 is another eclectic theory, which uses neurochemical and behavioristic factors to explain general substance use among youth. However, their focus is on youth identified as hyperactive.[9] Loney, his cotheorists Langhorne and Paternite, and others hypothesized that both childhood aggression and hyperactivity are psychological traits rather than psychiatric disorders. Individual children are susceptible to subsequent substance use as a result of childhood aggression; they are not susceptible to substance use because of childhood hyperactivity, either directly or indirectly (through the effect of hyperactivity on aggression). In their studies (Loney, Langhorne, & Paternite, 1978), the anticipated link between early hyperactivity and later delinquency was found to be missing. Although adolescent aggression was apparently exacerbated by negative environmental events, it did not appear to be a secondary result of primary or core hyperactivity. Rather, the link appears to be between early aggression and later delinquency; thus, childhood aggression was seen to be apparently primary. Thus, hyperactive children are not at risk for later substance use unless they are also aggressive; however, aggressive children are at risk for later substance use whether they are hyperactive or not (Loney, 1980, p. 133). Langhorne and Loney (1979) recommended that hyperactive children be prognostically separated in relation to aggressiveness from those who are exclusively hyperactive.

As further explained by Loney (1980):

> Childhood aggression and childhood hyperactivity are assumed to have different antecedents and different consequents both at referral and at followup. If valid, this theory also explains why treatment with central nervous system stimulants does not lead to improved adolescent behavior and reduced delinquency [see G. Weiss, Kruger, Danielson, & Ellman, 1975]. Although drug treatment reduces childhood inattention and hyperactivity, behavior outcome and subsequent delinquency are determined instead by childhood aggression and by its ecological antecedents—which are not affected by drug treatment. Thus, drug treatment for childhood hyperactivity is ineffective in reducing adolescent symptomatology because childhood hyperactivity is *not* the first link in a chain leading to teenage delinquency and deviant behavior. (p. 134)

Jessor and Jessor advanced the problem behavior theory (1977), which was derived from differential opportunity perspective (Cloward & Ohlin, 1960), field theory (Lewin, 1951; Yinger, 1965), anomie formulations (Merton, 1957), and social learning theory (Rotter, 1954; Rotter, Chance, & Phares, 1972). Classified as an eclectic theory integrating psychological (personality/learning/social psychology) and sociological (anomie orientations), the theory attempted to address alcohol and psychedelic (marijuana) use (as well as other deviant behavior) among adolescents. The theory revised and

---

[9] This mental disorder, currently referred to as "attention deficit hyperactivity disorder" (ADHD), has also been called "hyperkinesia" and "minimal brain dysfunction."

extended the earlier work of Jessor, Graves, Hanson, and Jessor (1968) and Jessor, Collins, and Jessor (1972).

The Tri-Ethnic Project, as summarized by Sadava (1987), studied adolescents of Anglo-American, Ute Indian, and Hispano-American backgrounds living in a small town in Colorado. Jessor, Graves, et al. (1968) sought to explain both intergroup differences and intragroup individual differences in deviant behavior within one integrated theoretical framework. Differences in ethnic group rates of problem drinking and other deviance were explained in terms of a set of group characteristics, a *sociocultural system*. Differences between individual adolescents in problem drinking, apart from their group membership, were explained in terms of a set of relevant individual characteristics, a *personality system*. Finally, linkages between characteristics of groups and of individuals were explained through relevant characteristics and practices of parents, a *socialization system* (the process by which a sociocultural system is transmitted to the adolescent and becomes incorporated within the individual as a personality system). Thus, by a set of logical linkages, person and environment were combined to form a field theory of problem drinking.[10] In contrast to subsequent work by R. Jessor, here the environment is conceived and measured as external to the perception of the person.[11] Jessor and Jessor (1977) describe their theory and its development:

> The study reported in this book is the second phase of a long-term program of research on problem behavior. Like the earlier study from which it grew, it has taken nearly a decade. . . . Initiated toward the end of the 1960s in the midst of the turmoil that marked that period of American history, the research focused on problem behavior in youth—on drug use, sexual activity, drinking and the problem use of alcohol, activism and protest, and deviant behavior generally. Our aim was to see whether a contribution could be made to understanding what was happening among young people by applying the theoretical perspectives developed in our earlier work. That perspective—problem-behavior theory—is from the intersection of the fields of social psychology, developmental psychology, and the psychology of personality. . . . The approach to theory testing involved a longitudinal design, a method that enabled us to follow the lives of young people over a significant portion of their adolescent years. It made it possible to plot trajectories of change over time in personality, the social environment, and behavior, and to use the theory to forecast important transitions—beginning to drink, starting to use marijuana, becoming a nonvirgin. Thus, in addition to learning more about the areas of behavior that occasioned the study, it became possible to see them as an integral part of psychosocial growth and development. (pp. xiii–xiv)

[10] As noted by Sadava (1987), extending several theories and a broad literature in developmental psychology, while the concepts and variables were not novel, and their individual relationships to problem drinking and deviant behavior were well established, their integration into a coherent multidisciplinary theory represented a new contribution (p. 95).

[11] The theory also was later extended by Sadava (1984), Orford (1985), and Tonkin (1987).

Among their results, the theorists conclude:

In relation to the personality system as a whole, the adolescent who is less likely to engage in problem behavior is one who values academic achievement and expects to do well academically, who is not concerned much with independence, who treats society as unproblematic rather than as deserving of criticism and reshaping, who maintains a religious involvement and is more uncompromising about transgression, and who finds little that is positive in problem behavior relative to the negative consequences of engaging in it. The adolescent who is more likely to engage in problem behavior shows an opposite personality pattern—a concern with personal autonomy, a relative lack of interest in the goals of conventional institutions (such as school and church), a jaundiced view of the larger society, and a more tolerant attitude about transgression.

The most salient finding about the perceived environment system is the powerful contribution it made to the explanation of variation in problem behavior. . . . Within the distal structure of perceived environment, the variables that indicate whether a youth is parent oriented or peer oriented are the most significant. In the proximal structure, the variables referring to peer models and support for problem behavior are most important. Together they suggest the character of a problem-prone environment; adolescents who are likely to engage in problem behavior perceive less compatibility between the expectations that their parents and their friends hold for them, they acknowledge greater influence of friends relative to parents, they perceive greater support for problem behavior among their friends, and they have more friends who provide models for engaging in problem behavior. (Jessor & Jessor, 1977, p. 237)

Zucker (1976) proposed a heuristic model for pathways of parent influence on the child's drinking, a psychological, personality (interactionism) theory, and extended work begun in the 1960s and work examining problem drinking among adolescent girls (Zucker & Devoe, 1975; see also Wilsnack & Wilsnack, 1979). Attention is given to adolescent alcohol use based on the assumption that the specifics connected with drinking are best understood by examining specific drinking influences in the child's environment. The model was further developed with attention to influencing structures affecting drinking behavior over developmental time by Zucker (1979), Zucker and Noll (1982), and Zucker et al. (1984).

Several concepts are identified, including: child's drinking, behavior system, need, and personality; family status (lifestyle, community involvement, and religious value influences on family) and environmental factors; parents' socioeconomic factors, behaviors (drinking, personality, and child-rearing), belief structures, ethnicity, interaction; and peer behavior, including peer choice relevant to drinking and peer deviance. The theory proposed offers a model for exploring the relationships among these direct and indirect parental influences and other personal and social factors associated with a child's alcohol use (Zucker, 1976, pp. 214–215). As such it provides: 1. an organizational framework for the multivariate determinants of adolescent alcohol use; 2. a heuristic device for the study of changes over time, particularly those of psychosocial development before, during, and after adolescence; and 3. a conceptual framework for several analytic reviews of the literature on adolescent drinking (e.g., Zucker, 1976, 1979). A multilevel influencing process within the family is proposed, with evidence supporting a multiple-pathway model of parental influence on heavy or abusive use of alcohol by youth. If earlier influencing processes are more severe, then later compensatory influences are less likely to have an effect. In detailing this process, two basic functions of the family as a group are distinguished: 1. *group maintenance functions* (those concerned with continuation of affectional relationships of a group) and 2. *task-oriented functions* (those concerned with socialization of offspring).

Zucker (1976) argues:

> The fact that developmental influences and parent socialization practices relating to the problem use of alcohol are best understood not in a medical framework but in a deviancy one makes the issue of intervention a difficult one. Physicians who encounter problems that are developmental markers of high risk, in either the parents or the children, are faced with several difficult problems. Since high-risk parenting has its most intimate connections with socialization for deviancy, high-risk signs are more likely to show themselves earlier in other contexts than the physician's office. Pediatric practice in the later years of middle childhood may encounter some, but earlier manifestations are far more likely to appear in marital counselors' offices and in contacts with clergymen, with employers, with welfare agency personnel, with the [teacher] principal, and occasionally in street contact with the police. Where high-risk signs for parents appear . . . it is likely that the situation has already gone too far for much in the way of effective intervention. . . . Given these difficulties and the reality that parenting behavior is still viewed as no one but the parents' responsibility in our society, those concerned with intervention are faced with three questions: What can be done? With whom? At what ages? . . . In fact, if deviancy theory is correct . . . to the extent that greater access to the opportunity structure is opened up (via job satisfaction, increasingly successful school performance, increased religious involvement, improved affectional patterns in the family) and the high-risk individual is able to perceive and respond to it, deviancy proneness and alcohol-abuse problems should be reduced. (pp. 234–235)

Focusing on psychological and sociocultural factors, Dembo (1979) proposed the environmental theory of drug involvement. This theory used personality and sociocultural factors to explain general substance use, including opiate, alcohol, solvent and inhalant, amphetamine, cocaine, LSD, and marijuana use, among black and Puerto Rican adolescent boys and girls living in the inner city.[12] Another of the few theories that addressed solvent use was

---

[12] This work was followed by Dembo and Shern's (1982) theoretical framework of relative deviance and processes of drug involvement.

that proposed by G. E. Barnes (1979), who focused on Native American adolescents in his theoretical (causal) model of adolescent solvent abuse, with attention to Wyse's (1973) four-stage theory of symptoms associated with inhalation of hydrocarbons.

As computerized data analysis became popularized, several other new directions were taken, including Huba and colleagues' interactive theory of drug use (Huba & Bentler, 1979, 1980; Huba et al., 1979a, 1979b, 1980a, 1980b, 1980c).

The 1980s

> Despite the length of time that this disorder [problematic patterns of substance use] has been known its origins are still not clearly understood, although recent decades of research have clarified the problem considerably [*sic*]. We know, for example, that alcoholism is a problem that frequently runs in families (Cotton, 1979). There is an accumulating and substantial body of literature that implicates genetic factors, and hence individual differences in biochemical factors as important elements in the etiological chain (Cloninger, Bohman, & Sigvardsson, 1981; Alterman & Tartar, 1983). Sociocultural differences in attitudes toward alcohol and individual differences in the availability of situations where alcohol is accessible clearly also play a role. What is currently missing in this puzzle, that is the research problem of the eighties, is the specification of the extent to which each of these elements is contributory, and the understanding of the way that these elements unfold and fit together over the life span of the individual. After all, even a toddler with a heavy genetic loading that predisposes toward alcoholism, growing up in a family where there is steady exposure to a heavy drinking environment, does not become alcoholic overnight. It may take 15 to 20 years, and some children even manage to totally avoid this tragic outcome. (Zucker et al., 1984, pp. 1–2)

While theorizing during the 1960s and 1970s was aimed at identifying the antecedents of adolescent and adult substance use, theorists during the 1980s began to focus increasingly on ethnicity, socioeconomic class, and other factors as they extended the pioneering work of Robins (e.g., Robins, 1978b; Robins et al., 1978) and others (e.g., Brook, Lukoff, & Whiteman, 1977a, 1977b, 1978, 1980). The majority of these theorists embraced positivistic views of science and sought to produce knowledge that would be cumulative and progressive (i.e., a unitary theory). However, as the limitations of positivism were increasingly acknowledged, other theorists embraced the assumptions inherent in early and late postpositivism. As ethnographies and narratives developed prominence amid the struggles of positivism to predict and control phenomena, several theorists, seemingly in anticipation of postmodern science, espoused nonrational and nonlogical explanations of why adolescents came to use or not use substances of abuse. The attempts of these various theorists are presented in this section.

Several prominent theorists made significant contributions during the 1980s. For example, developing the original work of Glueck and Glueck (1950, 1968), Vaillant (1983a) advanced his disease theory, the natural history of alcoholism. Other longitudinal work was completed by H. B. Kaplan et al. (1984) on the longitudinal model of adoption of drug use. Significant work addressing delinquency was produced by Orford (1985), who advanced his psychological model of excessive appetites. During this decade, biological theories continued to ignore adolescents per se, but a number of psychological and sociological theories were produced, including Elliott, Huizinga, and Ageton's (1985) integrated theory of delinquency and drug use. Eclectism, however, was king during the 1980s.

Biological Theories

Vaillant's (1983a, 1983b, 1983c, 1989/1992) natural history of alcoholism emphasized the illness/disease conceptualization of alcoholism with attention to college sophomores and Boston schoolboys. Focus was on initial use to compulsive use, resumed nonuse, and relapsed use. Based on the general assumptions inherent in illness/disease theories and medical practice, seven questions were posed for longitudinal study: 1. Is alcoholism a symptom or a disease? 2. Does alcoholism get progressively worse? 3. Before they begin to abuse alcohol, are alcoholics different from nonalcoholics? 4. Rather than being counterproductive, is abstinence a necessary goal of treatment for alcoholism? 5. Is a return to safe social drinking possible for alcoholics? 6. Does treatment alter the natural history of alcoholism? 7. Is AA helpful in the treatment of alcoholism?

A prospective longitudinal study, involving over 660 subjects (204 upper-middle-class elite college men and 456 less-privileged inner city boys of high school age), was conducted over 40 years (1940–80). A clinical sample of 100 alcohol-dependent men and women admitted for detoxification were also selected and followed for 8 years. Data collected included alcohol use data and life data. As noted by Vaillant (1983a), the development of the theory actually began during the late 1930s in that his sample included the sample obtained by Sheldon and Eleanor Glueck at the Harvard Law School for their study of juvenile delinquency (the Core City sample). Vaillant obtained a control (the college sample) by using the sample taken by Clark Heath and Arlie Bock at Harvard University Health Services, who were associated with the Grant Study of Adult Development. In 1972, the two research groups came together under the auspices of the Harvard Medical School as the Study of Adult Development. The research group, of which Vaillant was a member, attempted to contrast medical and social models of alcoholism in an effort to see whether they are congruent. The researchers concluded that alcoholism is a continuum of negative consequences, one end of which can best be viewed as a disease. Vaillant (1983a) recognized that the answer to the question, Why do people use alcohol? requires formal study so that rational treatment for alcoholism can be provided. "Information should come from meticulously conducted, long-term prospective studies, studies in which subjects are selected for study before they develop problems with alcohol and then followed for many years." In this regard, cross-sectional studies would not be able to adequately "capture the genesis of alcoholism" (p. 2).

Vaillant (1989/1992) reported the results of his multivariate analyses of data from a 33-year prospective study of the 456 nondelinquent controls from the Gluecks' delinquency study concluding that "both environment and genes may make important and quite different contributions to alcoholism":

> The data suggest that presence or absence of South European ethnicity (perhaps as a result of attitudes toward alcohol use and abuse) and the number of alcoholic relatives (perhaps more due to heredity rather than environment) accounted for most of the variance in adult alcoholism explained by childhood variables. Premorbid antisocial behavior also added significantly to the risk of alcoholism. However, an unstable family environment was a more important predictor of whether an individual loses control of alcohol at an early age and/ or has multiple symptoms, than whether he has many alcoholic relatives. (p. 71)

Although genetic effects in relation to substance use have not been entirely consistent across all studies, the bulk of the evidence, using adoption and twin methodologies, clearly indicates that "something is there." Research during this period began to refine the basic finding of increased risk, examining gender differences and potential multiple lines and types of genetic influences (see Alterman, 1987; Cloninger, 1987). Most studies showed specific risk for the development of alcoholism among boys, particularly when associated with sociopathy in their fathers.

A number of studies extended this line of research, including those of sons of alcoholics who are at high risk for developing alcoholism. This methodology seeks to elucidate differences between sons of alcoholics and sons of nonalcoholics that might mediate differences in risk status (see, e.g., the review by Sher, 1987). A variety of potential factors have been studied including alexithymia, cognitive style, electroencephalogram evoked potentials, impulsivity, learning, personality, and reasoning. In the area of personality, children of alcoholics tend to show patterns of behavioral undercontrol, or impulsivity, that have previously been associated with prospective risk for alcoholism (Zucker & Lisansky Gomberg, 1986). These differences have been replicated in several prospective studies (e.g., W. M. Cox, 1987; Zucker & Lisansky Gomberg, 1986) and have been incorporated into genetic theories of alcoholism proposed by such theorists as Cloninger (1987). This dimension of impulsivity appears to be one of the most significant personality characteristics that has been consistently associated with later addiction problems (W. M. Cox, 1987; Zucker & Lisansky Gomberg, 1986).

Another line of research has been the study of the responses to alcohol of children of alcoholics. Alcohol absorption, metabolism, and endocrine response may reflect genetic differences, as noted by Sher (1987). Sons of alcoholics seem to experience less subjective intoxication after consuming alcohol (for reviews see Newlin & Thomson, 1990; Sher 1987). Theoretically, those with less subjective intoxication will drink more to produce a desired effect, thus increasing the risk for addiction.

Sher and Levenson (1982), in a study in which subjects were exposed to a stressor, first demonstrated that individuals at risk for alcoholism, as assessed by personality type, exhibited attenuation of heart rate increase after consuming alcohol. Young adult sons of alcoholics also were shown to have similar attenuation of heart rate responses after consumption of alcohol when compared to children of nonalcoholics (Finn & Pihl, 1987, 1988; Levenson, Oyama, & Meek, 1987). Finn and Pihl (1988) have also shown that subjects with generational alcoholism on the father's side most clearly show the dampening effect.[13]

Psychological Theories

Personality theories. One of the few theories extended from Jungian psychoanalytic theory was proposed by Spotts and Shontz (1982, 1985), the theory of psychological individuation (theory of adolescent substance abuse). The theory addressed the use of opiates, sedative-hypnotics (barbiturates), amphetamines, and cocaine.

The representative case method (see Spotts & Shontz, 1980b) embraced and developed by the theorists requires an "intensive, holistic study of persons, who are not sampled from a population but are deliberately sought out because they epitomize a condition of theoretical or practical interest, or present an extraordinarily clear opportunity to critically examine hypotheses about an important human state or problem" (Spotts & Shontz, 1985, p. 119). As noted by the theorists, generalization proceeds from individuals who are studied as whole people to other individuals who are studied as whole people, not from individuals to group means, and thus findings take into account the "complexity and uniquenesses" of personal psychological structures. The method was also considered to be "a powerful and cost efficient way to conduct 'clinical' studies of individuals," and although the method does not primarily describe populations or test specific hypotheses, it generates findings that are particularly useful to practitioners who deal with people

---

[13] It is noteworthy that the dampening of the stress response can reinforce drinking without implying motivations for the modulation of negative affect or stress. Young people seldom report that they drink to cope with stress, yet stress is understood by most people as a negative experience. Conceptually, many positive settings create generalized stress (e.g., dating and parties). Most generally, difference in stress response with alcohol may reflect a person's experience of alcohol effects—one that is more pleasurable or reduces discomfort to a greater degree.

on an individual basis. It is also noted by the theorists that sequential selection of people permits participants to be combined into groups that may be described by summary statistics and quantitative comparisons among groups (Spotts & Shontz, 1985, p. 119; see also Shontz, 1993; Spotts & Shontz, 1980b, 1982, 1984a, 1984b).

In 1974, Spotts and Shontz began a series of NIDA-sponsored studies of people who were identified as heavy, chronic users of cocaine (Spotts & Shontz, 1980b). As described by Spotts and Shontz (1985), this research involved an interlocking series of intensive, multidimensional studies of people who reportedly were heavy chronic users of a variety of different substances of abuse (amphetamines, barbiturates, cocaine, and opiates). They also studied "nonusers." The research program was continued for 8 years. The theory of adolescent substance abuse was produced from the theoretical inferences drawn from this study. This theory asserted that the predisposition to commitment to heavy, chronic use of a specific substance of abuse or class of substances of abuse originated early in life and that these predispositions develop from failures, delays, blockages, or only partial successes in meeting challenges and crises of normal individuation. People who become committed to heavy, chronic use of specific substances do so because they induce a distinctive *ego state* that allows temporary escape from currently experienced problems or creates the illusion that these problems have been solved. Using concepts proposed by other theorists, their theory was expanded to include ideas about the overall structure and the process of individual psychological life. As such, they were not limited in their applicability to drug users, but could apply their ideas to all human beings, particularly those living in Western cultures (Spotts & Shontz, 1980b, p. 67).

According to the theorists, their research program led them to conclude that there was an aspect of human existence that quickly becomes apparent when an individual, rather than a group, is studied: the potential for *numinous* (i.e., spiritual) experience. Among substance users, numinous factors are not obvious when substances are used to produce some form of transcendent experience or are incorporated into quasi-religious rituals. However, numinous factors operate overtly or covertly in everyone's life, give human existence a mythic quality, and lie behind the search for meaning and the occasional feelings of being driven or possessed by life-shaping forces over which personal control is impossible (Spotts & Shontz, 1980b, p. 68).

A fundamental postulate of the theory is that

> there exists within each individual a counterpart of the Ego, which is called the Self. As the Ego perceptually and motorically relates to external reality, the Self intuitively and creatively relates to the realities of inner life. The *person* is both the battle ground upon which Ego and Self struggle for supremacy and the integrated structure within which the two may function harmoniously, at least from time to time. (Spotts & Shontz, 1980b, p. 68)

As such the ego must develop through encounters with the outer world, while the self must develop through encounters with the world of dreams, myth, and revelation. Intertwined, both must grow and develop if normal psychological individuation is to occur. Thus, successful personal growth runs a spiraling course that carries the person on a generally ascending path, back and forth between these two realities. This process is depicted in a diagrammatic representation provided by the theorists: the spiral of individuation as related to the core problems of heavy, chronic drug abusers (Shontz & Spotts, 1986, p. 69). Adolescent substance abusers are described as having difficulty "'putting away childish things,' letting go of past behaviors, and accepting the new ones of the future." As such, "adolescent substance abuse is anchored in the individuation process (particularly the Second Individuation Crisis [see Stages of Psychological Individuation in Spotts & Shontz, 1985, p. 123]) and is rooted in the failures, conflicts, and dysfunctional relationships with parental figures which make it impossible for individuation to proceed in a normal manner" (Spotts & Shontz, 1985, p. 131; see also Spotts & Shontz, 1980b, 1982, 1984a, 1984b, 1984c, 1984d).

Jungian theory was also extended by Zoja (1989), who proposed the initiatory model of drug abuse as a general explanation of addiction. Sadava proposed the generalized tendency toward psychoactive drug use in 1984 and the problem behavior theory in 1985, the latter of which extended the original theory proposed by Jessor and Jessor (1977) with emphasis on personality and social psychological constructs. A unified psychological theory, the psychological model of excessive appetites, was proposed by Orford (1985) to explain opiate and nicotine use among children and adolescents. Other psychological theories included Hull's (1981) self-awareness model of alcohol consumption.

Zoja (1989) proposed the initiatory model of drug abuse. This theory was based in Jungian psycho-anthropologic theory. Addressing substance use in general, the theory focused on adolescent and adult "drug addicts" based on those assumptions inherent in Jungian psychology and that: 1. the disappearance of *initiation* (initiation rituals) is one of the principal differences between the ancient and modern worlds; 2. death and regeneration are the keys to every process of initiation, or rebirth (in primitive societies, the relationship between initiation and death is so close that many initiatory processes are analogous to death rites); 3. modern Western society lacks meaningful initiation and death rituals (death and initiation have been repressed and belong to the same area of repression); 4. death and initiation are archetypically related terms; 5. when family affections, ideals, and values are dead, life experiences worthy of that name are sought, even those that are purely subjective experiences shared by a restricted few; 6. through the world of drugs, the themes of death and initiation are continually activated and reactivated (e.g., heavy drug users typically experience a sensation of death during periods of abstinence relieved only by reuse of the drug, a phenomenon that probably contributes to the exaggerated importance given to physical addiction); 7. there is an unconscious link between drug use and the theme of death and renewal; 8. drug use is an attempt to create a form of self-initiation (p. 58); and 9. drug addiction is the response to a natural universal need for initiation or, more generally, for rebirth (p. 68; i.e., an unconscious need for death experiences is inherent among drug addicts and less overtly in society as a whole and requires an archetypal perspective in order to be understood).

Several hypotheses are advanced: 1. People in modern Western society use drugs (or turn to membership in terrorist and other groups) in order to meet a latent need for initiation. 2. Individual drug users are prone to group phenomena (the ways group members acquire and use drugs have a practical and ritual function that enables them to unconsciously recall the ancient rites of entrance through which initiates are elevated into a more prestigious group or social class; Zoja, 1989, p. 13). 3. A personified archetypal reality known as the *negative hero* is present in drug addiction. 4. The archetypal need to transcend one's present state at any cost, even when it entails the use of physically harmful substances, is especially strong in those who find themselves in a state of meaninglessness, lacking both a sense of identity and a precise societal role. 5. Drug addiction is not an escape from society, but a desperate attempt to occupy a place in it. 6. Drug addicts have an unconscious need for death. 7. The consumerism of the modern Western world leads people to the initiatory process that begins with renewal and ends with the death experience.

From this theoretical perspective, it is apparent that therapy with drug addicts is more difficult than most and entails difficulties not encountered with other patients. The values and aims of medicine are different from those of analysis: In the case of drug addiction, medicine will seek to overcome a state of intoxication, and its goal will be to repair battered organs. Depth psychology strives to resolve certain contradictions and unconscious psychic sufferings. The use of a toxic substance is for medicine an evil in itself, while for depth psychologists it represents a symptom that may become chronic and that may exist independently of its cause—a psychic disturbance whose nature, development, and existence are hard to verify. A second element affecting the therapy of drug addicts is linked to the question of motivation. Organic medical treatment can be performed on an unwilling and uncooperative person, whereas, by definition, analytic therapy can only be conducted with deep personal motivation on the patient's part. From this perspective, one encounters problems in "forcing" drug addicts to undergo treatment.

Learning theories. Hull (1981), addressing adults, proposed the self-awareness model of alcohol consumption. This theory, an extension of Hull and Levy's (1979) self-awareness model, was based on information-processing constructs, including encoding and interference, and was extended to adolescent drinking by Chassin, McLaughlin Mann, and Sher (1988). Reflecting a psychological learning orientation, the theory assumed that: 1. self-awareness is associated with specific affective and behavioral consequences; 2. alcohol has effects on behavior by virtue of disrupting cognitive processes; 3. alcohol produces effects opposite to those affected by self-awareness; 4. self-awareness is often painful; and 5. one motive for consuming alcohol (to intoxication) is to avoid self-awareness.

Hull and Levy (1979) demonstrated that highly self-aware people encode self-relevant information at a deeper cognitive level than do less self-aware people and, thus, defined self-awareness in terms of the differential tendency of an individual to encode information in terms of its self-relevance. If alcohol interferes with such higher-order encoding-elaboration strategies, it follows that alcohol consumption should have behavioral effects opposite to those of variables that increase self-awareness. Support for the proposition that subjects drink in order to reduce self-awareness in the face of personal failure was found in two studies reported by Hull and Young (1983b; see also Hull & Young 1983a). In addition, Hull, Levenson, Young, and Sher (1983) demonstrated in two experiments that alcohol reduced self-awareness. Finally, a third study was designed to investigate the effects of alcohol on self-relevant encoding processes among individuals high and low in dispositional self-awareness. Using an incidental memory paradigm, it was found that highly self-conscious subjects recalled more self-relevant words than did less self-conscious subjects under placebo conditions; thus, the findings reported by Hull and Levy (1979) were replicated, and as predicted, alcohol eliminated differences between highly and less self-conscious subjects (Hull et al., 1983, p. 461).

Chassin et al. (1988) in two studies evaluated the predictive ability of the self-awareness theory in relation to adolescent drinking behavior in a natural environment and the ability of the theory to account for phenomena of clinical importance (e.g., indicators of adolescent problem drinking and drinking among offspring of problem drinkers). Results indicated that adolescent drinking was predictable as a function of demographic variables, self-awareness, failure feedback, and a family history of alcohol abuse. However, the predictions of the self-awareness theory were *not* supported. Nevertheless, boundary conditions within self-awareness theory were identified as useful for explaining alcohol consumption and were described.

As argued by Sher (1987), the self-awareness model posits that alcohol interferes with the cognitive processes underlying self-awareness. Thus, the impact of certain stressors (e.g., those conveying negative information about the self) is likely to be attenuated by alcohol-related reductions in self-awareness. Although Hull (1981) and Hull et al. (1983) argue convincingly and provide data in support of the hypothesis that people who have high self-consciousness might modulate their drinking more as a function of success and failure experiences, the hypothesis that highly self-conscious people are more likely to drink more when stressed by self-relevant stressors is *not* supported. The stress response dampening (SRD) model proposed by Sher (1987) and the self-awareness model appear to differ in their predictions concerning the type of people most likely to experience pronounced SRD effect. The SRD model posits that people who show certain undercontrolled personality traits (e.g., aggressiveness or impulsivity) are the most likely to experience SRD effects and to drink when stressed. The self-awareness model predicts that people high in dispositional self-awareness are most likely to experience stress-reducing effects of alcohol under stress. Although there is some evidence to suggest that highly self-aware recovering alcoholics might be more likely to relapse following self-relevant negative life events, and to drink when stressed, this general perspective does not seem consistent with other available data. Until direct tests of the self-awareness model and stress reduction from alcohol are undertaken, the relevance of the model for explaining alcohol-related SRD effects, particularly for adolescents, remains uncertain.

H. J. Shaffer (1987) continued the cognitive focus with the development of the three-component cognitive-behavioral model of treatment, as did G. R. Ross (1994) with the cognitive-behavioral theory of adolescent chemical dependency.

Sociological Theories

During this period, fewer than 10 sociological theories were found that purported to explain adolescent substance use. Represented in these theories are: Wister and Avison's (1982) social network perspective of marijuana use and Single's (1988) political and economic availability theory, which addressed alcohol access and other factors (e.g., advertising) on adolescent (and adult) consumption of alcohol. Fingarette (1988) proposed a counterargument to the classic disease theories of alcohol use with his idea of heavy drinking as a way of life; Battjes (1984), in his symbolic interactionism, extended, used Median concepts of symbolic interactionism to explain general adolescent (and adult) substance use (see also Battjes, 1985). Sociological constructs were also represented in eclectic theories, and attention to the family continued, as illustrated by the extensions of the work of Stanton and his colleagues on addiction as a family phenomenon (M. D. Stanton et al., 1978): for example, the familial interpersonal system model of addict suicide (addict as savior model; M. D. Stanton & Coleman, 1980; M. D. Stanton & Todd, 1982b), Coleman's (Coleman, 1980; Coleman & Stanton, 1978b) incomplete mourning theory, and S. Brown's (1988) integrated developmental theory. A model relating child-rearing factors, authoritarianism, drug use attitudes, and adolescent drug use was proposed by Mercer and Kohn (1980), using personality and social psychologic factors to explain alcohol, nicotine, and marijuana use.

According to Coleman (1980), substance use behavior occurs when an unusual number of traumatic or premature deaths, separations, or losses occur within critical or transitional stages of the family's developmental cycle and are not effectively resolved or mourned. Homeostatic family processes and interlocking transactional patterns make problematic patterns of substance use a response for coping with overwhelming stress associated with the loss experience. Substance use also serves to keep the using member helpless and dependent on the family, a process that unifies and sustains family intactness. However, within the complex set of interpersonal relationships is an overall sense of hopelessness, despair, and a lack of purpose or meaning in life (pp. 83–84).

Early development and support for the theory can be found in a pilot study that reported an unusually high prevalence of premature or untimely deaths among recovering heroin addicts and their families. Additional clinical evidence for the significance of death and death-related issues in addict families was also found in work with siblings of recovering addicts (Coleman, 1978, 1979a, 1979b). A sense of faith, religiosity, was seen as a major interface between death and the family's adaptive behavior. Thus, a sense of faith has been proposed as either alleviating or exacerbating the sorrow, rage, and guilt that accompany or follow the loss of a loved one (Coleman, 1980). Clinical findings were supported by statistical evidence that the incidence of death differed significantly across groups, with addicts having a more distinct orientation to death, being more suicidal, and having more premature and bizarre death experiences. It was also noted that during childhood, they had more family separations and developed a unique pattern of continuously separating from and returning to their families. Further, they were less likely to have a clearly defined purpose in life. In addition to these clinical studies, there was also systematic empirical research that supported the incomplete mourning theory, giving credence to the view that the etiology of substance use is due both to unpredictable, unexpected experiences of death and loss and to structural or functional imbalances in the family. Taking these results together, patterns of substance use cannot be described by a linear, cause-and-effect model but are best understood from the standpoint of the "new epistemology" or from a cybernetic model that views the family's relationship patterns and feedback system as essential to the "addictive symptoms" observed (Coleman, 1980, 1985).

Mercer and Kohn (1980) produced the child-rearing factors, authoritarianism, drug use attitudes, and adolescent drug use model. A more psychological (personality and social psychological) theory, attention is paid to polysubstance use (alcohol, nicotine, and psychedelic use) among adolescents. Focusing on such concepts as attitudes, authoritarianism, child-rearing practices, illicit drugs, and licit drugs, the theorists hypothesized that parental child-rearing practices produce within their children a personality that shapes their attitudes toward the use of substances of abuse, which in turn affects their use of alcohol, marijuana, and tobacco. As a predictive model of adolescent substance use, the model was found to be more successful in predicting illicit rather than licit drug use, with "love" on the part of the mother and "positive control" on the part of the father as the most salient dimensions with regard to parental child-rearing practices.

Theorists such as Jessor (1985) have implicated adult role demands (e.g., marriage, parenthood, and employment) as central in a natural process toward moderation of drinking. Although longitudinal research on illicit substance use has generated more theoretical specificity than that on alcohol, Yamaguchi and Kandel (1984, 1985a, 1985b) have provided evidence for two separate developmental processes: 1. *role selection* (those who use illicit drugs choose roles more consistent with their lifestyles, such as cohabitation instead of marriage and delayed entry into traditional roles) and 2. *role socialization* (once adopted, roles such as marriage and parenthood tend to be followed by reductions in illicit drug use).[14]

D. H. Olson proposed with his colleagues the circumplex model of marital and family systems (D. H. Olson, 1980, 1986; D. H. Olson, Russell, & Sprenkle, 1979, 1980; D. H. Olson, Sprenkle, & Russell, 1979). The theory reflects a sociological family systems orientation (D. H. Olson, Russell, & Sprenkle, 1979, 1980, 1983; D. H. Olson, Sprenkle, & Russell, 1979) and, as such, addresses general substance use among adolescents and their families using related concepts—boundaries, coalitions, decision making, emotional bonding, family, family adaptability (rigid, structured, flexible, or chaotic), family cohesion (disengaged, separated, connected, or enmeshed), family members, family power structure (assertiveness, control, or discipline), mutual interests, negotiation styles, relationship rules, role relationships, sharing of friends, sharing of recreation, space, stress (developmental or situational), and time.

The theory proposes two major concepts relevant to understanding marital and family functioning: cohesion and adaptability. *Family cohesion* is defined as the emotional bonding that family members have toward one another and ranges from *disengaged* (very low) to *separated* (low to moderate) to *connected* (moderate to high) to *enmeshed* (very high). *Family adaptability* is defined as the ability of a marital or family system to change its power structure, role relationships, and relationship rules in response to situational

---

[14] As noted by Baer (1991), role socialization may put pressure on the individual to reduce alcohol use, whereas role selection, because many social systems support heavy alcohol use, may be a more potent process for alcohol use. Heavier drinkers who wish to protect their heavy-drinking lifestyles may perceive threats from adult roles and choose living arrangements conducive to drinking (e.g., delayed marriage and parenthood and delayed entry into regular occupational pursuits).

and developmental stress (D. H. Olson, McCubbin, et al., 1983; D. H. Olson, Russell, & Sprenkle, 1983).

The theory was formalized in an unpublished manuscript and tested by several theorists, including L. S. Smart, Chibucos, and Didier (1990), who explored the relationship between levels of drug and alcohol use and adolescents' perceptions of family functioning and other individual risk factors. In addition to testing the circumplex model, L. S. Smart et al. (1990) showed that their findings could be useful for developing strategies that would decrease or prevent substance abuse among adolescents (p. 208). Several researchers have identified an association between extreme family closeness or distance and high levels of adolescent alcohol and drug use and have shown that extreme closeness precipitates drug use, especially alcohol use (e.g., Brook et al., 1980). Less clear evidence exists in the literature regarding the relevance of adaptability. For example, Hendin et al. (1981), among others, suggested that levels of alcohol and drug use are higher in rigidly structured, tightly controlled families that allow little deviation or independence (families expected to be low on adaptability). Other theorists concluded from comparing families that had members with problematic patterns of alcohol and drug use to those that did not that the latter displayed greater flexibility and adaptability (e.g., Brook et al., 1980; Brook, Nomura, & Cohen, 1989a, 1989b; Brook, Whiteman, & Gordon, 1985; Brook, Whiteman, Gordon, & Cohen, 1986).[15]

L. S. Smart et al. (1990) reported clear support for the hypothesis that extreme family functioning is related to greater risk of substance use among adolescents than balanced or midrange functioning. Although adolescents from extreme families consistently used more alcohol, depressants, marijuana, psychedelics, stimulants, and tobacco, the findings of the study also made clear that, except for alcohol, most of the adolescents in their sample do not use substances of abuse. Within extreme families, the presence or absence of a drinking problem within the family serves generally to increase or decrease the level of risk for alcohol or substance use. L. S. Smart et al.'s findings were identified as consistent with the view that family variables are important determinants of adolescent substance use. Other research reported adolescent substance use as especially likely to occur in families that would be classified as extreme by the circumplex model (D. H. Olson, 1986). Other research has substantiated that variables conceptually similar to cohesion (e.g., G. M. Barnes, 1984; G. M. Barnes & Welte, 1986) and adaptability (e.g., Pandina & Schuele, 1983) are related to substance use by adolescents.

In regard to other family-related variables, the presence of a drinking

[15] As noted by L. S. Smart et al. (1990), this ability to adapt flexibly to stress, particularly to stressors from outside the family and over which the family members have little control, may lead to fewer problems related to alcohol and drug use in regard to those stressors.

problem in the family was found to differentiate adolescent users from nonusers in extreme families.[16] Additional research suggested the importance of a combination of parental modeling and parental attitudes toward their children (e.g., Kandel & Andrews, 1987).

Family structure proved to be a less-important discriminator of substance use with extreme families. Among adolescents from extreme families who currently used alcohol, there were no differences associated with family structure. However, adolescents from extreme single-parent families were more likely to have previously used alcohol than those from extreme families with two parents (both biological or biological and step-parent) present. There are many potential explanations for these results. For example, perhaps adolescents from single-parent families have more opportunity to experiment with alcohol than do those who live in families with two parents present (see Richardson et al., 1989, who reported that eighth-grade children who cared for themselves for 11 or more hours a week were at twice the risk of substance use as those who did not care for themselves). As concluded by L. S. Smart et al. (1990), adolescents who perceive their families as being extremely high or low on cohesion and adaptability appear to be vulnerable to the use of substances of abuse as early as the ninth grade.

Eclectic Theories

One eclectic theory was the synthetic-dynamic theory of drug abuse proposed and later extended by Kim and Newman (1982). This theory incorporated concepts from humanism and sociology, as well as personality and social psychological factors, in an effort to explain general substance use among adolescent boys and girls. The revised theory focused more formally on explaining alcohol and other sedative-hypnotic use, including solvents and inhalants, as well as amphetamines, cocaine, nicotine, and "hallucinogens." This theory was further elaborated by Kim, Hoffman, Pike, and Gibson (1984) to produce the synthetic-dynamic model of student involvement, alcohol education evaluation instrument (AEEI).

The work of George Huba and his research group involved the investigation of patterns of causal influence, particularly by means of structural equation models. Whereas Richard Jessor treated this as one of a set of predictor variables to be entered in a linear additive regression equation, Huba and Bentler were interested in comparing causal paths by which peer drinking influences drinking behavior by the individual (e.g., investigating whether the influence on behavior is direct or is effected through changes in personal attitudes toward drinking). The domain model concerns adolescent behav-

---

[16] Although it could not be assumed that the family member with the problem was a parent, previous research has noted the importance of parental modeling on adolescent substance use (Jessor & Jessor, 1975; Kandel, 1978a, 1978b).

ioral styles. Drinking behavior is embedded in a larger set of general behavioral tendencies or lifestyles, which show some generality or consistency over time and situational contexts and which may include recreational activities, drug use, other illicit or criminal acts, compulsive eating, or gambling. Thus, the model is not specific to substance abuse (Sadava, 1987, pp. 100–101).

The interactive theory of drug use incorporated biological, psychological, and sociological perspectives and focused on alcohol, cocaine, and psychedelic (PCP and THC) use and other "habitual behaviors" (excessive shopping, gambling, and overeating) among adolescents and their parents (Huba et al., 1979a, 1979b, 1980a, 1980b; Wingard, Huba, & Bentler, 1979a, 1979b; see also Huba et al., 1980c, 1981a, 1981b). It hypothesizes that: 1. drug-taking behavior is caused by several large constellations of intraindividual and extraindividual forces; 2. domains of influence interact to modify each other while determining the presence or absence of a large variety of lifestyle behaviors, including drug and alcohol use; and 3. the intimate support system affects drug use through perceived behavioral pressure, but not directly.

This work was followed in 1981 by the latent variable causal model of adolescent drug use, which focused on biological (genetic and psychophysiological), psychological (personality/learning: interactionism/behaviorism), and sociological (sociocultural and interactionism) concepts. Attention was given to heroin, sedative-hypnotic, amphetamine, cocaine, and psychedelic use among adolescents (and adults).

Newcomb and Bentler (1988) advanced the large integrated model of adolescent drug use. The theory addressed general substance use with attention to patterns of nonuse to compulsive use and resumed nonuse. The group studied was adolescent boys and girls, as well as young adult men and women. The theory was based on the following assumptions, inherent in positivism and experimental psychology (evaluation and measurement): 1. The use of various drugs, the method of their use, or their metabolites interfere with or impair physical, psychological, or emotional functioning as a result of their direct psychotropic effects on affect, cognition, and behavior (p. 25). 2. Precocious development may result from an inability to delay gratification (there may be a strong drive and need to enjoy the positive aspects of adulthood—e.g., autonomy, drug use, and sex—without waiting for its natural occurrence and while avoiding the difficult tasks of adulthood, which are gained with experience and maturity; p. 38). 3. Adolescent drug use is acquired in a sequence of increasing involvement progressing from one drug to another (e.g., high levels of alcohol use precede initiation of cannabis use and high levels of cannabis use precede initiation of hard drug use, including cocaine; p. 60). 4. There are necessary conditions for interpreting causality (e.g., there must be a statistically reliable association between the cause and the effect, the cause must precede the effect in a temporal sequence, and cause and effect relationships must not be spurious or result from a third factor that antecedently predicts them; p. 63). 5. The long-term consequences of drug use and their impact on developmental achievements (e.g., family formation and career) tend to be more difficult to demonstrate in a scientifically rigorous manner than short-term or immediate effects and, as such, could have serious lifelong implications (e.g., failure to achieve successful transition to adulthood). 6. Such effects cannot be ethically induced and, thus, must be studied in naturally occurring circumstances (p. 64).

The model, developed during the early 1980s, includes four levels of characteristic factors thought to influence or be influenced by substance use: 1. *biological* (e.g., physiological processes), 2. *intrapersonal* (within the person), 3. *interpersonal* (social), and 4. *sociocultural* (community systems). According to the theorists, the potential consequences of substance use can be discussed according to each of these factors. In addition, specific areas requiring attention in regard to the young adult life period are subsumed under these four factor domains and include consequences of substance use related to physical health, emotional health, marriage and family formation, deviant attitudes and behavior, sexual behavior and involvement, social integration, and educational and job pursuits. Prior to Newcomb and Bentler's study, there was little solid research aimed at explaining the impact of adolescent substance use on these critical life areas. Although some attention had been given to the chronic and excessive use of various substances of abuse over longer periods of time, little research had emerged that examined the consequences of substance use during the critical developmental period of adolescence and young adulthood.

Newcomb and Bentler (1988) were also interested in exploring the question, "To what extent does adolescent drug use affect psychological development in later life?" Although they knew that the use and abuse of "psychoactive chemicals" was recognized as a major national and international problem affecting all segments of society and that enough anecdotal evidence on the devastating effects of substance use on health, social, and personal functioning existed to merit a strong effort at clinical intervention and prevention, scientific evidence on such consequences in relatively normal and unselected populations was meager. In addition, because use of a variety of substances rather than only a single one tended to be a common occurrence, evidence for the differential consequences of the use of particular substances tended to be even more scarce. Thus, they undertook their "pioneering attempt to evaluate the effects of general and specific drug use during adolescence on young adult functioning" (p. 7).

The concern of the theorists was not to pathologize the occasional and experimental use of drugs among adolescents, which they believed reflected normal developmental processes, but to better understand regular or committed use or abuse of substances among adolescents and their effects on achieving both adolescent and adult developmental goals (to determine the specific effects of frequent substance use on an adolescent, in relation to peers in their normal sample of adolescents, and on the quality, nature, and success of psychosocial functioning of the drug-using adolescent as a young adult; Newcomb & Bentler, 1988, p. 214). The results of their study characterized an adolescent lifestyle of regular substance use as also one of rebellion, nonconformity to traditional values, involvement with other deviant or illegal behavior together with other people who were engaged in such behavior, poor family connections, few educational interests, precocious involvement in sexual activities, experiences of emotional turmoil, lack of social connection, alienation, and precocious involvement with the workforce and earning money. Their characterization of a typical drug-involved lifestyle did not imply that every adolescent fit into this pattern; the correlations were weak, and thus, it is possible that many patterns exist, with a few adolescents being quite average except for their level of drug involvement. Further, their characterization was based on correlations and does not imply any causal priority based on across-time analyses. They did not suggest that there is a single common pathway or explanation for adolescent substance use. Just as there are several different causal factors related to substance use initiation (see Maddahian, Newcomb, & Bentler, 1988; Newcomb, Maddahian, & Bentler, 1986), substance use maintenance involves a complex of correlated factors, specific components of which may or may not characterize a particular individual (Newcomb & Bentler, 1988, p. 217).

Substance use creates a developmental trajectory that progresses into young adulthood and can be observed as the impact of adolescent drug use. Newcomb and Bentler's (1988) findings support the hypothesis that adolescent substance use affects young adult functioning in ways over and beyond those changes in lifestyle patterns characteristic of adolescents who use substances of abuse. Substance use during adolescence differentially influences certain life areas as adolescents mature into young adults. Similarly, different types of substances of abuse have different effects (e.g., for young adults, only the specific use of alcohol, and not other types of substances of abuse, decreased social conformity and religious commitment from levels reported during adolescence).

Newcomb and Bentler (1988) conclude that it is obvious that adolescent substance use disrupts both the timing of and competence at many of the critical developmental tasks associated with adolescence and adulthood. Timing is affected by a premature involvement with many tasks (e.g., childbearing and parenting, job responsibilities, and sex) prior to the acquisition of adequate competencies to handle these challenges. Adolescent substance use directly interferes with social integration and acceptance of adult civic and societal responsibilities. As a consequence, essential developmental tasks required during adulthood are not successfully completed. Although theories vary in regard to the claimed mechanism of interference, they generally acknowledge that adolescent substance use interferes with family development (increasing divorce), job instability (increasing the number of times fired), educational pursuits (reducing chances of completing high school and going on to college), cognitive functioning (increasing psychoticism and reducing deliberateness), survival attitudes (increasing suicide ideation), and social functioning (for "hard drug" use, increasing loneliness and reducing social support). These findings were identified as providing clear examples of the areas of young adulthood disturbed by adolescent substance use. Thus, the general theory that adolescent substance use interferes with various kinds of life functioning is supported by their analyses (Newcomb & Bentler, 1988, p. 227).

The Rutgers health and human development project working model (Pandina & Raskin White, 1981) was extended by Pandina, Labouvie, and Raskin White (1984) and, later, with V. Johnson (Pandina & Johnson, 1989, 1990). An eclectic theory derived from psychological (developmental—lifespan) and sociological concepts, the theory addresses general alcohol, marijuana, and other substance use. Attention is given to nonuse and initial use to compulsive use among children, adolescents, and young adults (11–24 years of age).

The theory assumes that: 1. sociocultural changes affect developmental patterns and functions; 2. developmental patterns and functions affect sociocultural changes; 3. such phenomena (as relationships 1 and 2) require short- and long-term study (e.g., a given developmental transition may seem problematic from a short-term perspective but beneficial from a long-term perspective); and 4. the use of a transactional model requires that the various developing systems be linked to each other through reciprocal interactions across time (Pandina et al., 1984, p. 256).

The theory addresses such concepts as developmental tasks (maintenance of health, development of identity, preparation for an occupation, development of social interactions, and preparation for marriage and parenthood), consummatory behaviors (frequency, quantity, and recency of substance use), supporting or sustaining behaviors (attitudes, beliefs, and perceptions of use practices), environment (proximal and distal—exposure to models of the behaviors, such as parents, siblings, peers, and media, and quality of parent-child relationships, conventional values and beliefs, and experience of strain), and motivations for use and nonuse (see also Labouvie, Pandina, Raskin White, & Johnson, 1990). Other work by Labouvie (1986a) provides some evidence that the experience of strained social relationships and a heightened sense of powerlessness/helplessness may induce adolescents to rely on substance (alcohol and marijuana) use as a means of emotional self-regulation requiring little effort and ability while offering instant effects and a sense of control. In a later study, Labouvie (1987) reported longitudinal evidence linking personality and substance use to adolescent ego strength and control. Above-average levels of use intensity and of coping use were exhibited by adolescents who maintained below-average levels of ego strength and ego control or who fell from average to below-average levels over the 3-year period.

Elliott et al. (1985) advanced an explanatory model that expanded and synthesized traditional strain, social control, and social learning theories in an effort to account for delinquent behavior and substance use. The individual level was the focus for explaining how adolescents become involved in delinquent acts, including substance use (the dependent variable in this causal model is the variation in individual rates of offending). The extension of the explanatory model to substance use was justified by the following observations: 1. The use of illicit substances may be considered a specific form of delinquent behavior in that their possession involves the violation of criminal statutes and carries the risk of formal legal sanction. 2. There is considerable empirical evidence that the use of alcohol and marijuana, the most frequently used substances of abuse, is part of a general deviance syndrome that involves a wide range of minor criminal acts and other forms of norm-violating behavior (as previously noted by Donovan & Jessor, 1984; Elliott & Ageton, 1976; Huizinga & Elliott, 1981; Jessor & Jessor, 1977a; Jessor, Carman, & Grossman, 1968; Kandel, 1980a, 1980b; Kandel, Kessler, & Margulies, 1978a, 1978b; Robins & Murphy, 1967; among others).

One of the major contributions of Elliott et al. (1985) is their recommendations based on research related to the proposed integrative model that emphasize the critical role that adolescent friends play in the production of delinquent behavior. According to the empirical testing of the model, adolescents involved with prosocial friends have a low risk for delinquency, whereas adolescents involved with delinquent friends have a high risk. Unfortunately, although strong bonds to the family and/or school help to diminish the pro-delinquent influences of delinquent friends, they do not totally protect adolescents from these influences.

Tarter (1983) proposed the diathesis-stress model for the prevention and treatment of alcohol and drug abuse, an eclectic theory focusing on genetic and personality factors. This theoretical direction was further explored by Tarter with Alterman and Edwards, as well as others, as the neurobehavioral theory of alcoholism etiology (vulnerability) (Tarter, Alterman, & Edwards, 1985, 1988; Tarter & Edwards, 1988; Tarter, Kabene, Escallier, Laird, & Jacob, 1990; Tarter, Laird, Kabene, Bukstein, & Kaminer, 1990). While the main focus was on adults, the results reported by Tarter, Laird, et al. (1990) had implications for prevention and treatment of adolescent substance use. Their finding that the adolescents who displayed problematic patterns of substance use demonstrated a mixture of temperament deviations found in later childhood psychiatric disorders concurred with prior research examining the etiology of substance use (Tarter et al., 1988) and has implications for primary prevention. Tarter et al. (1988) reported increased evidence suggesting that deviations in childhood temperament traits may increase the risk for adulthood alcoholism. Although not conclusive, certain temperament trait deviations (e.g., high behavioral activity level) have been commonly reported among boys who subsequently developed alcoholism and among the biological offspring of alcoholics (Tarter, Kabene, et al., 1990). Tarter, Alterman, & Edwards (1985) reported other temperament deviations (e.g., high emotionality, low attentional capacity, and low sociability) as indicating vulnerability to alcoholism. Because virtually no research had been published aimed at determining whether there was an association between substance abuse, other than alcoholism, and temperament, they sought: 1. to determine whether adolescent substance users differed from normal (non-substance-using, nonpsychiatric adolescents) in temperament and 2. to ascertain whether there was an association between the magnitude of temperament deviation and the severity of drug abuse and psychosocial maladjustment.

The results of their study supported the discrimination of substance-abusing adolescents from normal controls on seven of the nine scales composing the revised dimensions-of-temperament scales. However, aggregation of the scales into orthogonal dimensions using factor analysis resulted in the finding that only activity level was associated with severity of substance use. This behavioral trait was correlated with seven of ten scales composing the drug use screening inventory, which includes severity of substance use, behavior problems, psychiatric disorders, work, peer relationships, and leisure activities. Results indicated that substance-abusing adolescents were distinguishable from normal controls on a variety of temperament dimensions. However, these differentiating characteristics were closely linked to differences in behavioral activity regulation in as much as it is this aspect of temperament that almost exclusively correlated with severity of substance use involvement and associated disruption in psychosocial adjustment. Considered collectively, the researchers' findings indicate that disturbed behavioral activity regulation is associated with substance problem severity and associated psychosocial difficulties. The extent to which the temperament deviations presage or emerge consequential to the onset of substance abuse requires further investigation, as does their finding that unaffected male children of alcoholic men also exhibit deviation in behavioral activity regulation (Tarter, Kabene, et al., 1990), suggesting that this trait precedes the substance abuse and, when this latter outcome occurs in adolescence, covaries in magnitude of severity with degree of temperament trait deviation.

This demonstration that the temperament trait of high behavioral activity distinguishes substance abusers from normal controls has both theoretical and practical implications. With respect to the former, it suggests that substance use may for some people optimize or stabilize behavior (Tarter, Alterman, & Edwards, 1985). In this respect, the results concur with the long-held notion that the consumption of substances of abuse may have a self-regulatory effect (see also the discussion of eclectic theories of the 1990s).

Zuckerman (1983a, 1983b, 1983c) advanced the biological theory of sensation seeking (and the new biological theory of sensation seeking), which incorporates biological, genetic (neurochemical: neurotransmitters), and psychological (personality and social psychology) perspectives. The theory addresses sedative-hypnotic (alcohol and barbiturates), amphetamine, cocaine, and psychedelic (LSD and marijuana) initial use and polysubstance use. The focus is on the sensation seeker. The basic assumption is that a personality trait rooted in biological structure and function plays a major role in the "reckless willingness" to try and to use substances of abuse (Zuckerman, 1983b, p. 202). Central to the *new* model is the hypothesis that intense or varied sensations are sought because they affect the release of catecholamines in the reward or pleasure circuits of the limbic system. Arousal has been relegated to a secondary role in this theory.

Several hypotheses were advanced: 1. Intense or varied sensations, including the use of alcohol and other substances of abuse, are sought because they affect the release of catecholamines in the reward or pleasure circuits of the limbic system. 2. The central biological traits that underlie sensation seeking are the functional levels of the catecholamine neurotransmitters as influenced by their production and disposal and the enzymes, such as monoamine oxidase (MAO), that regulate these processes. 3. Sensation seekers are attracted to stimulants (stimulants are abused by sensation seekers for the same reasons that exciting stimulation and activities are sought: both the substance of abuse and stimulating activities increase the turnover of the neurotransmitters of the reward systems). 4. Other substances of abuse may be used because of their direct or indirect effects on neurotransmitter systems (e.g., LSD produces a rise in dopamine, but a fall in norepinephrine and it also appears to be an agonist for tryptamine and serotonin; the evidence that barbiturates and marijuana affect monoamine release is contradictory and inconclusive; there is evidence that alcohol increases synthesis and turnover for all monoamine systems, including norepinephrine and dopamine, although it may block receptor systems for norepinephrine; barbiturates may also block the turnover of monoamines, but barbiturates produce euphoric effects through reduction of pain or negative effect, rather than directly as do amphetamine and cocaine).

Noting that the results of B. Segal, Huba, and Singer (1980) provided little support for two common explanations of substance use (peer influence and anxiety reduction), Zuckerman found that opiate and psychedelic users more frequently said their reason for using was "to experience something new." "Curiosity" was given as a motive by 86 percent of marijuana users and was also frequently given by opiate and psychedelic users. "To get kicks" or "to get high," terms describing the euphoric arousal produced by substances of abuse, were cited by between 25 and 38 percent of the users. Getting "pep" or "energy" was a reason given for using substances of abuse that typically produce energizing effects, particularly the stimulants. However, of the various reasons given for substance use the most frequent was "to experience something new and different." This finding led Zuckerman (1979) to the identification of the trait of sensation seeking, which he defined as "the need for varied, novel, and complex sensations and experiences and the willingness to take physical and social risks for the sake of such experience" (Zuckerman, 1979, p. 10).

Zuckerman (1983b) advanced more formally the assertion that sensation seeking was an initial motive for "drug abuse":

> Theories of drug abuse typically offer social or intrapsychic causes for the initial experimentation with drugs and physiological and conditioning causes for maintenance of the addiction. In this paper a proposition will be presented: a personality trait that is rooted in biological structure and functions plays a major role in the reckless willingness to try drugs. (p. 202)

This theory (Zuckerman, 1971) was extended by Tonkin (1987, p. 215) as the risky behavior paradigm—sensation seeking may influence the feedback loop by modifying motivational state or by affecting the perceptual skills that depend on the level of arousal (see also Jessor & Jessor, 1977b). In that a biological approach to human traits is necessarily a comparative approach, a model for comparative study of the biological bases of personality was presented by Zuckerman (1984). This model relates mood, behavioral activity and sociability, and clinical states to activity of the central catecholamine neurotransmitters and to neuroregulators and other transmitters that act in opposite ways on behavior or that stabilize activity in the arousal systems. As further explained by Zuckerman (1987), as a marker for alcoholism, low MAO levels may indicate a disposition toward an impulsive, extroverted, sensation-seeking temperament—a risk factor for other drug abuse as well:

> Sensation seekers seek intense and novel external stimulation and use catecholamine-releasing drugs like amphetamine and cocaine in order to activate these systems. In an unstimulated state (producing boredom), high sensation seekers may be below an optimal level of activity in catecholaminergic systems. Low MAO levels may allow these monoamine systems to fluctuate within wide limits. Thus, a period of intense excitement could be followed by a depletion of catecholamines leading to further attempts to stimulate the system.
>
> How does this apply to alcohol use? . . . According to my new optimal catecholamine system activity (CSA) theory, moderate levels of CSAs are optimal and associated with rewarding or pleasurable effects, while very low or high levels are associated with dysphoria. Actually, such a theory is compatible with the effects of increasing doses of alcohol which show mild euphoria and disinhibition at lower doses and increased anxiety and depression at higher doses or after more prolonged drinking. The alcoholic seems to follow the maxim "if a

little is good a lot is better." Unfortunately, the central nervous system follows the maxim "moderation and homeostasis in all systems." (p. 298)

Marcos advanced the bonding/association model of drug use with R. E. Johnson (Marcos & Johnson, 1988). This eclectic theory attempted to explain adolescent substance use focusing on populations in Greece and the United States. The theorists were interested in correlates or predictors of substance use that were derived from major theories of deviant behavior and in whether the presumed causes had similar effects on adolescent substance use in cultures that were distinct in many ways. Thus, patterns of adolescent substance use in Greece and the United States were compared.

Given the observed differences in sample size, social patterns of alcohol and tobacco use in Athens and Arizona, and the different social attitudes toward and availability of other substances of abuse in these cities, it was considered reasonable by the theorists to expect major differences in the application of the causal model in the two cultures. Highlighting some of their findings, the model was found to have greater explanatory power, although weak, for American than for Greek students. Nevertheless, substance-using friends were the best predictor of alcohol use for students in both cultural samples, and effects were similar for both. The only other direct effect on alcohol use was a religious attachment effect for Arizona students. For cigarette smoking, substance-using friends were the most powerful influence, and effects were similar in strength for both samples. However, other differences were found in which variables had a direct effect on smoking behavior. For Greek students, parental attachment was almost as predictive of smoking behavior as substance-using friends. For other substances, Arizona student total effects were consistently higher than effects for Greek students, and the differences were greater than for alcohol and tobacco.

A causal model integrating variables from social control and social learning theories was found to work well in regard to predicting all types of substance use for Arizona students. However, the model only showed similar efficacy for Athens students in regard to cigarette smoking. Several possible explanations for these results were discussed by the theorists. For example, perhaps adolescent alcohol use by Greek students was not thought of as deviant, whereas the use of other substances of abuse was perhaps considered too deviant for the model to display predictive power. Statistically, there is a reduced chance of finding strong relationships with variables that have only minor variation. Substantively, variables derived from theories of deviant behavior do not apply as well in settings where the behavior in question is not defined as particularly deviant.

The testing of the model in the two groups of students emphasizes the need for the cross-cultural study of adolescent substance use patterns and related variables, which seem to be influenced by cultural group and setting.

American theories of adolescent substance use probably require revision before they can be used in any meaningful way in the study of adolescents living in other countries that differ in terms of substance availability and normative ambiguity regarding their use and response to users. Future cross-cultural studies should include larger and more diverse samples and incorporate measurement scales that allow for broader variation in dependent variables. Appropriate steps should be taken to obtain measures of the availability of substances to adolescents and of the punishments that are applied to adolescents when substances are used. These are important variables that are likely to vary across cultural groups and settings (Marcos & Johnson, 1988, pp. 570–571).

The 1990s

Recently, polysubstance use and its spread among all sectors of society has received significantly increased attention. Several theorists have advanced explanations of these phenomena, and greater emphasis has been placed on treatment approaches. During the early 1990s, several researchers and scholars attempted to pare down the eclecticism of the bio-psycho-social domains in an effort to address treatment issues more effectively, particularly those related to alcohol problems:

> The theoretical model I adopt is "biopsychosocial." In defence of a cumbersome term, "biopsychosocial" essentially communicates the idea that biological, psychological, and social factors are all important for the etiology of addiction. In an area of difficult theoretical challenges, and often competing theoretical approaches, it can be easy to adopt an integrated or multifaceted model. It allows one to avoid committing to a more specific model by saying "everything is important." A greater challenge involves selecting the most relevant or useful factors to include in an interactive model. (Baer, 1991, p. 51)

Attention also focused on explaining substance use among adolescents from increasingly diverse ethnic backgrounds (e.g., Beauvais, 1992a; Brook, 1993; Brook, Hamburg, Balka, & Wynn, 1992; Brook, Whiteman, Balka, & Hamburg, 1992).

Psychological Theories

The right brain model of substance abuse was proposed by Mace (1992) to explain adolescent and adult alcohol and other substance use. This theory reflected Freudian and Jungian psychoanalytic theory, as well as learning theory emphasizing lateral specialization. Also embracing those assumptions inherent in Eriksonian developmental stage theory, Kohlbergian and Piagetian theory, and family systems theory (i.e., that the family, as a system, must change to accommodate the change of any single member), Mace argued that mental health requires that people be truly in touch with their *nondomi-*

nant needs (right hemispheric needs). In addition, he argued that mental health professionals can better communicate with their clients' nondominant needs when they are in touch with their own nondominant needs. In regard to substance use, he hypothesized that: 1. drugs and alcohol are used by adolescents and adults to relieve stress from left brain tasks and to access right brain activities[17] and 2. accessing right brain activities satisfies developmental stage needs carried over from early childhood into adolescence and adulthood—*belonging needs* (oral), *self-control needs* (anal), and *power-seeking needs* (phallic) (Mace, 1992, p. 62).

As explained by Mace (1992), not all adolescents and adults are driven by the same developmental needs. Adolescents and adults who experiment with or use alcohol and drugs may be attempting to satisfy different developmental needs. Having linked the satisfactions of alcohol and drug use with developmental needs derived from childhood and recapitulated in adolescence and adulthood, the built-in conflict between the left and right hemispheres produces many incompatible needs and conflicting self-concepts. This conflict makes possible the changes that underlie personal growth and without which there would be no internal mechanisms for change. The left and right hemispheres develop independently and have their own stages of development that are displayed in adults as either left or right dominance. Early childhood education focuses generally on the rigid programming and development of the left brain, while little attention is paid to the right brain and its development. Thus, some people may develop a tendency to get stuck in the left hemisphere. These people may find that they are unable to obtain relief from the accompanying stress of being stuck in the left hemisphere or may be unable to access right hemisphere activities except by temporarily deadening the left hemisphere by using alcohol and drugs (Mace, 1992, pp. 62–63).

When the left hemisphere regains control after the right hemisphere has been accessed by the use of alcohol or drugs, anger, self-reproach, and partial amnesia can be experienced (e.g., people who are alcoholic cannot relate in a sober state to those experiences they had when they were drunk and vice versa—see discussion of state-dependent learning in Chap. 7). According to the theorist, this partial amnesia is a way for adolescents and adults to deal with low self-esteem and self-hatred. The right hemisphere splits and creates two personality parts: a *good guy* and a *bad guy.* The latter will have the problem of addiction and expresses all the anger and has all the fun. In fact, the right hemisphere is identified as sometimes being more mentally healthy

---

[17]The right brain is responsible for feelings, intuitive insights, artistic expression, personal relationships, and having fun. The left brain, which is considered the dominant hemisphere, is responsible for verbal expression, mathematics, cause-and-effect reasoning, and dealing analytically with one thing at a time (Mace, 1992, p. 62).

than the left hemisphere because the repressed bad guy part is more honest in regard to the inner self and the person's world. This amnesia can be viewed as a symptom of vertical repression or split personality, which helps adolescents and adults, particularly those who have above-average intelligence, to deal with severe conflict. These people can be helped by putting them in touch with the healthy part and awakening their *buried dreams*. Buried dreams are the wishes people have, what they want to do and what they want to be, that have been repressed. Mental health professionals can encourage these people to seek their dreams.

The left hemisphere also can split, with one part being *extraordinarily righteous* and having its roots in listening to and behaving in accordance with the wishes of significant others. This part thrives on outbreaks from the buried bad part, which in turn is fueled by repression from the righteous part, as they complement one another. The other part of the left hemisphere split is a *super sense of self,* a self that listens to the advice of others, but questions the advice and makes decisions that may or may not coincide with it.

Various integrative techniques can often help substance abusers bridge conflicting needs between the two hemispheres and help them find alternative ways to satisfy their nondominant right hemisphere needs without resorting to the use of alcohol or drugs. It is for this reason that mental health professionals and family members who use rational arguments to convince people to moderate the use of alcohol or drugs are frequently unsuccessful. Not only is the right hemisphere immune to advice from its own dominant left hemisphere, but also to any rational intervention offered by therapists, family members, and others. Thus, according to this theory, in order to be effective, mental health professionals need to achieve rapport with their clients' nondominant right hemispheres and legitimize their inner needs that have been carried over from childhood. Family members must also be taught this strategy (e.g., the client may want the family to provide respect, honesty, or praise).

Volkan (1994) proposed a theory of object relations and compulsive drug use. The theory addressed compulsive opiate, amphetamine, and psychedelic (LSD) use among adolescents and adults.

Based on assumptions inherent in Freudian psychoanalytic theory and modern object relations theory, three major hypotheses were advanced: 1. People who have satisfactory object relations will not feel the need to compulsively use substances of abuse, even those that are "highly addictive." 2. People who have poor object relations, weak ego formation, narcissistic disturbances, and introjective depression are likely to begin to use substances of abuse as reactivated transitional objects and continue to use them compulsively. 3. Eventually, people who use substances of abuse compulsively may increase ego destruction, schizoid pathology, and commit suicide. According to Volkan, because of a deficit in early object relations and the internalization of harsh and frustrating parental objects, drug addicts take drugs, which provide a regressive experience of a primary good object. The experience of this primary good object also masks the harsh, introjected (bad) objects and related dysphoric feelings of self-criticism and worthlessness. As the substance wears off, the affect of the bad object representations return *all the stronger for being repressed.* In this way the bad objects and the dysphoria they produce are linked to the substance of abuse. If more of the substance can be obtained, the dysphoria can be controlled, and thus, the cycle is complete as the user searches for the substance of abuse. The internalization of bad object representations allows substance users to be controlled while the influence of the substance of abuse is repressed. However, because the bad object representations carry tremendous aggressive energy, they threaten to surface and overpower the ego.[18]

According to Volkan, substance users report feeling a loss of control when under the influence of a substance of abuse. This feeling alternates with a feeling of being in control when the effects of the substance of abuse wear off. This cycle of control is very important. If the cycle of use and subsequent withdrawal from the substance is not maintained, it becomes difficult for the substance user to maintain control over his or her internalized bad object representations. This type of problem can be seen among recovering addicts. As noted by Volkan (1994), addicts who abstain from using can become intensely depressed, hostile, rageful, and suicidal. The substance of abuse serves to control their bad object representations, and when it is not used, the bad object representations threaten to surface.

Volkan (1994) outlined the basic tenets of developmental object relations theory and how it is manifested in substance use pathology:

> The phenomenology of compulsive drug users indicates that their object relations dynamics have aspects of the dynamics of good and bad object representations as described by Fairbairn (1952). In a more modern sense, Kernberg's (1967, 1975) conceptualization of borderline pathology shows that the drug user is unable to integrate good and bad object representations. Instead drugs are used in an attempt to maintain the defensive splitting between good and bad object representations. This type of compulsive drug use also serves to energize a cycle of introjection and projection of object representations. Seen in light of modern object relations theories, drugs serve as transitional objects, which reactivate a link to the good and bad aspects of the primary object. For most compulsive drug users, the transitional stage of object relations is not resolved. (pp. 77–78)

In regard to an object relations understanding of substance use, the task of the therapist would be one of maintaining a supportive neutral presence

---

[18] Fairbairn (1952) characterized this situation as an experience of "being possessed," a characterization also noted by Wurmser (1994; i.e., as an experience of being demonically possessed).

while helping the substance user to reestablish healthy object relations dynamics. The successful treatment of compulsive users would involve engendering a transference relationship with a positive role model. "Only when this relationship is established is there a chance to release or integrate the bad internalized object representations," that is, heal the split between the good and bad object representations (p. 116). As explained by Volkan (1994):

> Programs such as the twelve-step or co-dependency groups which include elements designed to bond drug abusers to a positive environment and role models may work for this reason. . . . Although it is recognized that some severely pathological patients may not tolerate the self-help approach, many patients will derive benefit from this type of supportive, contained environment. Also . . . self-help groups like AA (Alcoholics Anonymous), NA (Narcotic Anonymous) or CA (Cocaine Anonymous) force compulsive drug users to face the defensive denial and narcissism associated with their drug problem. Both the admission of addiction and the storytelling of drug experiences by patients in self-help groups may play a valuable psychodynamic role in overcoming these defenses. Nevertheless, without the deep insight engendered in psychoanalytic therapy, the success of the self-help approach alone may be transitory. Without the support of an external agency (e.g., supportive therapist or self-help group) the drug user will likely fall back into his old habits. Because the addict has relied on an external, reactivated transitional object for support, he does not necessarily have the motivation to internalize this support. This internalization comes about through introspective psychoanalytic work which requires some ability to tolerate painful affect. . . . Of course, this is why psychotherapeutic treatment with compulsive drug users is reported to be extremely difficult. . . . For this reason, it is perhaps best to do introspective work in combination with psychotherapies or self-help modalities which provide some external support. Although there is no good evidence which delineates the effectiveness of different types of drug treatment programs, this type of multimodal approach may have the best chance of success. (pp. 116–117)

While other psychoanalytic or other approaches may be valid for various types of substance users, the interpretation of substances of abuse as transitional objects may become a central issue in the prevention, treatment, and understanding of compulsive substance use.

Peele, Brodsky, and Arnold (1991) advanced the Life Process Program (LPP) theory of natural recovery. This cognitively based psychological theory addresses use of alcohol and other substances in addition to other "destructive habits" (e.g., codependence, gambling, overeating, excessive exercise, love and sex, and shopping). Attention is given to compulsive use, resumed nonuse, and relapsed use ("controlled use," "slips," and "relapse") by youth as well as adults. The focus is on self-help and, in regard to children and adolescents, the role of parents in instilling (directly or by example) healthful rather than addictive habits in their children.

The LPP theory proposes the following: 1. Belonging to a supportive social group—one with prosocial values that do not support addictive excesses—makes it unlikely that a person will be addicted. 2. Having a job and a family provides most people with a structure in life and a sense of value; conversely, addictions result when people's lives are structured and made to seem worthwhile by activities that harm them or those close to them, detract from their environments and relationships, and deepen their feelings of self-doubt. 3. Addictive activities, although a part of essential human experiences, subvert and substitute for genuine satisfactions. 4. The *addictive cycle* is the self-feeding reliance on feelings that the addiction makes harder to get in any other way (masking anxieties with substance use and not dealing with them constructively and depending more and more on the substance of abuse for this purpose as health is undermined). 5. Addiction is not an accident, but a consequence of the confluence of forces in people's lives, of their needs and available ways of satisfying them.

The LPP offers an alternative therapeutic approach for the treatment of problematic substance use and other "addictions to experience." Rejecting the disease theory because of its lack of therapeutic success and its basic assumptions, the theorists provide a nondisease self-help or therapist-assisted approach that emphasizes the natural processes of recovery, including building on individual strengths and developing and using those offered by the community. Rather than lifelong, treatment is finite. People are seen as evolving beings who require individualized treatment that is client centered. The development of coping abilities is seen as essential to the process of becoming nonaddicted. In this regard, the goal of treatment is personal efficacy, which is developed through motivation, identification of personal values, and development of life skills and life involvements, including those inherent in family, work, and community (Peele et al., 1991).

The LPP is proposed as a successful therapy for people who have destructive habits. The goal of the LPP is to change these habits. The focus of treatment is not the past, but the current situation—current rewards, satisfactions, and obstacles—and treatment is aimed at helping people mobilize their "assets." Thus, instead of focusing on past failures and weaknesses as is done with psychoanalytic therapy, the LPP draws on the personal strengths and resources that are available to the addicted person. The LPP also differs from behavioral techniques that shape behavior through contrived rewards and punishments in that it seeks rewards and punishments to encourage new behavior in the natural structure of the person's life. In essence the LPP is a values-based approach. Values are believed to be most crucial in orienting or reorienting a person's life. Developing and living by a set of values, expanding connections to the world, and aiming for and accomplishing worthwhile goals are key factors in the LPP. As described by Peele et al. (1991):

The Life Process Program presents a recipe for change through toning down overblown and frightening rhetoric about addictions and by instead appealing to the strength, intelligence, and instinct for self-preservation in every person. Addiction *is* a problem, and for some people a very severe problem. But you can best address that problem by reminding yourself of everything about you that is normal and healthy and by applying those strengths to your weakest areas of functioning.

Similarly, if your child is abusing drugs, you rightly worry about the potentially serious consequences of that behavior. But these immediate concerns do not obviate the need to address the values, relationships, and activities that constitute the young person's life. Whether it is you or a loved one who must cope with an addiction, don't discount your own resourcefulness. . . . The Life Process Program we recommend . . . does not focus exclusively or even primarily on addiction itself. You will certainly need to work on your addiction specifically, but the most crucial work you need to do is on the direction of your overall life, of which an addiction is just one expression. (pp. 167–168)

Sociological Theories

Several sociological theories were advanced from the family perspective, including the theory developed by Szapocznik, Kurtines, Santisteban, and Rio (1990), whose research program has been underway since 1970. This theory extended structural family systems theory, as proposed by Minuchin (1974) and others, to the problem of general substance use among Hispanic children and adolescents and their families and culturally appropriate intervention strategies, including brief strategic and one-person family therapy. For progress in the field of substance use, the theorists argue for the interplay of theory, research, and application. As described by Szapocznik et al. (1990):

Our program of research . . . provided a solid foundation from which to pursue new advances in the field. For example, the Structural Family System Rating Scale (SFSR) enabled us to evaluate the effectiveness of structural family therapy in a way that is immensely relevant to structural family theory and therapy. . . . Our refinement of structural family theory strategies and goals in the form of brief strategic family therapy (BSFT), in turn, enabled us to understand how to modify these strategies to achieve the same goals without having the entire family in therapy, thus making one-person family therapy possible. Our success in bringing about change in family interactions by working primarily through one person became the foundation of our breakthrough in engaging resistant families in treatment. Our findings that changes in family functioning are not necessary for reduction in symptom has challenged our most basic postulate regarding the relationship between family interaction and symptom change. Although it appears that family therapy "works," our findings raise more questions than they answer about the mechanisms through which family therapy brings about change. (p. 702)

Oetting and Beauvais (1990–91), also concerned with substance use among Hispanic as well as American Native adolescents, presented their orthogonal cultural identification theory by arguing its advantages as a model of cultural adaptation over previously proposed models (e.g., dominant majority, transitional, alienation, multidimensional, and bicultural [transcultural] models). According to Oetting and Beauvais (1990–91):

Identification with any culture is essentially independent of identification with any other culture. Instead of two cultures being placed at opposite ends of a single dimension or single line, cultural identification dimensions are at right angles to each other. At the origin of the angles is lack of identification with any culture, cultural anomie or cultural alienation. The change from the previous models may appear to be minor, but the differences are profound. All of the other models place limits on what patterns of cultural identification and on what adaptations to change are possible. The orthogonal identification model indicates that any pattern, any combination of cultural identification, can exist and that any movement or change is possible. There can be highly bicultural people, unicultural identification, high identification with one culture and medium identification with another, or even low identification with either culture. (pp. 661–662)

However, in regard to the general results obtained from their research program that has focused on the relationship between cultural identification and adolescent substance use, Oetting and Beauvais (1990–91) report:

While higher cultural identification seems to be consistently associated with greater personal and social resources, the links to drug use are inconsistent and seem to depend on many other intervening factors. There is no one simple relationship nor is there even one pattern of results that is consistent across groups. . . . It is apparent that if we are to truly understand how cultural identification and drug use are connected, we will have to carefully assess all of the intermeshing links, covering process (the general levels and patterns of identification with the cultures involved), content (covering cultural content including gender roles), peer relationships (links to peers and their behaviors), and environmental factors (such as isolation, epidemiology and access to drugs). . . . Orthogonal cultural identification theory has a number of obvious implications for theory and research, but it also suggests some ideas for new directions. (p. 677)

Natakusumah et al. (1992) examined the family dimensions of cohesion and adaptability and their relationship to substance use severity among American and Indonesian families of adolescent substance users. They were specifically concerned with studying the perceived levels of cohesion and adaptability of the individual members of these families, the manner and extent to which they differed from one another, and the extent to which their adaptability and cohesion were related to substance use severity (p. 390). The third version of the Family Adaptability and Cohesion Evaluation Scale (FACES III) was used as a cross-cultural measure of family functioning. As described by Natakusumah et al. (1992):

The development of the various versions of FACES is theoretically based on the
Circumplex Model of Family Functioning developed by Olson & Sprenkle et
al. (1979). This model postulated three important dimensions of family functioning: cohesion (the emotional bonding among family members), adaptability (flexibility of family structure, role relationships, and family rules), and communications (how family members relate to each other). FACES III measures the
dimensions of cohesion and adaptability. (p. 391)

Inherent in the model is the assumption that it is optimal for a family to have
a balance of cohesion between the extremes of enmeshment and disengagement, and a balance of adaptability between the extremes of rigidity and
chaos. However, the validity of this curvilinear hypothesis, as well as its cross-
cultural consistency in regard to nuclear versus extended families, has been
questioned by several researchers, including those who argue for a linear relationship for cohesion and adaptability—that is, the greater the cohesion and
adaptability displayed by a family, the better its functioning. Thus, Natakusumah et al. (1992) also sought to test its generalizability with culture as the
independent variable.

The findings seem to show cultural differences that may or may not be
related to the etiology of drug abuse itself. American adolescents may be
more likely to see their families as part of the problem than are their parents,
and Indonesian parents feel more guilt and responsibility for their child's
problem with drugs than do American parents. The greatest differences were
that Americans saw their families as considerably more extreme and more
dysfunctional, as reflected in the distance from center scores of the FACES III,
than did Indonesian family members. As described by the theorists, this may
mean that the American family is indeed more dysfunctional than the Indonesian family on the dimension of cohesion and adaptability or that the Indonesian family is more concerned with saving face than is the American
family. It may also mean that in most situations Indonesians are more moderate in their responses. Another difference was that the American substance
abusers were much more likely to see their families as disengaged (60 vs. 5
percent), while the Indonesians were more likely to see their families either
as balanced (separated or connected) or as enmeshed. These findings are
suggestive of possible interventions within the two cultures. The integrative
family therapy model that Natakusumah et al. (1992) have developed for
substance-abusing American adolescents strongly emphasizes getting parents involved with their children again. In this regard, an attempt is made to
decrease family disengagement by putting parents back in charge of their
teenagers. More culturally appropriate goals should take precedence with
Indonesian substance abusers, such as involving extended family members in
treatment (p. 406). In addition, while 16.7 percent of the Indonesian adolescents saw their families as enmeshed (the extreme end of cohesion), the theorists were hesitant to consider this finding necessarily dysfunctional within

that culture. "In a close-knit family system, as in Indonesia, family enmeshment may indeed be a positive characteristic that prevents adolescents from using drugs" (p. 406).

Adaptability was not found to predict the severity of substance use for Indonesian or American adolescents. Cohesion, however, had predictive power in both samples, although to a lesser extent in the American sample. The finding that family cohesion was related to substance use severity in these samples supports the link between close family relationships and substance use patterns among adolescents. While the theorists stressed that they would have to be sensitive to cultural differences in order to adequately understand adolescent substance use in different cultures, they also recognized that they should not neglect such commonalities.

Eclectic Theories

Brook and her colleagues (Brook, Brook, Scovell Gordon, Whiteman, & Cohen, 1990) proposed the family interactional theory for explaining the psychosocial aspects of adolescent drug use. Attention was given to marijuana as the paradigm for other substance use. The two-component development model emphasized three themes: 1. the extension of developmental perspectives on drug use; 2. the elucidation of family influences leading to drug use, particularly parental influences; and 3. the exploration of factors that increase or mitigate adolescents' vulnerability to drug use. The first component deals with adolescent pathways to drug use, while the second incorporates childhood factors. As described by the theorists:

> Our theoretical model is drawn from a number of conceptual orientations, such as social learning theory, attachment theory, psychoanalytic theory, and deviant behavior proneness. In our framework, which is psychobiologically based, we stress psychological issues while recognizing that growth and development occur on the basis of a biological, species-specific anlage. Such mechanisms as introjection and identification are emphasized because they affect parent-child attachment. Learning is important in the transgenerational passage of values and behavior. The child's attitudes and behavior not only reflect the parent-child interaction but also are influenced by the shaping power of peer group affiliations and influences. This latter process is particularly powerful if the peer group sanctions deviant behavior. The consequences of adolescent marijuana use thus ensue from both earlier and current parent-child relationships and from current peer interactions. . . . The parental peer socialization systems in which children develop interact with and influence each other uniquely. However, present knowledge about the interrelationship has not advanced. . . . We attempted to examine the nature of the conjoint influences from the parent and peer systems. (Brook et al., 1990, pp. 119–120)

The model was tested in two studies: one cross-sectional study of 649 college students and their fathers, and one longitudinal study of 429 children and their mothers. The subjects were given self-administered questionnaires containing scales measuring the personality, family, and peer variables relevant to the model. The results of each study supported the proposed model, with some differences between parental influences. The theorists noted that individual protective factors (e.g., adolescent conventionality and parent-child attachment) could offset risk factors (e.g., peer drug use) and enhance other protective factors, resulting in less adolescent marijuana use. As noted by Brook et al. (1990, p. 111) the results of their studies have implications for prevention and treatment, future research, and public policy.

McDonald and Towberman (1993) developed the four-factor model of adolescent drug involvement (psychosocial model of adolescent drug involvement). Noting that "no one model has been developed that fully explains the cause of substance abuse" and that "present theories are bound by reductionist interpretations from different disciplines," with "psychological theories tend[ing] to focus on the individual rather than on environmental and cultural contributors to individual behavior" and "sociological theories tend-[ing] to focus on external factors, which has the effect of ignoring individual differences," a four-factor model was presented based on a larger, multiyear psychosocial study of emergent adolescent drug involvement. McDonald and Towberman's study considered both the environment and the intrapsychic forces as they interact on the individual. The study tracked students from grade 5 through grade 9. The cross-sectional findings were derived from analysis of sample data collected when the subjects were in grades 7 and 8. As described by the theorists:

> In accordance with the theory that internal and external forces affect youths' decisions to experiment with or continue the use of substances, fourteen psychosocial measures were selected as independent variables. . . . Before submission for multiple regression analysis, the explanatory variables were factor analyzed to reduce multicollinearity and to produce a more efficient model of factors underlying drug involvement. . . . Analysis of the fourteen variables produced the four-factor model. (McDonald & Towberman, 1993, pp. 931–932)

The results of their study of the antecedents of adolescent drug use were identified as being important in several ways: 1. the psychosocial focus expanded the view of drug use causation, which, according to the theorists, was generally limited to either psychological or sociological theories; 2. causation is viewed in terms of both external and internal factors; and 3. interdisciplinary research cooperation is supported. Summarizing their work, McDonald and Towberman (1993) note:

> The explanatory potency of the four-factor model is a notable contribution to adolescent drug use research. The significant amount of variance in drug experimentation and the magnitude of drug use that is explained in this model may serve as a building block for further study. The fact that both internalized values and external influences were important in explaining adolescent drug use is not surprising. It is somewhat surprising, however, that the internality of

self-concept was not significantly associated with either drug experimentation or frequency of drug use. This finding is in contrast with others linking self-concept and adolescent drug use. Given the relatively young age or maturity level of the study sample, individuation may not have been developed to a point consistent with an integrated self-identity. It may be that self-concept factors may emerge as significant predictors of adolescent drug use in the later adolescent years. (p. 935)

The results of this work emphasize the importance of children bonding with parents, peers, and other people who have drug-resistant attitudes and their connection with, and achievement in, school.

Muisener (1994) proposed the biopsychosocial model in his text *Understanding and Treating Adolescent Substance Abuse.* This model presents five possible levels of causal interacting factors as important to an adolescent's susceptibility to developing a substance abuse disorder: 1. biological factors (genetic, neurological, and idiosyncratic physiological factors), 2. adolescent psychological development factors, 3. interpersonal (family functioning and peer relationship) factors, 4. community factors (schools, churches, criminal justice systems, prevention services and programs), and 5. societal factors (government policies, media). Of these factors, adolescent psychological development and interpersonal (family functioning and peer) relationships are emphasized. As the "toxic agent," the substance of abuse penetrates all five levels of factors resulting in what is manifested as the adolescent substance abuse disorder. As explained by the theorist:

> The interaction of psychoactive substance use with the adolescent's biological, psychological, and social systems can culminate in an addiction process. This addiction process simultaneously infiltrates every aspect of the young person's life . . . [as it unfolds] across three stages—initiation, escalation, and maintenance—and is composed of three dynamics: compulsion [the driving urge to obtain, use, and continue using drugs—the central addiction dynamic], relapse [involving four stages: immediate determinants stage, crossroads stage, breaking of abstinence stage, and abstinence violation coping stage], and denial [those systems and processes that most immediately and directly diminish their awareness of their chemical use and the effects of this use]. These three addiction dynamics can be understood as having biopsychosocial expressions. (pp. 52–53)

Muisener (1994) provides a metaphor to symbolize his model:

> The growing teenager is represented by an apple tree in an orchard. This tree is in the season of blossoming and is on the threshold of bearing fruit. A fire, like the toxic agent drugs, becomes a predator of the maturing tree. The origin of this fire—whether matches, or heat friction, or some random synergy of elements—cannot be easily determined. How this sprouting tree resists or succumbs to the fire is, in part, reflective of its overall combustibility—analogous to the adolescent's intrapsychic structure. Depending on this young tree's over-

all combustibility, it may be able to withstand the fire or be susceptible to severe burns. The endogenous constitution of the wood of the tree—similar to the biological factors of addiction—may, in part, contribute to the flourishing of the fire. The cluster of other trees surrounding the apple tree is similar to the teenager's interpersonal environment of family and peers. By fueling the fire, this cluster of surrounding trees may enable the fire to continue much in the way that family and peers can enable an adolescent's continued substance abuse. Larger environmental elements within and beyond the orchard—climate and weather conditions—can encourage or impede the burning of the tree, just as community and society factors can enable the teenager's continued chemical abuse. The addiction dynamics of compulsion, relapse, and denial also resemble some dynamics of this fire. Compulsion is akin to the driving symbiosis between the burning fire and the apple tree, relapse is analogous to smoldering roots of the tree that can reignite a later fire, and denial is similar to the smoke that billows from the fire, engulfing the tree so as to obscure awareness of the extent of the fire. The interplay of all of these factors will determine if the apple tree experiences only minor charring, much like a substance use problem, or suffers extensive fire damage, similar to a substance abuse disorder. (pp. 56–57)

According to the theorist, few adolescents progress to serious patterns of use. However, those who do usually require external intervention in order to regress to a less problematic pattern of use or cease altogether. Adolescents rarely experience spontaneous remission or practice self-prescribed abstinence for any length of time. Thus, Muisener rejects arguments for maturing out, natural recovery, or growing out of problematic patterns of substance use. Instead, he proposes an extension of his biopsychosocial model for recovery-oriented treatment with adolescent substance abusers. This model considers multiple and interacting systems that may require treatment and the multiple and interacting interventions that can be used. As emphasized by Muisener (1994), the possible factors that contribute to adolescent substance abuse can become a part of the solution (p. 99).

Thus, Muisener's recovery-oriented treatment embraces a hybrid combination of treatment approaches that integrate biomedical and mental health approaches with those offered by AA and other 12-step self-help programs: for example, AL-ANON for family members, including teens, of alcoholics; Alateen for teens with alcoholic parents; and Family Anonymous. The Adolescent Chemical Use Problem Index is provided by Muisener (1994) as a tool to assist in identifying an adolescent's substance use problem so that his or her difficulties can be effectively dealt with. The model also provides guidelines for promoting recovery among vulnerable adolescents (e.g., adolescents who have a dual diagnosis or who have been victims of physical or sexual abuse) for whom treatment seeks to "bring awareness, growth, and developmental insight" so that they may "thrive in recovery" (p. 198).

Continuing an eclectic focus, Tarter and Mezzich (1992) proposed the model of dynamic lifetime interplay among risk-enhancing and risk-attenuating factors interacting with genetic predisposition for substance abuse outcome. This interactive model focused on genetic and environmental effects on the development of substance abuse among children, adolescents, and adults (see also the discussion of eclectic theories in the 1980s). A diagrammatic representation of the conceptual model is provided by Tarter and Mezzich (1992, p. 160), which can be used for researching the etiology of and developmental pathways to a substance abuse outcome.

According to Tarter and Mezzich (1992), a genetic predisposition (ranging from low to high) is assumed to be normally distributed in the general population. Substance abuse, as a complex behavioral disorder, is thought to have its genetic basis in the additive effects of many genes located on several chromosomes. The theorists emphasize that genetic susceptibility is neither a necessary nor a sufficient condition for an adverse outcome. In fact, a person who has high genetic vulnerability (i.e., who has many of the genes) can be protected from a substance abuse outcome by a protective environment (e.g., low drug availability, cultural sanctions, and strong social support). On the other hand, a person who has low genetic susceptibility may have such an adverse outcome where drug exposure is high and the social environment is conducive.

Tarter and Mezzich (1992) argue that a substance abuse outcome can theoretically occur at any stage in life because it is contingent on the dynamic interplay among genetic and environmental factors:

> The risks for a drug-abuse outcome must be considered in the specific framework of unique and specific factors occurring throughout life. . . . Not only does the individual predisposed to drug abuse react to environmental contingencies, but such persons seek out specific environmental circumstances (e.g., high stimulus intensity, non-normative peers, etc.). The quality of these interactions additionally determines outcome throughout the life span. Therefore, there is some degree of risk for an adverse outcome at any stage in life. Depending on the changing contingencies involved in gene-environment interactions, the triggering of a drug abuse disorder at one stage in the life span (e.g., adolescence) may be different from the precipitating factors at another stage (e.g., late adulthood). Similarly, the factors that trigger drug-use initiation differ during the course of the life span; this consideration has important ramifications for the design of effective primary prevention programs. (p. 161)

The model proposed by Tarter and Mezzich (1992) provides a basis for understanding the variant rate of progression from drug initiation to substance abuse and the diverse pathways to this adverse outcome. Emphasizing genetic individuality, idiosyncratic developmental history, and unique micro- and macroenvironmental effects, the model implies also that everyone in a given population is theoretically at risk for substance abuse—an outcome contingent on changes in either the organism or the environment (see also Tarter, 1990; Tarter, Kabene, et al., 1990; Tarter, Laird, et al., 1990).

G. R. Ross (1994) proposed the cognitive-behavioral theory of adolescent chemical dependency. Integrating biological (illness/disease) and psychological (learning: neobehaviorism) orientations with the spiritual component inherent in AA, he addressed abuse and compulsive use patterns of substances of abuse among adolescent boys and girls. He also stated that the theories and techniques can be applied to adult substance abusers, to other forms of addiction, and to oppositional defiant and conduct disorders.

According to G. R. Ross (1994):

Whether the practitioner considers chemical dependency a disease or a behavior disorder, or attributes its cause to genetic factors, environmental, family, and cultural influences, or underlying personality conflicts; clinical evidence clearly suggests that a faulty cognitive structure, or "self-defeating self-talk," is a critical element in the assessment and treatment of adolescents suffering from the use and abuse of mind-altering substances. (p. 7)

Thus, he advanced several hypotheses and a conceptual model that consider the emerging personality and cognitive structure of the chemically dependent adolescent. Defining *chemical dependency* as "a disease of attitudes leading to the use and abuse of mind-altering substances" (e.g., alcohol, cocaine, and marijuana) culminating in "physical deterioration of the body, emotional instability, and spiritual bankruptcy," he advocates essential assessment and treatment guided by his theory.

Using Rokeach's (1970) definition of *attitude* (a relatively enduring organization of beliefs around an object or situation predisposing a person to respond in some preferential manner), G. R. Ross (1994) identifies two types of attitudes that contribute to the development of a *chemically dependent personality:* 1. *a priori attitude* (an enduring organization of beliefs around a perception or images of the environment that helps people to make sense of their external experiences) and 2. *a posteriori attitude* (an enduring organization of beliefs around autonomically mediated physiological responses, or emotions, that helps people to make sense out of their internal experiences). These two types of attitudes produce automatic emotional and behavioral responses that eventually result in the formation of distinct personality structures. According to Ross, chemical use, abuse, and dependency among adolescents occurs when a distinct set of a priori beliefs about the environment results in a multitude of self-defeating emotional responses. These responses activate a distinct set of a posteriori beliefs that, in turn, activate a distinct set of self-defeating behavioral responses.

Critical factors in the adolescent's environment (e.g., family, peer culture, media, and ready availability of substances of abuse) influence a priori beliefs. These beliefs and subsequent feelings create a distinct mind set conducive to substance use, abuse, and, when left unchallenged, habitual substance usage. Over time, the behavior of substance use reinforces a set of a posteriori beliefs. According to these beliefs, substance use is a way to seek stimulation, gain self and peer acceptance, and avoid/escape responsibility. With repeated substance use, the adolescent eventually develops an *erroneous obsessive thinking pattern* (what was once "a way" eventually becomes "the only way" to seek stimulation, gain self and peer acceptance, and avoid/escape responsibility). As use continues, the adolescent's life becomes increasingly unmanageable, as a sense of powerlessness or loss of control intensifies, fuelled by this erroneous obsession. The adolescent also finds that he or she is faced with such behavioral consequences as the violation of well-learned ethical, value, and legal standards; deterioration of cognitive, affective, and behavioral functioning; and the emergence of more pronounced psychological defenses. As the addictive personality develops, an added set of a priori beliefs emerge that concern the fear of discovery and possible punishment. This additional internal dialogue significantly increases the adolescent's anxiety level and creates an increased demand for emotional relief. The obsession becomes greater as the temporary emotional relief provided by substance use reinforces the erroneous a posteriori belief that the only way to find relief from unpleasant feelings is to get high. As this addictive process continues to repeat itself, a distinct personality pattern and cognitive structure emerge. The latter ultimately maintains a *cauldron of emotional pain* and self-defeating behavior patterns that culminate in physical deterioration of the body, emotional instability, and spiritual bankruptcy.

G. R. Ross (1994) provides a multimethod approach to assessment that includes screening for substance use, a signs and symptoms checklist, psychosocial assessment and family interviews, parental evaluation, teenage substance abuser interviews, medical examination, psychological and psychiatric evaluation, and clinical observations. Three dimensions used to formulate a diagnosis of an adolescent substance abuser are also provided and explained. The theorist offers treatment options and environments (treatment climate, staffing patterns, and supportive services), four distinct plateaus of recovery (admitting, submitting, committing, and transmitting), and 30 treatment strategies useful in helping adolescents develop healthier cognitive structures.

The development of healthier cognitive structures is thought to enable them to reach the four plateaus, and includes teaching them how to be more aware and honest with themselves, how to more effectively manage their feelings, how to change self-defeating emotions and behavior, and how to identify self-defeating self-talk, change it, and keep it from reoccurring. Codependency among parents and other family members is addressed, and treatment strategies are presented along with methods for developing more effective communication and interaction patterns. The attributes (character strengths, confidentiality, timing and tact, listenership, objectivity and discernment, empathy and understanding, honesty, genuine interest and love, and patience and perseverance) and requisite skills (e.g., basic one-on-one and group cognitive-behavioral substance abuse counseling skills, including a working knowledge of the steps and principles of AA; and knowledge of developmental, family systems, and other theories, especially gestalt, reality, and actualizing therapies) of an effective substance abuse counselor are outlined. Successful diagnosis and treatment involve helping substance-abusing adolescents identify and change the a priori and a posteriori attitudes that constitute a self-defeating personality and cognitive structure and that keep them in a state of intoxication and emotional and behavioral turmoil.

SUMMARY

This chapter has presented, in broad brush strokes, modern theories advanced in an effort to explain why children and adolescents use in various ways the substances of abuse. While rich and diverse in their contributions, causal understanding remains out of reach. Two decades ago, Kandel (1978b) noted in the preface of her classic text *Longitudinal Research on Drug Use:*

> Longitudinal studies are among the most powerful available to social scientists because they provide an optimal set of data for the testing of causal assumptions. Analyses of longitudinal data are complex, however, and the methods available for dealing with such data obtained from large-scale surveys are in their infancy. Recently, as social science has moved in the direction of complex mathematical techniques, such as path and regression analyses or the analysis of mean and covariance structure, interest has developed in the application of these techniques to panel data and the study of change. A variety of techniques has been proposed, but few have been applied empirically because longitudinal data are not readily available. (p. ix)

The chapters in her text were for the most part revisions of conference papers that, in her opinion, were "the most significant of their period" on the basis of "sample size, the richness of the information collected, the nature of the theoretical scheme underpinning a study, the sophistication of analysis, and the strength of the results" (pp. ix–x).[19] As noted by Kandel (1978b),

[19] Papers were presented at the Conference on Strategies of Longitudinal Research on Drug Use, which was organized and held April 7–9, 1976, in San Juan, PR, under the sponsorship of the Center of Socio-Cultural Research on Drug Use of Columbia University with the support of NIDA.

until this time most longitudinal data relevant to drug use were obtained in follow-ups of clinical populations of heroin addicts. Subjects were drawn from facilities specifically designed for addicts, or from institutions such as courts or social service agencies set up to deal with deviant or maladjusted people. These subjects represented the most extreme segment of the substance-using population. Research based on already-addicted people precluded the investigation of many issues relevant to the understanding of substance behavior, which takes many forms other than addiction. Furthermore, although longitudinal in character, studies of this nature do not permit a clear assessment of the antecedents and the consequences of drug use. Such an assessment requires contact with a population at risk for substance use and subsequent follow-up over time in regard to the variables related to the initiation and maintenance of substance use.

The results of the longitudinal studies selected for inclusion in Kandel's (1978b) text were reviewed and synthesized into a series of 19 propositions. These propositions addressed patterns of involvement in substance use, antecedents of substance use, and consequences of substance use. In regard to patterns of involvement in substance use in the form of illicit substance use, she identified the following:

1. The period of risk for initiation into substance use is over by a person's mid-20s.
2. A high proportion of adolescents who have tried marijuana will eventually go on to experiment with other substances of abuse.
3. Later age of onset is associated with lesser involvement with substance use and greater probability of discontinuing use.
4. There are clear-cut developmental steps and sequences in substance use behavior, so that the use of one of the legal substances almost always precedes use of illegal substances.
5. Addiction to heroin is not necessarily a permanent condition.
6. Occasional use of heroin does not necessarily lead to addiction.

In regard to the antecedents of substance use, 11 propositions were noted:

1. Different factors are involved in the transitions into different stages of substance use.
2. Personality factors, indicative of maladjustment, precede the use of marijuana and other illicit substances of abuse.
3. Poor school performance is a common antecedent of subsequent initiation into illicit substance use.
4. Delinquent and deviant activities precede involvement with illicit substance use.

5. A constellation of attitudes and values favorable to deviance precedes involvement with illicit substances of abuse.

6. There is a process of anticipatory socialization in which adolescents who will initiate the use of substances of abuse develop attitudes favorable to the use of legal and illegal substances of abuse prior to initiation.

7. Substance use behavior and related attitudes of peers are among the most potent predictors of involvement with substances of abuse.

8. Parental behaviors, attitudes, and closeness to their children have differential importance at different stages of involvement with substance use.

9. Sociodemographic variables hold little predictive power for initiation into marijuana use.

10. Age of onset of substance use declines as degree of proneness to deviance increases.

11. A social setting favorable to substance use reinforces and increases individual predisposition to use.

Finally, in regard to the consequences of substance use:

1. Nonaddictive illicit substance use has not been shown to lead to increased criminality.

2. Substance use has not been shown to lead to the amotivational syndrome.

These propositions would be tested over the next two decades and would stimulate much debate and research in that they identified several limitations and issues in regard to explaining substance use during childhood and adolescence. These issues included problems with the consistent definition and measurement of variables; immature research designs and analysis procedures (e.g., limitations of linear models in regard to studying the dynamic processes of change, interactional effects, and influences of cluster variables); cultural and historical conditions of change (e.g., subject maturation and variation in availability of substances of abuse or cultural values regarding their use); attrition among subjects who are heavy users of the substances of abuse; and limited attention to consequences, including positive effects (e.g., adaptive use of substances of abuse as a form of self-medication for depression or "incipient psychopathology," health benefits of alcohol or marijuana, and improved academic performance with stimulants) and negative health consequences (e.g., smoking-related heart disease and lung cancer).

A decade later, Newcomb and Bentler (1988) noted in their text *Consequences of Adolescent Drug Use:*

An extremely large body of data, speculation, and well-refined theories have emerged during the past 20 years to explain the processes of acquiring drug-using behaviors among adolescents. These are very crucial and critical issues and tasks. Certainly, it is imperative to understand the etiological or antecedent factors involved in drug use. Interestingly, however, very little effort has been devoted to determining the consequences of drug use.

Drugs, including psychoactive drugs, have been used by virtually all cultures in many different forms from time immemorial. More recently, public policy has been based on the proposition that the use of mind-altering drugs is bad. This concern, which is largely associated with the epidemic rise in drug use among youngsters and teenagers during the recent past, is appropriate. But as scientists, we must challenge the rather uncritical and unscientific assumption that drug use, in and of itself, is bad and should be prevented, understood, or treated. This may be true. But we need to demonstrate any conclusions in a scientifically rigorous manner, testing explicit theories and causal relationships, and evaluating or controlling spurious influences. How does drug use create bad or problematic outcomes? What areas of functioning are affected? Are there positive effects of drug involvement? These are the types of questions we address. . . .

The study of drug use consequences is a new area for the epidemiological study of drug use, as reflected in panel studies of adolescents (such as ours and other important research projects around the country involving Judith Brook, Ann Brunswick, Richard Clayton, the Jessors, Lloyd Johnston, Denise Kandel, Howard Kaplan, Robert Pandina, Gene Smith, Harwin Voss, and others). The primary initial task of most of these and related projects . . . has been the development and testing of theories of how drug use is acquired. In other words, they have been etiological in nature and have attempted to explain the essential antecedents of drug use among teenagers. Many important theories have been developed and tested . . . [and] have progressed from being rather vague and diffuse to being clear, concise, and well refined. The focus of these theories has been on family and peer influences . . . , numerous types of risk factors . . . , deviance, problem behavior, or lack of social conformity . . . , low self-esteem, depression, or psychological distress . . . , and stressful life change events. . . . Recently, theories have attempted to grapple with these diverse processes by proposing more complex frameworks that can integrate biological, psychological, and social factors . . . that may be tested in large, interactive models spanning many years. . . . More general theories have attempted to account for a broad range of deviant behaviors among the young, such as the structured strain perspective . . . , subcultural socialization . . . , control theories . . . , containment theories . . . , labeling theory . . . , social learning . . . , and an integrated control-strain model. . . . Discussion of these etiological theories [, however,] is beyond the scope of this book. (pp. 14–16)

As yet another decade comes to a close, we see both continuing and new theoretical directions developing, each reflecting its particular science in its aims, methods, and factual claims—its theories. Obviously we have come far, but not far enough, in our quest for knowledge of why children and adolescents come to use or not use the substances of abuse. Our journey continues into a new decade and new century as we endeavor to disentangle a multitude of interacting factors related to understanding substance use among children and adolescents.

> *My worthy friend, all theories are gray,*
> *And green alone Life's golden tree.*

Johann Wolfgang von Goethe, *Faust*

CHAPTER 3

Prenatal Exposure to Substances of Abuse

This chapter focuses on substances of abuse (Table 3.1) as human teratogens. A *teratogen* is broadly defined as any factor, for example, a drug, associated with the production of physical or mental abnormalities in the developing embryo or fetus. The term is derived from the Greek words *terato* (monster) and *genesis* (origin or beginning). It is estimated that some type of teratogenic effect can be found among 2–3 percent of all live births and that teratogenic effects, at least in part, account for 20 percent of the deaths that occur during the first 5 years of life. These effects, which can be acute and self-limiting or irreversible and long-term, may be displayed in a variety of ways (L. A. Pagliaro & Pagliaro, 1995b).

The type and degree of human teratogenesis has been associated with many factors, including unknown factors, genetic factors, and maternal/fetal environmental factors. The maternal/fetal environmental factors include radiation, disease, and infections. They also include substances of abuse.

This chapter summarizes the published literature examining the teratogenic effects associated with the maternal use of various substances of abuse during pregnancy. Attention is given only to human studies because of the inherent difficulties associated with extrapolating data from animal studies to humans, including the determination of physiological and genetic differences in teratogenic susceptibility and the establishment of comparable doses, stages of pregnancy, environmental conditions, ages, and maternal health status (Hemminki & Vineis, 1985). A classic example of the problems associated with the extrapolation of the results of animal studies to humans is the thalidomide tragedy. When thalidomide, a sedative-hypnotic drug, was tested on several pregnant rodent species, no teratogenic effects were noted. However, when thalidomide was used by women to treat anxiety and insomnia during the first trimester of pregnancy, devastating teratogenic effects were produced ("What Lessons," 1983).

MATERNAL SUBSTANCE USE

According to a recent survey conducted for the National Association for Perinatal Addiction Research and Education, 11 percent of all American babies

TABLE 3.1   Major Substances of Abuse[a]

Central Nervous System Depressants
  Opiates (e.g., codeine, heroin, meperidine, methadone, morphine, pentazocine)
  Sedative-hypnotics (e.g., alcohol [beer, wine, distilled spirits], barbiturates,
    benzodiazepines)
  Volatile solvents and inhalants (e.g., gasoline, glue)
Central Nervous System Stimulants
  Amphetamines (e.g., dextroamphetamine)
  Caffeine (e.g., caffeinated soft drinks, coffee, tea)
  Cocaine (e.g., cocaine hydrochloride, crack cocaine)
  Nicotine (e.g., tobacco cigarettes, tobacco cigars)
Psychedelics (partial list)
  Lysergic acid diethylamide (LSD)
  Mescaline (peyote)
  Phencyclidine (PCP)
  Psilocybin (hallucinogenic mushrooms)
  Tetrahydrocannabinol (THC; e.g., hashish, hashish oil, marijuana)

[a]Classification scheme from A. M. Pagliaro (1990a, 1991).

are born with evidence of drug exposure. We know that we are seeing just the first few months and years in the lives of an entire generation of children who are maimed and deformed physically, emotionally, and mentally by the drug addictions of their mothers. We will be mourning for decades if not generations the waste of human and financial resources that these children represent. (Gore, 1991, p. 99)[1]

Some authors (e.g., L. D. Gilchrist, Gillmore, & Lohr, 1990; Lohr, Gillmore, Gilchrist, & Butler, 1992) suggest that substance use declines "voluntarily and substantially during pregnancy." However, the preponderance of available data suggests that most adolescent girls and women still use one or more of the substances of abuse at some time during their pregnancies (Chasnoff, 1988; Deren, Frank, & Schmeidler, 1990; Kokotailo, Adger, Duggan, Repke, & Joffe, 1992; Marques & McKnight, 1991; Merrick, 1993; Newman & Buka, 1991; L. A. Pagliaro, 1995d; Sarvela & Ford, 1992); the likelihood of such use is determined primarily by such factors as age, race, and socioeconomic status (Cornelius et al., 1993; Jorgensen, 1992; Wheeler, 1993). Research has also identified additional risk factors for substance use by adolescent girls during pregnancy, including physical or sexual abuse during childhood.

Substance use was reported seven times more often in those with a history of combined physical and sexual assault, five times more frequently by those who had been sexually assaulted, and three times more often in those who had been

[1] Although not cited in the original article, the source for this research appears to be Gittler and McPherson (1990). A similar prevalence rate (11.35 percent) has also been noted by Vega (1992) in a statewide study in California.

physically assaulted than adolescents without a history of assault. (Berenson, San Miguel, & Wilkinson, 1992, p. 470)

See Chapter 5 for identification and discussion of additional risk factors.

Unfortunately, a reliable estimate of the nature and extent of substance use among this population group is not available. There are many reasons for this lack of data including the fact that many substances of abuse (e.g., cocaine, heroin, and marijuana) are illegal and, thus, their use is hidden or underreported. Of concern is the fact that although the moderate use of a particular substance of abuse may have limited harmful effects for the mother, it may be extremely toxic and pose high teratogenic risk to the developing embryo or fetus as a result of differences in maternal and fetal metabolism, concentration, tissue sensitivity, and a variety of other factors that preclude a single direct cause-effect relationship (Griffith, Azuma, & Chasnoff, 1994).[2]

Attention to the types of substances of abuse used by adolescent girls and women during pregnancy and their patterns of use before becoming pregnant is important in order to retrospectively identify teratogenic risk to the developing embryo and fetus.[3] Although there are limitations to this type of research, human teratogenic experiments cannot be ethically performed, and the results of experiments involving animal models, as previously noted, cannot be relied upon to determine human teratogenic potential. In order to better identify the teratogenic risk associated with maternal substance use, attention must also be given to the interaction of several factors, including maternal factors, placental factors, fetal factors, environmental factors, and

---

[2] It should be noted that maternal substance use raises a plethora of potential legal and ethical issues (S. Goldsmith, 1990; Madden, 1993). As noted by Garcia (1993), "some policies have pitted mothers against their fetuses and children . . . new paradigms [are required] to minimize conflict and to achieve just and therapeutic balances between the rights and needs of those involved" (p. 1311). We will not attempt to address or resolve these issues here. Our focus, however, will be on optimizing the health and well-being of the fetus and neonate in keeping with the focus and goal of this text.

[3] This information also is important in relation to perinatal health. For example:

For the period 1978–1984, the infant mortality rate for infants whose mothers were substance users (as indicated on birth certificates) was about three times higher than the citywide rate (46.7/1,000 vs 15.5/1,000 live births). The percentage of newborns of low birth weight (under 2,500 grams or less than 5½ lb) born to these women was more than three times the citywide rate (32.8/1,000 vs 9.6/1,000 live births). Recent information indicates that the infant mortality rate may be increasing in New York City, after more than a decade of decline, due to births to mothers who are abusing cocaine or who have AIDS. (Deren et al., 1990, p. 179)

In addition, it has been found that women who use substances of abuse while pregnant are significantly more likely to neglect, physically abuse, or sexually abuse their newborns and infants (see Chap. 8). Unfortunately, it appears that "the incidence and prevalence of perinatal drug exposure is substantial and rising" (Cole, Jones, & Sadofsky, 1990, p. 5).

specific substance of abuse factors (Cordier, Ha, Ayme, & Goujard, 1992; L. A. Pagliaro & Pagliaro, 1995b; Van Allen, 1992; see Fig. 3.1).

Maternal factors include uterine blood flow, concomitant medical conditions (e.g., diabetes, epilepsy, infections, and thyroid disorders), maternal dose, and general health. *Placental factors* include the size and thickness of the placenta; placental blood flow; ability of the placenta to metabolize the substance of abuse to an inactive, active, or teratogenic metabolite; and placental age. *Fetal factors* include the stage of fetal development, the status of hepatic drug-metabolizing systems, the amount of hepatic blood flow through the ductus venosus, fetal blood pH, genetic predisposition, and concomitant exposure to other potential teratogens. *Environmental factors* include food additives (e.g., aspartame and nitrates), pesticides (e.g., chlordane), air and water pollutants, radiation, and toxins (e.g., mercury and organic solvents). *Substance of abuse factors* include the amount, frequency, and method of maternal use; distribution (concentration), metabolism, excretion; physiochemical properties of the substance of abuse (e.g., lipid solubil-

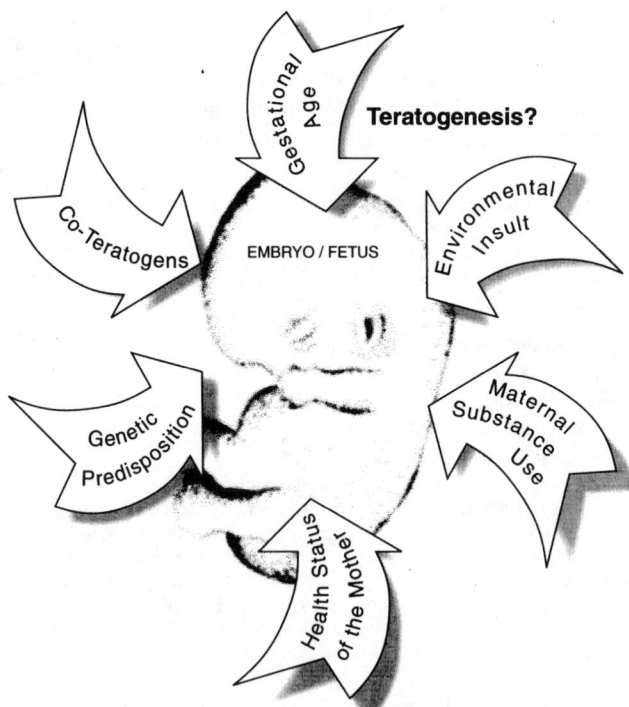

FIGURE 3.1   Multivariate determinants of teratogenesis

ity); and pharmacological effects (Gilbody, 1991; L. A. Pagliaro & Pagliaro, 1995b).

Of all the factors identified as being involved in producing a particular teratogenic effect, the most important factor is timing in regard to organogenesis (Fig. 3.2). There is a critical period of greatest teratogenic susceptibil-. ity. Although this critical period of susceptibility varies slightly among different organ systems, teratogenic effects associated with major physical malformations are generally induced during the first trimester. It is important to note that teratogenic effects will not occur if exposure to a particular substance of abuse, which is a known teratogen, occurs after organogenesis is complete. For example, the maternal use of diazepam (Valium) during pregnancy has been implicated in cleft palate anomaly. However, this teratogen would not cause this effect if it were used after the fetal palate had fused. Thus, when determining the possible teratogenic potential of a particular substance of abuse, it is essential to identify whether the substance, or another in the same class, has been implicated in producing a human teratogenic effect *and* the stage of embryo and fetal development at which time the exposure occurred.

SUBSTANCE-INDUCED TERATOGENESIS

The potential teratogenic effects associated with specific substances of abuse are summarized in the following sections. Substance use during pregnancy

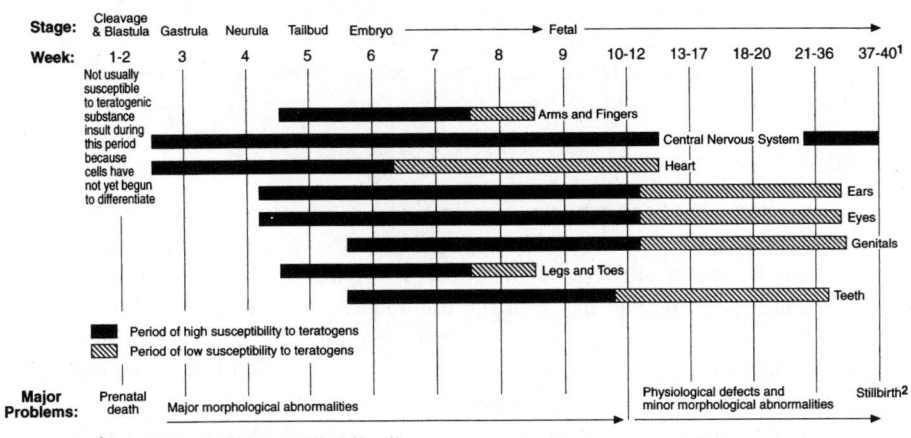

FIGURE 3.2   Organogenic variation in human teratogenic susceptibility

always involves some degree of risk to the developing embryo or fetus. Therefore, regardless of how safe a substance of abuse may appear to be, it should *not* be used during pregnancy unless it is clearly indicated and its benefits outweigh its potential risks. Adolescent girls and women who are pregnant or considering pregnancy should be encouraged to limit their substance use. Adolescent girls and women who display problematic patterns of substance use (e.g., abuse or compulsive use) should be referred to treatment programs aimed at promoting nonuse or, in the event that use has been discontinued, preventing relapse. In this regard, it also is important to note that, although not a direct teratogenic effect of substances of abuse, mother-to-infant transmission of HIV infection is a significant problem associated with intravenous and other substance use by pregnant adolescent girls and women (Deren, Beardsley, Davis, & Tortu, 1993; Hoegerman, Wilson, Thurmond, & Schnoll, 1990; Lyman, 1993; Nwanyanwu et al., 1993; A. M. Pagliaro et al., 1993; R. B. Van Dyke, 1991). This risk underscores the increased need for: 1. prevention and treatment programs specifically tailored to meet the needs of adolescent girls and women who are pregnant or thinking about becoming pregnant (see Chap. 10) and 2. early intervention for neonates and infants who have been exposed prenatally to substances of abuse (F. F. Russell & Free, 1991; see also Fig. 6.1).

Central Nervous System Depressants

The CNS depressants discussed in this section include the opiates and sedative-hypnotics. Although the CNS depressants have been associated with various levels of teratogenic risk, data accumulated over the last several decades only support a particularly strong relationship for the sedative-hypnotic alcohol. For this reason, a more comprehensive discussion of alcohol has been included in this section.

Opiates

Several cases have been reported implicating teratogenic insult with maternal opiate use during pregnancy. However, a review of this literature only provides weak support for teratogenic effects involving codeine, heroin, meperidine (Demerol), methadone, morphine, and pentazocine (Talwin). In addition, the use of these opiates near term may result in neonatal CNS depression, as indicated by decreased Apgar scores, and the opiate withdrawal syndrome, particularly when chronic high doses have been used.

Convulsions during unmedicated opiate withdrawal occur most frequently among neonates exposed in utero to methadone. Whenever possible, adolescent girls and women who use methadone, including those enrolled in methadone maintenance programs, should undergo detoxification before becoming pregnant. Methadone detoxification during the first trimester has been associated with an increased incidence of spontaneous abortions. When attempted during the third trimester, it has been associated with fetal distress. Thus, if methadone detoxification is to be implemented during pregnancy, it should be attempted between the 14th and 28th weeks of gestation with a slow tapering of the dosage. Intrauterine growth retardation may be noted but appears to be related to confounding variables such as poor maternal nutrition and concurrent alcohol and nicotine use.

Sedative-Hypnotics

The sedative-hypnotics include alcohol, barbiturates, benzodiazepines, and miscellaneous sedative-hypnotics (e.g., chloral hydrate). A more comprehensive discussion of alcohol is included in this section because of the increased accumulation of data regarding its teratogenic effects and related sequelae among affected infants, children, and adolescents.

Alcohol.   Alcohol (ethanol or ethyl alcohol) is a known human teratogen. As such, it has the potential to affect all fetuses of mothers who consume it during their pregnancies (Day & Richardson, 1991; Larroque, 1992). Once ingested and absorbed into the bloodstream, alcohol crosses readily from the maternal circulation to the fetal circulation (L. A. Pagliaro & Pagliaro, 1995b). It also is found in significant levels in the amniotic fluid even after the ingestion of a single moderate dose. Alcohol is "eliminated from the amniotic fluid at one-half the elimination rate from the maternal blood" and remains in the amniotic fluid and fetal circulation after "there is none present in the maternal blood stream" (Tranmer, 1985).

Unfortunately, many adolescent girls and women drink quantities of alcohol that are known to be harmful to their unborn babies (Cornelius et al., 1994; "Substance Abuse," 1994). The National Institute on Alcohol Abuse and Alcoholism (1987) has estimated that approximately 16 percent, or 1 out of 6 mothers, expose their fetuses to the harmful effects of alcohol. Based on a comprehensive and extensive review of the literature, this figure could be conservatively increased by 50–100 percent to approximately 1 out of every 3–4 mothers. However, even if there is a lack of agreement regarding the exact percentage of mothers who use alcohol during pregnancy, there is consensus that *fetal alcohol syndrome* (FAS) is currently the leading cause of mental retardation in North America and that it is totally preventable (L. A. Pagliaro & Pagliaro, 1995b).

The harmful effects associated with the use of alcohol during pregnancy have long been recognized (Table 3.2). However, the specific physical, mental, and developmental characteristics associated with FAS were not formally identified until the early 1970s (K. L. Jones, Smith, Ulleland, & Streissguth,

TABLE 3.2　A Brief History of Fetal Alcohol Syndrome[a]

1000 B.C.	Samson's mother was advised by an angel that she was about to become pregnant and should refuse alcohol: "Behold, thou shalt conceive and bear a son . . . and now drink no wine or strong drink." (Judges 13:7)
700 B.C.	Newly married Spartan couples were prohibited from consuming alcohol on their wedding nights so that conception would not occur during intoxication with resultant fetal damage.
384–322 B.C.	"Foolish, drunken, or hare-brain women for the most part bring forth children like unto themselves, morosos et languidos [irritable and weak]." (Aristotle)
1725 A.D.	"Half the train of chronic diseases, with which we see children afflicted . . . will be brought on infants by the debauchery of the mother. . . . The regulation of the mother, during her pregnancy, is an affair of the highest moment and consideration." (James Sedgewick, *A New Treatise on Liquors*)
1813	"If offspring should unfortunately be derived from such a [alcoholic] parentage, can we doubt that it must be diseased and puny in its corporeal parts; and beneath the standard of a rational being in its intellectual facilities?" (Thomas Trotter)
Mid-1800s	British House of Commons hearings on the "Effects of Drunkenness on the Nation" passed the Licensure Act that prohibited the sale of alcohol to pregnant women.
1849	"Facts abundantly show that the children of mothers who drink alcohol are more likely to become drunkards, and in various ways to suffer. Often they are not so large and healthy as other children. They have less keenness and strength of eyesight, less firmness and quietness of nerves, less capability of great bodily and mental achievement, and less power to withstand the attacks of disease, or the vicissitudes of climates and seasons." (Justin Edwards)
1890	"As the result of parental intemperance, children often lack physical strength and mental and moral power." (Ellen White)
1899	"Maternal inebriety is a condition peculiarly unfavourable to the vitality and to the normal development of the offspring. Its gravity in this respect is considerably greater than that of paternal alcoholism." Among a group of 120 female alcoholics in a Liverpool prison, Sullivan found the rate of stillbirth or death before 2 years of age to be 2.5 times that for sober blood relatives. (William Sullivan)
1907	"Alcohol acts in all three ways . . . by causing abortion, by predisposing to premature labor, and by weakening the infant by disease or deformity." (J. W. Ballantyne)
1968	Ten children, whose middle-class mothers drank heavily during pregnancy, suffered from growth and mental retardation. (E. Collins & Turner, 1978)

TABLE 3.2   (*Continued*)

1968	Physical anomalies were observed among 127 children of alcoholic parents; however, maternal and paternal alcohol dependence was not differentiated. (Lemoine, Harousseau, & Borteyru, 1968)
1972	Infants born to chronic alcoholic mothers commonly have growth retardation, failure to thrive, and mental retardation. (Ulleland, 1972)
1973	Pattern of anomalies and functional deficits were reported for eight unrelated children, all of whom were exposed to alcohol by their chronic alcoholic mothers who drank alcohol throughout their pregnancies. The pattern of malformations, which was based in large part on Ulleland's 1972 data and found to be similar to that reported by Lemoine, Harousseau, and Borteyru in 1968, was named the "fetal alcohol syndrome." (K. L. Jones et al., 1973)

[a]References include Coffey (1966), Edwards (1981), Hill, Hegemier, and Tennyson (1989), K. L. Jones et al. (1973), L. A. Pagliaro & Pagliaro (1995b), Plant (1985), Reid (1992), Warner and Rosett (1975), Warren and Bast (1988).

1973; see Table 3.3). Subsequently, clinicians and scientists have used this list of physical characteristics, particularly the associated craniofacial features (Fig. 3.3), to assist them with the identification of affected infants and children. Although the characteristic features of FAS vary among affected infants and children and can present difficulties in clinical identification (Edwards, 1981; B. B. Little, Snell, & Rosenfeld, 1990), the consistent use of these characteristic features has been found to be generally reliable (Abel, Martier, Kruger, Ager, & Sokol, 1993).

In addition to the use of these characteristic features, a consensus case definition for FAS was established by the Fetal Alcohol Study Group of the Research Society on Alcoholism (Sokol & Clarren, 1989). This consensus case definition includes the following three major criteria:

1. Prenatal and/or postnatal growth retardation (weight and/or length or height below the 10th percentile when corrected for gestational age);
2. CNS involvement (including neurological abnormality, developmental delay, behavioral dysfunction or deficit, intellectual impairment, and/ or structural abnormalities, such as microcephaly [head circumference below the 3rd percentile] or brain malformations found on imaging studies or autopsy); and
3. A characteristic face, currently qualitatively described as including short palpebral fissures, an elongated midface, a long and flattened philtrum, thin upper lip, and flattened maxilla.

The incidence of FAS in North America varies among cultural, ethnic, and socioeconomic groups with the highest incidence reported among blacks and

TABLE 3.3   Abnormalities Originally Associated with Fetal Alcohol Syndrome[a]

Category	Abnormality	Percentage Occurrence
Growth	Prenatal growth deficiency	100
Craniofacies	Short palpebral fissures	100
	Microcephaly	91
	Maxillary hypoplasia	64
	Epicanthal folds	36
	Micrognathia	27
	Cleft palate	18
Development	Developmental delay	100
	Postnatal growth deficiency	100
Limbs	Albered palmar crease pattern	73
	Joint anomalies	73
Heart	Cardiac anomalies	70
Other	Fine-motor dysfunction	80
	Anomalous external genitalia	36
	Capillary hemangiomata	36

[a]This original list from K. L. Jones et al. (1973) has been expanded by several authors (e.g., American Academy of Pediatrics, 1993; L. A. Pagliaro & Pagliaro, 1995b) in order to account for additional features (e.g., asymmetrical or low-set ears; flat or absent philtrum; hypoplastic, flat midface; short nose; and thin vermilion of the upper lip) commonly noted by other researchers (e.g., Clarren & Smith, 1978; Haddad & Messer, 1994).

Native Americans (Abel & Sokol, 1987, 1991; Bray & Anderson, 1989; Burd & Moffatt, 1994; Duimstra et al., 1993; "Fetal Alcohol Syndrome," 1991; Gordis & Alexander, 1992; see Table 3.4). However, its actual incidence is difficult to specify for a number of reasons. These reasons include the unreliability of self-reports of maternal drinking (i.e., consistently biased underreporting; Ernhart, Morrow-Tlucak, Sokol, & Martier, 1988); qualitative and quasi-experimental research methods (e.g., case report and retrospective studies; Abel & Sokol, 1987); and possible confusion, or overlap, with *fetal alcohol effects* (FAE) (Remkes, 1993; P. Wallace, 1991).

Fetal alcohol effects is a term that is used to identify neonates and children who exhibit fewer of the characteristics deemed necessary, by definition or convention, for the establishment of a proper diagnosis of FAS (Caruso & Bensel, 1993; Ginsburg, Blacker, Abel, & Sokol, 1991; Smitherman, 1994). Other terminologies have also been suggested and have been used in the clinical literature—for example, alcohol-related birth defects (ARBD) (Harris, Osborn, Weinberg, Loock, & Junaid, 1993; Jacobson et al., 1993; Sokol & Clarren, 1989). We strongly disagree with the use of these terminologies and argue that the infants and children who display fewer of the classic characteristics of FAS be diagnosed more appropriately as having a less severe form of FAS and not a different syndrome. We argue that this approach to diagnosing FAS

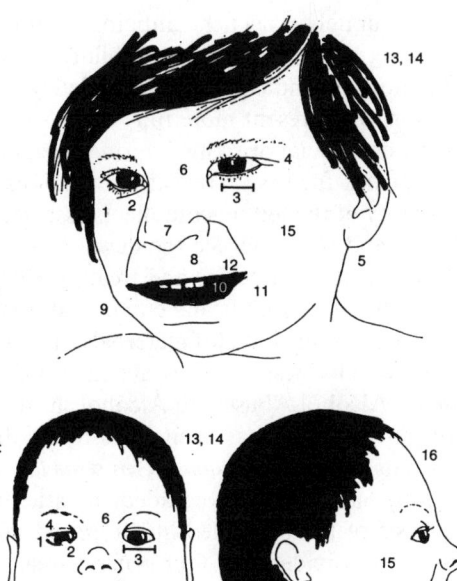

Eyes
1. ptosis (drooping lid)
2. strabismus (squint)
3. shortened palpebral fissure
   (opening between eyelids)
4. epicanthal fold

Ears
5. smaller or larger than normal,
   malformed, or low-set

Nose
6. low nasal bridge
7. short with high or
   up-turned nasal tip

Mouth
8. philtrum (groove in upper lip):
   underdeveloped or absent
9. micrognathia (small jaw) or
   retrognathia (posteriorly
   displaced jaw)
10. teeth: absent enamel,
    malformed, or maloccluded
11. wide mouth
12. thin vermilion border of
    upper lip

Head
13. microcephaly (small head size)
14. abnormally shaped cranium
15. mid-face hypoplasia (broad, flat face)
16. narrow receding forehead

FIGURE 3.3   Common craniofacial characteristics associated with fetal alcohol syndrome

TABLE 3.4   Reported Range of Incidence of Fetal Alcohol Syndrome

Incidence[a]	Country (Group)	Reference
1:8	Canada (Native Americans)	Robinson, Conry, & Conry, 1987
1:20–40	Canada (Native Americans)	Asante & Nelms-Matzke, 1985
1:125–250	U.S.A. (Native Americans)	Duimstra et al., 1993
1:333–500	Europe (mixed)	Hill et al., 1989
1:500	Worldwide (mixed)	Abel & Sokol, 1987
1:500–1000	Western world (mixed)	Clarren & Smith, 1978
1:700	U.S.A. (mixed)	Bertucci & Krafchik, 1994
1:1000	U.S.A. (mixed)	Rosett et al., 1983
1:1500–3000	Western world (mixed)	Abel & Sokol, 1991
1:3000	U.S.A. (mixed)	Shoemaker, 1993

[a]Per number of live births

would: 1. more accurately reflect the anticipated normal distribution of the effects of FAS among affected infants and children in the general population or its subpopulations, 2. indicate more completely the extent of FAS in the general population, 3. represent more fully the nature of FAS, 4. clearly identify that even "modest social drinking" during pregnancy places the exposed fetus at significant risk for FAS, 5. reflect the relationship of other factors in regard to the severity of the teratogenic effects associated with maternal alcohol use (Fig. 3.1), and 6. encourage the development of more rational and comprehensive prevention strategies and treatment programs aimed at optimizing the development of infants and children affected by maternal alcohol use. "There is no proven safe limit [of maternal alcohol use] that will eliminate all risk to the fetus. The best policy is abstinence during pregnancy" (National Institute on Alcohol Abuse and Alcoholism, 1987, p. 7).

While significant attention has been given to the diagnosis of FAS among neonates and young children, the *long-term sequelae* associated with such a diagnosis generally have not received adequate attention. A comprehensive review and analysis of the published literature indicates that the long-term sequelae of FAS can be divided into four general areas: 1. growth retardation, 2. developmental deficits in cognitive skills (see Chap. 7 for additional discussion), 3. developmental deficits in motor skills, and 4. mental disorders (Table 3.5). As noted in Table 3.5, the long-term sequelae appear to be quite stable. Thus, the effects associated with FAS do not end in infancy but persist into childhood, adolescence, and, unfortunately, throughout adulthood (Smitherman, 1994; Spohr, Willms, & Steinhausen, 1993). "The growth and neurological disabilities associated with alcohol consumption in pregnancy persist even when the child grows up in a good home" (Karp, Qazi, Hittleman, & Chabrier, 1993, p. 106). The lifelong effects of FAS on human growth and development should not be ignored. In this regard, we concur with Streissguth, Randels, and Smith (1992) that, for infants and children affected with FAS and their parents and caregivers, "more realistic expectations for performance during childhood and adolescence may result in the availability of more appropriate services, less frustration, and improved behavioral outcome in later adolescence and adulthood" (p. 587).

Alcohol is a known human teratogen that can cause significant, lifelong deficits in relation to physical growth, cognitive functioning, psychomotor skills, and psychological health. Although some authors (e.g., Knupfer, 1991; Walpole, Zubrick, Pontré, & Lawrence, 1991) disagree, we concur with the recommendation made by the National Institute of Child Health and Human Development, the American Academy of Pediatrics, and the U.S. Surgeon General (American Academy of Pediatrics, 1993; C. D. Johnson, Reeves, & Jackson, 1983; Schydlower & Perrin, 1993), and by others (e.g., Caruso & Bensel, 1993; C. H. Olson, 1994; H. C. Olson, Sampson, Barr, Streissguth, & Bookstein, 1992; Streissguth, Sampson, Barr, Bookstein, & Olson, 1994),

TABLE 3.5 Long-Term Sequelae of Fetal Alcohol Syndrome

Age	Number of Cases (sample size)	Comments	Reference
		Growth Retardation	
Birth	20	Exposure to alcohol in utero throughout the mother's entire pregnancy resulted in prenatal growth retardation affecting body length, weight, and head circumference.	Autti-Rämö & Granström, 1991
0, 8, 18, and 36 mo.	595	Smaller physical size noted among alcohol-exposed neonates, which did *not* demonstrate a postnatal "catch-up" by 3 years of age (the relative smaller size noted at birth was maintained).	Geva, Goldschmidt, Stoffer, & Day, 1993
5 mo. to 15 yr.	6	"All were small at birth, though their mothers were not underweight, and none has shown any catch-up in growth despite being offered adequate nutrition by their caring foster families."	E. Collins & Turner, 1978
6.5 and 13 mo.	412	Postnatal growth retardation was strongly correlated with maternal drinking during the second and third trimesters, but not with drinking at conception. Maternal nutrition during pregnancy did *not* appear to significantly influence postnatal growth. The findings support the contention "that symmetrical intrauterine growth retardation is most likely to be associated with persistently smaller size later in life."	Jacobson, Jacobson, & Sokol, 1994
18 mo.	505	"Prenatal alcohol exposure during the second and third trimesters was related to growth deficits (weight, height, and head circumference) in the offspring at 18 months of age."	Day, Goldschmidt, et al., 1991

TABLE 3.5 (*Continued*)

Age	Number of Cases (sample size)	Comments	Reference
		Growth Retardation	
5 yr.	2	Twin girls with FAS were followed from birth. Growth retardation was noted at birth and, by 5 years of age, they remained "both small for their ages."	Harris et al., 1993
6 yr.	152	Alcohol consumption during pregnancy was associated with "shorter mean height and smaller mean head circumference in children at age six."	M. Russell, Czarnecki, Cowan, McPherson, & Mudar, 1991
6 yr.	668	"At 6 years of age, children who were prenatally exposed to alcohol were significantly smaller in weight, height, head circumference, and palpebral fissure width."	Day, Richardson, Geva, & Robles, 1994
10 yr.	60	"We found that the craniofacial malformations of FAS diminish with time, but *microcephaly* and to a lesser degree, *short stature* and underweight (in boys) persist; in female adolescents body weight normalizes."	Spohr et al., 1993
10 yr. (mean)	11	"All children remained growth-deficient over time with respect to height, weight, and head circumference."	Streissguth, Clarren, & Jones, 1985
12–40 yr.	61	"Short stature and microcephaly appeared to be the most prominent growth deficiencies as the children got older . . . although their weight was somewhat closer to the mean."	Streissguth et al., 1991
		(Developmental) Deficits in Cognitive Skills	
13 mo.	382	Significant deficits were noted among infants whose mothers drank heavily. "Effects of second and third trimester drinking were as strong or stronger than those of drinking at the time of conception."	Jacobson et al., 1993

TABLE 3.5   (*Continued*)

Age	Number of Cases (sample size)	Comments	Reference
		(Developmental) Deficits in Cognitive Skills	
24 mo.	146	"Moderate levels of [maternal] alcohol [use] were significantly associated with lower mental scores [as assessed by the Bayley Scale of Infant Development] at 24 months of age."	Fried & Watkinson, 1988
27 mo. (mean)	60	The number of children with cognitive impairment (mental or verbal performance 2 standard deviations below normal) increased in relation to the duration of intrauterine alcohol exposure (i.e., exposure during all three trimesters was related to significantly increased numbers of children with cognitive impairment in comparison to exposure during only the first or first and second trimesters).	Autti-Rämö & Granström, 1991
5 yr.	2	Stanford-Binet IQs of 71 and 72 were determined at 5 years of age for twin sisters born with FAS. Note that an IQ range of 20–95 (with a mode of ~70) has been reported for children with FAS (Carney & Chermak, 1991; Robinson et al., 1987; Streissguth et al., 1991).	Harris et al., 1993
5–12 yr.	60	"The children with FAS/FAE were more intellectually impaired than were the normal and ADD children. The mean IQ in this sample of FAS/FAE children was 78."	Nanson & Hiscock, 1990
6 yr.	175	Verbal IQ, as measured by the Wechsler Preschool and Primary Scale of Intelligence, and linguistic ability, as measured by the Token Test for Children, were significantly lower among children born to mothers who drank alcohol during pregnancy.	M. Russell et al., 1991

TABLE 3.5   (*Continued*)

Age	Number of Cases (sample size)	Comments	Reference
		(Developmental) Deficits in Cognitive Skills	
6 yr.	68	"Cognitive scores on the K-ABC [Kaufman Assessment Battery for Children] are generally lower for the two alcohol-exposed groups; the group whose mothers reported continuing to drink had the lowest scores on all but one of the subtests. These scores are significantly lower in sequential processing, achievement and the mental processing composite (which is referred to as an equivalent to an IQ score on other standardized measures of intelligence)."	C. Coles et al., 1991
6–12 yr.	27	"The results of the present study are consistent with previous reports of expressive and receptive language deficits among FAS children."	Carney & Chermak, 1991
10 yr.	60	"Persistent mental retardation is the major sequela of intrauterine alcohol exposure in many cases, and environmental and educational factors do *not* have strong compensatory effects on the intellectual development of affected children."	Spohr et al., 1993
11 yr.	458	Academic performance problems were noted "in apparent linear fashion with the lowest non-zero alcohol scores and extending across the spectrum of maternal alcohol use." "Learning problems with the greatest salience for prenatal alcohol exposure include three items measuring information-processing and reasoning	H.C. Olson et al., 1992.

TABLE 3.5 (*Continued*)

Age	Number of Cases (sample size)	Comments	Reference
		(Developmental) Deficits in Cognitive Skills	
		problems, one item indicating a lack of interest in reading, and two items reflecting the teacher's overall impression that the child had a learning problem and did not do work well."	
12 yr. (mean)	8	"None of the eight children had normal intellectual development on followup . . . four appeared to be mildly handicapped and four were seriously handicapped [mean IQ score was 61]."	Streissguth et al., 1985
Children of "various ages"		Most children displayed some degree of cognitive deficit, with a large percentage classified as mentally retarded. The cognitive deficits and IQ bands appeared to be longitudinally stable (i.e., intelligence generally did *not* improve with age over time).	Steinhausen, Willms, & Spohr, 1993
14 yr.	464	"Earlier reports of prenatal, alcohol-related neurobehavioral deficits in childhood have now been extended into adolescence." The neurobehavioral deficits were related to "the acquisition of reading and arithmetic skills."	Streissguth, Barr, et al., 1994
14 yr.	462	"The 14-year attention/memory deficits observed in the present study appear to be the adolescent sequelae of deficits observed earlier in development."	Streissguth, Sampson, et al., 1994
12–40 yr.	61	"The developmental and cognitive handicaps persist as long in life as these patients have been studied . . . the average IQ was 68."	Streissguth et al., 1991

TABLE 3.5 (*Continued*)

Age	Number of Cases (sample size)	Comments	Reference
(Developmental) Deficits in Psychomotor Skills			
12 mo.	80	Significant retardation of gross motor development was noted in all groups of infants exposed to alcohol in utero. However, "it was more severe if alcohol consumption was continued towards the end of pregnancy."	Autti-Rämö & Granström, 1991
13 mo.	382	Significant deficits were noted among children whose mothers drank heavily. "Effects of second and third trimester drinking were as strong or stronger than those of drinking at the time of conception."	Jacobson et al., 1993
18 mo.	5	Psychomotor skills, as determined by Bayley Psychomotor Development Index, showed some variability over time, but ended being 1 to 3 standard deviations below normal for 60 percent of the infants studied who had FAS.	Harris et al., 1993
5 yr.	2	In terms of overall motor performance, twin girls with FAS were found to perform at 60–65 percent of their age level; "percentile scores were all at either the 1st or 2nd percentile, indicating that 98% to 99% of age-mates were performing at higher levels."	Harris et al., 1993
Mental Disorders			
4 yr.	128	"Children of moderate drinkers were more likely to display behaviors associated with a hyperactivity or attention deficit syndrome than were offspring of occasional or nondrinkers."	Landesman-Dwyer, Ragozin, & Little, 1981

TABLE 3.5 (*Continued*)

Age	Number of Cases (sample size)	Comments	Reference
		Mental Disorders	
7.5 yr.	486	"The learning problems [ADHD] evidenced by these children are the school-age sequelae of CNS dysfunction originating from in utero alcohol exposure."	Streissguth, Barr, & Sampson, 1990; Streissguth et al., 1986
6–15 yr.	6	"The children described in this paper manifested the physical phenotype of FAS and had a history of maternal alcohol abuse during pregnancy but had a very different behavioral phenotype, typical of autistic children, and characterized by more significant retardation of both their cognitive and social skills."	Nanson, 1992
Children of "various ages"	158	An "excess of psychopathology" was noted among children diagnosed with FAS. These mental disorders, particularly attention-deficit hyperactivity disorder and various affective and sleep disorders, were noted in almost 66 percent of the children and tended to persist over time.	Steinhausen et al., 1993
11 yr.	458	A number of problem classroom behaviors were noted among children prenatally exposed to alcohol "including seven items measuring distractibility, restlessness, lack of persistence, and reluctance to meet challenges . . . (all of which are consistent with a diagnosis of attention deficit [hyperactivity] disorder)."	H. C. Olson et al., 1992
3–17 yr.	46	Among the 46 children, 18 (39 percent) were diagnosed with ADHD.	Caruso & Bensel, 1993

that adolescent girls and women who are pregnant or planning to become pregnant totally abstain from alcohol use. This recommendation is based on the following observations: 1. no safe level of alcohol use has been demonstrated; and 2. there is no known cure for FAS. As noted by Karp et al. (1993), FAS is "not a treatable disease in the literal sense" (p. 103). In this regard, it is essential that prevention and treatment programs be developed to assist adolescent girls and women to abstain from alcohol use, particularly when pregnant. Attention must be given to mothers for whom abstinence may be difficult to achieve or maintain (i.e., adolescent girls and women who compulsively use alcohol).

Barbiturates.   The barbiturates discussed in this section include mephobarbital, pentobarbital, phenobarbital, and secobarbital. Although the use of the barbiturates has decreased dramatically over the past two decades as a result of the synthesis and use of the benzodiazepines, they are still generally available and may be used therapeutically for the treatment of seizure disorders among adolescent girls and women who are unresponsive to other anticonvulsant therapy. The use of the barbiturates during pregnancy has generally been associated with a number of teratogenic effects. However, confounding variables, particularly maternal epilepsy, have not yet been completely ruled out as principal or coteratogenic factors. The use of the barbiturates near term, particularly chronic, high doses, may result in neonatal respiratory depression and the barbiturate withdrawal syndrome.

Benzodiazepines.   The benzodiazepines include chlordiazepoxide, diazepam, lorazepam, nitrazepam, and oxazepam. The use of these substances during pregnancy has been associated with various degrees of teratogenic effects, particularly cleft lip and palate (Rivas, Hernandez, & Cantu, 1984; Shiono & Mills, 1984). However, data are conflicting (U. Bergman, Rosa, Baum, Wiholm, & Faich, 1992; Czeizel, 1988; L. Rosenberg et al., 1983), and overall, the use of benzodiazepines during pregnancy appears to have a low teratogenic risk. However, maternal use of the benzodiazepines near term has resulted in lethargy, poor muscle tone, and respiratory depression in the neonate. Fortunately, these effects are generally fully reversible with proper recognition and care (Chesley et al., 1991; Sanchis, Rosique, & Catala, 1991).

Volatile Solvents and Inhalants

Although volatile solvents and inhalants (e.g., gasoline and glue) are commonly used by adolescents and young adults, their potential teratogenic effects have not been widely researched. Only four studies were found in a review of the published literature. One report contained data "on 30 pregnancies in ten women with chronic glue- and paint-sniffing abuse" (Wilkins-Haug & Gabow, 1991), and another reviewed the case records "of 35 deliveries with antenatal exposure to toluene" (Arnold, Kirby, Langendoerfer, & Wilkins-Haug, 1994). The teratogenic effects identified in these studies as possibly related to the use of these volatile solvents and inhalants include preterm delivery, neonatal electrolyte disturbances (hypobicarbonatemia and hypokalemia), low birth weight, microcephaly, and postnatal growth retardation. Hersh (1989) was the first to describe five children with "toluene embryopathy." Toluene is a volatile solvent found in many different products, including glues and spray paint. The reported embryopathy, which has since been supported by Arnold et al. (1994) and Pearson, Hoyme, Seaver, and Rimsza (1994), includes growth retardation, developmental delays, and minor craniofacial anomalies (e.g., short palpebral fissures, flat [wide] nasal bridge, deficient philtrum, and micrognathia). These described teratogenic features are extremely similar to those associated with FAS. This similarity of features may be due to the pharmacological similarity between alcohol and the volatile solvents and inhalants or to the mother's possible concomitant use of alcohol. Pearson et al. (1994) has proposed "a common mechanism of craniofacial teratogenesis for toluene and alcohol, namely a deficiency of craniofacial neuroepithelium and mesodermal components due to increased embryonic cell death" (p. 211). More data are needed.

Central Nervous System Stimulants

The CNS stimulants discussed in this section include caffeine, cocaine, dextroamphetamine, methylphenidate, and nicotine (tobacco smoking). Research results are mixed in regard to the teratogenic effects associated with these substances of abuse, particularly dextroamphetamine and methylphenidate.

Caffeine

Caffeine, in the form of coffee, tea, and other beverages (e.g., caffeinated soft drinks), is probably consumed to a greater extent by pregnant adolescent girls and women than any other substance of abuse, including alcohol. Although research has not been as prolific as for alcohol, some studies have associated caffeine consumption with birth defects. The consumption of eight or more cups of coffee per day was related to fetal limb defects in three case reports, but more recent studies have shown that the only teratogenic effect associated with maternal caffeine use during pregnancy is reduced birth weight (Linn et al., 1982; T. Martin & Bracken, 1987; Olsen, Overvad, & Frische, 1991). This effect was associated with the consumption of three or more cups of coffee per day. However, a significant correlation between increased caffeine consumption during pregnancy and fetal loss also has been reported (Infante-Rivard, Fernandez, Gauthier, David, & Rivard, 1993). Although these data would generally support the relative safety of the use of caffeine during pregnancy, pregnant adolescent girls and women should be encouraged to minimize their caffeine use, particularly if they smoke tobacco cigarettes. Tobacco smoking, which is significantly correlated with coffee consumption, is an obvious confounding factor in the interpretation of data supporting the possible teratogenic effects of caffeine (see also the discussion of nicotine, below).

Cocaine

Cocaine use during pregnancy increased significantly during the 1980s, and cocaine continues to be, after marijuana, the most commonly used illicit substance among pregnant adolescent girls and women, particularly in North American inner cities. Cocaine use during pregnancy has been associated with intrauterine death (including spontaneous abortions), low birth weight, preterm delivery, neonatal seizures, neonatal tachycardia, intrauterine growth retardation, and a variety of fetal physical anomalies, particularly affecting the ophthalmic and urogenital systems (Bandstra & Burkett, 1991; Brouhard, 1994; Hannig & Phillips, 1991; Hume et al., 1994; Nucci & Brancato, 1994; Plessinger & Woods, 1991; Scanlon, 1991; Stafford, Rosen, Zaider, & Merriam, 1994). Autopsies of fetuses exposed to cocaine in utero often reveal cerebral hemorrhages (Gieron-Korthals, Helal, & Martinez, 1994; Kapur, Cheng, & Shephard, 1991). However, some researchers have attributed these effects to confounding factors associated with maternal cocaine use (e.g., poor nutrition and inadequate prenatal care; Bohan, Dominguez, Slopis, & Vila-Coro, 1992; Church, 1993; Hutchings, 1993; Koren, 1993; Neuspiel, 1992; Racine, Joyce, & Anderson, 1993; Snodgrass, 1994; see Table 3.6 for a list of obstetrical complications noted among cocaine-using pregnant adolescent girls).

TABLE 3.6   Obstetrical Complications Noted among Cocaine-Using Pregnant Adolescent Girls[a]

Abortion
Abruptio placentae
Breech presentation
Previous Caesarean delivery
Chorioamnionitis
Eclampsia
Gestational diabetes
Intrauterine death
Intrauterine growth retardation
Placental insufficiency
Postpartum hemorrhage
Pre-eclampsia
Preterm labor
Premature rupture of membranes
Septic thrombophlebitis

[a]From Lesar (1992, p. 38).

There also appears to be a significantly higher incidence of behavioral and learning disorders (e.g., ADHD and delays in receptive and expressive language skills) among preschoolers and school-age children exposed to cocaine in utero (K. L. Jones, 1991; L. A. Pagliaro, 1992b; Rivers & Hedrick, 1992; D. C. Van Dyke & Fox, 1990). However, the teratogenic effects associated with maternal use of cocaine during pregnancy remain inconclusive because of the difficulties associated with interpreting and evaluating research data. For example, the widely used retrospective case report methodology has several inherent limitations, including the possible inaccuracy of reported information. These limitations make definitive conclusions highly speculative (Dow-Edwards, 1993; Frank & Zuckerman, 1993; Konkol, 1994; Neuspiel, 1993; Slutsker, 1992; Spear, 1993). In addition, adolescent girls and women who use cocaine also commonly use alcohol, a known teratogen, to come down from a cocaine high. This additional factor further confounds the interpretation of data. However, the consensus seems to be that the use of high dosages of cocaine (e.g., injectable use or use of smokable crack or rock forms of cocaine) probably has a significant, but low, potential for inducing teratogenic effects (C. D. Coles, 1993; M. L. Martin, Khoury, Cordero, & Waters, 1992). When used by the mother near term, the neonate may experience CNS excitation.

Dextroamphetamine (Dexedrine)

Dextroamphetamine (crystal meth), used intravenously, is receiving renewed interest from adolescent girls and young women. It is also commonly prescribed as a component of weight reduction programs for these age groups. Although data are contradictory regarding the teratogenic effects of dextroamphetamine exposure in utero, it appears that there is a moderate risk for human teratogenesis. Maternal use of dextroamphetamine during the first trimester has been associated with neonatal biliary atresia, cleft lip and palate, congenital heart disease, prematurity, and small size for gestational age. However, a prospective study found no increase in fetal malformations. More data are needed. In the interim, it appears prudent to advise adolescent girls and women *not* to use dextroamphetamine during pregnancy.

Methylphenidate (Ritalin)

Methylphenidate is commonly prescribed for children and adolescents diagnosed with ADHD, and no teratogenic effects have been reported. However, only one study (with 11 neonates exposed prenatally to methylphenidate) could be found in the literature. More data are needed.

Nicotine: Tobacco Smoking

The mode of reported tobacco use among adolescent girls and women appears to be approximately 40 percent, although variation is noted among certain ethnic groups, geographical regions, and races (Nash & Persaud, 1988; L. A. Pagliaro & Pagliaro, 1993). Unfortunately, tobacco smoking during pregnancy is teratogenic to the fetus, and there is an inverse relationship between the number of cigarettes smoked per day and the birth weight of neonates. Neonates born to mothers who smoke are on average 200 g (100–400 g) smaller and have shorter body length than do neonates born to mothers who do not smoke (Nash & Persaud, 1988). Fortunately, a period of accelerated growth occurs during the first year of life, and generally, no differences in body weight or length are observed among these infants at 1 year of age. Adolescent girls and women who cease smoking during the first trimester generally have infants of normal size (Abel, 1980).

Adolescent girls and women who continue to smoke during pregnancy may have higher rates of spontaneous abortions, abruptio placentae, placenta previa, and higher perinatal mortality rates (DiFranza & Lew, 1995). In addition, mothers who smoke may have a higher fetal malformation rate (H. C. Miller, Hassanein, & Hensleigh, 1976; Seidman, Ever-Hadani, & Gale, 1990; Shiono, Klebanoff, & Berendes, 1986). The risk of the sudden infant death syndrome (SIDS) is estimated to be 4.4 times higher for infants born to mothers who smoke during pregnancy than for infants born to mothers who do not (Butler & Goldstein, 1973) and may account for over 2,000 SIDS deaths annually (DiFranza & Lew, 1995). Some studies (e.g., Olds, Henderson, & Tatelbaum, 1994) suggest that maternal smoking may cause among their children a neurodevelopmental impairment resulting in a reduction in IQ scores by 4–8 points. However, as with other substances of abuse, the teratogenic effects of heavy tobacco smoking are confounded by concurrent alcohol use (see alcohol discussion, above). Based on the available data, as a precaution, adolescent girls and women should be advised *not* to smoke during pregnancy.

Psychedelics

The psychedelics comprise a variety of substances that generally are used for their hallucinatory effects and to "expand consciousness." No studies were found that reported teratogenic effects associated with the maternal use of psilocybin or peyote during pregnancy. Several publications were found that discussed LSD, THC in various forms of cannabis, and PCP. For example, Fried and Watkinson (1990) noted that "at 48 months, significantly lower scores in verbal and memory domains were associated with maternal marijuana use" (p. 49). Fico and Vanderwende (1989) summarized several studies involving PCP use during pregnancy and noted "concern . . . that adult toxicity may be predictive of developmental toxicity" (p. 319). However, the use of LSD, THC, and PCP during pregnancy has not been clearly and consistently associated with major physical or developmental teratogenic effects in humans (Day,

Sambamoorthi, et al., 1991; Fried, 1982; L. A. Pagliaro 1991b; Tabor, Smith-Wallace, & Yonekura, 1990). Given the widespread use of the psychedelics by adolescent girls and women of child-bearing age and the relative paucity of reported teratogenic effects, the teratogenic potential of the psychedelics, if it does exist, appears to be low. More data are needed.

SUMMARY

Teratogenesis is a complex process that is influenced by many factors including maternal, placental, fetal, environmental, and substance of abuse factors. To minimize the risk for and incidence of substance-induced teratogenesis, it is necessary to recognize that all substances of abuse have the potential to cause teratogenic effects under certain conditions. Thus, as a precaution, adolescent girls and women who are pregnant, or thinking about becoming pregnant should be encouraged, whenever possible, to abstain from, or to minimize, their use of the substances of abuse. In particular, they should be advised to avoid alcohol because of the strong evidence associating its use with significant teratogenic effects (e.g., FAS; L. A. Pagliaro, 1991b; Tennes et al., 1985). It is also important to note that when substances of abuse are used during pregnancy, their respective withdrawal syndromes can be expected to occur among the resultant neonates. In addition, most substance use near term can cause expected pharmacological effects and toxicities among neonates. Fortunately, associated withdrawal syndromes and other pharmacologically related effects are generally reversible with proper recognition and care.

Mental health professionals concerned about children and adolescents should be aware of the teratogenic effects associated with the maternal use of the substances of abuse during pregnancy. Further research examining the relationship between substance use by pregnant adolescent girls and women and associated teratogenic effects is needed. There is extensive documentation relating maternal alcohol and tobacco use to serious risk for teratogenesis. However, a high percentage of pregnant adolescent girls and women continue to unnecessarily expose themselves and their unborn babies to the harmful effects associated with these substances of abuse. In this regard, adolescent girls and women should be advised regarding these possible harmful effects, including possible long-term effects on their unborn babies. In addition, greater attention needs to be given to the development and implementation of effective psychotherapeutic interventions designed to prevent or minimize substance use among adolescents and women of child-bearing age (see Chap. 10). Attention to relapse prevention among this group is also a major challenge.

CHAPTER 4

Exposure to and Use of Substances of Abuse during Infancy and Childhood

Many young people experiment with alcohol and drugs and a small minority meet the criteria for substance dependency. Yet substance misuse may be overlooked in children presenting with behavioural problems, difficulties at school and associated poor academic performance. (Dunne, 1993, p. 643)

A comprehensive review of the published literature supports the contention that most clinicians and researchers have focused on the study of substance use during adolescence with almost total disregard for the patterns displayed during infancy and childhood (i.e., birth to 12 years of age). In fact, G. W. Bailey (1992) noted, and we concur, that "substance abuse has been identified as the most commonly missed pediatric diagnosis" (p. 1015). However, the available published data concerning exposure to and use of substances of abuse during infancy and childhood, which are much more limited in number and scope than for adolescence (M. Farrell & Strang, 1991), suggest that such exposure and use are increasing among these age groups (Norwood, 1985; Swadi, 1992; Westermeyer, 1992). Increased exposure and use are primarily associated with: 1. maternal breast milk exposure, 2. secondhand smoke exposure, 3. foodstuff exposure, 4. medical exposure, primarily prescribed treatment for ADHD, and 5. experimental and other use (Fig. 4.1). This chapter discusses these various types of exposure and use. Unfortunately, many of these infants and children may have already been prenatally exposed to various substances of abuse (see Chap. 3).

MATERNAL BREAST MILK EXPOSURE

Over half of all new mothers in North America breast-feed their infants. Although breast milk is generally considered to be the best form of infant nutrition for the first months of life and breast-feeding is important to psychological development, breast-feeding can expose neonates and infants to various drugs and chemicals, including virtually all of the substances of abuse. In order to cross the blood-brain barrier and elicit their primary psy-

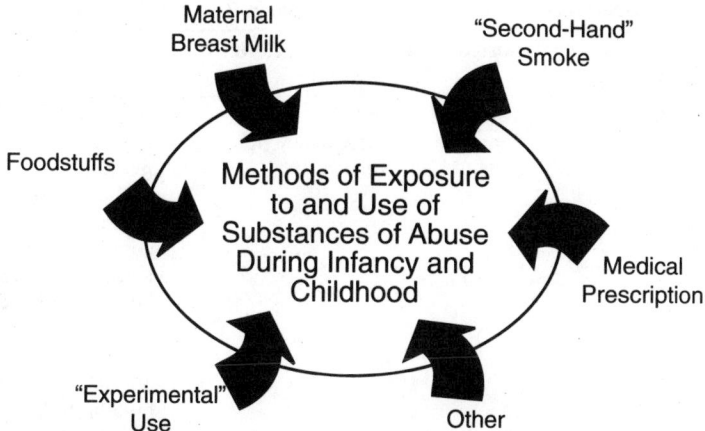

FIGURE 4.1   Methods of exposure to and use of substances of abuse during infancy and childhood

chotropic effects, the substances of abuse must be lipid soluble, a property that also assures that they are significantly excreted in human breast milk. In fact, for some substances of abuse (e.g., nicotine), concentrations in breast milk can be higher than in maternal serum (see Table 4.1). As identified in Table 4.1, chronic moderate to high maternal use of any of the substances of abuse places nursing neonates and infants at risk for the direct pharmacological effects of these substances, including addiction.

When mothers require a substance of abuse for acute, short-term use (e.g., a sedative-hypnotic for a few days), then the lowest effective dose should be used as long before breast-feeding as possible and the nursing neonate or infant carefully monitored for untoward effects. When mothers require a substance of abuse (particularly at moderate or high dosages) for chronic, long-term use (e.g., an opiate analgesic for a few weeks), then breast-feeding should be discontinued indefinitely or at least until the substance is no longer needed. For mothers who display abuse or compulsive use patterns (see Chap. 1 for a brief review), it is recommended that breast-feeding be discontinued and appropriate treatment or referral services be implemented for these mothers and their infants, as required.

EXPOSURE TO SECONDHAND SMOKE

Available data suggest that a large number of infants and children are exposed to cocaine, nicotine, and THC by means of secondhand smoke. This exposure usually occurs when they are confined to an automobile or room

TABLE 4.1   Substances of Abuse Excreted in Human Breast Milk[a]

Substance of Abuse	Reported Average Concentration in Breast Milk[b]	Effect on Neonate/Infant
Alcohol (e.g., beer, wine, and distilled liquor)	Variable (depends on number and frequency of drinks consumed)	Not significant at low to moderate levels of maternal use. May inhibit milk ejection and decrease neonatal milk consumption with higher levels of maternal use because of effects on the taste and smell of milk, which may decrease the amount ingested by nursing infants.
Amphetamines (e.g., dextroamphetamine)	100 μg/ml	Amphetamines are excreted in human breast milk. However, there is a paucity of reported data. Thus, the effects on nursing neonates and infants are unknown.
Barbiturates (e.g., pentobarbital and phenobarbital)	Variable (depends on specific barbiturate)	May cause sedation in nursing neonates and infants. Breast-feeding over extended periods of time by mothers who are using moderate to high doses of the barbiturates may result in addiction among their nursing neonates and infants. The barbiturate withdrawal syndrome may be observed among neonates and infants when breast-feeding or maternal use is discontinued.
Benzodiazepines (e.g., alprazolam, clonazepam, and diazepam)	Variable (depends on specific benzodiazepine)	Possible accumulation of benzodiazepine and its metabolites may occur among nursing neonates due to immature hepatic metabolism, particularly during the first week of life. Infants of mothers who use moderate to high doses of the benzodiazepines may develop addiction

TABLE 4.1   (*Continued*)

Substance of Abuse	Reported Average Concentration in Breast Milk[b]	Effect on Neonate/Infant
		and display benzodiazepine withdrawal syndrome (e.g., crying and irritability) when breast-feeding or maternal benzodiazepine use is discontinued.
Caffeine	5 µg/ml	Not significant at low to moderate levels of maternal use. May cause CNS excitation (e.g., irritability) among neonates and infants whose mothers have high levels of use.
Cocaine	—	Cocaine is detectable in breast milk for up to 36 hours after maternal use. However, because of the paucity of reported data, the effects on neonates and infants are unknown (see also secondhand smoke).
Nicotine	50 ng/ml	Nicotine and cotinine (a metabolite) are found in higher concentrations in breast milk than in maternal serum. Symptoms of CNS excitation (e.g., increased heart rate and restlessness) may be noted among neonates and infants of mothers who use nicotine (see also secondhand smoke). A nicotine withdrawal syndrome may occur when breast-feeding or maternal use of nicotine is discontinued.

TABLE 4.1 (*Continued*) .

Substance of Abuse	Reported Average Concentration in Breast Milk[b]	Effect on Neonate/Infant
Opiates (e.g., codeine, heroin, meperidine, morphine, and oxycodone)	Variable (depends on specific opiate)	All of the opiates are excreted in human breast milk. Accumulation can occur over several days and cause respiratory depression among neonates and infants of mothers who use opiates. In addition, an opiate withdrawal syndrome may occur when breast-feeding or maternal opiate use is discontinued.
THC (e.g., hashish, hashish oil, and marijuana)	200 ng/ml	May cause drowsiness among nursing neonates and infants whose mothers use THC. However, because of the paucity of reported data, the effects upon these neonates and infants are largely unknown (see also secondhand smoke).

[a]Adapted from O'Mara and Nahata (1995).
[b]Note that neonates who are fed exclusively on breast milk consume, on average, approximately 150 ml of breast milk per kg of body weight per day. Concentration is dependent on several factors including dose and frequency of use.

where an older sibling, parent, or other care giver is smoking one, or a combination of, these substances of abuse. This exposure can be deliberate (the sibling, parent, or care giver may want to get the infant high to "see what he or she will do"; A. M. Pagliaro & L. A. Pagliaro, 1982, clinical patient file notes; R. H. Schwartz, Peary, & Mistretta, 1986). "Eleven percent of teenage girls in one drug treatment reported that they deliberately intoxicated infants and children in their care by giving them beer or blowing marijuana smoke into their noses or mouth" (Bays, 1990, p. 886). Most of this exposure, however, can be considered unintentional. Generally, siblings, parents, and other care givers do not realize that an infant or child might be inhaling their smoke just by being in close proximity. However, exposed infants and children can inhale enough secondhand smoke to display the major effects of cocaine, nicotine, and THC. Exposure to each of these substances of abuse is discussed.

Cocaine

As the use of smokable (freebase) forms of cocaine, particularly crack, increased over the past decade, so did the exposure of infants and young children to their psychotropic and other effects (Bateman & Heagarty, 1989; Hicks, Morales, & Soldin, 1990; Kharasch, Vinci, & Reece, 1990). These neonates, infants, and children, ranging in age from less than 1 month to over 4 years, were reported to display various (expected) toxic CNS and respiratory effects, such as seizures and pulmonary edema (Batlle & Wilcox, 1993; N. M. Rosenberg, Meert, Knazik, Yee, & Kauffman, 1991). While the long-term effects of secondhand cocaine smoke have not been well documented, it is expected that infants and children experiencing such exposure will be at risk for respiratory diseases and, perhaps, other effects directly related to their cocaine exposure (e.g., learning disabilities).

THC

After inhalation into the lungs, THC, the principal active cannabinoid in marijuana or hashish smoke, is readily absorbed into the bloodstream of exposed infants and children. Although a number of studies have identified THC in the blood and urine of adolescents and adults exposed to secondhand smoke, there is a paucity of studies examining the effects of such exposure among infants and young children. In fact, there was only one study found. This study used a random, convenience sample of 360 children and sought to prospectively identify occult cocaine and THC among children exposed to these substances of abuse by secondhand smoke. Although this study found cocaine in blood and urine samples, it failed to detect THC (N. M. Rosenberg et al., 1991).

Nicotine

During the 1990s, many changes were made to public policies regarding when and where people could smoke tobacco because of the tremendous amount of research and data that conclusively demonstrated the health risks associated with secondhand smoke (e.g., smoking was generally prohibited in airplanes, many public buildings, and hospitals). The wealth of available data addressed all age groups, from neonates to spouses exposed to secondhand tobacco smoke. For neonates, the research evidence indicated that: 1. nicotine and cotinine (a metabolite) levels are significant among neonates whose mothers smoke when compared to those whose mothers do not; and 2. nicotine and cotinine levels among neonates are even higher when their mothers both smoke and breast-feed (Luck & Nau, 1985).

Maternal tobacco smoking has been directly associated with SIDS and several childhood respiratory diseases (DiFranza & Lew, 1995; Young, 1992). In fact, it has been suggested that the relative risk of asthma, bronchitis, or lower respiratory tract infections is more than twice as high among children whose mothers smoke when compared to those whose mothers do not (Stone, 1992; Ugnat et al., 1990; Weitzman et al., 1990; P. Young, 1992).

MEDICAL EXPOSURE

Substances of abuse (e.g., opiates and sedative-hypnotics) are rarely prescribed to infants and children. The only clear and pervasive exception to this rule involves, for children, the use of the CNS stimulants (dextroamphetamine, methylphenidate, and pemoline) for the treatment of ADHD. ADHD is reportedly the most prevalent mental disorder among North American children, with estimates as high as 10 percent among boys. Medical treatment of this disorder has generally involved the use of various types of CNS stimulants, with Ritalin (methylphenidate) being the most widely used drug of choice. Stimulant therapy has generally resulted in observed improvement in classroom manageability. However, questions have consistently been raised about the potential negative effect(s) associated with the use of methylphenidate and other stimulants on cognition, learning, and memory. A review of the literature examining this issue provides mixed results (see Chap. 7).

Children who have been prescribed methylphenidate for ADHD require individual evaluation. The factors that appear to be related to a higher incidence of cognition, learning, and memory impairment in this clinical context include: 1. the use of higher than optimal therapeutic doses and 2. the use of methylphenidate for children who do not fully meet the diagnostic criteria for ADHD. In regard to the latter, ADHD is misdiagnosed (overdiagnosed) in a significant number of children. In addition, in those cases in which it is correctly diagnosed, treatment is frequently inappropriate. Until better evidence to the contrary is accumulated, the prescription of methylphenidate for ADHD must be given special attention because of its potential long-term effects on cognition, learning, and memory (L. A. Pagliaro, 1992b). In addition, although the data are not conclusive, several studies (e.g., Johnston, O'Malley, & Bachman, 1987) suggest that children who are prescribed substances of abuse, including methylphenidate, have higher subsequent rates of substance use as adolescents than those children who are not.

Although not well documented in the literature, one other rather common form of substance exposure and use during infancy and childhood involves a form of "lay medication" (Bays, 1990). In these situations, the parent or care giver, often themselves compulsive users of a substance of abuse (particularly the CNS depressants), may administer some of the drug to their infant (usually) or child to quiet their crying or discomfort, which is frequently associated in these cases with childhood conditions such as colic or teething. This is not only done by "drug addict mothers." For example, we have encountered, on several occasions, Ukrainian grandmothers ("Babas") who, following traditional folk cures, would make a sachet filled with opium poppy pods and seeds and give this to their infant grandchildren to suck on in order to ease teething pain (A. M. Pagliaro & L. A. Pagliaro, 1977, 1981, 1989, clinical patient file notes).

Another, more devious and vile, form of lay medication involves the administration of substances of abuse to children by adolescents or adults in order to facilitate their sexual victimization. Bean (1992–93), for example, in a qualitative study of "adolescent girl victims of sexual abuse" noted this behavior in several cases:

> Suzanne was a victim of repeated rapes from the time she was 5 years old by her mother's live-in boyfriend. Suzanne's father never married her mother; he was only 14 at the time of her birth. Suzanne's mother was 18 when she gave birth to Suzanne. Soon after Suzanne's birth, Suzanne's mother began living with Suzanne's perpetrator. . . . Suzanne reported on her questionnaire that she was 7 years old when she had her first drink, which was with her perpetrator. She only reports agreeing with one "benefit" of drinking, "Drinking helps me feel like an adult." (p. 69)

> I had my first drink at 8 years old. Jeff [the victim's 17-year-old brother] conned me into it with some of his friends. It was peach schnapps. I thought it was pretty disgusting, but Jeff made me drink it. These "conned" drinking sessions occurred at the same time as the sexual abuse. (p. 67)

FOODSTUFF EXPOSURE

Although foodstuff exposure of infants and children to various substances of abuse is invariably unintentional, it can be more or less deliberate. For example, "less deliberate" exposure occurs when an infant or young child, most frequently between the ages of 6 months and 5 years, picks up an item such as a tablet or cigarette butt from the floor and ingests it (Klein-Schwartz & Oderda, 1995). As noted by Baldridge and Bessen (1990), "Children often become intoxicated by ingesting the butts of used PCP-impregnated cigarettes." Similar cases have been presented for an 8-month-old infant and a 21-month-old child, who reportedly accidentally ingested cocaine powder or the chemical ingredients used to make crack cocaine (Reece, 1990). When this occurs, the exposure is treated as are other cases of accidental childhood poisoning. A more "deliberate," although still predominantly unintentional, exposure occurs when the infant or child ingests a foodstuff, such as a caffeinated soft drink (see also discussion of maternal breast milk exposure, above).

TABLE 4.2   Mean Daily Caffeine Intake: Bogalusa Heart Study[a]

		Boys		Girls	
Age (years)	*n*	White	Black	White	Black
0.5	125	1.5	1.0	1.2	0.3
1	99	4.6	2.2	3.9	2.3
4	219	4.1	2.3	4.5	2.5
10	185	1.8	0.7	2.0	0.7
15	108	1.7	0.5	2.0	0.6
Percentage of sample		32	20	28	20

[a]Data from Arbeit et al. (1988).

Caffeine

Caffeine is one of the most widely consumed substances of abuse in the world (L. A. Pagliaro, 1989b). It has become so ubiquitously associated with foods and beverages, such as chocolate, coffee, tea, and caffeinated soft drinks, that many people do not consider it to be a substance of abuse. Among infants and children, caffeine consumption (on a mg/kg basis) is reportedly highest among those children under 5 years of age (see Table 4.2).

Although caffeine is found in some prescription and nonprescription drugs and is excreted in breast milk, virtually all of the caffeine consumed by infants and children is in foodstuffs. Fortunately, "caffeine, at levels consumed by most children, does not appear to produce adverse effects" (Leviton, 1992), despite: 1. the relatively high intake of caffeine by infants and children; 2. its known pharmacological effects as a CNS stimulant, which can increase arousal and nervousness and produce other effects; and 3. its addiction potential (the development of tolerance and a relatively mild withdrawal syndrome when chronic exposure or use is abruptly discontinued).

EXPERIMENTAL AND OTHER USE

Among children, social factors (e.g., cultural norms, homelessness, peers, socioeconomic status, and single-parent families) appear to be the most significant predictors of initial or experimental use (Caputo, 1993; Swadi, 1992; Wagner, Melragon, & Menke, 1993; Westermeyer, 1992). More serious use patterns, including the intravenous injection of opiates by children, as well as adolescents, have been related to such factors as maternal loss through separation by abandonment, divorce, or death. For example, as reported by a child interviewed during one of the authors' research studies:

> I was 3 months away from my 12th birthday. I went home for my mom's funeral and I saw my stepdad fixing. I asked him what it was for, he said to make

himself feel better. . . . I asked him if it would make me feel better about mom dying and he said it would. He got into the habit of fixing me at least once a day. (A. M. Pagliaro & Pagliaro, 1994)

The experimental and other use of substances of abuse is increasing among children (Norwood, 1985; Swadi, 1992; Westermeyer, 1992) who may also experiment with other substances—for example, anticholinergics (Carlini, 1993) and cinnamon oils (Norwood, 1985). However, of all of the substances of abuse, alcohol, tobacco, and volatile solvents and inhalants are most commonly used during childhood (Van Kammen, Loeber, & Stouthamer-Loeber, 1991). Each of these commonly used substances of abuse is briefly discussed (see also Chaps. 1 and 2 for additional discussion).

Alcohol

Several studies have reported initiation of alcohol use to occur, on average, by 10 or 11 years of age (Catalano et al., 1992; Leite & Parrish, 1994; Okwumabua, Okwumabua, Winston, & Walker, 1989). However, perhaps more disturbing is the finding that significant use of alcohol (~5 percent during the previous 6 months and ~10 percent lifetime) has been reported from a large sample of first-grade boys (mean age 6.9 years; Van Kammen et al., 1991). In addition, a large longitudinal study of children and adolescents in several cities (Denver, Pittsburgh, and Rochester) noted that approximately 18 percent of first-grade boys and 10 percent of first-grade girls (mean age 7 years) used alcohol (Huizinga et al., 1993, p. 93).

Some studies have noted that factors such as geographical region (e.g., Torabi, Bailey, & Majd-Jabbari, 1993) and ethnic or racial group (e.g., Katims & Zapata, 1993) may contribute to variability in use. Catalano et al. (1992), for example, found alcohol use to be significantly higher in fifth-grade boys than girls. They also found that among sampled fifth-grade students in Seattle, alcohol was highest for whites, followed by blacks, and lowest for Asians. However, perhaps surprisingly, reports of alcohol use by children have been few overall (Famularo et al., 1985). Based on the available published data and clinical experience, it appears that alcohol use is significantly increasing among children, with over 40 percent of fifth- and sixth-graders reporting alcohol use within the previous month and over 20 percent of boys reporting one or more binges within the previous month (Pierce, Broste, & Layde, 1991).

In 1990, approximately 60 percent of sixth-graders reported significant "peer pressure to try alcohol." Indeed, "trying to 'fit in' was the reason most often given by elementary school children to explain their use of a drug" ("Trends in Drug," 1993). However, the influence of parents in relation to both drinking intentions and actual drinking behavior among a sample of fifth-graders was also reported to be significantly correlated (Quine & Stephenson, 1990).

> In my family my mother was a drug addict, she died. It was accepted. Drugs, booze, prostitution, robbery, theft, murder, it was accepted. It was all general knowledge. Like when I was 10 years old I found a dead body in my basement it was no big deal. I went to school, what the hell's the difference, who cares, they hauled him away. . . . They said they didn't care. Here, what're you whining about, go drink. (A. M. Pagliaro & L. A. Pagliaro, 1983, clinical patient file notes)

(See also discussion of family alcohol and other substance use in Chap. 5).

Nicotine (Tobacco)

The adverse health consequences associated with tobacco use have been well documented (see Chap. 1). Unfortunately, although tremendous public health strides have been made in relation to significantly reducing tobacco use among adults, no similar reduction has been noted for children. The annual use of tobacco among a statewide sample of approximately 1,600 eighth-graders was reported to be over 40 percent (41.8 percent) for cigarettes and over 20 percent (22.8 percent) for smokeless tobacco (e.g., moist snuff; Torabi et al., 1993).

Various studies of smoking behavior among children in grades 4–6 have related findings to geographic factors. For example, a study in southern California found that male Hispanic youths were most likely to smoke cigarettes (Morris, Vo Bassin, Savaglio, & Wong, 1993), while a study in rural New Hampshire found that male Caucasian youths were most likely to use smokeless tobacco (Stevens, Freeman, Mott, Youells, & Linsey, 1993). General commonalities noted among other studies and reports concerning childhood smoking include: 1. a higher incidence of new smokers among girls, 2. girls most often reporting smoking "to appear older," 3. few problems associated with purchasing cigarettes at convenience stores near schools (often merely across the street), and 4. significant peer pressure and a certain sense of camaraderie (often meeting at the local convenience store, or in its parking lot, before and after school to smoke and socialize; Kohut, 1995; A. M. Pagliaro & L. A. Pagliaro, unpublished data; Quine & Stephenson, 1990; Stevens et al., 1993; Torabi et al., 1993; Vanderschmidt, Lang, Knight-Williams, & Vanderschmidt, 1993).

Volatile Solvents and Inhalants

Solvents and inhalants are used by adolescents and young adults, particularly those who are socioeconomically disadvantaged (e.g., Native Americans living on reserves or reservations; Fornazzari, 1990; K. Martin, 1993). However, they are primarily the "drug of choice" among children, with use decreasing with increasing age, as older children and adolescents go on to use other available substances of abuse (e.g., alcohol and marijuana; McHugh, 1987; N. S. Miller & Gold, 1990).

The children who use volatile solvents and inhalants are typically 8–12 years of age, but may be as young as 4 or 5 years of age (Beauvais & Oetting, 1989; "It's an Important," 1986; Westermeyer, 1987). The factors that tend to encourage volatile solvent and inhalant use and make them particularly attractive to children include: 1. their rapid onset of effect (desired effects can be expected within a few minutes), 2. alcohol-like high, 3. low cost (affordable), 4. easy and widespread availability (various solvents and inhalants can be obtained in virtually every home and school), 5. convenient packaging (small packages that make concealment easy, features that also make shoplifting easier), and 6. legal status (solvents and inhalants are the only substances of abuse for which purchase and possession by children are generally legal; McHugh, 1987).

SUMMARY

Although the topic of exposure to and use of the various substances of abuse during infancy and childhood has not received adequate attention, clinical experience and the available data suggest that it is a significant and growing problem. Prominent patterns of exposure and use among this age group include: 1. maternal breast milk exposure, 2. secondhand smoke exposure, 3. foodstuff exposure, 4. medical exposure, and 5. experimental and other use. An awareness and recognition of these patterns of exposure and use will enable adults, including parents and health care professionals, to: 1. decrease substance exposure among infants and children, 2. recognize and appropriately deal with related behavior when observed among exposed infants and children, and 3. better attend to common patterns of substance use among children.

CHAPTER 5

Adolescent Substance Use

Adolescence, a time of transition from childhood to adulthood, is a period of significant physical and psychological change. During this period, adolescents are faced with several major developmental challenges, including developing their own personal identities, values, and relationships and separating from their parents and families as they increasingly assume adult responsibilities and roles. Adolescence also is a period when youth establish or consolidate their sexual identities and deal with such issues as their sexual orientations and feelings of attractiveness to desirable sexual partners. In addition, they are confronted with decisions regarding social mores; religious doctrines; and family, cultural, and societal taboos and expectations (Botvin & Dusenbury, 1992; L. A. Pagliaro, 1995e; L. A. Pagliaro & Pagliaro, 1993).

Amid these challenges, virtually all adolescents yearn for just one thing— to be happy. As noted by George Santayana (1863–1952): "Happiness is the only sanction of life; where happiness fails, existence remains a mad and lamentable experiment." In the adolescents' transition to adulthood, where happiness fails developmental problems prevail (Rolf, Masten, Cicchetti, Nuechterlein, & Weintraub, 1990). These problems include delinquency; eating disorders; parental conflict; truancy; dropping out of school; sexual promiscuity, with an increased risk for unwanted pregnancies and infection with STDs; and various patterns of substance use ("Adolescents as Victims," 1993; Glantz, 1992; A. M. Pagliaro & Pagliaro, 1995; L. A. Pagliaro & Pagliaro, 1993). Of concern in this chapter are the data supporting the relationships among selected developmental problems and substance use.

FACTORS RELATED TO SUBSTANCE USE
AMONG ADOLESCENTS

No single biological, psychological, or sociological factor has been found to account for the significant patterns of substance use observed among adolescents (see Chap. 2). In this regard, it appears that a unique combination of biological, psychological, and sociological factors are required (see Chap. 1). However, to date, the identification of this unique combination of factors remains elusive. Age seems to be associated with initial use and the number and types of substances used. Race and ethnicity have been related to severity

138

of patterns of use. Gender also has been related to the number and types of substances used. However, demographic factors, in general, have not been consistently associated with explaining the variance observed among adolescents in regard to their specific patterns of substance use (Chassin, 1984; R. G. Smart, Adlaf, Porterfield, & Canale, 1990).

Within the myriad of possible factors, there is, however, a remarkable similarity among the factors associated with adolescent suicide and substance use. Virtually all of the factors associated with adolescent suicide (L. A. Pagliaro, 1995e), with the exception of access to firearms and previous suicide attempts (see Chap. 8, Table 8.3), have been significantly associated with adolescent substance use.[1] A brief discussion of each of these risk factors and their association with adolescent substance use follows. In order to organize discussion and to facilitate conceptual application, each of these risk factors has been grouped under two of the major variable dimensions of MIMSEUICA—the infant/child/adolescent dimension and the societal dimension (see Table 5.1).[2] In addition, as noted by others (e.g., J. S. Brook, Cohen, Whiteman, & Gordon, 1992), we believe that an interactional perspective offers a fuller, more accurate understanding of these risk factors (L. A. Pagliaro & Pagliaro, 1993). Therefore, readers are encouraged to consider, interpret, and apply these factors in the full context of MIMSEUICA (see Fig. 1.3).

INFANT/CHILD/ADOLESCENT DIMENSION

The infant/child/adolescent dimension comprises physical, psychological, and social variables. The psychological and social variables are considered in regard to adolescent substance use.

[1] Other authors (e.g., Vitaro, Dobkin, Janosz, & Pelletier, 1992) similarly have identified groups of factors associated with adolescent substance use. These similar groupings have contained many of the same factors identified here but generally have been less comprehensive.

[2] Many, but not all, of these high-risk factors could be categorized according to DSM-IV taxonomy. However, we are of the opinion that to do so would require a forced fit because the risk factors were not originally conceptualized in this manner. Others have also noticed the problem of forcing a fit to DSM-IV. For example, in commenting on "the alcoholic family," S. Brown and Lewis (1995) noted:

> These dual or even multiple frameworks raise critical, more complicated questions than we have ever before addressed. If parental alcoholism is also a "family disease," does every individual suffer the consequences of the traumatic environment and family systems pathology, and if so, how? When do we focus on the family as a whole, and when do we address the individuals? Do we need to do both? If so, when? What is the diagnosis? Do we incorporate the complexities of these multiple tracks into the dominant, individually based DSM-IV, or do we push for additional tracks, which would require separate assessment and diagnosis? We argue for the latter. (p. 282)

We too, in this case, would argue for "the latter." However, where DSM-IV taxonomy can make a significant contribution (e.g., for extricating clinical diagnoses from semantic debate) we recommend its use (see, e.g., Chap. 6).

TABLE 5.1   Major Variables Associated with Substance Use among Adolescents

Infant/Child/Adolescent Dimension
  Psychological Variables
    Conduct disorder
    Depression
    External locus of control (see discussions of peer pressure and media
      influences)
    Gender identity crisis
    Hopelessness (see discussion of depression)
    Lack of reasons for living or meaning in life (see discussion of depression)
    Loneliness
    Low self-esteem
    Previous substance use
    Serious early childhood losses
  Social Variables
    Absence of maternal figure
    Dissatisfaction with family relationships
    Family alcohol and other substance use
    Peer pressure
    Physical or sexual abuse
    Previous psychiatric inpatient treatment
Societal Dimension
  Societal Variables
    Social programs and services (treatment availability and accessibility)
    Media messages

Psychological Variables

A number of the psychological variables, alone and in combination (see Table 5.1), have been purported to account for adolescent substance use. Each of these variables is discussed, in alphabetical order.[3]

Conduct Disorder

A repetitive and persistent pattern of behavior involving early aggression, destruction of property, deceitfulness, theft, and violation of parental rules (e.g., running away from home) is indicative of conduct disorder (CD) (American Psychiatric Association, 1994). As noted by Chassin (1984), "The implication of this pattern is that adolescents who are at risk [for] initiating drug use are less socially adapted to the demands of the mainstream normative culture." Thus, substance use may result from CD (Boyle et al., 1992; Lavin & Rifkin, 1993). J. S. Brook, Cohen, et al. (1992) also noted the significant positive relationship between "early childhood aggression" and "heavy use or

---

[3] Although the focus of this chapter is on antecedents of adolescent substance use, where appropriate, brief discussion of each factor as a possible consequence is included and reflects the complex nature of the relationship among these variables in regard to adolescent substance use. The "chicken versus egg" controversy remains largely unresolved.

abuse of drugs" during adolescence. In addition, a prerequisite for the diagnosis of antisocial personality disorder in adults, which is highly correlated with substance use, is the appearance of symptoms of CD (e.g., cruelty to animals, initiation of physical fights, forced sexual activity, and theft) during childhood or adolescence (American Psychiatric Association, 1994). As noted by Hodgins (1992), "Antisocial behavior in childhood significantly increased the risk of persistent adult criminality and of early onset, severe substance abuse in both males and females" (p. 41).

Conversely, it also appears that the chronic regular use of various substances of abuse can presage or contribute to the development of CD, as noted by R. H. Schwartz, Hoffmann, and Jones (1987) in their study of adolescent marijuana use (see the related discussion of FAS in Chaps. 3 and 7). In addition, as noted by Gabel and Shindledecker (1990), "Children with parents who have had substance abuse problems are themselves likely to be at high-risk for conduct disorder, later substance abuse, and early psychiatric hospitalization" (p. 922). (See the discussion of family alcohol and other substance use in the social variables section of this chapter; see also Chap. 6 for additional discussion of CD.)

ADHD, which has been closely related to CD as a concurrent disorder, an antecedent, or, according to the International Classification of Diseases (ICD-10), a variant (Barkley, 1990; Lavin & Rifkin, 1993), is also a risk factor for the development of problematic patterns of substance use among adolescents, particularly boys (Claude & Firestone, 1995; Hellgren, Gillberg, Gillberg, & Enerskog, 1993; G. Weiss & Hechtman, 1986; Wilens et al., 1994; Windle, 1990). Hechtman, Weiss, and Perlman (1984) observed that "young adults who had been diagnosed as hyperactive in childhood were found to have had greater involvement with alcohol and drug use" (p. 415). In addition, "post hoc analyses suggest that behavior problems resulting from drug use in early adolescence have graver consequences for previously hyperactive children than normal subjects" (Mannuzza, Klein, Bonagura, Konig, & Shenker, 1988, p. 13). These effects appear to be particularly significant when the adolescent has met diagnostic criteria during childhood for both ADHD and CD. As noted by Barkley (1990), "The mixed hyperactive-CD subjects [ages 4–12 years] used these substances [alcohol, cigarettes, or marijuana] at a rate two to five times that of the pure hyperactives or normals" (p. 118). (See Chap. 7; see also the discussion of previous substance use, below.)

Depression

The nature of the relationship between depression and substance use is complex and incompletely understood (J. Block & Gjerde, 1990; see Chap. 2). Depression can be either an antecedent to, or a consequence of, substance use (L. A. Pagliaro, 1990b; R. H. Schwartz et al., 1987; R. G. Smart et al., 1990). For example, some adolescents who are depressed may drink alcohol in an effort to forget their problems. Conversely, other adolescents may drink to "party" or to celebrate their team's victory, only to subsequently become depressed as a direct result of alcohol's pharmacological action as a sedative-hypnotic. In these situations, a vicious cycle can begin in which depression leads to drinking (and further depression) or drinking leads directly to depression; either way, each situation encourages additional drinking for relief.

Whatever its cause, depression is commonly associated with the use of various substances of abuse by adolescents. As noted by D. Miller (1986), "The most common reason for using drugs is to avoid the depressive affect associated with emotional deprivation, mood disorders, or both" (p. 207). Perez-Bouchard, Johnson, and Ahrens (1993) similarly stated that "drug abuse can provide a depressed youngster with a way of coping with overwhelming feelings and/or stresses in his/her environment" (p. 486). Of increasing concern, regardless of the cause of depression, is the significant relationship among depression, substance use, and adolescent suicide (L. A. Pagliaro, 1995e). For an overview and discussion of adolescent suicide and its relationship to substance use, see Chapter 8.

Gender Identity Crisis

Gender identity crises typically occur during early childhood and adolescence and are frequently accompanied with problematic patterns of substance use. Generally, as noted by Unks (1995):

> LGB [lesbian, gay, and bisexual] adolescents—and even those unsure of their sexual identity—are at a higher risk for substance abuse, clinical depression, prostitution, AIDS, running away, truancy, academic difficulties, and dropping out of school. They experience more psychological stress and lower self-esteem than other teens their age. . . . As conflicts arise over issues of sexual orientation, young people often turn to substances to reduce the pain and anxiety. One study found that fifty-eight percent of young gay males interviewed could be classified as having a substance abuse disorder as defined in the Diagnostic and Statistical Manual III. (pp. 86, 217)

Although gender identity and sexual orientation are established during early childhood (D. W. Kaplan & Mammel, 1993a), they are largely irrelevant to children until puberty. It is generally during adolescence that boys and girls begin self-selected sexual activity. It is during this time that gay, lesbian, or bisexual youth first typically identify that they "feel different." This feeling is generally followed by a period of time during which they may notice a particular and pervasive sexual attraction to others of the same gender. Finally, for many, a "coming-out" phase may occur during which they may come to terms with, and accept, their own sexual identity. As they become more accepting of their own sexual identity they may feel more comfortable revealing it to others. As described by Unks (1995), "adolescence and young adulthood are times of sexual exploration and, at times, confusion. . . . The percentage of adolescent boys who admit to being gay can be lower than one percent, but the number who report homosexual behaviors can be as high as twenty-five percent" (p. 178). When gender identity is unclear (e.g., in cases where denial or homosexual experimentation has occurred), adolescents may doubt their true gender identity. A crisis may result, characterized by severe homophobia or maladaptive coping mechanisms, including substance use.

Often, multiple factors appear to work in concert with gender identity crisis to encourage the development of problematic patterns of substance use. Consider, for example, the following reported case:

> Carlos' earliest memory is being shot in the left eye with a pellet gun by a drunken uncle when he was four years old. He had to have several operations to repair the damage, and he endured years of disfigurement before he received a replacement glass eye. He was continually teased by other children at school. As he got older, he got into fights and finally dropped out of school in the eighth grade.
>
> Eventually, Carlos drifted onto the streets. He started to hang out with a group of boys with whom he felt accepted and secure. They also turned him onto drugs. In the beginning, Carlos was happy hanging out and "partying" with his new-found friends. He drank a lot and smoked pot, but he promised himself that he would stay away from crack and heroin. He saw what the crack was doing to his friends, and he knew what the heroin did to his mother. Carlos doesn't remember why he smoked crack for the first time around his fifteenth birthday. He does know why he continues to smoke it: "It makes me feel better than I ever felt before."
>
> As Carlos' drug abuse continued to increase, he experimented with a variety of drugs. His drug of choice remained crack. When he began to run out of ways to pay for the crack, a friend taught him how to hustle (prostitute) in a local park. Carlos found that hustling was the easiest way for him to get all the money he needed to support his crack habit. Carlos' good looks and outgoing personality made him very popular in the park. He also started to become addicted to the excitement and notoriety he got from hustling in the park. Before he was arrested, he was "scoring" ten to fifteen times a day with mainly anonymous older men who frequented the park. He was engaging in both unprotected oral and anal intercourse. This was undoubtedly how he became HIV infected.
>
> Carlos had been sexually active with only two neighborhood girls before he started to hustle. As he became more drug involved, he only engaged in male-to-male sex. Carlos admits enjoying sex with men, but does not feel he is gay. His dream is to "marry a nice girl and have a family." A strong ethnic and social bias against homosexuality might be the cause of Carlos' confusion regarding his sexual identity. (Reulbach, 1991, pp. 35–36)

Stress, as a general factor, has also been related to substance use among adolescents who display a gender identity crisis. In this context, stress has been primarily associated with: 1. fear of infection with HIV and developing AIDS, 2. being "in the closet," and 3. verbal and physical abuse aimed by others at the adolescent's gender identity (e.g., gay-bashing).

AIDS remains a uniformly fatal disease with no effective cure and no preventative vaccine. As a result of the following factors, anyone can become infected with HIV and develop AIDS: 1. transfusion with infected blood, blood products, or equipment; 2. unprotected sex with multiple partners; or 3. unsafe needle-sharing behaviors (see Fig. 6.1 in the following chapter). However, the population group with the most reported cases and highest risk for infection with HIV, excluding intravenous drug users, is male homosexuals. Male homosexuals have been, and remain, at extremely high risk for infection with HIV and development of AIDS. This high risk for infection is a direct result of their preferred sexual behavior (unprotected insertive and receptive anal intercourse with multiple partners).[4] Adolescent boys who are gay are constantly reminded of this risk by media campaigns largely organized and developed through gay communities and networks. In addition, these adolescents are reminded by their own personal risks, having had acquaintances, friends, lovers, or partners who have become HIV positive or who have died of AIDS (A. M. Pagliaro, Pagliaro, Thauberger, Hewitt, & Reddon, 1990; A. M. Pagliaro et al., 1993). However, these reminders do not seem to diminish their risk-taking sexual behaviors: "I'm always amazed when gay men who have seen many friends and loved ones die, who teach and talk about AIDS and its prevention, tell me they themselves sometimes forget to practice safe sex" (Sack & Streeter, 1992, p. 64).

Stress associated with "being in the closet" appears to be particularly acute for gay and lesbian adolescents. Gay and lesbian adolescents, because they are generally living at home with heterosexual parents, are particularly loathe or unable to come out of the closet. These adolescents often fear rejection by their parents and other heterosexuals who are important to them (e.g., teachers and family members). Often this rejection takes the overt form of verbal and physical abuse that can run the gamut from name-calling (e.g., "dyke," "fag," "homo," or "queer") to physical assault (e.g., gay-bashing or murder; Freiberg, 1995; see also the discussion of physical or sexual abuse, below). As noted by Savin-Williams (1994):

> A common theme identified in empirical studies and clinical reports of lesbian, gay male, and bisexual youths is the chronic stress that is created by the verbal

---

[4] Gay adolescents who are monogamous with an HIV-negative partner are at extremely low risk (as per the general population) for becoming HIV positive and developing AIDS. This is true regardless of the nature and frequency of their sexual intercourse. However, we have had gay patients undergoing treatment for dual diagnosis (see Chap. 6) who have experienced severe peer pressure from other gay men to abandon their monogamous gay life-styles. They have been told that they are "Uncle Toms"; "monogamy is an unnatural myth of heterosexuals"; "one cannot be both truly gay and monogamous"; and "the whole concept of marriage is heterosexual bullshit" (A. M. Pagliaro & L. A. Pagliaro, 1987, clinical patient file notes). Obviously, this peer pressure becomes an additional source of stress for gay adolescents who are monogamous and wish to remain so.

and physical abuse they receive from peers and adults. . . . [This] is often associated with several problematic outcomes including . . . substance abuse. (p. 261)

In summary, it should be noted that a significant percentage of gay and lesbian adolescents use alcohol and other substances of abuse to deal with (self-medicate) the stress associated with the acknowledgment of their gender identities. In addition, the use of alcohol and other substances of abuse is a largely formalized part of the established gay and lesbian culture (gays and lesbians meet and socialize with other gays and lesbians for social and sexual purposes at gay bars; Lauritsen, 1993). It should be noted that substance use in this context significantly increases the risk for the development of problematic patterns of substance use and infection with HIV as a result of high-risk sexual behavior resulting from the cognitive dysfunction associated with intoxication (J. L. Martin & Hasin, 1991; A. M. Pagliaro et al., 1993; Stall, 1988). As discussed by Sack and Streeter (1992):

> We've used the term bisexual, meaning someone who has sex with both men and women. Now there's a new term—trisexual. This refers to people who are so attached or addicted to alcohol and drugs that the substance is actually a third presence in their relationship. When under its influence, they may try anything sexually. We counsel people not to have sex when they are drunk or high because they may make irresponsible choices in partners and sexual practices and don't always remember how to put on a condom properly, if at all. (p. 69)

Or, as noted by Faltz and Rinaldi (1987):

> Additionally, there is the factor of increased sexual risk and needle-using behavior while under the influence of alcohol or drugs [i.e., *disinhibition*]. Persons who have made promises to themselves or others concerning behaviors that may increase risk of exposure to AIDS, who have alcohol or drug abuse problems, often, despite the best of intentions, are not able to keep these promises consistently. (p. 19)

Loneliness

Loneliness among adolescents is most often associated with feelings of rejection or isolation from family and peer groups. As noted by Watts and Wright (1990a) in regard to a sample of adolescent Mexican Americans, "Feeling rejected by parents and without adequate parental supervision . . . they join a peer group [often a gang] that supports drug use" (p. 153). (See discussion of depression, above; see also Chap. 9.)

Low Self-Esteem

Low self-esteem has been frequently found to be associated with substance use among children (M. Young, Werch, & Bakema, 1989) and adolescents. For example, Dembo, Williams, Schmeidler, and Wothke (1993) found that the use of "marijuana/hashish . . . tends to be a vehicle for the expression of personal difficulties in the areas of self-esteem" (p. 1045). Harrison and Luxenberg (1995) noted that adolescent students with "three or more adverse consequences of substance use . . . were also two to fifteen times more likely than other students to report such correlates as low self-esteem" (p. 137). M. Young et al. (1989) found that "area specific self-esteem [i.e., school and home] is associated with reported substance use, and intended use" (p. 253).

Virtually all of the other factors listed in Table 5.1 can adversely affect self-esteem. Thus, interpretation of the relationship between self-esteem and adolescent substance use may be confounded. Indeed, results of studies examining this factor have yielded inconsistent and sometimes contradictory results. However, the nature of this relationship has been explored by Howard B. Kaplan in some detail and his explanation does intuitively appear sound. As described by Chassin (1984):

> Kaplan suggests that the adolescents who are at risk to begin substance use are those whose experiences within the normative membership group have resulted in feelings of self-rejection. The basic postulate of the theory is that individuals are motivated to behave in ways that maximize their sense of self-esteem and self-worth. If an adolescent has low self-esteem within the normative group, he or she will lose motivation to conform to their expectations and will attempt to seek other behavioral alternatives. A deviant behavior (such as substance use) can serve a variety of self-enhancing functions by symbolically attacking the normative group, by resulting in acceptance and positive feedback from a new group of peers, or by providing pharmacological relief. Thus Kaplan's theory predicts that substance use will be preceded by low self-esteem but that esteem will rise after drug use is established. (p. 113)

Interestingly, low self-esteem has been consistently reported among pregnant adolescent girls who use substances of abuse. These adolescent girls reportedly have significantly lower self-esteem than matched pregnant adolescent girls who do not use substances of abuse (Degen, Myers, Williams-Petersen, Knisely, & Schnoll, 1993; Williams-Petersen et al., 1994).

Previous Substance Use

Consonant with the old adage that the best predictor of future behavior is past behavior, a number of studies (e.g., A. D. Farrell, Anchors, Danish, & Howard, 1992; A. D. Farrell, Danish, & Howard, 1992; Vanderburg, Weekes, & Millson, 1995; Windle, 1990) have demonstrated a positive relationship between previous and subsequent substance use. Such substance use may involve either the same or different substance(s) of abuse. A corollary of this finding is that the earlier the initiation into the use of substances of abuse, the more likely use will continue and become problematic.

Serious Early Childhood Losses

Serious losses during childhood, including the loss of parents because of death or other separation (e.g., abandonment, divorce, or incarceration), have been related to substance use among adolescents, as well as younger children (see Chap. 4). As reported by one adolescent girl interviewed by A. M. Pagliaro and Pagliaro (1994) in their study of hard-core intravenous drug users, "I was 14, that was the first time [I used intravenous drugs], and I did it once and started using probably because I was under stress. I had just lost my parents a year before that" (see also discussion of absence of maternal figure, below).

Social Variables

Social variables include influences in the adolescents' proximal environment that could affect, in various ways, their initial or continued use of substances of abuse. These variables include the adolescents' family, peers, and usual contexts of social interaction (e.g., school, treatment center, or work setting). As Freeman (1990) declared:

> The source of the drug problem in North America is not in Colombia, it is in our society's desire to use drugs. Although the drug problem is complex and has many roots, the largest single root is the decay of stable families as the basic unit of society. (p. 796)

Research results increasingly support relationships between family functioning and adolescent substance use (Burnside, Baer, McLaughlin, & Pickering, 1986; Daly & Wilson, 1985; Flewelling & Bauman, 1990; D. W. Murray, 1994; Needle, Su, & Doherty, 1990). For example, Prange et al. (1992) found that perceptions by adolescents (and their parents) of "their family relations as more disengaged and less connected" were found to be significantly correlated with measures of adolescent psychopathology such as "alcohol/marijuana" use, "conduct disorder," and depression. Along the same line, Perez-Bouchard et al. (1993) identified that "the dysfunctional family environment that often results from alcoholism or other substance abuse fosters a depressogenic attributional style [among the children]" (p. 476). (See earlier discussions of both conduct disorder and depression.)[5] J. S. Brook, Cohen, et al. (1992) stated that "lack of parent-child mutual attachment" resulted in the adolescent "turning to the peer group to satisfy developmental needs not met in the parent-child relationship" (p. 385; see discussion of peer pressure, below). A general lack of parental support also has been related to adolescent substance use (Barrera, Chassin, & Rogosch, 1993; Muller, Fitzgerald, Sullivan, & Zucker, 1994). As noted by Hsu (1993): "Strengthening

---

[5] These findings are open to other interpretations; e.g., some studies have found "a higher risk of having children with a history of major depression or dysthymia, substance abuse, or conduct disorder . . . [in] families in which at least one parent had an affective illness" (C. E. Schwartz, Dorer, Beardslee, Lavori, & Keller, 1990, p. 244).

the social network and families' coping mechanisms may reduce the demand for and the consequences of substance abuse by family members" (p. 237).

A brief review follows of the major social variables identified in MIMSEUICA that have been significantly associated, both positively and negatively, with adolescent substance use.

Absence of Maternal Figure

The absence of a maternal figure has reportedly been associated with adolescent substance use and several other developmental problems, including gang involvement. The maternal figure may be absent from the home of an adolescent because of death, divorce, or imprisonment (Gabel & Shindledecker, 1993).[6] Increased homelessness among women, in addition to their substance use, also significantly contributes to the absence of a maternal figure. As noted by Robertson (1991):

> Clearly, alcohol and other drug use may impair a woman's ability to compete for scarce resources, and thereby threaten family integrity. Also, drug or alcohol abuse is likely to place a homeless woman at higher risk of losing custody of her children. Separation may occur when the mother informally places a child with a friend or relative—often the child's grandparent. Other separations occur when children are placed in foster care, either voluntarily by the mother or as a result of intervention by authorities, such as county child protective services. (pp. 1200–1201)

However, more often than not, the maternal figure is absent from an adolescent's life because the adolescent, dissatisfied with family relationships, has run away from home (Sherman, 1992; R. G. Smart & Adlaf, 1991; see also discussions of family alcohol and other substance use, dissatisfaction with family relationships, and physical or sexual abuse).

Dissatisfaction with Family Relationships

For a variety of reasons, including abandonment, death, divorce, illegitimacy, imprisonment, neglect, or separation (including kidnapping) many adolescents have grown up without the stability provided by a traditional family (see Fig. 5.1). D. W. Murray (1994) has written:

> America is becoming a nation of bastards. Thirty percent of the children born in 1991 were out of wedlock, up from 5 percent in 1960. Families are no longer simply breaking apart—with one in two marriages ending in divorce. More and more parents today aren't marrying at all. . . . Legitimacy is nothing more

---

[6] The absence of a father figure is also related to adolescent psychopathology. In this regard, it is important to note that only approximately 10 percent of the children involved in divorces are assigned by the courts to the custody of their fathers (Schwartzberg, 1992) and incarcerated fathers reportedly outnumber incarcerated mothers by a ratio of 10 to 1 (Kemper & Rivara, 1993).

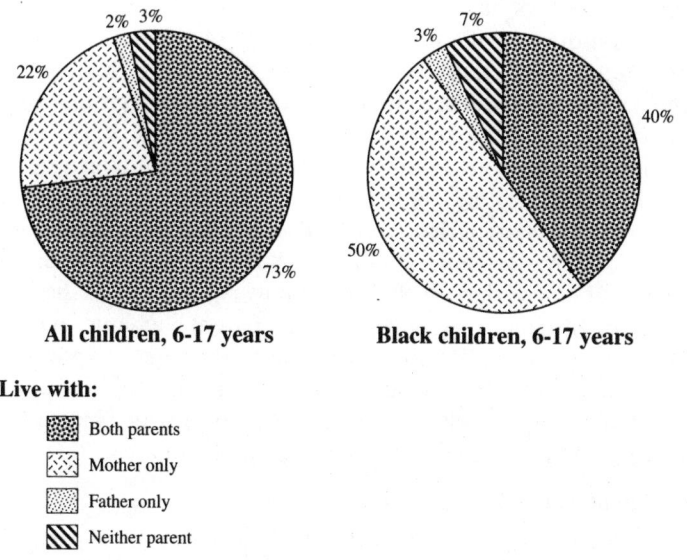

All children, 6-17 years   **Black children, 6-17 years**

Live with:

Both parents

Mother only

Father only

Neither parent

FIGURE 5.1   Percentage of children living with biological parents
Note: Data from U.S. Bureau of the Census (1991).

or less than the orderly transfer of social meaning across the generations . . .
so legitimacy is not just the concern of judgmental moralists, but a problem for
every human group. (p. B5)

Divorce has been consistently rated by adolescents as one of the most stress-
ful life events and can contribute to, or exacerbate, their substance use
(Needle et al., 1990; Schwartzberg, 1992; Sherman, 1992; Wallerstein, 1987).
In this regard it has been noted that:

The child of divorce faces intensified problems associated with separation;
problems of identification with parental figures, especially in families marked
by enduring parental hostility; and distinctive problems associated with visita-
tion, parent absence, and remarriage [see discussion of absence of maternal
figure]. All problems are exacerbated by protracted legal battles and custody
disputes. (Schwartzberg, 1992, p. 635)

As one of our patients described:

I brought up 5 kids, all of them experimented with all types of drugs, some
pretty heavily at different times. The only one that had serious difficulties was
J. . . . He was the youngest, he was the one who came to maturity while my wife
and I were having our worst difficulties and going through our divorce. . . . He
was the only one who got into it seriously where he had to be hospitalized.
(A. M. Pagliaro & L. A. Pagliaro, 1983, clinical patient file notes)

Several researchers have suggested developmental variation in regard to the relative importance of various contributory factors related to substance use. For example, S. L. Bailey and Hubbard (1990) found that "only parental attachment measures influence initiation for the youngest group," while "only measures of peer attachment" became important as adolescents mature and become more autonomous from their parents. These findings would appear to be consistent with other empirical findings and the concept of developmental psychopathology (Glantz, 1992; Rolf et al., 1990). In addition, some researchers (e.g., W. Feigelman et al., 1990) have noted that, for many adolescents, living at home with both parents actually contributed to their increased substance use, particularly when significant "parent enabling" existed within the family environment. We, too, have noted this potential problem in the family dynamics of several of our adolescent patients and have developed and used the "family flowchart" (see Fig. 5.2) to provide clinical assistance in identifying and dealing with this potential problem area.

Family Alcohol and Other Substance Use

Rebeta-Burditt (1977) observed that "alcoholism is not a spectator sport, eventually, the whole family gets to play." This observation can probably be extended to all forms of substance use, as noted by one of our patients:

> I was around 13 or 14 and the old lady was firing it [heroin] up. I said, "Hey, if you're gonna be doing that in front of me, give me some or I'll go do it by myself." She said, "Okay, if you're gonna fix, do it around here, then if you OD [overdose] I can get you to the hospital." It was accepted around my house. Accepted behavior to get high. I think there are a lot of other kids like that out there in the same position. Their parents don't give a shit one way or another. (A. M. Pagliaro & L. A. Pagliaro, 1983, clinical patient file notes)

Lending support to our patient's observation is the report from Lewandowski and Westman (1991): "Family activities for some [adolescents] involved the use of hard drugs together or the condoning of use" (p. 353).

Children and adolescents appear to be at significantly greater risk of developing their own problems with alcohol or other substances of abuse if their parents were heavy users (Rowe, 1989; Rubio-Stipec, Bird, Canino, Bravo, & Alegria, 1991; Schinke, Botvin, & Orlandi, 1991; R. G. Smart et al., 1990; Woodside, Coughey, & Cohen, 1993). Much of the research in this area (e.g., Mathew, Wilson, Blazer, & George, 1993) involves adult children of alcoholics and provides a particularly strong gender-based risk for the development, particularly among boys, of subsequent problematic patterns of substance use (Kosten, Rounsaville, Kosten, & Marikangas, 1991).

This increased risk appears to be mediated through biological (e.g., genetic predisposition), psychological (e.g., "pro-use" attitudes), and sociological (e.g., socially learned behavior) variables (Chassin, Pillow, Curran, Mol-

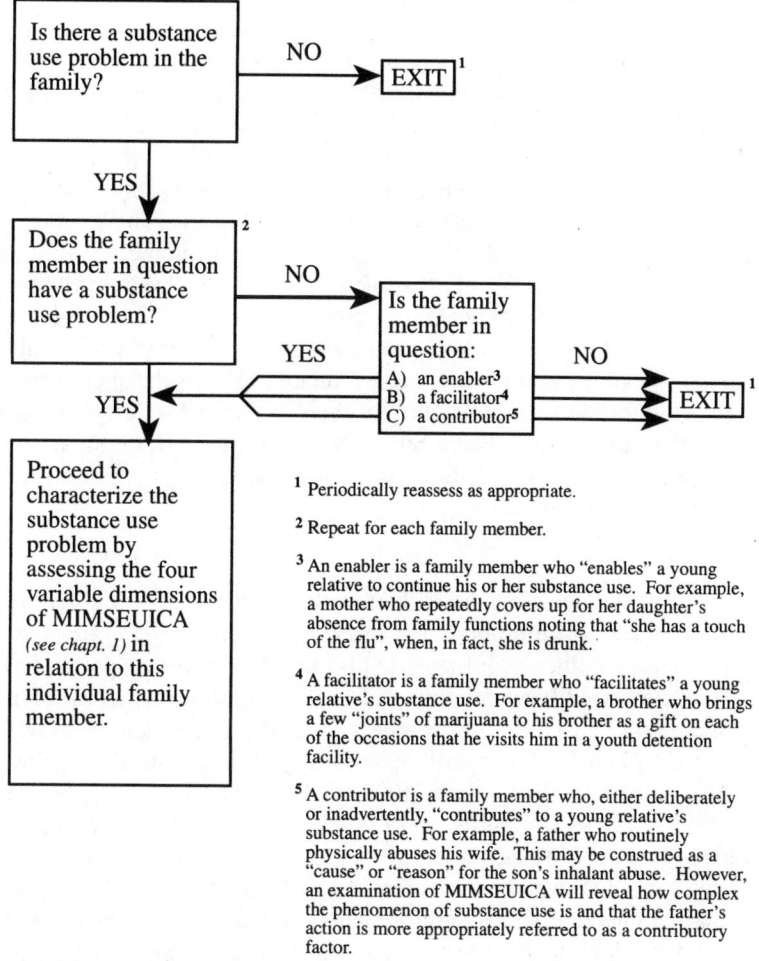

FIGURE 5.2   Family flowchart

ina, & Barrera, 1993). Most studies, in this regard, have focused on genetic predisposition, with several investigators reporting consistent results. For example, sons of alcoholic fathers have been shown to have significantly higher rates of CD and associated problematic patterns of substance use (Frick et al., 1992; Gabel & Shindledecker, 1990, 1992). In relation to socially learned behavior, one study (McDermott, 1984) found not only that parental attitude was important but that it was even more important than the parents' own substance use in relation to subsequent substance use by their adolescent offspring. However, for the most part, the role set by parents appears to be particularly important to the development of adolescent substance use (McMurran, 1991; see Chap. 2 for a more complete discussion).

It has been noted that 44 percent of homeless street youth reportedly run away from home because of parental substance use ("Homelessness," 1989; see discussion of physical or sexual abuse, below). These youth are at significant risk of using substances of abuse themselves (R. G. Smart & Adlaf, 1991; Wagner et al., 1993). It has been estimated that between 500,000 and 1 million adolescents in North America run away from home annually (this involves approximately 1 out of 10 adolescents who run away from home at least once; Council of Scientific Affairs, 1989; Sherman, 1992). These adolescents, and the other hundreds of thousands of adolescents simply labeled "homeless," have a significantly higher incidence of substance use than do their counterparts who remain in their homes (McCarty, Argeriou, Huebner, & Lubran, 1991; R. G. Smart & Adlaf, 1991; R. G. Smart et al., 1990; see also discussions of dissatisfaction with family relationships and physical or sexual abuse).[7]

Peer Pressure

Adolescents become more independent in thinking and decision making as they move closer to adulthood. However, they remain susceptible to the behavior-shaping influence of their friends and acquaintances, particularly if they have an external locus of control. For these adolescents, external influences, including substance use by peers (J. S. Brook, Cohen, et al., 1992; A. D. Farrell, Danish, & Howard, 1992; Leary, Tchividjian, & Kraxberger, 1994; McDonald & Towberman, 1993; Oetting & Beauvais, 1986, 1987; Swadi, 1992) and media messages (DiFranza et al., 1991; Whitaker, 1989; see discussion of media influences, below), appear to be the most prominent factors in determining the nature and extent of their substance use. Even though all normal "adolescent social developments are marked by increasing independence from the family and increasing involvement in peer relationships" (Healy & Stewart, 1984), those adolescents who have an external locus of control are, by their very nature, particularly susceptible to substance use and related problems: "Drug dealing by older peers becomes an important issue in early adolescent drug abuse. That is, early adolescents use older peers as identification models, and so they are particularly apt to mimic the older adolescents' behavior" (D. Miller, 1986, p. 200). In addition, as noted by Botvin and Botvin (1992):

---

[7] It should be noted that government surveys of adolescent substance use typically sample from high school students. Thus, these data would be expected to be biased and to significantly underrepresent the actual nature and extent of use by homeless or other adolescents who do not attend school and, hence, adolescents overall.

Vulnerability to peer pressure to engage in the use of one or more psychoactive substances is greater for adolescents who have fewer effective coping strategies in their repertoire, fewer skills for handling social situations, and greater anxiety about social situations. For these adolescents, the range of options for achieving personal goals is restricted at the same time that discomfort in interpersonal situations is high, motivating them to take some action in an effort to alleviate that discomfort. (p. 293)

Adolescent peer pressure also includes participation in related high-risk behaviors. For example, Escobedo (1994), in reviewing several drinking-and-driving studies involving adolescents, noted that among samples of adolescents 14–18 years of age, 32–45 percent reported that they "rode in a vehicle driven by someone who had been drinking alcohol at least once in the past month." This behavior is particularly disturbing in view of the well-recognized and publicized fact that alcohol-related motor vehicle crashes are a leading cause of death among adolescents (National Center for Health Statistics, 1991; see Chap. 8 for additional discussion of substance use related to motor vehicle crashes).

Peer and other external influences, such as the media, appear to play an even greater role in the lives of adolescents who lack family support and quality interaction (positive time spent together in school work and recreational activities; Varenhorst, 1981/1983). For example, in families in which one or both parents are alcoholics, "negative affect and impaired parental monitoring were associated with adolescents' membership in a peer network that supported drug use behavior" (Chassin et al., 1993, p. 3).

Physical or Sexual Abuse

Corporal punishment of adolescents by their parents has been associated with the subsequent development of several significant psychological problems (e.g., problematic patterns of alcohol use, depression, and suicide). Although varying greatly in severity and extent, this form of punishment appears to be quite commonly practiced by parents in North America:

Over 90% of parents of toddlers spank or use other forms of corporal punishment. Although the rate declines each year from about age five, this study of a large national sample of U.S. adults found that almost half recalled having been corporally punished during their teen years. (M. A. Straus & Kantor, 1994, p. 543)

In addition, other forms of abuse, particularly severe physical and sexual abuse during childhood and adolescence have frequently been reported as an antecedent to significant psychopathology (e.g., problematic patterns of alcohol use and major depression) in adulthood ("Adolescents as Victims," 1993; B. E. Carlson, 1991; Hendricks-Mathews, 1993; Hernandez, 1992; Hernandez, Lodico, & DiClemente, 1993; Hussey & Singer, 1993; Malinosky-Rummell & Hansen, 1993; Pribor & Dinwiddie, 1992). For example,

Triffleman, Marmar, Delucchi, and Ronfeldt (1995) noted that among a "sample of male veteran substance abuse inpatients . . . seventy-seven percent of [the] subjects had been exposed to severe childhood trauma . . . which in turn was related to multiple substance dependence" (p. 172). As described by Nemeth (1993):

> Theresa grew up in Saint John, N.B., where, she says, her alcoholic father used to beat her mother and brothers and they, in turn, would beat her. Then, when she was 14 and a virgin, her boyfriend raped her. Soon, she says, she started dabbling in drugs—and prostitution. Her friends introduced her to men who paid $20 for oral sex. "After the rape happened," she explains, "I thought sex didn't matter so I didn't really care. And I needed the money." (p. 49)

A significant positive correlation between a previous history of physical or sexual abuse and subsequent substance use also has been noted among various groups of adolescents (e.g., adolescents hospitalized with dual diagnosis, juvenile detainees, pregnant teenagers, and street youth) that suggests self-medicating behavior (Bayatpour, Wells, & Holford, 1992; Burgess, Hartman & McCormack, 1987; Cavaiola & Schiff, 1988; Dembo et al., 1988, 1989; Malinosky-Rummell & Hansen, 1993; B. A. Miller, 1990; Sherman, 1992; Van Hasselt, Ammerman, Glancy, & Bukstein, 1992). Consider, for example, Shara's all-too-common story:

> My step-father abused me from the time I was five years old until I was fourteen. He used to trap me in my bedroom or the bathroom, when no one else was home. Then I left home. I wanted to be far away from what my step-father did to me.
>
> Before I started drinking, I always felt different from other people. But drinking helped me fit in. Drinking helped me forget my abuse. . . . I could go on drinking for days at a time. The thing was, though, I couldn't forget. When I woke up from a wild night of drinking, I could still remember what my step-father did to me. *Drinking just kept me from facing it.* ("Making the Links," 1990, pp. 2–3)

Estimates have been made that approximately 40 percent of homeless street youth have run away from home because of severe physical or sexual abuse ("Homelessness," 1989; Janus, Burgess, & McCormack, 1987; Powers, Eckenrode, & Jaklitsch, 1990; Seng, 1989). Sadly, these adolescents often run away to exactly what they were running from:

> From age three to eight, Patsy was molested by an older brother. He was nine when he started touching her "down there," usually late at night in her bedroom while their parents were "out drinking or downstairs sobering up." Patsy explains, apologetically, that although she resisted her brother, she didn't understand that what he did to her was wrong—even when touching escalated to penetration.
>
> "I was seven when the rapes started. . . . My parents were into alcohol and

my brother was into incest. As far as I knew, my family was normal and what my brother did to me was what all families did to their girls. If anything was wrong, I would have figured it was my fault anyway."

When Patsy was eight, her mother walked in on a rape. How did she react: "Left the room till my brother finished and we had our clothes back on. Then she came back into my bedroom, asked him to go outside. 'You slut,' she hollered at me. 'Why are you doing this to your brother?'"As Patsy recalls the scene now, her brown eyes fire with rage, and her voice quavers. . . .

By the time she was ten, Patsy had discovered the pain-dulling benefits of alcohol. By eleven, she had started sniffing typists' correction fluid. By thirteen, she knew how to make the cash she needed to bribe older kids to buy her beer: just hitch-hike to the next town in the Kootenays and "do favours for dirty old men." By her teens, she was a seasoned runaway. "I didn't understand why I started running away when I was seven and sleeping in the bushes, but looking back I know I ran to get away from the sex abuse. At the time, I used to say that God told me to run away. When I got a bit older and into a cult, I used to say that Satan made me do it. Now I know it was me making me run." (Webber, 1991, pp. 80–81)

Most of the attention in the area of adolescent physical and sexual abuse has focused on girls. Indeed, by comparison, empirical data on the nature and consequences of the physical and sexual abuse of boys is scarce and frequently overlooked. However, available data suggest a similar scenario, particularly in relation to the risk for the development of problematic patterns of substance use and other psychopathology:

Boys in this chemical dependency treatment population who admit to histories of sexual abuse are characterized by a number of psychological and social problems similar to those experienced both by abused girls and by abused male runaways. Specifically, they and other family members have been variously physically and sexually abused; they show psychological distress, especially agitation, and are markedly suicidal; they have abused alcohol and other chemicals regularly and from a very young age, at least in part to self-medicate their distress; and they have been in more and more serious trouble with the law than their peers. (Harrison, Edwall, Hoffman, & Worthen, 1990, p. 64)

Among survivors, the severe psychological trauma associated with physical and sexual abuse is correlated, directly and indirectly, with various patterns of substance use. As noted by Rew (1989), "survivors of childhood sexual exploitation experience a variety of long-term effects, including low self-esteem, posttraumatic stress disorder, depression, suicidal attempts, and drug and alcohol abuse" (p. 229). Study after study (e.g., Bennett & Kemper, 1994; M. A. Straus & Kantor, 1994) tends to support the same conclusions in relation to the consequences of severe childhood physical or sexual abuse. For example, Berenson et al., (1992), in a study of pregnant adolescents, found that substance use was reported seven times more often in those with a history of combined physical and sexual assault, five times more frequently by those who had been sexually assaulted, and three times more often in those who had been physically assaulted than adolescents without a history of assault. (p. 470)

Parental alcoholism is commonly found among children and adolescents who have been physically or sexually abused and is a contributory factor in need of more controlled study (Burgess et al., 1987; Malinosky-Rummell & Hansen, 1993; Rose, Peabody, & Stratigeas, 1991a; Yama, Tovey, Fogas, & Teegarden, 1992; see discussion of family alcohol and other substance use, above; see also Chap. 8).

Previous Psychiatric Inpatient Treatment

Dual diagnosis among adolescents who have previously received psychiatric inpatient treatment is relatively common. As noted by Singer and White (1991), "Our findings from two years of consecutive adolescent psychiatric admissions lend further support to the association between psychiatric disorders and substance abuse in this population" (p. 13; see Chap. 6).

SOCIETAL DIMENSION

The societal dimension of MIMSEUICA comprises those variables that reflect services provided by a society to its members. It also reflects customs, mores, and the laws of the land.

Societal Variables

The societal variables related to adolescent substance use include, in particular, social programs and services and mass media messages.

Social Programs and Services (Treatment Availability)

Social programs and services include the availability and accessibility of preventive and treatment services for adolescents (Buber, 1992; Esman, 1992; M. R. Kennedy, 1991). The need for such services is paramount and is just now being modestly addressed. Broader services are also required, including those addressing the needs of increasing numbers of homeless adolescents and their families (DeAngelis, 1994; Robertson, 1991; Yates, Mackenzie, Pennbridge, & Swofford, 1991).

Media Messages

The media, in the form of antisubstance use messages, can play an important role in preventing or reducing the incidence of adolescent substance use (Zastowny, Adams, Black, Lawton, & Wilder, 1993). These efforts have been encouraged over the last decade in large part by a coordinated program organized by the Entertainment Industry Council in cooperation with the Office for Substance Abuse Prevention (see Chap. 10). However, North American society, more often than not, appears to actively encourage substance use through its extensive media messages (e.g., televised beer commercials), entertainment (e.g., glamorization of substance use in music videos and movies), and news reporting (e.g., stories about popular drug-using sports and rock stars, particularly in teen and "grocery checkout-counter" magazines; Atkin, 1990; Leite & Parrish, 1994; L. Wallace, Breed, & Cruz, 1987; Whitaker, 1989). As Coombs, Paulson, and Palley (1988) observed:

> Advertisements promote the concept that popularity, friendship, adventure, achievement, sex appeal, and true love are enhanced by substance use. Other enticing messages suggest exclusive status in elite friendship groups whose substance using members are associated with wealth, high status, and social sophistication. Such seductive messages are especially alluring to adolescents during a developmental life period marked by profound social insecurities and self-doubts. (p. 20)

In addition, as noted by Newcomb and Bentler (1989):

> The United States is a drug culture. Drugs are used commonly and acceptably to wake up in the morning (coffee or tea), get through the stresses of the day (cigarettes), and relax in the evening (alcohol). The Marlboro Man and the Virginia Slims woman are widely seen models, and licit drugs are pushed to remedy all of the ills one may face—stress, headaches, depression, physical illness, and so on. Children face a monumental task of sorting out the many images and messages regarding both licit and illicit drugs. Adolescents are quite adept at spotting hypocrisy and may have difficulty understanding a policy of "saying no to drugs" when suggested by a society that clearly says "yes" to the smorgasbord of drugs that are legal as well as the range of illicit drugs that are widely available and used. (p. 242)

SUMMARY

Adolescent substance use has many varied antecedents and consequences. In this chapter we have identified and briefly discussed the major variables that appear to be related in an etiological manner to the development of significant problematic patterns of substance use among adolescents. The discussion of these variables has been organized according to the infant/child/adolescent and societal dimensions of MIMSEUICA (see Chap. 1). Accordingly, even though these variables have for the most part been discussed in isolation, a complete and accurate appreciation and understanding of their nature requires consideration within the interactive context of this model.

Substance use by adolescents can result in virtually all of the many well-recognized physical, psychological, and social sequelae noted at younger (childhood) and older (adulthood) ages (L. A. Pagliaro & Pagliaro, 1992b, 1993). However, substance use by adolescents can also cause developmentally related effects that are unique to this age group (Glantz, 1992; Muramoto & Leshan, 1993). As noted by S. Cohen (personal communication, 1984), "Use of drugs and alcohol among adolescents can disrupt the transition from childhood to adulthood, not the physical transition, but the psychological one." Or, as stated by Bentler (1992), another prominent theorist and researcher:

> Heavy drug use as a teenager in turn further interferes with the mastery of critical developmental tasks, such as formation of a prosocial identity, gaining interpersonal and educational skills, and learning to take on family and work role responsibilities. It also fosters precocious development; i.e., it accelerates development by leading to premature adoption of adult roles of jobs and family, without the necessary growth and development typically needed to ensure success with these roles. Thus drug users may develop a pseudomaturity that does not adequately prepare them for the real difficulties of adult life. (p. 57)

CHAPTER 6

Dual Diagnosis among Adolescents

"Dual diagnosis" is a term that refers quite simply and literally to the occurrence of two mental disorders within the same person at the same time (L. A. Pagliaro, 1990b). Other closely related terms in common use include "dual addiction," which has been used to refer to "concomitant alcoholism and drug abuse" (Kreek & Stimmel, 1984),[1] "comorbidity," which has been used to refer to "cases of two diagnosable entities in the realm of substance abuse and mental illness" (Belfer, 1993), and "dual disorder," which has been used to refer to "concurrent diagnoses of alcoholism plus a psychiatric diagnosis" (Daley, Moss, & Campbell, 1987, p. 3). Definitions also vary. For example, N. S. Miller (1994) defines dual diagnosis as the co-occurrence of "another disorder (psychiatric or medical) exist[ing] *independent* of an addictive disorder" (p. 8). This diversity in terms, usage, and definitions has contributed to semantic confusion in the literature and in the clinical setting (Fields, 1995).

As used in the context of this text, *dual diagnosis* is defined as the occurrence in an adolescent of one, or more,[2] mental disorders (e.g., anxiety disorder, CD, major depressive disorder, and panic disorder) in addition to a substance use disorder (SUD),[3] which may or may not be directly related (Moss, Kirisci, & Mezzich, 1994). In those cases in which the co-occurring disorders are directly related, the SUD(s) can be either an antecedent or a consequence of the mental disorder(s) (see Table 6.1; Lehman, Myers, Corty, & Thompson, 1994; L. A. Pagliaro, 1995d). An example of a direct relationship, in which a SUD was consequential, is one in which a young man used cocaine as

[1] In this regard, we prefer the use of the term "polysubstance use," which is more accurate and less confusing (see Chap. 1).

[2] The presence of more than one additional mental disorder is not uncommon. For example, Keller et al. (1992) noted that of the adolescents diagnosed with a substance use disorder, almost three-quarters (74 percent) had between two and four other diagnosable non-substance-use mental disorders.

[3] Although DSM-IV diagnostic categories have generally been used in this definition, dual diagnosis is not dependent on adherence to the DSM-IV taxonomy. Indeed, the term "dual diagnosis" is not even officially used in DSM-IV (American Psychiatric Association, 1994).

TABLE 6.1   Mental Disorders That Are Commonly Associated with the Use of Substances of Abuse[a]

Substance of Abuse	Mental Disorder[b]						
	Amnestic Disorders	Anxiety Disorders	Delirium	Mood Disorders	Psychotic Disorders	Sexual Dysfunctions	Sleep Disorders
CNS Depressants							
Opiates			✔	✔		✔	✔
Sedative-hypnotics	✔	✔	✔	✔		✔	✔
Solvents and inhalants	✔	✔	✔	✔			✔
CNS Stimulants							
Amphetamines		✔	✔	✔	✔	✔	✔
Caffeine		✔					✔
Cocaine		✔	✔	✔	✔	✔	✔
Nicotine		✔					✔
Psychedelics		✔	✔	✔	✔		

[a]Modified from American Psychiatric Association (1994, p. 177).
[b]In addition to substance use disorders.

a means of self-medication to treat his undiagnosed depression, with tragic results (for details of this case, see Chap. 8, pp. 196–197, see also L. A. Pagliaro, Jaglalsingh, & Pagliaro, 1992).

A significant percentage of adolescents and adults who present with a *primary* diagnosis of a SUD *or* a mental disorder can be expected to have a dual diagnosis.[4] Several studies and reports have suggested that a dual diagnosis can be expected in approximately 10–20 percent of patients who have mental disorders. The authors' clinical experiences and the literature (e.g., N. S. Miller, Belkin, & Gibbons, 1994) have also suggested that the incidence of dual diagnosis is significantly higher when only those patients whose primary disorder is a significant SUD (e.g., compulsive substance use or polysubstance use) are considered. In this regard, greater than 50 percent (and often close to 100 percent) of patients whose primary disorder is a SUD can be expected to have a dual diagnosis.

Adolescents who have a dual diagnosis necessarily have significant health care requirements (Galanter, Egelko, Edwards, & Vergaray, 1994). In addition, those adolescents who present with a SUD *and* another mental disorder (e.g., CD) have a significantly poorer prognosis than those who present with only a SUD *or* another mental disorder (Bell, 1995). However, as expected,

[4]In the authors' clinical practice, which specializes in the treatment of dual diagnosis patients, it has been noted that the vast majority of the patients themselves are generally unaware that they have a dual diagnosis. The dual diagnosis has not been previously diagnosed, and they are consciously aware only that they are depressed or that they have a drinking problem (i.e., the reason for their referral). They are not aware, however, that they have two, and generally more, of these problems and that these problems are likely related.

even those adolescents who have a dual diagnosis respond better to treatment when their multiple problems are adequately addressed with treatment appropriately tailored to their particular needs (Chatlos, 1994). As R. J. Frances and Allen (1986) wrote, "It is better to cut the shoes to fit the feet rather than the other way around."

Indeed, dual diagnosis is commonly reported among adolescents who have substance use problems (Chatlos, 1989; Eisen, Youngman, Grob, & Dill, 1992; Goldbloom, 1993; see Chap. 5), and increasingly, *tridiagnosis* (dual diagnosis plus associated HIV infection; L. A. Pagliaro, 1991c) is being recognized (Fisher, 1991; K. L. Irwin et al., 1995; Morrison, Smith, Wilford, Ehrlich, & Seymour, 1993; Pennbridge, Freese, & MacKenzie, 1992; Siegel, 1988; Silberstein et al., 1994; Swofford, 1991), particularly among runaway homeless adolescents:

> Risk of human immunodeficiency virus (HIV) infection exacerbates the already difficult lives of 1.5 million homeless adolescents in the United States. Homeless youths engage in sexual and substance-abuse behaviors that place them at increased risk of contracting HIV, and they demonstrate other problem behaviors that reduce their coping responses. (Rotheram-Borus, Koopman, & Ehrhardt, 1991, p. 1188)[5]

The nature of the relationship between substance use and HIV infection is clear but can be indirect (see Fig. 6.1). Several studies and reports (e.g., E. M. Johnson, McColgan, & Denniston, 1991; A. M. Pagliaro et al., 1993) have noted that substance use functions as an antecedent risk factor placing adolescents at significant risk of HIV infection in several specific ways, including: 1. "sharing unclean needles and other drug paraphernalia with infected persons" and 2. "loosening inhibitions and increasing the likelihood that adolescents will engage in unprotected sex or trade sex for drugs or money" (E. M. Johnson, McColgan, & Denniston, 1991, p. 6). (See also the previous discussion of gender identity crisis in Chap. 5.)

Although the availability of appropriate treatment services for dually diagnosed adolescents has increased significantly during the 1990s, it remains all too common for them to be refused admission to a drug abuse treatment center because of their other mental disorder (e.g., clinical depression or schizophrenia) or to be refused admission to a mental health facility because of their problematic substance use (e.g., compulsive use of alcohol or cocaine; Ponce & Jo, 1990). This catch-22 reflects a general lack of appropriate education and training for mental health care professionals (Belfer, 1993), particularly in the field of substance abusology. A survey by Adger, McDonald, and

---

[5] Likewise, E. Cohen, MacKenzie, and Yates (1991), in a large study of "homeless/runaway youths . . . [who had] demonstrated all forms of drug abuse," found that "they were 6 times more likely to be at risk for HIV infection" (p. 539).

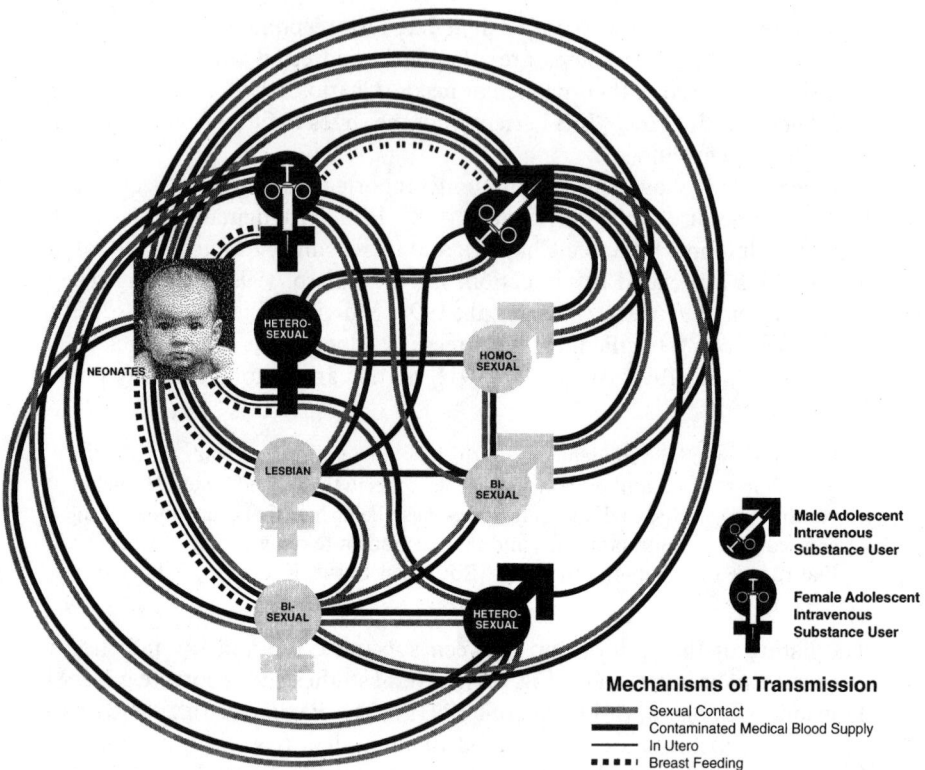

FIGURE 6.1   Transmission of HIV among adolescent intravenous substance users and their family members, friends, and other contacts

DeAngelis (1990) "of all pediatric programs in the United States was conducted to assess the current status of alcohol/drug education in pediatrics." The authors found that

> at the medical student and residency training levels, only 44% and 40% of programs, respectively, required any formal instruction, and only 27% and 34%, respectively, offered an elective for medical students or residents. Although most respondents endorsed the inclusion of both required and elective alcohol and drug education in the curriculum, few programs that did not include it already had a future plan for it. (p. 555)

Treatment services also reflect the widespread and common practice of using people who have histories of SUD (e.g., recovering alcoholics) as drug counselors for the treatment of adolescents who have dual diagnoses. Although these people have an important role to play in the complex treatment

of SUDs, they are not qualified academically or clinically as primary therapists. For example, as noted by Penick et al. (1990):

> Many of the traditional caregivers in the substance abuse field are, themselves,
> recovering from chemical dependency; [these individuals] tend to know and use
> only one approach to treatment. If they are recovering themselves, the ap-
> proach taken is usually the one that "worked" for them. When confronted with
> failure, substance abuse workers typically have no "fall back" position to draw
> upon, continuing instead to do "more of the same" rather than shift to a differ-
> ent treatment strategy. (pp. 7–8)

Adolescents can present with any of a number of possible dual diagnoses;
there is a seemingly unending number of combinations and permutations of
mental disorders and SUDs. In fact, "dual diagnosis patients are [generally]
heterogeneous as to their psychiatric diagnoses, as well as the various substances they abuse" (Stowell, 1991, p. 98). However, a review of the literature
suggests that the majority of cases of dual diagnosis among adolescents involve problematic patterns of alcohol, amphetamine, cocaine, marijuana, and
nicotine use concurrent with a mental disorder from one or more of the following four categories: 1. *mood disorders* (e.g., major depressive disorder), 2.
personality disorders (e.g., borderline personality disorder), 3. *psychotic disorders* (e.g., schizophrenia), and 4. *sexual or gender identity disorders* (e.g., sexual dysfunction; Fields, 1995; Gold & Slaby, 1991). Each of these mental
disorders and related patterns of substance use are briefly discussed, with
attention to their occurrence during adolescence.[6]

SUBSTANCE USE AND MOOD DISORDERS

Major depressive disorders are likely the most common mental disorders that
occur concurrently with SUDs (Burke, Burke, & Rae, 1994; Coryell, 1991;
Deykin, Buka, & Zeena, 1992; Faraco-Hadlock, 1990; Greenbaum, Prange,
Friedman, & Silver, 1991; Gregorius & Smith, 1991; Hughes, Preskorn,
Wrona, Hassanein, & Tucker, 1990; Keller et al., 1992; Stowell & Estroff,
1992). This combination of mental disorders is particularly common among
adolescent girls and women (Bukstein, Glancy, & Kaminer, 1992). D. B.

---

[6] ADHD is closely associated with SUDs but is not discussed in this chapter. As noted by Wilens et
al. (1994), although ADHD and SUDs appear to be significantly related, "the two disorders differ
in the timing of their developmental expression—ADHD manifests itself at a younger age than
the substance use disorders" (p. 421). ADHD appears to be an important antecedent to a SUD, and
it has been noted that children with ADHD, particularly boys, are much more likely to develop a
SUD as adolescents and adults (even though, for most, ADHD does not persist into adulthood).
However, interpretation is confounded by the comorbidity of CD with ADHD (Comings, 1990; see
Chap. 5).

Clark et al. (1995), reporting on hospitalized adolescents with alcohol use disorders, confirmed that mood disorders occur most commonly and also that anxiety disorders are also commonly identified (i.e., in 40 percent of the hospitalized adolescents—note that 88 percent of these patients "had a comorbid affective disorder"; p. 619). Unfortunately, because the nature of our present health care system tends to compartmentalize disorders (e.g., making a distinction between "substance use disorder" and other "mental disorders") and, consequently, their treatment, all too often the commonly co-occurring depressive disorders are "miss"-diagnosed. Consider, for example, the sample of drug-using "homicidal adolescents" reported by Malmquist (1990):

> Impressive besides the past history connected with drug usage was the finding that only one of the 44 subjects was ever diagnosed as depressed before the acts that led to their being included in this study. The difficulty is partly explained by where they made contact, such as in a court probation system, a chemical dependency referral, a clinic, or a hospital unit. The few times depression was considered, it was viewed as secondary to the primary problem of chemical dependency. A related finding was that 10 of the males and three of the females had previously been through chemical dependency treatment programs. (p. 29)

Clinical depression can exist as either an antecedent or consequence of substance use, particularly the use of any of the CNS depressants. Of these substances of abuse, alcohol and the other sedative-hypnotics (e.g., benzodiazepines) are the most prominent in this regard: "Among the dually diagnosed, controversy exists as to whether substance abuse is a symptom of an underlying mental health problem or conversely, whether the mental health problem is symptomatic of alcohol or drug use" (Greenbaum et al., 1991, p. 582).

Suggested reasons for a consequential association between a SUD and another mental disorder (e.g., depression) include "physiological symptoms of withdrawal, the apathy of the alcoholic personality, the state of chronic intoxication, and concomitant drug use" (Slaby, 1991). In this regard, it is important to note that the direct pharmacological effect of alcohol and the other sedative-hypnotics is depression (L. A. Pagliaro, 1995d). Several reasons also have been suggested for an antecedent association. Children whose parents have problematic patterns of substance use have been identified as having a proclivity for developing depressive symptoms. As noted by Perez-Bouchard et al. (1993), "The dysfunctional family environment that often results from alcoholism or other substance abuse fosters a depressogenic attributional style . . . that can be a risk factor for future depression" (p. 476). In addition, among adolescents who have not yet been diagnosed as being depressed, a tendency to self-medicate with either cocaine to treat their depression (R. D. Weiss, Griffin, & Mirin, 1992) or alcohol to temporarily diminish its distressing features (Deykin, Levy, & Wells, 1987; Slaby, 1991) also has been noted. As described by Boyle and Offord (1991), "The risks for drug and alcohol abuse are high among young adults experiencing depression or anxiety who are not undergoing treatment" (p. 699). Or as identified by Burke et al. (1994), "Age at onset for drug abuse and dependence . . . appears to peak in the age interval of 15 to 19 if there is a pre-existing mood or anxiety disorder" (p. 454). However, as Breslau, Kilbey, and Andreski (1993) pointed out, other underlying variables may be involved: "Neuroticism and the correlated psychologic vulnerabilities may commonly predispose to nicotine dependence *and* major depression or anxiety disorders" (p. 941). In addition, some personality disorders, such as antisocial personality, are highly correlated with both substance use and depression (Coryell, 1991).

Of particular concern is the fact that regardless of the nature of the association (as antecedent or consequence), a dual diagnosis is frequently accompanied by suicide attempts (Fowler et al., 1986; Gregorius & Smith, 1991; Kirkpatrick-Smith, Rich, Bonner, & Jans, 1991; L. A. Pagliaro, 1995e; Runeson & Rich, 1992; A. J. Ward, 1992) and completed suicide. As noted by Berman and Schwartz (1990), "It is generally agreed that there is a progressive increase in depressive mood from abstainer to substance user and a corresponding increase in suicide attempts among adolescents with depression, substance abuse, or both" (p. 310). This observation is also supported by Runeson and Rich (1992), who note that "depressive and substance use disorders predominate in the psychopathological backgrounds of suicides of all ages. In five published studies of consecutive suicides by adolescents and young adults, the average reported rates are 41% for major depression and 48% for substance abuse" (p. 197). (See Chap. 8 for additional discussion of depression and suicide among adolescents.)

SUBSTANCE USE AND PSYCHOTIC DISORDERS

Substance-use-related disorders have been commonly found among a significant proportion of cohorts of schizophrenics in several studies. In addition, several substances of abuse have the direct ability to pharmacologically cause psychotic effects. Although usually of a transitory nature, these psychotic effects are characteristically associated with acute intoxication (see Table 6.1). For example, the stimulants (amphetamines and cocaine) and the psychedelics (LSD and PCP) can cause symptoms of psychosis—that is, delusions, hallucinations, disorganized speech, and grossly disorganized or catatonic behavior—that are virtually indistinguishable from those associated with acute schizophrenia (American Psychiatric Association, 1994). In fact, the psychedelics have been commonly referred to in the pharmacology literature as *psychotomimetics* or *psychotogens,* that is, drugs that mimic or cause psychosis.

Although schizophrenia is usually first observed among affected people during early adulthood with a worldwide prevalence of approximately 1 percent, premorbid mental abnormalities (e.g., significant negatively skewed variance in relation to cognition, emotional and neurological maturation, and social competence) and prodromal manifestations (e.g., incipient psychosis) may occur during adolescence (Stowell & Estroff, 1992). These adolescents may be at a particularly high risk for depression, a SUD, CD, and suicide—all of which appear to be interrelated (see Chap. 5).

SUBSTANCE USE AND PERSONALITY DISORDERS

People who have antisocial or borderline personality disorders appear to be at greater risk for dual diagnosis (Coryell, 1991; Fields, 1995; Norris & Extein, 1991; Slaby, 1991). Both of these personality disorders have their onset during adolescence[7] and include a proclivity for potentially self-damaging impulsive behavior, including the binge use of substances of abuse (see also Chap. 9).

A gender effect in relation to substance use and borderline personality disorder has been observed:

> The borderline female is often on a spectrum of affective disorders, whereas the borderline male more often overlaps with severe conduct disorders, sociopathy, drug addiction and alcoholism, the episodic dyscontrol syndrome, or the attention deficit hyperactivity disorder with learning disabilities. (Andrulonis, 1991, p. 23)

Of note is the observation that virtually every disorder or condition identified by Andrulonis in regard to borderline personality disorder also has been associated with problematic patterns of substance use (e.g., CD; Boyle & Offord, 1991; Bukstein et al., 1992; Greenbaum et al., 1991). From a developmental perspective, Bates and Pandina (1991) reported that adolescent boys undergoing "substantial changes in personality needs would be more likely to (1) experience higher levels of perceived stress in response to disruptive life prob-

---

[7]According to DSM-IV criteria, antisocial personality disorder is not diagnosed prior to 18 years of age. However, a very closely related and required antecedent is CD. CD is rather commonly encountered among dually diagnosed adolescents and often displays gender differences in incidence (more common in males) and nature. E.g., Mezzich et al. (1994) found that adolescent girls with a dual diagnosis including CD were more likely than matched adolescent boys to experiment with "nonprescription diet pills," fulfill the criteria for nicotine dependence, start drinking alcohol at a later date, and have a shorter time interval between initial use of alcohol and diagnosis of alcohol abuse or dependence (p. 289). (See Chap. 9 for additional discussion of CD.)

TABLE 6.2   Substance Use and Sexual Behavior[a]

1. Sexual dysfunction may be directly related to the pharmacological effect(s) of the substance of abuse.
2. Stress may lead independently to both sexual dysfunction and substance use.
3. Substances of abuse may be used to facilitate sexual behavior/performance.
4. Substances of abuse may be used to cope or deal with inadequate or undesirable sexual behavior/performance (e.g., to self-medicate sexual and gender identity disorders or feelings related to childhood sexual victimization).
5. Cognitive impairment, including reasoning impairment associated with mental disorders (e.g., schizophrenia), may lead independently to substance use and sexual disorders.
6. Substance use may result from the pattern of socialization required to meet sexual partners (e.g., adolescent boys or girls seeking homosexual or lesbian sex at gay bars).
7. Sexual behavior may be used in order to obtain substances of abuse or the money necessary to purchase substances of abuse (e.g., adolescent girls engaging in sex at crack houses in order to obtain crack).

[a]Modified from Harrison et al. (1990), L. A. Pagliaro (1995c), and Slaby (1991).

lems and (2) engage in more intensive alcohol and other drug use behaviors than others" (p. 471; see also Chap. 5).

SUBSTANCE USE AND SEXUAL OR GENDER IDENTITY DISORDERS

Adolescents who have been victims of severe sexual abuse as children or who have gender identity disorders are at risk for SUDs (Bayatpour et al., 1992; Gardner & Cabral, 1990; Harrison et al., 1990; see Chap. 5 for additional discussion). In addition, substance use and sexual behavior/performance can be related in several different ways (see Table 6.2), as illustrated by the following quotations from Ogden Nash (1902–1971), "Candy is dandy, but liquor is quicker," and William Shakespeare (1564–1616), "It [alcohol] provoketh the desire, but taketh away the performance."

TREATMENT

Effective treatment begins with proper attention to the potential for dual diagnosis and its subsequent appropriate diagnosis. Once a dual diagnosis has been made, treatment can be provided by an appropriately qualified health care provider (e.g., clinical psychologist or psychiatrist) and other qualified professionals specializing in the treatment of SUDs and the other mental disorders (e.g., major depression; O'Connell, 1990).

Several approaches have been developed for treating adolescents and adults who have dual diagnoses. Examples of these varied approaches include the treatment models proposed by Daley and Salloum (1995), Gorski (1995), and Chatlos (1994).

The treatment model proposed by Daley and Salloum (1995) is based on an integrated approach emphasizing the necessity not only to recognize dual disorders but to treat them accordingly. The treatment model is based on the rationale that integrated treatment is the best approach for helping clients who have dual diagnoses. Specific clinical interventions involving education, referral, compliance with pharmacotherapy, and self-help programs, among others, are used with the acknowledgment that change occurs as a result of the client-counselor and treatment-team relationships. The context of treatment may vary, depending on the client's specific needs at a particular time (e.g., admission to a substance detoxification unit to initiate abstinence and set the foundations for recovery or hospitalization in a psychiatric unit for severe "suicidality"). Treatment focuses on balancing issues associated with mental disorders and SUDs with changes in client symptomatology. The model assumes that there are six possible phases of treatment that clients may progress through over time: transition and engagement; stabilization; early, middle, and late recovery; and maintenance. Each of these phases has its own possible therapeutic issue, interventions, and criteria for progress, and each provides guidelines that can be used to delineate common issues that clients must deal with in regard to their mental and substance use disorders at various points in recovery. The overall strategy of treatment is to maintain adequate focus on all disorders. As described by Daley and Salloum (1995):

> Dual disorders recovery counselling [DDRC] is one treatment model developed specifically to treat clients with dual diagnoses. DDRC draws upon information from the substance abuse, psychiatric and dual diagnosis literature and over a decade of experience in treating a wide range of combinations of disorders. DDRC views psychiatric and substance use disorders as biopsychological conditions caused and/or maintained by a variety of biological, psychological and social factors. Disorders are seen as "no fault" with a multiplicity of possible relationships between the psychiatric and substance use disorder. DDRC can be used in individual, group and family treatment contexts in inpatient, residential, partial-hospital, outpatient and aftercare programs. (p. 16)

Gorski (1995) described treatment planning and step-by-step interventions for "dual recovery" patients, emphasizing the need for the development of a disorder-specific treatment plan that addresses the unique symptoms of each disorder and a general holistic treatment plan for the general problems related to all disorders (e.g., proper diet, exercise, stress management, communication effectiveness, and balanced living). According to Gorski, treatment planning for dual diagnosis patients begins with a comprehensive assessment designed to determine the type of treatment and the level of care required by the client. The assessment information is reviewed, and a problem list developed that identifies short- and long-term problems using a problem severity rating measure (a 10-point scale with 10 being the most severe). The treatment plan identifies the target problems (primary issues that will be the focus of the current episode of treatment), the primary goal of treatment (the anticipated outcome of the current episode of treatment), and the specific interventions (the sequence of steps) that will be used to accomplish the goal. The actual outcomes describe the real results of the current treatment. Progress reporting identifies the target problems and goals for the current treatment episode. As noted by Gorski (1995):

> Effective treatment plans for dual diagnosis patients integrate the following components: (1) *disorder specific clinical models* for managing the symptoms of the target disorders (the chemical dependence and specific related mental and personality disorders); (2) *physical interventions* for managing physical problems related to the target disorders; (3) *cognitive therapy* for changing the irrational thoughts that drive the target disorders; (4) *affective therapy* for changing unmanageable feelings that drive the target disorders; (5) *behavioral therapy* for changing self-defeating behaviors that drive the target disorders; and (6) *social/ situational therapy* for changing lifestyle factors that drive the target disorders. (p. 52)

Gorski (1995) provided standard treatment interventions for guiding clinical reasoning about the progressive treatment process. These guidelines can be adapted to the individual needs of each patient.

A developmental model specifically addressing the treatment of adolescents who have dual diagnoses is provided by Chatlos (1994): the developmental biopsychosocial disease model (DBDM). Offered as a guide for therapists, this model depicts prevention, intervention, and treatment on a continuum integrating substance use and mental disorders into a similar process. The DBDM, which can also be used in community education and prevention settings, identifies three factors central to the development of problematic patterns of substance use: 1. *predisposition* (genetic, constitutional, psychological, and sociocultural factors that lead to an attitude about substance use); 2. *initiation* (substance availability, peer influence, and perceived harmfulness associated with use of the substance of abuse among other factors such as parental substance use); and 3. *progression,* comprising four stages (experimentation/learning the mood swing, regular use/seeking the mood swing, daily preoccupation/preoccupation with the mood swing, and harmful dependency/using to feel normal).

Progression of substance use occurs in relation to the interaction of such factors as the strong reinforcement of euphoria associated with the substance of abuse, negative reinforcement associated with the abstinent syndrome, and genetic and biochemical effects of the substance of abuse on the adolescent's developing brain. The final factor in the equation is the enabling or maintenance system. This system includes all people, places, and things surrounding the adolescent that knowingly or unknowingly enable the progression of substance use to increasingly more problematic patterns of use.

The mental disorder is the other factor central to the DBDM. The initiation of a mental disorder is triggered by a biological or life event rather than a substance of abuse and progresses and is maintained by the enabling system (e.g., a significant family member who has a substance use or mental disorder or who is physically or emotionally unavailable). According to the model, substance use and mental disorders are best considered as two parallel biopsychosocial processes in constant interaction. Distinctions as to the source and the temporal sequence along the continuum will indicate specific interventions.

The recovery process follows the reverse order of the SUD/mental disorder process. Initial abstinence requires an intervention into the enabling system that may involve admitting the adolescent to an inpatient treatment program, involving the school and courts, or performing a family intervention. Adolescents entering treatment are asked to make a "commitment to abstinence." Parents are also required to commit to treatment. Following the initial intervention, continued work with the adolescent, family, and school are thought to strengthen other parts of the recovery environment and ultimately transform the enabling system.

The following list, modified from R. E. Meyer (1986), summarizes the possible combinations of relationships that may occur between the disorders constituting the dual diagnosis and may help to plan appropriate treatment:

1. Mental disorders may serve as risk factors for SUDs.
2. Mental disorders may modify the course of SUDs.
3. Signs and symptoms associated with various mental disorders may occur in the course of chronic intoxication with various substances of abuse.
4. Mental disorders may develop as a result of the use of various substances of abuse and persist despite cessation of use.
5. Substance use and the signs and symptoms of a mental disorder may become meaningfully linked over time.
6. A mental disorder and a SUD may occur in the same adolescent but not be related (cited in R. D. Weiss, 1992, p. 138).

SUMMARY

Dual diagnosis is defined as the concurrent presentation within an adolescent of one or more substance use disorders (SUDs) and one or more other mental disorders (e.g., CD and major depressive disorder). Dual diagnosis is frequently encountered among adolescents seeking treatment for a SUD or another significant mental disorder and, thus, should always be considered and either appropriately ruled out or confirmed so that appropriate treatment can be implemented. Although adolescents can present with any number of combinations of SUDs and other mental disorders, they most frequently present with a problematic pattern of alcohol, cocaine, marijuana, or nicotine use in the context of a mood disorder, personality disorder, psychotic disorder, or gender identity disorder. Proper diagnosis of dual diagnoses among adolescents is essential in regard to planning and providing appropriate treatment, which may commonly involve an integration of both pharmacotherapy and psychotherapy. Examples of the several approaches available for the treatment of adolescents with dual diagnoses have been briefly presented in this chapter. The choice of therapy will depend on the unique needs of the patient, the clinical training and abilities of the therapist, and the availability of additional treatment or referral services (e.g., Alateen). Regardless of which treatment modalities are chosen, it is essential to ensure that each of the adolescent's diagnoses is provided with adequate and appropriate treatment. As noted by Daley and Salloum (1995), "A dual focus of treatment reduces the chances that an untreated disorder will increase vulnerability to relapse to another disorder" (p. 16). (See Chap. 10 for additional discussion of prevention and treatment.)

CHAPTER 7

Effects of Substance Use on Learning and Memory among Children and Adolescents

The nature and extent of substance use by children and adolescents has been clearly associated with academic performance. For virtually all of the substances of abuse, increased use is associated with lowered attendance at classes, poorer academic performance (compared to preuse levels), lowered educational aspirations, and an increased drop-out rate (failure to complete high school; Franklin, 1992; Friedman, Bransfield, & Kreisher, 1994; Hawkins, Lishner, Catalano, & Howard, 1985; Paulson, Coombs, & Richardson, 1990). The associations between substance use and academic performance are not spurious. They may be mediated by an underlying covariable, such as CD, or may be directly related to the pharmacological effects of various substances of abuse on cognition, learning, and memory.[1]

The effects of substance use on learning and memory are currently of particular interest to educational psychologists, teachers, policymakers, and others involved in the education and care of children and adolescents. This interest is derived from the nature and extent of exposure to and use of substances of abuse among children and adolescents and their apparent effects on the basic mechanisms of learning and memory.[2] Interest also exists in distinguishing between the symptoms of "true" learning disorders and those elicited by the acute and chronic effects of substance use. As noted by Fox and Forbing (1991):

> The effects of substance abuse have produced a population of students who exhibit behaviors similar to the behaviors of many youth with learning problems. . . . To differentiate between behavior resulting from a learning handicapped condition and that resulting from substance abuse, trained diagnosticians need to evaluate both the potential causes and the context in which these behaviors are exhibited. (p. 24)

---

[1] Parental substance use can also adversely affect learning among children and adolescents by means of the emotional and social disruption related to "inadequate or inconsistent parenting, emotional neglect, and potential [or actual] physical and psychological abuse" (G. H. Smith, 1993, p. 1435).

[2] This chapter is based on a cognitive approach to, and understanding of, learning and memory.

A significant amount of knowledge has accrued over the past decade in relation to learning and memory. However,

> unequivocal causal relations between a change in cell structure or function and learning still remain to be demonstrated . . . [and] terms encountered in this field, such as memory, learning, perception, attention, and cognition, need to be recognized as essentially abstract constructs used to name phenomena that can be "observed" only in behavioral experiments. (J. R. Cooper, Bloom, & Roth, 1978/1991, p. 428)

Hence, many somewhat varied definitions of learning reflective of a diversity of theoretical orientations have been proposed and utilized. We would suggest the following definition. This definition has been developed and used over the last decade in our lectures on learning and appears to be consonant with both the available research data and the majority of definitions in current use: *Learning* is defined as a change in mental associations (i.e., acquisition of new information), which is usually accompanied by a change in related behavior, due to experience (i.e., related to sensory input).

As such, learning is a complex process. The macrovariables affecting this process are identified in Figure 7.1 (L. A. Pagliaro, 1979). The Mega Inter-

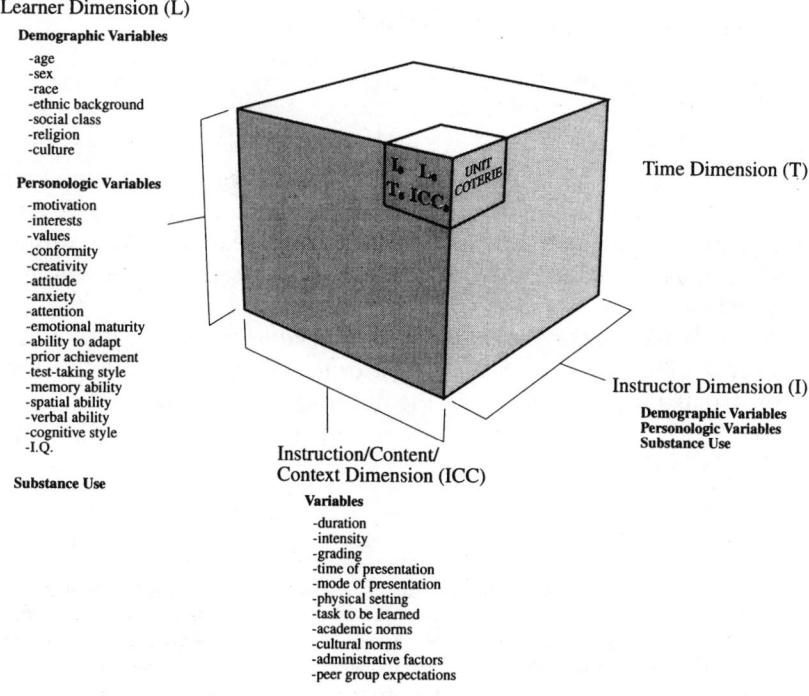

FIGURE 7.1   Mega Interactive Model of Instruction (MIMI)

active Model of Instruction illustrates the simultaneous interaction of three variable dimensions within the instructional milieu (represented by the cube) coincident with the additional dimension of time. The instructional milieu is further represented as comprising a number of groups of interacting subsets of the four variable dimensions (I_S, L_S, ICC_S, T_S) referred to collectively as unit coteries. The microvariables in the learning process that are potentially affected by substance use include the interpretation, processing, and encoding of sensory input. The exact molecular or neurochemical mechanism(s) by which substances elicit their effects on learning is not yet clearly established; however, significant advances based on animal data and models have been proposed (J. R. Cooper et al., 1978/1991; Erinoff, 1990).[3]

ANTECEDENT FACTORS

Although the exact molecular mechanism(s) by which substance use affects learning remains unclear, a significant amount of human data have been accumulated. These data document demonstrated effects on basic factors or processes (attention, cognitive processing, motivation, and perception) that are integrally related to learning. These factors, each of which is necessary for optimal learning to occur, are briefly discussed.

Attention

Attention may be defined as the process of preferentially responding to a stimulus or range of stimuli. As such, attention is integral to learning (even if learners are motivated to learn, have their senses intact and properly functioning, and have adequate intelligence, they cannot learn optimally without paying adequate attention to what is being taught; see, e.g., discussion of ADHD, below).

Various substances of abuse have been studied in relation to their ability to affect attention and, consequently, learning. For example, it has been reported that long-term cannabis use adversely affects selective attention (Solowij, Michie, & Fox, 1991). However, the majority of research in this area has focused on the CNS depressants and the CNS stimulants.

---

[3] We are inclined, as previously stated in this text (e.g., see Chap. 3), to largely disregard animal data because of the difficulty inherent in extrapolating, with a significant degree of confidence, the results of these data to humans. Although many psychologists would disagree, we are of the opinion that until an adequate animal model is discovered that has the same degree of morphological development of the cerebral cortex as do humans and recognizable language development (i.e., can talk), it is inappropriate to directly extrapolate observations of complex behavior from laboratory animal models to humans. Accordingly, all of the data in this chapter are derived exclusively from human studies.

In general, the CNS depressants (e.g., alcohol, benzodiazepines, and opiates) decrease the ability to attend to sensory input (it is increasingly difficult to pay attention as a child or adolescent becomes more and more sleepy). For example, as noted by C. R. Rush, Higgins, Bickel, and Hughes (1993), the benzodiazepines "dose-dependently disrupted learning and psychomotor performance and increased subject ratings of sedation" (p. 1218). Conversely, the CNS stimulant nicotine can moderately increase attention and, hence, facilitate learning (Graham, 1988).[4] Perhaps surprisingly, caffeine use alone has not been associated consistently with effects on learning or memory. However, its use may attenuate (slightly) the learning and memory decrements associated with sedative-hypnotic use (Loke, Hinrichs, & Ghoneim, 1985; C. R. Rush et al., 1993), presumably by attenuating the sedative-hypnotic-induced CNS depression.

Cognitive Processing

In the context of learning, *cognitive processing* refers to the process that occurs between input of data (sensory input) and output of new mental associations (behavioral demonstration of the acquisition of new information). While it is commonly recognized and agreed that this process involves the input, recording (encoding), and analysis (interpretation) of sensory input, the exact molecular, or even neuronal, mechanism(s) is still in debate and includes many theories to explain what is commonly observed (e.g., Hebb's theory of perceptual learning involving reverberatory neuronal circuits within the CNS; Hebb, 1949).

Virtually all of the substances of abuse can impair cognitive processing. Much of the research in this area has focused on the related factors of reduced global cerebral metabolic rate and state-dependent learning. Each of these factors will be briefly discussed.

Reduced Global Cerebral Metabolic Rate

Reduction in the global cerebral metabolic rate will result initially in slowing of cognitive processing, followed, at high dosages of substances of abuse, by disruption of cognitive processing. This type of effect on learning is typically associated with the use of the CNS depressants (e.g., alcohol, barbiturates such as Seconal, benzodiazepines such as Valium, and opiate analgesics such as Demerol). Consider, for example, the acute progressive decrease in the rate and ability of cognitive processing noted among people as they consume additional alcoholic beverages over the continuum from sobriety to inebriation (L. A. Pagliaro & Pagliaro, 1995b). This effect also has been demon-

---

[4] Use of the other CNS stimulants (e.g., amphetamines and cocaine), as well as high doses of caffeine and nicotine, can actually decrease attention by overstimulating the CNS.

strated when the substances of abuse are used in a therapeutic capacity, such as for the treatment of children and adolescents who have been diagnosed with epilepsy or other seizure disorders (Corbett, Trimble, & Nichol, 1985; Leiderman, Balish, & Bromfield, 1991; Trimble & Thompson, 1983).

State-Dependent Learning

> Tasks learned in the presence of a psychotropic drug may subsequently be performed better in the drug state. Conversely, learning acquired in the nondrug state may be more available in the nondrugged state. This phenomenon has been called "state dependent learning" and demonstrates the inability to transfer learning from a drugged to a nondrugged condition. An example of this is the alcoholic who during a binge hides his supply of liquor for later consumption but is unable to find it while he is sober (in the nondrugged state). Once he has returned to the alcoholic state, he can readily locate his cache. (R. S. Feldman & Quenzer, 1984, p. 22)

Although state-dependent learning in humans was originally demonstrated by observation and studies involving the use of alcohol, it has been known for some time that other substances of abuse, including amobarbital, amphetamine, diazepam, marijuana, and methylphenidate, also can produce state-dependent learning (Craig, 1985; Reus, Weingartner, & Post, 1979). In this regard, the CNS depressants and CNS stimulants can potentially have negative effects on learning not only when used for recreational reasons but also when used for therapeutic reasons. For example, methylphenidate (Ritalin), which can produce state-dependent learning, is widely and routinely used to treat ADHD among children and adolescents. As such, the potential exists (although not yet widely studied in a controlled systematic manner) that a significant amount of the learning acquired by a child receiving methylphenidate does not transfer to the nonuse state when the methylphenidate is routinely discontinued during adolescence[5] (for additional details, see the discussion of ADHD below).

Motivation

Motivation can be simply defined as that factor that is intrinsically responsible for orientation toward goal attainment. Thus, children and adolescents who are not sufficiently motivated toward the goal of learning will not be able to achieve optimal learning, even if all other necessary factors (e.g., sufficient intelligence) and conditions (e.g., optimal learning environment) are present.

Motivation can be adversely affected by the use of virtually any of the substances of abuse. On the basis of available research data, however, this

---

[5] Could this contribute to the learning disorders noted in some adolescents with ADHD whose predominant symptoms have remitted and whose pharmacotherapy has been discontinued?

effect appears to be particularly significant for the barbiturates and the cannabis formulations. The amotivational syndrome, "characterized by great difficulty rousing oneself from profound self-absorption to return to reinvolve oneself with friends, work, family, and school" (Wilson, O'Leary, & Nathan, 1991, p. 282), had previously been associated with the chronic heavy use of barbiturates by youth and over the past 20 years with the chronic heavy use of cannabis in its various forms (Baumrind & Moselle, 1985; Tunving, 1987; see the discussion of amotivational syndrome in Chap. 1 for additional details). Lack of motivation may also, at least partially, help account for the positive correlation between "teenage drug usage and school dropout" (Eggert, Seyl, & Nicholas, 1990).

Perception

If a person's perception of sensory input is distorted, so too, by definition, will learning be distorted. The psychedelics (e.g., LSD, mescaline, and THC) have the intrinsic ability, at usual pharmacological dosages, to distort perception. Consider, for example, the experiences of Alice in Wonderland. The perceptual distortions may include misinterpretations, illusions, or hallucinations.[6] In addition, intoxication with the CNS stimulants (amphetamines and cocaine) and the CNS depressants (e.g., alcohol) can also result in perceptual distortion. For a complete list, see the "Delirium" column in Table 6.1 of Chap. 6).

Memory

Memory, in the context of learning, can be simply defined as the ability to store and retrieve experienced mental associations (see Fig. 7.2). The use of various substances of abuse, including alcohol, benzodiazepines, and marijuana, can adversely affect memory.

Alcohol

Acute alcohol intoxication may cause anterograde amnesia for the period of intoxication (L. A. Pagliaro & Pagliaro, 1995b). Consider, for example, the alcoholic blackouts that are commonly experienced and frequently reported

---

[6] Misinterpretations involve the incorrect interpretation of sensory input (e.g., the sudden lifting of the arm of a teacher to scratch her head is interpreted by a nearby student as an imminent threatening gesture prefatory to being struck). Illusions involve the perceptual distortion of existing stimulus patterns (e.g., a straight pencil placed in a glass of water appears to bend at the waterline). Hallucinations involve false perceptions that are not merely distortions of reality, but the generation by the mind of the individual of a different perceptual reality (e.g., seeing and talking to a large, pink, rabbit friend named Harvey). Although primarily involving the sense of vision, the various perceptual distortions may involve any of the five senses.

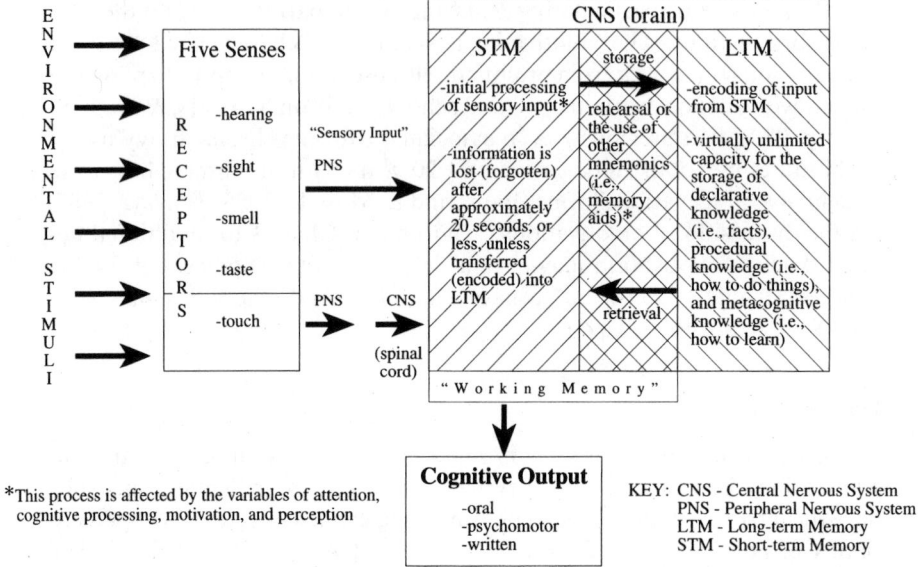

FIGURE 7.2   Cognitive input-output memory model

by children and adolescents who drink alcohol. Memory impairment associated with chronic alcohol intoxication may result from the accumulation of multiple episodes of anterograde amnesia. It can also be associated with alcohol-induced Wernicke-Korsakoff syndrome[7] (Kopelman, 1991; Parkin, Dunn, Lee, O'Hara, & Nussbaum, 1993). Although this syndrome is still predominantly associated with older chronic alcoholics, its occurrence has been reported among younger and younger people, and we have seen several adolescents in their late teens with this diagnosis (A. M. Pagliaro & L. A. Pagliaro, clinical patient file notes). These patients typically present with both impairment to short-term current memory and significant retrograde amnesia. The decrease in short-term memory is believed to be due, at least in part, "to a 20% decrease in the rate of brain metabolism in the alcoholics" (McCann, 1992). The retrograde amnesia is believed to be due to brain changes associated with chronic thiamine (vitamin B_1) deficiency.

Benzodiazepines

The effects of substance use on memory have been more widely studied with the benzodiazepines than with any of the other substances of abuse. This is because benzodiazepines are widely used therapeutically, primarily as anxio-

[7]This condition is also referred to, according to DSM-IV classification, as alcohol-induced persisting amnestic disorder.

lytics, and because memory impairment has been frequently noted in the context of their therapeutic use.

There appears to be a general consensus that benzodiazepine use can impair explicit memory, which involves contextual and associative information and is related to conscious recollection (Danion et al., 1992; Ghoneim, Block, Ping, el-Zahaby, & Hinrichs, 1993; Mallick, Kirby, Martin, Philp, & Hennessy, 1993; Polster, McCarthy, O'Sullivan, Gray, & Park, 1993; Vidailhet et al., 1994), and can cause anterograde amnesia (affect long-term visual and verbal episodic memory storage; Barbee, 1993; Roehrs, Merlotti, Zorick, & Roth, 1994; Unrug-Neervoort, van Luijtelaar, & Coenen, 1992). Although contradictory studies can be found in the literature (e.g., Ghoneim et al., 1993), it appears that explicit memory, which does not require conscious awareness, and semantic memory are not significantly and consistently affected by benzodiazepine use (Curran, Gardiner, Java, & Allen, 1993; Knopman, 1991; Mallick et al., 1993; Polster et al., 1993; Weingartner, Hommer, Lister, Thompson, & Wolkowitz, 1992).

The acute adverse effects of benzodiazepine use on memory appear to be mediated through the gamma-aminobutyric acid (GABA) receptor complex, which contains the benzodiazepine receptor binding site (Barbee, 1993; Izquierdo & Medina, 1991). The ability of flumazenil (Anexate), a benzodiazepine receptor blocker, to reverse both the sedative and memory effects of the benzodiazepines (Ghoneim et al., 1993) lends further support to this hypothesis. Consonant with this hypothesis, the reported research data have indicated that the effects of benzodiazepines on memory are dose related and directly associated with the degree of CNS depression induced by the benzodiazepines (Barbee, 1993; Hindmarch, Sherwood, & Kerr, 1993; Roehrs et al., 1994).

In relation to long-term use of the benzodiazepines it has been observed that "tolerance to the memory effects never fully develops" (Gorenstein, Bernik, & Pompeia, 1994) and "cognitive deficits [including demonstrable effects on learning and memory may persist] after withdrawal from long-term benzodiazepine use" (Tata, Rollings, Collins, Pickering, & Jacobson, 1994). This area of work has obvious potential significance for learning and memory among youth, particularly adolescents, who may have started benzodiazepine use, either experimentally or therapeutically (e.g., pharmacotherapy for a seizure disorder), during childhood.

Cocaine

The data on the effects of cocaine use on memory are less extensive than for the other listed substances of abuse. However, several studies (e.g., Manschreck et al., 1990; Mittenberg & Motta, 1993) have reported significant residual memory impairment among former cocaine-using subjects who, at the time of testing, had been abstinent from cocaine use for varying periods of time ranging from 1 week to 3 months.

Marijuana

The use of cannabis in its various forms can impair memory (Millsaps, Azrin, & Mittenberg, 1994), presumably by adversely affecting the incorporation (encoding) of short-term memory into long-term memory. The negative effects of marijuana use on human cognition and learning appear to be dose related (depend on the amount and frequency of marijuana use) and, as such, are most pronounced among heavy chronic users (R. I. Block & Ghoneim, 1993). The effects of marijuana on memory have been clearly and widely documented. Thus, even articles in magazines favoring marijuana legalization and use, such as *High Times,* now accept and publish this fact: "Clearly, cannabis acts . . . on memory by way of the receptors in the limbic system's hippocampus, which 'gates' information during memory consolidation" (Gettman, 1995, p. 29).

DISEASES OR MENTAL DISORDERS AS CONFOUNDING VARIABLES

As noted in the previous chapters, substance use is frequently related in an etiological fashion to major diseases or mental disorders, in addition to the substance-related disorders (e.g., alcohol abuse). Among these various major diseases and mental disorders, three (depression, FAS, and ADHD) have particular relevance and importance in relation to effects on learning.

Depression

Depression is a common consequence of the use of CNS depressants (e.g., alcohol and benzodiazepines; see discussion in Chaps. 5 and 6). There appears to be a growing consensus among several theoretical approaches to depression (e.g., the cognitive model of depression proposed by A. T. Beck, 1967) that "emphasize information processing concepts as being at the core of depressive symptomatology" (Ingram & Holle, 1992).

In this regard, it has been noted that cognitive processing (such as that which occurs during problem solving) and memory are both severely impaired among people experiencing major depression (Austin et al., 1992; Query & Megran, 1984; J. D. Smith, Tracy, & Murray, 1993). This negative effect of depression on memory may be subject to gender effects, being more relevant for males than for females (Turner, 1993). It may also be associated with specific types or contexts of memory, such as "implicit memory" (Turner, 1993), "positive memories" (Moffitt, Singer, Nelligan, Carlson, & Vyse, 1994), and "positively valenced words" (Denny & Hunt, 1992).

Fetal Alcohol Syndrome

Alcohol is a known human teratogen capable of causing CNS dysfunction, growth retardation, characteristic facies, and associated morphological abnormalities in the developing fetus (L. A. Pagliaro & Pagliaro, 1995c). Most of these effects, which are present at birth, persist through childhood and adolescence and into adulthood (see Chap. 3 for a comprehensive discussion). Perhaps the most serious enduring consequences of FAS are varying degrees of mental retardation and a high incidence of attention deficit disorder with or without hyperactivity.[8] Specific cognitive-processing-related learning deficits associated with FAS that have been observed among school-aged children include deficits for sequential processing (short-term memory and encoding; "Attention," 1994; M. Becker, Warr-Leeper, & Leeper, 1990; C. Coles et al., 1991; L. A. Pagliaro, 1992b). As noted by Streissguth et al. (1990), these deficits are not restricted to the offspring of mothers who drank heavily throughout their entire pregnancies:

> Learning problems were associated with the alcohol "BINGE" pattern of five or more drinks on at least one occasion. This study shows that alcohol use patterns within the social drinking range can have long lasting effects on IQ and learning problems in young school aged children. (p. 662)

Attention Deficit Hyperactivity Disorder

ADHD is reportedly the most prevalent psychological disorder of childhood in North America. Its incidence is generally estimated at 3–5 percent of school-aged children (American Psychiatric Association, 1994), but it is found in approximately 5–10 times as many boys as girls, with estimates of prevalence reportedly as high as 10 percent among boys.

> Attention deficit hyperactivity disorder is not simply a random group of rambunctious children whose behavior happens to irritate parents and teachers. It is a distinct genetic, behavioral syndrome which is expressed as ADHD in children, and may be a lifelong problem resulting in antisocial personality and alcoholism in adult men, and in a hysteric-histrionic personality in adult women. (Comings, 1990, p. 87)

---

[8] By this we do not mean to imply that all children with FAS are mentally retarded. As noted in the literature, "although FAS is considered one of the leading causes of mental retardation in the western world, not all children with FAS/FAE are affected in this way. Intelligence quotients (IQs) have a wide range from 60 to 110" ("Fetal Alcohol," 1994, p. 1). However, the negative effects of FAS on IQ are present, even in those children whose IQ scores fall within the normal range, by means of a shift in the "population" curve to the left. Thus, assuming that all other things remain constant, the child with FAS and an IQ of 110 would be expected to have had a significantly higher IQ score if he or she had not been affected by FAS.

TABLE 7.1   Attention Deficit Hyperactivity Disorder: Purported Causative Factors

Alcohol consumption during pregnancy (i.e., FAS)
Altered neurochemical processes
Diet
Early childhood trauma
Genetic disorder
Lead poisoning
Parental behavior (e.g., poor parenting)
Physical brain damage
Psychological factors
Social factors (e.g., marital discord)
Temperament (personality)

Although the etiology of ADHD is currently unknown, many different causative factors have been suggested (see Table 7.1). The authors' clinical experience and the literature suggest a strong association between FAS and ADHD (Nanson & Hiscock, 1990; L. A. Pagliaro, 1992b; Spohr & Steinhausen, 1984; Streissguth, Barr, Sampson, & Bookstein, 1994). Students with ADHD invariably have learning disorders (Golden, 1991; L. A. Pagliaro, 1992b; Shaywitz & Shaywitz, 1991). As observed by Biederman, Newcorn, & Sprich (1991):

> Studies have consistently shown that children with attention deficit hyperactivity disorder perform more poorly in school than control subjects, as evidenced by more grade repetitions, poorer grades in academic subjects, more placement in special classes, and more tutoring. Findings also indicate that children with attention deficit hyperactivity disorder perform more poorly than control subjects on standard measures of intelligence and achievement. Follow-up studies have found that the academic and learning problems of children with attention deficit hyperactivity disorder persist into adolescence and are associated with chronic underachievement and school failure. (p. 572)

The relationship(s) between ADHD and learning disorders is complex and controversial—Is the relationship one of an antecedent or consequential nature or do these disorders merely co-occur in an unrelated manner? However, the specific behaviors that contribute to learning disorders are self-evident and can be readily identified in the list of common ADHD signs and symptoms (see Table 7.2).

Learning among children and adolescents who have ADHD can also be adversely affected by the pharmacotherapy commonly prescribed for the treatment of this disorder (Allen & Drabman, 1991; L. A. Pagliaro, 1994; Swanson, Cantwell, Lerner, McBurnett, & Hanna, 1991). These adverse drug effects will be discussed because the most prevalent pharmacotherapy of

TABLE 7.2   Signs and Symptoms of Attention Deficit Hyperactivity Disorder[a]

Inattention

Often fails to give close attention to details or makes careless mistakes in schoolwork, work, or other activities

Often has difficulty sustaining attention in tasks or play activities

Often does not seem to listen when spoken to directly

Often does not follow through on instructions and fails to finish schoolwork, chores, or duties in the workplace (not due to oppositional behavior or failure to understand instructions)

Often has difficulty organizing tasks and activities

Often avoids, dislikes, or is reluctant to engage in tasks that require sustained mental effort (such as schoolwork or homework)

Often loses things necessary for tasks or activities (e.g., toys, school assignments, pencils, books, or tools)

Often is easily distracted by extraneous stimuli

Often is forgetful in daily activities

Hyperactivity

Often fidgets with hands or feet or squirms in seat

Often leaves seat in classroom or in other situations in which remaining seated is expected

Often runs about or climbs excessively in situations where it is inappropriate (among adolescents, may be limited to subjective feelings of restlessness)

Often has difficulty playing or engaging in quiet leisure activities

Often is on the go or often acts as if "driven by a motor"

Often talks excessively

Impulsivity

Often blurts out answers before questions have been completed

Often has difficulty awaiting turn

Often interrupts or intrudes on others (e.g., butts into conversations or games)

[a]According to DSM-IV criteria (American Psychiatric Association, 1994), the signs and symptoms of ADHD have been divided into three groups: inattention, hyperactivity, and impulsivity.

ADHD involves the use of the CNS stimulants, including amphetamine, dextroamphetamine, methylphenidate, and pemoline (all of which are substances of abuse).

Pharmacological treatment of this disorder has generally involved the use of various types of CNS stimulants, with methylphenidate (Ritalin) being the most widely used drug of choice. This type of treatment has generally resulted in observed improvement in classroom manageability. However, questions have consistently been raised concerning the potential negative effect(s) that methylphenidate use may have on learning.

A review of the literature indicates that methylphenidate's reported effects on learning and memory have been mixed and must be individually evaluated. The factors that appear to be related to a higher incidence of learning and memory impairment in this clinical context include the use of: 1. higher than optimal therapeutic doses of methylphenidate and 2. methylphenidate for children who do not fully meet diagnostic criteria for ADHD (Swanson et al., 1991).

ADHD is misdiagnosed in a significant number of cases (it is frequently overdiagnosed), and in those cases in which it is appropriately diagnosed, it is frequently inappropriately treated. Because of the potential cognitive impairment associated with the inappropriate use of methylphenidate among children and other potential physical and psychological adverse effects, its prescription and use must be given special attention and should never be taken lightly (L. A. Pagliaro, 1994).

SUMMARY

The use (experimental or therapeutic) of substances of abuse can have significant effects on learning and memory among children and adolescents. Teachers and mental health professionals must be aware of the nature and extent of these effects and be able to differentiate, for therapeutic reasons, between behavior resulting from organically (e.g., genetically or pathologically) based learning disorders and those resulting from the use of various substances of abuse.

To facilitate the work of teachers and mental health professionals, this chapter has identified and briefly reviewed the basic factors or processes related to learning (attention, cognitive processing, motivation, and perception) and the substances of abuse that can significantly affect these processes. In addition, three major diseases or mental disorders (depression, FAS, and ADHD) that are related to substance use and capable of affecting learning and memory have also been discussed.

CHAPTER 8

Substance-Related Accidents and Violence: Children and Adolescents as Victims

Accidents and acts of violence account for more deaths during childhood and adolescence than all other causes combined (D. C. Clark, Sommerfeldt, Schwarz, Hedeker, & Watel, 1990; L. A. Pagliaro & Pagliaro, 1993; Shanks, 1990). As noted by V. J. Gilchrist (1991):

> Adolescents represent the only segment of the population with an increasing mortality rate. The majority of deaths are due to accidents, homicide and suicide. The risks for these events are associated with developing sexuality and the use of drugs and alcohol. (p. 869)

Accidents and acts of violence also result in significant morbidity and, likewise, are frequently associated with substance use (L. A. Pagliaro, 1993b; Windle, 1994; see Chap. 1). In this context, children and adolescents suffer significantly more victimization than do adults (Finkelhor & Dzuiba-Leatherman, 1994). For example, as cited by Werblin (1995): "Each year since 1985 nearly 1 million adolescents have been victims of violent crime" (p. 44), including over 10 percent of all adolescent students, who annually are "crime victims in or around their school[s]" (Bastian & Taylor, 1991, p. 1). Cousineau, Grenier, and Allard (1994) reported similar rates of victimization among their large sample of adolescents. In addition, they found that "students, especially young women, who consume illegal drugs are more likely to be victims of violence than those who do not" (p. 703).

The purpose of this chapter is to examine the increasing number of substance-related accidents and acts of violence that have been related to the significant rates of mortality and morbidity among North American children and adolescents. Attention is given to accidents, particularly accidental falls and motor vehicle crashes, and acts of violence, particularly assaults, homicides, and suicides (see Table 8.1). The focus of the chapter is on children and adolescents as *victims;* for a discussion of children and adolescents as *perpetrators,* see Chapter 9.

TABLE 8.1   Substance-Related Violent Physical Injuries among Children and Adolescents

Accidents
    Falls
    Motor vehicle crashes

Assaults
    Battery during pregnancy
    Dating violence
    Fights
    Physical abuse/assault
    Sexual abuse/assault

Homicides
    Intentional (e.g., drug dealing or gang related)
    Unintentional (e.g., fatal motor vehicle crashes)

Suicides
    Attempted
    Completed

ACCIDENTS

The most common substance-related accidents involving children and adolescents are falls and motor vehicle crashes. Substance-related accidents that are a major source of morbidity and mortality among adults (e.g., industrial or worksite accidents associated with alcohol and marijuana use) are not as frequently reported for children and adolescents because they are not, as yet, a significant part of the workforce. In situations where children and adolescents are working, they are generally involved in less hazardous jobs than adults. However, children and adolescents are often among the victims of public transportation (e.g., airplane, bus, and train) crashes associated with adult pilots and drivers who were intoxicated.

Falls

Substance use can contribute to a variety of accidents involving falls. These falls range from infants rolling off their change tables after being left unattended by their mothers who were intoxicated with alcohol to adolescents jumping from condominium balconies in order to fly after a "hit" of LSD. Significant alcohol consumption before a fall has been reported for children as young as 10 years of age and for 28 percent of patients 15 years of age and older (Hussain, Wijetunge, Grubnic, & Jackson, 1994, p. 36). Death can also result from neglect related to substance use by parents or other care givers (e.g., children less than 5 years of age being left unattended and drowning in a bathtub; Budnick & Ross, 1985).

Motor Vehicle Crashes

Children and adolescents constitute a significant group of victims of motor vehicle crashes as passengers in cars and trucks, bicycle riders, and pedestrians. "One estimate is that every fifty minutes a teenager dies in an alcohol-related accident" (Royce, 1989, p. 24). Substance use appears to contribute to motor vehicle crashes as a consequence of the direct pharmacological effects of the substances of abuse (e.g., the "euphorogenic activity of ecstasy"; Hooft & van de Voorde, 1994, p. 328) and because their use tends to be highly correlated with reckless and risk-taking behavior among adolescents (D. C. Clark et al., 1990; V. Johnson & White, 1989; Jonah & Dawson, 1987; see Fig. 8.1). For example, in a study of Native American adolescents, R. W. Blum, Harmon, Harris, Bergeisen, and Resnick (1992) found that in relation to "injury risk behaviors," 37.9 percent of 10th- through 12th-graders who drive "drank and drove" and 21.8 percent of 7th- through 12th-graders "rode with a driver who had been drinking" (p. 1637).

Although various substances of abuse, alone and in combination, have been implicated in "driving under the influence" (Poklis et al., 1987, p. 57), most motor vehicle crashes involving adolescents are directly correlated with alcohol consumption (Hussain et al., 1994; N. E. Jones, Pieper, & Robertson, 1992; Simpson, Mayhew, & Warren, 1982). As noted by Shanks (1990), in this regard adolescents are at particular risk:

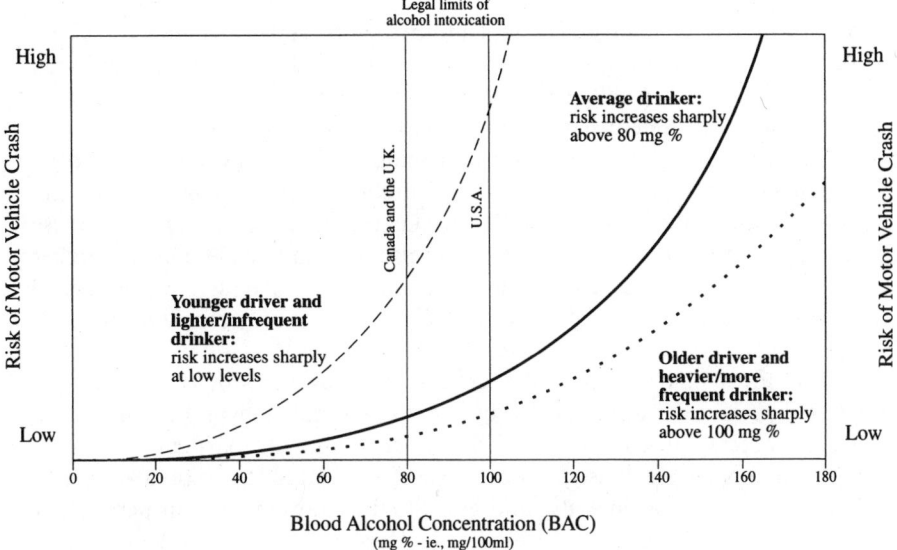

FIGURE 8.1   Risk of motor vehicle crash: Relationship to blood alcohol concentration, driving experience, and drinking experience
Note: Modified from Shanks (1990, p. 239).

The commonest form of alcohol-related trauma is a road accident. . . . Compared with adults, teenagers are more often involved in fatal crashes at night, particularly weekend nights: about 30% of fatal crashes involving 18-year-old drivers in the USA occur between 8 p.m. and 4 a.m. on Friday and Saturday nights compared to only 18% of similar crashes involving older people. Alcohol use is high at this time. (p. 238)

In addition, it also has been found that reduced rates of alcohol consumption by adolescents are significantly correlated with "lowered involvement in alcohol-related fatal crashes among drivers under 21 [years of age]" (P. M. O'Malley & Wagenaar, 1991; see also discussion of homicide, below).[1]

The use of marijuana has also been associated with motor vehicle crashes involving children and adolescents. In fact, THC has been found in the systems of many adolescents involved in fatal motor vehicle crashes (see Chap. 1). Marijuana decreases performance on a variety of driving tasks (e.g., emergency response and lane position variability; Smiley et al., 1985) and is often used along with alcohol. However, precisely for this reason, it is difficult to implicate the exact role of marijuana in motor vehicle crashes because "the increased accident risk of THC-positive drivers may be largely explained by alcohol use" (Gieringer, 1988, p. 99).

ASSAULTS

An assault can be defined as a violent physical or verbal personal attack on another person—an infant, child, adolescent, or adult. Although children and adolescents can be perpetrators, more commonly they are victims. In fact, it has been noted that "81 percent of the victims of violent crimes are preteens or teenagers" (Gore, 1991). Excluding sibling assault, it has been estimated that approximately one-third of children in the United States are assaulted annually (Finkelhor & Dziuba-Leatherman, 1994). In most of these cases the parent or care giver is the perpetrator, and in a significant number of these cases, the assault results in serious physical injury. Psychological sequelae, which can be significant (see Chap. 5), are only recently being addressed.

The direct pharmacological effects of the substances of abuse (e.g., decreased social inhibitions caused by the use of sedative-hypnotics; increased aggressiveness caused by alcohol or amphetamine use, particularly among males; and paranoia caused by cocaine use) account for the significant correlation between substance use and assaults. In addition, certain personality

[1] The corollary of this finding is not that one should drink less and drive, but that one should not drink at all and drive. As noted by Royce (1989): "One need not be legally drunk to kill somebody with an automobile. Nor must one be an alcoholic" (p. 325). (See Fig. 8.1.)

types (e.g., antisocial personality) and mental disorders (e.g., CD), which typically have their onset during childhood or adolescence, are commonly observed among perpetrators who are also often diagnosed with SUDs and include among their symptomatology "aggression to people and animals" and "repeated physical fights or assaults" (American Psychiatric Association, 1994, pp. 90, 650; see Chaps. 5 and 6). "Alcohol and other drugs, used alone or in combination, dramatically increase the risk of violent behavior and contribute significantly to the prevalence of adolescent suicide, fighting, homicide, accidental death and disability, robbery, rape, and assault" (Valois, Vincent, McKeown, Garrison, & Kirby, 1993, p. 141).

Assaults, which are related to substance use and involve children and adolescents, have been placed into the following nonexclusive categories for discussion: battery during pregnancy, dating violence, fights, gang- or drug-dealing-related violence, physical abuse/assault, and sexual abuse/assault. The published literature pertaining to each of these categories will be briefly reviewed and discussed.

Battery during Pregnancy

Battery during pregnancy has been established as an important risk to the health of pregnant girls and women and their unborn babies and has been correlated with "anxiety, depression, housing problems, inadequate prenatal care, and drug and alcohol use" (Campbell, Poland, Waller, & Ager, 1992, p. 219). As noted by Berenson et al. (1992):

> The strong association that we observed between violence and drug use in pregnant adolescent victims increases the possibility of an adverse outcome for both the mother and infant. The increased incidence of self-destructive behaviors, such as suicide attempts and accidents, in abused adolescents place the fetus at additional risk. (p. 473)

(See also Chap. 3 for a discussion of the possible teratogenic effects associated with substance use by pregnant adolescents.)

Dating Violence

"Dating violence," also referred to as "courtship violence" or "premarital abuse," is relatively common among adolescents, with estimates involving adolescents exceeding 25 percent of high school students (O'Keefe, Brockopp, & Chew, 1986). As noted by Koval (1989), "Research has indicated that a fairly substantial number of adolescents may experience violence in a dating relationship" (p. 298). The incidence of dating violence can be explained, in part, developmentally (Metzger & Steffen, 1995). In this regard, when adolescents are compared to older age groups, they generally date more, are less experienced in interpersonal relationships, have lower autonomy, are more compulsive, have less self-esteem (are still trying to "prove" themselves), are less experienced in anger control and conflict resolution, and are less mature. These factors help explain why adolescents are commonly involved in dating violence, and why they frequently remain in violent dating relationships instead of simply walking away.

Although adolescent boys have been generally implicated more frequently as the perpetrators in dating violence, these findings are inconsistent and inconclusive (Koval, 1989). A number of researchers (e.g., Billingham & Sack, 1986; Deal & Wampler, 1986) have found that adolescents involved in dating violence are rarely "typecast" as aggressor only or as victim only, but rather, the majority report mutually violent behaviors.

As occurs in other types of assaults, substance use has been implicated as a contributory factor in approximately half of the reported cases of dating violence (Bogal-Allbritten & Allbritten, 1985; Laner, 1983). This contribution can occur in several ways, such as increasing aggressive behavior in the user and also increasing high-risk behaviors for victimization (e.g., hitchhiking or going on a blind date; Windle, 1994).[2] In addition, the coincidence of substance use and sexual intercourse also confounds interpretation. Consider, for example, the report that "over 70 percent of teenagers have their first sexual encounter under the influence of alcohol" (Royce, 1989, p. 325).

Some authors (e.g., Gelles & Pedrick-Cornell, 1985) have argued that substance use is more of an excuse for, rather than a cause of, dating violence. In this regard, substance use among adolescents involved in dating violence can be considered as a maladaptive coping mechanism aimed at both diminishing personal responsibility for the aggressor and allowing the victim to justify his or her date's behavior. As noted by Aramburu and Leigh (1991): "Research on attributions about drunken violence has suggested that intoxication serves to decrease responsibility attributed to aggressors while increasing responsibility attributed to victims" (p. 31). This theory helps to explain how the victim can remain in the abusive relationship. For example, one of our patients stated that he hit his girlfriend "only gently" and only when she needed "a therapy slap." His girlfriend concurred that he only hit her when she was "out of line" and "deserved it." However, when he drank alcohol or "cranked" amphetamines, the "therapy slaps" would become more severe and result in bruising and black eyes. When confronted, the girlfriend would simply respond, "He really didn't mean it; he was drunk," or "He was high and I shouldn't have bothered him," or "I should have stayed out of his way" (A. M. Pagliaro & L. A. Pagliaro, 1992, clinical patient file notes). Dating violence also includes sexual abuse/assault such as date rape (Christoffel,

---

[2] These findings are confounded by the occurrence of dual diagnoses (see Chap. 6).

1990; Erickson & Rapkin, 1991; see the discussion of sexual abuse/assault, below).

Fights

As noted previously, substance use is integrally related to violent behavior. A majority of people who present to emergency rooms with serious craniofacial trauma, and their assailants, were intoxicated at the time of the assault (Dannenberg, Parver, & Fowler, 1992; Hall & Ofodile, 1991; Hussain et al., 1994; Ord & Benian, 1995). As noted by Hall & Ofodile (1991):

> The rising incidence of drug addiction and the violence associated with it has led in recent years to a changing pattern of facial fractures in the inner cities of the United States. Trauma from fists, kicks, and blunt objects, such as baseball bats, are now the primary cause of mandibular fractures. (pp. 422–423)

A study of 2,300 11th- and 12th-graders from several schools in South Carolina provided evidence that "being black, male, sexually active, and engaging in binge drinking and drug use were significant predictors of fighting" (Valois et al., 1993, p. 141). These fights and associated injuries are not limited to older adolescents who live in urban areas but are also observed among younger adolescents living in rural areas. For example, a study of 1,000 8th- and 10th-graders from a number of rural, small central Texas communities found that over 50 percent of the boys and over 20 percent of the girls had been involved in at least one physical fight during the previous year (Kingery, Mirzaee, Pruitt, Hurley, & Heuberger, 1991). On the basis of the data collected, the authors concluded that "rural schools are not safe havens from the violence and drug problems seen in the large urban areas nearby [i.e., Houston]" (Kingery et al., 1991, p. 48). Substance use was found to be significantly correlated with both frequency of fighting and frequency of victimization:

> Drug users, compared to nonusers, fought more, took more risks which predisposed them to assault, and were assaulted more both at school and outside school supervision. Adolescents who were victims at school were also more likely to be victimized outside of school supervision. This study clearly demonstrates that the aggressor may also be the victim, and that illegal drug/alcohol use is related to victimization. (Kingery, Pruitt, & Hurley, 1992, p. 1445)

Physical Abuse/Assault

> The U.S. Advisory Board on Child Abuse and Neglect declared in a recent report that the overwhelming increase in cases of child maltreatment has created a national emergency and that the national system for responding to child maltreatment is failing. ("Child Abuse," 1991, p. 101)

Approximately two-thirds of parents use violence against their children, and substance use contributes to this violent behavior (Lujan, DeBruyn, May, & Bird, 1989, B. A. Miller, 1990; Suh & Abel, 1990; Wolfner & Gelles, 1993), with estimates suggesting that over 1.5 million children in North America are abused each year by family members or other intimates (Aday, 1994).[3] This form of abuse, generally a combination of both physical and verbal abuse, is typified in the story of seven-year-old Sharon:

> "You can't do anything right, you stupid bitch," my mother would holler at me while smacking me across the head with her open hand. "Stupid bitch" and "bad girl" were practically the only words she ever said to me.
>
> From age six, I did all the housework. Nothing I did, from peeling potatoes to scrubbing floors, was ever good enough. I got no thanks, just beatings and threats that she'd kill me if I complained to my father. . . . Our lives went down the toilet faster than the booze went down her throat. . . .
>
> She needed more than his earnings and the welfare for necessities—booze, cigarettes, and the odd loaf of bread. So, she got domestic jobs in rich Rosedale homes. She got the wages; I did the labour. She'd keep me out of school, where I was in trouble anyway, to go with her to houses she had keys for, where the lady wasn't home. She'd watch the soaps and help herself at the overstocked bars, spiking the half-empty bottles with water, while I cleaned. When she'd inspect my work, she'd complain that it wasn't good enough, smack me, and curse me out. (Webber, 1991, pp. 65–67)

However, the full nature and extent of the relationship between parental violence aimed at children and substance use by parents (and other care givers) has not been adequately studied and remains inconclusive. As noted by

---

[3] Although not discussed in this chapter, attention should also be given to the abuse that children and adolescents suffer as a result of parental neglect directly related to substance use (Ney, Fung, & Wickett, 1992). This form of abuse, although difficult to specifically define in terms of its nature and extent, is believed to be widespread and a significant contributor to morbidity and mortality among children and adolescents of all ages. Consider, e.g., the following:

> Last year, in an article on the youngest victims of the crack epidemic, the *Oakland Tribune* reported that police, making a routine drug bust, "found a crack mother passed out on her bed, with her seven-month-old baby sitting in a pool of vomit, chewing on cigarettes. A glass crack pipe was nestled between mother and child." Readers of almost every major urban newspaper have read similar stories about preschool children forced to beg food from neighbors, premature infants born addicted to crack, and babies who remain in hospitals for months because their mothers have abandoned them. (DeBettencourt, 1990, p. 17)

The abuse and neglect found in families with chronic compulsive patterns of substance use, particularly alcohol, continues past infancy and throughout childhood. As noted by one of our patients, "I was born and raised in the 'sticks.' . . . We had no heat in the house, no food, but we always had two gallons of St. George's wine to get up and have at breakfast. . . . My brother and I would have to go and beg for food from our neighbors. . . . I was big for my age and started drinking heavy with the best of them around 11 years. . . . My parents encourage drinking" (A. M. Pagliaro & L. A. Pagliaro, 1994, clinical patient file notes).

B. A. Miller (1990), "Our data on the importance of parental alcohol and drug problems to the willingness to use parental violence toward children was less clear [than the effect of this violence in subsequently contributing to substance use among the children as they get older]" (p. 195; see also Chap. 5).

Although "alcohol and drug use" among perpetrators are commonly associated with their physical abuse of children (Famularo, Kinscherff, & Fenton, 1992; Kelley, 1992; Muller et al., 1994), "no physical child abuse perpetrator typology has been adequately validated" in the general population (Milner & Chilamkurti, 1991, p. 345). Additional factors, such as poverty, stress, and lack of social support, also appear to contribute significantly to this form of violent behavior (Christoffel, 1990). However, in alcoholic families, "for both fathers and mothers, lifetime alcohol problems predicted extent of child maltreatment" (Muller et al., 1994, p. 438). In addition, in high-risk multiproblem families (e.g., Native American families living in poverty on reservations), "alcohol abuse is present in virtually all families that abuse/neglect children" (DeBruyn, Lujan, & May, 1992, p. 305). Although this association may not be unique or causal, it is significant and requires appropriate consideration, particularly in regard to the increasing incidence of serious cases of childhood physical abuse (Donnelly, 1991; see also the related discussions of sexual abuse/assault and homicide, below).

Sexual Abuse/Assault

> When I was about eleven years old, my teacher abused me. He never actually raped me, but he would sit me on his lap and hug and kiss me. I could feel him getting a hard-on. Then, when I was about sixteen, I was at a party. I'd had a few beers so I was feeling pretty relaxed. I ended up in a bedroom with a guy. At first we were just necking, but then he got more pushy. I didn't want to have sex with him, but he wouldn't stop. It was awful. I was so scared; I felt like I was 11 years old again, with that teacher. I froze and he raped me. After that I felt worthless and dirty. ("Making the Links," 1990, pp. 12–13; see also discussion of dating violence, above)

Sexual abuse/assault of children and adolescents can occur at any age, including the neonatal period,[4] and perpetrators can be family members, acquaintances, or total strangers (see Fig. 8.2). The reported incidence of sexual abuse/assault during childhood or adolescence, which has been generally based on recollected self-reports by adults, has increased 10-fold from 6 to

---

[4]For example, Chasnoff et al. (1986) described several cases of "mother-child incest initiated during the neonatal period. . . . The mothers all were estranged from their sexual partners, had demonstrated some confusion regarding sexual identity, and had sought assistance with chemical dependency during pregnancy" (p. 577).

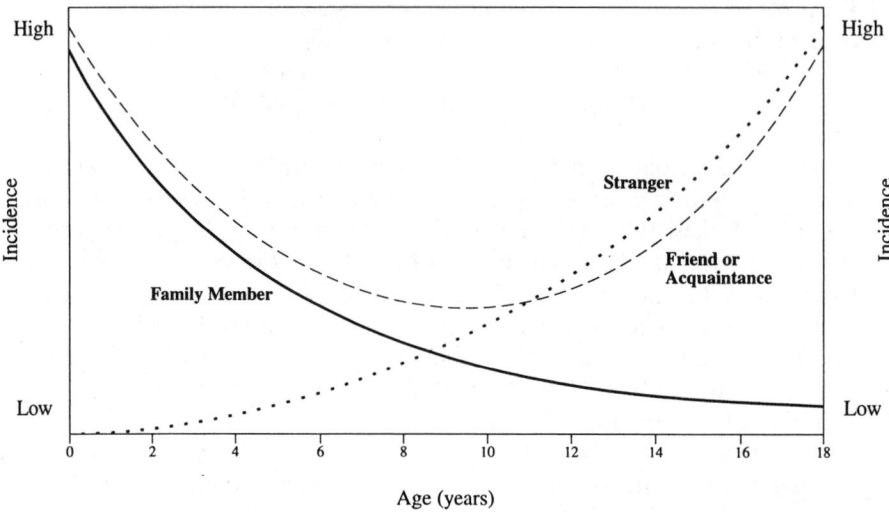

FIGURE 8.2   Sexual abuse and homicide: Incidence and relationship to perpetrator according to age of victim

60 percent. The actual incidence is probably closer to 12 percent (W. Feldman et al., 1991; Finkelhor & Dziuba-Leatherman, 1994).

Substance use, particularly of alcohol, appears to play a significant role in these sexual offenses by disinhibiting social taboos against child molestation, particularly that involving incest, and in males also increasing testosterone levels and, consequently, sexual aggressiveness (L. A. Pagliaro, 1993b). Sociological variables, such as social class, do not appear to be significantly related to childhood sexual abuse (Finkelhor, Hotaling, Lewis, & Smith, 1990; Wyatt, 1985). However, other sociological factors, such as ethnicity, do appear to be related, with lower risk reported for Jews and higher risk reported for Hispanics (Christoffel, 1990). Age has also been found to be a significant factor. Children do molest other children. For example, in a study of child perpetrators, T. C. Johnson (1988) reported that "the mean age of the children at the time of their first known sexual perpetration was 8 years, 9 months. The range was 4 to 12 years of age" (p. 222).

Overall, it has been estimated that up to 50 percent of rapes (including date rapes) and child molestations are perpetrated by adolescents (Deisher, Wenet, Paperney, Clark, & Fehrenbach, 1982), and the "influence of drugs/ alcohol" in these cases is significant (Erickson & Rapkin, 1991). In addition, intervening variables, such as previous sexual victimization of the perpetrator (boy or girl) by an adult, usually the father (or father figure, e.g., stepfather, mother's boyfriend, etc.), and positive family histories of problematic patterns of substance use, have been found to be highly correlated with this abnormal violent sexual behavior perpetrated by children and adolescents (Eisenman, 1995; T. C. Johnson, 1988).

Adults who perpetrate child molestation or rape vary considerably in relation to psychological and social variables, but most display problematic patterns of alcohol use (Hillbrand, Foster, & Hirt, 1990; Ritter, 1989; Stiffman, 1989). In addition, a number of studies have proposed a "cycle of alcohol abuse in men leading to domestic violence and sexual abuse in women and children" (Yellowlees & Kaushik, 1992, p. 197). Although these studies have, almost exclusively, focused on men as the perpetrators of sexual abuse, a parallel scenario can occur involving women, as noted in the following excerpt from the diary of one of our patients:

A dresser was next to the window, with a woman's hand mirror, tissues, and lipstick littered on top. One small cut glass tumbler was always there, it seemed, half-filled with the clear yellow liquid visible through the flying ducks etched in the side of the glass.

The young boy tentatively was in one bed, pretending to sleep. His black hair and deep set eyes, visible above the covers, accentuated his sad, perpetually unsmiling, face. The woman sat on the side of the other bed, her housecoat open with only a bra underneath. Her disheveled hair and sagging facial muscles framed the wild, uncaring look in her eyes. The bottles were on the floor beside her.

"C—," she said, "come and sleep with me." The older boy tentatively entered the room, not knowing what to expect.

"Come and sleep with me, you can sleep next to the wall." The boy looked at his mother, looked at her eyes, with their crazy, unloving gaze. He was lonely, his father on one of his interminable "business trips," no friends in this new neighborhood, the cleaning lady gone home.

He looked at his mother's open housecoat, with her naked body showing. She looked so different than she did in the mornings, fully clothed and acting "normally." Then he knew she loved him. Now he wasn't sure, but he knew he couldn't trust her.

The boy was afraid. Why was she acting so crazy? Why did she not seem to love him now? Why did no one else seem to notice? Why did no one else say anything about this craziness?

"Come on, you've got your pajamas on, just climb into bed here."

He walked over towards her, she grabbing him when he got close, and holding him close to her breasts. He struggled away and, climbing over her, lay down on the other side of the bed next to the wall.

"Don't you love me, C—? Don't you want me to hold you?"

The tears started to well up inside, as the numbness set in on the outside. He wanted her love, but hated her craziness, hated her like this.

"Yeh," he said.

He lay facing the wall, legs curled up, in a position that was to become etched in his memory, an image that would come blazing back years later.

She snuggled up close to him, her breasts touching his back, her arm around him. Her sickening menstrual breath, saturated with alcohol, enveloped him. He felt paralyzed, too numb and afraid to move.

The feelings came flooding in. What if he left her bed? What would she do to his little brother in the next bed? Would she smother him like she did with little E—? He mustn't leave his brother alone here with her. What was she doing: Why was she touching him when she didn't love him now?

He felt the security of her touch, but the fear and hatred of her craziness. Afraid to move, afraid to tell her he hated her, he felt her hand move down his body. Wanting her touch, but paralyzed with fear, he lay there, staring at the wall, screaming with despair and loneliness inside. (A. M. Pagliaro & L. A. Pagliaro, 1992, clinical patient file notes)

As noted by O'Hagan (1993), in her discussion of the "case of Tony, aged 7" and his alcoholic mother, these children repeatedly experience their mother's "drunken anger, drunken threats, and drunken physical affection and protestations of love," which, in turn, cause anger, embarrassment, humiliation, shame, stress, and the "pervasive apprehension that mother will be drunk again" (pp. 67–68). It is then perhaps not surprising that childhood victims of sexual abuse are at increased risk of developing subsequent problematic patterns of substance use (Famularo et al., 1992; Van Hasselt et al., 1992; see related discussion concerning sexual abuse as an antecedent of substance use, in Chap. 5).

HOMICIDE

Homicide can be defined as the unlawful taking of another person's life. It can be intentional (e.g., drive-by shooting in retribution for "moving into a gang's drug turf") or unintentional (e.g., driving while under the influence of alcohol and running over a child in a crosswalk). In a majority of cases, both intentional and unintentional homicides are related to substance use (Lindenbaum et al., 1989; L. A. Pagliaro & Pagliaro, 1993; Royce, 1989). This scenario has been repeated to us countless times by adolescents during our forensic psychological assessments. The following is a typical case that illustrates the effects of cocaine and the tragic consequences that occur all too frequently:

> I worked hard all day on several large orders until 7 p.m. when I got paid by my boss and headed home. On the way home I thought it might be nice to have a taste of cocaine . . . went to the dealer's home and bought one gram. Got a box of new rigs from the dealer and fixed half. Wrapped the remaining one-half gram and put it in my pocket. Got into my GMC half-ton and started driving away. By this point I'm paranoid and think someone is in the box of my truck and they're waiting until I slow down to get [i.e., arrest] me . . . so I start running over curbs and drive around corners fast so that I can shake the guy out of the back of my truck. . . . Police cruiser started to follow me. I had to get away at any cost. I was running for my life. . . . I remember hitting hard a

couple of times [running into other vehicles], but I don't remember the third hit at all . . . don't remember all the details . . . when they caught me, one cop said "two people died there because of you." (A. M. Pagliaro & L. A. Pagliaro, 1991, clinical patient file notes)[5]

Those who think of homicide as an adult phenomenon should consider the following and think again:

Violence, including homicide, child abuse and neglect, and assault by peers and others, causes over 2000 deaths a year to U.S. children aged 0 to 19 years. Homicide is a leading cause of death for U.S. children. (Christoffel, 1990, p. 697)

Homicide is the 11th leading cause of death in the United States and is increasingly prevalent among youth; between 1980 and 1989, more than 11,000 persons died as a result of homicides committed by high school-aged youths who used a weapon of some type. (U.S. Department of Justice, 1994b, p. 1)

Violence, particularly African American on African American crime, is another type of victimization that occurs as a result of the drug trade. The homicide rate for African American males ages 15–24 has risen by more than two-thirds in recent years: 40 percent of all deaths in this age group are homicides. Homicide is the leading cause of death for African American teenagers, mostly attributable to gunfire. . . . The literature does show a relationship between abuse of drugs and homicidal violence. And studies of combined alcohol and drug related homicides indicate a positive relationship, particularly among males. (Bass & Kane-Williams, 1993, p. 81)

Homicide is now the leading cause of death among children in many American cities—and half the assailants are other youths. (Laird, Keister, & Tiberi, 1993, p. 22)

Almost half of all deaths among African American male teenagers now involve firearms. (O'Donnell, 1995, p. 771)

Homicide is the leading cause of death among young non-white males [in the United States]. According to the Centers for Disease Control, homicides associated with firearms accounted for nearly one half of the deaths of young black males between 1978 and 1987. . . . The interaction of poverty, family violence, substance abuse, drug dealing, and the cultural acceptance of violent behavior contributes to rising statistics on adolescent violent crime. (Busen, 1992, p. 194)

Nonadult homicides can be divided into two major categories: 1. those that occur during infancy or early childhood and 2. those that occur during adolescence. The first group includes predominantly infants and young children who die as a direct result of severe abuse or neglect by their parents or care givers (e.g., infants being thrown against the wall or being asphyxiated

---

[5] The two people who died were recent high school graduates who had just become engaged to be married. The adolescent driver was subsequently convicted of vehicular manslaughter.

with a pillow, "shaken to death," or choked because they soiled themselves or would not stop crying; Christoffel, 1990). In most cases the cause of death is related to the infliction of a severe head injury with "alcohol or drug abuse" being a significant contributory factor (B. Goldstein, Kelley, Bruton, & Cox, 1993; see discussion of physical abuse/assault, above). Cavaliere (1995), citing a 1995 report commissioned by the U.S. Advisory Board on Child Abuse and Neglect, noted that "at least 2,000 children a year—five each day—die at the hands of their parents or caretakers. More preschool children are killed by their parents than die from falls, choking, suffocation, drowning or fires" (1995, p. 34).

The second group of homicides includes predominantly adolescents involved in drug-dealing or gang-related activities (E. Cohen et al., 1991; R. Fennell, 1994; "Firearms," 1994; Sheley, McGee, & Wright, 1992; Swan, 1995b; Washburn, 1994; G. K. Weisman, 1993). In these cases, risk of homicide has been highly correlated with substance use (particularly alcohol and cocaine) and the involvement of firearms (particularly handguns; McGonigal et al., 1993; Tardiff et al., 1994). A study by M. L. Levy et al. (1993) of "gunshot wounds to the brain" included 105 children (aged 6 months to 17 years). "Occipital or assassination-type wounds" were the type most frequently encountered in this age group, and 72 percent were reportedly gang related (p. 1018).

> Existing data indicate that approximately 10% of male, urban, African-American early adolescents report having engaged in drug trafficking, with a higher percent of youths reporting having been asked to sell drugs and/or indicating that they expect to become involved in drug trafficking. Rates increase with advancing age. . . . Drug trafficking is associated with increased mortality, accounting for one third to one half of homicide-related deaths in some studies. (B. Stanton & Galbraith, 1994, p. 1039)

"Firearms [usually handguns] are the leading means of homicide for victims aged 12 years and over" (Christoffel, 1990, p. 697). Homicide is positively correlated with substance use by perpetrators and victims (Garriott, 1993; Swan, 1995). Several explanations have been advanced to account for this finding, the most plausible of which appears to be that children and adolescents who become intoxicated with one or more of the substances of abuse: 1. take more risks and, hence, place themselves in more dangerous situations and 2. are less able to extricate themselves from high-risk situations as a direct result of the effects of their substance use on cognitive and psychomotor function (Windle, 1994).

SUICIDE

Adolescence is a period of relatively little serious physical disease (common childhood diseases have been survived and heart disease and other diseases

TABLE 8.2 **Reported Suicide Rates over the Past Decade: Canada and the United States**[a]

Year	Country	Rate[b]	Sample Population	Comments	Reference
1991	USA	11.1	15–19 y.o. (all)	Canada's rate of adolescent suicide is reportedly the third highest among major countries (after New Zealand [15.7] and Finland [15]).	Nemeth, 1994
	Canada	13.5	15–19 y.o. (all)		
1991	USA	3	15–19 y.o. (all)	The suicide rate for white ♂ appears to be leveling off over the past several years, while the rate for other ♂ is showing a significant increasing trend.	D. Shaffer, Gould, & Hicks, 1994
	USA	12	15–19 y.o. black ♂		
	USA	13	15–19 y.o. Oriental and Hispanic ♂		
	USA	18	15–19 y.o. white ♂		
1986	USA	10.2	15–19 y.o. (all)	The rate of suicides reported for ♂ (15–19 y.o.) was 400 percent higher than for ♀ and among ♂ was highest for white ♂.	Hathaway, Groothuis, Hay, & Paisley, 1993
	USA	18.2	15–19 y.o. white ♂		
1985	USA	2	15–19 y.o. non-white ♀		Holinger, 1990
	USA	4	15–19 y.o. white ♀		
	USA	10	15–19 y.o. nonwhite ♂		
	USA	17	15–19 y.o. white ♂		
1984–88	Canada	3	15–19 y.o. ♀		Bagley et al., 1990
	Canada	20	15–19 y.o. ♂		

[a]Abbreviations: y.o., years old; ♂, boys; ♀, girls.
[b]Rates are per 100,000 individuals.

of adulthood, which are generally associated with poor life-style choices, are not yet commonly encountered). Among this relatively healthy group, one of the major sources of mortality is suicide, which is generally ranked, after accidents and before homicide, as the second leading cause of death (Bagley et al., 1990; Ellis & Range, 1992; Felts, Chenier, & Barnes, 1992; Holinger, 1990; Kaplan & Mammel, 1993b; O'Donnell, 1995; Samy, 1993; M. P. Stanton, 1990).

Suicide rates reported for North American adolescents are presented in Table 8.2. These data provide evidence that over the past 10 years, adolescent suicide rates have been consistently higher for: 1. Canada in comparison to the United States, 2. males in comparison to females, and 3. Caucasians in comparison to other races. In Canada, adolescent suicide rates are highest in the Yukon and the Northwest Territories (Bagley et al., 1990; Pronovost, Coté, & Ross, 1990). Available data for suicide rates among Native American adolescents tend to be incomplete and conflicting. However, they suggest that suicide rates for "off-reserve" Native American adolescents are similar to those for non–Native American adolescents, while "on-reserve" suicide rates are often found to be significantly higher (Aldridge & St. John, 1991; M. Cooper, Corrado, Karlberg, & Adams, 1992; Gotowiec & Beiser, 1993/94; Moncher et al., 1990). For example, in a large study of Native American adolescents from eight Indian health service areas, R. W. Blum et al. (1992) found that "eleven percent of the teens surveyed knew someone who had killed himself or herself, and 17% had attempted suicide themselves" (p. 1637). Several explanations have been offered for this observation including a greater degree of poverty and fewer jobs for Native American adolescents living on reserves.

In comparison to completed suicides, it is generally estimated that 50–100 times as many adolescents attempt suicide (one adolescent attempts suicide approximately every 60 seconds in North America), with estimates of at-risk adolescents as high as 1 million (M. B. Straus, 1994). Adolescent girls attempt suicide 3 or 4 times more frequently than do adolescent boys. However, they generally use less lethal means (e.g., substance overdose versus firearm) and, consequently, have a significantly higher rate of survival (Bagley et al., 1990; Pronovost et al., 1990; Rich, Kirkpatrick-Smith, Bonner, & Jans, 1992). These failed attempts at suicide often have been viewed as desperate cries for attention or help as illustrated in the words of the following suicide note, which was found near the unconscious body of a 15-year-old girl who had tried to kill herself with a prescription overdose: "Dear Mom, I know that you'll be sad to find me dead. You'll be sorry when I'm gone. I hope you'll be happy with no more fights. I love you, Susan" (M. B. Straus, 1994, p. 33). Regardless of the reason for their attempted suicide, these adolescents require immediate and appropriate intervention, particularly because of their risk for repeated attempts (Brent, 1989; Thibault, 1992).

A comprehensive search of the computerized Medline, CINAHL, and Psy-INFO databases (1990–95) was conducted to identify those factors reported in the literature as being associated with adolescent suicides and suicide attempts. Nineteen major risk factors were identified (L. A. Pagliaro, 1995e). These risk factors are presented in alphabetical order in Table 8.3. Perhaps unexpectedly, several factors that are commonly associated with problematic adolescence (e.g., cancer, low socioeconomic status, pregnancy, and infection with STDs) were not found to be significantly related to risk for suicide or suicide attempts (L. C. Bernard & Krupat, 1994; de Anda, Javidi, Jefford, Komorowski, & Yanez, 1991; Perrone, 1993).

Depression was found to be the most frequently reported factor associated with adolescent suicide or suicide attempts. An examination of this factor

TABLE 8.3   Major Risk Factors Associated with Adolescent Suicide Ideation and Attempts[a]

Absence of maternal figure
Access to firearms
Alcoholic family
Conduct disorder
Depression
Dissatisfaction with family relationships
External locus of control
Gender identity crisis: gay, lesbian, or bisexual sexual orientation
Hopelessness
Lack of reasons for living
Lack of social support
Loneliness
Low self-esteem
Physical or sexual abuse
Previous psychiatric inpatient treatment
Previous suicide attempt
Serious early childhood losses
Substance use

[a]From L. A. Pagliaro (1995e).

and its relationship to the other identified risk factors revealed that it was significantly correlated with suicide ideation and attempts and most of the other identified risk factors. This finding supports the notion that depression should probably be considered as a "general" factor. Although, retrospectively, depression is strongly correlated with suicide ideation and attempts (most adolescents who attempt suicide are depressed), prospective correlations are much lower (most depressed adolescents do not attempt suicide; Kienhorst, de Wilde, Diekstra, & Wolters, 1991). Thus, the predictive power of depression for identifying adolescents who may be at significant risk for suicide is limited.

Substance use (e.g., the use of crack cocaine; Berman & Schwartz, 1990; Felts et al., 1992; Marzuk et al., 1992) is considered to be a major risk factor for suicide attempts during adolescence (Hoberman & Garfinkel, 1988; van Aalst et al., 1992; L. S. Wright, 1985b). Use of the sedative-hypnotics (e.g., alcohol and diazepam [Valium]) decreases social inhibitions that might otherwise dissuade the adolescent from committing suicide.[6] In addition, the substances of abuse are often used, more often by girls than boys, as the

[6]The sedative-hypnotics can also cause depression, which as previously noted, is associated with adolescent suicide attempts (Madianos, Gefou-Madianou, & Stefanis, 1994; L. A. Pagliaro & Pagliaro, 1993).

actual means of suicide attempt by overdose (Coleridge, Cameron, Drummer, & McNeil, 1992; Downey, 1991; L. A. Pagliaro, 1990b).

Although any adolescent can attempt suicide, knowledge of the reported risk factors can increase the ability of adult contacts (e.g., parents, schoolteachers, counselors, psychologists, or other health care professionals) to appropriately identify those adolescents who appear to be at particular risk. Once identified, a program of effective intervention can be developed and implemented. Appropriate clinical intervention is always predicated on careful and comprehensive assessment. Specific psychometric instruments (e.g., the Multi-Attitude Suicide Tendency Scale) have been developed and used to assess suicidal tendencies among adolescents (Lamb & Pusker, 1991); however, most such measures (e.g., the Beck Depression Inventory and the Child Depression Inventory) are limited by their focus on depression as the major underlying construct (Morgan, 1994; Wozencraft & Ellegrin, 1991).

The literature (e.g., Garrison, Lewinsohn, Marsteller, Langhinrichsen, & Lam, 1991) and the authors' clinical experience indicate that a good clinical interview provides the best available method for assessment. In this regard, schoolteachers, counselors, psychologists, and other health care professionals might begin by: 1. identifying adolescents at risk (those who possess several of the risk factors noted in Table 8.3), 2. looking for clues (e.g., the adolescent begins giving away prized possessions), 3. conducting a complete evaluation for additional suicide risk factors, and 4. asking specifically about suicide (e.g., ideation, previous attempts, or specific suicide plan). Once the suicidal risk has been identified and characterized, appropriate intervention strategies must be implemented (Brent, 1989).

A diagnosis of AIDS has been recognized as a factor for suicide risk among adults (Coté, Biggar, & Dannenberg, 1992). Although not yet recognized as such among adolescents, it can be expected that as the incidence of HIV infection and AIDS continues to increase in this age group (see Chap. 6), HIV-infection-related suicide risk will significantly increase and will need to be added to the list of factors identified in Table 8.3.

> *There are said to be occasions when a wise man chooses suicide—but generally speaking, it is not in an excess of reasonableness that people kill themselves. Most men and women die defeated.*

> Voltaire

So too, do most children and adolescents.

SUMMARY

The use of the various substances of abuse is integrally related to the occurrence of accidents and acts of violence, including homicides and suicides, among children and adolescents. Accidental injuries are most commonly associated with substance-related falls and motor vehicle crashes. However, serious morbidity and mortality are also associated with assaults, including those occurring most commonly in the context of battery during pregnancy, dating violence, fights, physical abuse, and sexual abuse. Of additional concern, homicide rates among children and adolescents have continued to rise during the 1990s to a current all-time record, with the highest incidence noted among black adolescent boys. Similarly during this period, suicide rates have tended to rise, particularly among black adolescent boys and girls; however, the adolescents typically at the greatest risk for suicide remain white adolescent boys. "Violence has been characterized as a 'public health epidemic' in the United States" (Osofsky, 1995, p. 782). However, adults tend frequently to view this epidemic as a problem affecting adults. Clearly, the data presented in this chapter indicate that accidents and violence associated with substance use pose a clear and present problem for the health and well-being of North American children and adolescents.

CHAPTER 9

Substance-Related Crime: Children and Adolescents as Perpetrators

According to 1991 FBI statistics, almost 18 percent of urban crime is committed by youngsters under the age of 18. Out of 8.4 million urban arrests in 1991, 1.5 million were kids. (Lubinski, 1995, p. 31)

From 1983 to 1992, arrests of youths for murder increased by about 128%, while arrests of adults for murder increased by only 9 percent. In 1983, about 1 in every 13 arrests for murder was a minor; by 1992, that fraction had increased to 1 in every 7 arrests for murder. (*National Archive of Criminal Justice Data Newsletter,* 1994, p. 1)

Regardless of whether the relationship is causal, spurious, or reciprocal, serious juvenile offenders are involved disproportionately in substance abuse. (Fagan, 1990, p. 184)

A number of research studies support a relationship between crimes perpetrated by children and adolescents and their substance use (e.g., Abram, 1989; Carpenter, Glassner, Johnson, & Loughlin, 1988; Cornell, 1990; Daniel & Dodd, 1990; Dembo, Williams, Getreu, et al., 1991; Fagan, 1990; Newcomb & McGee, 1989; M. J. Russell, 1993). However, the nature of this complex relationship, as suggested by Fagan (1990), is incompletely understood (see Fig. 9.1) and gives rise to several rudimentary questions (Abram, 1989; Bradford, Greenberg, & Motayne, 1992; Dembo et al., 1992). For example, in regard to children and adolescents: Does substance use contribute to crime? Does crime contribute to substance use? What part do other variables (e.g., antisocial personality) play in the relationship between substance use and crime? Are certain types of crime more strongly related to substance use (e.g., violent vs. nonviolent crime)? Is the use of certain substances of abuse more strongly related to crime? This chapter will attempt to address these and other related questions. The general nature of the relationship between childhood and adolescent substance use and violent and nonviolent crime is first considered. This overview is followed by a discussion of commerce- and pharmacopsychology-related crime as associated with substance use by children and adolescents.

$$SU \Rightarrow Crime$$

$$(SU + y) \Rightarrow Crime$$

$$SU \Rightarrow y \Rightarrow Crime$$

$$Crime \Rightarrow SU$$

$$SU \Longleftrightarrow Crime$$

$$SU \nLeftrightarrow Crime$$

FIGURE 9.1   Substance use (SU) and crime: Proposed relationships

SUBSTANCE USE AND CRIME

> Even though persons under age 18 constitute only about 15 percent of the U.S. population, they commit about 25 percent of serious crimes such as homicide, rape, robbery, aggravated assault, and arson—10 percent of all murders, 19 percent of rapes, 32 percent of robberies, 17 percent of aggravated assaults, and 32 percent of cases of arson. . . . In addition, violent adolescents are at risk for violent death, which is often associated with alcohol use. (Marohn, 1992, p. 622)

It is commonly thought that substance use, particularly the "hustling" and other activities required to maintain a particular pattern of use, is a major contributor to crime. It is widely believed that "crack heads," "pot heads," and "heroin addicts" commit serious physical or sexual assaults, robberies, and other crimes in order to maintain their habits. However, this notion, popularized in the media, has not been clearly substantiated by the available research data (Benson & Holmberg, 1984; Bradford et al., 1992; J. J. Collins, 1981; Spunt, Goldstein, Brownstein, & Fendrich, 1994). These data indicate that, while adolescents often commit crimes to maintain their substance use, these adolescents are not involved in more serious crimes than other groups and they do not pose a significant risk for engaging in violent crimes (Dembo, Williams, Wish, et al., 1990; Dembo, Williams, Wothke, et al., 1990; "Drugs," 1994; N. S. Miller & Gold, 1994; Nurco, Cisin, & Ball, 1985). When children and adolescents are involved in crimes, their crimes more often than not involve breaking and entering, drug dealing, prostitution, and theft rather than violent crimes. As reflected by an 18-year-old adolescent boy addicted to heroin:

> I don't stick-up, I don't snatch ladies' pocketbooks, man. My mother brought me up to know better than that. . . . We have what we call a "boostin' crew." There are three girls and four of us, and we look out for each other in stores. We go boostin', stealin' meat and coffee and things like that, mainly just run-nin' back and forth to the stores. (B. Hanson, Beschner, Walters, & Bovelle, 1985, p. 36)

Although violent (e.g., homicide and rape) and nonviolent (e.g., prostitu-tion and shoplifting) crimes are committed by children and adolescents who use substances of abuse, several researchers (e.g., Cornell & Wilson, 1992; P. L. Taylor & Albright, 1981) concur with Weisz, Martin, Walter, and Fer-nandez (1991) that "the distinction between perpetrators of personal and property crimes is rarely definitive" (p. 791). As concluded by Abram (1989):

> There is substantial evidence that drug users tend to engage in income-generating crime. . . . The relationship between drug use and violent crime, however, has been inconsistently reported and is less well documented. . . . Al-though drug users commit violent offenses, they engage in fewer violent offenses than [their] non-drug using counterparts. (p. 135)

This finding has been corroborated by a summary report from the Office of National Drug Control Policy:

> Inmates incarcerated for robbery, burglary, larceny, and drug trafficking most often committed their crime to obtain money for drugs. Inmates who commit-ted homicide, sexual assault, assault, and public-order offenses were least likely to commit their offense to obtain money for drugs. (Chaiken, 1995, p. 8)

However, the use of one particular substance of abuse, alcohol, has been consistently associated with aggressive behavior and violent crime, particu-larly among boys (Bradford et al., 1992; Labouvie & McGee, 1986; Lau & Pihl, 1994; A. M. Weisman & Taylor, 1994; Yarvis, 1994). J. J. Collins (1981) noted that "the consistency and strength of the alcohol-crime empirical asso-ciation is sufficient to justify the inference that alcohol is sometimes causally implicated in the occurrence of serious crime" (p. 289).

Alcohol Use and Violent Crime

"Alcohol and other drugs, used alone or in combination, dramatically in-crease the risk of violent behavior and contribute significantly to the preva-lence of adolescent suicide, fighting, homicide, accidental death and disabil-ity, robbery, rape, and assault" (Valois et al., 1993, p. 141). A consistent and positive relationship between the use of alcohol and violent crime involving aggressive behavior has been identified (Milner & Chilamkurti, 1991; L. A.

TABLE 9.1   Alcohol Use and Criminal Behavior: Methodological Limitations[a]

Biased sampling (e.g., delinquent adolescents, incarcerated inmates, and students)

Failure to control relevant variables (e.g., gender and race)

Lack of interactional studies

Lack of longitudinal studies

Lack of prospective studies

Lack of sufficient attention to the nature of the targets (victims) of the crime

Lack of uniformity in the definitions of alcohol use

Lack of uniformity in the definitions of crime

Poorly described context within which drinking and crime co-occurred

Unclear distinction between subgroups of alcohol users and perpetrators

Use of law enforcement statistics (which by their nature are biased toward reporting
  only the most extreme cases)

[a]Modified from Bradford et al. (1992, p. 607), Pelletier and Coutu (1992, p. 9), Volavka, Martell, and Convit (1992, pp. 246–247), and Westermeyer (1990, p. 53).

Pagliaro & Pagliaro, 1992a). As noted by Holcomb and Anderson (1983), "A relationship between violence and alcohol intoxication has been recognized for centuries" (p. 159). Unfortunately, although much empirical data exist,[1] research examining this relationship has been plagued by several methodological limitations (see Table 9.1). These limitations serve to confound the interpretation of results and limit their generalization. For example, some researchers (e.g., Tomori, 1994; White, Brick, & Hansell, 1993) have suggested that an aggressive personality is an antecedent of alcohol use, which then leads to alcohol-related aggression. Others (e.g., Roman, 1981) suggest that *situational factors* (see Table 9.2) influence in various ways the relationship between alcohol use and crime. However, the commonly associated relationship between alcohol use and violent crime, including aggravated sexual assault and homicide, can be explained, for the most part, by two pharmacological mechanisms (direct effects of alcohol and cofactor effects) and

---

[1] E.g., the analysis of emergency room and coroner data consistently suggests a significant positive relationship between alcohol consumption and violent-crime-related morbidity and mortality. As noted by Cherpitel in 1993:

> Those with violence-related injuries were more likely than those with other injuries to have positive breathalyzer readings and to report drinking prior to the event, frequent heavy drinking, consequences of drinking, experiences associated with alcohol dependence and loss of control and prior treatment for an alcohol problem. (p. 79)

Again, in 1994, Cherpitel found that "violence-related fatalities were more likely to involve alcohol (47%) than non-fatal injuries (19%)" (p. 211). As noted by Klatsky and Armstrong (1993):

> In adjusted analyses, persons reporting intake of 6 or more drinks daily were at greatly increased risk of death from suicide (6 times) and homicide (7 times), and at moderately increased risk of death from MVAs [motor vehicle accidents] (2 times). Lighter and ex-drinkers were not at significantly increased risk for all unnatural deaths or any of its subsets. (p. 1156)

TABLE 9.2   Alcohol Use and Crime: Situational Factors[a]

Drinker
  Drinking alone
  Drinking with others
    Relatives
    Acquaintances
    Strangers
  Drinking in presence of other drinkers
    Relatives
    Acquaintances
    Strangers
  Drinking in presence of nondrinkers
    Relatives
    Acquaintances
    Strangers

Role Relationships vis-à-vis Expected Aggressive Behavior
  Dominant relationships in which aggression is or is not expected from drinker
  Submissive relationships in which aggression is or is not expected from drinker
  Equal-power relationships in which aggression may be directed from or received
    by drinker

Mobility
  Drinker remains in drinking environment
  Drinker moves from drinking environment to another environment

Definition of Drinking Situation
  Drinking for escape or other desired effects
  Recreational/"time-out" drinking
  Religious/ceremonial drinking

Drinking Environment
  Home
  Private nonhome setting
  Tavern/bar
  Open space (e.g., park)

Weapons
  Absence of aggression-related weaponry (e.g., gun or knife)
  Drinker's or other's possession of aggression-related weaponry (e.g., gun or knife)
  Drinker's *and* other's possession of aggression-related weaponry (e.g., gun or
    knife)

Social Control
  Absence of labeling/social control factors
  Presence of labeling/social control factors

[a]Modified from Roman (1981, p. 150).

one social mechanism (cognitive social learning; Graham, 1980; Pernanen, 1981).[2]

Pharmacological Mechanisms

The first pharmacological mechanism involves the direct effect of alcohol as a sedative-hypnotic (see Chap. 1; see also the related discussion of substance-induced automatism, below). As a sedative-hypnotic, alcohol depresses the CNS, decreasing social inhibitions (it functions as a disinhibitor) and impairing cognitive processing (it affects problem solving and, hence, the ability to develop strategies to effectively deal with frustrating or threatening situations). For example, aggressive and sexual behavior, or thoughts about such behavior, that have been suppressed because of acquiescence to social norms or concern for associated consequences (e.g., adverse publicity, harm to self or others, or incarceration) are released from conscious control, making them more likely to be acted on (Pihl, Peterson, & Lau, 1993; Sayette, Wilson, & Elias, 1993; Zeichner, Allen, Giancola, & Lating, 1994). As noted by R. H. Blum (1981):

> Alcohol may alter perceptions, cognitive performance, moods/emotions, and response capabilities and preferences. Less adaptive solutions, such as violence, can occur with decrements in judgment. Violence may also be adaptive, or perceived as such. Meanings imposed on the environment may change. Violence variability may be a function of cues that are subliminal to the observer but are notably altered perceptions within the person. (pp. 115–116)

Obviously, this pharmacological mechanism would significantly interact with the personality of the user—assuming that two adolescents drank alcohol to the same level of intoxication, the disinhibitory effects would most likely result in an increased risk for violent behavior in the adolescent who had such a predisposition (e.g., an adolescent with CD or oppositional defiant disorder) in comparison to the adolescent who did not (Abram, 1989; Fishbein, Jaffe, Synder, Haertzen, & Hickey, 1993; M. Irwin, Schuckit, & Smith, 1990).

In addition, available data suggest that the effect of social inhibition is more pronounced for children and adolescents who have lower IQ scores. This notion was supported by Busch, Zagar, Hughes, Arbit, and Bussell (1990), who, in their study of "adolescents who kill," observed that their subjects had significantly higher levels of "alcohol abuse" and significantly "lowered full IQ scores" (mean of 80.4; p. 476). Conversely, as noted by Hodgins (1992), "Intellectual capacity is a factor that appears to protect otherwise high-risk boys [e.g., those with a "diagnosis of substance abuse/dependence"]

---

[2] These explanations provide assistance in regard to better understanding of the phenomenon. However, it is quite likely that various mechanisms may account for the relationship between alcohol use and violent crime and that, in specific instances, one mechanism may account for more of the data than another.

from criminal involvement" (p. 477). Both observations are consistent with the conclusion of Lau and Pihl (1994) "that acute alcohol intoxication interferes with the ability to integrate previously acquired knowledge in the formulation of behavioral strategies" (p. 701). These observations also are consistent with the more general notion that statelike psychometric variables (e.g., mood) are more readily influenced by substance use than are traitlike variables (e.g., IQ and personality; R. H. Blum, 1981).

The second suggested pharmacological mechanism involves an interaction between alcohol use and another variable that also is related to violent behavior. For example, assuming that level of frustration is positively related to violent behavior, there may be situations in which the level of frustration in a particular situation is insufficient to lead to violent behavior (the critical threshold has not been exceeded). Similarly, a situation could exist in which the level of alcohol use was insufficient to lead to violent behavior. However, if these two risk factors, level of frustration and alcohol use, are combined in a predisposed child or adolescent, then violent behavior is likely to occur because the threshold for such behavior is much more likely to be exceeded as a result of the interaction of these two variables.

For example, I.U., a 17-year-old Native American adolescent boy, was referred to us for a forensic pharmacopsychological assessment. He had been charged with beating his brother to death with a baseball bat after a night of partying, which included heavy alcohol and marijuana use. I.U. was the younger of two brothers and often had been slapped around by his older brother. He always took this abuse without saying or doing much about it. However, on this particular evening, after being slapped around and questioned about where the rest of the marijuana was, he calmly got up, went to his bedroom closet, got a baseball bat, returned, and began hitting his brother on the head (approximately 20 times) until his mother, who had been called by other boys who were at the party, came into the room and stopped him. Our subsequent analysis, based on police breathalyzer samples, indicated that I.U.'s blood alcohol concentration (BAC) at the time of the incident was approximately 210 mg%, or over twice the legal level of intoxication.[3] In response to a question regarding possible problems with controlling his temper, I.U. responded: "Whenever I'm not drinking, I'm not mad or anything. I don't lose my temper. It's only when I'm drinking" (A. M. Pagliaro & L. A. Pagliaro, 1992, clinical patient file notes).[4]

---

[3] No other forensic samples were obtained by the police at the time of the arrest; therefore, we were unable to determine I.U.'s THC blood level. There was no evidence that indicated the use of any other substances of abuse at the party (e.g., amphetamine, cocaine, or PCP).

[4] This case illustrates the difficulty noted earlier in this chapter in regard to determining the nature of the association between alcohol use and violent crime. In this case, alcohol use was obviously related to the violent crime (at least in a temporal sense). However, the nature of the relationship can be explained in several ways. For example: the alcohol directly induced the

Another proposed variant of this second suggested mechanism involves the interaction between alcohol and endogenous hormones or neurotransmitters and their functions. For example, B. Bergman and Brismar (1994), in a study of "abusive and suicidal male alcoholics" reported that "the violent subgroup . . . had elevated levels of serum testosterone and low levels of cortisol when compared with the rest of the sample" (p. 311). In an earlier related study, Buydens-Branchey and Branchey (1992) found the opposite (*increased* cortisol levels in violent male alcoholics), but a similar underlying mechanism: "that individuals displaying severe forms of violence could have a dysregulated HPA [hypothalamus-pituitary-adrenal] axis function revealed by exposure to excessive amounts of alcohol" (p. 45). Other researchers (e.g., Coccaro, Silverman, Klar, Horvath, & Siever, 1994; Linnoila & Virkkunen, 1992) have noted a central serotonergic (5-hydroxytryptamine) deficit among male alcoholics with "a tendency to exhibit impulsive violent behavior under the influence of alcohol" (Virkkunen & Linnoila, 1993, p. 163). While the available evidence in support of these theories is insufficient, they do demonstrate a possible interaction involving alcohol use, neuroendocrine function, and violent crime.

Social Mechanism

The third mechanism, the social mechanism, involves intervening psychological and sociological variables, including cognitive social learning variables (e.g., expectations; see Chap. 2 for additional related explanation and discussion). When drinking alcohol, children and adolescents anticipate certain effects from the alcohol and behave in a manner that they have learned is expected of them (George & Dermen, 1988; Lindman & Lang, 1994). For example, if men drink to feel more "strong," "manly," or "powerful," and if the social role expectation of being strong, manly, or powerful is to be more aggressive, then adolescents, particularly boys, will be more likely, when drinking, to act in accordance with this expectation (Aramburu & Leigh, 1991; Dermen & George, 1989).[5] This relationship was described by MacAn-

---

violent behavior by means of neuroendocrine effects (e.g., elevation of serum testosterone); or the alcohol interacted with I.U.'s level of frustration (or anger) causing the violent behavior; or the alcohol interacted with an underlying personality disorder contributing to the behavior (see discussion later in chapter); or the alcohol use in the context of a unique set of situational (social) variables caused the violent physical assault. Obviously, determining the nature of the relationship between alcohol use and violent crime remains difficult.

[5] This phenomenon appears also to help explain the use of high doses of PCP (angel dust or hog) by some Hispanic adolescent gang members. When questioned about why they use a substance of abuse well known for its unpredictable and frequently violent effects on behavior, they respond because it is "macho" (a manly activity that demonstrates courage; A. M. Pagliaro & L. A. Pagliaro, 1990, clinical patient file notes). Of course, other possible explanations and factors (e.g., disinhibition, risk-taking behavior, adolescent feeling of unique invulnerability, and peer influence) could also be involved.

drew and Edgerton (1969) in their cross-cultural ethnographic study of drinking behavior that rejected the disinhibition theory of drunken comportment and advanced the "time-out hypothesis."

As noted by Labouvie and McGee (1986), "Alcohol and drug use may be adopted because it facilitates the overt expression of otherwise latent or covert needs" (p. 292). In this context, the associated drunkenness may be an "excuse" for sexual promiscuity or aggressive behavior. "Alcohol/drugs seem to set the stage for aggressive sexual behavior by reducing the perpetrator's inhibitions and providing an 'excuse' for the abuse" (Milgram, 1993, p. 58). Accordingly, as the Roman philosopher Seneca (5 B.C.–65 A.D.) wrote, "drunkenness is nothing but a form of insanity deliberately assumed." This mechanism of alcohol-related violent crime appears to be particularly common and relevant in relation to gang activity (see the discussion of commerce-related crime, below). However, regardless of the mechanism involved, it is clear that, at least for some children and adolescents, alcohol use is a significant antecedent for involvement in violent crime, including physical assault, sexual assault, and homicide (J. J. Collins, 1981; Joffe, 1988). This relationship between alcohol use and violent crime appears to be particularly significant for children and adolescents who have a positive past history of violent behavior (Pincus & Lewis, 1991).

Alcohol Use, Violent Crime, and Antisocial Personality Disorder

It is worse to be sick in soul than in body, for those afflicted in body only suffer, but those afflicted in soul both suffer and do ill.

Plutarch, *Afflictions of Soul and Body*

Diagnostic criteria for antisocial personality disorder include "aggressiveness," "deceitfulness," "impulsivity," "irresponsibility," "lack of remorse," "repeated arrests," and "repeated physical fights." As noted by the American Psychiatric Association (1994), "The essential feature of Antisocial Personality Disorder is a pervasive pattern of disregard for, and violation of, the rights of others that begins in childhood or early adolescence and continues into adulthood" (p. 645). According to DSM-IV criteria, children and adolescents prior to 15 years of age also must display signs and symptoms of this disorder and have a previous diagnosis of CD (American Psychiatric Association, 1994). Given the nature of antisocial personality disorder, it is not surprising that researchers have identified strong positive relationships among this disorder, alcohol use, and violent crime (Abram, 1989; M. Irwin et al., 1990; Penick et al., 1984; H. E. Ross, Glaser, & Germanson, 1988). As reported by Abram (1989):

> This study suggests that pure alcoholics have a lower likelihood of criminal recidivism than alcoholics with an accompanying drug or antisocial disorder.

Moreover, pure drug users, or even alcoholic drug users have a lower likelihood of committing a violent crime than their antisocial counterparts. (p. 144)

Such violent crime also may be perpetrated against family members: "Particularly high rates of violence are found in those [families] where alcoholism is combined with antisocial personality disorder" (Bland & Orn, 1986, p. 129). In this context "parents also are frequently victims of violence at the hands of their adolescents" (Pelletier & Coutu, 1992, p. 6).

Alcohol Use, Violent Crime, and Conduct Disorder

CD is one of the most prevalent mental diagnoses among children. The incidence of this disorder has been increasing over the last three decades and currently may be as high as one out of every seven or eight children. The incidence among boys is approximately double the incidence among girls and is correlated with having "substance abusing parents" (Gabel & Shindledecker, 1992). "The essential feature of Conduct Disorder is a repetitive and persistent pattern of behavior in which the basic rights of others or major age-appropriate societal norms or rules are violated" (American Psychiatric Association, 1994, p. 85). Van Kammen et al. (1991) noted that substance use (e.g., alcohol, glue, marijuana, or tobacco) by first-, fourth-, and seventh-graders was strongly correlated with behavior consistent with the diagnostic criteria for CD, including "physical aggression towards people," "cruelty to animals," "destruction of property," "theft," "truancy," and "running away from home."

CD among children and adolescents, both girls and boys, typically has been found to predict antisocial personality and problematic patterns of substance use in adult life (Hodgins, 1992; Robins & Price, 1991). The definitive signs and symptoms associated with this disorder generally occur by 8 years of age (American Psychiatric Association, 1994; Lavin & Rifkin, 1993)[6] and, as recorded by Gore (1991), are reflected in the comments of an 8-year-old homeless boy:

When our baby die we start to sit by the window. We just sit and sit all wrapped up quiet in old shirts an' watch pigeons. That pigeon she fly so fast. She move nice. A real pretty flier. She open her mouth and take in the wind. We just spread out crumbs, me and my [4-year-old] brother. And we wait. Sit and wait, there under the window sill. She don't even see us till we slam down the window. And she break. She look with one eye. She don't die right away. We dip her in, over and over, in the water pot we boils on the hot plate. We wanna see how it be to die slow like our baby die. (p. 95)

---

[6] CD has a high coincidence with ADHD. "Children who have both disorders [CD and ADHD] appear to have a particularly severe form of ADHD" (Lavin & Rifkin, 1993, p. 878; for a discussion of ADHD, see Chap. 7).

TABLE 9.3   Types of Substance-Related Crime[a]

Commerce-Related Crime
  Crimes related to drug trafficking
    Production, distribution, sale, purchase, and possession
    Corruption of law enforcement and political officials
  Crimes related to maintaining substance use
    Possession and use
    Drug trafficking, prostitution, and robbery to obtain money to purchase the
      substance(s) of abuse
Pharmacopsychology-Related Crime
  Crimes related to substance intoxication
    Driving while intoxicated, homicide, physical assault, sexual assault, and
      vehicular and other manslaughter
  Substance-induced automatism
    Homicide, physical assault, sexual assault, and manslaughter

[a]Note that there is some overlap between categories, depending on who is committing the crime and his or her reason for doing so.

SUBSTANCE USE AND COMMERCE- AND PHARMACOPSYCHOLOGY-RELATED CRIME

Crimes related to substance use can be broadly divided into two groups: those related to commerce and those related to the pharmacopsychological effect(s) of the involved substance of abuse (see Table 9.3). Except for those crimes related to the pharmacopsychological effects of specific substances of abuse, which are predominantly of a violent nature, most substance-related crime is nonviolent (Hoffman & Goldfrank, 1990).[7]

Commerce-Related Crime

Most commerce-related crime is accounted for by drug trafficking. Drug trafficking includes the various activities associated with the production, distribution, sale, purchase, and possession of illicit substances of abuse. Each of these activities is a criminal offense that can be perpetrated by a child or adolescent commonly by their association with, and membership in, gangs.

[7]Although a comprehensive discussion of drug legalization is beyond the scope of this chapter, a general perusal of Table 9.3 would suggest that, while most substance-related crime could be eliminated by drug legalization, violent crime, which is related to the intrinsic pharmacopsychological effects of selected substances of abuse, would likely increase (see discussion of alcohol use and violent crime, above).

Before proceeding, we would like to note that the entire issue of drug legalization is obviously quite complex and involves many factors (e.g., the potential generation of considerable additional tax revenues for governments in desperate need of such revenues). However, with an appreciation of the complexity of this issue and having carefully considered the arguments in favor and against, we do *not* currently favor drug legalization.

This striking array of changes in juvenile crime since 1985—a doubling of the homicide rate, a doubling of the number of homicides committed with guns, and a doubling of the arrest rate of nonwhites for drug offenses, all after a period of relative stability in these rates—cries out for an explanation that will link them all together. The explanation that seems most reasonable can be traced to the rapid growth of the crack markets in the mid-1980s. To service that growth, juveniles were recruited, they were armed with guns that are standard tools of the drug trade, and these guns then were diffused into the larger community of juveniles. (Blumstein, 1995)

Drug trafficking also occurs on a large, international scale, which, to be successful, requires the corruption of law enforcement and political officials. This aspect of drug trafficking almost exclusively involves adults and, thus, will not be discussed in this text.

Gangs

Gangs in North America are formed predominantly on the basis of race and ethnic origin (see Table 9.4; C. Johnson, Webster, & Connors, 1995). Approximately 90 percent of the estimated one-quarter million current gang members are black or Hispanic (see Fig. 9.2), and most are adolescent boys (less than 5 percent of gang members are girls; Curry, Ball, & Fox, 1994). Many of these gang members, particularly those of Hispanic heritage, are second or third (sometimes fourth) generation gang members (their fathers and grandfathers belonged to the same barrio gang). However, children and adolescents join gangs, not primarily because their fathers or grandfathers were members, but because of inadequate parental attention and emotional support (Hardy, 1995; Washburn, 1994). The average age for formally joining a gang is 14 years of age ("Drugs," 1994). Peer pressure is also a major factor in fostering gang membership and, once a child or adolescent has joined a gang, becomes the predominant social mediating influence on subsequent behavior, including substance use and the perpetration of crime (Maki, 1995; D. Miller, 1986; Watts & Wright, 1990a).

Gangs have become a major social problem in communities nationwide. In Los Angeles alone, estimates of 25,000 gang members and nearly 700 gang-related homicides were tallied during one recent year. San Diego County figures indicated more than 100 gangs and more than 8,000 gang members, spanning most every ethnic group. . . . A surprising large number of violent crimes are committed by a comparatively small number of hard-core gang members. (Maki, 1995, p. 30)

Extreme violence, which often involves drug trafficking, has become an integral element of the gang subculture (C. Johnson et al., 1995, p. 3). As can be seen in Table 9.4, violent crime and drug trafficking are common behaviors among gang members (Fagan, 1990). In 1992 alone, gangs were responsible for over 1,000 homicides in North America (Curry et al., 1994). Although

TABLE 9.4 Percentages of Gangs Involved in Substance Use, Violent Crime, and Drug Trafficking, by Type of Gang[a]

Type of Gang[b]	Substance Use	Violent Crime	Drug Trafficking
Locally based, black[c]	98 cocaine 24 heroin 60 marijuana 12 other	88	88
Motorcycle[d]	67 cocaine 22 heroin 65 marijuana 60 other	65	88
Hispanic[e] (Latino, Mexican)	86 cocaine 40 heroin 79 marijuana 22 other	90	84
White Supremacy[f]	55 cocaine 8 heroin 63 marijuana 24 other	66	20
Asian[g] (Hong Kong, Thai, Vietnamese)	78 cocaine 57 heroin 16 marijuana 20 other	91	43
Los Angeles based, black[h]	99 cocaine 17 heroin 53 marijuana 17 other	83	94
Caribbean origin, black[i] (Dominican Republic, Jamaica)	98 cocaine 15 heroin 38 marijuana 19 other	73	100

[a]Modified from C. Johnson et al. (1995, p. 4).

[b]Arranged in descending order of prevalence in relation to North American membership and distribution (i.e., number of cities).

Although not yet widely recognized, or large enough in percentage terms to be included separately in this table, other ethnic/racial gangs are beginning to be formed and involved in violent crime and drug trafficking on both local and national levels (e.g., East Indian gangs such as the Brown Nation and Native American gangs such as the Indian Posse [IP]).

[c]E.g., Black Disciples, Black Dragons, Black Gorilla Family (BGF), Colors, and Niggers in Action (NIA).

[d]E.g., Devil's Disciples, Hell's Angels, Grim Reapers, Outlaws, Rebels, Rocker's, and Rock Machine.

[e]E.g., 43rd Avenue, 57th Street, Latin Kings, and Miami Boys.

[f]E.g., Aryan Nation, Chosen Ones, and Ku Klux Klan (KKK).

[g]E.g., 14K, Big Circle Gang (BCG), Flying Dragons, Sun Yee On, and Wo Group.

[h]E.g., Bloods, Crips, and Grape Street.

[i]E.g., Jamaican posses such as Montego Bay, Power House Posse, Shower, Spanish Town, and Tivoli Gardens.

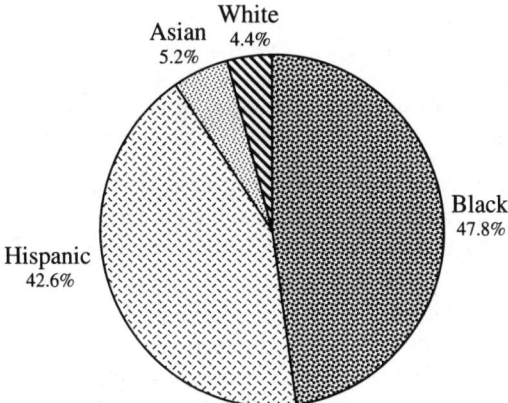

FIGURE 9.2   Gang membership in the United States by race, 1991
Note: Data from Curry, Ball, and Fox (1994, p. 9).

several types of illicit substances of abuse (e.g., cocaine, heroin, marijuana, methamphetamine, and PCP) have been and continue to be sold by gangs, cocaine in its crack form is currently the substance of abuse most widely involved in this form of trafficking. While not confined to gangs or engaged in by all gangs (Klein & Maxson, 1994), commerce in crack cocaine—its manufacture, sale, and distribution—is frequently associated with violent crime (Inciardi, 1990; Inciardi & Pottieger, 1991; Rhodes & Fischer, 1993).

Although the purported relationship between crack cocaine and violent crime receives much supporting evidence from general observation (e.g., T. Fennell, Ajello, & Howse, 1994; Morganthau et al., 1988) and research investigation (e.g., Inciardi, 1990; G. K. Weisman, 1993), some researchers (e.g., Klein & Maxson, 1994; Meehan & O'Carroll, 1992) question the legitimacy of the relationship. The concerns of the latter may largely be due to semantics. For example, C. R. Block and Block (1993), in a study of street gang crime in Chicago, "found that the city's four largest street gangs were identified with most of the street gang crime and that most of the violence and homicides were related to battles over 'turf' rather than drugs" (p. 1). However, turf is integrally related to a gang's commerce in illicit substances of abuse (whoever controls the turf also controls drug sales and other gang-related crimes, such as extortion and robbery). As noted by one sheriff in the 1994 National Institute of Justice survey (McEwen, 1995), "Most of the violent crimes are gang-related. . . . Most of the gang problems are over drug selling territories" (p. 1).

Not all gang-related violence associated with substances of abuse involves specifically drug trafficking. As reported by Inciardi (1990), a significant amount of violence involves crack cocaine use by individual gang members:

It doesn't seem to matter whether you're on or off crack . . . you're crazy both times. If you're high, you think someone's goin' ta do something to you, or try an' take your stuff. If you're comin' down or are waiting to make a buy or just get off, you seem to get upset easy. . . . A lot of people been cut just because somebody looked at them funny or said somethin' stupid. (pp. 98–99)

Although gangs are heavily involved in drug trafficking, the "typical," or most common, drug trafficker is not a gang member nor a member of a drug cartel. The typical drug trafficker is an adolescent involved in substance use, who deals not so much to make large amounts of money, but to maintain his or her own habit. A common example might be a 17-year-old high school student who is not involved in any additional serious crime or delinquent behavior, but sells marijuana in order to make enough profit to pay for his or her own marijuana use (R. G. Smart, Adlaf, & Walsh, 1992). These drug traffickers usually deal with relatively small quantities of substances of abuse (e.g., an ounce of marijuana, which is divided for sale into quarter-ounce bags, or a gram of cocaine, which is divided into several "lines").[8]

In this regard, drug trafficking is generally related to the need to generate income and can be expected to occur more frequently among adolescents who have an income insufficient to maintain their substance use; a more serious pattern of substance use (e.g., compulsive use) and, hence, a need for more money to maintain it; previous experience with crime as an income producer; and other tendencies toward antisocial behavior (Dembo, Williams, Wish, et al., 1990; Dembo, Williams, Wothke, et al., 1990; R. G. Smart et al., 1992). As Hunt (1991) observed:

Even among cocaine users who commit no other crime, dealing small amounts of cocaine is common. Frequent users deal as a way of obtaining consistent supplies, larger quantities, or quantities at a reduced price. Even occasional users may buy more than they need and sell or share a portion with other using friends as a way to defray costs or "treat" others. The frequent user may also

---

[8] By definition, every child and adolescent who has used an illicit substance of abuse has committed a crime (simple possession) and most (e.g., a teenager who gives a joint of marijuana to a schoolfriend) have committed several crimes (possession for the purpose of drug trafficking and drug trafficking). These crimes, although of relevance to the literature on delinquent behavior, are not part of the primary focus of this chapter. While some delinquent behavior is addressed in this chapter, delinquency per se is not. As noted by Fagan (1990): "Few adolescent substance users, however, are involved in serious delinquency. Because the drugs-delinquency relationship is skewed, knowledge of drug use is better predicted by delinquency than knowledge of delinquency is predicted by drug use" (p. 218). Most of what can be considered delinquent behavior by children and adolescents can also be considered as symptoms of CD (see earlier discussion). For additional discussion of the nature of the relationship between substance use by children and adolescents and delinquent behavior, see Dembo, Williams, Getreu, et al. (1991), Dembo, Williams, Wish, et al. (1990), Dembo, Williams, Wothke, et al. (1990), Dembo, Williams, Schmeidler et al. (1991), Fagan (1990), Fagan, Weis, and Cheng (1990), Huizinga et al. (1993), B. D. Johnson, Wish, Schmeidler, and Huizinga (1991), and Watts and Wright (1990a, 1990b).

find dealing cocaine the only way to maintain an adequate supply affordably. (p. 145)

Other crimes related to maintaining particular patterns of substance use primarily include prostitution and robbery.

Prostitution

Prostitution has long been a readily available means for people, including children and adolescents, to support their drug habits (A. M. Pagliaro et al., 1993). Most of these prostitutes work from street corners or parks. However, an increasing trend, concurrent with the increasing spread of crack cocaine, has been the direct exchange of sex for crack (Ratner, 1993; Rolfs et al., 1990; Schwarcz et al., 1992). As noted by M. F. Goldsmith (1988): "Organized prostitution is no longer necessary; the exchange is more direct" (p. 2009). This exchange occurs more formally in crack houses, many of which have special rooms or areas set aside specifically for these exchanges and their own live-in "crack whores." As noted by Inciardi (1993) in an ethnographic study of the sex-for-crack exchange phenomenon in Miami:

> Upon entering a room in the rear of the crack house (what I later learned was called a freak room), I observed what appeared to be the gang-rape of an unconscious child. Emaciated, seemingly comatose, and likely no older than 14 years of age, she was lying spread-eagled on a filthy mattress while four men in succession had vaginal intercourse with her. After they had finished and left the room, however, it became readily clear that it had not been forcible rape at all. She opened her eyes and looked about to see if anyone was waiting. When she realized that our purpose there was not for sex, she wiped her groin with a ragged beach towel, covered herself with half of a tattered sheet affecting a somewhat peculiar sense of modesty, and rolled over in an attempt to sleep. Almost immediately, however, she was disturbed by the door man, who brought a customer to her for oral sex. He just walked up to her with an erect penis in his hand, said nothing to her, and she proceeded to oblige him.
>
> Upon leaving the crack house a few minutes later, the dealer/informant explained that she was a house girl, a person in the employ of the crack house owner. He gave her food, a place to sleep, and all the crack she wanted in return for her providing sex—any type and amount of sex—to his crack house customers. (pp. 39–40)

Exchanging sex for crack occurs much more frequently among adolescents in a less formal manner. In these cases adolescent girls and boys typically choose their "dates," not because of good looks, a fancy car, love, or other characteristic reasons, but because the date, who could be of the same or opposite gender, has cocaine and is willing to "share it." In most of these cases, the terms of the barter are not formally stated, but are socially understood.

Robbery

Robbery, including theft and burglary, is another common method used by adolescents, particularly boys, to obtain the funds necessary to support their illicit substance use (Mott, 1986).

Pharmacopsychology-Related Crime

Pharmacopsychology-related crime is crime that is directly related to the effects of the substances of abuse on those parts of the brain (amygdala, hippocampus, and related structures of the limbic system) associated with human cognition, learning and memory, and emotion. Pharmacopsychology-related crimes are crimes related, directly or indirectly, to intoxication by the substances of abuse. As noted earlier in this chapter, the use of some substances of abuse (e.g., alcohol) has been demonstrated to be closely associated with criminal behavior, particularly violent crimes, such as homicide (Spunt et al., 1994; Zagar, Arbit, Sylvies, Busch, & Hughes, 1990), physical assault (Pelletier & Coutu, 1992), sexual assault (Lightfoot & Barbaree, 1993; Vinogradov, Dishotsky, Doty, & Tinklenberg, 1988), and vehicular manslaughter.[9] This section will briefly discuss some possible mechanisms underlying these phenomena, particularly substance-induced automatism.

Substance-Induced Automatism

The relationship between automatism and violent crime was popularly characterized in 1886 by Robert Louis Stevenson's *The Strange Case of Dr. Jekyll and Mr. Hyde:*

> It was the curse of mankind that these incongruous fagots were thus bound together—that in the agonized womb of consciousness, these polar twins would be continuously struggling. How, then, were they dissociated? . . . I declare, at least, before God, no man morally sane could have been guilty of that crime upon so pitiful a provocation, and that I struck in no more reasonable spirit than that in which a sick child may break a plaything.

Several closely related definitions can be found for the term *automatism* (Beran, 1992; D'Orban, 1989; Fenwick, 1990). The one that we find to be the most useful and clear is the definition provided by *Taber's Cyclopedic Medical Dictionary* (Thomas, 1993):

> Automatic actions or behavior without conscious volition or knowledge. The subject, though (generally) amnesic, appears normal to an observer, but the real personality is latent during a secondary state or period of automatism. . . .

---

[9] Driving while intoxicated, or, as it also is known, driving under the influence, and its related sequelae in terms of morbidity and mortality are discussed in Chap. 8.

Such patients are not responsible for their acts and must not be left alone. They may carry out complicated acts without remembering having done so. (p. 180)

Automatism has been associated with several physical (e.g., diabetes mellitus and epilepsy) and psychological (e.g., post-traumatic-stress disorder and severe psychological blow) conditions (Bisson, 1993; Febbo, Hardy, & Finlay-Jones, 1993–94; Hindler, 1989; Treiman, 1986; van Rensburg, Gagiano, & Verschoor, 1994). Somnambulism, or sleepwalking, may be considered to be one of the most common and well known forms of automatism (Beran, 1992; Fenwick, 1987). However, the characterization of automatism and explanations of its possible mechanism of action in relation to the commission of violent crimes have been most studied in the context of epilepsy. As noted by van Rensburg et al. (1994):

Ictal aspects include the specific part of the brain from which the seizure originates, the loss of integration of incoming sensorial stimuli with motor-emotional output, the loss of higher control associated with a reversion to primitive automatic behaviour and the emergence of repressed feelings and aggressive instincts. Post-ictal violent behaviour may stem from the epileptic's misinterpretation of well-meant attempts by bystanders to protect him or her against the consequences of his or her confused conduct—and is usually characterized by a clouded consciousness, paranoid ideas and hallucinations. (p. 373)

Drug-induced automatism is, as the name implies, a condition of automatism that occurs as a direct result of the pharmacological action of a drug. Several types and classifications of drugs can cause drug-induced automatism. These include substances of abuse (e.g., alcohol, barbiturates, benzodiazepines, and cocaine), nonabusable substances (e.g., clomipramine [Anafranil] and fluoxetine [Prozac]), and several other diverse groups of drugs, for example anabolic steroids (e.g., oxandrolone), several antineoplastics (e.g., chlorambucil [Leukeran]), cimetidine (Tagamet), and the corticosteroids (e.g., prednisone; L. A. Pagliaro & Foster, 1990). The likelihood of occurrence and the potential severity of drug-induced automatism tends to increase directly in relation to both the dosage and the number of drugs used that are capable of producing automatism.

Previously, the term has been used, most notably and generally inappropriately, to narrowly refer to automatic, nondeliberate (i.e., accidental) behavior associated with fatal barbiturate overdosing. However, drug-induced automatism is not limited to, and generally does not even concern, this type of situation. In the current context, it refers to any nonreflexive, directed, and apparently purposive motor behavior that is performed without full consciousness of what is being done and is followed by grossly incomplete recollection or insight.

Although probably occurring fairly commonly, drug-induced automatism is frequently overlooked by both clinical psychologists and psychiatrists, who are generally neither aware of, nor alert to, this real drug-induced psychological effect. Further contributing to overlooked diagnoses of drug-induced automatism is the fact that the affected person may engage in complicated acts and appear, for all practical intents and purposes, normal to the observer.

Clinical features that should alert astute clinicians to the potential for drug-induced automatism include: 1. lack of apparent motive for a particular behavior in an otherwise normal person (i.e., a nonpsychotic, nonsociopathic person, with normal intelligence), 2. total or partial amnesia of the event, and 3. consumption of a sufficient amount of one, or more, drugs that are capable of causing automatism. In addition, a higher incidence of drug-induced automatism may be noted among people who have a past history of epilepsy, personality disorders, post-traumatic-stress disorder, psychoses, sleep disorders, or severe head trauma (L. A. Pagliaro, 1992a, 1995a; L. A. Pagliaro & Pagliaro, 1991).[10]

Perhaps the concept of drug-induced automatism in the context of violent crime can best be illustrated by examples from two cases for which we performed forensic pharmacopsychological evaluations and provided expert testimony.[11]

Case 1.   A.L. had been away on a 2-day hunting trip with friends that had turned into a drinking trip. A.L. "ran into an old friend that I hadn't seen for four or five years. He suggested that we have a couple drinks . . . and that was it." During this 2-day trip, A.L. consumed a significant amount of alcohol. On returning home, he went to his neighbors' home where his wife was visiting and proceeded to verbally and physically assault her. The neighbors tried without success to calm him down and, fearing for his wife's and their own personal safety,[12] called the police. Although his wife refused to press charges, he was arrested and charged with assault causing bodily harm and uttering a threat.

---

[10] Alcohol-related automatism also has been referred to legally as "extreme drunkenness" (L. A. Pagliaro, 1995a) or "pathologic intoxication" (Lange, 1987). As noted by Pincus and Lewis (1991):

> Pathologic intoxication is not associated with slurred speech or incoordination and may last for only a few minutes. It usually occurs when alcohol is imbibed under circumstances "conducive" to violence, that is, at a bar or a party, and it has been difficult to reproduce this state of intoxication by administering alcohol in a laboratory setting. Those who become pathologically intoxicated are usually heavy drinkers. The condition may be more common in criminals. In a sense, it is an alcoholic "blackout" during which violence is committed. (p. 148)

[11] These two cases involve adults but illustrate relevant early childhood and adolescent experiences while serving as examples of this phenomenon.

[12] A.L. is a large (6 foot tall, 250 pound) athletic man, and during the violent episode, he broke one of the neighbors' chairs and their dinette table.

Assessment of A.L. revealed a 41-year-old married male Caucasian of normal, average intelligence with a mental status within normal limits. He was fully cooperative and at no time during the assessment displayed or suggested any psychotic symptoms or ideation. Initial diagnoses of active psychological problems or mental disorders included: 1. alcoholism, 2. adult child of an alcoholic, 3. low self-esteem, 4. panic disorder with agoraphobia, 5. anxiety disorder, and 6. severe childhood neglect.

A.L.'s family history was positive for alcoholism involving both parents. His mother was committed to a mental psychiatric facility at age 36 years, reportedly due to alcohol-induced dementia. His father died at 51 years of age, reportedly due to alcoholic cirrhosis. His only sibling, a brother, also had a positive history of alcoholism. There was no recollected history of physical or sexual abuse. However, as might be expected in a rural alcoholic family, there was a severe history of childhood neglect:

> I was born and raised in an alcoholic family out in the sticks. . . . We had no heat in the house, no food, but we always had 2 gallons of St. George's wine to get up and have at breakfast. . . . My brother and I often would have to go to the neighbors for food.

There was also a history of alcohol-related family violence between his parents:

> My mother and father would always be fighting when they were drunk and then make up. . . . Sometimes my father would be so drunk and stumbling around and she would hit him on the head with a cast-iron frying pan and knock him out. She would grab his arms and I would grab his legs and we'd lift him on the couch where he'd sleep it off until he sobered up.

Psychometric assessment failed to detect a violent or antisocial personality, and A.L. did not fit the profile of a perpetrator of spousal abuse. These findings were consistent with his previous police record (no previous violence-related charges) and family history (his wife noted that this incident was the only time in 10 years of marriage that A.L. had assaulted her and that he had never assaulted any of their six children).[13]

During the day and a half immediately preceding the reported incident of assault causing bodily harm and uttering a threat, A.L. had consumed a significant amount of alcohol, which conservatively calculated would yield a BAC in excess of 550 mg% (over 5 times the legal level of intoxication and equivalent to an amount that would cause death in the overwhelming majority of adult males).

As we testified in court, this level of blood alcohol would render all indi-

---

[13] In addition, testimony of several friends and acquaintances, at the preliminary inquiry and trial, consistently indicated that this incident of violent behavior was completely out of character for A.L.

viduals incapable of any higher-level cognitive processing (e.g., problem solving and integration and synthesis of data), including the ability to form intent. At this level of intoxication, all individuals would be in a condition of drug-induced automatism in which they may appear normal to the casual observer, but in which their usual personalities are latent. These individuals may carry out complicated actions, generally without remembering having done so. In this case, we felt that it was quite likely that A.L. was, under this state of extreme intoxication, reliving (acting out) the social interaction (fights) between his mother and his father that he had witnessed innumerable times as a child and adolescent.

Drug-induced automatism appeared to be particularly probable in this case because A.L. was using other drugs, which were prescribed for him by his physician (clomipramine [Anafranil] and lorazepam [Ativan], according to his physician's direction), either of which alone also is capable of causing aggression and drug-induced automatism (Alarcon, Johnson, & Lucas, 1992; J. D. Little & Taghavi, 1989; L. Meyer, Wiklund, & Lidberg, 1991).

Following a lengthy trial, A.L. was acquitted of all charges on the basis of "extreme drunkenness" (Chisholm, 1994).[14]

---

[14] Before proceeding, we would like to address two questions that are frequently posed to expert forensic witnesses: 1. Should psychologists be involved in court cases assisting "guilty" people to escape punishment? 2. Is this ethical?

Provision of expert testimony by psychologists is a well-recognized and valuable service to society that is an integral part of forensic psychology. Psychologists have been involved in providing expert testimony for about as long as the profession and the courts have existed. The rationale for this activity goes back to the roots of current American and Canadian laws (i.e., both Roman law and English common law) and is based on the assumption of free will and the related capacity of people to make choices. Thus, in addition to a guilty, or answerable, act (*actus reus*), a person also requires a guilty, or answerable, mind (*mens rea*) in order to fulfill the requirement for criminal culpability under existing laws.

Expert witnesses should be knowledgeable and in good professional standing with their relevant professional psychological associations; avoid possible conflicts of interest and dual relationships; be aware of and consciously attempt to minimize any biases or value components in their deliberations and conclusions; provide reasonable and probable conclusions that are based on a thorough and complete evaluation of all available related data; and provide a comprehensive, objective, and honest presentation of data. Psychologists, as expert witnesses, do not determine whether a person charged with a particular crime is guilty or not guilty. This function is left to the hearer of facts (the trial judge or jury). Thus, psychologists who are functioning as expert witnesses in court-related proceedings should be concerned not with "getting someone off" or "getting someone convicted," but rather with providing to the courts sound scientific testimony that will facilitate the work of the hearer of facts to correctly determine whether in a specific case and under specific circumstances the accused is guilty or not guilty (L. A. Pagliaro, 1995a).

Psychologists, as well as psychiatrists, are, by the very nature of their education and training, those professionals who are best qualified to provide the courts with expert knowledge and opinion regarding such psychological factors as personality, human motivation, cognitive function, memory, ability to form intent, and propensity for recidivism, which are absolutely essen-

Case 2. E.U. and a group of others, including R. (the victim) had been involved for a period of time in such criminal activities as trafficking in cocaine, breaking and entering, and armed robbery. As appears to be typical for most dealers, E.U. and R. eventually started to use significant amounts of cocaine themselves. E.U. had recently been involved in an argument with R. over their coke dealing and girlfriends. R.'s ex-girlfriend went to E.U.'s apartment with her new boyfriend for protection from R. They were afraid that R. was "going to get some bikers and have us killed." The ex-girlfriend and her new boyfriend were also afraid to go to R.'s apartment to retrieve her belongings before leaving town. E.U. offered to assist them in regard to retrieving the belongings. However, during this time, and for half a day previously, E.U. and his associates were using large amounts of cocaine intravenously, which they were supplementing with cocaine freebase. E.U. got his 357 magnum revolver "for protection since R.'s a big violent guy" and drove with the others to R.'s apartment. During the drive, E.U. and the others felt sure that they were being followed.

On entering the apartment, they found several acquaintances, including R., who was in the bathroom fixing cocaine with a young woman. As R. turned to see who was there, M. (an acquaintance of E.U. who accompanied him to the apartment for protection) yelled out, "That's it, he's got a gun!" and jumped out of the way. E.U. started shooting and hit R. several times, fatally wounding him. E.U. then entered the bathroom and shot R. once again and then attempted to shoot the woman who had been fixing cocaine with him in the bathroom. Pointing the gun at the woman, he pulled the trigger twice, but the gun was empty. E.U. and M. then left the apartment. They were arrested several days later. Both E.U. and M. were charged with first-degree murder. E.U. was also charged with attempted murder.

A pharmacopsychological assessment of E.U. revealed a 27-year-old male Caucasian of normal, above-average intelligence with a mental status within normal limits (he was fully cooperative, and at no time during the assessment did he display or suggest any psychotic symptoms or ideation). Initial diagnoses of active psychological problems or mental disorders included: 1. alcoholism, 2. compulsive use of cocaine, 3. compulsive use of opiates, 4. CD, and 5. antisocial personality disorder. Family history was negative for alcoholism and other major mental disorders. His parents were divorced when E.U. was 17 years old. He maintains a positive relationship with both parents but is closer to his mother. E.U. has no recollected history of either physical or sexual abuse. A younger brother has none of E.U.'s antisocial or substance use characteristics.

---

tial in order for the courts to render a fair and just verdict. In consideration of these factors, citizens facing trial might well ask if it would be ethical for psychologists to deny their expertise to the courts and the societies that they serve.

E.U.'s history for CD and antisocial behavior was positive. He started using substances of abuse when he was 10 years old, including glue, marijuana, and tobacco. This was also the age at which he was first arrested on charges of breaking and entering and vandalism. Although he has since used virtually all of the various substances of abuse, his preferred drug is heroin "because it's the most pleasurable trip." He also periodically binges on cocaine ("¹/₈ to ¹/₄ gram [intravenously] every 20 to 30 minutes for at least one day"). Since first being placed in a youth detention center when he was in sixth grade, E.U. has done time at over a dozen different youth detention centers and jails for a variety of mostly drug-related nonviolent crimes. He has served a total of approximately 7 years in closed custody during which time he was charged with over 30 "institutional charges," including two that were violence related. However, E.U. has never had a history of violent behavior in the community. These observations from his police and institutional records were consistent with our psychometric assessment that revealed a low ranking (within the normal range for the general population) in measures of anger and aggression. E.U. appeared to have a strong external locus of control. From an early age he interacted, almost exclusively, with peers involved in the drug trade as users or dealers. This peer group from childhood through adolescence to adulthood apparently served as his principal means of support and self-validation (as a drug dealer and as an "enforcer").

Our testimony at trial focused on the adverse effects of cocaine, including irrational thought, facilitation of aggressive behavior, and paranoia. The probability of cocaine-induced paranoid psychosis, given the amount of cocaine ingested, and the support provided by the available physical and psychological evidence, including eyewitness reports, were presented for this forensic diagnosis.[15]

On the basis of our evidence presented at trial, M. was acquitted of all charges. In addition, the charge of murder against E.U. was dismissed, but he was found guilty of the lesser offense of manslaughter. He was found not guilty of attempted murder because "doubt prevails as to his ability to form such intent."

---

[15] Paranoid psychosis is frequently involved in cases of drug-induced automatism during which a violent crime has been committed (Manschreck et al., 1990; Osran & Weinberger, 1994). The paranoia appears to be a central feature in these cases. Even in subjects without a history of violent behavior, the paranoia seems to elicit violent behavior, thought to be "self-defensive" by the perpetrator. As noted by Pincus and Lewis (1991): "The specific causes of psychoses or organic brain syndromes are probably not relevant variables in determining violence. It seems to be the *paranoia* with which these conditions are associated that is the crucial ingredient" (p. 150).

Several substances of abuse are capable of inducing psychosis (see Table 6.1 in Chap. 6). The most common are alcohol (Yudofsky, Stevens, Silver, Barsa, & Williams, 1984), amphetamines (L.A. Pagliaro, 1989a), cocaine (Manschreck et al., 1988; Tueth, 1993), and PCP (Grover, Yera-

SUMMARY

Substance use, particularly alcohol use, has long been associated with violent and nonviolent crime perpetrated by children and adolescents, particularly when antisocial personality disorder and CD are present. Proposed mechanisms for this association include direct pharmacological mechanisms resulting in disinhibition (decreased impulse control) and resultant increased aggressiveness. Social mechanisms have also been postulated. However, commerce- and pharmacopsychology-related crime, including substance-induced automatism, drug trafficking and gang crime, prostitution, and robbery have also been related to crime perpetrated by children and adolescents. Pharmacopsychological crime associated with drug-induced automatism appears to provide an important explanation for much of the violence observed that has been related to substance use and has been largely overlooked.

This chapter has reviewed substance-related crime perpetrated by children and adolescents. As noted by several responses to the 1994 National Institute of Justice survey (McEwen, 1995, pp. 1–2), the relationship between substance use and violent crime remains a serious, and apparently escalating, social problem:

> Overall the survey found that like most other Americans, criminal justice system directors were concerned with violence, drugs, and firearms—particularly as they affected young people, both as victims of crime and as offenders.
>
> Drug activity is the one factor most affecting our court. (judge)
>
> Most crime is related to drug use. (judge)
>
> Domestic violence, child abuse, larceny, and robbery cases are increasing due to drug abuse. (police chief)
>
> Most of the violent crimes are gang-related. They are difficult to investigate due to lack of cooperation [from victims and witnesses]. Most of the gang problems are over drug selling territories. (sheriff)
>
> Our workload problems are a result of the overwhelming number of cases that are a direct or indirect result of drugs. (sheriff)

---

gani, & Keshavan, 1986; Pradhan, 1984; see Chap. 1 for a more detailed discussion of the related pharmacology).

CHAPTER 10

Preventing and Treating Substance Use among Children and Adolescents

Exposure to and use of substances of abuse is related to significant harm among infants, children, and adolescents. Therefore, it is obvious that exposure to substances of abuse and their use should be prevented, or at least minimized. The purpose of this chapter is to describe primary, secondary, and tertiary prevention strategies that are aimed at: 1. preventing children and adolescents from beginning substance use; 2. minimizing the harmful effects of substance use when it has begun and, perhaps, also achieving resumed nonuse; and 3. helping children and adolescents achieve abstinence and minimize associated harmful effects when they have come to abuse or compulsively use substances of abuse (Fig. 10.1). As noted in Chapters 1 and 2, substance use among children and adolescents is a long-standing, complex, and pervasive human concern. Therefore, it is illogical and naive to expect that a singular, and often simplistic, prevention approach (e.g., knowledge concerning the danger associated with substance use) will be effective. As Botvin and Botvin (1992) noted in their review of this issue:

> Traditional approaches to substance abuse prevention relying on the provision of factual information about the adverse consequences of substance use/abuse or attempting to foster the development of self-esteem and responsible decision making have produced disappointing results. These approaches are ineffective because they are based on faulty assumptions about the causes of substance abuse. The existing literature suggests that substance abuse is the result of the complex interaction of a number of etiologic determinants. Knowledge concerning the dangers of substance use appears to play a much less prominent role than previously believed. Considerably more important are the social influences that promote substance use and the psychological factors that help determine susceptibility to these influences. (p. 299)

Thus, a wide range of prevention programs utilizing various techniques and services in the context of primary, secondary, and tertiary prevention models is required (Hawkins, Catalano, & Miller, 1992). In this regard, as observed by Shedler and Block (1990), the "current efforts at drug prevention are misguided to the extent that they focus on symptoms, rather than on the

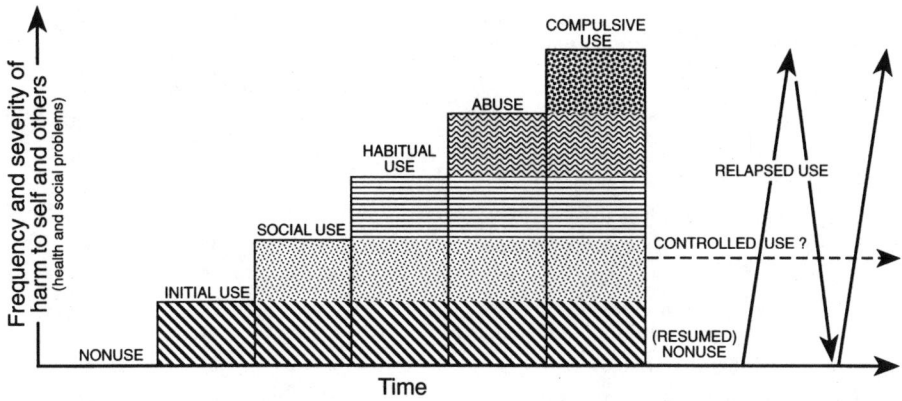

Prevention

FIGURE 10.1   Prevention in relation to the patterns of substance use

psychological syndrome underlying drug abuse" (p. 612). These underlying factors were identified in Chapter 5, and their amenability to primary, secondary, or tertiary prevention techniques are noted in Table 10.1, where data indicate that virtually all of the risk factors are amenable to primary, secondary, and tertiary prevention techniques.

PRIMARY PREVENTION

Primary prevention (prevention of substance use among children and adolescents before it begins) appears to be the ideal goal (G. W. Bailey, 1989; Weissberg, Caplan, & Harwood, 1991). Thus, many of the efforts at primary prevention have involved preschool and elementary school programs (Schaps & Battistich, 1991). However, although much substance use starts early in life (see Chap. 4), primary prevention should continue across the life span for those who have not yet started to use a particular substance of abuse. For example, just because a 15-year-old began to drink alcohol at 10 years of age and smoke tobacco at 11 years of age does not preclude the use of primary prevention techniques in relation to preventing cocaine use.

The goals for the primary prevention of substance use should include reducing the number of antecedent risk factors, reducing the acquisition of vulnerabilities, and increasing the number of protective factors (Felner, Silverman, & Adix, 1991). A review of Table 10.1 indicates that some traitlike variables associated with substance use (e.g., CD and external locus of con-

TABLE 10.1   Variables Associated with Substance Use and Amenability to Primary, Secondary, or Tertiary Prevention Techniques

Variable	Prevention Technique[a]		
	Primary	Secondary	Tertiary
Infant/Child/Adolescent Dimension			
Psychological Variables			
Conduct disorder	n/a	✔	✔
Depression	✔	✔	✔
External locus of control (see also peer pressure and media messages)	n/a	✔	✔
Gender identity crisis	✔	✔	✔
Hopelessness (see depression)	✔	✔	✔
Lack of reasons for living or meaning in life (see depression)	✔	✔	✔
Loneliness	✔	✔	✔
Low self-esteem	✔	✔	✔
Previous substance use	✔	✔	✔
Serious early childhood losses	(✔)	✔	✔
Social Variables			
Absence of maternal figure	✔	✔	✔
Dissatisfaction with family relationships	✔	✔	✔
Family alcohol and other substance use	(✔)	✔	✔
Peer pressure	(✔)	✔	✔
Physical or sexual abuse	(✔)	✔	✔
Previous psychiatric inpatient treatment	(✔)	✔	✔
Societal Dimension			
Societal Variables			
Social programs and services (treatment availability and accessibility)	✔	✔	✔
Media messages	✔	✔	✔

[a]Key: ✔, amenable; (✔), partially amenable; n/a, not amenable.

trol) are not amenable to primary prevention; they cannot be predicted or controlled prior to their occurrence, and once they have occurred, it is too late for primary prevention. Other variables (e.g., serious early childhood losses, family alcohol and other substance use, peer pressure, physical or sexual abuse, and previous psychiatric inpatient treatment) are only partially amenable to primary prevention techniques.

Most of the attempts to achieve the goals of primary prevention have ended in failure. As expressed in many studies and reports (e.g., Kozlowski, Coambs, Ferrence, & Adlaf, 1989; Logan, 1991; Tobler, 1992; Wallack & Corbett, 1990), "the 'vaccine' to prevent [children and] adolescents from using cigarettes, alcohol, and other drugs has not yet been found" (Norman & Turner, 1993, p. 3). Several reasons have been suggested for this failure, including: 1. the lack of appropriate focus and goals (M. B. Goldstein & Engwall, 1992; Shedler & Block, 1990), 2. the lack of appropriate theory to develop and guide prevention strategies, and 3. the lack of political or social resolve (Clayton & Leukefeld, 1992; DuPont, 1987). Each of these reasons for failure is briefly described.

Lack of Appropriate Focus and Goals

In general, the purpose of programs aimed at preventing substance use by children and adolescents is to increase awareness and understanding among stakeholders (youth, parents, teachers, and community); provide accurate information regarding the nature and extent of substance use; and, having recognized the harm associated with substance use, positively change the related attitudes and behaviors of targeted groups. However, the focus and priorities of these primarily government-sponsored programs appear to be particularly sensitive to public opinion and pressure and, hence, are often educationally unsound and short lived (DuPont, 1987; Goodstadt, 1989; see also the related discussion regarding lack of political or social resolve, below).

M. B. Goldstein and Engwall (1992) in their documentary analysis found a decided change in the public's perception of the problem of substance use among children and adolescents over the past several decades and, consequently, in the government's approach to primary and secondary prevention. During the 1970s and early 1980s, the public did not perceive the drug problem as a major social problem, and the approach to prevention was "soft" (although abstinence from substance use was considered ideal, the promotion of safe or responsible use was seen as sufficient). Programs that encouraged decision making regarding safe and responsible substance use were funded and developed. These programs included, for example, the Don't Drink and Drive program and the designated driver program. However, by the mid-1980s the public's perception changed, as substance use among children and adolescents became the leading social problem in North America. In response, the government hardened its policy. As identified by M. B. Goldstein and Engwall (1992), the perspective clearly changed from safe and responsible use to no use or "zero tolerance"—the slogan "Drug-Free America" supported this message (p. 76).[1]

---

[1] We favor and encourage a more hybrid approach. In terms of primary prevention, we concur that the goal should be abstinence. This conflicts with the more liberal position of M. B. Goldstein and Engwall (1992) and perhaps also with other researchers, who, although in a de-

Lack of Appropriate Theory to Guide Prevention

The problem here has not been a lack of theories, but conversely the existence of a plethora of theories, many of which are philosophically incompatible and untested in the clinical arena (see Chap. 2). However, it appears that most previous programs designed to prevent substance use among children and adolescents can be classified into one of four models: 1. the information-only model, 2. the alternatives model, 3. the affective educational/social competency model, and 4. the social environmental/learning model (Norman & Turner, 1993). The models are listed in their chronological order of predominant use (the information-only model was the first widely used model and the social environmental/learning model is the most recent). However, each of these models continues to be used in various contexts and will be briefly discussed.

Information-Only Model

The information-only model was the first model widely used to prevent substance use by children and adolescents. It was the predominant model of the 1960s and 1970s and was predicated on two assumptions: 1. Youth were ignorant of the harmful effects of the substances of abuse. 2. If aware of the harmful effects, youth would refrain from substance use.[2] Unfortunately, both assumptions tended, in large measure, to be incorrect. While the model positively affected knowledge acquisition (Tobler, 1986), attitudes and behavior were, for the most part, not significantly affected (D. J. Hanson, 1982; National Institute on Drug Abuse, 1984; Schaps, DiBartalo, Moskowitz, Palley, & Churgin, 1981; Tobler, 1992). In some cases, experimentation reportedly increased as a result of increased knowledge, and hence curiosity (B. Bernard, Fafoglia, & Perone, 1987; Hawkins et al., 1985).

---

cided minority, have suggested a positive relationship between a low level of substance use by adolescents and overall psychological adjustment. E.g., Shedler and Block (1990), utilizing a sample of 101 18-year-olds, found that "adolescents who had engaged in some degree of experimentation (primarily with marijuana) were the best-adjusted in the sample" (p. 404). This appears to be in sharp contrast to the observation by Logan (1991) that "even minimal use of illicit substances may be an indicator of an adolescent's willingness to engage in potentially harmful high-risk behaviors" (p. 27). These contrasting views and results are indicative of the current lack of consensus within the field.

However, for those children and adolescents for whom abstinence is untenable, in keeping with secondary and tertiary models of prevention and health promotion, we encourage safe and responsible use that minimizes the risk of harm to self or others. The levels of substance use, which were described in Chap. 1 are suggested as a guide in this regard (see also discussion later in this chapter).

[2] The roots of this model can be traced back much further, perhaps to almost a century earlier, when during the late 1800s most states mandated some form of school instruction on the "evil and harmful" effects of alcohol and opiates (Wallack & Corbett, 1990).

In an effort to counteract this "curiosity effect" and associated youthful experimentation with the substances of abuse, teacher-led information programs were emphasized. However, as a result of poorly prepared and scientifically inaccurate training materials, teachers often found themselves (in most cases unknowingly) exaggerating the negative effects of substance use (claiming, e.g., that marijuana use is addictive and causes insanity or that LSD use during pregnancy will cause severe birth defects) or using fear tactics (e.g., showing a picture of a black, tarry, cancerous lung from a deceased tobacco smoker and then blowing tobacco smoke through a white handkerchief to display the solid material in smoke that is not removed by the cigarette filter or the lungs) that were later found to be largely ineffective. For example, students who had already experimented with marijuana quickly recognized that their teachers did not know what they were talking about or assumed that teachers were lying. In this context, misinformation about even one of the negative consequences associated with even one substance of abuse tended to undermine the teacher's credibility in regard to everything else that was subsequently said in the program, whether or not it was correct.

In response to the growing concern about the lack of efficacy of these programs, the White House Special Action Office for Drug Abuse Prevention called for an end to the use of federally funded drug information material that used scare tactics, stereotyping of drug users, and dogmatic statements (e.g., "use of substance X always causes problem Y"; Resnick, 1978). In addition, attention was given to ensuring that the information provided was age-appropriate and not inadvertently directed at teaching students how to acquire, make, or use the substances of abuse.

Another major flaw of the information-only model was its restricted focus, which discounted, or ignored, other significant variables (e.g., parent, peer, and media influences or individual personality characteristics). In an effort to address these inadequacies, information-only programs aimed at preventing substance use among children and adolescents were replaced by programs that focused on the characteristics of the user, particularly self-esteem.[3]

Alternatives Model

The alternatives model was primarily used during the late 1970s. This model had seven basic assumptions:

1. People take drugs because they want to;
2. People use drugs to "feel better" or to "get high." Individuals experiment

---

[3] The shift in the focus of programs aimed at preventing substance use was so complete that most later programs never mentioned substances of abuse at all. These later programs were based in large part on the humanistic psychology movement of the 1970s and its general philosophy that if children and adolescents could just be happy with themselves, they would have no reason to use substances of abuse.

with drugs out of curiosity or hope that using drugs can make them feel better;

3. People have been taught by cultural example, media, etc. that drugs are an effective way to make them feel better;

4. "Feeling better" encompasses a huge range of mood or consciousness change, including such aspects as oblivion-sleep, emotion shift, energy modification and visions of the Divine, etc.;

5. With many mind or mood-altering drugs, taken principally for that purpose, individuals may temporarily feel better. However, drugs have substantial short and long term disadvantages related to the motive for their use. These include possible physiological damage, psychological deterioration and cognitive breakdown. Drugs also tend to be temporary, relatively devoid of satisfying translations to the ordinary non-drug state of life, and siphon off energy for long term constructive growth;

6. Basically, individuals do not stop using drugs until they discover "something better"; and

7. The key to meeting problems of drug abuse is to focus on the "something better," and maximize opportunities for experiencing satisfying nonchemical alternatives. The same key can be used to discourage experimentation or, more likely, keep experimentation from progressing to dependency. (A. Y. Cohen, 1974, pp. 3–4)

This model sought to provide alternative activities for children and adolescents that would meet their needs, which, in turn, would presumably alleviate their need to use substances of abuse. Although most alternative programs focused on physical and recreational activities (e.g., mountain climbing, skydiving, or sports) to help children and adolescents build self-confidence as well as be busy and productive, some focused more specifically on increasing self-esteem and the development of prosocial community values. An example of one of the more comprehensive applications of alternative programs was developed by A. Y. Cohen (1974; see Table 10.2). Unfortunately, alternative programs did not, in general, prove effective in preventing substance use among children and adolescents (Schaps, Moskowitz, Malvin, & Schaeffer, 1986; Tobler, 1992).

Affective Educational/Social Competency Model

The development of this model was based, in large part, on the problem behavior theory advanced by Jessor and Jessor (1977b). According to this theory,

adolescents engage in problem behaviors such as substance use and premature sexual behavior, because these behaviors help the adolescent achieve desired personal goals. To the extent that adolescents perceive these behaviors as functional, they will be motivated to engage in them. For example, problem behaviors may serve as a way of coping with real or anticipated failure, boredom, social anxiety, unhappiness, rejection, social isolation, low self-esteem, and a lack of self-efficacy. These behaviors may also serve as a way of gaining admission to a particular peer group. For adolescents who are not achieving academically, the use of psychoactive substances may provide a way of achieving social status. Adolescents may believe that smoking, drinking, or using drugs will enhance their public image by making them look "cool" or by demonstrating independence from authority figures. Adolescents at the greatest risk of becoming substance users are those who perceive that alternative ways of achieving these same goals are unavailable. (Botvin & Botvin, 1993, p. 293)

The affective educational/social competency model, which shares many of the assumptions of the alternatives model,[4] was primarily used during the mid-1970s to the mid-1980s. Social competency in this context was defined as the ability of students to disagree, refuse, make requests, and initiate conversations. The model was based on two assumptions: 1. Children and adolescents use substances of abuse because of low self-esteem and inappropriate social values. 2. If self-esteem is increased and children and adolescents are taught "values clarification" and related problem-solving, decision-making, and communication skills, then they will, of their own volition, choose not to use substances of abuse. Thus, as with the alternatives model, the issue of nonuse of the substances of abuse was generally not directly addressed by programs based on this model. Instead, the focus of these programs was on: 1. choosing an alternative after having carefully considered all other available behaviors together with their related consequences, 2. publicly affirming the alternative selected and feeling positive about ("prizing") it, and 3. acting on one's own positive beliefs and choices consistently and regularly (Harmin, Kirschenbaum, & Simon, 1973). This values clarification process was often reinforced by the use of classroom role playing and a private "values journal," which was maintained by each student.

Overall, these programs demonstrated a poor success rate (Botvin, 1986; Del Greco, Breitbach, Rumer, McCarthy, & Suissa, 1986; DuPont, 1987; Petersen, 1987; Schaps et al., 1981). This lack of success was probably due to several factors. One factor was the inadequate training of teachers in regard to the methods inherent in this model. The high school teachers involved in these programs were, generally, not particularly experienced or competent in teaching self-esteem and values clarification. The results of these programs may have been significantly different had they been provided by specially trained school psychologists.

In spite of the solid research evidence contradicting information-only or alternatives programs (and even those combining these two approaches), far too many programs are still based on these ineffective modalities. The critical component (of successful programs) is the direct emphasis on behavior

---

[4] Some authors actually categorize the alternatives model as a subset, or specialized example, of the affective educational/social competency model.

TABLE 10.2　A Comprehensive Alternatives Model[a]

Level of Experience	Examples of Corresponding Motives for Substance Use	Examples of Possible Alternatives
Physical	Physical satisfaction; physical relaxation; relief from sickness; more energy; maintenance of physical dependency	Athletics; dance; exercise; hiking; diet; health training; carpentry or outdoor work
Sensory	To stimulate sight, sound, touch, taste; sensual-sexual stimulation; to magnify sensorium	Sensory awareness training; sky diving; experiencing sensory beauty of nature
Emotional	Relief from psychological pain; to solve personal perplexities; relief from bad mood; escape from anxiety; emotional insight; liberation of feeling; emotional relaxation	Competent individual counseling; well-run group therapy; instruction in psychology of personal development
Interpersonal	To gain peer acceptance; to break through interpersonal barriers; to "communicate," especially nonverbally; to defy authority figures; to cement two-person relationships; to relax interpersonal inhibition; to solve interpersonal hangups	Expertly managed sensitivity and encounter groups; well-run group therapy; instruction in social customs; confidence training; social-interpersonal counseling; emphasis on assisting others in distress via education; marriage
Social (including sociocultural and environmental)	To promote social change; to find identifiable subculture; to tune out intolerable environmental conditions, e.g., poverty	Social service; community action in positive social change; helping the poor, aged, infirm, young; tutoring handicapped; ecology action
Political	To promote political change; to identify with antiestablishment subgroup; to change drug legislation; out of desperation with the social-political order; to gain wealth, affluence, or power	Political service; political action; nonpartisan projects such as ecological lobbying; field work with politicians and public officials

TABLE 10.2   (*Continued*)

Level of Experience	Examples of Corresponding Motives for Substance Use	Examples of Possible Alternatives
Intellectual	To escape mental boredom; out of intellectual curiosity; to solve cognitive problems; to gain new understanding in the world of ideas; to study better; to research one's own awareness; for science	Intellectual excitement through reading, through discussion; creative games and puzzles; self-hypnosis; training in concentration; synectics—training in intellectual breakthroughs; memory training
Creative-aesthetic	To improve creativity in the arts; to enhance enjoyment of art already produced, e.g., music; to enjoy imaginative mental productions	Nongraded instruction in producing and/or appreciating art, music, drama, crafts, handiwork, cooking, sewing, gardening, writing, singing
Philosophical	To discover meaningful values; to grasp the nature of the universe; to find meaning in life; to help establish personal identity; to organize a belief structure	Discussions, seminars, courses in the meaning of life; study of ethics, morality, the nature of reality; relevant philosophical literature; guided exploration of value systems
Spiritual-mystical	To transcend orthodox religion; to develop spiritual insights; to reach higher levels of consciousness; to have divine visions; to communicate with God; to augment yogic practices; to get a spiritual shortcut; to attain enlightenment; to attain spiritual powers	Exposure to nonchemical methods of spiritual development; study of world religions; introduction to applied mysticism, meditation; yogic techniques
Miscellaneous	Adventure, risk, drama, "kicks," unexpressed motives; prodrug general attitudes	"Outward Bound" survival training; combinations of alternatives above; pronaturalness attitudes; brain-wave training; meaningful employment

[a]From A. Y. Cohen (1974, pp. 6–7).

through the teaching of refusal skills and other direct behavior skills, such as communication and problem solving (B. Bernard, 1988).

Social Environmental/Learning Model

The social environmental/learning model,[5] largely based upon cognitive-social learning theory (Bandura, 1977; Evans, Rozelle, Mittlemark, & Hansen, 1978), has been used from the mid-1980s to date with an overall moderate degree of success.[6] The assumptions of the social environmental/learning model are that: 1. social influences (e.g., parents, peers, and media) have a significant effect on substance use; and 2. children and adolescents can be trained to become aware of and resist social situational pressures (e.g., user-parent, peer pressure, and media messages) to use substances of abuse. Using the primary prevention metaphor that children and adolescents can be "inoculated" against subsequent substance use, this approach has been generally referred to in the literature as *psychosocial inoculation* or *social inoculation training,* that is, training that will protect children and adolescents from "infection" by future social influences to use substances of abuse. Examples of the numerous programs based on this model include: ALERT, DARE, Here's Looking at You, Just Say No, Life Skills Training, PALS, and SMART Moves (De Jung, 1987; Dusenbury & Botvin, 1992; Ellickson & Bell, 1990; Gelb, 1984; A. P. Goldstein, Reagles, & Amann, 1990; Kim, 1988; Sweet, 1991; Van Hasselt, Hersen, et al., 1993). Often these programs have used student peers as coleaders with a teacher or school counselor. In addition to teaching students about the adverse consequences of substance use, the peer-focused programs have generally attempted to integrate the following objectives:

- Create a school climate that encourages the development of responsible independence and a positive identity;
- Create opportunities for students to learn how to actively and intentionally use their experiences to gain new levels of confidence and competence;
- Encourage opportunities for early intervention to deal with adolescent difficulties; and
- Involve students in identifying and meeting student-perceived needs. ("Alberta's," 1987, p. 23)

In addition, much of the focus of these programs has been directed at: 1. socially normed education (e.g., "It's *not* true that everybody does drugs" and "Most people do *not* smoke tobacco") and 2. cognitive-behavioral train-

---

[5] This model also has been referred to as a *cognitive/behavioral* or *social influences* model.
[6] It has clearly been demonstrated to be more successful in preventing substance use among children and adolescents than the information-only, alternatives, or affective educational/social competency models (Norman & Turner, 1993).

ing (i.e., strategies to resist the pressure to use substances of abuse are developed, modeled, and rehearsed).

The student peer facilitators, if appropriately trained and committed to the goals of the program, serve as important role models for the other students in the program and contribute significantly to its success (Botvin, Baker, Renick, Filazzola, & Botvin, 1984; Logan, 1991; D. Murray, Pirie, Luepker, & Pallonen, 1989; Perry et al., 1989). However, as asserted by Tobler (1992), peers do not take the place of well-trained, well-qualified teachers or counselors and, if not appropriately monitored, may do more harm than good: "A peer leader does not make a peer program. Peer leaders may or may not be able to facilitate the necessary interaction. In many cases, the peer leader benefits from his more active role than do the group members" (p. 21).[7]

Although not universally successful (e.g., H. K. Becker, Agopian, & Yeh, 1992; Hansen & Graham, 1991), the social environmental/learning model has been demonstrated in a number of studies to be effective in preventing or decreasing the use of selected substances of abuse among children and adolescents, including alcohol (e.g., Botvin, Baker, Botvin, Filazzola, & Millman, 1984; Perry et al., 1989), tobacco (e.g., Biglan et al., 1987; Botvin, Renick, & Baker, 1983), and polysubstance use (e.g., Botvin, Baker, Dusenbury, Tortu, & Botvin, 1990; Hansen, Johnson, Flay, Graham, & Sobel, 1988). The most success demonstrated with this approach to date has been in relation to tobacco smoking. However, even in this context, the programs "can [at best] be effective some of the time. However, [even] this conclusion seems somewhat fragile, given the considerable differences between studies in the patterns of reported results" (Flay, 1985, p. 473).

None of the four models of prevention has demonstrated widespread, long-lasting effectiveness.[8] As governments continue to downsize and reduce

[7] Commonly, those students actively involved as peer educators or student counselors have noted significant gains in their own self-esteem. In addition, leadership and teaching skills are developed or notably improved. While we view these as positive outcomes, which should be encouraged, care must be taken by the group leader (teacher or professional counselor) that these outcomes occur together with, and not at the expense of, benefits for the other students in the group.

[8] A quick perusal of the variables listed in Table 10.1 helps explain the success, or lack thereof, experienced by the four models previously discussed. For example, "lack of knowledge about the substances of abuse" is not listed. It is no wonder, then, that the information-only model, which focused on knowledge acquisition, had virtually no effect. Similarly, the appearance of "low self-esteem" as a listed risk factor helps to explain the limited success of the alternatives and the affective educational/social competency models, both of which had self-esteem as a focus. A similar analysis with future prevention models would be expected to predict, a priori, their propensity for success. To obtain an even more accurate and complete representation of the effects of the various prevention programs, they should be considered within the multifactorial interactional context of MIMSEUICA (see Chap. 1).

spending during the late 1990s, it appears likely that less and less funding will be available for preventing substance use among children and adolescents. In this context, ineffective, or marginally effective, programs that waste time and money will have no place in an increasingly stressed school curriculum or budget.

With some indication of the prevention strategies that work, and the ones that do not, we can begin to develop more effective programs, but many pressing questions remain. For example, as noted by Norman and Turner (1993):

1. Do we target high risk youth or the general population? Some researchers contend that the prevention programs currently most widely used may be affecting prevalence of alcohol and other drug use in the general population, but they are failing to reach the 5–15% of the adolescent population who are at greatest risk for becoming substance abusers. Although high risk youth are in the minority, they may account for the majority of young adults in the criminal justice system and of those involved in drug-related traffic accidents.

2. Do we focus on primary or secondary prevention? Currently the majority of New York State prevention resources are allocated for secondary prevention or counseling those youth who already have problems related to substance use. Some experts believe that if we continue to do secondary prevention we will never have any significant impact on overall substance use and abuse, and that we will be continuing to put bandaids on problems that already exist, as opposed to trying to eliminate the problems through primary prevention strategies.

3. Do we concentrate on First Order or Second Order Change? Most of the prevention efforts of the 1980s have aimed at trying to change the behavior of individuals (second order change). An increasing number of prevention planners believe that the emphasis should be on first order change—that is, addressing the societal problems that are influencing individuals to become substance abusers. Increasing the price of legal substances, banning cigarette and alcohol advertising, and raising the legal drinking age are examples of first order change. (p. 17)

Lack of Political or Social Resolve

Examples of lack of political or social resolve abound but are probably clearest in the area of tobacco. As noted in Chapter 1, tobacco has no defined safe level of use and individually causes more deaths in North America than any other single substance of abuse. However, the use of tobacco, a so-called soft drug, remains legal.[9] In addition, tobacco farmers continue to receive

---

[9] We have steadfastly refrained from using in this text the term "soft drug," which we find to be an oxymoron.

government subsidies and export tobacco as a cash crop to countries such as China where use is on the rise. In this context, it is not surprising that regulations concerning the distribution and sale of tobacco are generally weak and infrequently enforced, with over 80 percent of convenience stores and pharmacies sampled reporting illegal sale of tobacco products to minors (L. J. Brown & DiFranza, 1992; DiFranza, 1989; DiFranza & Brown, 1992).[10] In fact, legal promotional advertising campaigns, designed and produced specifically to encourage adolescents to start smoking, continue to be widely used across North America (DiFranza et al., 1991). However, in schools and communities that have developed the necessary political or social resolve, tobacco use by children and adolescents has decreased significantly (DiFranza, 1992). Such successful outcomes demonstrate that proactive community involvement, extended to communities across North America, can be a significant factor in reducing problematic patterns of substance use among children and adolescents. Most of these successful community programs will begin with or involve school-based prevention strategies.

School-Based Prevention Strategies

A variety of strategies have been aimed at preventing substance use among children and adolescents. These programs have been developed at local community, city, state or provincial, national, or international levels.[11] Most efforts, in this regard, have focused on, or have involved, school-based approaches (e.g., Kantor, Caudill, & Ungerleider, 1992; McLaughlin et al., 1993; Moskowitz, Schaps, Schaeffer, & Malvin, 1984; Schaps & Battistich, 1991; Sexter, Sullivan, Wapner, & Denmark, 1984). Table 10.3 lists several problems that have been identified with school-based prevention programs. These limitations must be recognized and addressed by school boards and concerned community members in order to maximize the potential benefits of these programs.

School-based prevention programs should begin in the early primary grades and continue through grade 12 with attention to the specific needs of the children (e.g., inner city vs. urban, ethnicity, socioeconomic level, and community substance use patterns) served by the school and the school district. The developmental leveling of programs from kindergarten to grade 12 is also essential. This tailoring of programs requires well-defined, realistic goals (e.g., a program that begins in junior high school and attempts to do everything for everyone is quite likely to do little for anyone). These goals

[10] The reader need only take an early morning drive by the nearest convenience store adjacent to a junior high school to see firsthand how easily minors can purchase cigarettes.

[11] Worker safety promotion campaigns or employee assistance programs (EAPs) have served as models for the development of student assistance programs (SAPs) (Palmer & Paisley, 1991).

TABLE 10.3   Major Problems Commonly Encountered
in School-Based Prevention Programs

Ill-defined target audience
Improper leveling/timing
Lack of active student involvement
Limited linkage to the community
Limited scope
Limited time
Poorly qualified teachers
Simplistic design
Unrealistic goals
Use of ineffective techniques

should be based on an accurate knowledge of the nature and extent of substance use encountered generally among the particular cohort of students targeted (e.g., a particular school or school district). These data should be collected and then further refined based on a well-designed local needs assessment study followed by a pilot study to test the efficacy of planned interventions. The pilot study can identify areas that require revision before the program is developed and implemented for use at the broader community level or with other comparable cohorts of students in other geographic regions. A prototype of this approach can be found in Table 10.4.[12] Although this approach may require much time and costly preparatory work, the untenable alternative, as previously noted, is to provide "ineffective programs [that] waste time and money . . . [and] occupy space in a stressed curriculum" (Kozlowski et al., 1989, p. 454).[13] While local community-based interventions

---

[12] Additional examples of this general approach are presented in the U.S. Department of Education (1992).

[13] For schools without the necessary resources to develop their own tailored curriculum model for substance use prevention or that would like to begin with a basically sound program that can be modified to better meet local needs, we would recommend the Learning to Live Drug Free model developed by Flatter and McCormick (1992) for the U.S. Department of Education. As noted in its introduction:

This drug prevention curriculum model provides a framework for prevention education from kindergarten through 12th grade. It provides the basics for starting or expanding drug education; it includes information about drugs, background for teachers on child growth and development, sample lesson plans and activities, and suggestions on working with parents and the community. The format is expandable, so that school districts and individual classroom teachers can add or update information—and create their own lesson plans and activities.

Written primarily for school teachers, administrators, and principals, the curriculum model is also useful for health and social services professionals, parents, business leaders, and other people who want to help prevent drug use among youth. (Flatter & McCormick, 1992, Pt. 1, p. 1)

TABLE 10.4   Plan for Achieving Schools without Drugs[a]

Parents

1. Teach standards of right and wrong, and demonstrate these standards through personal example.
2. Help children to resist peer pressure to use drugs by supervising their activities, knowing who their friends are, and talking with them about their interests and problems.
3. Be knowledgeable about drugs and signs of drug abuse. When symptoms are observed, respond promptly.

Schools

4. Determine the extent and character of drug use and establish a means of monitoring that use regularly.
5. Establish clear and specific rules regarding drug use that include strong corrective actions.
6. Enforce established policies against drug use fairly and consistently. Implement security measures to eliminate drugs on school premises and at school functions.
7. Implement a comprehensive drug prevention curriculum for kindergarten through grade 12, teaching that drug use is wrong and harmful and supporting and strengthening resistance to drugs.
8. Reach out to the community for support and assistance in making the school's antidrug policy and program work. Develop collaborative arrangements in which school personnel, parents, school boards, law enforcement officers, treatment organizations, and private groups work together to provide necessary resources.

Students

9. Learn about the effects of drug use, the reasons why drugs are harmful, and ways to resist pressures to try drugs.
10. Use an understanding of the danger posed by drugs to help other students avoid them. Encourage other students to resist drugs, persuade those using drugs to seek help, and report those selling drugs to parents and the school principal.

Communities

11. Help schools fight drugs by providing them with the expertise and financial resources of community groups and agencies.
12. Involve local law enforcement agencies in all aspects of drug prevention, assessment, enforcement, and education. The police and courts should have well-established and mutually supportive relationships with the schools.

[a]From U.S. Department of Education (1986, p. vii).

may suffice for the short term, long-range planning is also needed at the broader levels.

Once the desired goals have been properly identified, effective techniques to achieve these goals should be selected and integrated into the program delivery model (e.g., it has been clearly demonstrated that the information-only and alternatives models are almost invariably ineffective and, thus, should not be selected). Quick-fix, uncoordinated programs (e.g., a 1-hour per week "drug education class") should be replaced with integrated programs throughout the school that have clearly established community linkages (e.g., through parent groups and community agencies). In this context, several hours per week in lectures, discussions, and community activities can be planned and undertaken—for example, a school-sponsored health walk could be organized, with fees generated from sponsors and donations given to local smoking research, prevention, or treatment programs. Another example of a positive link between schools and their communities is the establishment of drug-free zones around schools. In this approach, school officials and community organizers work together to have local city ordinances passed that make the possession or sale of an illicit substance of abuse within a specified area around a school (e.g., a two- or three-block radius) subject to significantly increased penalties in terms of fines and imprisonment. This approach serves as a deterrent to drug dealers and can significantly reduce the availability of illicit substances of abuse on school grounds. It also decreases the likelihood of students being approached by dealers on the way to school, at recess, in the school parking lot, or on the way home from school.[14]

Finally, the school-based prevention programs will only be as good as the teachers who are involved with the programs. As noted by Tobler (1992) in a review of "153 adolescent drug prevention programs": "Evidence obtained indicates implementation factors, in particular the effect of the leader, may impact the success of the program as much as the type or strategy of the program" (p. 2). Because most teachers have not received adequate preparation in relation to childhood and adolescent substance use—that is, formalized courses in the pharmacological, psychological, and sociological factors affecting use—their knowledge and beliefs are often subject to significant bias and error, being influenced by personal experience, media reporting, or

---

[14] This approach can also be used with substances of abuse such as tobacco, which may actually be legal in some areas for adolescents to use. DiFranza (1992), e.g., suggests the following school policies as a model for dealing with tobacco use:

1. Students shall not be allowed to possess tobacco products on school grounds. Tobacco products brought onto school grounds shall be confiscated.
2. Use of tobacco products by students, staff, and visitors shall be prohibited in school buildings, on school property, and at school functions.
3. If students possess tobacco products, their parents shall be notified and invited to meet with school personnel concerning the matter.
4. Students possessing tobacco products shall be offered treatment for potential nicotine addiction.
5. Help with smoking cessation shall be offered to students in school on a regular basis.
6. Students possessing tobacco products shall face appropriate disciplinary action.
7. All grades, K through 12, shall receive instruction concerning tobacco on an annual basis. (p. 754)

other nonobjective resources. It is imperative that teachers be provided with formal courses in these areas during their basic education and that they attend periodic continuing education programs taught by experts in the area of childhood and adolescent substance use. Such educational strategies have the potential to help dispel any myths or misconceptions that the teachers may have developed in relation to substance use, update the teachers regarding changing patterns of use and prevention or treatment modalities, and alleviate the teachers' concerns that the students already know more than they do regarding drug use. Such programs will prepare teachers to more effectively meet their expanded roles in the educational arena and provide them with a forum to share their experiences and ideas. As noted by Weissberg et al. (1991): "Regardless of a program's quality, its potential for positive effects is diminished when program implementors are poorly trained, have inadequate organizational support for program delivery or lack the necessary skills to provide effective training" (p. 837). Appendix III lists a number of agencies and groups that can offer professional and expert advice regarding the prevention or treatment of substance use among children and adolescents. These agencies and groups may serve as an initial source of contact for teachers and others interested in developing better school-based programs.[15]

Perhaps the greatest problem encountered by school-based prevention programs, and the most difficult to effectively deal with, is that children and adolescents who may need such programs the most are not likely to benefit because they do not attend school (Tobler, 1992). As noted earlier in this text, a significant number of children and adolescents cut classes, drop out of school, or become homeless runaways each year in North America (see Chap. 5). These children and adolescents are at significant risk of developing problematic patterns of substance use and, generally, would not have access to school-based programs.

SECONDARY PREVENTION

Secondary prevention is concerned with early intervention among children and adolescents who have already begun substance use but for whom the

[15] An alternative, although generally much more expensive and often more difficult logistically, is to use drug and substance use professionals to deliver the programs to students directly. In spite of the difficulties, this approach generally has met with a significant increase in the success rate of prevention programs, primarily because of the specialized, in-depth training, education, and clinical abilities of these professionals (often clinical psychologists). In addition, these professionals are seen as outside experts by the students, who find that they do not need to contend with unrelated issues (e.g., what grade the teacher gave a student in social studies the previous term; Tobler, 1992). Several private companies now offer such programs on a contractual basis, including a student assistance counselor for the school district and a 24-hour telephone help line for students.

serious related adverse effects have not yet occurred—for example, programs aimed at convincing high school students, most of whom drink alcohol, not to drink and drive (e.g., Mothers against Drunk Driving and Students against Drunk Driving) or providing intravenous substance users with sterile injection equipment or with bleach kits to clean their needles to eliminate or decrease the risk of spreading HIV (e.g., the Health Education Resource Organization). In general, the government does not support or fund these secondary prevention programs as widely as primary prevention programs because their goals focus on the minimization of harm related to substance use rather than on abstinence from substance use.

Secondary prevention techniques could be used for all of the variable risk factors identified in Table 10.1. For example, if an adolescent is observed to be depressed, perhaps in relation to a gender identity crisis (see Chap. 5), then a referral for appropriate counseling, psychotherapy, and other necessary therapy should be made. This intervention may help the adolescent (a "social drinker") resolve his or her gender identity crisis, resolve the accompanying depression, and consequently prevent the development of problematic patterns of substance use. Similarly, a young girl, "who drinks only with friends," whose mother has recently died in a motor vehicle crash, and who is now living with her alcoholic father should be recognized as being at risk for the subsequent development of problematic patterns of substance use. This child should be preventively monitored for grief resolution and provided, along with her father, with appropriate counseling, psychotherapy, and other services, as needed.

TERTIARY PREVENTION

Tertiary prevention involves the prevention of secondary sequelae among children and adolescents who have already engaged in problematic patterns of substance use (abuse or compulsive use). Aspects of tertiary prevention typically involve active medical or psychological treatment, including residential treatment and rehabilitation involving relapse prevention (Hohman & Buchik, 1994). It often has been noted that "traditional models of addiction and treatment work better with older populations than with younger ones" (Baer, 1991, p. 51). This observation can be explained, in part, by the general characteristics of childhood and adolescent development (see Table 10.5).[16] However, the observed difficulties associated with tertiary prevention are probably explained to a greater degree by the relative lack of well-controlled

[16] An additional factor is the difference in legal requirements regarding consent for treatment by a minor. As noted by Thompson (1989), in regard to the state of Texas:

> A minor may consent to counseling or counseling in conjunction with treatment by a physician, psychologist, counselor, or social worker for sexual abuse, physical abuse, suicide prevention, or chemical addiction, dependency, or abuse. Such counseling may be rendered by

TABLE 10.5   Developmental Characteristics of Adolescents Relevant to the Treatment of Alcohol and Other Substance Use[a]

Dependent position in family and society
Frequent coexisting mental disorders
Frequent polysubstance use
Greater influence by peers and popular culture
Limits imposed by cognitive, physical, and social development
Need for educational or vocational training

[a]Modified from Bukstein (1994, p. 297).

empirical studies aimed at providing treatment approaches for these age groups. As noted by Catalano, Hawkins, Wells, & Miller, (1990–91):

> A review of controlled evaluations of adolescent and other drug abuse treatment programs concludes that some treatment is better than no treatment, that few comparisons of treatment method have consistently demonstrated the superiority of one method over another, that posttreatment relapse rates are high, and that more controlled studies of adolescent treatment which allow evaluation of the elements of treatment are needed. (p. 1086)

Thus, the focus of this section will be to provide an overview of the various approaches used for the treatment of children and adolescents who have

---

a physician and the above professionals on the basis of the appropriate written statement by the minor and may be divulged to the parent if so desired. Liability for counseling will not attach except as a result of negligence or willful misconduct. (p. 57)

However, these regulations vary among legal jurisdictions and some states and provinces do not provide exceptions to the general principle that minors are legally incapable of giving consent for treatment. Thus, clinicians must apprise themselves of the related legal requirements in the jurisdiction in which they are practicing. In addition, clinicians must be particularly sensitive to assuring that the treatment provided to children and adolescents is not only legal, but ethical. As noted by I. M. Schwartz (1989):

> There is also mounting evidence that many of these inpatient placements are inappropriate, that large numbers of young people are being deprived of their liberty under the guise of receiving medical treatment without the benefit of due process or procedural safeguards, and that the quality of care in many hospitals is poor and abusive. (p. 473)

In recognition of this fact and the lack of conclusive demonstration of the superior efficacy of inpatient hospitalization (Butts & Schwartz, 1991), it has been recommended that the following four factors be considered prior to the recommendation of any child or adolescent for referral for inpatient treatment:

1. The patient is unable to discontinue his or her abuse in spite of appropriate interventions by the physician [or other health services provider] and the patient's family.
2. The patient is no longer in control and is exhibiting abusive or dangerous behavior toward himself/herself, siblings, parents, or others.
3. The patient displays runaway behavior or is suicidal.
4. The patient's physical and emotional condition has deteriorated to a level that threatens his or her life. (Pruitt, Jacobs, Schydlower, Stands, & Sutton, 1990, p. 139)

problematic patterns of substance use, with attention to their reported success or lack there of.[17]

Types of Treatment

Although numerous programs exist to treat adolescents who have problematic patterns of substance use, the methods used can be conveniently grouped into six major categories: 1. pharmacotherapy, 2. psychotherapy, 3. family therapy, 4. social skills training, 5. AA and other 12-step programs, and 6. therapeutic communities. Each of these treatment approaches will be briefly discussed.

Pharmacotherapy

Pharmacotherapy, involving a variety of drugs, has been and continues to be the mainstay of the medical treatment of acute overdoses involving substances of abuse and their respective withdrawal syndromes. Pharmacotherapy also has proved to be a useful adjunct to cessation (through drug-assisted abstinence), maintenance (through drug substitution), and relapse prevention programs. In addition, pharmacotherapy is often a necessary and integral component of the treatment of children and adolescents who have dual diagnoses, particularly for the management of ADHD, anxiety, and depression (see Chap. 6). As noted by L. A. Pagliaro and Pagliaro (1993):

> The widespread and variable use of abusable psychotropics [substances of abuse] by North Americans is of concern to clinical pharmacologists who practice or conduct research in a variety of settings. Although clinical pharmacologists have traditionally been concerned with this class of drugs primarily because of the inherent interest in related psychopharmacologic (e.g., mechanisms of action; therapeutic applications) and toxicologic (e.g., drug-induced psychosis, overdose, teratogenesis) effects, they are increasingly interested in the development of effective pharmacologic intervention strategies aimed at the prevention and treatment of abusable psychotropic use patterns exemplified by abuse and compulsive use. In this regard, attention has been directed at cessation of or modification of use patterns, detoxification and therapeutic support during withdrawal, and relapse prevention.
>
> Past advances in this regard are considerably variable and include, for example, in relation to the opiates, the use of: methadone maintenance programs as a substitute for illicit opiate use; naltrexone for the treatment of opiate addiction; clonidine-aided opiate detoxification; and naloxone for the treatment of

---

[17] Several researchers (e.g., R. W. Blum, 1987; Tartar, 1990; Wodarski, 1990) have noted the need for multiple therapeutic approaches to effectively deal with the varied nature of substance use problems encountered among children and adolescents. In this regard, as previously noted in Chap. 1, we recommend that the individual approaches to treatment described in this chapter be considered and applied in the context of MIMSEUICA.

opiate overdose. Other examples of pharmacologic intervention include the use of flumazenil for the treatment of benzodiazepine overdose and disulfiram (Antabuse) for the treatment of problematic patterns of alcohol use. Attention has been given also to the pharmacologic management of the withdrawal phenomenon associated with the use of cocaine and nicotine (e.g., bromocriptine-aided cocaine withdrawal; buspirone-aided nicotine withdrawal).

Another direction of therapeutics and research by clinical pharmacologists has been the active development of dosage forms and drug delivery systems that can help to prevent or to reduce undesired patterns of abusable psychotropic use. For example, a highly successful approach has been the development of combination pentazocine/naloxone tablets (Talwin-Nx) for the reduction of illicit intravenous abuse of pentazocine. As a result of this pharmacologic strategy, the illicit intravenous use of pentazocine has been all but eliminated in the United States. Likewise, the transdermal nicotine delivery systems have become important adjuncts to smoking cessation programs and have demonstrated positive effects in relation to decreasing tobacco smoking. On the horizon are a number of promising developments in pharmacology, including several aimed at the pharmacologic prevention and treatment of cocaine addiction. As polysubstance or, more accurately, polyabusable psychotropic use becomes even more prominent in North America, clinically significant interactions involving the abusable psychotropics and their methods of use certainly will be increasingly addressed.

Although pharmacologists have been successful in developing useful knowledge of the pharmacology, toxicology, abuse potential, and addiction liability of the abusable psychotropics among adult population groups, increased attention must be directed toward the prevention and treatment of abusable psychotropic use among youth, whose use of the abusable psychotropics is increasingly significant. In this regard, clinical pharmacologists, and other health care providers, must recognize that:

1. Certain abusable psychotropics hold particular attraction to youth and are selected and used preferentially for a variety of reasons. . . .

2. Youth are at particular risk for social problems associated with abusable psychotropic use. . . .

3. Because of their heterogeneity, youth require individualized and diverse prevention and treatment approaches. (pp. 676–677)

In relation to the prevention and treatment of substance use among children and adolescents, the major applications of pharmacotherapy involve acute overdoses, withdrawal, abstinence, substitution, and dual diagnoses. Each of these applications is presented.

Acute overdoses.   Two groups of the substances of abuse classified as CNS depressants, opiates and benzodiazepine sedative-hypnotics, have available specific pharmacological antagonists that can be used to reverse their toxic and other pharmacological effects. These antagonists are, respectively, naloxone and flumazenil.

Naloxone (Narcan) is an essentially pure opiate antagonist that has virtually no direct observable effects other than its antagonistic effects. These effects are elicited within the CNS by competitive inhibition; that is, it selectively competes with opiate analgesics for binding sites on endogenous endorphin receptors. By displacing the opiate from its binding sites, naloxone immediately inhibits the pharmacological activity of the opiates, including, in cases of severe overdose, life-threatening respiratory depression. If administered to a person who is physiologically dependent on the opiates, naloxone can precipitate an opiate withdrawal syndrome (e.g., increased blood pressure, nausea, tachycardia, and vomiting). The onset of action for naloxone is generally within 2 minutes of administration. Effects last for approximately 1–2 hours. In this regard, naloxone may need to be periodically readministered in cases of overdose in which long-acting opiates such as methadone have been used.

Flumazenil (Anexate and Mazicon) is an essentially pure benzodiazepine receptor antagonist. Flumazenil elicits its antagonistic effects within the CNS by means of competitive inhibition. The onset of action for flumazenil is generally within 2 minutes of intravenous injection with effects lasting for approximately 1 hour. Although flumazenil effectively antagonizes the sedative and hypnotic effects (conscious sedation or general anesthesia) produced by the benzodiazepines, it is less effective at reversing their respiratory depressive effects. The use of flumazenil for a person who is physiologically dependent on the benzodiazepines may sometimes precipitate convulsions ("Flumazenil," 1992; Karavokiros & Tsipis, 1990).

Withdrawal syndromes. Several drugs have been used, with varying degrees of success, to reduce the unpleasant physiological and psychological signs and symptoms associated with substance withdrawal syndromes, including those associated with the cessation of alcohol, opiate, and cocaine use (W. A. Taylor & Slaby, 1992).[18] Alcohol withdrawal often is treated quite successfully with a long-acting benzodiazepine, usually chlordiazepoxide (Librium), the dosage of which is gradually reduced over a 1–2 week period. When appropriately used, chlordiazepoxide can make the alcohol withdrawal syndrome virtually symptomless. However, to prevent cross-addiction, benzodiazepine use should be discontinued once detoxification is complete (Mirin, 1995).[19]

Although less efficacious, clonidine (Catapres), an alpha-adrenergic ago-

[18] Generally, the signs and symptoms associated with substance withdrawal are simply the opposite of those normally expected as the desired pharmacological effects. For example, the desired effects of the sedative-hypnotics are calmness, muscle relaxation, and sleep; the signs and symptoms associated with sedative-hypnotic withdrawal syndromes include, conversely, such effects as anxiety, muscle tremor (or convulsion), and insomnia.

[19] Other drugs (e.g., clonidine and propranolol) have been used to diminish elevated blood pressure and heart rate, as well as tremors, associated with alcohol withdrawal. We generally do not

nist used clinically for its antihypertensive effects, has been used increasingly to manage opiate—heroin and methadone—withdrawal syndromes (M. S. Gold & Dackis, 1984; Kleber, 1994; Washton et al., 1985). The signs and symptoms of withdrawal are effectively managed by gradually decreasing the clonidine dosage over a 1–2-week period.[20]

Amantadine (Symmetrel), bromocriptine (Parlodel), carbidopa/levodopa (Sinemet), pergolide mesylate (Permax), and other drugs that possess dopaminergic activity have been used to treat the psychological craving associated with the cocaine withdrawal syndrome (Jonas & Gold, 1992; Tutton & Crayton, 1993). However, results have been varied, and further research is required before the widespread clinical use of these drugs for the treatment of cocaine craving can be recommended.

Abstinence.   Several drugs have been developed to encourage abstinence among people who have ceased abusive or compulsive use of a substance of abuse.[21] These drugs exert generally unpleasant effects when the substance of abuse is used. Thus, their ability to promote abstinence is by means of their association with adverse stimuli. The prototype drug with the longest history of use in this regard is disulfiram (Antabuse).

Disulfiram blocks the metabolism of alcohol at the acetaldehyde stage by means of inhibition of the enzyme acetaldehyde dehydrogenase. Consequently, when alcohol is consumed, even in small quantities, acetaldehyde accumulates in the bloodstream, eliciting a number of unpleasant effects, including blurred vision, chest pain, confusion, copious vomiting, dyspnea, flushing, hyperventilation, hypotension, nausea, respiratory difficulty, syncope, tachycardia, throbbing headache, vertigo, and weakness. The intensity of this reaction, which is known as the disulfiram-alcohol reaction (or more commonly as the "Antabuse reaction"), is generally proportional to the amount of disulfiram used as a component of the alcohol abstinence promo-

---

recommend their use because they have no effect on preventing seizures that may accompany severe alcohol withdrawal.

[20] We would not recommend pharmacological adjuncts for the management of the heroin withdrawal syndrome because it is generally relatively mild and can usually be handled "cold turkey"; signs and symptoms of the withdrawal syndrome resemble those of a bad case of influenza. However, the methadone withdrawal syndrome can be quite severe, with convulsions and other physiological effects that require appropriate treatment under medical supervision. Even when not required medically, we strongly recommend inpatient withdrawal, particularly for patients with long-standing or high-dose use of a substance of abuse, in order to provide appropriate psychological support and to significantly increase the chances that the patient successfully completes the withdrawal process. The average stay for people in detoxification units or centers in these situations is approximately 3 days (B. Rush & Ekdahl, 1990).

[21] Abstinence, in this context, is actually a form of relapse prevention (see discussion of relapse prevention, below).

tion program and the amount of alcohol consumed at a particular drinking session.[22]

Therapy is begun following at least 1 day of abstinence from alcohol use in order to avoid precipitating the disulfiram-alcohol reaction. Subsequently, disulfiram is orally ingested on a daily basis each morning for a period of months to years until abstinence can be maintained without the aid of the drug.[23] Patients must be properly educated regarding the necessity for complete abstinence (even from alcohol-containing cough syrups) in order to avoid the disulfiram-alcohol reaction.

A more recent pharmacological approach to promoting abstinence is the use of naltrexone (ReVia). Naltrexone, a long-acting oral opiate antagonist, was originally developed and marketed under the brand name Trexan for the treatment of abusive and compulsive patterns of opiate use (Greenstein et al., 1984). However, it was discovered by serendipity that it also blocked the "euphorogenic" effect of alcohol.[24] When used as an adjunct to effective psychotherapy, naltrexone has been found to demonstrate significant clinical utility with reports of less craving for alcohol, a lower rate of relapse, and, when drinking, the consumption of fewer drinks per occasion (S. S. O'Malley et al., 1992; Volpicelli, Clay, Watson, & Volpicelli, 1994). However, long-term safety and efficacy have not yet been clearly established.[25] Caution must be exercised when naltrexone is used for people who have alcoholism and also are abusing the opiates because naltrexone can precipitate an acute opiate withdrawal syndrome among these people. Likewise, people who use opiate analgesics for the management of chronic cancer or other malignant pain would require alternative pain relief measures until the effects of naltrexone dissipate because it is a potent opiate antagonist ("Naltrexone," 1995; Volpicelli et al., 1995).

Several selective serotonin re-uptake inhibitors (e.g., citalopram, fluoxetine, and sertraline) also have been investigated in relation to their possible effects on alcohol euphoria and craving. Results, in the absence of depres-

---

[22] Clinicians should be cognizant that disulfiram also interferes with the metabolism of other drugs (e.g., benzodiazepines and tricyclic antidepressants), and consequently the dosage of these drugs, if used concurrently, will need to be appropriately modified.

[23] We have found disulfiram to be effective in highly motivated compliant patients as an initial adjunct to the AA 12-step program and weekly psychotherapy. The youngest patients for whom we have successfully used disulfiram have been in their early 20s. However, the successful use of disulfiram therapy for adolescents has been reported in the clinical literature (e.g., Myers, Donahue, & Goldstein, 1994).

[24] The CNS depressant effects, including alcohol-related effects on cognition, do not appear to be significantly affected by naltrexone ("Naltrexone," 1995). Thus, it is *not* a "sobriety pill."

[25] E.g., until additional data are available, the potential for naltrexone to potentiate the possible hepatotoxicity of disulfiram makes the concurrent use of these two drugs relatively contraindicated.

sion, have been mixed, with a tendency toward being "weakly efficacious" (Anton, 1994).

Substitution.   Substitution is based on the principle of harm reduction, which is an integral component of tertiary prevention (see earlier discussion). As such, substitution does not attempt to stop the use of substances of abuse but, rather, attempts to change the level of harm associated with the use of a particular substance of abuse, including its method of use. Two major examples of this approach are currently used in North America: 1. the substitution of methadone for heroin and 2. the substitution of alternative methods of nicotine use (e.g., chewing gum and transdermal delivery systems) for tobacco smokers.

Methadone (Dolophine) has been used for over 30 years in North America to maintain people who have compulsive patterns of heroin use so that they do not have to use heroin in order to ward off the withdrawal syndrome or resort to hustling and other illegal means of supporting their heroin habits. Methadone maintenance "keeps the edge off" for these people and, thus, allows them to maintain parenting, work, and other social responsibilities. Although maintaining a person's dependence on opiates, methadone offers several benefits in that it is effective orally, decreases heroin craving, produces neither euphoria nor excessive sedation, is relatively inexpensive, and is legal. Unfortunately, the withdrawal syndrome associated with methadone is actually more severe than that associated with heroin. L-alpha-acetyl-methadol (LAAM or ORLAAM), a long-acting (i.e., 3 days) methadone derivative, is also in current clinical use ("LAAM," 1994). Many people who choose to enroll in methadone maintenance programs remain on the programs for long periods of time (several years), and those people who do not remain on them usually revert to their original heroin use (Des Jarlais & Dole, 1981).

The widest use of substitution in North America involves the use of nicotine chewing gum and nicotine transdermal patches as part of tobacco smoking cessation programs. Whereas methadone maintenance is just that, it is generally expected that nicotine substitutes be used over the short term as a means to help people cease their nicotine use. Although primarily intended for adults, a survey of adolescent smoking behaviors and attitudes indicated that a significant percentage (~30 percent) of this age group believes that the use of nicotine substitutes would make quitting smoking easier (Tuakli et al., 1990, p. 372). While potentially beneficial, studies have repeatedly demonstrated that the use of nicotine substitutes is only effective when combined with psychotherapy programs. For example, as noted by Covey and Glassman (1991), "Evidence of the addictive nature of chronic tobacco use suggests that pharmacologic interventions, in conjunction with behaviorally oriented therapy, may present the best hope for achieving smoking cessation in refractory smokers" (p. 69). Or, as observed by Generali (1992): "Smoking cessation rates associated with nicotine transdermal patch therapy have varied in clinical trials. However, appropriate patient instruction and an extensive behavioral modification program ensure optimal response to transdermal nicotine therapy" (p. 34). The use of nicotine substitutes is meant as a temporary adjunct to smoking cessation. These drug substitutes should be gradually terminated with dosage reductions over a 2–3 month period.

Dual Diagnoses.   Appropriate pharmacotherapy for mental disorders is a common and integral component of the treatment of problematic patterns of substance use among people who have a dual diagnosis (see Chap. 6). The two most commonly treated categories of mental disorders, in this regard, are anxiety disorders and depression (Anton, 1994; Ryan & Puig-Antich, 1987). Many of the following treatment modalities can be used, in addition to pharmacotherapy, for treating children and adolescents who have dual diagnoses. However, as stated by Kaminer and Frances (1991), "No single therapeutic intervention has been proven to be superior to others in the inpatient treatment of adolescents with concomitant substance abuse and mental illness" (p. 896). Thus, treatment approaches must be highly individualized, and often multimodal, in order to obtain optimal therapeutic response (see Chap. 6).

Psychotherapy

Cognitive therapy is probably the most commonly used form of psychotherapy in the treatment of problematic patterns of substance use among children and adolescents. Cognitive therapy, in this context, is based on the assumption that problematic patterns of substance use are reflective of maladaptive coping, that the child or adolescent has not learned other ways to cope with her or his problems or meet certain individual needs. Cognitive therapy is, therefore, directed at the correction or modification of irrational belief systems, maladaptive or deficient coping skills, and faulty thinking patterns or styles.

Training in self-observation, the sharing of thoughts and emotions with the therapist, the systematic analysis of the validity of negative and irrational self-statements, and the gradual substitution of positive logical thinking patterns based on rational belief systems are attempted as part of the cognitive therapy process. Through this process, children and adolescents are gradually made more aware of their problems, which may have been denied or avoided, and helped to develop the strategies, skills, and abilities they need to effectively deal with them.

The development, or strengthening, of specific intrapersonal and interpersonal skills, including anger control, leisure time management, problem solving, and resistance training (see Table 10.6 for a more comprehensive list), is an integral component of cognitive therapy. Cognitive therapy is often ap-

**TABLE 10.6   Intrapersonal and Interpersonal Skills Training
Elements**[a]

Intrapersonal Skills
    Managing thoughts about alcohol or other substance use
    Problem solving
    Decision making
    Relaxation training
    Becoming aware of anger
    Managing anger
    Becoming aware of negative thinking
    Managing negative thinking
    Increasing pleasant activities
    Planning for emergencies
    Coping with persistent problems

Interpersonal Skills
    Refusing offers to use substances of abuse
    Starting conversations
    Using body language
    Giving and receiving compliments
    Assertiveness training
    Refusing requests
    Communicating emotions
    Communicating in intimate relationships
    Giving criticism
    Receiving criticism
    Receiving criticism about using substances of abuse
    Enhancing social support networks

[a]Modified from Kadden (1994, p. 281).

plied in the context of relapse prevention in order to help to assure that the positive gains achieved during early abstinence are maintained. A central component to the achievement of this goal involves teaching children and adolescents how to identify high-risk situations that may lead to relapsed use and apply previously learned and rehearsed techniques to effectively avoid or deal with them.

Group psychotherapy for children and adolescents also can be extremely effective. As noted by Azima and Richmond (1989):

There is little doubt that group psychotherapy is the treatment of choice for most adolescents who are in the process of separation from parents and who rely strongly on influential peers for identification and direction. The peer group is the natural developmental habitat in which the adolescent manifests his struggle for independence, a separate identity, and a transitional model for adulthood. The stimulation, activity, and self-disclosure provided by the group creates the therapeutic climate in which adolescents can come to grips with and work through their problems, angers, and frustrations in an acceptable, meaningful way. (p. xi)

However, not all psychotherapists are equally adept at effectively practicing group psychotherapy. Bratter (1989) observed that "those psychotherapists who can work with addicted adolescents effectively in a group setting possess a quintessential quality that the theologian, Paul Tillich, has defined as 'caritas,' which connotes a noncompromising and nonpossessive form of caring" (p. 167). Additional details of group therapy will be discussed within the contexts of the following sections on family therapy, social skills training, AA, and therapeutic communities. Some general guidelines that can assist family therapists, regardless of their specific orientations, are presented in Table 10.7.

Family Therapy

The family often plays a significant role in the etiology and maintenance of problematic patterns of substance use among children and adolescents as identified throughout this text and particularly in Chapters 4 and 5. As noted by Bukstein and Van Hasselt (1993), "Intervention with substance-abusing adolescents that fails to proactively involve the family in treatment is unlikely to yield significant short- or long-term improvements" (p. 465). Cognizant of this association, family therapy attempts to correct the dysfunctional behavior of family members, both individually and as a group (see Table 10.8; Friedman & Granick, 1990; Joanning, Thomas, Newfield, & Lamun, 1991; Kaufman, 1990; Reilly, 1978).[26] Lewis et al. (1990, p. 88) described the Purdue Brief Family Therapy Model, a "mixed" family therapy model, noting its seven major goals, which we believe are applicable to many types of family therapy:

1. To decrease a family's resistance to treatment;
2. To redefine substance use as a family problem;

---

[26] When the concept of circular or reciprocal causality is applied, this approach is also commonly referred to as a *systemic* (family systems oriented) approach or model (Lewis, Piercy, Sprenkle, & Trepper, 1990). This approach or model should not be confused with "systemic family therapy," a particular model of family therapy that uses a cybernetic process. Systemic intervention or treatment differs from psychological and pharmacological approaches because of the inherent focus of these intervention strategies. Whereas the focus of the latter is on the child or adolescent as an individual, the focus of the former is on the entire family as a group that includes a member(s)—the child or adolescent—who displays problematic patterns of substance use. In this regard, the substance-using member is often identified as the "thermostat" of family health and functioning. Thus, therapists attempt (optimally) to assess and treat all the members of the family, including nuclear and extended family members or significant others, as a group.

TABLE 10.7 General Guidelines for the Family Therapist[a]

- When appropriate, respect the hierarchical structure of the family; if inappropriate, help the family reestablish a functional hierarchy.
- Listen to what is being said and not said, asking relevant questions for both.
- Do not interrupt a family member to ask for clarification while he or she is still speaking. Wait until he or she has finished.
- Closely observe nonverbal behavior in order to better understand family relationships and the possible need for intervention.
- Give equal attention to each family member.
- Be honest and open with the family and do not attempt to minimize its problems.
- Empathize with the stated family issues.
- Be nonjudgmental so that the family feels it can discuss problems without fear of censure.
- Establish open communication patterns early in therapy.
- Be aware of personal biases (and countertransference tendencies).
- Be flexible enough to shift your approach if you find that it is not working.
- Do not give advice, only suggestions as they fit the plan of operation.
- Do not allow yourself to be "triangled" or manipulated. *You* are the therapist.
- Evaluate each individual member of the family in terms of depression, guilt, self-esteem, and so forth.
- For a family that feels it has failed, bring up past successful experiences as reinforcement.
- Become a role model for the family.
- Allow the family to see you as a person who can make mistakes and own up to them. Allow them to see you as a person with feelings.
- Try to have a purpose and reason for all your actions or lack of action.
- Do not copy another therapist's style. Be yourself. Act in a manner that is comfortable for you and fits your personality.
- Provide options for the family from which it can select those that it would like to pursue. Plant seeds for positive growth that will foster the therapeutic process and help to bring about positive change.

[a]Modified from Frankel (1990, p. 263).

3. To reestablish appropriate parental influence;
4. To interrupt dysfunctional family sequences of behavior;
5. To assess the interpersonal function of the substance use;
6. To implement change strategies consistent with the family's interpersonal functioning; and
7. To provide assertion training skills for child and adolescent family members to resist peer pressures to engage in substance use.

Behavioral and strategic-structural family therapies are the most commonly used, excluding mixed therapies, and will be briefly discussed in the

TABLE 10.8　Types of Family Therapy[a] and Their Major Components or Focus[b]

Behavioral
　　Assertiveness training
　　Contingency contracting
　　Parent management training
　　Problem-solving skills training

Contextual (functional)
　　Integration of emotional, behavioral, cognitive, and spiritual aspects of family

Strategic-Structural
　　Restructure maladaptive patterns

Systemic
　　Address behavioral limit setting and intergenerational conflicts

Mixed
　　Various combinations of family therapy components

[a]While this categorization has been selected to facilitate organization and discussion, it is recognized that other, perhaps more comprehensive or detailed, categorizations of types of family therapy also are available.
[b]Modified from Bukstein (1994, p. 298).

context of application to the treatment of problematic patterns of substance use among children and adolescents.

Behavioral family therapy.　Behavioral family therapy for children and adolescents who display problematic patterns of substance use and their families consists predominantly of those techniques that were developed and validated by empirical study with children and adolescents who were identified as delinquent (e.g., Alexander, Waldon, Newberry, & Liddle, 1990; Bry, Conboy, & Bisgay, 1986; Rueger & Liberman, 1984). These techniques typically include contingency and behavioral contracting and training.

Contingency or behavioral contracting involves identifying, operationally defining, and agreeing to a set of desired child or adolescent target behaviors: for example, completing household chores such as taking out the garbage or cleaning one's room, getting homework done well and on time, and complying with time schedules for coming home after school or returning from an evening date. Consequences (punishment, such as "grounding") for breaking these "contracts" and rewards (reinforcement, such as an allowance) for complying with them are defined and used in order to positively modify the child's or adolescent's behavior.

The training component of behavioral family therapy is often directed toward assertion, parent management, and problem-solving skills training. Assertion training assists children and adolescents to learn and rehearse skills and techniques that can help them to resist peer pressure to use substances of abuse. Parent management training helps parents to improve their communication with their children, establish common goals, and reestablish their appropriate influence within the family structure. Parent training focuses on altering inappropriate parental behavior(s) and teaching parents, using role playing and practice, new skills for managing positive and negative behaviors noted in their children or adolescents (Wells, 1988; Wells & Forehand, 1981). Problem-solving skills training is aimed at assisting all family members to learn to become less dogmatic and more accepting of alternative strategies and solutions to family problems. The problem-solving approach has four principal components: 1. define the problem, 2. generate a number of alternative solutions for the defined problem,[27] 3. evaluate the positive and negative aspects of each alternative solution, and 4. select and implement the best available (practical and "doable") solution (Robin & Foster, 1988).

Strategic-structural family therapy. Strategic-structural, or simply structural, family therapy attempts to restructure maladaptive family boundaries that separate parents and their children or adolescents (Joanning et al., 1991). For example, a mother and son may form a close, protective alliance that excludes the father from the knowledge that his son is a homosexual and displays problematic patterns of alcohol use. In reaction to this exclusion, the father may feel alienated from his family and become increasingly indifferent to his wife and unsupportive of, or antagonistic toward, his son. In another example, parents may be involved in constant, bitter conflict with each other and engage one or more of their children or adolescents in this conflict by asking them to take sides or use them as a scapegoat for their anger, frustration, and blame. Such engagement may result in the child or adolescent withdrawing socially or seeking comfort and support from peers who may, in turn, facilitate his or her initiation or exacerbation of substance use.

The general approaches used with the strategic-structural model of family therapy include reframing, validation, facilitated communication, and paradoxical directives. *Reframing,* which also is used as a method with cognitive psychotherapy, simply refers to the process of conceptualizing a problem in a new and different way. The purpose of reframing is generally to: 1. put a problem in proper (generally smaller) perspective and 2. lessen the negative views that the family members have regarding their perceived notion of the cause of the problem. For example, the therapist may reframe more accurately an adolescent's marijuana use, which has been perceived by the parents as an act of parental defiance, as an expression of insecurity and low self-esteem. This reframing of the reasons related to the adolescent's marijuana

---

[27] This component process is often referred to as "brainstorming" and is conceptually equivalent to what has been referred to in the scientific context as the generation of multiple working hypotheses.

use may then shift the treatment approach from one of punishment to one of understanding and support.

Validation refers to the process by which the therapist, in acting as a role model for the family members, acknowledges and expresses understanding for each individual family member's feelings and desires. This process encourages the hearing out of individual family member's concerns before they are reacted to or judged.

In order to facilitate communication among family members, various techniques are taught and used during therapy sessions. For example, in relation to statements regarding feelings, individual family members may be taught to use the term "I feel" as opposed to "you feel." This technique avoids casting blame based on "mind-reading" and allows the other family members to clarify their own feelings. In response they can state for themselves what they feel as opposed to what a family member thinks they feel. This technique also tends to engender more empathetic responses than the use of "you feel" communications, which tend to elicit decidedly more defensive responses.

Paradoxical directives involve the encouragement of at least one of the family members to engage in behavior that he or she believes will exacerbate an identified family problem. For example, if an adolescent runs away from home because her parents have been fighting and threatening divorce and she refuses their attempts to talk to her or bring her back into the household, then the therapist may suggest, in the presence of the adolescent, that the parents stop making such attempts. In this situation, the adolescent is told explicitly to maintain the symptomatic behavior—in the example, running away—while being told implicitly to change it. This strategy, in turn, provides the adolescent with an opportunity for some self-control over her problem behavior, thereby removing its need and function. When carefully chosen and properly used, this technique has been found to be quite effective.[28]

Social Skills Training

Social skills training attempts to help children and adolescents deal more effectively with their families, peers, teachers, or employers. Social skills

---

[28] This technique is not to be confused with "tough love," an approach to parenting that uses an uncompromising refusal to let children be manipulative or break rules (Pieper & Pieper, 1992). E.g., parents may tell their adolescent daughter that if she returns home from a date after midnight, the door will be locked, requiring her to stay out all night. While this approach to problematic adolescent behavior may work in a few selected situations (B. Newton, 1985), its uncompromising nature (e.g., it may be just 1 minute after midnight or the curfew may have been missed because of a valid reason out of the control of the adolescent such as a flat tire or a bridge closure due to a motor vehicle crash) leads us to refrain from recommending tough love as a therapeutic option. In fact, when uncompromisingly practiced by parents, tough love can actually remove the necessary family support required by adolescents and inadvertently compel them to seek support from a peer group that may actively encourage substance use.

training is accomplished by detailed, focused training sessions that typically deal with common problems related to the child's or adolescent's lack of sufficiently developed social skills and include nonverbal expression, refusing unreasonable requests, making difficult requests, expressing and receiving positive emotions, replying appropriately to criticism, and initiating social conversations (Oei & Jackson, 1980).

This treatment approach is based on the observation that many children and adolescents who engage in problematic patterns of substance use have interpersonal, family, and vocational problems that appear to be related to deficits in social skills. Generally, individual and group training programs rely on therapist role modeling, role playing, and homework assignments to help children and adolescents develop effective methods of dealing with anger and frustration, reducing high levels of social anxiety, communicating with other people, being assertive, and avoiding peer pressure (Van Hasselt, Hersen, & Milliones, 1978; Van Hasselt, Null, Kempton, & Bukstein, 1993).[29]

Alcoholics Anonymous

AA was started in 1935 in Akron, Ohio, by Bill W. (a stockbroker) and Bob S. (a physician), who were its first two members. AA has since spread across North America and now holds meetings worldwide. As noted by Trice (1983), AA has become, particularly in North America, the most frequently used form of alcohol treatment. According to several other researchers and therapists (e.g., Room & Greenfield, 1993; Weisner, Greenfield, & Room, 1995), the popularity of AA is due in large part to its "American" themes of individualism, equality, and spirituality, which are embodied in the Twelve Steps (see Table 10.9). As noted by Kurtz (1988, 1993), the organizational structure of AA also supports these themes in that there is no central authority or hierarchy, the only officer in AA groups is a secretary, and members avoid the use of last names.

AA is regarded as neither a medical nor a psychological approach to treatment. As such the organization maintains that alcoholism is a disease without cure and that treatment is social.[30] AA relies on a rather informal form of group therapy and social support, with frequent meetings of recovering members, and a "buddy" system in which sponsors who have remained sober for a period of time by working the 12 steps show newcomers the way to sobriety. As part of the group therapy, members hear from other members that they are not alone and that they share common, painful experiences in relation to their alcohol use. In addition, in conjunction with Step 1, members learn to overcome their strong denial of their own drinking problems.

---

[29] The technique of social skills training also has been widely applied in juvenile correctional settings.

[30] In this regard, AA has often been labeled a "social" form of treatment.

TABLE 10.9   Twelve Steps of Alcoholics Anonymous[a]

1. We admitted that we were powerless over alcohol, that our lives had become unmanageable.
2. We came to believe that a Power greater than ourselves could restore us to sanity.
3. We made a decision to turn our will and our lives over to the care of God as we understood Him.
4. We made a searching and fearless moral inventory of ourselves.
5. We admitted to God, to ourselves, and to another human being the exact nature of our wrongs.
6. We were entirely ready to have God remove all these defects of character.
7. We humbly asked Him to remove our shortcomings.
8. We made a list of all persons we had harmed, and became willing to make amends to them all.
9. We made direct amends to such people wherever possible, except when to do so would injure them or others.
10. We continued to take personal inventory and when we were wrong promptly admitted it.
11. We sought through prayer and meditation to improve our conscious contact with God as we understood Him, praying only for knowledge of His will for us and the power to carry that out.
12. Having had a spiritual awakening as a result of these steps, we tried to carry this message to alcoholics and to practice these principles in all our affairs.

[a]From *The Little Red Book* (1986).

The confrontation of denial is clearly reflected in the members' introductions of themselves at AA group meetings: "Hello, my name is _____ and I'm an alcoholic."

Members are encouraged to work through and practice the 12 steps daily and, because the AA model asserts that there is no cure for alcoholism,[31] maintain lifelong abstinence by continued membership in the AA fellowship. For many alcoholics, including children and adolescents (Alford, Koehler, & Leonard, 1991; S. Beck & Olivet, 1988; Ehrlick, 1987; Lawson, 1992; Marshall, Marshall, & Heer, 1994; Sipe, 1984), AA provides both the social support necessary to maintain abstinence and an effective surrogate for their previously patterned drinking time or familiar bar scene; AA meetings serve as a place to go on evenings, weekends, and holidays for socialization with "friends" who, in addition to other benefits, provide understanding and help in alleviating social isolation and loneliness.[32]

[31] This AA belief would be consonant with what we describe as "compulsive use" in the levels of substance use (see Fig. 10.1 and Chap. 1 for additional details). In this regard, we would concur with the AA philosophy that treatment, to be successful, must include a lifetime of total abstinence—an often severe acknowledgment for children and adolescents.

[32] The number of AA meetings that a current member attends generally ranges from one daily to one weekly and is dictated, in large part, by factors such as the amount of time that a member

The overall effectiveness of AA is difficult to ascertain because AA maintains no formal records, research is not an AA mandate, the amount of time that members remain active in AA is extremely variable, and drop-out rates are high (Alford et al., 1991; Fingarette, 1988; W. R. Miller & McCrady, 1993).[33]

Therapeutic Communities

Therapeutic communities (TCs) are based on the assumption that substance use is primarily symptomatic of psychosocial maladaptation to society, often as a result of incompetence in dealing with stress or social privation and alienation. As enumerated by O'Brien and Biase (1984), the goals of TC programs are:

1. To eliminate the addict/abuser's drug-taking behavior,
2. To assist the addict/abuser in learning to respond to distress (personal and environmental) in a more healthful manner, and
3. To assist in readjusting and returning the resident to the outside community as a functioning, independent individual. (p. 16)

These goals are achieved by providing residential care for children and adolescents who have problematic patterns of substance use. The residential care is usually provided for 9–18 months and gives children and adolescents the opportunity to live with other children and adolescents who have similar problems in a highly structured homelike environment. As such, the TC pro-

---

has been sober (e.g., 1 day vs. 1 year), the personality of the member (e.g., avoidant, dependent, or compulsive), and accessibility (e.g., is the scheduled meeting nearby; does the member require and have available transportation; is the style of the meeting compatible with the member's needs?). However, in some cases an individual member will develop a "cultlike" relationship with AA; he or she will become obsessive and compulsive regarding AA doctrine, will limit social interaction to AA meetings and members, and will increasingly become estranged from other social groups such as family and colleagues (A. M. Pagliaro & L. A. Pagliaro, 1992, 1995, clinical patient file notes). These situations, although relatively infrequently encountered, should be appropriately monitored for and dealt with as part of the patient's program of psychotherapy.

[33] Obviously, the approach used by AA will not be suitable for all children and adolescents and, because of the paucity of data to substantiate its effectiveness with these age groups, we would *not* recommend it as the sole approach to therapy. However, for patients who are willing to attend the AA meetings, we have found it to be an effective and useful adjunct to individual psychotherapy and family therapy and can highly recommend it in this regard. In addition, the efficacy of AA programs appears to be substantiated de facto by the large number of members who speak positively about it and the use of the AA approach by similar groups (e.g., Cocaine Anonymous, Gamblers Anonymous, and Narcotics Anonymous). It also has been extended to other 12-step self-help groups for adolescents and families who have parents or members, respectively, that display problematic patterns of substance use (e.g., Alateen, AL-ANON, and Families of Alcoholics; Room & Greenfield, 1993). In addition, AA has consistently been rated highly by health care professionals (e.g., Chang, Astrachan, & Bryant, 1994).

vides a setting where everyone shares in the work and responsibility to see that community problems are minimized. Ideally, during their residential treatment, children and adolescents will be able to develop increasing skills and responsibilities, which they can transfer to the larger community on their completion of the program. Regular meetings are held throughout the day in informal settings (e.g., sitting around the kitchen table). These meetings serve to facilitate the running of the TC (e.g., division of work and provision of feedback on the quality of residents' work performance) and provide a format for decision-making processes. A significant amount of therapy also occurs informally throughout the day, during which residents learn to take responsibility for and perform their tasks while interacting with the other residents. Recreational and leisure activities also provide a means for socializing and learning to interact more positively with others.

Most TCs practice a form of egalitarianism (Freudenberger & Carbone, 1984). For example, in regard to deciding how to handle a resident who is having difficulty "getting on the program" or in dealing with setting a program policy, all residents have an equal opportunity to share input and have an equal vote with the staff members.[34] All TCs require total abstinence from the use of alcohol, cocaine, heroin, LSD, and marijuana, but many still allow caffeine and nicotine use.

The TCs have served as a model for many "halfway house" programs, which have been designed to ease a child's or adolescent's transition to the community after being released from a locked residential treatment facility or correctional facility. Such children and adolescents often require more supervision and monitoring than can be provided by their families or outpatient treatment services.

Children and adolescents who complete TC programs have been found to "show a success rate of more than 75%" (Rosenthal, 1984, p. 55). However, most patients (~75%) do not complete the entire course of treatment provided by a TC (S. Cohen, 1982). For these patients "outcome results indicate that reduction of illicit drug use, crime, and unemployment is commensurate to the length of time an addict participates in a therapeutic community" (Coombs, 1981, p. 199).[35]

---

[34] Primary clinical and custodial staff employed by TCs are generally paraprofessionals who have successfully rehabilitated themselves from previous substance use with the assistance of a TC program. Ancillary staff include professionals from various disciplines (e.g., law, medicine, and psychology) who are generally used on a contractual basis (De Leon, 1985). Although this staffing pattern is beginning to change with the use of more certified counselors and social workers, the utilization of clinical psychologists and other university-educated social and health care professionals generally remains low in these programs.

[35] Similarly, "day-care" programs have been developed for adolescents who have problematic patterns of substance use in order to facilitate their transition from residential treatment back to the home and family environment (e.g., B. Feigelman & Jaquith, 1992; W. Feigelman, 1987).

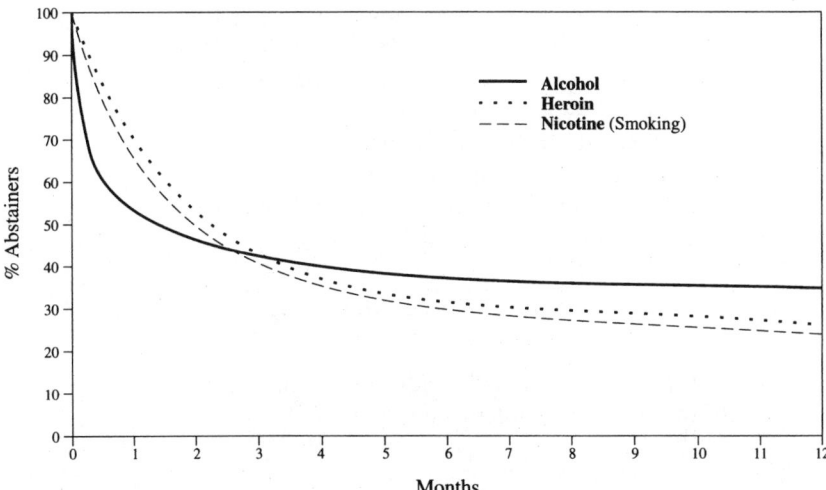

FIGURE 10.2   Typical relapse rates following treatment for problematic patterns of substance use

RELAPSE

The rate of relapse, or recidivism, following the "successful" treatment of problematic patterns of substance use among children and adolescents is quite high (see Fig. 10.2). Although much research has examined treatment factors such as involvement of family in treatment, provision of special services, staff characteristics, and time in treatment, these factors have not been able to account for the majority of variance in posttreatment return to substance use (Catalano et al., 1990–91). Obviously, much more research is required in this area.

Our own clinical experience and the currently available research data would suggest that the use of the following three recommendations would at least minimize the potential for relapsed use:

1. Individualize treatment to the needs and characteristics of the child or adolescent ("cut the shoe to fit the foot");[36]
2. Use specific indicators or performance goals to objectively evaluate the success of treatment outcome and, subsequently, the degree of relapse or efficacy of relapse prevention (see Table 10.10); and

[36] The use of "patient-treatment matching" has significantly increased in recent years (e.g., Kaminer & Frances, 1991; Mattson, 1994; "Project MATCH," 1993).

TABLE 10.10   Performance Goals/Criteria in Relation to Evaluation of Treatment Success and Relapse Prevention[a]

1. Interviewer's clinical evaluation of improvement
2. Job/school and social adjustment
3. Self-reported reduction in substance use
4. Reduction in sociopathy
5. Intrapersonal adjustment (e.g., with family and friends)
6. Social involvement
7. Abstinence

[a]From Foster, Horn, and Wanberg (1972, p. 1079).

3. Periodically, as individually indicated, prophylactically reassess patients and proactively intervene to prevent relapse.[37]

SUMMARY

Much effort has been directed toward finding effective programs and techniques to prevent or treat substance use among children and adolescents. However, to date, only marginal success has been achieved in these areas, as demonstrated by: 1. the increasing numbers of children and adolescents who engage in problematic patterns of substance use and 2. the extremely high recidivism rates that accompany virtually all current treatment programs.

An overview of the major available prevention and treatment programs has been presented together with general guidelines to assist practitioners (see Table 10.11). The theme that is consistently and repeatedly found in the research literature is that different children and adolescents who have problematic patterns of substance use respond differently to different treatment approaches—what works best for one child or adolescent may not work

[37] Some of this periodic monitoring is addressed, e.g., in "aftercare" programs and in continued attendance at AA meetings, both of which have been positively correlated with significant post-treatment abstinence (E. Johnson & Herringer, 1993; B. P. Kennedy & Minami, 1993; McBride, 1991). We would suggest, particularly for children and adolescents who have engaged in compulsive patterns of substance use, that (as in the AA model discussed above and our previous discussion of patterns of use in Chap. 1) the propensity for substance use be considered a lifelong problem. Whenever possible, once children and adolescents are abstinent, we gradually decrease the frequency and length of their psychotherapy sessions (e.g., from biweekly, to weekly, to every other week, to monthly, to every other month, to telephone contact every six months). This strategy helps to maintain a communication linkage and "lifeline" (help line) for each patient that demonstrates continued concern and provides an opportunity for the early detection of problems by the therapist and for patients to request needed assistance *before* problems get out of control. In our practice, this strategy has resulted in a long-term (as long as we can maintain patient contact, generally in excess of five years) relapse rate of less than 20 percent (A. M. Pagliaro & L. A. Pagliaro, unpublished research data).

TABLE 10.11   General Guidelines for the Treatment of Children and Adolescents Who Use Substances of Abuse

- Conduct a comprehensive assessment prior to initiating treatment.
- Be nonjudgmental in approaching treatment.
- Individualize treatment approaches.
- Recognize that different types of treatment may be required—the type of treatment that works best for one child or adolescent may not necessarily work best for another.
- Remember that success or failure is ultimately the child's or adolescent's responsibility—do not become co-dependent.
- Assess for, treat, or refer appropriately for treatment any accompanying mental disorders (i.e., dual diagnoses).
- Break the denial of problems associated with substance use.
- Respect children and adolescents; do not treat them in a condescending manner.
- Provide education in a straightforward, nonbiased way that is appropriately tailored to the developmental, learning, and social needs and cognitive abilities of the child or adolescent.
- Work toward realistic and achievable goals that have been mutually agreed upon.
- Remember that reasons for substance use may differ from one child or adolescent to another and even for the same child or adolescent over time.
- Appropriately address underlying problems (e.g., lack of self-esteem or poor coping skills).
- Involve family, friends, and others as appropriate in confrontation, treatment planning, and program implementation.
- Use peer groups (i.e., group children and adolescents according to age and gender).
- Use community social agencies designed for children and adolescents.
- Make referrals to other appropriate health and social care professionals and agencies.
- Provide appropriate followup or aftercare services and collaborate, as appropriate, with schools and other community resources during this process.

best, or in some cases, at all, for a different child or adolescent. Thus, instead of attempting to find and use the single "best" program, it is recommended that mental health and other professionals become familiar with the various types and approaches to prevention and treatment and then select the one(s) that is (are) best suited to the specific needs of their patients, be that patient an individual (e.g., treatment of a 16-year-old cocaine user) or a group (e.g., prevention of the initiation of cocaine use among a group of fifth-grade students attending an inner-city school). In this regard, MIMSEUICA can serve as a particularly useful heuristic device (see Chap. 1).

APPENDIX I

Abbreviations Used in the Text

AA	Alcoholics Anonymous	**MAO**	monoamine oxidase
ADD	attention deficit disorder	**MDMA**	3,4-methylenedioxy-methamphetamine
ADHD	attention deficit hyperactivity disorder		
AIDS	acquired immunodeficiency syndrome	**MIMSEUICA**	Mega Interactive Model of Substance Exposure and Use among Infants, Children, and Adolescents
ARBD	alcohol-related birth defect		
BAC	blood alcohol concentration	**mo.**	month(s)
CD	conduct disorder	**NIDA**	National Institute on Drug Abuse
CNS	central nervous system	**PCP**	phencyclidine
DSM-IV	*Diagnostic and Statistical Manual of Mental Disorders,* 4th ed.	**pH**	hydrogen ion concentration
		pka	degree of ionization
FACES III	Family Adaptability and Cohesion Evaluation Scale, Version 3	**SIDS**	sudden infant death syndrome
FAE	fetal alcohol effect	**STD**	sexually transmitted disease
FAS	fetal alcohol syndrome		
HIV	human immunodeficiency virus	**SUD**	substance use disorder
		T_s	teacher subset
I_s	instructor subset	**TC**	therapeutic community
ICC_s	instructor-content-context subset	**THC**	tetrahydrocannabinol
		TTY	teletype for the hearing impaired
IQ	intelligence quotient		
L_s	learner subset	**UC**	unit coterie
LAAM	L-alpha-acetyl-methadol	**y.o.**	years old
LSD	lysergic acid diethylamide		

Generic, Trade, and Common Names of the Substances of Abuse

APPENDIX II Generic, Trade and, Common Names of the Substances of Abuse

Generic Name	Trade Name	Classification	Subclassification	Common Street Names
Alcohol (ethanol)	Various brand names of beer, wine, and distilled liquor	CNS depressant: sedative-hypnotic	Alcohol	Alleviator, angel's food, apple fritter, Bacchus, bamboo juice, barley-bree, barley broth, barley-corn, beggar boy's, beggar boy's ass, belsh, belt, berpwater, bit of blink, bitters, blue ribbon, blue ruin, blue stone, blue tape, bob, boilermaker, booze, bracer, brew, brewer's fizzle, Brian O'Flinn, Brian O'Linn, Brian O'Lynn, bush girlfriend, cat's water, cheerer, cheerer-upper, chit-chat, clap of thunder, cocktail, cocky's joy, cold one, cooler, corker, courage in a bottle, cream of the valley, cream of the wilderness, cup of cheer, cup of comfort, dago red, daily mail, day and night, deadeye, demon vino, drink, drinkypoo, eye-opener, eyewash, eyewater, flash of lightning, frog's wine, Geneva, Geneva courage, giggle and titter, golden cream, Gordon, Gordon water, grape, grapes, grapes of wrath, grappo, Gunga Din, gunpowder, hair of the dog, hair of the dog that bit one, happy sale, heart's ease, hi-ball, highball, Holland tape, hops, Huckleberry Finn, hum, hum cap, humming October, in-jay, jackey, jacky, Jersey lightning, jigger, jinny, johnnie, joy-juice, juice, jolt, jump-steady, juniper, juniper-juice, just what the doctor ordered, kick in the guts, kill-cobbler, kill-priest, knock down, knock-me-down, leg-opener, light blue, lunatic broth, lunatic soup, lush, mad dog, madman's broth, merry-go-down, mother's milk, mother's ruin, mouthwash, nap, nappy, nightcap, nip, nipper, old boy, old red goofy, old Tom, one for the road, paint, panther piss, pharaoh, pharo, pink-eye, pinkie, pissticide, pistol shot, porter, porter's ale, quencher, rag water, ribbon, right sort, rosy, rouge, royal poverty, ruby, ruin, satin, short one, short snort, shot, sky blue, tall one, the grape, the grapes, the vine, Tom, tonic, twankay, water of life

Alfentanil	Alfenta	CNS depressant: analgesic	Opiate	
Alprazolam	Apo-Alpraz, Novo-Alprazol, Nu-Alpraz, Xanax	CNS depressant: sedative-hypnotic	Benzodiazepine	
Amobarbital	Amytal	CNS depressant: sedative-hypnotic	Barbiturate	Amies, blue, blue angel, blue birds, blue clouds, blue devils, blue dolls, blue dots, blue heavens, blue jackets, blues, blue tips, blue velvet, double blue, jack-ups
Amphetamine	Benzedrine, Biphetamine	CNS stimulant	Amphetamine	Amps, **B, B-Bomb,** beans, benj, bennies, benny, benz, benzadrina, benzies, brother Ben, bomber pilot, cartwheels, copilot, crasses, drin, greenies, hearts, hi-ball, minibennie, peaches, roses, whites
Anileridine	Leritine	CNS depressant: analgesic	Opiate	
Aprobarbital	Alurate	CNS depressant: sedative-hypnotic	Barbiturate	Aprobarbs, barbs
Benzphetamine	Didrex	CNS stimulant	Amphetamine	
Bromazepam	Lectopam	CNS depressant: sedative-hypnotic	Benzodiazepine	
Butabarbital	Barbased, Busodium, Buta-Barb, Butalan, Butatran, Buticaps, Butisol, Mebutal	CNS depressant: sedative-hypnotic	Barbiturate	
Butorphanol	Stadol-NS	CNS depressant: analgesic	Opiate	

APPENDIX II (*Continued*)

Generic Name	Trade Name	Classification	Subclassification	Common Street Names
Cannabis (hashish, hashish oil, marijuana)	Not commercially available	Psychedelic		Acapulco, Acapulco gold, Acapulco red, African black, African bush, Angola black, Aunt Mary, baby buds, bad green, bale, bhang, bhang ganjah, black, black Columbus, black ganja, black gold, black gungeon, black gungi, black gunion, black gunny, black hash, black mo, black moat, black mold, black mole, black monte, black mota, black mote, black Russian, block, blond, blond hash, blond hashish, blond Lebanese, blue cheese, blue sage, bo-bo, bo-bo bush, brick, broccoli, brown, brown weed, bud, bull jive, bullet Thai, bush, cam, cam red, cam trip, Cambodian red, Cambodian trip weed, Canadian black, candy bar, charas, chocolate, chunkies, Colombian, Colombian gold, Colombian green, Columbian gold, Columbian pink, Columbian red, Congo brown, Congo dirt, Congo mataby, cube, dagga, dagha, ditch dope, dreamstick, ganga, ganja, ganjah, gold, gold bud, gold Colombian, gold Columbian, golden leaf, grass, green bud, green goddess, green moroccan, hash, hash oil, Hawaiian, hemp, herb, herbs, Indian hay, Indian hemp, Indian rope, Indian weed, Jamaica ganga, Jamaica gold, Jamaican, Jamaican red, Jane, Jary Jane, jay, joint, keef, kef, keff, keif, khif, kief, kif, killer weed, Kona gold, leaf, leaves, Lebanese hash, Lebanese red, Lebanon red, Lipton's Tea, loco weed, Mary J, Mary Jane, Maryjane, Maui Waui, Maui wowee, Maui wowie, Mex, Mexican, monster weed, murder weed, Panama, Panama gold, Panamanian gold, Panama red, Panamanian red, pot, pukalolo, puna butter, red leb, red Lebanese, reefer, righteous bush, roach, rope, sense, sinse, sinsemilla, smoke, stash, supergrass, superweed, sweet Mary, T, Texas tea, Thai pot, Thai-weed, Thaistick, THC, the herb, the weed, trip weed, turnip greens, weed

Chloral hydrate	Aquachloral, Noctec, Novo-Chlorhydrate, PMS-Chloral Hydrate	CNS depressant: sedative-hypnotic	Chlorals, corals, knockout drops, Mickey Finn (when mixed with alcohol)
Chlordiaze-poxide	Apo-chlordiaze-poxide, Libritabs, Librium, Limbitrol, Limbitrol DS, Lipox-ide, Medilium, Men-rium, Novo-Poxide, Reposans-10, Solium	CNS depressant: sedative-hypnotic	Benzodiazepine
Chlorphenter-mine	Pre-sate	CNS stimulant	
Clobazam	Frisium	CNS depressant: sedative-hypnotic	Benzodiazepine
Clonazepam	Klonopin, PMS-Clonazepam, Rivotril	CNS depressant: sedative-hypnotic	Benzodiazepine
Clorazepate	Apo-chlorazepate, Gen-Xene, Novo Clorazepate, Novo-Clopate, Tranexene, Tranexene-SD Half Strength Tablets, Tranexene T-TAB, Tranxene	CNS depressant: sedative-hypnotic	Benzodiazepine

APPENDIX II (*Continued*)

Generic Name	Trade Name	Classification	Subclassification	Common Street Names
Cocaine	Cocaine Topical Solution	CNS stimulant		Angel, angie, baking soda base, base, bernese, Bernice, Bernies, Bernies flake, big bloke, big-C, bloke, blow, bump, C, Cadillac, California cornflakes, candy, Cecil, cee, C-game, chalk, coca, cocaina, cocanuts, cocunut, coka, Coke, cola, cookie, Corine, Corinne, Corrine, flake, free base, frisky, frisky powder, girl, girlfriend, girli, girly, glad stuff, gold dust, golden girl, happy trails, heaven leaf, her, Inca message, incentive, initiative, joy dust, joy flakes, joy powder, lady, Lady Snow, Lady White, leaf, line, magic flake, Mama coca, nose candy, nose powder, nose stuff, number three, old lady White, paradise, perico, Peruvian flake, pimp dust, pogo pogo, rich man's drug, rock, rock candy, rocks, sleighride, sniff, snow, snow stuff, snow-caine, snowball, snowflakes, sophisticated lady, star spangled powder, star stuff, stardust, superblow, sweet stuff, talc, the leaf, the pimp's drug, the ultimate drug, toot, tootonium, tootuncommon, uptown, WC, whiff, white, white cross, white nurse, white stuff, white tornado
Codeine (methylmorphine)	Various combination products (e.g., acetaminophen with codeine or aspirin with codeine)	CNS depressant: analgesic	Opiate	Cement, cod, cods, codys, deens, deines, denes, fours, schoolboy
Dextroamphetamine (dexamphetamine)	Biphetamine, Dexedrine, Ferndex, Oxydess II, Spancap No. 1	CNS stimulant	Amphetamine	Beans, benn, bennies, black beauties, blues, brown, brown & clears, brownies, browns, Christmas tree, copilots, crank, crystal meth, dexie, dexo, dexies, dex, green & clears, hearts, horse hearts, ice, jolly beans, orange, oranges, peaches, pep pills, pink football, purple hearts, purple passion, truck-drivers

Drug	Trade/other names	Classification	Type	Street names
Diazepam	Apo-diazepam, Diazemuls, E-pam, Meval, Novo-Dipam, PMS-Diazepam, T-Quil, Valium, Valrelease, Vazepam, Vivrol, Zetran	CNS depressant: sedative-hypnotic	Benzodiazepine	BB, blue, blue bombers, blues, dies, dis, dyes, ums, V, Vs, vals, vees
Diethylpropion	M-Orexic, Nobesine-75, Nu-Dispoz, Regebon, Ro-Diet, Tenuate, Tepanil	CNS stimulant		
Estazolam	Prosom	CNS depressant: sedative-hypnotic	Benzodiazepine	
Fenfluramine	Ponderal, Pondimin	CNS stimulant		
Fentanyl	Duragesic, Innovar, Sublimaze	CNS depressant: analgesic	Opiate	Fen
Flurazepam	Apo-flurazepam, Dalmane, Durapam, Novo-Flupam, Novoflurazepam, PMS-Flurazepam, Som-Pam, Somnol	CNS depressant: sedative-hypnotic	Benzodiazepine	
Halazepam	Paxipam	CNS depressant: sedative-hypnotic	Benzodiazepine	

APPENDIX II (*Continued*)

Generic Name	Trade Name	Classification	Subclassification	Common Street Names
Heroin (diacetylmorphine)		CNS depressant: analgesic	Opiate	8, A-bomb, antifreeze, Aunt Hazel, balloon, balot, big boy, big daddy, big Harry, big time, big-H, black stuff, black tar, blanca, blanco, bomb, boy, bozo, brother, brown, brown dope, brown rock, brown sugar, caballo, caca, capital H, China white, Chinese red, Chinese white, deck, dope, downtown, eight, gato, girl, H, Harry, Hazel, hero, heroina, horse, jack, jazz, junk, kabayo, kaka, lady, Mexican brown, Mexican horse, mojo, Persian brown, Persian dust, poison, poppy, red chicken, red rock, scag, scat, schmack, shit, shmack, skag, skid, smack, smak, stuff, yen-shee
Hydrocodone	Codone, Dicodid, Hycodan, Robidone, Vicodin	CNS depressant: analgesic (antitussive)	Opiate	
Hydromorph-one	Dilaudid, PMS-Hydromorphone	CNS depressant: analgesic	Opiate	Big-D, D, Ds, dees, dids, dilies, dillies, dilly, drugstore stuff, footballs, hospital heroin, juice, junk, little-D, lords, shit, white stuff
Ketazolam	Loftram	CNS depressant: sedative-hypnotic	Benzodiazepine	
Levorphanol	Levo Dromoran	CNS depressant: analgesic	Opiate	
Lorazepam	Alzapam, Apo-lorazepam, Ativan, Loraz, Novo-Lorazem, Novolorazepam, Nu-Loraz, PMS-Lorazepam, Pro-Lorazepam	CNS depressant: sedative-hypnotic	Benzodiazepine	

Drug	Trade names/Availability	Classification	Category	Street names
Lysergic acid diethylamide	Not commercially available	Psychedelic		A, acid, acid cube, barrel, barrels, black acid, black tabs, blotter, blotter acid, blue, blue acid, blue angelfish, blue barrel, blue cheer, blue dot, blue doubledomes, brown acid, brown caps, brown dots, California sunshine, candy, cap, contact lens, crackers, cube, dome, domes, dots, Hoffmann's bicycle, LBJ, LDJ, LSD, Lucy in the Sky with Diamonds, mickey mouse, microdot, mind-detergent, mind-tripper, orange, orange crystal, orange cube, orange micro, orange Owsley, orange sunshine, orange wafers, orange wedges, osley, Owsley, Owsley acid, ozzy, paisley caps, paper acid, pink swirl, pink wafers, pink wedges, pink witches, purple, purple barrels, purple dot, purple dragon, purple flats, purple haze, purple microdots, purple Owsley, Raggedy Ann, red dot, red dragon, strawberries, strawberry fields, sugar, sugar cube, sunshine pill, the chief, the cube, trips, wedge, wedges, wedgies, white domes, white double domes, white lightning, white Owsley, windowpane
Mazindol	Mazanor, Sanorex	CNS stimulant		
Meperidine (pethidine)	Demerol, Merpergan	CNS depressant: analgesic	Opiate	Demies, demis, dems, junk, meps, morals
Mephobarbital	Mebaral, Mephoral	CNS depressant: sedative-hypnotic	Barbiturate	
Mescaline	Not commercially available	Psychedelic		Beans, big chief, biscuits, button, cactus, cactus buttons, chief, chocolate mesc, dog biscuits, dry whiskey, footballs, full moons, half moons, hikori, hikuli, magic pumpkin, mesc, mescal, mescal bean, mescal button, mescalina, mescalito, moon, P, peyote, peyote button, peyotl
Methabarbital	Gemonil	CNS depressant: sedative-hypnotic	Barbiturate	

Generic Name	Trade Name	Classification	Subclassification	Common Street Names
Methadone	Dolophine, Methadose	CNS depressant: analgesic	Opiate	Biscuits, chalk, dollies, dolls, dollys, dolo, done, medicine, meth, phy, water
Methamphet-amine	Desoxyn, Desoxyn Gradumets, Methedrine	CNS stimulant	Amphetamine	Crank, crystal, go fast, ice, meth, speed, West Coast
Methohexital	Brevimytal, Brevital, Brietal	CNS depressant: sedative-hypnotic	Barbiturate	
3,4-Methylenedi-oxymethamphet-amine	Not commercially available	Psychedelic		EA-1475, ecstasy, MDMA, XTC
Methylphen-idate	PMS-Methylphenidate, Ritalin, Ritalin-SR	CNS stimulant		Rs, rits
Midazolam	Versed	CNS depressant: sedative-hypnotic	Benzodiazepine	
Morphine	Astramorph, Duramorph, Epimorph, Infumorph, M-Eslon, Morphine HP, Morphitec, MS Contin, MS.IR, Oramorph SR, Rescudose, RMS Uniserts, Roxanol, Statex	CNS depressant: analgesic	Opiate	Aunt Emma, big-M, dreamer, eli lilly, em, emm, emsel, GOM, good old M, junk, M, MS, M sul, Mary, medicine, Miss Emma, Miss Morph, mojo, monkey, monkey morf, monkey-medicine, morfina, morph, morphema, morphi, morphia, morphie, morphina, morphinum, morpho, morphy, morshtop, mort, old Steve, pins and needles, racehorse Charley, red cross, red cross M, sister, slumber medicine, slumber party, snow, snowball, stuff, sweet Jesus, sweet Morpheus, tab, white merchandise, white nurse, white silk, white stuff, witch
Nalbuphine	Nubain	CNS depressant: analgesic	Opiate	

Drug	Trade name	Classification	Type	Street names
Nitrazepam	Mogadon	CNS depressant: sedative-hypnotic	Benzodiazepine	
Oxazepam	Apo-oxazepam, Novoxapam, Oxpam, PMS-Oxazepam, Serax, Zapex	CNS depressant: sedative-hypnotic	Benzodiazepine	
Oxycodone	Percodan, Roxicodone, Supeudol	CNS depressant: analgesic	Opiate	Percs, perks
Oxymorphone	Numorphan	CNS depressant: analgesic	Opiate	
Pemoline	Cylert	CNS stimulant		
Pentazocine	Talcen, Talwin	CNS depressant: analgesic	Opiate	Big T, poor man's heroin, Ts, tea, tee
Pentobarbital	Nembutal, Nova Rectal, Novo-Pentobarb	CNS depressant: sedative-hypnotic	Barbiturate	Abbot, amarilla, blockbuster, canary, jacket, neb, nem, nemb, nembies, nemishes, nemmies, nimbies, nimbly, yellow angels, yellow bams, yellow birds, yellow bullets, yellow dolls, yellow jackets, yellows
Phencyclidine	Not commercially available	Psychedelic		Angel death, angel dust, angel hair, angel mist, angel puke, animal tranquilizer, aurora borealis, bad grass, black whack, busy bee, buzz, CJ, cannabinol, ciclon, ciclon de cristal, cosmos, cozmos, crystal, crystal flake, crystal joint, crystal weed, cyclone, DOA, death wish, devil dust, dipper, double dipper, dummy dust, dust joint, dust of angels, elefante, elephant, elephant tranquilizer, fairy dust, heaven dust, hercules, hog, hog tranquilizer, horse trank, horse tranquilizer, PCP, PeaCe Pill, pig killer, pig tranquilizer, whack, yerba mala, zombie buzz

APPENDIX II (*Continued*)

Generic Name	Trade Name	Classification	Subclassification	Common Street Names
Phendime-trazine	Adipost, Anorex, Appecon, Bacarate, Bontril PDM, Dital, Nolahist, Nolanine Timed-Release, Obalan, Obezine, Panrexin, Parazine, Phendiet, Phenzine, Prelu-2, Sprx-1, Sprx-2, Sprx-3, Statobex, Timecelles, Trimtabs, Wehless-105	CNS stimulant		BI-64s, green and yellows
Phenobarbital	Barbita, Gardenal, Luminal, Solfoton	CNS depressant: sedative-hypnotic	Barbiturate	Barbs, goofballs, pheno, phennies, purple hearts
Phentermine	Adipex, Adipex-P, Anoxine-AM, Dapex, Dapex-37.5, Fastin, Ionamin, Obe-Nix, Obephen, Obermine, Obestin, Obestin-30, Oby-Trim, Panshape, Parmine, Phentercot, Phentrol 4, Phentrol 5, Phentride, Phentrol Z, T-Diet, Teramin, Wilpowr, Zantryl	CNS stimulant		
Prazepam	Centrax	CNS depressant: sedative-hypnotic	Benzodiazepine	

Drug	Trade names	Category	Class	Street names
Primidone (metabolized to phenobarbital)	Apo-Primidone, Myidone, Mysoline, Primoline, Sertan	CNS depressant: sedative-hypnotic	Barbiturate	
Propoxyphine	642, Darvocet-N, Darvon-N, Darvon, Dolene, Doraphen, Doxaphene, Novo-Propoxyn, Profene, Propoxycon, ProPox	CNS depressant: analgesic	Opiate	Football, yellow, vons
Psilocybin	Not commercially available	Psychedelic		God's flesh, hombrecitos, las mujercitas, los ninos, magic mushrooms, Mexican mushrooms, mushrooms, sacred mushrooms, schrooms, spores
Quazepam	Doral	CNS depressant: sedative-hypnotic	Benzodiazepine	
Secobarbital	Barbasec, Novosecobarb, Seconal	CNS depressant: sedative-hypnotic	Barbiturate	40s, apple, bala, billys, blunt, border, border red, bullet, bullet head, Canadian bouncer, cardenales, colorado, devil, diablo rojas, dolls, F-forties, forties, gumdrop, hors d'oeurves, ju-ju, juju, lillys, M&Ms, marshmallow reds, Mexican jumping beans, Mexican red, perla, pink ladies, pink marshmallow reds, pinks, prescription reds, RD, red, red birds, red bullets, red dolls, red jackets, red lillies, reds, rojas, rojita, roll of reds, round head, sec, seccies, seccy, secs, seggies, seggy, sex, sickey, suckonal
Sufentanil	Sufenta	CNS depressant: analgesic	Opiate	

APPENDIX II (*Continued*)

Generic Name	Trade Name	Classification	Subclassification	Common Street Names
Temazepam	Razepam, Restoril, Temaz	CNS depressant: sedative-hypnotic	Benzodiazepine	
Thiopental	Pentothal	CNS depressant: sedative-hypnotic	Barbiturate	
Triazolam	Apo-Triazo, Gen-Triazolam, Halcion, Novo-Triolam, Nu-Triazo	CNS depressant: sedative-hypnotic	Benzodiazepine	

APPENDIX III

Directory of Major North American Child and Adolescent Substance Use Treatment Centers, Referral Agencies, and Information Sources

In order to facilitate use, this directory has been arranged in three parts. Part I lists major local and regional treatment centers, referral agencies, and information sources in alphabetical order by the state or province in which they are located. Part II lists the major national treatment centers, referral agencies, and information sources in alphabetical order by name. Part III lists separately, in alphabetical order by state or province, the major AIDS information hotlines (telephone numbers) in North America.

While it is recognized that this list is apt to be incomplete and subject to change, it is hoped that the names and telephone numbers listed may at least provide an initial source of contact(s) for the interested reader.

Note: Most major active treatment hospitals have poison control/treatment facilities that are able to deal with substance overdoses. For telephone numbers not listed in this appendix, readers should consult their local telephone directory assistance.

PART I. Directory of Major Local and Regional Treatment Centers, Referral Agencies, and Information Sources Listed by State or Province

Alabama AL

Alabama Department of Mental Health/
　Mental Retardation
Montgomery AL
205-270-4640

Alabama Poison Control System, Inc.
Tuscaloosa AL
800-462-0800 (Alabama only)
205-345-0600

Children's Hospital of Alabama Regional
　Poison Control Center
Birmingham AL
800-292-6678 (Alabama only)
205-933-4050
205-939-9201
205-939-9202

Division of Mental Illness and Substance
　Abuse
Community Programs
Department of Mental Health
PO Box 3710
200 Interstate Park Drive
Montgomery AL 36193
205-271-9250

Drug Education Program
State Department of Education
50 North Ripley Street
Montgomery AL 36130
205-242-8083

Alaska AK

Alaska Council on Prevention of Alcohol
　and Drug Abuse, Inc.
Anchorage AK
907-258-6021

Alaska Department of Education
Division of Education Program Support
801 West 10th Street, Suite 200
Juneau AK 99801-1894
907-465-8730/2843

Anchorage Poison Center
Anchorage AK
800-478-3193 (Alaska only)
907-261-3193

Office of Alcoholism and Drug Abuse
Department of Health and Social Services
Pouch H-05-F
Juneau AK 99811
907-586-6201

Alberta AB

Alberta Alcohol and Drug Abuse
　Commission (AADAC) Counselling Services
Stephenson Building, 2nd Floor
1177 11 Avenue SW
Calgary AB T2R 0G5
403-297-3071

Alberta Alcohol and Drug Abuse
　Commission (AADAC) Downtown
　Treatment Centre
10010 102A Avenue
Edmonton AB T5J 3G2
403-427-2736

Alberta Alcohol and Drug Abuse
　Commission (AADAC) Library
10909 Jasper Avenue, Room 200
Edmonton AB T5J 3M9
403-427-7303

Alberta Alcohol and Drug Abuse
　Commission (AADAC) Northern
　Addictions Centre
11333 106 Street
Grande Prairie AB T8V 6T7

Alberta Alcohol and Drug Abuse
　Commission (AADAC) Poundmaker's Lodge
Box 34007 Kingsway Mall Post Office
Edmonton AB T5G 3G4
403-458-1884

Alberta Alcohol and Drug Abuse
　Commission (AADAC) Poundmaker's Lodge
Outpatient and Adolescent
10010 102A Avenue, 2nd Floor
Edmonton AB T5J 3G2
403-420-0356

Alberta Alcohol and Drug Abuse
　Commission (AADAC) Recovery Centre
10302 107 Street
Edmonton AB T5J 1K2
403-427-4291

Alberta Alcohol and Drug Abuse
Commission (AADAC) Training and
Professional Development
10909 Jasper Avenue, 7th Floor
Edmonton AB T5J 3M9
403-427-7305

Calgary Poison and Drug Information
Services
Calgary AB
800-332-1414 (Alberta only)
403-670-1414

Clinical Drug Consultants and Associates
c/o Substance Abusology Research Unit
Faculty of Nursing, University of Alberta
Suite 500, University Extension Center
8303 112 Street
Edmonton AB T6G 2T4
403-492-2856

Substance Abusology Research Unit
Faculty of Nursing, University of Alberta
Suite 500, University Extension Center
8303 112 Street
Edmonton AB T6G 2T4
403-492-2856

American Samoa AS
Alcohol and Drug Program
Human Services Program
LBJ Tropical Medical Center
Pago Pago AS 05799
684-633-4485

Alcohol and Drug Program
Social Services Division
Government of American Samoa
Pago Pago AS 96799
684-633-4485

Department of Education
Office of Pupil Services
Government of American Samoa
Pago Pago AS 96799
684-633-1246

Arizona AZ
Alcoholism and Drug Abuse
Office of Community Behavioral Health
Department of Health Services
411 North 24th Street
Phoenix AZ 85008
602-220-6455

Arizona Department of Education
Comprehensive Health Unit
1535 West Jefferson
Phoenix AZ 85007
602-542-3051

Arizona Department of Health Services
Office of Community Behavioral Health
1740 West Adams, Room 001
Phoenix AZ 85007
602-255-1152

Arizona Poison and Drug Information
Center
University of Arizona
Arizona Health Sciences Center
Tucson AZ
800-362-0101 (Arizona only)
602-626-6016

Arizona Prevention Resource Center
Arizona State University
Tempe AZ
602-965-9666

Samaritan Regional Poison Center
Good Samaritan Medical Center
Phoenix AZ
602-253-3334

Arkansas AR
Arkansas Department of Education
Drug Education
Four Capitol Mall, Room 405-B
Little Rock AR 72201-1071
501-682-5170

Arkansas Poison and Drug Information
Center
Little Rock AR
800-482-8948 (MDs and hospitals, Arkansas
only)
501-661-6161
501-666-5532 (MDs and hospitals)

Bureau of Alcohol and Drug Abuse
Prevention
Freeway Medical Center
Little Rock AR
501-280-4506

Office on Alcohol and Drug Abuse
Prevention
Donaghey Plaza North, Suite 400
PO Box 1437
Little Rock AR 72203-1437
501-682-6650

British Columbia BC

BC Drug and Poison Information Centre
Vancouver BC
604-682-5050

Poison Control
Victoria BC
800-567-8911 (BC only)
604-595-9211 (Victoria only)
604-682-5050 (lower mainland)

California CA

Alcohol Research Group
Epidemiology and Behavioral Medicine
Institute of Medical Research
San Francisco CA
510-642-5208

California Department of Education
Healthy Kids, Healthy California
PO Box 944272
Sacramento CA 94244-2720
916-657-2810

Department of Alcohol and Drug Programs
State of California
Sacramento CA
916-327-3009

Fresno Regional Poison Control Center
Fresno CA
800-346-5922 (Fresno, Kern, Kings, Madera,
  Mariposa, Merced, and Tulare counties
  only)
209-445-1222

Los Angeles County Regional Poison
  Control Center
Los Angeles CA
800-777-6476 (Los Angeles, Santa Barbara,
  and Ventura counties only)
800-825-2722 (MDs and hospitals,
  California only)
213-484-5151
213-664-2121 (MDs and hospitals)

Marin Institute Resource Center for the
  Prevention of Alcohol and Other Drug
  Problems
San Rafael CA
415-456-5692

San Diego Regional Poison Center
San Diego CA
800-876-4766 (Imperial and San Diego
  counties only)
619-543-6000

San Francisco Bay Area Regional Poison
  Control Center
San Francisco CA
800-523-2222 (Alameda, Contra Costa, Del
  Norte, Humboldt, Marin, Mendocino,
  Napa, San Francisco, San Mateo, and
  Sonoma counties only)
415-476-6600

Santa Clara Valley Medical Center Regional
  Poison Control Center
San Jose CA
800-662-9886 (Monterey, San Benito, San
  Luis, Obispo, Santa Clara, and Santa
  Cruz counties only)
408-299-5112

UC-Davis Medical Center Regional Poison
  Control Center
Sacramento CA
800-342-9293 (northern California only)
916-734-3692

UC-Irvine Regional Poison Center
Orange CA
800-544-4404 (Inyo, Mono, Orange,
  Riverside, and San Bernardino counties
  only)
714-634-5988
714-634-6665 (hazardous materials hotline)

Colorado CO

Alcohol and Drug Abuse Division
Department of Health
4210 East 11th Avenue
Denver CO 80220
303-331-8201

Colorado Department of Education
High Risk Intervention
201 East Colfax Avenue
Denver CO 80203
303-866-6766

Colorado Department of Human Services
Denver CO
303-692-2930

Rocky Mountain Poison and Drug Center
Denver CO
800-332-3073 (Colorado only)
800-525-5042 (Montana only)
800-446-6179 (Las Vegas NV only)
303-629-1123

Connecticut CT
Connecticut Alcohol and Drug Abuse
  Commission
999 Asylum Avenue, 3rd Floor
Hartford CT 06105
203-566-4145

Connecticut Clearinghouse
Plainville CT
203-793-9791

Connecticut Department of Education
PO Box 2219, Room G-32
Hartford CT 06145
203-566-6645

Connecticut Poison Control Center
Farmington CT
800-343-2722 (Connecticut only)
203-679-3473 (administration)
203-679-4346 (TTY)

Delaware DE
Delaware Division of Alcoholism, Drug
  Abuse and Mental Health
1901 North DuPont Highway
Newcastle DE 19720
302-421-6101

Department of Public Instruction
Health Education and Services
Townsend Bldg., PO Box 1402
Dover DE 19903
302-739-4886

Department of Services for Children, Youth,
  and Their Families
Office of Prevention
Wilmington DE
302-633-2682

District of Columbia DC
Health Planning and Development
1660 L Street NW
Washington DC 20036
202-673-7481

National Capital Poison Center
Washington DC
202-625-3333
202-784-4660 (TTY)

Resource Center on Substance Abuse
Prevention and Disability
Washington DC
202-783-2900

Florida FL
Alcohol and Drug Abuse Program
Department of Health and Rehabilitative
  Services
1317 Winewood Boulevard
Tallahassee FL 32301
904-488-0900

Florida Alcohol and Drug Abuse
  Association, Inc.
Tallahassee FL
904-878-2196

Florida Poison Information Center at
  Tampa General Hospital
Tampa FL
800-282-3171 (Florida only)
813-253-4444

Manatee Palms Adolescent Specialty
  Hospital
1324 37th Avenue East
Bradenton FL 34208
800-367-7007

Prevention Center
Florida Department of Education
325 West Gaines Street, Suite 414
Tallahassee FL 32399-0400
904-488-6304

Georgia GA
Alcohol and Drug Services
878 Peachtree Street NE, Suite 318
Atlanta GA 30309
404-894-6352

Center for Health Promotion and Education
Centers for Disease Control
1600 Clifton Road
Building 1 South, Room SSB249
Atlanta GA 30333
404-320-3492

Georgia Regional Poison Control Center
Atlanta GA
800-282-5846 (Georgia only)
404-589-4400
404-525-3323 (TTY)

Georgia State Board of Education
Health and Physical Education
2054 Twin Towers East
Atlanta GA 30334-5040
404-651-9406

Georgia State Crime Lab
Division of Forensic Science/Crime Lab
Decatur GA
404-244-2666

Substance Abuse Services
Georgia Prevention Resource Center
Atlanta GA
404-657-2296

Guam GU
Department of Education
Government of Guam
Office of the Director
PO Box DE
Agana GU 96910
671-472-8901 ext. 307

Department of Mental Health and
    Substance Abuse
PO Box 8896
Tamuning GU 96911
671-646-9260

Hawaii HI
Alcohol and Drug Abuse Division
Department of Health
PO Box 3378
Honolulu HI 96801
808-548-4280

Coalition for Drug Free Hawaii
Prevention Resource Center
Honolulu HI
808-593-2221

Department of Education
Assistant Superintendent
PO Box 2360
Honolulu HI 96804
808-586-3446

Hawaii Poison Center
Honolulu HI
800-362-3585 (outer islands of Hawaii only)
800-362-3586
808-941-4411

Idaho ID
Department of Health and Welfare
450 West State Street
Boise ID 83720
208-334-5935

Drug Education Consultant
Idaho Department of Education
Len B. Jordan Bldg.
Boise ID 83720
208-334-2165

Idaho Poison Center
Boise ID
800-632-8000 (Idaho only)
208-378-2707

Idaho RADAR Network Center
Boise State University
Boise ID
208-385-3471

Spokane Poison Center
Interstate Centers ID
800-572-5842 (northern Idaho only)

Illinois IL
Alexian Brothers Medical Center
800 Biesterfield Road
Elk Grove IL 60007
800-431-5005

Cardinal Glennon Children's Hospital
    Regional Poison Center
Interstate Centers IL
800-366-8888 (western Illinois only)

Central and Southern Illinois Regional
    Poison Resource Center
Springfield IL
800-252-2022 (Illinois only)
217-753-3330

Chicago and Northeastern Illinois Regional
    Poison Control Center
Chicago IL
800-942-5969 (northeastern Illinois only)
312-942-5969

Department of Alcoholism and Substance
    Abuse
100 West Randolph Street, Suite 5-600
Chicago IL 60601
312-814-3840

Midwest Regional Center for Drug Free
    Schools and Communities
Oakbrook IL
708-571-4710

Prevention Resource Center Library
Springfield IL
217-525-3456

Indiana IN
Bloomington Meadows Hospital/Child and
  Adolescent Treatment Programs
3600 North Prow Road
Bloomington IN 47404
800-972-4410

Charter Hospital of Terre Haute
1400 East Crossing Blvd.
Terre Haute IN 47802
812-299-4196
800-245-4196

Department of Education
Center for School Improvement
State House, Room 229
Indianapolis IN 46204-2798
317-232-6984

Division of Addiction Services
Department of Mental Health
117 East Washington Street
Indianapolis IN 46204
317-232-7816

Fairbanks Hospital/The Turning Point
8102 Clearvista Parkway
Indianapolis IN 46256
317-849-8222
800-225-HOPE (Indianapolis residents)

Indiana Poison Center
Indianapolis IN
800-382-9097 (Indiana only)
317-929-2323
317-929-2336 (TTY)

Indiana Prevention Resource Center
Indiana University
Bloomington IN
812-855-1237

Kentucky Regional Poison Center of Kosair
  Children's Hospital
Interstate Centers IN
502-589-8222 (southern Indiana only)

Mulberry Center/Parkside
420 Mulberry Street
Evansville IN 47710
812-426-8201
800-788-6541

St. Vincent Stress Center Youth Services
8401 Harcourt Road
Indianapolis IN 46280
317-338-4800
800-872-2210

Iowa IA
Division of Substance Abuse and Health
  Promotion
Department of Public Health
Lucas State Office Bldg., 4th Floor
Des Moines IA 50319
515-281-3641

Iowa Substance Abuse Information Center
Cedar Rapids Public Library
Cedar Rapids IA
319-398-5133

Mercy Hospital Chemical Dependency
  Services
800 Mercy Drive
Council Bluffs IA 51503
712-328-5113
402-398-6866
800-432-9211 (Iowa)
800-831-4140 (Nebraska)

Poison Control Center
Interstate Centers IA
800-955-9119

Poison Control Center
Iowa City IA
800-272-6477 (Iowa only)
319-356-2922

St. Mary's Adolescent Substance Abuse/
  Mercy Health Center
1111 3rd Street SW
Dyersville IA 52040
319-875-2951

Substance Education Consultant
Iowa Department of Education
Grimes State Office Bldg.
Des Moines IA 50319
515-281-3021

Kansas KS
Alcohol and Drug Abuse Services
Department of Social and Rehabilitation
  Services
300 SW Oakley, Biddle Bldg.
Topeka KS 66606-1861
913-296-3925

Cardinal Glennon Children's Hospital
  Regional Poison Center
Interstate Centers KS
800-366-8888 (Topeka only)

Kansas State Board of Education
120 East 10th Street
Topeka KS 66612
913-296-4946

Mid-America Poison Control Center
University of Kansas Medical Center
Kansas City KS
800-332-6633 (Kansas only)
913-588-6633

Parkview Hospital of Topeka
3707 SW 6th Avenue
Topeka KS 66606
913-235-3000

St. Joseph Medical Center
3600 East Harry
Wichita KS 67218
316-689-4850

Kentucky KY
Department of Education
Alcohol/Drug Unit
1720 Capitol Plaza Tower
Frankfort KY 40601
502-564-6720

Division of Substance Abuse
Department for Mental Health and Mental
  Retardation Services
275 East Main Street
Frankfort KY 40621
502-564-2880

Drug Information Services for Kentucky
  (DISK)
Division of Substance Abuse
Frankfort KY
502-564-2880

Kentucky Regional Poison Center of Kosair
  Children's Hospital
Louisville KY
800-722-5725 (Kentucky only)
502-637-8309 (metropolitan Louisville and
  southern Indiana only)

Knoxville Poison Control Center
Interstate Centers KY
615-544-9400 (southern Kentucky only)

Southeast Regional Center for Drug-Free
  Schools and Communities
Louisville KY
502-852-0052

Louisiana LA
Division of Alcohol and Drug Abuse
Office of Human Services
PO Box 3868
1201 Capitol Access Road
Baton Rouge LA 70821-3868
504-342-9354
504-342-9352

Louisiana Department of Education
Bureau of Student Services
PO Box 94064
Baton Rouge LA 70804-9064
504-342-3480

Office of Prevention and Recovery from
  Alcohol and Drug Abuse
2744-B Woodale Blvd.
Baton Rouge LA 70892
504-922-0725

Maine ME
Affiliated Chemical Dependency Services
489 State Street
Bangor ME 04401
201-945-7267

Department of Education
State House Station 57
Augusta ME 04333
207-624-6500

Maine Poison Control Center at Maine
  Medical Center
Portland ME
800-442-6305 (Maine only)
207-871-2381 (emergency room)

Office of Alcoholism and Drug Abuse
  Prevention
Bureau of Rehabilitation
State House Station 11
Augusta ME 04333
207-289-2781

Office of Substance Abuse Information
  Resource Center
Augusta ME
207-624-6528

Manitoba MB
Provincial Poison Information Centre
Winnipeg MB
204-787-2591

Maryland MD
Alcohol and Drug Abuse Administration
Department of Health and Mental Hygiene
Baltimore MD
410-225-6914

Maryland Poison Center
Baltimore MD
800-492-2414 (Maryland only)
410-528-7701

Residents Initiatives Drug Information and
   Strategy Clearinghouse
Rockville MD
301-251-5546

State Department of Education
Drug-Free Schools Program
200 West Baltimore Street
Baltimore MD 21201
410-333-2307

Massachusetts MA
Division of Substance Abuse Services
150 Tremont Street
Boston MA 02111
617-727-8614

Governor's Alliance against Drugs
John W. McCormack State Office Bldg.
One Ashburton Place, Room 611
Boston MA 02108
617-727-0786

Massachusetts Poison Control System
Boston MA
800-682-9211 (Massachusetts only)
617-232-2120

Prevention Support Services
The Medical Foundation
Boston MA
617-451-0049

Michigan MI
Blodgett Regional Poison Center
Grand Rapids MI
800-632-2727 (517/616/906 area codes only)
800-356-3232 (TTY)
616-774-2963

Comprehensive School Health Unit
Department of Education
PO Box 30008
Lansing MI 48909
517-373-2589

Michigan Substance Abuse and Traffic
   Safety Information Center
Lansing MI
517-482-9902

Office of Substance Abuse Services
Department of Public Health
PO Box 30206
2150 Apollo Drive
Lansing MI 48909
517-335-8809

Office of Substance Abuse Services
Public Information Office
PO Box 30035
3500 North Logan Street
Lansing MI 48909
519-373-8345

Poison Control Center
Children's Hospital of Michigan
Detroit MI
313-745-5711

Poison Information Center of Northwest
   Ohio
Interstate Centers MI
800-589-3897 (southeastern Michigan only)

Minnesota MN
Chemical Dependency Program Division
Department of Human Services
444 Lafayette Road
St. Paul MN 55155-3823
612-296-4610

Drug Abuse Program
State Department of Education
Learner Support Systems
994 Capitol Square Bldg.
St. Paul MN 55101
612-296-3925

Hazelden Center for Youth and Families
11505 36th Avenue North
Plymouth MN 55441
619-559-2022

Hennepin Regional Poison Center
Minneapolis MN
612-347-3141

Minnesota Prevention Resource Center
St. Paul MN
612-427-5310

Minnesota Regional Poison Center
St. Paul MN
800-222-1222 (Minnesota only)
612-221-2113

Mississippi MS
Division of Alcohol and Drug Abuse
Department of Mental Health
Robert E. Lee State Office Bldg., 11th Floor
Jackson MS 39201
601-359-1288

Health Related Services
Mississippi Department of Education
550 High Street
Jackson MS 39205
601-359-2459

Mississippi Regional Poison Control Center
Jackson MS
601-354-7660

Missouri MO
Arthur Center/Audrain Medical Center
100 Nifong, Bldg. 5, Suite 120
Columbia MO 65203-5661
314-875-7995 (local)
314-581-1785 (Mexico)
800-530-5465 (USA)

Cardinal Glennon Children's Hospital
  Regional Poison Center
St Louis MO
800-366-8888 (Missouri, western Illinois, and
  Topeka KS)
800-392-9111 (Missouri only)
314-772-5200
314-577-5336 (TTY)

Charter Hospital of Columbia
200 Portland Street
Columbia MO 65201
314-876-8000
800-343-4673

Department of Elementary and Secondary
  Education
PO Box 480
Jefferson City MO 65102
314-751-5386

Hyland Child and Adolescent Center of St.
  Anthony's Medical Center
10018 Kennerly Road
St. Louis MO 63128
314-525-3400
800-525-2032

Missouri Division of Alcohol and Drug
  Abuse
Department of Mental Health
PO Box 687
1915 South Ridge Drive
Jefferson City MO 65102
314-751-4942

Poison Control Center
Interstate Centers MO
800-955-9119

Montana MT
Alcohol and Drug Abuse Division
Department of Corrections and Human
  Services
Helena MT 59601
406-444-2827

Chemical Dependency Bureau
Department of Institutions
Helena MT
406-444-1202

Department of Education
Office of Public Instruction
Capitol Bldg.
Helena MT 59620
406-444-4434

Mission Mountain School for Adolescent
  Females
PO Box 980
Guest Ranch Road
Condon MT 59826
406-754-2580

Rocky Mountain Poison and Drug Center
Interstate Centers MT
800-525-5842

Spokane Poison Center
Interstate Centers MT
800-572-5842 (western Montana only)

Wilderness Treatment Center
200 Hubbart Dam Road
Marion MT 59925
406-854-2832

Nebraska NE
Administrator of Instructional Strategies
Nebraska State Department of Education
301 Centennial Mall South
Lincoln NE 68509-4987
402-471-4332

Alcohol and Drug Abuse Clearinghouse
Nebraska Council to Prevent Alcohol and
  Drug Abuse
Lincoln NE
402-474-1992

Division of Alcoholism and Drug Abuse
Department of Public Institutions
PO Box 94728
Lincoln NE 68509
402-471-2851 ext. 5583

Poison Center
Omaha NE
800-955-9119 (Nebraska, Iowa, Missouri,
South Dakota, and Wyoming)
402-390-5555

Nevada NV
Bureau of Alcohol and Drug Abuse
Department of Human Resources
505 East King Street
Carson City NV 89710
702-687-6239

Department of Education
Office of Public Instruction
Capitol Complex
Carson City NV 89710
702-687-3100

Rocky Mountain Poison and Drug Center
Interstate Centers NV
800-446-6179 (Las Vegas NV only)

New Brunswick NB
Bathurst Poison Control
Bathurst NB
506-546-4666

Moncton Poison Control
Moncton NB
506-857-5555

Saint John Poison Control
Saint John NB
506-648-6222

Newfoundland NF
Provincial Poison Control Centre
St John's NF
709-722-1110

St Anthony Poison Control
St Anthony NF
709-454-3333 ext. 149

New Hampshire NH
Department of Education
State Office Park South
101 Pleasant Street
Concord NH 03301
603-271-2717

New Hampshire Office of Alcohol and Drug
  Abuse Prevention
Health and Welfare Bldg.
Hazen Drive
Concord NH 03301
603-271-4627
603-271-6100

New Hampshire Poison Information Center
Lebanon NH
800-562-8236 (New Hampshire only)
603-650-5000

New Jersey NJ
Center of Alcohol Studies
Rutgers University
Smithers Hall, Busch Campus
Piscataway NJ 08854
201-932-2190

Department of Health
CN 360
Trenton NJ 08625
609-292-3147

Division of Alcoholism and Drug Abuse
New Jersey State Department of Health
Trenton NJ
609-984-6961

Division of Narcotic and Drug Abuse
  Control
129 East Hanover Street
Trenton NJ 08625
609-292-5760

New Jersey Poison Information and
Education System
Newark NJ
800-962-1253 (New Jersey only)
201-923-0764
201-926-8008 (TTY)

New Jersey State Department of Education
Office of Educational Programs and Student
Services
240 West State Street, CN500
Trenton NJ 08625
609-292-5780

Rutgers Center of Alcohol Studies
Piscataway NJ
908-932-4442

New Mexico NM
Department of Health/BHSD/DSA
Santa Fe NM
505-827-2601

New Mexico Poison and Drug Information
Center
Albuquerque NM
800-432-6866 (New Mexico only)
505-843-2551

State Department of Education
300 Don Gaspar Avenue
Santa Fe NM 87501
505-827-6648

Substance Abuse Bureau
190 St. Francis Drive, Room 3350 North
Sante Fe NM 87503
505-827-2589

New York NY
Central New York Poison Control Center
Syracuse NY
800-252-5655 (New York only)
315-476-4766

Division of Alcoholism and Alcohol Abuse
194 Washington Avenue
Albany NY 12210
518-474-5417

Division of Substance Abuse Services
Executive Park South, Box 8200
Albany NY 12203
518-457-7629

Hudson Valley Regional Poison Center
Nyack NY
800-336-6997 (New York only)
914-353-1000

Life Line/Finger Lakes Regional Poison
Control Center
Rochester NY
800-333-0542 (Ontario and Wayne counties
only)
716-275-5151
716-275-2700 (TTY)

Long Island Regional Poison Control Center
East Meadow NY
516-542-2323/2324/2325
516-542-3813
516-747-3323 (TTY)

New York City Poison Control Center
New York NY
212-340-4494
212-764-7667

New York State Office of Alcoholism and
Substance Abuse Services
Albany NY
518-473-3460

Northeast Regional Center for Drug-Free
Schools and Communities
Sayville NY
516-589-7022

State Education Department
Washington Avenue, Room 964EBA
Albany NY 12234
518-474-1491

North Carolina NC
Alcohol and Drug Abuse Section
Division of Mental Health and Mental
Retardation Services
325 North Salisbury Street
Raleigh NC 27611
919-733-4670

Department of Public Instruction
Alcohol and Drug Defense Section
301 North Wilmington Street
Raleigh NC 27601-2825
919-715-1676

Duke University Regional Poison Control
Center
Durham NC
800-672-1697 (North Carolina only)
919-684-8111

Mercy Hospital Poison Control Center
Charlotte NC
704-379-5827

North Carolina Alcohol and Drug Resource
Center
Durham NC
919-493-2881

Triad Poison Center
Greensboro NC
800-722-2222 (Alamance, Forsyth, Guilford,
Rockingham, and Randolph counties
only)
919-379-4105

Western North Carolina Poison Control
Center
Asheville NC
800-542-4225 (North Carolina only)
704-255-4490

North Dakota ND
Department of Public Instruction
Guidance/Drug-Free Schools
State Capitol, 9th Floor
Bismarck ND 58505-0440
701-224-2269

Division of Alcoholism and Drug Abuse
Department of Human Services
State Capitol/Judicial Wing
Bismarck ND 58505
701-224-2769

North Dakota Prevention Resource Center
Bismarck ND
701-224-2769

Nova Scotia NS
Poison Control Center
Halifax NS
902-428-8161

Ohio OH
Akron Regional Poison Control Center
Akron OH
800-362-9922 (Ohio only)
216-379-8562
216-379-8446 (TTY)

Central Ohio Poison Center
Columbus OH
800-682-7625 (Ohio only)
614-228-1323
614-228-2272 (TTY)

Department of Education
Division of Education Services
65 South Front Street, Room 719
Columbus OH 43266-0308
614-466-3708

Mahoning Valley Poison Center
St. Elizabeth Hospital Medical Center
Youngstown OH
800-426-2348 (Ohio, and Mercer and
Lawrence counties in Pennsylvania only)
216-746-2222
216-746-5510 (TTY)

Northwest Regional Poison Center
Interstate Centers OH
800-822-3232 (northeastern Ohio only)

Ohio Department of Alcohol and Drug
Addiction Services
Columbus OH
614-466-6379

Poison Information Center of Northwest
Ohio
Medical College of Ohio Hospital
Toledo OH
800-589-3897 (northwestern Ohio and
southeastern Michigan only)
419-381-3897

Regional Poison Control System and Drug
and Poison Information Center
Cincinnati OH
800-872-5111 (Ohio only)
513-558-5111

Saint Luke's Medical Center
11311 Shaker Blvd.
Cleveland OH 44104
216-368-7970

Oklahoma OK
Comprehensive Health
Department of Education
2500 North Lincoln Blvd.
Oklahoma City OK 73105-4599
405-521-2106

Department of Mental Health and
  Substance Abuse Services
PO Box 53277 Capitol Station
Oklahoma City OK 73152
405-522-3810

Laureate Psychiatric Clinic and Hospital
6655 South Yale Avenue
Tulsa OK 74136
918-481-4000
800-322-5173

Morning Star Adolescent Treatment Unit
PO Box 500
Marietta OK 73448
405-276-5443

Southwest Regional Center for Drug-Free
  Schools and Communities
Norman OK
405-325-1454

Tulsa Regional Medical Center/Behavioral
  Health Services
744 West 9th Street
Tulsa OK 94127
918-599-5880

Ontario ON
Addiction Research Foundation
Toronto ON
416-595-6059

Children's Hospital of Eastern Ontario
Ottawa ON
800-267-1373 (area code 807 call collect)
613-737-1100

Hospital for Sick Children
Toronto ON
800-268-9017 (area code 807 call collect)
416-813-5900

Oregon OR
Department of Education
Division of Special Student Services
700 Pringle Parkway SE
Salem OR 97310
503-378-2677

Office of Alcohol and Drug Abuse Programs
Oregon Prevention Resource Center
1178 Chemeketa Street NE, Suite 102
Salem OR 97310
503-378-8000

Oregon Poison Center
Portland OR
800-452-7165 (Oregon only)
503-494-8968

Spokane Poison Center
Interstate Centers OR
800-572-5842 (northwestern Oregon only)

Western Center for Drug-Free Schools and
  Communities
Northwest Regional Education Laboratory
Portland OR
503-275-9500

Western Regional Center for Drug-Free
  Schools and Communities
101 Southwest Main Street, Suite 500
Portland OR 97204
503-275-9479
800-547-6339 (outside Oregon)

Pennsylvania PA
Caron Adolescent Treatment Center
Galen Hall Road, Box A
Wernersville PA 19565
215-678-2332
800-678-2332

Central Pennsylvania Poison Center
Hershey PA
800-521-6110
717-531-6111
717-531-6039

Delaware Valley Mental Health Foundation
1833 Butler Avenue
Doylestown PA 18901
215-345-0444

Division of Student Services
Department of Education
333 Market Street
Harrisburg PA 17126-0333
717-783-2949

Drug and Alcohol Programs
Department of Health
PO Box 90
Harrisburg PA 17108
717-787-9857

Lehigh Valley Poison Center
Allentown PA
215-433-2311

Mahoning Valley Poison Center
Interstate Centers PA
800-426-2348 (Lawrence and Mercer
   counties only)

Northwest Regional Poison Center
Erie PA
800-822-3232 (northwestern Pennsylvania,
   northeastern Ohio, and southwestern New
   York)
814-452-3232

PENNSAIC
Erie PA
814-459-0245

Pittsburgh Poison Center
Pittsburgh PA
412-681-6669

Poison Control Center
Philadelphia PA
215-386-2100
215-590-2003

Susquehanna Poison Center
Danville PA
800-352-7001 (Pennsylvania only)

Puerto Rico PR
Administracion de Servicios de Salud
   Mental y Contra la Addicion
San Juan PR
809-767-5990

Department of Anti-Addiction Services
Box 21414 Rio Piedras Station
Rio Piedras PR 00928-1414
809-764-3795

Department of Education
Office of Federal Affairs
PO Box 759
Hato Rey PR 00919
809-4949 ext. 6047

Quebec PQ
Poison Control Line
Centre de Toxicologie de Québec
Québec City PQ
800-463-5060
418-656-8090

Rhode Island RI
Brown University Center for Alcohol and
   Addiction Studies
Box G, Brown University Butler Hospital
Providence RI 02912
401-863-3173

Department of Education
School Support Services
22 Hayes Street
Providence RI 02908
401-277-2638

Division of Substance Abuse
Department of Mental Health, Retardation
   and Hospitals
PO Box 20363
Cranston RI 02920
401-464-2091

Rhode Island Department of Substance
   Abuse
Cranston RI
401-464-2191

Rhode Island Poison Center
Rhode Island Hospital
Providence RI
401-277-5727

Saskatchewan SK
Poison Control Centre
Regina SK
306-359-4545

Poison Control Centre
Saskatoon SK
306-966-1010
306-966-1012

South Carolina SC
Drug-Free Schools and Communities
Department of Education
1429 Senate Street, Room 912
Columbia SC 29201
803-734-8566

Drug Store Information Clearinghouse
South Carolina Commission on Alcohol and
   Drug Abuse
Columbia SC
803-734-9559

South Carolina Commission on Alcohol and
   Drug Abuse
3700 Forest Drive
Columbia SC 29204
803-734-9520

South Dakota SD
Department of Education
700 Governors Drive
Pierre SD 57501-3182
605-773-4670

Rapid City Regional Hospital Addiction
   Recovery Center
915 Mountain View Road
Rapid City SD 57702
605-399-7200

South Dakota Division of Alcohol and Drug
   Abuse
Joe Foss Bldg., 523 East Capitol
Pierre SD 57501
605-773-3123

Tennessee TN
Alcohol and Drug Abuse Services
Department of Mental Health and Mental
   Retardation
706 Church Street, 4th Floor
Nashville TN 37219
615-741-1921

Drug-Free Schools Program
Tennessee Department of Education
Gateway Plaza, 6th Floor
710 James Robertson Parkway
Nashville TN 37243-0375
615-741-3248

Knoxville Poison Control Center
Knoxville TN
615-544-9400 (eastern Tennessee and
   southern Kentucky only)

Middle Tennessee Regional Poison/Clinical
   Toxicology Center
Nashville TN
800-288-9999 (mid-Tennessee only)
615-322-6435 (Nashville and adjacent
   counties only)

Southern Poison Center Inc.
Memphis TN
901-528-6048
901-522-5985 (administration)

Tennessee Alcohol and Drug Association
   Statewide Clearinghouse
Nashville TN
615-244-7066

Texas TX
Drug Abuse Prevention Program
Texas Education Agency
1701 North Congress Avenue
Austin TX 78701-1494
512-463-9006

El Paso Poison Control Center
El Paso TX
915-533-1244 (southwestern Texas and
   southern New Mexico only)

North Texas Poison Center
Dallas TX
800-441-0040 (Texas only)
214-590-5000

Texas Commission on Alcohol and Drug
   Abuse
1705 Guadalupe Street
Austin TX 78701
512-463-5510

Texas Commission on Alcohol and Drug
   Abuse Resource Center
Austin TX
512-867-8821

Texas State Poison Control Center
Galveston TX
800-392-8548 (MDs and ambulance
   personnel, Texas only)
409-772-1420
713-654-1701 (Houston only)
409-765-1420
409-539-7700

U.S.-Mexico Border Health Association
El Paso TX
915-581-6645

Utah UT
Charter Provo Canyon School
4501 University Avenue
Provo UT 84604
801-227-2088

Drug-Free Schools Program
Office of Education
250 East 500 South
Salt Lake City UT 84111
801-538-7713

Intermountain Regional Poison Control
    Center
Salt Lake City UT
800-456-7707 (Utah only)
801-581-2151

Utah Alcoholism Foundation
2880 South Main Street, Suite 210
Salt Lake City UT 84115
801-487-3276

Utah State Division of Substance Abuse
Department of Social Services
PO Box 45500
120 North 200 West, 4th Floor
Salt Lake City UT 84145-0500
801-538-3939

Vermont VT
FAS/FAE Prevention Program
Vermont Department of Health
1193 North Avenue
PO Box 70
Burlington VT 05401
802-863-7330

Office of Alcohol and Drug Abuse Programs
103 South Maine Street
Waterbury VT 05676
802-241-2170/2175
802-241-2178

Vermont Poison Center
Burlington VT
802-658-3456 (Vermont and bordering New
    York counties only)
802-656-2721 (education programs)

Virgin Islands VI
Alcoholism and Drug Dependency
Department of Health
Division of Mental Health
PO Box 520
Christiansted, St. Croix VI 00820
809-773-5150

Department of Education
44-56 Kongens Gade
St. Thomas VI 00802
809-774-4976

Virginia VA
Blue Ridge Poison Center
Charlottesville VA
800-451-1428 (Virginia, West Virginia, North
    Carolina, District of Columbia, Tennessee,
    and Maryland)
804-924-5543

Center for Health Promotion
George Mason University
Fairfax VA
703-993-3697

Office of Substance Abuse Services
Department of Mental Health, Mental
    Retardation and Substance Services
PO Box 1797
109 Governor Street
Richmond VA 23214
804-786-3906

Virginia Department of Mental Health
Office of Prevention
Richmond VA
804-371-7564

Virginia Poison Center
Richmond VA
800-552-6337 (Virginia only)
804-786-9123

Washington WA
Alcohol and Drug Abuse Institute Library
University of Washington
Seattle WA
206-543-0937

Bureau of Alcoholism and Substance Abuse
Washington Department of Social and
    Health Services
Mail Stop OB 44W
Olympia WA 98504
206-753-5866

Mary Bridge Poison Center
Tacoma WA
800-542-6319 (Washington only)
206-594-1414

St. Peter Chemical Dependency Center
4800 College Street
Lacey WA 98503
800-332-0465

Seattle Poison Center
Seattle WA
800-732-6985 (Washington only)
206-526-2121
206-526-2223 (TTY)

Spokane Poison Center
Spokane WA
800-572-5842 (eastern Washington, northern
  Idaho, western Montana, and
  northwestern Oregon only)
509-747-1077

Substance Abuse Education
Department of Public Instruction
Old Capitol Building, MS/FG-11
Olympia WA 98504
206-753-5595

Washington State Substance Abuse
  Coalition
Bellevue WA
206-637-7011

West Virginia WV
Division of Alcohol and Drug Abuse
State Capitol
1800 Washington Street East, Room 451
Charleston WV 25305
304-348-2276

RADAR Network Clearinghouse
West Virginia Library Commission
Charleston WV
304-558-2041

Student Services and Assessment
State Department of Education
Capitol Complex, B-057
Charleston WV 25305
304-558-2546

West Virginia Poison Center
Charleston WV
800-642-3625 (West Virginia only)
304-348-4211

Wisconsin WI
Bureau for Pupil Services
Program Development
Department of Public Instruction
125 South Webster Street
Madison WI 53707
608-266-0963

Office of Alcohol and Other Drug Abuse
PO Box 7851
1 West Wilson Street
Madison WI 53707
608-266-3442

St. Agnes Hospital Adolescent and
  Addiction Services
682 Western Avenue
Fond Du Lac WI 54935
414-923-6554
414-929-1381

University of Wisconsin Hospital Regional
  Poison Control Center
Madison WI
608-262-3702

Wisconsin Clearinghouse
Madison WI
608-262-9157

Wyoming WY
Alcohol and Drug Abuse Programs
Hathaway Building
Cheyenne WY 82002
307-777-7115 ext. 7118

CARE Program Wyoming
University of Wyoming
Laramie WY
307-766-4119

Department of Education
Office of Public Instruction
Hathaway Building
2300 Capitol Avenue
Cheyenne WY 82002
307-777-6202

Poison Control Center
Interstate Centers WY
800-955-9119 (Wyoming and Nebraska)
402-390-5555

PART II. Directory of National Treatment Centers, Referral Agencies, and Information Sources Listed in Alphabetical Order

ACTION Drug Prevention Program
806 Connecticut Avenue NW, Suite M513
Washington DC 20525
202-634-9380

Addiction Research Foundation (ARF)
33 Russell Street
Toronto ON M5S 2S1
416-595-6059
416-595-6072
416-595-6144 (library)

Adult Children of Alcoholics (ACOA)
Interim World Service Organization
PO Box 3216
2522 West Sepulveda Blvd.
Torrance CA 90505
213-534-1815

AL-ANON Family Groups, Inc.
World Service Office
PO Box 862 Midtown Station
New York NY 10018
212-302-7240
800-344-2666

Alcohol and Drug Abuse Institute Library
University of Washington
Seattle WA 98105
206-543-0937

Alcohol and Drug Abuse Services
  Administration
Office of Information, Prevention and
  Education
Washington DC 20018
202-576-7315

Alcohol and Drug Problems Association of
  North America
444 North Capitol Street NW, Suite 706
Washington DC 20001
202-737-4340

Alcohol Research Group
Epidemiology and Behavioral Medicine
Institute of Medical Research
San Francisco CA
510-642-5208

Alcoholics Anonymous (AA)
15 East 26th Street, Room 1810
New York NY 10010
212-683-3900

Alcoholics Anonymous (AA)
General Services Office
Box 459 Grand Central Station
New York NY 10163
212-686-1100

Alcoholics Anonymous (AA)
World Service Office
475 Riverside Drive
New York NY 10115
212-870-3400

Alcoholics Anonymous (AA)
4530 Connecticut Avenue NW, Suite 111
Washington DC 20008
202-966-9115

Alcoholism and Alcohol Abuse
194 Washington Avenue
Albany NY 12210
518-474-5417

Alexian Brothers Medical Center
800 Biesterfield Road
Elk Grove IL 60007
800-431-5005

American Academy of Health Care
  Providers in the Addictive Disorders
260 Beacon Street
Somerville MA 02143
617-661-6248

American Academy of Psychiatrists in
  Alcoholism and Addictions (AAPAA)
PO Box 376
Greenbelt MD 20768
301-220-0951

American College Health Association
  (ACHA) Task Force on Alcohol and Other
  Drugs
1300 Piccard Drive, Suite 200
Rockville MD 20850
301-963-1100

American Council for Drug Education
204 Monroe Street, Suite 110
Rockville MD 20850
301-294-0600
800-488-3784

American Medical Association (AMA)
Department of Mental Health
Division of Substance Abuse
535 North Dearborn Street
Chicago IL 60610
312-645-5000

American Nurses' Association (ANA)
2420 Pershing Road
Kansas City MO 64108
816-474-5720

American Public Health Association (APHA)
Section on Alcohol and Drugs
1015 15th Street NW
Washington DC 20005
202-789-5600

American Society of Addiction Medicine
  (ASAM)
12 West 21st Street
New York NY 10010
202-244-8948

American Society of Addiction Medicine
  (ASAM)
5225 Wisconsin Avenue NW, Suite 409
Washington DC 20016
212-206-6770

Anesthetists in Recovery (AIR)
5626 Preston Oaks Road, Unit 40D
Dallas TX 75240
214-960-7296
913-383-2878

Arthur Center/Audrain Medical Center
100 Nifong, Bldg. 5, Suite 120
Columbia MO 65203-5661
314-875-7995 (local)
314-581-1785 (Mexico)
800-530-5465 (USA)

Association of Halfway House Alcoholism
  Programs of North America (AHHAP)
786 East 7th Street
St. Paul MN 55106
613-227-7818

Association of Labor, Management
  Administrators, and Consultants on
  Alcoholism (ALMACA)
1800 North Kent Street, Suite 907
Arlington VA 22209
703-522-6272

Association for Medical Education and
  Research in Substance Abuse (AMERSA)
Center for Alcohol and Addiction Services
Box G, Brown University Butler Hospital
Providence RI 02912
401-863-3173

Black Children of Alcoholic and Drug
  Addicted Persons (BCOADAP)
c/o National Black Alcoholism Council
417 Dearborn Street
Chicago IL 60605
312-663-5780

Boys and Girls Clubs of America
771 1st Avenue
New York NY 10017
212-351-5900

Brown University Center for Alcohol and
  Addiction Studies
Box G, Brown University Butler Hospital
Providence RI 02912
401-863-3173

Canadian Centre on Substance Abuse
Ottawa ON K1P 5E7
613-235-4048

Caron Adolescent Treatment Center
Galen Hall Road, Box A
Wernersville PA 19565
215-678-2332
800-678-2332

CDC's National AIDS Information
  Clearinghouse
Rockville MD 20849-6003
800-458-5231

Center for Education in Maternal and Child
  Health
38th and R Streets NW
Washington DC 20057
202-625-8400

Center for Health Promotion
George Mason University
Fairfax VA
703-993-3697

Center for Health Promotion and Education
Centers for Disease Control
1600 Clifton Road
Building 1 South, Room SSB249
Atlanta GA 30333
404-320-3492

Center for Substance Abuse Prevention
(CSAP)
Parklawn Bldg.
5600 Fishers Lane
Rockville MD 20857
301-443-0365

Center of Alcohol Studies
Rutgers University
Smithers Hall, Busch Campus
Piscataway NJ 08854
201-932-2190

Centers for Disease Control and Prevention
National AIDS Clearinghouse
PO Box 6003
Rockville MD 20849-6003
800-342-AIDS

Centers for Disease Control and Prevention
National HIV/AIDS Hotline
800-662-HELP

Charter Hospital of Columbia
200 Portland Street
Columbia MO 65201
314-876-8000
800-343-4673

Charter Hospital of Terre Haute
1400 East Crossing Blvd.
Terre Haute IN 47802
812-299-4196
800-245-4196

Charter Provo Canyon School
4501 University Avenue
Provo UT 84604
801-227-2088

Children of Alcoholics Foundation, Inc.
PO Box 4185 Grand Central Station
New York NY 10163-4185
212-754-0656
800-359-COAF

Cities in Schools, Inc.
Alexandria VA 22314
703-519-8999

Clearinghouse on Child Abuse and Neglect
Information
PO Box 1182
Washington DC 20013
703-385-7565

Clinical Drug Consultants and Associates
c/o Substance Abusology Research Unit
Faculty of Nursing, University of Alberta
Suite 500, University Extension Center
8303 112 Street
Edmonton AB T6G 2T4
403-492-2856

Coalition of Hispanic Health and Human
Services Organizations (COSSMHO)
1030 15th Street NW, Suite 1053
Washington DC 20005
202-371-2100

CoAnon Family Groups
PO Box 64742 66
Los Angeles CA 90064
213-859-2206

Cocaine Anonymous (CA)
3740 Overland Avenue, Suite G
Los Angeles CA 90034
213-559-5833
800-347-8998

Cocaine Helpline
800-COCAINE

CompCare Publications
PO Box 27777
2415 Annapolis Lane
Minneapolis MN 55441

CSAP's National Resource for the Prevention
of Alcohol, Tobacco, Other Drug Abuse
and Mental Illness in Women
Alexandria VA
800-354-8824

DARE America
PO Box 2090
Los Angeles CA 90051
800-223-DARE

David M. Winfield Foundation
Turn It Around Program
One Bridge Plaza, Suite 400
Fort Lee NJ 07024
201-592-5031

Delaware Valley Mental Health Foundation
1833 Butler Avenue
Doylestown PA 18901
215-345-0444

Drug and Alcohol Nursing Association, Inc.
(DANA)
113 West Franklin Street
Baltimore MD 21201
301-752-3318

Drug Enforcement Administration (DEA)
600 Army Navy Drive
Arlington VA 20537
202-307-7977 (public affairs)
202-307-8932 (library)

Drug Store Information Clearinghouse
South Carolina Commission on Alcohol and
   Drug Abuse
Columbia SC 29204
803-734-9559

Drugs and Crime Data Center and
   Clearinghouse
1600 Research Blvd.
Rockville MD 20850
800-666-3332

Elks Drug Awareness Program
Jackson's Gap AL
205-825-4690

Employee Assistance Professionals
   Association (EAPA)
4601 North Fairfax Drive, Suite 1001
Arlington VA 22203
703-522-6272

Fair Oaks Hospital
PO Box 100
Summit NJ 07902-0100
800-COCAINE

Fairbanks Hospital/The Turning Point
8102 Clearvista Parkway
Indianapolis IN 46256
317-849-8222
800-225-HOPE (Indianapolis residents)

Families Anonymous, Inc.
PO Box 548
Van Nuys CA 91408
818-989-7841
800-736-9805

Food and Drug Administration
Legislative, Professional, and Consumer
   Affairs Branch (HFD-365)
5600 Fishers Lane
Rockville MD 20857
301-295-8012

Hazelden Center for Youth and Families
11505 36th Avenue North
Plymouth MN 55441
619-559-2022

Hazelden Foundation
Box 11
Center City MN 55012
800-822-0800 (training and education)
800-328-9000 (educational materials)

Health Communications, Inc.
3201 SW 15th Street
Deerfield Beach FL 33442

Healthy Nations National Program Office
UCHSC University North Pavilion
Denver CO 80236
303-372-3272

Indian Health Service
Colorado River Service
Route 1, Box 12
Parker AZ 85344
602-669-2137

Institute on Black Chemical Abuse (IBCA)
   Resource Center
2616 Nicollet Avenue South
Minneapolis MN 55408
612-871-7878

Inter-American Drug Information System
OAS/CICAD
Washington DC
202-458-3809

International Doctors in Alcoholics
   Anonymous (IDAA)
7250 France Avenue South, Suite 400C
Minneapolis MN 55435
612-835-4421

International Institute on Inhalant Abuse
Englewood CO 80110
303-788-1951

International Lawyers in Alcoholics
   Anonymous (ILAA)
1092 Elm Street, Suite 201
Rocky Hill CT 06067
203-529-7474

International Nurses Anonymous (INA)
1020 Sunset Drive
Lawrence KS 66044
913-842-3893

Johnson Institute
7205 Ohms Lane
Minneapolis MN 55439-2159
800-231-5165
800-247-0484
800-447-6660 (Canada)

Join Together—A National Resource for
Communities Fighting Substance Abuse
Boston MA
617-437-1500

Just Say No Foundation
1777 North California Blvd., Room 210
Walnut Creek CA 94596
415-939-6666
800-258-2766

Just Say No International
2101 Webster Street, Suite 1300
Oakland CA 94612
800-258-2766

Manatee Palms Adolescent Specialty
Hospital
1324 37th Avenue East
Bradenton FL 34208
800-367-7007

Marin Institute Resource Center for the
Prevention of Alcohol and Other Drug
Problems
24 Belvedere Street
San Rafael CA 94901
415-456-5692

Mercy Hospital Chemical Dependency
Services
800 Mercy Drive
Council Bluffs IA 51503
712-328-5113
402-398-6866
800-432-9211 (Iowa)
800-831-4140 (Nebraska)

Midwest Regional Center for Drug Free
Schools and Communities
Oakbrook IL 60521
708-571-4710

Mission Mountain School for Adolescent
Females
PO Box 980
Guest Ranch Road
Condon MT 59826
406-754-2580

Morning Star Adolescent Treatment Unit
PO Box 500
Marietta OK 73448
405-276-5443

Mothers against Drunk Driving (MADD)
511 East John Carpenter Freeway, Suite 700
Irving TX 75062
214-744-6233
800-GET-MADD

Nar-Anon Family Groups
PO Box 2562
Palos Verdes Peninsula CA 90274
213-547-5800

Narcotics Anonymous (NA)
PO Box 9999
Van Nuys CA 91409
818-780-3951

Narcotics Anonymous (NA)
PO Box 9863
Washington DC 20016
202-399-5316

National Asian Pacific American Families
against Drug Abuse
6303 Friendship Court
Bethesda MD 20817
301-530-0945

National Asian Pacific American Families
against Substance Abuse, Inc.
420 East 3rd Street, Suite 909
Los Angeles CA 90013-1647
213-617-8277

National Association for Children of
Alcoholics (NACOA)
11426 Rockville Pike
Rockville MD 20852
301-468-0985

National Association for Children of
Alcoholics, Inc. (NACOA)
31582 Coast Highway, Suite B
Laguna Beach CA 92677
714-499-3889

National Association for Native American
Children of Alcoholics (NANACOA)
PO Box 18736
Seattle WA 98114
206-467-7686

National Association of Alcoholism and
Drug Abuse Counselors (NAADC)
3717 Columbia Pike, Suite 300
Arlington VA 22204
703-920-4644

National Association of Perinatal Addiction
Research and Education (NAPARE)
11 East Hubbard Street, Suite 200
Chicago IL 60611
312-329-2512
800-638-BABY

National Association of Social Workers
(NASW)
7981 Eastern Avenue
Silver Spring MD 20910
301-565-0333

National Association of State Alcohol and
Drug Abuse Directors (NASADAD)
444 North Capitol Street NW, Suite 642
Washington DC 20001
202-783-6868

National Black Alcoholism Council (NBAC)
1629 K Street NW, Suite 802
Washington DC 20006
202-296-2696

National Catholic Council on Alcoholism
1200 Varnum Street NE
Washington DC 20017-2796
202-737-8122

National Center for Education in Maternal
and Child Health
3520 Prospect Street NW, Suite 1
Washington DC 20057
202-625-8410

National Certification Reciprocity
Consortium/Alcohol and Other Drug
Abuse (NCRC)
PO Box 157
Atkinson NH 03811
603-898-1516

National Clearinghouse for Alcohol and
Drug Information (NCADI)
PO Box 2345
Rockville MD 20847-2345
301-468-2600
800-729-6686

National Clearinghouse for Primary Care
Information
8201 Greensboro Drive, Suite 600
McLean VA 22102
703-821-8955

National Coalition of Hispanic Health
Services Organization (COSSMHO)
1501 16th Street NW
Washington DC 20036
202-387-5000

National Cocaine Hotline
800-COCAINE

National Consortium of Chemical
Dependency Nurses, Inc. (NCCDN)
975 Oak, Suite 675
Eugene OR 97401
800-87-NCCDN
503-485-4421

National Council on Alcoholism
12 West 21st Street, 7th Floor
New York NY 10010
212-206-6770

National Council on Alcoholism and Drug
Dependence, Inc. (NCADD)
12 West 21st Street
New York NY 10010
212-206-6770
212-777-8923
800-NCA-CALL

National Crime Prevention Council
1700 K Street NW, 2nd Floor
Washington DC 20006
202-466-6272

National Criminal Justice Reference Service
(NCJRS)
Box 6000
Rockville MD 20850
301-251-5500

National Families in Action
2296 Henderson Mill Road, Suite 300
Atlanta GA 30345
404-934-6364

National Federation of Parents for Drug-
Free Youth
11159B South Towne Square
St. Louis MO 63123
314-845-1933

National Health Information Clearinghouse
PO Box 1133
Washington DC 20013-1133
703-522-2590 (Virginia)
800-336-4797

National Institute on Alcohol Abuse and
Alcoholism (NIAAA)
5600 Fishers Lane, Room 14C-17
Rockville MD 20857
301-443-2954

National Institute on Drug Abuse (NIDA)
5600 Fishers Lane, Room 10-04
Rockville MD 20857
301-443-4577
800-662-HELP (English language)
800-66A-YUDA (Spanish language)

National Network of Runaway and Youth
Services, Inc.
Washington DC
202-783-7949

National Nurses' Society on Addictions
(NNSA)
5700 Old Orchard Road, 1st Floor
Skokie IL 60077-1024
708-966-5010

National Prevention Network
444 North Capitol Street NW, Suite 642
Washington DC 20001
202-783-6868

National PTA
700 North Rush Street
Chicago IL 60611
312-787-0977
312-549-3253

National Rural Institute on Alcohol and
Drug Abuse
Eau Claire WI
715-836-2031

National Safety Council
444 North Michigan
Chicago IL 60611
312-527-4800

National Self-Help Clearinghouse
25 West 43rd Street
New York NY 10036
212-642-2944

Northeast Regional Center for Drug-Free
Schools and Communities
Sayville NY 11782-0403
516-589-7022

Office of National Drug Control Policy
Executive Office of the President
Washington DC 20500
202-395-6792

Office of Science Policy, Education, and
Legislation
National Institute on Drug Abuse (NIDA)
5600 Fishers Lane, Room 10A-55
Rockville MD 20857
301-443-6071

Office on Smoking and Health
3005 Rhodes Bldg. (Koger Center)
Chamblee GA 30341
404-488-5705

Office for Substance Abuse Prevention
(OSAP)
5600 Fishers Lane, Room 9A-54
Rockville MD 20857
301-443-0365

Parent's Resource Institute for Drug
Education, Inc. (PRIDE)
50 Hurt Plaza, Suite 210
Atlanta GA 30303
404-577-4500
800-677-7433

Phoenix House
164 West 74th Street
New York NY 10023
212-595-5810

Prevention Support Services
The Medical Foundation
Boston MA
617-451-0049

Project Cork Institute
Dartmouth Medical School
Hanover NH 03755
603-646-3935

Psychologists Helping Psychologists (PHP)
23439 Michigan Avenue
Dearborn MI 48124
313-565-3821

Rational Recovery Systems
PO Box 800
Lotus CA 95651
916-621-2667

Recovered Alcoholic Clergy Association
(RACA)
5615 Midnight Pass Road, Siesta Key
Sarasota FL 54242

Residents Initiatives Drug Information and
Strategy Clearinghouse
Rockville MD
301-251-5546

Resource Center on Substance Abuse
Prevention and Disability
Washington DC
202-783-2900

RID USA (Remove Intoxicated Drivers)
PO Box 520
Schenectady NY 12301
518-372-0034

Rutgers Center of Alcohol Studies
Piscataway NJ 08854
908-932-4442

Scott Newman Center (Preventing Drug
Abuse through Education)
6255 Sunset Blvd., Suite 1906
Los Angeles CA 90028
213-469-2029

Secular Organizations for Sobriety (SOS)
PO Box 5
Buffalo NY 14215
716-834-2922

Smokers Anonymous (SA) World Services
2118 Greenwich Street
San Francisco CA 94123
415-922-8575

Social Workers Helping Social Workers
Route 63
Goshen CT 06756
203-489-3808

Society of Teachers of Family Medicine
(STFM)
PO Box 8729
Kansas City MO 64114
800-274-2237

Southeast Regional Center for Drug-Free
Schools and Communities
Louisville KY 40292
502-852-0052

Southwest Regional Center for Drug-Free
Schools and Communities
Norman OK 73037
405-325-1454

St. Agnes Hospital Adolescent and
Addiction Services
682 Western Avenue
Fond Du Lac WI 54935
414-923-6554
414-929-1381

St. Mary's Adolescent Substance Abuse/
Mercy Health Center
1111 3rd Street SW
Dyersville IA 52040
319-875-2951

St. Peter Chemical Dependency Center
4800 College Street
Lacey WA 98503
800-332-0465

St. Vincent Stress Center Youth Services
8401 Harcourt Road
Indianapolis IN 46280
317-338-4800
800-872-2210

Students Against Driving Drunk (SADD)
200 Pleasant Street
Marlboro MA 01752
508-481-3568

Substance Abuse Librarians and
Information Specialists (SALIS)
Alcohol Research Group
1816 Scenic Avenue
Berkeley CA 94702

Substance Abusology Research Unit (SARU)
Faculty of Nursing, University of Alberta
Suite 500, University Extension Center
8303 112 Street
Edmonton AB T6G 2T4
403-492-2856

TARGET
National Federation TARGET Program
Kansas City MO
816-464-5400

The Challenge
Department of Education
Office of Alcohol and Drug Education
Washington DC 20202-3726
202-732-4161

Toughlove
PO Box 1069
Doylestown PA 18901
215-348-7090

U.S. Congress, House Select Committee on
  Narcotics Abuse and Control
H2-234 House Annex 2
Washington DC 20515
202-226-3040

U.S. Congress, Senate Committee on Labor
  and Human Resources, Subcommittee on
  Children
Washington DC 20510
202-224-5630

U.S. Department of Education
Drug-Free Schools Staff
400 Maryland Avenue SW
Washington DC 20202
202-401-1599

U.S. Department of Education
Drug Planning and Outreach Staff
Office of Elementary and Secondary
  Education
400 Maryland Avenue SW, Room 1073
Washington DC 20202-6123
202-401-3030

U.S. Department of Education
Schools without Drugs
800-624-0100

U.S. Department of Health and Human
  Services
200 Independence Avenue SW
Washington DC 20201
202-245-6296

U.S. Department of Housing and Urban
  Development
Office for Drug-Free Neighborhoods
451 7th Street SW
Washington DC 20241
202-708-1197

U.S. Department of Justice
Drug Enforcement Administration
Office of Public Affairs
Prevention Program Coordinator
1405 I Street NW, Room 1209
Washington DC 20537
202-633-1469
202-633-1230

U.S. Department of Transportation
National Highway Traffic Safety
  Administration
400 7th Street SW
Washington DC 20590
202-426-9550

U.S.-Mexico Border Health Association
El Paso TX
915-581-6645

Western Center for Drug-Free Schools and
  Communities
Northwest Regional Education Laboratory
Portland OR 97204
503-275-9500
800-547-6339 (outside Oregon)

Wilderness Treatment Center
200 Hubbart Dam Road
Marion MT 59925
406-854-2832

Women for Sobriety
PO Box 618
Quakertown PA 18951
215-536-8026

Part III. Major North American AIDS Hotlines Listed by State or Province

CDC National AIDS Hotline
800-342-AIDS

Alabama
Alabama AIDS Hotline
Montgomery
800-228-0469

Alaska
Alaska AIDS Hotline
Juneau
800-478-2437

Alberta
Alberta Health—STD Control
403-427-2830 (Edmonton)
800-772-AIDS (throughout Alberta)

Arizona
Arizona AIDS Hotline
Phoenix
800-334-1540

British Columbia
British Columbia Ministry of Health
604-872-6652 (Vancouver)
800-972-2437 (throughout BC)

California
Southern California AIDS Hotline
Los Angeles
800-922-2437
800-553-2437 (TTY)

Northern California AIDS Hotline
San Francisco
800-FOR-AIDS
415-864-6606 (TTY)

Colorado
Colorado Department of Health
Denver
800-252-2437

Connecticut
Connecticut AIDS Hotline
Hartford
203-566-1157

Delaware
Delaware AIDS Hotline
Wilmington
800-422-0429

District of Columbia
District of Columbia AIDS Hotline
Washington
202-332-2437

Florida
Florida AIDS Hotline
Tallahassee
800-545-SIDA (Spanish hotline)
800-352-2437 (English hotline)
800-AID-S101 (Haitian Creole hotline)

Georgia
Georgia AIDS Hotline
800-551-2728
404-876-9944
404-876-9950 (TTY)

Hawaii
Hawaii AIDS Hotline
Honolulu
808-922-1313

Idaho
Idaho AIDS Hotline
Boise
800-677-2437

Illinois
Illinois AIDS Hotline
Chicago
800-243-2437
800-782-0423 (TTY)

Indiana
Indiana AIDS Hotline
Indianapolis
800-848-2437

Iowa
Iowa AIDS Hotline
Des Moines
800-445-2437

Kentucky
Kentucky AIDS Information Service
Frankfort
800-654-2437

Louisiana
Louisiana AIDS Hotline
New Orleans
800-992-4379

Maine
Maine AIDS Hotline
Portland
800-851-2437

Manitoba
AIDS Infoline
Manitoba Department of Health
204-945-AIDS (Winnipeg)
800-782-AIDS (throughout Manitoba)

Maryland
Maryland AIDS Hotline
Baltimore
800-638-6252
800-553-3140 (TTY)

Massachusetts
Massachusetts AIDS Hotline
Boston
800-235-2331
800-235-2331 (TTY)
617-262-7248 (Spanish hotline)

Michigan
Michigan AIDS Hotline
Royal Oak
800-872-2437
800-332-0849 (TTY)

Minnesota
Minnesota AIDSline
Minneapolis
800-248-2437

Mississippi
Mississippi AIDS Hotline
Jackson
800-537-0851

Missouri
Missouri AIDS Hotline
Jefferson City
800-533-2437

Montana
Montana AIDS Hotline
Helena
800-233-6668

Nebraska
Nebraska AIDS Hotline
Omaha
800-782-2437

Nevada
Nevada AIDS Hotline
Carson City
800-842-2437

New Brunswick
New Brunswick Department of Health
506-453-2536

AIDS New Brunswick
506-459-7518
800-561-4009 (throughout NB)

Newfoundland
Newfoundland Department of Health and
   Disease Control
709-576-3430

New Hampshire
New Hampshire AIDS Information Line
Concord
800-872-8909

New Jersey
New Jersey AIDS Hotline
Trenton
800-624-2377

New Mexico
New Mexico AIDS Hotline
Santa Fe
800-545-2437

New York
New York AIDS Hotline
Buffalo
800-541-2437 (English hotline)
800-233-SIDA (Spanish hotline)

North Dakota
North Dakota AIDS Hotline
Bismarck
800-472-2180

Northwest Territories
AIDS Information Line
403-873-7017
800-661-0795 (throughout NT)

Nova Scotia
Nova Scotia Department of Health
Epidemiology Division
902-424-8698

Ohio
Ohio AIDS Hotline
Columbus
800-332-2437
800-DEA-FTTY (TTY)

Oklahoma
Oklahoma AIDS Hotline
Oklahoma City
800-522-9054
800-522-9054 (TTY)

Ontario
Ontario Ministry of Health
AIDS Section
416-668-6066
800-668-2437 (throughout Ontario; English
    and other languages)
800-267-7432 (throughout Ontario; French)

Oregon
Oregon AIDS Hotline
Portland
800-777-2437

Pennsylvania
Pennsylvania AIDS Hotline
Harrisburg
800-445-7720

Prince Edward Island
PEI Department of Health
902-368-4530

Puerto Rico
Linea de Auxilio SIDA y Enfermedades de
    Transmision Sexual
Rio Piedras
809-765-1010

Quebec
Quebec Department of Health
418-643-9395
800-463-5656 (throughout Quebec)

Rhode Island
Rhode Island AIDS Hotline
Providence
800-726-3010

Saskatchewan
Saskatchewan Health Education Line
306-787-3148
800-667-7766 (throughout Saskatchewan)

South Carolina
South Carolina AIDS Hotline
Columbia
800-322-2437

South Dakota
South Dakota AIDS Hotline
Sioux Falls
800-592-1861

Tennessee
Tennessee AIDS Hotline
Nashville
800-525-2437

Texas
Texas AIDSLINE
Austin
800-299-2437
800-252-8012 (TTY)

Utah
Utah AIDS Hotline
Salt Lake City
801-538-6094

Vermont
Vermont AIDS Hotline
Burlington
800-882-AIDS

Virginia
Virginia AIDS Hotline
Richmond
800-533-4148
800-533-4148 (TTY)

Virgin Islands
Virgin Islands AIDS Hotline
Christiansted
809-773-1311

Washington
Washington AIDS Hotline
Olympia
800-272-AIDS

West Virginia
West Virginia AIDS Hotline
Charleston
800-642-8244

Wisconsin
Wisconsin AIDSline
Milwaukee
800-334-2437

Wyoming
Wyoming AIDS Hotline
Cheyenne
800-327-3577

Yukon
Yukon Ministry of Health
403-668-9444 (Whitehorse)
800-661-0507 (throughout Yukon)

References

Abel, E. L. (1980). Smoking during pregnancy: A review of effects on growth and development of offspring. *Human Biology, 52,* 593–625.

Abel, E. L., Martier, S., Kruger, M., Ager, J., & Sokol, R. J. (1993). Ratings of fetal alcohol syndrome facial features by medical providers and biomedical scientists. *Alcoholism, Clinical & Experimental Research, 17,* 717–721.

Abel, E. L., & Sokol, R. J. (1987). Incidence of fetal alcohol syndrome and economic impact of FAS-related anomalies. *Drug and Alcohol Dependence, 19,* 51–70.

Abel, E. L., & Sokol, R. J. (1991). A revised conservative estimate of the incidence of FAS and economic impact. *Alcoholism, Clinical & Experimental Research, 15,* 514–524.

Abram, K. M. (1989). The effect of co-occurring disorders on criminal careers: Interaction of antisocial personality, alcoholism, and drug disorders. *International Journal of Law & Psychiatry, 12,* 133–148.

Accessibility of cigarettes to youths aged 12–17 years—U.S., 1989. (1992). *Annals of Pharmacotherapy, 26,* 1191–1192.

Aday, L. A. (1994). Health status of vulnerable populations. *Annual Review of Public Health, 15,* 487–509.

Adger, H. (1991). Problems of alcohol and other drug use and abuse in adolescents. *Journal of Adolescent Health Care, 12,* 606–613.

Adger, H., Jr., McDonald, E. M., & DeAngelis, C. (1990). Substance abuse education in pediatrics. *Pediatrics, 88,* 555–560.

Adler, T. (1992). Prenatal cocaine exposure has subtle, serious effects. *American Psychological Association Monitor, 23*(11), 17.

Adolescents and substance abuse: Trends in treatment. (1991, December). *AADAC Profile* (Reference No. 1000/.06). Edmonton, AB: Alberta Alcohol and Drug Abuse Commission.

Adolescents as victims of family violence. (1993). *Journal of the American Medical Association, 270,* 1850–1856.

Agurell, S., Halldin, M., Lindgren, J., Ohlsson, A., Widman, M., Gillespie, M., & Hollister, L. (1986). Pharmacokinetics and metabolism of delta-1-tetra-hydrocannabinol and other cannabinoids with emphasis on man. *Pharmacological Review, 38,* 21–43.

Akers, R. L. (1977). *Deviant behavior: A social learning approach* (2nd ed.). Belmont, CA: Wadsworth.

Akers, R. L., Krohn, M. D., Lanza-Kaduce, L., & Radosevich, M. (1979). Social learning and deviant behavior: A specific test of a general theory. *American Sociological Review, 44,* 636–655.

Alarcon, R. D., Johnson, B. R., & Lucas, J. P. (1992). Paranoid and aggressive behavior in two obsessive-compulsive adolescents treated with clomipramine. *Journal of the American Academy of Child & Adolescent Psychiatry, 30,* 999–1002.

Alberta's peer support program. (1987). *Health Promotion, 26,* 23.

Alcohol-related traffic fatalities among youth and young adults—United States, 1982–1989. (1991). *Morbidity & Mortality Weekly Report, 40,* 178–179, 185–187.

Aldridge, D., & St. John, K. (1991). Adolescent and pre-adolescent suicide in Newfoundland and Labrador. *Canadian Journal of Psychiatry, 46,* 432–436.

Alexander, J., Waldon, H. B., Newberry, A. M., & Liddle, N. (1990). The functional family therapy model. In A. S. Friedman & S. Granick (Eds.), *Family therapy for adolescent drug abuse* (pp. 183–199). New York: Lexington.

Alford, G. S., Koehler, R. A., & Leonard, J. (1991). Alcoholics Anonymous-Narcotics Anonymous: Model inpatient treatment of chemically dependent adolescents: A 2-year outcome study. *Journal of Studies on Alcohol, 52,* 118–126.

Allen, J. S., & Drabman, R. S. (1991). Attributions of children with learning disabilities who are treated with psychostimulants. *Learning Disability Quarterly, 14,* 1991.

Alterman, A. I. (1987). Patterns of familial alcoholism, alcoholism severity, and psychopathology. *Journal of Nervous & Mental Disease, 176,* 167–175.

Alterman, A., & Tarter, R. (1986). An examination of selected typologies: Hyperactivity, familial, and antisocial alcoholism. In M. Galanter (Ed.), *Recent developments in alcoholism* (Vol. 4, pp. 169–189). New York: Plenum.

Alterman, A. I., Tarter, R. E., Baughman, T. G., Bober, B. A., & Fabian, S. A. (1985). Differentiation of alcoholics high and low in childhood hyperactivity. *Drug and Alcohol Dependence, 15*(1–2), 111–121.

Amble, F. R. (1990). Drug abuse by adolescents. *Journal of Texas Medicine, 86*(11), 58–63.

American Academy of Pediatrics, Committee on Adolescence and Committee on Substance Abuse. (1991). Marijuana: A continuing concern for pediatricians. *Pediatrics, 88,* 1070–1072.

American Academy of Pediatrics, Committee on Substance Abuse and Committee on Children with Disabilities. (1993). *Pediatrics, 91,* 1004–1006.

American Psychiatric Association. (1994). *Diagnostic and statistical manual of mental disorders* (4th ed.). Washington, DC: Author.

Andrews, L. S., & Snyder, R. (1991). Toxic effects of solvents and vapors. In M. O. Amdur, J. Doull, & C. D. Klaassen (Eds.), *Casarett and Doull's toxicology: The basic science of poisons* (4th ed., pp. 681–722). New York: Pergamon.

Andrulonis, P. A. (1991). Disruptive behavior disorders in boys and the borderline personality disorder in men. *Annals of Clinical Psychiatry, 3,* 23–26.

Anton, R. F. (1994). Medications for treating alcoholism. *Alcohol, Health & Research World, 18,* 265–271.

Aramburu, B., & Leigh, B. C. (1991). For better or worse: Attributions about drunken aggression toward male and female victims. *Violence & Victims, 6,* 31–41.

Arbeit, M. L., Nicklas, T. A., Frank, G. C., Webber, L. F., Miner, M. H., & Bernenson, G. S. (1988). Caffeine intakes of children from a biracial population: The Bogalusa heart study. *Journal of the American Dietetic Association, 88,* 466–471.

Arnold, G. L., Kirby, R. S., Langendoerfer, S., & Wilkins-Haug, L. (1994). Toluene embryopathy: Clinical delineation and developmental follow-up. *Pediatrics, 93,* 216–220.

Asante, K., & Nelms-Matzke, J. (1985). Survey of children with chronic handicaps and fetal alcohol syndrome in the Yukon and Northwest B. C. Ottawa: National Native Advisory Council on Alcohol and Drug Abuse, Health and Welfare Canada. Unpublished report.

Atkin, C. K. (1990). Effects of televised alcohol messages on teenage drinking patterns. *Journal of Adolescent Health Care, 11*(1), 10–24.

Attention, memory deficits still apparent in FAS adolescents. (1994). *Brown University Digest of Addiction Theory and Application, 13*(8), 6.

Austin, M.-P., Ross, M., Murray, C., O'Carroll, R. E., Ebmeier, K. P., & Goodwin, G. M. (1992). Cognitive function in major depression. *Journal of Affective Disorders, 25,* 21–30.

Ausubel, D. P. (1958). *Drug addiction: Physiological, psychological, and sociological aspects.* New York: Random House.

Ausubel, D. P. (1961). Causes and types of drug addiction: A psychosocial view. *Psychiatric Quarterly, 35,* 523–531.

Autti-Rämö, I., & Granström, M.-L. (1991). The psychomotor development during the first year of life of infants exposed to intrauterine alcohol of various duration: Fetal alcohol exposure and development. *Neuropediatrics, 22,* 59–64.

Autti-Rämö, I., Korkman, M., Hilakivi-Clarke, L., Lehtonen, M., Halmesmäki, E., & Granström, M.-L. (1992). Mental development of 2-year-old children exposed to alcohol in utero. *Journal of Pediatrics, 120,* 740–746.

Azima, F. J. C., & Richmond, L. H. (Eds.). (1989). *Adolescent group psychotherapy.* Madison, CT: International Universities Press.

Baer, J. S. (1991). Implications for early intervention from a biopsychosocial perspective on addiction. *Behaviour Change, 8*(2), 51–59.

Bagley, C., Durie, D., Hall, R., Harrington, G., Hunter, W., Kiddey, K., & Tanney, B. (1990). *Facing the Facts: Suicide in Canada* [Brochure]. Ottawa: Suicide Information and Education Centre.

Bailey, G. W. (1989). Current perspectives on substance abuse in youth. *Journal of the American Academy of Child and Adolescent Psychiatry, 28,* 151–162.

Bailey, G. W. (1992). Children, adolescents, and substance abuse. *Journal of the American Academy of Child and Adolescent Psychiatry, 31,* 1015–1018.

Bailey, S. L., & Hubbard, R. L. (1990). Developmental variation in the context of marijuana initiation among adolescents. *Journal of Health and Social Behavior, 31,* 58–70.

Baldridge, E. B., & Bessen, H. A. (1990). Phencyclidine. *Emergency Medicine Clinics of North America, 8,* 541–550.

Balshem, M., Oxman, G., van Rooyen, D., & Girod, K. (1992). Syphilis, sex and crack cocaine: Images of risk and mortality. *Social Science and Medicine, 35,* 147–160.

Bandstra, E. S., & Burkett, G. (1991). Maternal-fetal and neonatal effects of in utero cocaine exposure. *Seminars in Perinatology, 15*(4), 288–301.

Bandura, A. (1969). *Principles of behavior modification.* New York: Holt, Rinehart and Winston.

Bandura, A. (1977). *Social learning theory.* Englewood Cliffs, NJ: Prentice-Hall.

Bandura, A. (1986). *Social foundations of thought and action: A social cognitive theory.* Englewood Cliffs, NJ: Prentice-Hall.

Banner, W., & Walson, P. D. (1983). Systemic toxicity following gasoline aspiration. *American Journal of Emergency Medicine, 3,* 292–294.

Barbee, J. G. (1993). Memory, benzodiazepines, and anxiety: Integration of theoretical and clinical perspectives. *Journal of Clinical Psychiatry, 54*(Suppl. 86–97), 98–101.

Barkley, R. A. (1990). *Attention-deficit hyperactivity disorder: A handbook for diagnosis and treatment.* New York: Guilford.

Barnes, G. E. (1979). Solvent abuse: A review. *International Journal of the Addictions, 14,* 1–26.

Barnes, G. M. (1984). Evaluation of alcohol education: A reassessment using socialization theory. *Journal of Drug Education, 14*(2), 133–150.

Barnes, G. M., & Welte, J. W. (1986). Patterns and predictors of alcohol use among 7–12th grade students in New York State. *Journal of Studies on Alcohol, 47*(1), 53–62.

Barr, H. L., Langs, R. J., Holt, R. R., Goldberger, L., & Klein, G. S. (1972). LSD: *Personality and experience.* New York: Wiley.

Barrera, M., Jr., Chassin, L., & Rogosch, F. (1993). Effects of social support and conflict on adolescent children of alcoholic and nonalcoholic fathers. *Journal of Personality and Social Psychology, 64,* 602–612.

Bass, L. E., & Kane-Williams, E. (1993). Stereotype or reality: Another look at alcohol and drug use among African American children. *Public Health Reports, 108,* 78–84.

Bastian, L. D., & Taylor, B. M. (1991). *School crime: A national crime victimization survey report* (NCJ No. 131645). Washington, DC: U.S. Department of Justice.

Bateman, D. A., & Heagarty, M. C. (1989). Passive free-base cocaine ("crack") inhalation by infants and toddlers. *American Journal of Diseases of Children, 143,* 25–27.

Bates, M. E., & Pandina, R. J. (1991). Personality stability and adolescent substance use behaviors. *Alcoholism, Clinical & Experimental Research, 15,* 471–477.

Bateson, G. (1971). The cybernetics of "self": A theory of alcoholism. *Psychiatry, 34,* 1–18.

Batlle, M. A., & Wilcox, W. D. (1993). Pulmonary edema in an infant following passive inhalation of free-base ("crack") cocaine. *Clinical Pediatrics, 32,* 105–106.

Battjes, R. J. (1984). Symbolic interaction theory: A perspective on drug abuse and its treatment. *International Journal of the Addictions, 19,* 675–688.

Battjes, R. J. (1985). Prevention of adolescent drug abuse [Review]. *International Journal of the Addictions, 20,* 1113–1134.

Bauman, K. E. (1994). Peer influence on adolescent drug use. *American Psychologist, 49,* 820–822.

Baumrind, D., & Moselle, K. A. (1985). A developmental perspective on adolescent drug abuse. *Advances in Alcohol and Substance Abuse, 4,* 41–67.

Bayatpour, M., Wells, R. D., & Holford, S. (1992). Physical and sexual abuse as predictors of substance use and suicide among pregnant teenagers. *Journal of Adolescent Health, 13,* 128–132.

Bays, J. (1990). Substance abuse and child abuse: Impact of addiction on the child. *Pediatric Clinics of North America, 37,* 881–904.

Bean, N. M. (1992–93). Elucidating the path toward alcohol and substance abuse by adolescent victims of sexual abuse. *Journal of Applied Social Sciences, 17,* 57–94.

Beauvais, F. (1992a). An integrated model for prevention and treatment of drug abuse among American Indian youth. *Journal of Addictive Diseases, 11*(3), 63–80.

Beauvais, F. (1992b). Trends in Indian adolescent drug and alcohol use. *American Indian Alaskan Native Mental Health Research, 5*(1), 1–12.

Beauvais, F., & Oetting, E. R. (1988). Inhalant abuse by young children. In R. A. Crider & B. A. Rouse (Eds.), *Epidemiology of inhalant abuse: An update* (NIDA Research Monograph No. 85, pp. 30–33). Rockville, MD: U.S. Department of Health and Human Services, National Institute on Drug Abuse.

Beauvais, F., Oetting, E. R., Wolf, W., & Edwards, R. W. (1989). American Indian youth and drugs, 1976–1987: A continuing problem. *American Journal of Public Health, 79,* 634–636.

Beck, A. T. (1967). *Depression: Clinical, experimental and theoretical aspects.* New York: Harper and Row.

Beck, S., & Olivet, D. C. (1988). Adapting the Alcoholics Anonymous model in adolescent alcohol treatment. *Holistic Nursing Practice, 2*(4), 28–33.

Becker, H. K., Agopian, M. W., & Yeh, S. (1992). Impact evaluation of drug abuse resistance education (DARE). *Journal of Drug Education, 22,* 283–291.

Becker, H. S. (1967). History, culture and subjective experience: An exploration of the social bases of drug-induced experiences. *Journal of Health and Social Behavior, 8,* 163–176.

Becker, M., Warr-Leeper, G. A., & Leeper, H. A. (1990). Fetal alcohol syndrome: A description of oral motor, articulatory, short-term memory, grammatical, and semantic abilities. *Journal of Communicative Disorders, 23,* 97–124.

Bejerot, N. (1972). *Addiction: An artificially induced drive.* Springfield, IL: Thomas.

Belfer, M. L. (1993). Substance abuse with psychiatric illness in children and adolescents: Definitions and terminology. *American Journal of Orthopsychiatry, 63*(1), 70–79.

Bell, T. (1995, October). Pay attention to this: ADD may be crucial factor in recovery. *Professional Counselor,* p. 12.

Bennett, E. M., & Kemper, K. J. (1994). Is abuse during childhood a risk factor for developing substance abuse problems as an adult? *Journal of Developmental & Behavioral Pediatrics, 15,* 426–429.

Benowitz, N. L. (1988). Pharmacologic aspects of cigarette smoking and nicotine addiction. *New England Journal of Medicine, 319,* 1318–1330.

Benson, G., & Holmberg, M. B. (1984). Drug-related criminality among young people. *Acta Psychiatrica Scandinavica, 70,* 487–502.

Bentler, P. M. (1992). Etiologies and consequences of adolescent drug use: Implications for prevention. *Journal of Addictive Diseases, 11*(3), 47–61.

Beran, R. G. (1992). Automatisms: The current legal position related to clinical practice and medicolegal interpretation. *Clinical & Experimental Neurology, 29,* 81–91.

Berenson, A. B., San Miguel, V. V., & Wilkinson, G. S. (1992). Violence and its relationship to substance use in adolescent pregnancy. *Journal of Adolescent Health, 13,* 470–474.

Bergman, B., & Brismar, B. (1994). Hormone levels and personality traits in abusive and suicidal male alcoholics. *Alcoholism, Clinical & Experimental Research, 18,* 311–316.

Bergman, U., Rosa, F. W., Baum, C., Wiholm, B.-E., & Faich, G. A. (1992). Effects of exposure to benzodiazepine during fetal life. *Lancet, 340,* 694–696.

Berlin, I. N. (1986). Psychopathology and its antecedents among American Indian adolescents. *Advances in Clinical Child Psychology, 9,* 125–152.

Berman, A. L., & Schwartz, R. H. (1990). Suicide attempts among adolescent drug users. *American Journal of Diseases of Children, 144,* 310–314.

Bernard, B. (1988, January). Peer programs: The lodestone to prevention. *Prevention Forum,* pp. 6–12.

Bernard, B., Fafoglia, B., & Perone, J. (1987). Knowing what to do and not to do reinvigorates drug education. In *Schools and drugs: A guide to drug and alcohol abuse prevention* (pp. 1–18). Sacramento, CA: Office of the Attorney General of California.

Bernard, L. C., & Krupat, E. (1994). *Health psychology: Biopsychosocial factors in health and illness.* Fort Worth, TX: Harcourt Brace.

Bertucci, V., & Krafchik, B. R. (1994). Diagnosis: Fetal alcohol syndrome. *Pediatric Dermatology, 11,* 180.

Biederman, J., Newcorn, J., & Sprich, S. (1991). Comorbidity of attention deficit hyperactivity disorder with conduct, depressive, anxiety, and other disorders. *American Journal of Psychiatry, 148,* 564–577.

Biglan, A., Glasgow, E., Avy, D., Thompson, E., Ary, D., Thompson, R., Severson, H., Lichtenstein, E., Weissman, W., Faller, C., & Gallison, C. (1987). How generalizable are the effects of smoking prevention programs? Refusal skills training and parent messages in a teacher-administered program. *Journal of Behavioral Medicine, 10,* 613–628.

Billingham, R., & Sack, A. (1986). Courtship violence and the interactive status of the relationship. *Journal of Adolescent Research, 1,* 315–325.

Bisson, J. I. (1993). Automatism and post-traumatic stress disorder. *British Journal of Psychiatry, 163,* 830–832.

Bland, R., & Orn, H. (1986). Family violence and psychiatric disorder. *Canadian Journal of Psychiatry, 31,* 129–137.

Blane, H. T., & Leonard, K. E. (Eds.). (1987). *Psychological theories of drinking and alcoholism.* New York: Guilford.

Blankstein, K. R., Flett, G. L., & Johnston, M. E. (1992). Depression, problem-solving ability, and problem-solving appraisals. *Journal of Clinical Psychology, 48,* 749–759.

Block, C. R., & Block, R. (1993). *Street gang crime in Chicago* (NCJ No. 144782). Washington, DC: U.S. Department of Justice.

Block, J., & Gjerde, P. F. (1990). Depressive symptoms in late adolescence: A longitudinal perspective on personality antecedents. In J. Rolf, A. S. Masten, D. Cicchetti, & K. H. Nuechterlein (Eds.), *Risk and protective factors in the development of psychopathology* (pp. 334–360). New York: Cambridge University Press.

Block, R. I., & Ghoneim, M. M. (1993). Effects of chronic marijuana use on human cognition. *Psychopharmacology, 110,* 219–228.

Blum, K. (Ed.). (1977). *Alcohol and opiates: Neurochemical and behavioral mechanisms.* New York: Academic.

Blum, R. H. (1981). Violence, alcohol, and setting: An unexplored nexus. In J. J. Collins, Jr., & M. E. Wolfgang (Eds.), *Drinking and crime: Perspectives on the relationships between alcohol consumption and criminal behavior* (pp. 110–142). New York: Guilford.

Blum, R. W. (1987). Adolescent substance abuse: Diagnostic and treatment issues. *Pediatric Clinics of North America, 34,* 523–537.

Blum, R. W., Harmon, B., Harris, L., Bergeisen, L., & Resnick, M. D. (1992). American Indian-Alaska Native youth health. *Journal of the American Medical Association, 267,* 1637–1644.

Blumstein, A. (1995, August). Violence by young people: Why the deadly nexus? *National Institute of Justice Journal,* pp. 1–9.

Bogal-Allbritten, R. B., & Allbritten, W. L. (1985). The hidden victims: Courtship violence among college students. *Journal of College Student Personnel, 26,* 201–204.

Bohan, T., Dominguez, R., Slopis, J., & Vila-Coro, A. A. (1992). Cocaine-associated abnormalities may not be causally related [Reply to letter to the editor]. *American Journal of Diseases of Children, 146,* 278.

Botvin, G. J. (1986). Substance abuse prevention research: Recent developments and future directions. *Journal of School Health, 56,* 370.

Botvin, G. J., Baker, E., Botvin, E. M., Filazzola, A. D., & Millman, R. B. (1984). Prevention of alcohol misuse through the development of personal and social competence: A pilot study. *Journal of Studies on Alcohol, 45,* 550–552.

Botvin, G. J., Baker, E., Dusenbury, L., Tortu, S., & Botvin, E. M. (1990). Preventing adolescent drug abuse through a multimodal cognitive-behavioral approach: Results of a 3-year study. *Journal of Consulting and Clinical Psychology, 58,* 437–446.

Botvin, G. J., Baker, E., Renick, N., Filazzola, A., & Botvin, E. M. (1984). A cognitive-behavioral approach to substance abuse prevention. *Addictive Behavior, 9,* 137–147.

Botvin, G. J., & Botvin, E. M. (1992). Adolescent tobacco, alcohol, and drug abuse: Prevention strategies, empirical findings, and assessment issues. *Developmental and Behavioral Pediatrics, 13,* 290–301.

Botvin, G. J., & Dusenbury, L. (1992). Substance abuse prevention: Implications for reducing risk of HIV infection. *Psychology of Addictive Behaviors, 6,* 70–80.

Botvin, G. J., Renick, N. L., & Baker, E. (1983). The effect of scheduling format and booster sessions on a broad spectrum psychosocial approach to smoking prevention. *Journal of Behavioral Medicine, 6,* 359–379.

Boyle, M. H., & Offord, D. R. (1991). Psychiatric disorder and substance use in adolescence. *Canadian Journal of Psychiatry, 36,* 699–705.

Boyle, M. H., Offord, D. R., Racine, Y. A., Szatmari, P., Fleming, J. E., & Links, P. S. (1992). Predicting substance use in late adolescence: Results from the Ontario child health study follow-up. *American Journal of Psychiatry, 149,* 761–767.

Bradford, J. M. W., Greenberg, D. M., & Motayne, G. G. (1992). Substance abuse and criminal behavior. *Psychiatric Clinics of North America, 15,* 605–622.

Bratter, T. E. (1989). Group psychotherapy with alcohol and drug addicted adolescents: Special clinical concerns and challenges. In F. J. C. Azima & L. H. Richmond, (Eds.), *Adolescent group psychotherapy* (pp. 163–189). Madison, CT: International Universities Press.

Bray, D. L., & Anderson, P. D. (1989). Appraisal of the epidemiology of fetal alcohol syndrome among Canadian Native peoples. *Canadian Journal of Public Health, 80,* 42–45.

Brecher, E. M. (1972). *Licit and illicit drugs.* Mt. Vernon, NY: Consumers Union.

Brent, D. A. (1989). Suicide and suicidal behavior in children and adolescents. *Pediatrics in Review, 10,* 269–275.

Breslau, N., Kilbey, M. M., & Andreski, P. (1993). Vulnerability to psychopathology in nicotine-dependent smokers: An epidemiologic study of young adults. *American Journal of Psychiatry, 150,* 941–946.

Brill, H., & Hirose, T. (1969). The rise and fall of a methamphetamine epidemic: Japan 1945–1955. *Seminars in Psychiatry, 1*(2), 179–194.

Brook, J. S. (1993). Interactional theory: Its utility in explaining drug use behavior among African-American and Puerto Rican youth [Review]. In M. R. De La Rosa & J.-L. R. Adrados (Eds.), *Drug abuse among minority youth: Methodological issues and recent research advances* (NIDA Research Monograph No. 130, pp. 79–101). Rockville, MD: U.S. Department of Health and Human Services, National Institute on Drug Abuse.

Brook, J. S., Brook, D. W., Scovell Gordon, A. S., Whiteman, M., & Cohen, P. (1990). The psychosocial etiology of adolescent drug use: A family interactional approach. *Genetic, Social, & General Psychology Monographs, 116*(2), 111–267.

Brook, J. S., Cohen, P., Whiteman, M., & Gordon, A. S. (1992). Psychosocial risk factors in the transition from moderate to heavy use or abuse of drugs. In M. Glantz & R. Pickens (Eds.), *Vulnerability to abuse* (pp. 359–389). Washington, DC: American Psychological Association.

Brook, J. S., Hamburg, B. A., Balka, E. B., & Wynn, P. S. (1992). Sequences of drug involvement in African-American and Puerto Rican adolescents. *Psychological Reports, 71*(1), 179–182.

Brook, J. S., Lukoff, I. F., & Whiteman, M. (1977a). Correlates of adolescent marijuana use as related to age, sex and ethnicity. *Yale Journal of Biology and Medicine, 50,* 383–390.

Brook, J. S., Lukoff, I. F., & Whiteman, M. (1977b). Peer, family, and personality domains as related to adolescents' drug behavior. *Psychological Reports, 41,* 1095–1102.

Brook, J. S., Lukoff, I. F., & Whiteman, M. (1978). Family socialization and adolescent personality and their association with adolescent use of marijuana. *Journal of Genetic Psychology, 133,* 261–271.

Brook, J. S., Lukoff, I. F., & Whiteman, M. (1980). Initiation into adolescent marijuana use. *Journal of Genetic Psychology, 137*(1st Half), 133–142.

Brook, J. S., Nomura, C., & Cohen, P. (1989a). A network of influences on adolescent drug involvement: Neighborhood, school, peer, and family. *Genetic, Social, & General Psychology Monographs, 115*(1), 123–145.

Brook, J. S., Nomura, C., & Cohen, P. (1989b). Prenatal, perinatal, and early childhood risk factors and drug involvement in adolescence. *Genetic, Social, & General Psychology Monographs, 115*(2), 221–241.

Brook, J. S., Whiteman, M., Balka, E. B., & Hamburg, B. A. (1992). African-American and Puerto Rican drug use: Personality, familial, and other environmental risk factors. *Genetic, Social, & General Psychology Monographs, 118*(4), 417–438.

Brook, J. S., Whiteman, M., & Gordon, A. S. (1985). Father absence, perceived family characteristics and stage of drug use in adolescence. *British Journal of Developmental Psychology, 2,* 87–94.

Brook, J. S., Whiteman, M., Gordon, A. S., & Cohen, P. (1986). Dynamics of childhood and adolescent personality traits and adolescent drug use. *Developmental Psychology, 22,* 403–414.

Brouhard, B. H. (1994). Cocaine ingestion and abnormalities of the urinary tract. *Clinical Pediatrics, 33,* 157–158.

Brown, L. J., & DiFranza, J. R. (1992). Pharmacy promotion of tobacco use among children in Massachusetts. *American Pharmacy, NS32*(5), 45–48.

Brown, R. T., & Braden, N. J. (1987). Hallucinogens. *Pediatric Clinics of North America, 34,* 341–347.

Brown, S. (1988). *Treating adult children of alcoholics: A developmental perspective.* New York: Wiley.

Brown, S., & Lewis, V. (1995). The alcoholic family: A developmental model of recovery. In S. Brown & I. D. Yalom (Eds.), *Treating alcoholism* (pp. 279–315). San Francisco: Jossey-Bass.

Bry, B. H., Conboy, C., & Bisgay, K. (1986). Decreasing adolescent drug use and school failure: Long-term effects of targeted family problem-solving training. *Child and Family Behavior Therapy, 8,* 43–59.

Buber, M. (1992). The current state of affairs: Flaws in the system. In S. J. Levy & E. Rutter, *Children of drug abusers* (pp. 93–126). New York: Lexington.

Budnick, L. D., & Ross, D. A. (1985). Bathtub-related drownings in the United States, 1979–81. *American Journal of Public Health, 75,* 630–633.

Bukstein, O. G. (1994). Treatment of adolescent alcohol abuse and dependence. *Alcohol, Health & Research World, 18,* 296–301.

Bukstein, O. G., Glancy, L. J., & Kaminer, Y. (1992). Patterns of affective comorbidity in a clinical population of dually diagnosed adolescent substance abusers. *Journal of the American Academy of Child and Adolescent Psychiatry, 31,* 1041–1045.

Bukstein, O. G., & Van Hasselt, V. B. (1993). Alcohol and drug abuse. In A. S. Bellack & M. Hersen (Eds.), *Handbook of behavior therapy in the psychiatric setting* (pp. 453–475). New York: Plenum.

Bukstein, O. G., & Van Hasselt, V. B. (1995). Substance use disorders. In V. B. Van Hasselt & M. Hersen, (Eds.), *Handbook of adolescent psychopathology* (pp. 384–406). New York: Lexington.

Burd, L., & Moffatt, M. E. K. (1994). Epidemiology of fetal alcohol syndrome in American Indians, Alaskan Natives, and Canadian aboriginal peoples: A review of the literature. *Public Health Reports, 109,* 688–693.

Burgess, A. W., Hartman, C. R., & McCormack, A. (1987). Abused to abuser: Antecedents of socially deviant behaviors. *American Journal of Psychiatry, 144*(11), 1431–1436.

Burke, J. D., Jr., Burke, K. C., & Rae, D. S. (1994). Increased rates of drug abuse and dependence after onset of mood or anxiety disorders in adolescence. *Hospital and Community Psychiatry, 45,* 451–455.

Burnside, M. A., Baer, P. E., McLaughlin, R. J., & Pickering, A. D. (1986). Alcohol use by adolescents in disrupted families. *Alcoholism, Clinical & Experimental Research, 10,* 272–278.

Busch, K. G., Zagar, R., Hughes, J. R., Arbit, J., & Bussell, R. E. (1990). Adolescents who kill. *Journal of Clinical Psychology, 46,* 472–485.

Busen, N. H. (1992). Counseling the high-risk adolescent. *Journal of Pediatric Health Care, 6,* 194–199.

Butler, N. R., & Goldstein, H. (1973). Smoking in pregnancy and subsequent child development. *British Medical Journal, 4,* 573–575.

Butts, J. A., & Schwartz, I. M. (1991). Access to insurance and length of psychiatric stay among adolescents and young adults discharged from general hospitals. *Journal of Health & Social Policy, 3,* 91–116.

Buydens-Branchey, L., & Branchey, M. H. (1992). Cortisol in alcoholics with a disordered aggression control. *Psychoneuroendocrinology, 17,* 45–54.

Campbell, J. D., Poland, M. L., Waller, J. B., & Ager, J. (1992). Correlates of battering during pregnancy. *Research in Nursing & Health, 15,* 219–226.

Caputo, R. A. (1993). Volatile substance misuse in children and youth: A consideration of theories. *International Journal of the Addictions, 28,* 1015–1032.

Carlini, E. A. (1993). Preliminary note: Dangerous use of anticholinergic drugs in Brazil. *Drug and Alcohol Dependence, 32*(1), 1–7.

Carlson, B. E. (1991). Outcomes of physical abuse and observation of marital violence among adolescents in placement. *Journal of Interpersonal Violence, 6,* 526–534.

Carlson, R. G., & Siegal, H. A. (1991). The crack life: An ethnographic overview of crack use and sexual behavior among African-Americans in a Midwest metropolitan city. *Journal of Psychoactive Drugs, 23,* 11–20.

Carney, L. J., & Chermak, G. D. (1991). Performance of American Indian children with fetal alcohol syndrome on the test of language development. *Journal of Communicative Disorders, 24,* 123–134.

Carpenter, C., Glassner, B., Johnson, B. D., & Loughlin, J. (1988). Research methods and respondent characteristics. In C. Carpenter, G. Glassner, B. D. Johnson, & J. Loughlin, *Kids, drugs, and crime* (pp. 15–26). Toronto, ON: Heath.

Carroll, J. F., Malloy, T. E., Hannigan, P., Santo, Y., & Kenrick, F. M. (1977). The meaning and evolution of the term "multiple substance use." *Contemporary Drug Problems, 6,* 101–134.

Caruso, K., & Bensel, R. (1993). Fetal alcohol syndrome and fetal alcohol effects: The University of Minnesota experience. *Minnesota Medicine, 76,* 25–29.

Catalano, R. F., Hawkins, J. D., Wells, E. A., & Miller, J. (1990–91). Evaluation of the effectiveness of adolescent drug abuse treatment, assessment of risks for relapse, and promising approaches for relapse prevention. *International Journal of the Addictions, 25,* 1085–1140.

Catalano, R. F., Morrison, D. M., Wells, E. A., Gillmore, M. R., Iritani, B., & Hawkins, J. D. (1992). Ethnic differences in family factors related to early drug initiation. *Journal of Studies on Alcohol, 53,* 208–217.

Cavaiola, A. A., & Schiff, M. (1988). Behavioral sequelae of physical and/or sexual abuse in adolescents. *Child Abuse & Neglect, 12,* 181–188.

Cavaliere, F. (1995, August). Parents killing kids: A nation's shame. *American Psychological Association Monitor,* p. 34.

Chaiken, J. M. (1995). *Drugs and crime facts, 1994* (NCJ No. 154043). Washington, DC: U.S. Department of Justice.

Chang, G., Astrachan, B. M., & Bryant, K. J. (1994). Emergency physicians' ratings of alcoholism treaters. *Journal of Substance Abuse Treatment, 11,* 131–135.

Chasnoff, I. J. (1988). Drug use in pregnancy: Parameters of risk. *Pediatric Clinics of North America, 35,* 1403–1412.

Chasnoff, I. J., Burns, W. J., Schnoll, S. H., Burns, K., Chisum, G., & Kyle-Spore, L. (1986). Maternal-neonatal incest. *American Journal of Orthopsychiatry, 56,* 577–580.

Chassin, L. (1984). Adolescent substance use and abuse. In P. Karoly & J. J. Steffen (Eds.), *Adolescent behavior disorders: Foundations and contemporary concerns* (pp. 99–152). Lexington, MA: Heath.

Chassin, L., McLaughlin Mann, L., & Sher, K. J. (1988). Self-awareness theory, family history of alcoholism, and adolescent alcohol involvement. *Journal of Abnormal Psychology, 97*(2), 206–217.

Chassin, L., Pillow, D. R., Curran, P. J., Molina, B. S., & Barrera, M., Jr. (1993). Relation of parental alcoholism to early adolescent substance use: A test of three mediating mechanisms. *Journal of Abnormal Psychology, 102,* 3–19.

Chatlos, J. C. (1989). Adolescent dual diagnosis: A 12-step transformational model. *Journal of Psychoactive Drugs, 21,* 189–201.

Chatlos, J. C. (1994). Dual diagnosis in adolescent populations. In N. S. Miller (Ed.), *Treating coexisting psychiatric and addictive disorders: A practical guide* (pp. 85–110). Center City, MN: Hazelden Educational Materials.

Chaudron, C. D., & Wilkinson, D. A. (Eds.). (1988). *Theories on alcoholism.* Toronto, ON: Addiction Research Foundation.

Chein, I., Gerard, D. L., Lee, R. S., & Rosenfeld, E. (1964). *The road to H: Narcotics, delinquency, and social policy.* New York: Basic Books.

Cherpitel, C. J. (1993). Alcohol and violence-related injuries: An emergency room study. *Addiction, 88,* 79–88.

Cherpitel, C. J. (1994). Alcohol and casualties: A comparison of emergency room and coroner data. *Alcohol & Alcoholism, 29,* 211–218.

Chesley, S., Lumpkin, M., Schatzki, A., Galpern, W. R., Greenblatt, D. J., Shader, R. I., & Miller, R. G. (1991). Prenatal exposure to benzodiazepine—I. *Neuropharmacology, 30*(1), 53–58.

Chick, J., Gough, K., Falkowski, W., Kershaw, P., Hore, B., Mehta, B., Ritson, B., Ropner, R., & Torley, D. (1992). Disulfiram treatment of alcoholism. *British Journal of Psychiatry, 161,* 84–89.

Child abuse and neglect a national emergency, U.S. advisory board declares in first report. (1991). *Hospital and Community Psychiatry, 42,* 101–102.

Chirgwin, K., DeHovitz, J. A., Dillon, S., & McCormack, W. M. (1991). HIV infection, genital ulcer disease, and crack cocaine use among patients attending a clinic for sexually transmitted disease. *American Journal of Public Health, 81,* 1576–1579.

Chisholm, P. (1994). Sobering questions: An Alberta case raises new debate over the so-called drunk defence. *Maclean's, 107,* 100–102.

Christoffel, K. K. (1990). Violent death and injury in U.S. children and adolescents. *American Journal of Diseases of Children, 144,* 697–706.

Church, M. W. (1993). Does cocaine cause birth defects? *Neurotoxicology and Teratology, 15,* 289.

Clark, D. B., Bukstein, O. G., Smith, M. G., Kaczynski, N. A., Mezzich, A. C., & Donovan, J. E. (1995). Identifying anxiety disorders in adolescents hospitalized for alcohol abuse or dependence. *Psychiatric Services, 46,* 618–620.

Clark, D. C., Sommerfeldt, L., Schwarz, M., Hedeker, D., & Watel, L. (1990). Physical reckless-ness in adolescence: Trait or byproduct of depressive/suicidal states? *Journal of Nervous and Mental Disease, 178*, 423–433.

Clarren, S. K., & Smith, D. W. (1978). Medical progress: The fetal alcohol syndrome. *New England Journal of Medicine, 298*, 1063–1067.

Claude, D., & Firestone, P. (1995). The development of ADHD boys: A 12-year follow-up. *Canadian Journal of Behavioural Science, 27*, 226–249.

Clayton, R. R. (1986). Multiple drug use: Epidemiology, correlates, and consequences. *Recent Developments in Alcoholism, 4*, 7–38.

Clayton, R. R., & Leukefeld, C. G. (1992). The prevention of drug use among youth: Implications of "legalization." *Journal of Primary Prevention, 12*, 289–302.

Clayton, R. R., & Ritter, C. (1985). The epidemiology of alcohol and drug abuse among adolescents. *Advances in Alcohol and Substance Abuse, 4*, 69–97.

Cloninger, C. R. (1987). Neurogenetic adaptive mechanisms in alcoholism. *Science, 236*, 410–416.

Cloward, R. A., & Ohlin, L. E. (1960). *Delinquency and opportunity.* New York: Free Press.

Coccaro, E. F., Silverman, J. M., Klar, H. M., Horvath, T. B., & Siever, L. J. (1994). Familial correlates of reduced central serotonergic system function in patients with personality disorders. *Archives of General Psychiatry, 51*, 318–324.

Coffey, T. G. (1966). Beer Street: Gin Lane. Some views of 18th-century drinking. *Quarterly Journal of Studies on Alcohol, 27*, 669–692.

Coghlan, A. J., Gold, S. R., Dohrenwend, E. F., & Zimmerman, R. S. (1973). A psychobehavioral residential drug abuse program: A new adventure in adolescent psychiatry. *International Journal of the Addictions, 8*, 767–777.

Cohen, A. Y. (1974). *The journey beyond trips: Alternatives to drugs.* Edmonton, AB: Alberta Alcohol and Drug Abuse Commission.

Cohen, E., MacKenzie, R. G., & Yates, G. L. (1991). HEADSS, a psychosocial risk assessment instrument: Implications for designing effective intervention programs for runaway youth. *Journal of Adolescent Health, 12*, 539–544.

Cohen, M. A. A., Palacios, A., Aladjem, A., Hernandez, I., Horton, A., Lefer, J., Lima, J., & Mehta, P. (1991). How can we combat excess mortality in Harlem: A one-day survey of substance abuse in adult general care. *International Journal of Psychiatry in Medicine, 21*, 369–378.

Cohen, S. (1967). *The beyond within* (2nd ed.). Kingsport, TN: Kingsport.

Cohen, S. (1981). Adolescence and drug abuse: Biomedical consequences. In D. J. Lettieri & J. P. Ludford (Eds.), *Drug abuse and the American adolescent* (NIDA Research Monograph No. 38, pp. 104–112). Rockville, MD: U.S. Department of Health and Human Services, National Institute on Drug Abuse.

Cohen, S. (1982). Therapeutic communities for substance abusers. *Drug Abuse & Alcoholism Newsletter, 11*(2), 1–4.

Cohen, S. (1985). LSD: The varieties of psychotic experience. *Journal of Psychoactive Drugs, 17*, 291–296.

Coke emergencies up, DAWN report. (1992). *Journal, 21*, 3.

Cole, C. K., Jones, M., & Sadofsky, G. (1990). Working with children at risk due to prenatal substance abuse. *PRISE Reporter, 21*, 5.

Coleman, S. B. (1978). Sib group therapy: A prevention program for siblings from drug-addicted families. *International Journal of the Addictions, 13*, 115–127.

Coleman, S. B. (1979a). Cross-cultural approaches to addict families. *Journal of Drug Education, 9*(4), 293–299.

Coleman, S. B. (1979b). Siblings in session. In E. Kaufman & P. Kaufmann (Eds.), *Family therapy of drug and alcohol abuse* (pp. 131–143). New York: Gardner.

Coleman, S. B. (1980). Incomplete mourning and addict/family transactions: A theory for understanding heroin abuse. In D. J. Lettieri, M. Sayer, & H. Wallenstein Pearson (Eds.), *Theories on drug abuse: Selected contemporary perspectives* (NIDA Research Monograph No. 30, pp. 83–89). Rockville, MD: U.S. Department of Health and Human Services, National Institute on Drug Abuse.

Coleman, S. B. (1985). The surreptitious power of the sibling cohort: An echo of sin and death. In S. B. Coleman (Ed.), *Failures in family therapy* (pp. 27–72). New York: Guilford.

Coleman, S. B., & Davis, D. I. (1978). Family therapy and drug abuse: A national survey. *Family Process, 17,* 21–29.

Coleman, S. B., & Stanton, M. D. (1978a). An index for measuring agency involvement in family therapy. *Family Process, 17*(4), 479–483.

Coleman, S. B., & Stanton, M. D. (1978b). The role of death in the addict family. *Journal of Marriage and Family Counselling, 4*(1), 79–90.

Coleridge, J., Cameron, P. A., Drummer, O. H., & McNeil, J. J. (1992). Survey of drug-related deaths in Victoria. *Medical Journal of Australia, 157,* 459–462.

Coles, C., Brown, T., Smith, I., Plantzman, K., Erickson, S., & Falek, A. (1991). Effects of prenatal alcohol exposure at school age. I. Physical and cognitive development. *Neurotoxicity and Teratology, 13,* 357–367.

Coles, C. D. (1993). Saying "goodbye" to the "crack baby." *Neurotoxicology and Teratology, 15,* 290–292.

Collins, E., & Turner, G. (1978). Six children affected by maternal alcoholism. *Medical Journal of Australia, 2,* 606–608.

Collins, J. J., Jr. (1981). Alcohol use and criminal behavior: An empirical, theoretical and methodological overview. In J. J. Collins, Jr. (Ed.), *Drinking and crime* (pp. 288–316). New York: Guilford.

Collishaw, N., & Leahy, K. (1991). Mortality attributable to tobacco use in Canada. *Chronic Diseases in Canada, 12,* 46.

Comings, D. E. (1990). *Tourette syndrome and human behavior.* Duarte, CA: Hope Press.

Consensus report: Drug concentration and driving impairment. (1985). *Journal of the American Medical Association, 254,* 2618–2621.

Coombs, R. H. (1981). Back on the streets: Therapeutic communities' impact upon drug users. *American Journal on Drug and Alcohol Abuse, 8,* 185–201.

Coombs, R. H., Paulson, M. K., & Palley, R. (1988). The institutionalization of drug use in America: Hazardous adolescence, challenging parenthood. In R. H. Coombs (Ed.), *The family context of adolescent drug use* (pp. 9–56). New York: Haworth.

Cooper, J. R., Bloom, F. E., & Roth, R. H. (1991). *The biochemical basis of neuropharmacology.* New York: Oxford University Press.

Cooper, M., Corrado, R., Karlberg, A. M., & Adams, L. P. (1992). Aboriginal suicide in British Columbia: An overview. *Canada's Mental Health, 40*(3), 19–23.

Corbett, J. A., Trimble, M. R., & Nichol, T. C. (1985). Behavioral and cognitive impairments in children with epilepsy: The long-term effects of anticonvulsant drugs. *Journal of the American Academy of Child Psychiatry, 24,* 17–23.

Cordier, S., Ha, M.-C., Ayme, S., & Goujard, J. (1992). Maternal occupational exposure and congenital malformations. *Scandinavian Journal of Work Environment Health, 18,* 11–17.

Cornelius, M. D., Day, N. L., Cornelius, J. R., Geva, D., Taylor, P. M., & Richardson, G. A. (1993). Drinking patterns and correlates of drinking among pregnant teenagers. *Alcoholism, Clinical & Experimental Research, 17,* 290–294.

Cornelius, M. D., Richardson, G. A., Day, N. L., Cornelius, J. R., Geva, D., & Taylor, P. M. (1994). A comparison of prenatal drinking in two recent samples of adolescents and adults. *Journal of Studies on Alcohol, 55,* 412–419.

Cornell, D. G. (1990). Prior adjustment of violent juvenile offenders. *Law and Human Behavior, 14,* 569–577.

Cornell, D. G., & Wilson, L. A. (1992). The PIQ > VIQ discrepancy in violent and nonviolent delinquents. *Journal of Clinical Psychology, 48,* 256–261.

Cornwall, T. P. (1990). Comorbidity of psychiatric disorders in adolescents. *American Journal of Psychiatry, 147,* 681.

Coryell, W. (1991). Genetics and dual diagnosis. In M. S. Gold, & A. E. Slaby (Eds.), *Dual diagnosis in substance abuse* (pp. 29–41). New York: Dekker.

Coté, T. R., Biggar, R. J., & Dannenberg, A. L. (1992). Risk of suicide among persons with AIDS: A national assessment. *Journal of the American Medical Association, 268,* 2066–2068.

Council of Scientific Affairs. (1989). Health care needs of homeless and runaway youth. *Journal of the American Medical Association, 262,* 1358–1361.

Cousineau, D., Grenier, J. L., & Allard, D. (1994). Violence and the consumption of illicit drugs in Quebec adolescents: An analysis of their perceptions. *Canadian Family Physician, 40,* 703–707.

Covey, L. S., & Glassman, A. H. (1991). New approaches to smoking cessation. *Physician Assistant, 15,* 69–70, 73–74, 77.

Cox, J. M., D'Angelo, L. J., & Silber, T. J. (1992). Substance abuse and syphilis in urban adolescents: A new risk factor for an old disease. *Journal of Adolescent Health, 13,* 483–486.

Cox, W. M. (1987). Personality theory and research. In H. T. Blane & K. E. Leonard (Eds.), *Psychological theories of drinking and alcoholism* (pp. 55–89). New York: Guilford.

Crabtree, B. L. (1984). Review of naltrexone, a long-acting opiate antagonist. *Clinical Pharmacy, 3,* 273–280.

Craig, R. D. (1985). State-dependent learning produced by diazepam ingestion in human subjects. *Dissertation Abstracts International, 46*(5-B), 1679.

Crites, L. S., Fischer, K. L., McNeish-Stengel, M., & Siegel, C. J. (1992). Working with families of drug-exposed children: Three model programs. *Transdisciplinary Journal, 2*(1), 13–23.

Cullen, J. W. (1982). Behavioral, psychological, and social influences on risk factors, prevention, and early detection. *Cancer, 50,* 1946–1953.

Curran, H. V., Gardiner, J. M., Java, R. I., & Allen, D. (1993). Effects of lorazepam upon recollective experience in recognition memory. *Psychopharmacology, 110,* 374–378.

Curry, D. G., Ball, R. A., & Fox, R. J. (1994). *Gang crime and law enforcement recordkeeping.* Washington, DC: U.S. Department of Justice.

Curtis, P. A., & McCullough, C. (1993). The impact of alcohol and other drugs on the child welfare system. *Child Welfare, 72,* 533–542.

Czeizel, A. (1988). Lack of evidence of teratogenicity of benzodiazepine drugs in Hungary. *Reproductive Toxicology, 1,* 183–188.

Daley, D. C., Moss, H., & Campbell, F. (1987). *Dual disorders: Counseling clients with chemical dependency and mental illness.* Center City, MN: Hazelden.

Daley, D. C., & Salloum, I. M. (1995, October). Focusing on dual disorders. *Professional Counselor,* pp. 15–16, 24–26.

Daly, M., & Wilson, M. (1985). Child abuse and other risks of not living with both parents. *Ethology & Sociobiology, 6,* 197–210.

Daniel, C., & Dodd, C. (1990). Covert sensitization treatment in the elimination of alcohol-related crime in incarcerated young offenders: A study of two cases. *Journal of Offender Rehabilitation, 16,* 123–137.

Danion, J. M., Peretti, S., Grange, D., Bilik, M., Imbs, J. L., & Singer, L. (1992). Effects of chlorpromazine and lorazepam on explicit memory, repetition priming and cognitive skill learning in healthy volunteers. *Psychopharmacology, 108,* 345–351.

Dannenberg, A. L., Parver, L. M., & Fowler, C. J. (1992). Penetrating eye injuries related to assault. *Archives of Ophthalmology, 110,* 849–852.

Davis, R. (1995, September 7). "Meth" use in the '90s: A growing "epidemic." *USA Today,* p. 7A.

Dawson, G. W., & Vestal, R. E. (1982). Smoking and drug metabolism. *Pharmacology and Therapeutics, 15,* 207–221.

Day, N., Sambamoorthi, U., Taylor, P., Richardson, G., Robles, N., Jhon, Y., Scher, M., Stoffer, D., Cornelius, M., & Jasperse, D. (1991). Prenatal marijuana use and neonatal outcome. *Neurotoxicology and Teratology, 13,* 329–334.

Day, N. L., Goldschmidt, L., Robles, N., Richardson, G., Cornelius, M., Taylor, P., Geva, D., & Stoffer, D. (1991). Prenatal alcohol exposure and offspring growth at 18 months of age: The predictive validity of two measures of drinking. *Alcoholism, Clinical and Experimental Research, 15,* 914–918.

Day, N. L., & Richardson, G. A. (1991). Prenatal alcohol exposure: A continuum of effects. *Seminars in Perinatology, 15,* 271–279.

Day, N. L., Richardson, G. A., Geva, D., & Robles, N. (1994). Alcohol, marijuana, and tobacco: Effects of prenatal exposure on offspring growth and morphology at age six. *Alcoholism, Clinical & Experimental Research, 18,* 786–794.

Deal, J. E., & Wampler, K. (1986). Dating violence: The primacy of previous experience. *Journal of Social and Personal Relationships, 3,* 457–471.

de Anda, D., Javidi, M., Jefford, S., Komorowski, R., & Yanez, R. (1991). Stress and coping in adolescence: A comparative study of pregnant adolescents and substance abusing adolescents. *Children and Youth Services Review, 13,* 171–182.

DeAngelis, T. (1994). Homeless families: Stark reality of the '90s. APA *Monitor, 25,* 1, 38.

DeBarona, M. S., & Simpson, D. D. (1984). Inhalant users in drug abuse prevention programs. *American Journal of Drug and Alcohol Abuse, 10,* 503–518.

DeBettencourt, K. B. (1990). The wisdom of Solomon: Cutting the cord that harms. *Children Today, 19,* 17–20.

DeBruyn, L. M., Lujan, C. C., & May, P. A. (1992). A comparative study of abused and neglected American Indian children in the Southwest. *Social and Scientific Medicine, 35,* 305–315.

Degen, H. M., Myers, B. J., Williams-Petersen, M. G., Knisely, J. S., & Schnoll, S. S. (1993). Social support and anxiety in pregnant drug abusers and nonusers: Unexpected findings of few differences. *Drug & Alcohol Dependence, 32*(1), 37–44.

De Jung, W. (1987). A short-term evaluation of Project DARE Drug Abuse Resistance Education: Preliminary indications of effectiveness. *Journal of Drug Education, 17,* 279–294.

De Leon, G. (1985). The therapeutic community: Status and evolution. *International Journal of the Addictions, 20,* 823–844.

Del Greco, L., Breitbach, L., Rumer, S., McCarthy, R. H., & Suissa, S. (1986). Four-year results of a youth smoking prevention program using assertiveness training. *Adolescence, 21,* 631–640.

Dembo, R. (1979). Substance abuse prevention programming and research: A partnership in need of improvement. *Journal of Drug Education, 9,* 189–208.

Dembo, R., Farrow, D., Schmeidler, J., & Burgos, W. (1979). Testing a causal model of environmental influences on the early drug involvement of inner city junior high school youths. *American Journal of Drug and Alcohol Abuse, 6*(3), 313–336.

Dembo, R., Pilaro, L., Burgos, W., Des Jarlais, D. C., & Schmeidler, J. (1979). Self-concept and drug involvement among urban junior high school youths. *International Journal of the Addictions, 14,* 1125–1144.

Dembo, R., & Shern, D. (1982). Relative deviance and the process(es) of drug involvement among inner-city youths. *International Journal of the Addictions, 17,* 1373–1399.

Dembo, R., Williams, L., Getreu, A., Genung, L., Schmeidler, J., Berry, E., Wish, E. D., & La Voie, L. (1991). A longitudinal study of the relationships among marijuana/hashish use, cocaine use and delinquency in a cohort of high-risk youths. *Journal of Drug Issues, 21,* 271–312.

Dembo, R., Williams, L., La Voie, L., Berry, E., Getreu, A., Wish, E. D., Schmeidler, J., & Washburn, M. (1989). Physical abuse, sexual victimization, and illicit drug use: Replication of a structural analysis among a new sample of high-risk youths. *Violence & Victims, 4,* 121–138.

Dembo, R., Williams, L., Schmeidler, J., Berry, E., Wothke, W., Getreu, A., Wish, E. D., & Christensen, C. (1992). A structural model examining the relationship between physical child abuse, sexual victimization, and marijuana/hashish use in delinquent youth: A longitudinal study. *Violence & Victims, 7*(1), 41–62.

Dembo, R., Williams, L., Schmeidler, J., Wish, E. D., Getreu, A., & Berry, E. (1991). Juvenile crime and drug abuse: A prospective study of high-risk youth. *Journal of Addictive Disorders, 11*(2), 5–31.

Dembo, R., Williams, L., Schmeidler, J., & Wothke, W. (1993). A longitudinal study of the predictors of the adverse effects of alcohol and marijuana/hashish use among a cohort of high-risk youths. *International Journal of the Addictions, 28,* 1045–1083.

Dembo, R., Williams, L., Wish, E. D., Berry, E., Getreu, A., Washburn, M., & Schmeidler, J. (1990). Examination of the relationships among drug use, emotional/psychological problems, and crime among youths entering a juvenile detention center. *International Journal of the Addictions, 25,* 1301–1340.

Dembo, R., Williams, L., Wothke, W., Schmeidler, J., Getreu, A., Berry, E., Wish, E. D., & Christensen, C. (1990). The relationship between cocaine use, drug sales, and other delinquency among a cohort of high-risk youths over time. In M. De La Rosa, E. Y. Lambert, & B. Gropper (Eds.), *Drugs and violence: Causes, correlates, and consequences* (NIDA Research Monograph No. 103, pp. 112–125). Rockville, MD: U.S. Department of Health and Human Services, National Institute on Drug Abuse.

Dembo, R., Wish, E. D., Dertke, M., Berry, E., Getreu, A., Washburn, M., & Schmeidler, J. (1988). The relationship between physical and sexual abuse and illicit drug use: A replication among a new sample of youths entering a juvenile detention center. *International Journal of the Addictions, 23,* 1101–1123.

Denny, E. B., & Hunt, R. R. (1992). Affective valence and memory in depression: Dissociation of recall and fragment completion. *Journal of Abnormal Psychology, 101,* 575–580.

Deren, S., Beardsley, M., Davis, R., & Tortu, S. (1993). HIV risk factors among pregnant and non-pregnant high-risk women in New York City. *Journal of Drug Education, 23*(1), 57–66.

Deren, S., Frank, B., & Schmeidler, J. (1990, April). Children of substance abusers in New York State. *New York State Journal of Medicine,* 179–184.

Dermen, K. H., & George, W. H. (1989). Alcohol expectancy and the relationship between drinking and physical aggression. *Journal of Psychology, 123,* 153–161.

Des Jarlais, D. C., & Dole, J. H. (1981). Long-term outcomes after termination from methadone maintenance treatment. *Annals of the New York Academy of Science, 362,* 231–238.

Dewey, W. L. (1986). Cannabinoid pharmacology. *Pharmacological Reviews, 38,* 151–178.

DeWitt, C. B. (1991, June). Drug use forecasting. In *Research in action* (pp. 1–8). Washington, DC: U.S. Department of Justice.

DeWitt, C. B., O'Neil, J. A., & Baldau, V. (1991, August). Drug use forecasting: Drugs and crime 1990 annual report. In *Research in action* (pp. 1–24). Washington, DC: U.S. Department of Justice.

Deykin, E. Y., Buka, S. L., & Zeena, T. H. (1992). Depressive illness among chemically dependent adolescents. *American Journal Psychiatry, 149,* 1341–1347.

Deykin, E. Y., Levy, J. C., & Wells, V. (1987). Adolescent depression, alcohol and drug abuse. *American Journal of Public Health, 77,* 178–182.

Deisher, R. W., Wenet, G. A., Paperney, D. M., Clark, R. F., & Fehrenbach, P. A. (1982). Adolescent sexual offense behavior: The role of the physician. *Journal of Adolescent Health Care, 2,* 279–286.

DiFranza, J. R. (1989). School tobacco policy: A medical perspective. *Journal of School Health, 59,* 398–400.

DiFranza, J. R. (1992). Preventing teenage tobacco addiction. *Journal of Family Practice, 34,* 753–756.

DiFranza, J. R., & Brown, L. J. (1992). The Tobacco Institute's "It's the Law" campaign: Has it halted illegal sales of tobacco to children? *American Journal of Public Health, 82*(9), 1272–1273.

DiFranza, J. R., & Lew, R. A. (1995). Effect of maternal cigarette smoking on pregnancy complications and sudden infant death syndrome. *Journal of Family Practice, 40,* 385–394.

DiFranza, J. R., Richards, J. W., Paulman, P. M., Wolf-Gillespie, N., Fletcher, C., Jaffe, R. D., & Murray, D. (1991). RJR Nabisco's cartoon camel promotes camel cigarettes to children. *Journal of the American Medical Association, 266,* 3149–3153.

Dole, V. P. (1971). Methadone maintenance treatment for 25,000 heroin addicts. *Journal of the American Medical Association, 215,* 1131–1134.

Dole, V. P., & Nyswander, M. E. (1980). Methadone maintenance: A theoretical perspective. In D. J. Lettierei, M. Sayers, & H. W. Pearson (Eds.), *Theories on drug abuse: Selected contemporary perspectives* (NIDA Research Monograph No. 30, pp. 256–261). Rockville, MD: U.S. Department of Health and Human Services, National Institute on Drug Abuse.

Donnelly, A. H. C. (1991). What we have learned about prevention: What we should do about it. *Child Abuse & Neglect, 15,* 99–106.

Donovan, J. E., & Jessor, R. (1984). *The structure of problem behavior in adolescence and young adulthood* (Research Report No. 10, Young Adult Follow-up Study). Boulder, CO: University of Colorado, Institute of Behavioral Studies.

D'Orban, P. T. (1989). Automatism: A medico-legal conundrum. *Irish Journal of Psychological Medicine, 6,* 71–80.

Dow-Edwards, D. (1993). The puzzle of cocaine's effects following maternal use during pregnancy: Still unsolved. *Neurotoxicology and Teratology, 15,* 295–296.

Downey, A. M. (1991). The impact of drug abuse upon adolescent suicide. *Omega, 22,* 261–275.

Drugs and crime facts, 1993 (NCJ No. 146246). (1994). Washington, DC: U.S. Department of Justice.

Duimstra, C., Johnson, D., Kutsch, C., Wang, B., Zentner, M., Kellerman, S., & Welty, T. (1993). A fetal alcohol syndrome surveillance pilot project in American Indian communities in the Northern Plains. *Public Health Reports, 108,* 225–229.

Dunne, F. J. (1993). Substance misuse in the young. *British Journal of Hospital Medicine, 50,* 643–649.

Dunne, F. J., & Schipperheijn, J. A. (1989). Alcohol and the young. *Alcohol and Alcoholism, 24,* 213–215.

DuPont, R. L. (1987). Prevention of adolescent chemical dependency. *Pediatric Clinics of North America, 34,* 495–505.

Dupuis, L. L., Smith, J., & Kowalczyk, A. (1995). Drug dosing in infants, children, and adolescents. In L. A. Pagliaro & A. M. Pagliaro (Eds.), *Problems in pediatric drug therapy* (3rd ed., pp. 813–1071). Hamilton, IL: Drug Intelligence.

Durell, J., & Bukoski, W. (1984). Preventing substance abuse: The state of the art. *Public Health Reports, 99,* 23–31.

Dusenbury, L., & Botvin, G. J. (1992). Substance abuse prevention: Competence enhancement and the development of positive life options. *Journal of Addictive Diseases, 11,* 29–45.

Edwards, M. S. (1981). Fetal alcohol syndrome. *Journal of Nursing Care, 11,* 6–14.

Eggert, L. L., Seyl, C. D., & Nicholas, L. J. (1990). Effects of a school-based prevention program for potential high school dropouts and drug abusers. *International Journal of the Addictions, 25,* 773–801.

Ehrlick, P. (1987). 12-Step principles and adolescent chemical dependence treatment. *Journal of Psychoactive Drugs, 19,* 311–317.

Eisen, S. V., Youngman, D. J., Grob, M. C., & Dill, D. L. (1992). Alcohol, drugs, and psychiatric disorders: A current view of hospitalized adolescents. *Journal of Adolescent Research, 7,* 250–265.

Eisenman, R. (1995). Adolescent sex offenders: Do kids learn to rape? *Adolescence, 8*(2), 29–31.

Ellickson, P. L., & Bell, R. M. (1990). Drug prevention in junior high: A multi-site longitudinal test. *Science, 247,* 1299–1305.

Elliott, D. S., & Ageton, R. A. (1976). *The relationship between drug use and crime among adolescents. Drug use and crime: Report of panel on drug use and criminal behavior.* Research Triangle, NC: Research Triangle Institute.

Elliott, D. S., Huizinga, D., & Ageton, S. S. (1985). *Explaining delinquency and drug use.* Newbury Park, CA: Sage.

Ellis, J. B., & Range, L. M. (1992). Mood influences on reasons for living in older adolescents. *Psychiatry, 55,* 216–222.

Epps, R. P., & Manley, M. W. (1991). A physician's guide to preventing tobacco use during childhood and adolescence. *Pediatrics, 88,* 140–144.

Erickson, P. I., & Rapkin, A. J. (1991). Unwanted sexual experiences among middle and high school youth. *Journal of Adolescent Health, 12,* 319–325.

Eriksson, M., Larsson, G., Winbladh, B., & Zetterstrom, B. (1978). The influence of amphetamine addiction on pregnancy and the newborn infant. *Acta Paediatrica Scandinavica, 67,* 95–99.

Erinoff, L. (1990). *Neurobiology of drug abuse: Learning and memory* (NIDA Research Monograph No. 97). Rockville, MD: U.S. Department of Health and Human Services, National Institute on Drug Abuse.

Ernhart, C. B., Morrow-Tlucak, M., Sokol, R. J., & Martier, S. (1988). Underreporting of alcohol use in pregnancy. *Alcoholism, Clinical & Experimental Research, 12,* 506–511.

Escobedo, L. G. (1994). Drinking and driving among U.S. high-school students [Letter to the editor]. *Lancet, 343,* 421.

Esman, A. H. (1992). Treatment and services for adolescents: An introduction. *Hospital and Community Psychiatry, 43,* 616.

Evans, R., Rozelle, R., Mittlemark, M., & Hansen, W. (1978). Deterring the onset of smoking in children: Knowledge of immediate physiological effects and coping with peer pressure, media pressure, and parent modeling. *Journal of Applied Social Psychology, 8,* 126–135.

Fagan, J. (1990). Social processes of delinquency and drug use among urban gangs. In C. R. Huff (Ed.), *Gangs in America* (pp. 183–219). Newbury Park, CA: Sage.

Fagan, J., Weis, J. G., & Cheng, Y. (1990). Delinquency and substance use among inner-city students. *Journal of Drug Issues, 20,* 351–402.

Fairbairn, W. H. D. (1952). *Psychoanalytic studies of the personality.* London: Routledge & Kegan Paul.

Faltz, B. G., & Rinaldi, J. (1987). *A training manual for health care professionals:* AIDS *and substance abuse.* San Francisco: University of California.

Famularo, R., Kinscherff, R., & Fenton, T. (1992). Parental substance abuse and the nature of child maltreatment. *Child Abuse & Neglect, 16,* 475–483.

Famularo, R., Stone, K., & Popper, C. (1985). Preadolescent alcohol abuse and dependence. *American Journal of Psychiatry, 142,* 1187–1189.

Faraco-Hadlock, G. G. (1990). Adolescent depression and substance abuse. *Journal of Psychology and Christianity, 9*(4), 64–71.

Farley, T. A., Hadler, J. L., & Gunn, R. A. (1990). The syphilis epidemic in Connecticut: Relationship to drug use and prostitution. *Sexually Transmitted Diseases, 17,* 163–168.

Farrell, A. D., Anchors, D. M., Danish, S. J., & Howard, C. W. (1992). Risk factors for drug use in rural adolescents. *Journal of Drug Education, 22,* 313–328.

Farrell, A. D., Danish, S. J., & Howard, C. W. (1992). Risk factors for drug use in urban adolescents: Identification and cross-validation. *American Journal of Community Psychology, 20,* 263–286.

Farrell, M., & Strang, J. (1991). Substance use and misuse in childhood and adolescence. *Journal of Child Psychology and Psychiatry, 32*(1), 109–128.

Febbo, S., Hardy, F., & Finlay-Jones, R. (1993–94). Dissociation and psychological blow automatism in Australia. *International Journal of Mental Health, 22,* 39–59.

Feigelman, B., & Jaquith, P. (1992). Adolescent drug treatment, a family affair: A community day center approach. *Social Work in Health Care, 16,* 39–52.

Feigelman, W. (1987). Day-care treatment for multiple drug abusing adolescents: Social factors linked with completing treatment. *Journal of Psychoactive Drugs, 19,* 335–344.

Feigelman, W., Hyman, M. M., Amann, K., & Feigelman, B. (1990). Correlates of persisting drug use among former youth multiple drug abuse patients. *Journal of Psychoactive Drugs, 22,* 63–75.

Feldman, J., Shenker, I. R., Etzel, R. A., Spierto, F. W., Lilienfield, D. E., Nussgaum, M., & Jacobson, M. S. (1991). Passive smoking alters lipid profiles in adolescents. *Pediatrics, 88,* 259–264.

Feldman, R. S., & Quenzer, L. F. (1984). *Fundamentals of neuropsychopharmacology.* Sunderland, MA: Sinauer.

Feldman, W., Feldman, E., Goodman, J. T., McGrath, P. J., Pless, R. P., Corsini, L., & Bennett, S. (1991). Is childhood sexual abuse really increasing in prevalence? An analysis of the evidence. *Pediatrics, 88,* 29–33.

Felner, R. D., Silverman, M. M., & Adix, R. (1991). Prevention of substance abuse and related disorders in childhood and adolescence: A developmentally based, comprehensive ecological approach. *Family Community Health, 14,* 12–22.

Felts, W. M., Chenier, T., & Barnes, R. (1991). Drug use and suicide ideation and behavior among North Carolina public school students. *American Journal of Public Health, 82,* 870–872.

Fennell, T., Ajello, R., & Howse, J. (1994, May 9). In the cross fire: Gang-related violence claims innocent lives. *Maclean's,* 19–20.

Fenwick, P. (1987). Somnambulism and the law: A review. *Behavioral Sciences and the Law, 5,* 343–357.

Fenwick, P. (1990). Automatism, medicine and the law. *Psychological Medicine, 17,* 1–27.

Fetal alcohol syndrome. (1991). *In Alcohol Alert* (PH297, no. 13, pp. 1–4). Rockville, MD: National Institute on Alcohol Abuse and Alcoholism.

Fetal alcohol syndrome. (1994). *Alberta Child Development Newsletter, 2*(5).

Fico, R. A., & Vanderwende, C. (1989). Phencyclidine during pregnancy: Behavioral and neurochemical effects in the offspring. In D. E. Hutchings (Ed.), *Prenatal abuse of licit and illicit drugs* (pp. 319–326). New York: New York Academy of Sciences.

Fields, R. (1995). Dual diagnosis: Definition, population, treatment. *Professional Counselor, 10*(2), 16.

Finestone, H. (1957). Cats, kicks, and color. *Social Problems, 5,* 3–13.

Fingarette, H. (1988). *Heavy drinking: The myth of alcoholism as a disease.* Berkeley and Los Angeles: University of California Press.

Finkelhor, D., & Dzuiba-Leatherman, J. (1994). Victimization of children. *American Psychologist, 49,* 173–183.

Finkelhor, D., Hotaling, G., Lewis, I. A., & Smith, C. (1990). Sexual abuse in a national survey of adult men and women: Prevalence, characteristics, and risk factors. *Child Abuse & Neglect, 14,* 19–28.

Finn, P. R., & Pihl, R. O. (1987). Men at high risk for alcoholism: The effect of alcohol on cardiovascular response to unavoidable shock. *Journal of Abnormal Psychology, 96,* 230–236.

Finn, P. R., & Pihl, R. O. (1988). Risk for alcoholism: A comparison between two different groups of sons of alcoholics on cardiovascular reactivity and sensitivity to alcohol. *Alcoholism, Clinical & Experimental Research, 12,* 742–747.

Firearms and crimes of violence (NCJ No. 146844). (1994). Washington, DC: U.S. Department of Justice.

Fishbein, D. H., Jaffe, J. H., Synder, F. R., Haertzen, C. A., & Hickey, J. E. (1993). Drug users' self-reports of behaviors and affective states under the influence of alcohol. *International Journal of the Addictions, 28,* 1565–1585.

Fisher, D. G. (Ed.). (1991). AIDS and alcohol/drug abuse: Psychosocial research. New York: Harrington Park.

Flatter, C. H., & McCormick, K. (1992). *Learning to live drug free: A curriculum model for prevention.* Washington, DC: U.S. Department of Education (ED/OESE92-36R).

Flay, B. R. (1985). Psychosocial approaches to smoking prevention: A review of findings. *Health Psychology, 4,* 449–488.

Flewelling, R. L., & Bauman, K. W. (1990). Family structure as a predictor of initial substance use and sexual intercourse in early adolescence. *Journal of Marriage and the Family, 52,* 171–181.

Fligiel, S. E., Venkat, H., Gong, H., & Tashkin, D. P. (1988). Bronchial pathology in chronic marijuana smokers: A light and electron microscopic study. *Journal of Psychoactive Drugs, 20,* 33–42.

Flumazenil. (1992). *Medical Letter, 34,* 66–68.

Fornazzari, L. (1990). The neurotoxicity of inhaled toluene [Letter to the editor]. *Canadian Journal of Psychiatry, 35,* 723.

Foster, F. M., Horn, J. L., & Wanberg, K. W. (1972). Dimensions of treatment outcome. *Quarterly Journal of Studies on Alcohol, 33,* 1079–1098.

Fournet, G. P., Estes, R. E., & Martin, G. L. (1990). Drug and alcohol attitudes and usage among elementary and secondary students. *Journal of Alcohol and Drug Education, 35,* 81–86.

Fowler, R. C., Rich, C. L., & Young, D. (1986). San Diego suicide study. II. Substance abuse in young cases. *Archives of General Psychiatry, 43,* 962–965.

Fox, C., & Forbing, S. (1991). Overlapping symptoms of substance abuse and learning handicaps: Implications for educators. *Journal of Learning Disabilities, 24,* 24–31.

Frances, R. J., & Allen, M. H. (1986). The interaction of substance-use disorders with nonpsychotic psychiatric disorders. In R. Michels, & J. O. Cavenar, Jr. (Eds.), *Psychiatry* (Vol. 1). New York: Basic Books.

Frank, D. A., & Zuckerman, B. S. (1993). Children exposed to cocaine prenatally: Pieces of the puzzle. *Neurotoxicology and Teratology, 15,* 298–300.

Frankel, L. (1990). Structural family therapy for adolescent substance abusers and their families. In A. S. Friedman & S. Granick (Eds.), *Family therapy for adolescent drug abuse* (pp. 47–61). New York: Lexington.

Franklin, C. (1992). Family and individual patterns in a group of middle-class dropout youths. *Social Work, 37,* 338–344.

Frederick, C. J. (1972). Drug abuse as self-destructive behavior. *Drug Therapy, 2,* 49–68.

Frederick, C. J. (1973). Drug abuse: A self-destructive enigma. *Maryland State Medical Journal, 22,* 19–21.

Frederick, C. J., & Resnik, H. L. P. (1971). How suicidal behaviors are learned. *American Journal of Psychotherapy, 25,* 37–55.

Frederick, C. J., Resnik, H. L., & Wittlin, B. J. (1973). Self-destructive aspects of hard core addiction. *Archives of General Psychiatry, 28*(4), 579–585.

Freeman, G. R. (1990). Kinetics of nonhomogeneous processes in human society: Unethical behaviour and societal chaos. *Canadian Journal of Physiology, 68,* 794–798.

Freiberg, P. (1995). Psychologists examine attacks on homosexuals. APA *Monitor, 26,* 30–31.

Freudenberger, H. J., & Carbone, J. (1984). The reentry process of adolescents. *Journal of Psychoactive Drugs, 16,* 95–99.

Frick, P. J., Lahey, B. B., Loeber, R., Stouthamer-Loeber, M., Christ, M. A. G., & Hanson, K. (1992). Familial risk factors to oppositional defiant disorder and conduct disorder: Parental psychopathology and maternal parenting. *Journal of Consulting and Clinical Psychology, 60,* 49–55.

Fried, P. (1982). Marijuana use by pregnant women and effects on offspring: An update. *Neurobehavioral Toxicity and Teratology, 4,* 451–454.

Fried, P. A., & Watkinson, B. (1988). 12- and 24-month neurobehavioural follow-up of children prenatally exposed to marijuana, cigarettes, and alcohol. *Neurotoxicology and Teratology, 10,* 305–313.

Fried, P. A., & Watkinson, B. (1990). 36- and 48-month neurobehavioral follow-up of children prenatally exposed to marijuana, cigarettes, and alcohol. *Developmental and Behavioral Pediatrics, 11*(2), 49–58.

Friedman, A. S., Bransfield, S., & Kreisher, C. (1994). Early teenage substance use as a predictor of educational-vocational failure. *American Journal on Addictions, 3,* 325–336.

Friedman, A. S., & Granick, S. (Eds.). (1990). *Family therapy for adolescent drug abuse.* New York: Lexington.

Gabel, S., & Shindledecker, R. (1990). Parental substance abuse and suspected child abuse/maltreatment predict outcome in children's impatient treatment. *Journal of the American Academy of Child and Adolescent Psychiatry, 29,* 919–924.

Gabel, S., & Shindledecker, R. (1992). Behavior problems in sons and daughters of substance abusing parents. *Child Psychiatry and Human Development, 23,* 99–115.

Gabel, S., & Shindledecker, R. (1993). Characteristics of children whose parents have been incarcerated. *Hospital & Community Psychiatry, 44,* 656–660.

Galanter, M., Egelko, S., Edwards, H., & Vergaray, M. (1994). A treatment system for combined psychiatric and addictive illness. *Addiction, 89,* 1227–1235.

Garcia, S. A. (1993). Maternal drug abuse: Laws and ethics as agents of just balances and therapeutic interventions. *International Journal of the Addictions, 28,* 1311–1339.

Gardner, J. J., & Cabral, D. A. (1990). Sexually abused adolescents: A distinct group among sexually abused children presenting to a children's hospital. *Journal of Paediatrics and Child Health, 26,* 22–24.

Garriott, J. C. (1993). Drug use among homicide victims: Changing patterns. *American Journal of Forensic Medicine & Pathology, 14,* 234–237.

Garrison, C. Z., Lewinsohn, P. M., Marsteller, F., Langhinrichsen, J., & Lam, I. (1991). The assessment of suicidal behavior in adolescents. *Suicide & Life-Threatening Behavior, 21,* 217–230.

Garvey, M. (1991). Information and alternatives: The role of a youth non-government organization in drug abuse control. *Bulletin of Narcotics, 43,* 29–33.

Gay, M., Meller, R., & Stanley, S. (1982). Drug abuse monitoring: A survey of solvent abuse in the County of Avon. *Human Toxicology, 1*(3), 257–263.

Gelb, L. N. (1984). *Just say no.* Washington, DC: U.S. Government Printing Office.

Gelles, R., & Pedrick-Cornell, C. (1985). *Intimate violence in families.* Beverly Hills, CA: Sage.

Generali, J. A. (1992). Nicotine transdermal patches. *Facts and Comparisons Drug Newsletter, 11,* 33–34.

George, W. H., & Dermen, K. H. (1988). Self-reported alcohol expectancies for self and other as a function of behavior type and dosage set. *Journal of Substance Abuse, 1,* 71–78.

Gettman, J. (1994, December). Heroin returning to center stage. *High Times,* p. 23.

Gettman, J. (1995, March). Highwitness news: Marijuana and the human brain. *High Times,* pp. 26–29.

Geva, D., Goldschmidt, L., Stoffer, D., & Day, N. L. (1993). A longitudinal analysis of the effect of prenatal alcohol exposure on growth, *Alcoholism, Clinical & Experimental Research, 17,* 1124–1129.

Ghoneim, M. M., Block, R. I., Ping, S. T., el-Zahaby, H. M., & Hinrichs, J. V. (1993). The interactions of midazolam and flumazenil on human memory and cognition. *Anesthesiology, 79,* 1183–1192.

Gibb, B. (1987). Sex, drugs, and alcohol: A losing combination. *Listen, 40,* 11–14.

Gieringer, D. H., (1988). Marijuana, driving, and accident safety. *Journal of Psychoactive Drugs, 20*(1), 93–101.

Gieron-Korthals, M. A., Helal, A., & Martinez, C. R. (1994). Expanding spectrum of cocaine induced central nervous system malformations. *Brain & Development, 16,* 253–256.

Gilbody, J. S. (1991). Effects of maternal drug addiction on the fetus. *Adverse Drug Reactions and Acute Toxicology Reviews, 10,* 77–88.

Gilchrist, L. D., Gillmore, M. R., & Lohr, M. J. (1990). Drug use among pregnant adolescents. *Journal of Consulting and Clinical Psychology, 58,* 402–407.

Gilchrist, V. J. (1991). Preventive health care for the adolescent. *American Family Practice, 43,* 969–878.

Ginsberg, K. A., Blacker, C. M., Abel, E. L., & Sokol, R. J. (1991). Fetal alcohol exposure and adverse pregnancy outcomes. *Contributions to Gynecology and Obstetrics, 18,* 115–129.

Gittler, J., & McPherson, M. (1990). Prenatal substance abuse. *Children Today, 14*(4), 3–7.

Glantz, M. D. (1992). A developmental psychopathology model of drug abuse vulnerability. In M. Glantz & R. Pickens (Eds.), *Vulnerability to drug abuse* (pp. 389–418). Washington, DC: American Psychological Association.

Glantz, M., & Pickens, R. (Eds.). (1992). *Vulnerability to drug abuse.* Washington, DC: American Psychological Association.

Glueck, S., & Glueck, E. (1950). *Unravelling juvenile delinquency.* New York: Commonwealth Fund.

Glueck, S., & Glueck, E. (1968). *Delinquents and nondelinquents in perspective.* Cambridge, MA: Harvard University Press.

Glynn, T. J., & Haenlein, M. (1988). Family theory and research on adolescent drug use: A review. *Journal of Chemical Dependency Treatment, 1*(2), 39–56.

Gold, M. S., & Dackis, C. A. (1984). New insights and treatments: Opiate withdrawal and cocaine addiction. *Clinical Therapeutics, 7,* 6–21.

Gold, M. S., & Slaby, A. E. (1991). *Dual diagnosis in substance abuse.* New York: Dekker.

Gold, S. R. (1980). The CAP control theory of drug abuse. In D. J. Lettieri, M. Sayer, & H. Wallenstein Pearson (Eds.), *Theories on drug abuse: Selected contemporary perspectives* (NIDA Research Monograph No. 30, pp. 8–11). Rockville, MD: U.S. Department of Health and Human Services, National Institute on Drug Abuse.

Gold, S. R., & Coghlan, A. J. (1975–76). Locus of control and self-esteem among adolescent drug abusers: Effects of residential treatment. *Drug Forum, 5*(2), 185–191.

Goldberg, L. (1968). Drug abuse in Sweden. *Bulletin on Narcotics, 20,* 1–12.

Goldbloom, D. S. (1993). Alcohol misuse and eating disorders: Aspects of an association. *Alcohol & Alcoholism, 28,* 375–381.

Golden, G. S. (1991). Role of attention deficit hyperactivity disorder in learning disabilities. *Seminars in Neurology, 11*(1), 35–41.

Goldsmith, M. F. (1988). Sex tied to drugs = STD spread. *Journal of the American Medical Association, 260,* 2009.

Goldsmith, S. (1990). Prosecution to enhance treatment. *Children Today, 19,* 13–16.

Goldstein, A. P., Reagles, K. W., & Amann, L. L. (1990). *Refusal skills: Preventing drug use in adolescents.* Champaign, IL: Research Press.

Goldstein, B., Kelly, M. M., Bruton, D., & Cox, C. (1993). Inflicted versus accidental head injury in critically injured children. *Critical Care Medicine, 21,* 1328–1332.

Goldstein, M. B., & Engwall, D. B. (1992). The politics of prevention: Changing definitions of substance use/abuse. *Journal of Health & Social Policy, 3,* 69–83.

Goodstadt, M. S. (1989). Substance abuse curricula vs. school drug policies. *Journal of School Health, 59,* 246–250.

Gordis, E., & Alexander, D. (1992). From the National Institutes of Health: Progress toward preventing and understanding alcohol-induced fetal injury. *Journal of the American Medical Association, 268,* 3183.

Gore, T. (1991). A portrait of at-risk children. *Journal of Health Care for the Poor and Underserved, 2*(1), 95–105.

Gorenstein, C., Bernik, M. A., & Pompeia, S. (1994). Differential acute psychomotor and cognitive effects of diazepam on long-term benzodiazepine users. *International Clinical Psychopharmacology, 9,* 143–153.

Gori, G. B., Benowitz, N. L., & Lynch, C. J. (1986). Mouth versus deep airways absorption of nicotine in cigarette smokers. *Pharmacology, Biochemistry and Behavior, 25,* 1181–1184.

Gorski, T. T. (1995, August). Brief therapy for dual recovery: II. Treatment planning and step-by-step interventions. *Professional Counselor,* pp. 27, 52–53.

Gorsuch, R. L. (1980). Interactive models of nonmedical drug use. In D. J. Lettieri, M. Sayers, & H. Wallenstein Pearson (Eds.), *Theories on drug abuse: Selected contemporary perspectives* (Research Monograph No. 30, pp. 18–23). Rockville, MD: U.S. Department of Health and Human Services, National Institute on Drug Abuse.

Gorsuch, R. L., & Butler, M. C. (1976a). Initial drug abuse: A review of predisposing social psychological factors. *Psychological Bulletin, 83*(1), 120–137.

Gorsuch, R. L., & Butler, M. C. (1976b). Toward developmental models of non-medical drug use. In S. B. Sells (Ed.), *The effectiveness of drug abuse treatment* (Vol. 3, pp. 29–76). Cambridge, MA: Ballinger.

Gotowiec, A., & Beiser, M. (1993–94). Aboriginal children's mental health: Unique challenges. *Canada's Mental Health, 41*(4), 7–11.

Graham, K. (1980). Theories of intoxicated aggression. *Canadian Journal of the Behavioural Sciences, 12,* 141–158.

Graham, K. (1988). Reasons for consumption and heavy caffeine use: Generalization of a model based on alcohol research. *Addictive Behaviors, 13,* 209–214.

Greaves, G. (1974). Toward an existential theory of drug dependence. *Journal of Nervous and Mental Disease, 159,* 263–274.

Greaves, G. (1980). An existential theory of drug dependence. In D. J. Lettieri, M. Sayer, & H. Wallenstein Pearson (Eds.), *Theories on drug abuse: Selected contemporary perspectives* (NIDA Research Monograph No. 30, pp. 24–28). Rockville, MD: U.S. Department of Health and Human Services, National Institute on Drug Abuse.

Greenbaum, P. E., Prange, M. E., Friedman, R. M., & Silver, S. E. (1991). Substance abuse prevalence and comorbidity with other psychiatric disorders among adolescents with severe emotional disturbances. *Journal of the American Academy of Child and Adolescent Psychiatry, 30,* 575–583.

Greenstein, R. A., Arndt, I. C., McLellan, A. T., O'Brien, C. P., & Evans, B. (1984). Naltrexone: A clinical perspective. *Journal of Clinical Psychiatry, 45,* 25–28.

Gregorius, H. H., & Smith, T. S. (1991). The adolescent mentally ill chemical abuser: Special considerations in dual diagnosis. *Journal of Adolescent Chemical Dependency, 1*(4), 79–113.

Griffith, D. R., Azuma, S. D., & Chasnoff, I. J. (1994). Three-year outcome of children exposed prenatally to drugs. *Journal of American Child and Adolescent Psychiatry, 33,* 20–27.

Gritz, E. R., & Crane, L. A. (1991). Use of diet pills and amphetamines to lose weight among smoking and nonsmoking high school seniors. *Health Psychology, 10,* 330–335.

Grover, D., Yeragani, V. K., & Keshavan, M. S. (1986). Improvement of phencyclidine-associated psychosis with ECT. *Journal of Clinical Psychiatry, 47,* 477–478.

Groves, W. E. (1974). Students' drug use and life styles. In E. Josephson & E. Carroll (Eds.), *Drug use: Epidemiological and sociological approaches.* New York: Winston-Wiley.

Haddad, J., & Messer, J. (1994). Fetal alcohol syndrome: Report of three siblings. *Neopediatrics, 25,* 109–111.

Hall, S. C., & Ofodile, F. A. (1991). Mandibular fractures in an American inner city: The Harlem Hospital Center experience. *Journal of the National Medical Association, 83,* 421–423.

Handal, K. A., Schauben, J. L., & Salamone, F. R. (1983). Naloxone. *Annals of Emergency Medicine, 12,* 438–445.

Hannig, V. L., & Phillips, J. A. (1991). Maternal cocaine abuse and fetal anomalies: Evidence for teratogenic effects of cocaine. *Southern Medical Journal, 84,* 498–499.

Hansen, W. B., & Graham, J. W. (1991). Preventing alcohol, marijuana, and cigarette use among adolescents: Peer pressure resistance training versus establishing conservative norms. *Preventive Medicine, 20,* 414–430.

Hansen, W. B., Johnson, C. A., Flay, B. R., Graham, J. W., & Sobel, J. (1988). Affective and social influences approaches to the prevention of multiple substance abuse among seventh grade students: Results from project SMART. *Preventive Medicine, 17,* 135–154.

Hanson, B., Beschner, G., Walters, J. M., & Bovelle, E. (1985). *Life with heroin.* Lexington, MA: Lexington.

Hanson, D. J. (1982). The effectiveness of alcohol and drug education. *Journal of Alcohol and Drug Education, 27,* 4.

Harding, W. M., Zinberg, N. E., Stelmack, S. M., & Barry, M. (1980). Formerly-addicted-now-controlled opiate users. *International Journal of the Addictions, 15,* 47–60.

Hardy, N. G. (1995, January). Dying without cause: Kids who kill. *Adolescence, 8.*

Harmin, M., Kirschenbaum, H., & Simon, S. B. (1973). *Clarifying values through subject matter: Applications for the classroom.* Minneapolis, MN: Winston Press.

Harper, C. G., & Kril, J. J. (1990). Neuropathology of alcoholism. *Alcohol & Alcoholism, 25,* 207–216.

Harris, S. R., Osborn, J. A., Weinberg, J., Loock, C., & Junaid, K. (1993). Effects of prenatal alcohol exposure on neuromotor and cognitive development during early childhood: A series of case reports. *Physical Therapy, 73,* 608–617.

Harrison, P. A., Edwall, G. E., Hoffman, N. G., & Worthen, M. D. (1990). Correlates of sexual abuse amongst boys in treatment for chemical dependency. *Journal of Adolescent Chemical Dependency, 1*(1), 53–67.

Harrison, P. A., & Luxenberg, M. G. (1995). Comparisons of alcohol and other drug problems among Minnesota adolescents in 1989 and 1992. *Archives of Pediatrics & Adolescent Medicine, 149,* 137–144.

Hathaway, W. D., Groothuis, J. R., Hay, W. W., & Paisley, J. W. (Eds.). (1993). *Current pediatric diagnosis and treatment.* Norwalk, CT: Appleton and Lange.

Hauschildt, E. (1992, October/November). Massive U.S. drug 'war' a failure: Policy group. *Journal, 21,* 5.

Hawkins, J. D., Catalano, R. F., & Miller, J. (1992). Risk and protective factors for alcohol and other drug problems in adolescence and early adulthood: Implications for substance abuse prevention. *Psychological Bulletin, 112,* 64–105.

Hawkins, J. D., Lishner, D. M., Catalano, R. F., & Howard, M. O. (1985). Childhood predictors of adolescent substance abuse: Toward an empirically grounded theory. *Journal of Children in a Contemporary Society, 18,* 11–48.

Healy, J. M., Jr., & Stewart, A. J. (1984). Adaptation to life changes in adolescence. In P. Karoly & J. J. Steffen (Eds.), *Adolescent behavior disorders: Foundations and contemporary concerns* (pp. 39–60). Lexington, MA: Heath.

Hebb, D. O. (1949). *The organization of behavior.* New York: Wiley.

Hechtman, L., Weiss, G., & Perlman, T. (1984). Hyperactives as young adults: Past and current substance abuse and antisocial behavior. *American Journal of Orthopsychiatry, 54,* 415–425.

Hellgren, L., Gillberg, C., Gillberg, I. C., & Enerskog, I. (1993). Children with deficits in attention, motor control and perception (DAMP) almost grown up: General health at 16 years. *Developmental Medicine and Child Neurology, 35,* 881–892.

Hemminki, K., & Vineis, P. (1985). Extrapolation of the evidence on teratogenicity of chemicals between humans and experimental animals: Chemicals other than drugs. *Teratogenesis, Carcinogenesis, and Mutagenesis, 5,* 251–318.

Hendin, H. (1973a). College students and LSD: Who and why? *Journal of Nervous and Mental Disease, 156,* 249–258.

Hendin, H. (1973b). Marijuana abuse among college students. *Journal of Nervous and Mental Disease, 156,* 259–270.

Hendin, H. (1974a). Amphetamine abuse among college students. *Journal of Nervous and Mental Disease, 158,* 256–267.

Hendin, H. (1974b). Beyond alienation: The end of the psychedelic road. *American Journal of Drug and Alcohol Abuse, 1,* 11–23.

Hendin, H. (1974c). Students on heroin. *Journal of Nervous and Mental Disease, 158,* 240–255.

Hendin, H. (1975). *The age of sensation.* New York: Norton.

Hendin, H. (1980). Psychosocial theory of drug abuse: A psychodynamic approach. In D. J. Lettieri, M. Sayer, & H. Wallenstein Pearson (Eds.), *Theories on drug abuse: Selected contemporary perspectives* (NIDA Research Monograph No. 30, pp. 195–200). Rockville, MD: U.S. Department of Health and Human Services, National Institute on Drug Abuse.

Hendin, H., & Haas, A. P. (1985). The adaptive significance of chronic marijuana use for adolescents and adults. *Advances in Alcohol and Substance Abuse, 5,* 99–115.

Hendin, H., Pollinger, A., Ulman, R., & Carr, A. C. (1981). *Adolescent marijuana abusers and their families* (NIDA Research Monograph No. 40). Rockville, MD: U.S. Department of Health and Human Services, National Institute on Drug Abuse.

Hendricks-Mathews, M. K. (1993). Survivors of abuse: Health care issues. *Primary Care, 20,* 391–406.

Hernandez, J. T. (1992). Substance abuse among sexually abused adolescents and their families. *Journal of Adolescent Health, 13,* 658–662.

Hernandez, J. T., Lodico, M., & DiClemente, R. J. (1993). The effects of child abuse and race on risk-taking in male adolescents. *Journal of the National Medical Association, 85,* 593–597.

Herridge, P., & Gold, M. S. (1988). Pharmacological adjuncts in the treatment of opioid and cocaine addicts. *Journal of Psychoactive Drugs, 20,* 233–242.

Hersh, J. H. (1989). Toluene embryopathy: Two new cases. *Journal of Medical Genetics, 26,* 333–337.

Hershey, C. O., & Miller, S. (1982). Solvent abuse: A shift to adults. *International Journal of the Addictions, 17,* 1085–1089.

Hertzman, M., & Bendit, E. A. (1975). Alcoholism and destructive behavior. In A. R. Roberts (Ed.), *Self-destructive behavior* (pp. 164–187). Springfield, IL: Thomas.

Hibbs, J. R., & Gunn, R. A. (1991). Public health intervention in a cocaine-related syphilis outbreak. *American Journal of Public Health, 81,* 1259–1262.

Hickl-Szabo, R. (1987, January 24). Crying infants sedated with gasoline fumes, Manitoba official says. *Globe and Mail,* pp. A1–A2.

Hicks, J. M., Morales, A., & Soldin, S. J. (1990). Drugs of abuse in a pediatric outpatient population. *Clinical Chemistry, 36,* 1256–1257.

Hill, R. M., Hegemier, S., & Tennyson, L. M. (1989). The fetal alcohol syndrome: A multihandi-capped child. *Neurotoxicology, 10,* 585–596.

Hillbrand, M., Foster, H., Jr., & Hirt, M. (1990). Rapists and child molesters: Psychometric comparisons. *Archives of Sexual Behavior, 19*(1), 65–71.

Hilleman, D. E., Mohiuddin, S. M., Del Core, M. G., & Sketch, M. H., Sr. (1992). Effect of buspirone on withdrawal symptoms associated with smoking cessation. *Archives of Internal Medicine, 152,* 350–352.

Hindler, C. G. (1989). Epilepsy and violence. *British Journal of Psychiatry, 155,* 246–249.

Hindmarch, I., Sherwood, N., & Kerr, J. S. (1993). Amnestic effects of triazolam and other hyp-notics. *Progress in Neuro-Psychopharmacology & Biological Psychiatry, 17,* 407–413.

Hoberman, H. M., & Garfinkel, B. D. (1988). Completed suicide in youth. *Canadian Journal of Psychiatry, 33,* 494–504.

Hobfoll, S. E., & Segal, B. (1983). A factor analytic study of the relationship of experience seeking and trait anxiety to drug use and reasons for drug use. *International Journal of the Addictions, 18,* 539–549.

Hochhauser, M. (1978a). Adolescent drug abuse and the development of behavior. *International Journal of Addictions, 13*(6), 1013–1019.

Hochhauser, M. (1978b). Chronobiological factors in drug abuse. In A. J. Schecter (Ed.), *Drug dependence and alcoholism: Vol. 2. Social and behavioral issues* (pp. 855–864). New York: Plenum.

Hochhauser, M. (1978c). Drugs as agents of control. *Journal of Psychedelic Drugs, 10*(1), 65–69.

Hochhauser, M. (1980). A chronobiological control theory. In D. J. Lettieri, M. Sayer, & H. Wallenstein Pearson (Eds.), *Theories on drug abuse: Selected contemporary perspectives* (NIDA Research Monograph No. 30, pp. 262–268). Rockville, MD: U.S. Department of Health and Human Services, National Institute on Drug Abuse.

Hodgins, S. (1992). Status at age 30 of children with conduct problems. *Studies on Crime & Crime Prevention, 3,* 41–62.

Hoegerman, G., Wilson, C. A., Thurmond, E., & Schnoll, S. H. (1990). Drug-exposed neonates. *Western Journal of Medicine, 152,* 559–564.

Hoffman, D., & Wynder, E. L. (1986). Chemical constituents and bioactivity of tobacco smoke. *IARC Scientific Publications, 74,* 145–165.

Hoffman, R. S., & Goldfrank, L. R. (1990). The impact of drug abuse and addiction on society. *Emergency Medicine Clinics of North America, 8,* 467–480.

Hohman, M., & Buchik, G. (1994). Adolescent relapse prevention. In C. W. LeCroy (Ed.), *Hand-book of child and adolescent treatment manuals* (pp. 200–239). New York: Lexington.

Holcomb, W. R., & Anderson, W. P. (1983). Alcohol and multiple drug abuse in accused murder-ers. *Psychological Reports, 52,* 159–164.

Holinger, P. C. (1990). The causes, impact, and preventability of childhood injuries in the United States: Childhood suicide in the United States. *American Journal of Diseases of Children, 144,* 670–676.

Hollister, L. E. (1986). Health aspects of cannabis. *Pharmacological Reviews, 38,* 1–20.

Hollister, L. E. (1988). Cannabis—1988. *Acta Psychiatrica Scandinavica, 345* (Suppl.), 108–118.

Homelessness: Homeless and runaway youth receiving services at federally funded shelters. (1989). In *gaolgrd* (pp. 90–145). Gaithersburg, MD: U.S. General Accounting Office.

Hooft, P. J., & van de Voorde, H. P. (1994). Reckless behaviour related to the use of 3,4-methylenedioxymethamphetamine (ecstasy): Apropos of a fatal accident during car-surfing. *International Journal of Legal Medicine, 106,* 328–329.

Hsu, L. N. (1993). Family health and the use of psychoactive substances. *World Health Statistics Quarterly, 46*, 237–241.

Huba, G. J., & Bentler, P. M. (1979). Phencyclidine use in high school: Tests of models. *Journal of Drug Education, 9*, 285–291.

Huba, G. J., & Bentler, P. M. (1980). The role of peer and adult models for drug taking at different stages in adolescence. *Journal of Youth and Adolescence, 9*, 465–499.

Huba, G. J., Wingard, J. A., & Bentler, P. M. (1979a). Adolescent drug use and intentions to use drugs in the future: A concurrent analysis. *Journal of Drug Education, 9*(2), 145–151.

Huba, G. J., Wingard, J. A., & Bentler, P. M. (1979b). Beginning adolescent drug use and peer and adult interaction patterns. *Journal of Consulting and Clinical Psychology, 47*(2), 265–276.

Huba, G. J., Wingard, J. A., & Bentler, P. M. (1980a). Applications of a theory of drug use to prevention programs. *Journal of Drug Education, 10*(1), 25–38.

Huba, G. J., Wingard, J. A., & Bentler, P. M. (1980b). Framework for an interactive theory of drug use. In D. Lettieri, M. Sayers, & H. Wallenstein Pearson (Eds.), *Theories on drug abuse: Selected contemporary perspectives* (NIDA Research Monograph No. 30, pp. 95–101). Rockville, MD: U.S. Department of Health and Human Services, National Institute on Drug Abuse.

Huba, G. J., Wingard, J. A., & Bentler, P. M. (1980c). Longitudinal analysis of the role of peer support, adult models, and peer subcultures in beginning adolescent substance use: An application of setwise canonical correlation methods. *Multivariate Behavioral Research, 15*, 259–279.

Huba, G. J., Wingard, J. A., & Bentler, P. M. (1981a). A comparison of two latent variable causal models for adolescent drug use. *Journal of Personality and Social Psychology, 40*(1), 180–193.

Huba, G. J., Wingard, J. A., & Bentler, P. M. (1981b). Intentions to use drugs among adolescents: A longitudinal analysis. *International Journal of the Addictions, 16*, 331–339.

Hughes, C. W., Preskorn, S. M., Wrona, M., Hassanein, R., & Tucker, S. (1990). Follow-up of adolescents initially treated for prepubertal-onset major depressive disorder with imipramine. *Psychopharmacology Bulletin, 26*, 244–248.

Huizinga, D., & Elliott, D. S. (1981). *A longitudinal study of drug use and delinquency in a national sample of youth: An assessment of causal order* (Project Report No. 16, National Youth Survey). Boulder, CO: University of Colorado, Behavioral Research Institute.

Huizinga, D., Loeber, R., & Thornberry, T. P. (1993). Longitudinal study of delinquency, drug use, sexual activity, and pregnancy among children and youth in three cities. *Public Health Reports, 108*, 90–96.

Hull, J. G. (1981). A self-awareness model of the causes and effects of alcohol consumption. *Journal of Abnormal Psychology, 90*(6), 586–600.

Hull, J. G. (1987). Self-awareness model. In H. T. Blane & K. E. Leonard (Eds.), *Psychological theories of drinking and alcoholism* (pp. 272–304). New York: Guilford.

Hull, J. G., Levenson, R. W., Young, R. D., & Sher, K. J. (1983). Self-awareness-reducing effects of alcohol consumption. *Journal of Personality and Social Psychology, 44*(3), 461–473.

Hull, J. G., & Levy, A. S. (1979). The organizational functions of the self: An alternative to the Duval and Wicklund model of self-awareness. *Journal of Personality and Social Psychology, 37*(5), 756–768.

Hull, J. G., & Young, R. D. (1983a). The self-awareness-reducing effects of alcohol: Evidence and implications. In J. Suls & A. G. Greenwald (Eds.), *Psychological perspectives on the self* (Vol. 2, pp. 159–190). Hillsdale, NJ: Erlbaum.

Hull, J. G., & Young, R. D. (1983b). Self-consciousness, self-esteem, and success-failure as determinants of alcohol consumption in male social drinkers. *Journal of Personality and Social Psychology, 44*, 1097–1109.

Hume, R. F., Jr., Gingras, J. L., Martin, L. S., Hertzberg, B. S., O'Donnell, K., & Killam, A. P. (1994). Ultrasound diagnosis of fetal anomalies associated with in utero cocaine exposure: Further support for cocaine-induced vascular disruption teratogenesis. *Fetal Diagnosis and Therapy, 9,* 239–245.

Hunt, D. (1991). Stealing and dealing: Cocaine and property crimes. In S. Schober & C. Schade (Eds.), *The epidemiology of cocaine use and abuse* (NIDA Research Monograph No. 110, pp. 139–150). Rockville, MD: U.S. Department of Health and Human Services, National Institute on Drug Abuse.

Hunter, S. M., Vizelberg, I. A., & Berenson, G. S. (1991). Identifying mechanisms of adoption of tobacco and alcohol use among youth: The Bogalusa heart study. *Social Networks, 13,* 91–104.

Hurlbut, K. M. (1991). Drug-induced psychoses. *Emergency Medicine Clinics of North America, 9,* 31–52.

Hussain, K., Wijetunge, D. B., Grubnic, S., & Jackson, I. T. (1994). A comprehensive analysis of craniofacial trauma. *Journal of Trauma, 36,* 34–47.

Hussey, D. L., & Singer, M. (1993). Psychological distress, problem behaviors, and family functioning of sexually abused adolescent inpatients. *Journal of the American Academy of Child and Adolescent Psychiatry, 32,* 954–961.

Hutchings, D. E. (1993). The puzzle of cocaine's effects following maternal use during pregnancy: Are there reconcilable differences. *Neurotoxicology and Teratology, 15,* 281–286.

Huxley, A. (1960). *The doors of perception: Heaven & hell.* London: Chatto & Windus.

Iannotti, R. J., & Bush, P. J. (1992). Perceived vs. actual friends' use of alcohol, cigarettes, marijuana, and cocaine: Which has the most influence. *Journal of Youth and Adolescence, 21,* 375–389.

Inciardi, J. A. (1990). The crack-violence connection within a population of hard-core adolescent offenders. In M. De La Rosa, E. Y. Lambert, & B. Gropper (Eds.), *Drugs and violence: Causes, correlates, and consequences* (NIDA Research Monograph No. 103, pp. 93–111). Rockville, MD: U.S. Department of Health and Human Services, National Institute on Drug Abuse.

Inciardi, J. A. (1993). Kingrats, chicken heads, slow necks, freaks, and blood suckers: A glimpse at the Miami sex-for-crack market. In M. S. Ratner (Ed.), *Crack pipe as pimp: An ethnographic investigation of sex-for-crack exchanges* (pp. 37–67). New York: Lexington.

Inciardi, J. A., & Pottieger, A. E. (1991). Kids, crack, and crime. *Journal of Drug Issues, 21,* 257–270.

Infante-Rivard, C., Fernandez, A., Gauthier, R., David, M., & Rivard, G. E. (1993). Fetal loss associated with caffeine intake before and during pregnancy. *Journal of the American Medical Association, 270,* 2940–2943.

Ingram, R. E., & Holle, C. (1992). Cognitive science of depression. In D. J. Stein & J. E. Young (Eds.), *Cognitive science and clinical disorders* (pp. 187–209). New York: Harcourt Brace Jovanovich.

Irwin, K. L., Edlin, B. R., Wong, L., Faruque, S., McCoy, H. V., Word, C., Schilling, R., McCoy, C. B., Evans, P. E., & Holmberg, S. D. (1995). Urban rape survivors: Characteristics and prevalence of human immunodeficiency virus and other sexually transmitted infections. *Obstetrics & Gynecology, 85,* 330–336.

Irwin, M., Schuckit, M., & Smith, T. L. (1990). Clinical importance of age at onset in Type 1 and Type 2 primary alcoholics. *Archives of General Psychiatry, 47,* 320–324.

It's an important form of entertainment for kids: Winnipeg solvent sniffers receiving little aid. (1986). *Addiction Research Foundation Journal, 15*(8), 3.

Izquierdo, I., & Medina, J. H. (1991). GABA receptor modulation of memory: The role of endogenous benzodiazepines. *Trends in Pharmacological Sciences, 12,* 260–265.

Jacobson, J. L., Jacobson, S. W., & Sokol, R. J. (1994). Effects of prenatal exposure to alcohol, smoking, and illicit drugs on postpartum somatic growth. *Alcoholism, Clinical & Experimental Research, 18,* 317–323.

Jacobson, J. L., Jacobson, S. W., Sokol, R. J., Martier, S. S., Ager, J. W., & Kaplan-Estrin, M. G. (1993). Teratogenic effects of alcohol on infant development. *Alcoholism, Clinical and Experimental Research, 17,* 174–183.

Janus, M.-D., Burgess, A. W., & McCormack, A. (1987). Histories of sexual abuse in adolescent male runaways. *Adolescence, 22,* 405–417.

Jessor, R. (1985). Bridging etiology and prevention in drug abuse research. In C. LaRue Jones & R. J. Battjes (Eds.), *Etiology of drug abuse: Implications for prevention* (NIDA Research Monograph No. 56, A RAUS Review Report, pp. 257–268). Rockville, MD: U.S. Department of Health and Human Services, National Institute on Drug Abuse.

Jessor, R., Carman, R., & Grossman, P. H. (1968). Expectations of need satisfaction and drinking patterns of college students. *Quarterly Journal of Studies on Alcohol, 29,* 101–116.

Jessor, R., Collins, M. I., & Jessor, S. L. (1972). On becoming a drinker: Social-psychological aspects of an adolescent transition. In F. A. Seixas (Ed.), *Nature and nurture in alcoholism* (pp. 199–213). New York: New York Academy of Sciences.

Jessor, R., Graves, T. D., Hanson, R. C., & Jessor, S. L. (1968). *Society, personality and deviant behavior: A study of a tri-ethnic community.* New York: Holt, Rinehart and Winston.

Jessor, R., & Jessor, S. L. (1973). A social psychology of marihuana use. *Journal of Personality and Social Psychology, 26,* 1–15.

Jessor, R., & Jessor, S. L. (1975). Adolescent development and onset of drinking: A longitudinal study. *Journal of Studies on Alcohol, 36*(1), 27–51.

Jessor, R., & Jessor, S. (1977a). A multivariate appraisal of problem-behavior theory. In R. Jessor & S. Jessor (Eds.), *Problem behavior and psychosocial development: A longitudinal study of youth* (pp. 127–142). New York: Academic.

Jessor, R., & Jessor, S. (1977b). *Problem behavior and psychosocial development: A longitudinal study of youth.* New York: Academic.

Jessor, R., & Jessor, S. L. (1978). Theory testing in longitudinal research on marijuana use. In D. B. Kandel (Ed.), *Longitudinal research on drug use* (pp. 41–71). New York: Wiley.

Joanning, H., Thomas, F., Newfield, N., & Lamun, B. (1991). Organizing a coordinated family treatment model for the inpatient and outpatient treatment of adolescent drug abuse. *Journal of Family Psychotherapy, 1,* 29–47.

Joffe, A. (1988). Adolescent suicide, homicide, and unintentional injuries. *Maryland Medical Journal, 37,* 955–958.

Johns, A. (1991). Volatile solvent abuse and 963 deaths. *British Journal of Addiction, 86,* 1053–1056.

Johnson, B. D. (1973). *Marijuana users and drug subcultures.* New York: Wiley.

Johnson, B. D. (1980). Toward a theory of drug subcultures. In D. J. Lettieri, M. Sayers, & H. Wallenstein Pearson (Eds.), *Theories on drug abuse: Selected contemporary perspectives* (NIDA Research Monograph No. 30, pp. 110–127). Rockville, MD: U.S. Department of Health and Human Services, National Institute on Drug Abuse.

Johnson, B. D., Wish, E. D., Schmeidler, J., & Huizinga, D. (1991). Concentration of delinquent offending: Serious drug involvement and high delinquency rates. *Journal of Drug Issues, 21,* 205–229.

Johnson, C., Webster, B., & Connors, E. (1995, February). Prosecuting gangs: A national assessment. In *National Institute of Justice: Research in Brief* (NCJ No. 151785, pp. 1–10). Washington, DC: U.S. Department of Justice.

Johnson, C. D., Reeves, K. O., & Jackson, D. (1983). Alcohol and sex. *Heart and Lung, 12*(1), 93–97.

Johnson, E., & Herringer, L. G. (1993). A note on the utilization of common support activities and relapse following substance abuse treatment. *Journal of Psychology, 127,* 73–77.

Johnson, E. M. (1990). Chemical dependency and black America: The government responds. *Journal of the National Black Nurses Association, 4*(2), 47–56.

Johnson, E. M., Davis, D. J., & Denniston, R. W. (1991). *Prevention plus II: Assessing alcohol and other drug prevention programs at the school and community level* (DHHS Publication No. ADM 91-1817). Rockville, MD: U.S. Department of Health and Human Services, Office for Substance Abuse Prevention.

Johnson, E. M., McColgan, B. R., & Denniston, R. W. (1991). *Preventing HIV infection among youth* (DHHS Publication No. ADM 91-1774). Rockville, MD: U.S. Department of Health and Human Services.

Johnson, T. C. (1988). Child perpetrators—children who molest other children: Preliminary findings. *Child Abuse & Neglect, 12,* 219–229.

Johnson, V., & White, H. R. (1989). An investigation of factors related to intoxicated driving behaviors among youth. *Journal of Studies on Alcohol, 50,* 320–330.

Johnston, L. D., Bachman, J. G., & O'Malley, P. M. (1983). *Student drug use, attitudes and beliefs: National trends 1975–1983.* Rockville, MD: U.S. Department of Health and Human Services, National Institute on Drug Abuse.

Johnston, L. D., O'Malley, P. M., & Bachman, J. G. (1987). Psychotherapeutic, licit, and illicit use of drugs among adolescents: An epidemiological perspective. *Journal of Adolescent Health Care, 8,* 36–51.

Jonah, B. A., & Dawson, N. E. (1987). Youth and risk: Age differences in risky driving, risk perception, and risk utility. *Alcohol, Drugs and Driving, 3,* 13–29.

Jonas, J. M., & Gold, M. S. (1992). The pharmacologic treatment of alcohol and cocaine abuse: Integration of recent findings into clinical practice. *Pediatric Psychopharmacology, 15,* 179–190.

Jones, C. L., & Battjes, R. J. (1985). *Etiology of drug abuse: Implications for prevention* (NIDA Research Monograph No. 56). Rockville, MD: U.S. Department of Health and Human Services, National Institute on Drug Abuse.

Jones, K. L. (1991). Developmental pathogenesis of defects associated with prenatal cocaine exposure: Fetal vascular disruption. *Clinics in Perinatology, 18,* 139–146.

Jones, K. L., Smith, D. W., Ulleland, C. N., & Streissguth, P. (1973). Pattern of malformation of offspring of chronic alcoholic mothers. *Lancet, 1,* 1267–1271.

Jones, N. E., Pieper, C. F., & Robertson, L. S. (1992). The effect of legal drinking age on fatal injuries of adolescents and young adults. *American Journal of Public Health, 82,* 112–115.

Jorgensen, K. M. (1992). The drug-exposed infant. *Critical Care Nursing Clinics of North America, 4,* 481–485.

Kadden, R. M. (1994). Cognitive-behavioral approaches to alcoholism treatment. *Alcohol, Health & Research World, 18,* 279–286.

Kalant, O. J., Fehr, K. O., Arras, D., & Anglin, L. (1983). *Cannabis health risks: A comprehensive annotated bibliography (1844–1982).* Toronto, ON: Addiction Research Foundation.

Kaminer, Y., & Frances, R. J. (1991). Inpatient treatment of adolescents with psychiatric and substance abuse disorders. *Hospital and Community Psychiatry, 42,* 894–896.

Kandel, D. (1975). Stages in adolescent involvement in drug use. *Science, 190,* 912–914.

Kandel, D. B. (1978a). Convergence in prospective longitudinal surveys of drug use in normal populations. In D. B. Kandel (Ed.), *Longitudinal research on drug use: Empirical findings and methodological issues* (pp. 3–38). Washington, DC: Hemisphere.

Kandel, D. B. (Ed.). (1978b). *Longitudinal research on drug use: Empirical findings and methodological issues.* Washington, DC: Hemisphere.

Kandel, D. B. (1980a). Developmental stages in adolescent drug involvement. In D. J. Lettieri, M. Sayers, & H. Wallenstein Pearson (Eds.), *Theories on drug abuse: Selected contemporary perspectives* (NIDA Research Monograph No. 30, pp. 120–127). Rockville, MD: U.S. Department of Health and Human Services, National Institute on Drug Abuse.

Kandel, D. B. (1980b). Drug and drinking behavior among youth. *Annual Review of Sociology, 6,* 235–285.

Kandel, D. B. (1986). Processes of peer influences in adolescence. In R. K. Silbereisen, K. Eyferth, & G. Rudinger (Eds.), *Development as action in context: Problem behavior and normal youth development* (pp. 203–227). Berlin: Springer.

Kandel, D. B., & Andrews, K. (1987). Processes of adolescent socialization by parents and peers. *International Journal of the Addictions, 22,* 319–342.

Kandel, D. B., & Davies, M. (1991). Cocaine use in a national sample of U.S. youth (NLSY): Ethnic patterns, progression, and predictors. In S. Schober & C. Schade (Eds.), *The epidemiology of cocaine use and abuse* (NIDA Research Monograph No. 110, pp. 151–188). Rockville, MD: U.S. Department of Health and Human Services, National Institute on Drug Abuse.

Kandel, D. B., & Faust, R. (1975). Sequence and stages in patterns of adolescent drug use. *Archives of General Psychiatry, 32,* 923–932.

Kandel, D. B., Kessler, R. C., & Margulies, R. Z. (1978a). Antecedents of adolescent initiation into stages of drug use: A developmental analysis. *Journal of Youth and Adolescence, 7*(1), 13–40.

Kandel, D. B., Kessler, R. C., & Margulies, R. Z. (1978b). Antecedents of adolescent initiation into stages of drug use: A developmental analysis. In D. B. Kandel (Ed.), *Longitudinal research on drug use: Empirical findings and methodological issues* (pp. 73–99). New York: Wiley.

Kandel, D. B., Treiman, D., Faust, R., & Single, E. (1976). Adolescent involvement in legal and illegal drug use: A multiple classification analysis. *Social Forces, 55*(2), 439–458.

Kantor, G. K., Caudill, B. D., & Ungerleider, S. (1992). Project impact: Teaching the teachers to intervene in student substance abuse problems. *Journal of Alcohol and Drug Education, 38,* 11–29.

Kaplan, D. W., & Mammel, K. A. (1993). Adolescence. In W. E. Hathaway, W. W. Hay, Jr., J. R. Groothuis, & J. W. Paisley (Eds.), *Current pediatric diagnosis & treatment* (pp. 85–138). San Mateo, CA: Appleton and Lange.

Kaplan, D. W., & Mammel, K. A. (1993). Adolescence. In G. B. Merenstein, D. W. Kaplan, & A. A. Rosenberg (Eds.), *Handbook of pediatrics* (pp. 235–295). Norwalk, CT: Appleton and Lange.

Kaplan, H. B. (1975a). Increase in self-rejection as an antecedent of deviant responses. *Journal of Youth and Adolescence, 4,* 438–458.

Kaplan, H. B. (1975b). *Self-attitudes and deviant behavior.* Pacific Palisades, CA: Goodyear.

Kaplan, H. B. (1980a). *Deviant behavior in defense of self.* New York: Academic.

Kaplan, H. B. (1980b). Self-esteem and self-derogation theory of drug abuse. In D. J. Lettieri, M. Sayers, & H. Wallenstein Pearson (Eds.), *Theories on drug abuse: Selected contemporary perspectives* (NIDA Research Monograph No. 30, pp. 128–131). Rockville, MD: U.S. Department of Health and Human Services, National Institute on Drug Abuse.

Kaplan, H. B., Martin, S. S., & Robbins, C. (1984). Pathways to adolescent drug use: Self-derogation, peer influence, weakening of social controls, and early substance use. *Journal of Health and Social Behavior, 25,* 270–289.

Kapur, R. P., Cheng, M. S., & Shephard, T. H. (1991). Brain hemorrhages in cocaine-exposed human fetuses. *Teratology, 44,* 11–18.

Karavokiros, K. A. T., & Tsipis, G. B. (1990). Flumazenil: A benzodiazepine antagonist. *Drug Intelligence and Clinical Pharmacy, Annals of Pharmacotherapy, 24,* 976–981.

Karp, R. J., Qazi, Q., Hittleman, J., & Chabrier, L. (1993). Fetal alcohol syndrome. In R. J. Karp (Ed.), *Malnourished children in the United States: Caught in the cycle of poverty* (pp. 101–108). New York: Springer.

Katims, D. S., & Zapata, J. T. (1993). Gender differences in substance use among Mexican-American school-age children. *Journal of School Health, 69,* 397–401.

Kaufman, E. (1990). Adolescent substance abusers and family therapy. In A. S. Friedman & S. Granick (Eds.), *Family therapy for adolescent drug abuse* (pp. 47–61). New York: Lexington.

Kelleher, K. J., Rickert, V. I., Hardin, B. H., Pope, S. K., & Farmer, F. L. (1992). Rurality and gender: Effects on early adolescent alcohol use. *American Journal of Diseases of Children, 146,* 317–322.

Keller, M. B., Lavori, P. W., Beardslee, W., Wunder, J., Drs, D. L., & Hasin, D. (1992). Clinical course and outcome of substance abuse disorders in adolescents. *Journal of Substance Abuse Treatment, 9,* 9–14.

Kelley, S. J. (1992). Parenting stress and child maltreatment in drug-exposed children. *Child Abuse & Neglect, 16,* 317–328.

Kemper, K. J., & Rivara, F. P. (1993). Parents in jail. *Pediatrics, 92,* 261–264.

Kennedy, B. P., & Minami, M. (1993). The Beech Hill Hospital/Outward Bound Adolescent Chemical Dependency Treatment Program. *Journal of Substance Abuse Treatment, 10,* 395–406.

Kennedy, M. R. (1991). Homeless and runaway youth mental health issues: No access to the system. *Journal of Adolescent Health, 12,* 576–579.

Kernberg, O. (1967). Borderline personality organization [Review]. *Journal of the American Psychoanalytic Association, 15*(3), 641–685.

Kharasch, S., Vinci, R., & Reece, R. (1990). Esophagitis, epiglottitis, and cocaine alkaloid ("crack"): "Accidental" poisoning or child abuse? *Pediatrics, 86,* 117–119.

Kienhorst, C. W. M., de Wilde, E. J., Diekstra, R. F. W., & Wolters, W. H. G. (1991). Construction of an index for predicting suicide attempts in depressed adolescents. *British Journal of Psychiatry, 159,* 676–682.

Kim, S. (1988). A short and long-term evaluation of Here's Looking at You alcohol education program. *Journal of Drug Education, 18,* 171–184.

Kim, S., Hoffman, I. R., Pike, M. A., & Gibson, J. (1984). An outcome evaluation instrument for alcohol education, prevention, and intervention programs. *Journal of Drug Education, 14*(4), 331–346.

Kim, S., & Newman, S. H. (1982). Synthetic-dynamic theory of drug abuse: A revisit with empirical data. *International Journal of the Addictions, 17,* 913–923.

Kingery, P. M., Mirzaee, E., Pruitt, B. E., Hurley, R. S., & Heuberger, G. (1991). Rural communities near large metropolitan areas: Safe havens from adolescent violence and drug use? *Health Values, 15,* 39–48.

Kingery, P. M., Pruitt, B. E., & Hurley, R. S. (1992). Violence and illegal drug use among adolescents: Evidence for the U.S. National Adolescent Student Health Survey. *International Journal of the Addictions, 27,* 1445–1464.

Kirkpatrick-Smith, J., Rich, A. R., Bonner, R., & Jans, F. (1991–92). Psychological vulnerability and substance abuse as predictors of suicide ideation among adolescents. *Omega Journal of Death and Dying, 24*(1), 21–33.

Klatsky, A. L., & Armstrong, M. A. (1993). Alcohol use, other traits, and risk of unnatural death: A prospective study. *Alcoholism, Clinical & Experimental Research, 17,* 1156–1162.

Kleber, H. D. (1994). Opioids: Detoxification. In M. Galanter & H. D. Kleber (Eds.), *Textbook of substance abuse treatment.* Washington, DC: American Psychiatric Press.

Klein, M. W., & Maxson, C. L. (1994). Gangs and crack cocaine trafficking. In D. L. MacKenzie & C. D. Uchida (Eds.), *Drugs and crime: Evaluating public policy initiatives* (pp. 42–58). Thousand Oaks, CA: Sage.

Klein-Schwartz, W., & Oderda, G. M. (1995). Pediatric poisoning. In L. A. Pagliaro & A. M. Pagliaro (Eds.), *Problems in pediatric drug therapy* (3rd ed., pp. 337–392). Hamilton, IL: Drug Intelligence.

Knopman, D. (1991). Unaware learning versus preserved learning in pharmacologic amnesia: Similarities and differences. *Journal of Experimental Psychology: Learning, Memory, & Cognition, 17,* 1017–1029.

Knupfer, G. (1991). Abstaining for foetal health: The fiction that even light drinking is dangerous. *British Journal of Addiction, 86,* 1063–1073.

Kohut, K. (1995, June 2). Teens ignoring anti-smoking message: MD. *Edmonton Examiner,* p. 6.

Kokotailo, P. K., Adger, H., Jr., Duggan, A. K., Repke, J., & Joffe, A. (1992). Cigarette, alcohol, and other drug use by school-age pregnant adolescents: Prevalence, detection, and associated risk factors. *Pediatrics, 90,* 328–334.

Konkol, R. J. (1994). Is there a cocaine baby syndrome? *Journal of Child Neurology, 9,* 225–226.

Kopelman, M. D. (1991). Frontal dysfunction and memory deficits in the alcoholic Korsakoff syndrome and Alzheimer-type dementia. *Brain, 114,* 117–137.

Koren, G. (1993). Cocaine and the human fetus: The concept of teratophilia. *Neurotoxicology and Teratology, 15,* 301–304.

Korsten, M. A., & Lieber, C. S. (1985). Medical complications of alcoholism. In J. H. Mendelson & N. K. Mello (Eds.), *The diagnosis and treatment of alcoholism* (2nd ed., pp. 21–64). New York: McGraw-Hill.

Kosten, T. R., Rounsaville, B., Kosten, T., & Marikangas, K. (1991). Gender differences in the specificity of alcoholism transmission among the relatives of opioid addicts. *Journal of Nervous and Mental Disease, 179,* 392–400.

Koval, J. E. (1989). Violence in dating relationships. *Journal of Pediatric Health Care, 3,* 298–304.

Kozlowski, L. T., Coambs, R. B., Ferrence, R. G., & Adlaf, E. M. (1989). Preventing smoking and other drug use: Let the buyers beware and the interventions be apt. *Canadian Journal of Public Health, 80,* 452–456.

Kreek, M. J., & Stimmel, B. (Eds.) (1984). *Dual addiction: Pharmacological issues in the treatment of concomitant alcoholism and drug abuse.* New York: Haworth.

Kurtz, E. (1988). AA: *The story.* San Francisco: Harper & Row.

Kurtz, E. (1993). Research on Alcoholics Anonymous: The historical context. In B. S. McCrady & W. R. Miller (Eds.), *Research on Alcoholics Anonymous* (pp. 13–26). New Brunswick, NJ: Rutgers Center of Alcohol Studies.

LAAM—A long-acting methadone for treatment of heroin addiction. (1994). *Medical Letter, 36,* 52.

Labouvie, E. W., (1986a). Alcohol and marijuana use in relation to adolescent stress. *International Journal of the Addictions, 21,* 333–345.

Labouvie, E. W. (1986b). The coping function of adolescent alcohol and drug use. In R. K. Silbereisen, K. Eyferth, & G. Rudinger (Eds.), *Development as action in context: Problem behavior and normal youth development* (pp. 229–240). Berlin: Springer.

Labouvie, E. W. (1987). Relation of personality to adolescent alcohol and drug use: A coping perspective. *Pediatrician, 14*(1/2), 19–24.

Labouvie, E. W., & McGee, C. R. (1986). Relation of personality to alcohol and drug use in adolescence. *Journal of Contemporary Clinical Psychology, 4,* 289–293.

Labouvie, E. W., Pandina, R. J., Raskin White, H., & Johnson, V. (1990). Risk factors of adolescent drug use: An affect-based interpretation. *Journal of Substance Abuse, 2*(3), 265–285.

Lacombe, S., Stanislav, S. W., & Marken, P. A. (1991). Pharmacologic treatment of cocaine abuse. *Annals of Pharmacotherapy, 25,* 818–823.

Laird, M., Keister, S. C., & Tiberi, T. M. (1993, September). Stop the violence in schools. *Adolescence,* 20–25.

Lamb, J., & Pusker, K. R. (1991). School-based adolescent mental health project survey of depression, suicide ideation, and anger. *Journal of Child & Adolescent Psychiatric & Mental Health Nursing, 4,* 101–104.

Lamminpaa, A., Vilska, J., Korri, U. M., & Riihimaki, V. (1993). Alcohol intoxication in hospitalized young teenagers. *Acta Paediatrica, 82,* 783–788.

Landesman-Dwyer, S., Ragozin, A. S., & Little, R. E. (1981). Behavioral correlates of prenatal alcohol exposure: A four-year follow-up study. *Neurobehavioral Toxicology and Teratology, 3,* 187–193.

Laner, M. R. (1983). Courtship abuse and aggression: Contextual aspects. *Sociological Spectrum, 3,* 69–83.

Lange, E. (1987). The "semiconscious" form of pathologic alcoholic intoxication, its characteristics and differences from "classical" forms of pathologic intoxication. *Psychiatrie, Neurologie un Medizinische Psychologie, 39,* 193–201.

Langhorne, J. E., Jr., & Loney, J. (1979). A four-fold model for subgrouping the hyperkinetic/ MBD syndrome. *Child Psychiatry and Human Development, 9,* 153–159.

Larroque, B. (1992). Alcohol and the fetus. *International Journal of Epidemiology, 21*(Suppl. 1), S8-S16.

Lau, M. A., & Pihl, R. O. (1994). Alcohol and the Taylor aggression paradigm: A repeated measues study. *Journal of Studies on Alcohol, 55,* 701–706.

Lauritsen, J. (1993). Political-economic construction of gay male clone identity. *Journal of Homosexuality, 24,* 221–232.

Lavin, M. R., & Rifkin, A. (1993). Diagnosis and pharmacotherapy of conduct disorder. *Progress in Neuro-Psychopharmacology and Biological Psychiatry, 17,* 875–885.

Lawson, G. W. (1992). Twelve-step programs and treatment of adolescent substance abuse. In G. W. Lawson & A. W. Lawson (Eds.), *Adolescent substance abuse: Etiology, treatment, and prevention* (pp. 219–229). Gaithersburg, MD: Aspen.

Leary, M. R., Tchividjian, L. R., & Kraxberger, B. E. (1994). Self-presentation can be hazardous to your health: Impression management and health risk. *Health Psychology, 13,* 461–470.

Lehman, A. F., Myers, C. P., Corty, E., & Thompson, J. W. (1994). Prevalence and patterns of "dual diagnosis" among psychiatric inpatients. *Comprehensive Psychiatry, 35,* 106–112.

Leiderman, D. B., Balish, M., & Bromfield, E. B. (1991). Effect of valproate on human cerebral glucose metabolism. *Epilepsia, 32,* 417–422.

Leikin, J. B., Krantz, A. J., Zell-Kanter, M., Barkin, R. L., & Hryhorczuk, D. O. (1989). Clinical features and management of intoxication due to hallucinogenic drugs. *Medical Toxicology and Adverse Drug Experience, 4,* 324–350.

Leite, J. S., & Parrish, J. K. (1994). Why kids are the way they are. *Adolescence, 7*(3), 52–54.

Lemoine, P., Harousseau, H., & Borteyru, J. P. (1968). Children of alcoholic parents: Observed anomalies (127 cases). *Ouest Medical, 21,* 476–478.

Lesar, S. (1992). Prenatal cocaine exposure: The challenge to education. *Infant-Toddler Intervention. The Transdisciplinary Journal, 2*(1), 37–52.

Lesmes, G. R., & Donofrio, D. K. (1992). Passive smoking: The medical and economic issues. *American Journal of Medicine, 93*(Suppl. 1A), 38S–42S.

Lettieri, D. J. (1985). Drug abuse: A review of explanations and models of explanation. In J. S. Brook, D. J. Lettieri, D. W. Brook, & B. Stimmel (Eds.), *Alcohol and substance abuse in adolescence* (pp. 9–40). New York: Haworth.

Lettieri, D. J., Sayers, M., & Wallenstein Pearson, H. (Eds.). (1980). *Theories on drug abuse: Selected contemporary perspectives* (NIDA Research Monograph No. 30). Rockville, MD: U.S. Department of Health and Human Services, National Institute on Drug Abuse.

Levenson, R. W., Oyama, O. N., & Meek, P. S. (1987). Greater reinforcement from alcohol for those at risk: Parental risk, personality risk, and sex. *Journal of Abnormal Psychology, 96,* 242–253.

Levin, J. N. (1971). Amphetamine ingestion with biliary atresia. *Journal of Pediatrics, 79,* 130–131.

Leviton, A. (1992). Behavioral correlates of caffeine consumption by children. *Clinical Pediatrics, 31,* 742–750.

Levy, M. (1992). Alcohol and addictions [Letter]. *American Journal of Psychiatry, 149*(8), 1117–1118.

Levy, M. L., Masri, L. S., Levy, K. M., Johnson, F. L., Martin-Thomson, E., Couldwell, W. T., McComb, J. G., Weiss, M. H., & Apuzzo, M. L. (1993). Penetrating craniocerebral injury resultant from gunshot wounds: Gang-related injury in children and adolescents. *Neurosurgery, 33,* 1018–1025.

Lewandowski, L. M., & Westman, A. S. (1991). Drug use and its relation to high school students' activities. *Psychological Reports, 68,* 363–367.

Lewin, K. (1951). Field theory in social science. In D. Cartwright (Ed.), *Social science: Selected theoretical papers.* New York: Harper and Row.

Lewis, R. A., Piercy, F. P., Sprenkle, D. H., & Trepper, T. S. (1990). Family-based interventions for helping drug-abusing adolescents. *Journal of Adolescent Research, 5,* 82–95.

Lightfoot, L. O., & Barbaree, H. E. (1993). The relationship between substance use and abuse and sexual offending in adolescents. In H. E. Barbaree, W. L. Marshall, & S. M. Hudson (Eds.), *The juvenile sex offender* (pp. 203–224). New York: Guilford.

Lindberg, M. C., & Oyler, R. A. (1990). Wernicke's encephalopathy. *American Family Physician, 41,* 1205–1209.

Lindenbaum, G. A., Carroll, S. F., Daskal, I., & Kapusnick, R. (1989). Patterns of alcohol and drug abuse in an urban trauma center: The increasing role of cocaine abuse. *Journal of Trauma, 29,* 1654–1658.

Lindesmith, A. R. (1947). *Opiate addiction.* Bloomington, IN: Principia.

Lindman, R. E., & Lang, A. R. (1994). The alcohol-aggression stereotype: A cross-cultural comparison of beliefs. *International Journal of the Addictions, 29,* 1–13.

Linn, S., Schoenbaum, S. C., Monson, R. R., Rosner, R., Stubblefield, P. C., & Ryan, K. S. (1982). No association between coffee consumption and adverse outcomes of pregnancy. *New England Journal of Medicine, 306,* 141–145.

Linnoila, V. M., & Virkkunen, M. (1992). Aggression, suicidality, and serotonin. *Journal of Clinical Psychiatry, 53,* 46–51.

Little, B. B., Snell, L. M., & Rosenfeld, C. R. (1990). Failure to recognize fetal alcohol syndrome in newborn infants. *American Journal of Diseases of Children, 144,* 1142–1146.

Little, J. D., & Taghavi, E. H. (1991). Disinhibition after lorazepam augmentation of antipsychotic medication. *American Journal of Psychiatry, 148,* 1099–1100.

The little red book. (1986). Center City, MN: Hazelden.

Littrell, J. (1991). *Understanding and treating alcoholism.* Hillsdale, NJ: Erlbaum.

Logan, B. N. (1991). Adolescent substance abuse prevention: An overview of the literature. *Community Health, 13,* 25–36.

Lohr, M. J., Gillmore, M. R., Gilchrist, L. D., & Butler, S. S. (1992). Factors related to substance use by pregnant school-age adolescents. *Journal of Adolescent Health, 13,* 475–482.

Loke, W. H., Hinrichs, J. V., & Ghoneim, M. M. (1985). Caffeine and diazepam: Separate and combined effects on mood, memory, and psychomotor performance. *Psychopharmacology, 87,* 344–350.

Loney, J. (1980). The Iowa theory of substance abuse among hyperactive adolescents. In D. J. Lettieri, M. Sayers, H. Wallenstein Pearson (Eds.), *Theories on drug abuse: Selected contemporary perspectives* (NIDA Research Monograph No. 30, pp. 132–136). Rockville, MD: U.S. Department of Health and Human Services, National Institute on Drug Abuse.

Loney, J., Langhorne Jr., J. E., & Paternite, C. E. (1978). An empirical basis for subgrouping the hyperkinetic/minimal brain dysfunction syndrome. *Journal of Abnormal Psychology, 87,* 431–441.

Long, J. V., & Scherl, D. J. (1984). Developmental antecedents of compulsive drug use: A report on the literature [Review]. *Journal of Psychoactive Drugs, 16*(2), 169–182.

Lubinski, B. (1995). Street law: Where kids learn the basics. *Professional Counselor, 10,* 31.

Luck, W., & Nau, H. (1985). Nicotine and cotinine concentrations in serum and urine of infants exposed via passive smoking or milk from smoking mothers. *Journal of Pediatrics, 107,* 816–820.

Lujan, C., DuBruyn, L. M., May, P. A., & Bird, M. E. (1989). Profile of abused and neglected American Indian children in the southwest. *Child Abuse & Neglect, 13,* 449–461.

Lukoff, I. F. (1972). *Social and ethnic patterns of reported heroin use and contiguity with drug users.* New York: Addiction Research and Treatment Corporation Evaluation Team.

Lukoff, I. F. (1974). Issues in the evaluation of heroin treatment. In E. Josephson & E. E. Carroll (Eds.), *Drug use: Epidemiological and sociological approaches* (pp. 129–157). New York: Wiley.

Lukoff, I. F. (1977). Consequences of use: Heroin and other narcotics. In J. D. Rittenhouse (Ed.), *The epidemiology of heroin and other narcotics* (NIDA Research Monograph No. 16, pp. 195–227). Rockville, MD: U.S. Department of Health and Human Services, National Institute on Drug Abuse.

Lukoff, I. F. (1980). Toward a sociology of drug use. In D. J. Lettieri, M. Sayers, H. Wallenstein Pearson (Eds.), *Theories on drug abuse: Selected contemporary perspectives* (NIDA Research Monograph No. 30, pp. 201–211). Rockville, MD: U.S. Department of Health and Human Services, National Institute on Drug Abuse.

Lyman, W. D. (1993). Perinatal AIDS: Drugs of abuse and transplacental infection. In H. Friedman et al. (Eds.), *Drugs of abuse, immunity, and AIDS* (pp. 211–217). New York: Plenum.

MacAndrew, C., & Edgerton, R. B. (1969). *Drunken comportment: A social explanation.* Chicago: Aldine.

MacDonald, D. I. (1984). Drugs, drinking, and adolescence. *American Journal of Diseases of Children, 138,* 117–125.

MacDonald, D. I. (1989). Diagnosis and treatment of adolescent substance abuse. *Current Problems in Pediatrics, 19,* 394–444.

MacDonald, D. I., & Newton, M. (1981). The clinical syndrome of adolescent drug abuse. *Advances in Pediatrics, 28,* 1–25.

Mace, W. (1992). A right brain model of substance abuse. *Family Dynamics of Addiction Quarterly, 2*(1), 60–68.

Maddahian, E., Newcomb, M. D., & Bentler, P. M. (1988). Adolescent drug use and intention to use drugs: Concurrent and longitudinal analyses of four ethnic groups. *Addictive Behaviors, 13*(2), 191–195.

Madden, R. G. (1993). State actions to control fetal abuse: Ramifications for child welfare practice. *Child Welfare, 72,* 129–140.

Madianos, M. G., Gefou-Madianou, D., & Stefanis, C. N. (1994). Symptoms of depression, suicidal behaviour and use of substances in Greece: A nationwide general population survey. *Acta Psychiatrica Scandinavica, 89,* 159–166.

Maier, S. F., & Seligman, M. E. P. (Eds.). (1976). Learned helplessness: Theory and evidence. *Journal of Experimental Psychology: General, 105,* 3–46.

Maki, R. J. (1995). Gangs: What can we do about them? *Professional Counselor, 10,* 30, 32.

Making the links: A book for young women about sexual violence, drugs, and alcohol. (1990). Kingston, ON: Action on Women's Addictions—Research and Education (AWARE).

Malinosky-Rummell, R., & Hansen, D. J. (1993). Long-term consequences of childhood physical abuse. *Psychological Bulletin, 114*(1), 68–79.

Mallick, J. L., Kirby, K. C., Martin, F., Philp, M., & Hennessy, M. J. (1993). A comparison of the amnesic effects of lorazepam in alcoholics and non-alcoholics. *Psychopharmacology, 110,* 181–186.

Malmquist, C. P. (1990). Depression in homicidal adolescents. *Bulletin of the American Academy of Psychiatry and Law, 18*(1), 23–36.

Mannuzza, S., Klein, R. G., Bonagura, N., Konig, P. H., & Shenker, R. (1988). Hyperactive boys almost grown up. *Archives of General Psychiatry, 45,* 13–18.

Manschreck, T. C., Laughery, J. A., Weisstein, C. C., Allen, D., Humblestone, B., Neville, M., Poslewski, H., & Mitra, N. (1988). Characteristics of freebase cocaine psychosis. *Yale Journal of Biology & Medicine, 61,* 115–122.

Manschreck, T. C., Schneyer, M. L., Weisstein, D. D., Laughery, J., et al. (1990). Freebase cocaine and memory. *Comprehensive Psychiatry, 31,* 369–375.

Marcos, A. C., Bahr, S. J., & Johnson, R. E. (1986). Test of a bonding/association theory of adolescent drug use. *Social Forces, 65*(1), 135–161.

Marcos, A. C., & Johnson, R. E. (1988). Cultural patterns and causal processes in adolescent drug use: The case of Greeks versus Americans. *International Journal of the Addictions, 23,* 545–572.

Marohn, R. C. (1992). Management of the assaultive adolescent. *Hospital and Community Psychiatry, 43,* 622–624.

Marques, P. R., & McKnight, A. J. (1991). Drug abuse risk among pregnant adolescents attending public health clinics. *American Journal of Drug and Alcohol Abuse, 17,* 399–413.

Marra, E. F. (1967). *Intoxicant drugs.* Buffalo, NY: State University of New York at Buffalo.

Marshall, M. J., Marshall, S., & Heer, M. J. (1994). Characteristics of abstinent substance abusers who first sought treatment in adolescence. *Journal of Drug Education, 24,* 151–162.

Martin, C. S., Arria, A. M., Mezzich, A. C., & Bukstein, O. G. (1993). Patterns of polydrug use in adolescent alcohol abusers. *Journal of Drug & Alcohol Abuse, 19,* 511–521.

Martin, J. L., & Hasin, D. S. (1991). Drinking, alcoholism, and sexual behavior in a cohort of gay men. In D. G. Fisher (Ed.), *AIDS and alcohol/drug abuse: Psychosocial research* (pp. 49–67). New York: Harrington Park.

Martin, K. (1993, April). Solvent use "part of a larger problem." *Journal,* pp. 5–6.

Martin, M. L., Khoury, M. J., Cordero, J. F., & Waters, G. D. (1992). Trends in rates of multiple vascular disruption defects, Atlanta, 1969–1989: Is there evidence of a cocaine teratogenic epidemic? *Teratology, 45,* 647–653.

Martin, T., & Bracken, M. (1987). Maternal caffeine use and low birth weight. *American Journal of Epidemiology, 126,* 813–821.

Marzuk, P. M., Tardiff, K., Leon, A. C., Stajic, M., Morgan, E. B., & Mann, J. J. (1992). Prevalence of cocaine use among residents of New York City who committed suicide during a one-year period. *American Journal of Psychiatry, 149,* 371–375.

Masi, M. A., Hanley, J. A., Ernst, P., & Becklaki, M. R. (1988). Environmental exposure to tobacco smoke and lung function in young adults. *American Review of Respiratory Disease, 138,* 296–299.

Mathew, R. J., Wilson, W. H., Blazer, D. G., & George, L. K. (1993). Psychiatric disorders in adult children of alcoholics: Data from the epidemiologic catchment area project. *American Journal of Psychiatry, 150,* 793–800.

Mattson, M. E. (1994). Patient-treatment matching: Rationale and results. *Alcohol, Health & Research World, 18,* 287–295.

McBride, J. L. (1991). Abstinence among members of Alcoholics Anonymous. *Alcoholism Treatment Quarterly, 8,* 113–121.

McCann, B. (1992, March). Alcoholism ages brain by up to 20 years. *Journal,* p. 2.

McCarty, D., Argeriou, M., Huebner, R. B., & Lubran, B. (1991, November). Alcoholism, drug abuse, and the homeless. *American Psychologist,* 1139–1148.

McCord, W., & McCord, J. (1960). *Origins of alcoholism.* Stanford, CA: Stanford University Press.

McDermott, D. (1984). The relationship of parental drug use and parents' attitude concerning adolescent drug use to adolescent drug use. *Adolescence, 19,* 89–97.

McDonald, R. M., & Towberman, D. B. (1993). Psychosocial correlates of adolescent drug involvement. *Adolescence, 28*(112), 925–936.

McEwen, T. (1995). *National assessment program: 1994 survey results* (NCJ No. 153517). Washington, DC: U.S. Department of Justice.

McGonigal, M. D., Cole, J., Schwab, C. W., Kauder, D. R., Rotondo, M. F., & Angood, P. B. (1993). Urban firearm deaths: A five-year perspective. *Journal of Trauma, 35,* 532–536.

McHugh, M. J. (1987). The abuse of volatile substances. *Pediatric Clinics of North America, 34,* 333–340.

McKenzie, J. D. (1969). *Trends in marijuana use.* College Park, MD: University of Maryland Counseling Center.

McLaughlin, R. J., Vlasak, J. W., McClanahan, K. K., Holcomb, J. D., Kingery, P. M., Gibbins, A. D., & Quentin, W. S. (1993). Reducing substance abuse risk factors among children through a teacher as facilitator program. *Journal of Drug Education, 23,* 137–150.

McMurran, M. (1991). Young offenders and alcohol-related crime: What interventions will address the issues? *Journal of Adolescence, 14,* 245–253.

Meade, L. (Author), Hirliman, G. (Producer), & Gasnier, L. (Director). (1937). *Reefer madness* [Film]. Mt. Morris, IL: High Times Video.

Meehan, P. J., & O'Carroll, P. W. (1992). Gangs, drugs, and homicide in Los Angeles. *American Journal of Diseases of Children, 146,* 683–687.

Menninger, K. A. (1938). *Man against himself.* New York: Harcourt, Brace.

Mercer, G. W., Hundleby, J. D., & Carpenter, R. A. (1978). Adolescent drug use and attitudes toward family. *Canadian Journal of Behavioral Science, 10*(1), 79–90.

Mercer, G. W., & Kohn, P. M. (1980). Child-rearing factors, authoritarianism, drug use attitudes, and adolescent drug use: A model. *Journal of Genetic Psychology, 136,* 159–171.

Mercer, G. W., & Smart, R. G. (1974). The epidemiology of psychoactive and hallucinogenic drug use. In R. J. Gibbons, Y. Israel, H. Kalant, R. E. Popham, W. Schmidt, & R. G. Smart (Eds.), *Research advances in alcohol and drug problems* (Vol. 1, pp. 303–307). New York: Wiley.

Merrick, J. C. (1993). Maternal substance abuse during pregnancy: Policy implications in the United States. *Journal of Legal Medicine, 14,* 57–71.

Merton, R. K. (1957). *Social theory and social structure* (Rev. ed.). New York: Free Press.

Metzger, L., & Steffen, L. L. (1995). When teen love turns to tainted love. *Adolescence, 8*(2), 25–27.

Meyer, L., Wiklund, N., & Lidberg, L. (1991). Does clomipramine in combination with alcohol provoke violent crimes? *Lakarttidningen, 88,* 2768–2769.

Meyer, R. E. (1986). How to understand the relationship between psychopathology and addictive disorders: Another example of the chicken and the egg. In R. E. Meyer (Ed.), *Psychopathology and addictive disorders* (pp. 3–16). New York: Guilford.

Mezzich, A. C., Moss, H., Tarter, R. E., Wolfenstein, M., Hsieh, Y., & Mauss, R. (1994). Gender differences in the pattern and progression of substance use in conduct-disordered adolescents. *American Journal on Addictions, 3,* 289–295.

Milgram, G. G. (1993). Adolescents, alcohol and aggression. *Journal of Studies on Alcohol, 11,* 53–61.

Milich, R., & Loney, J. (1979). The role of hyperactive and aggressive symptomatology in predicting adolescent outcome among hyperactive children. *Journal of Pediatric Psychology, 4,* 93–112.

Miller, B. A. (1990). The interrelationships between alcohol and drugs and family violence. In M. De La Rosa, E. Y. Lambert, & B. Gropper (Eds.), *Drugs and violence: Causes, correlates, and consequences* (NIDA Research Monograph No. 103, pp. 177–207). Rockville, MD: U.S. Department of Health and Human Services, National Institute on Drug Abuse.

Miller, D. (1986). Adolescent substance abuse. In D. Miller (Ed.), *Attack on the self: Adolescent behavioral disturbances and their treatment* (pp. 197–255). Northvale, NJ: Aronson.

Miller, H. C., Hassanein, K., & Hensleigh, P. A. (1976). Fetal growth retardation in relation to maternal smoking and weight gain in pregnancy. *American Journal of Obstetrics and Gynecology, 125,* 55–60.

Miller, N. S. (1994). The interactions between coexisting disorders. In N. S. Miller (Ed.), *Treating coexisting psychiatric and addictive disorders: A practical guide* (pp. 7–21). Center City, MN: Hazelden Educational Materials.

Miller, N. S., Belkin, B. M., & Gibbons, R. (1994). Clinical diagnosis of substance use disorders in private psychiatric populations. *Journal of Substance Abuse Treatment, 11,* 387–392.

Miller, N. S., & Gold, M. S. (1990). Organic solvents and aerosols: An overview of abuse and dependence. *Annals of Clinical Psychiatry, 2,* 85–92.

Miller, N. S., & Gold, M. S. (1994). Criminal activity and crack addiction. *International Journal of the Addictions, 29,* 1069–1078.

Miller, W. R., & McCrady, B. S. (1993). The importance of research on Alcoholics Anonymous. In B. S. McCrady & W. R. Miller (Eds.), *Research on Alcoholics Anonymous* (pp. 3–11). New Brunswick, NJ: Rutgers Center of Alcohol Studies.

Miller-Tutzauer, C., Leonard, K. E., & Windle, M. (1991). Marriage and alcohol use: A longitudinal study of "maturing out." *Journal of Studies on Alcohol, 52,* 434–440.

Millsaps, C. L., Azrin, R. L., & Mittenberg, W. (1994). Neuropsychological effects of chronic cannabis use on the memory and intelligence of adolescents. *Journal of Child & Adolescent Substance Abuse, 3*(1), 47–55.

Milner, J. S., & Chilamkurti, C. (1991). Physical child abuse perpetrator characteristics: A review of the literature. *Journal of Interpersonal Violence, 6,* 345–366.

Mirin, S. M. (1995). Practice guidelines for the treatment of patients with substance use disorders: Alcohol, cocaine, opioids. *American Journal of Psychiatry, 152,* 1–59.

Minuchin, S. (1974). *Families and family therapy.* Cambridge, MA: Harvard University Press.

Mittenberg, W., & Motta, S. (1993). Effects of chronic cocaine abuse on memory and learning. *Archives of Clinical Neuropsychology, 8,* 477–483.

Moffitt, K. H., Singer, J. A., Nelligan, D. W., Carlson, M. A., & Vyse, S. A. (1994). Depression and memory narrative type. *Journal of Abnormal Psychology, 103,* 581–583.

Moncher, M. S., Holden, G. W., & Trimble, J. E. (1990). Substance abuse among Native-American youth. *Journal of Consulting and Clinical Psychology, 58,* 408–415.

Morgan, I. S. (1994). Recognizing depression in the adolescent. *American Journal of Maternal Child Nursing, 19,* 148–155.

Morganthau, R., Lerner, M. A., Sandza, R., Abbott, N., Gonzalez, D. L., & King, P. (1988, March). The drug gangs. *Newsweek,* 20–27.

Morra, L. G. (1992). *Drug education: Rural programs have many components and most rely heavily on federal funds* (GAO/HRD Publication No. 92-34). Gaithersburg, MD: U.S. General Accounting Office.

Morris, G. S. D., Vo Bassin, S., Savaglio, D., & Wong, N. D. (1993). Prevalence and sociobehavioral correlates of tobacco use among Hispanic children: The tobacco resistance activity program. *Journal of School Health, 63,* 391–396.

Morrison, M. A., Smith, D. E., Wilford, B. B., Ehrlich, P., & Seymour, R. B. (1993). At war in the fields of play: Current perspectives on the nature and treatment of adolescent chemical dependency. *Journal of Psychoactive Drugs, 25,* 321–330.

Moskowitz, J. M., Schaps, E., Schaeffer, G. A., & Malvin, J. H. (1984). Evaluation of a substance abuse prevention program for junior high school students. *International Journal of the Addictions, 19,* 419–430.

Moss, H. B., Kirisci, L., & Mezzich, A. C. (1994). Psychiatric comorbidity and self-efficacy to resist heavy drinking in alcoholic and nonalcoholic adolescents. *American Journal on Addictions, 3,* 204–212.

Mott, J. (1986). Opioid use and burglary. *British Journal of Addiction, 81,* 671–678.

Muisener, P. P. (1994). *Understanding and treating adolescent substance abuse.* Thousand Oaks, CA: Sage.

Muller, R. T., Fitzgerald, H. E., Sullivan, L. A., & Zucker, R. A. (1994). Social support and stress factors in child maltreatment among alcoholic families. *Canadian Journal of Behavioural Science, 26,* 438–461.

Muramoto, M. L., & Leshan, L. (1993). Adolescent substance abuse: Recognition and early intervention. *Primary Care, 20*(1), 141–154.

Murray, D., Pirie, P., Luepker, R., & Pallonen, V. (1989). Five and six-year follow-up results from four seventh-grade smoking prevention strategies. *Journal of Behavioral Medicine, 12,* 207–218.

Murray, D. W. (1994, July 13). Every society is threatened by the disappearance of legitimate marriage. *Chronicle of Higher Education,* B5.

Myers, W. C., Donahue, J. E., & Goldstein, M. R. (1994). Disulfiram for alcohol use disorders in adolescents. *Journal of the American Academy of Child & Adolescent Psychiatry, 33,* 484–489.

Naltrexone for alcohol dependence. (1995). *Medical Letter, 37,* 64–66.

Nanson, J. L. (1992). Autism in fetal alcohol syndrome: A report of six cases. *Alcoholism, Clinical & Experimental Research, 16,* 558–565.

Nanson, J. L., & Hiscock, M. (1990). Attention deficits in children exposed to alcohol prenatally. *Alcoholism, Clinical & Experimental Research, 14,* 656–661.

Nash, J. E., & Persaud, T. V. N. (1988). Embryopathic risks of cigarette smoking. *Experimental Pathology, 33,* 65–73.

Natakusumah, A., Irwanto, Piercy, F., Lewis, R., Sprenkle, D., & Trepper, T. (1992). Cohesion and adaptability in families of adolescent drug abusers in the United States and Indonesia. *Journal of Comparative Family Studies, 23*(3), 389–411.

National Archive of Criminal Justice Data Newsletter. (1994, Fall). Washington, DC: U.S. Department of Justice.

National Center for Health Statistics. (1991). *Health, United States, 1990* (DHHS Publication No. 91-1232). Bethesda, MD: U.S. Department of Health and Human Services.

National Institute on Alcohol Abuse and Alcoholism. (1987). *Program strategies for preventing fetal alcohol syndrome and alcohol-related birth defects* (DHHS Publication No. ADM 87-1482). Washington, DC: U.S. Government Printing Office.

National Institute on Drug Abuse. (1984). *Drug abuse and drug abuse research, 43* (DHHS Publication No. ADM 85-1372). Washington, DC: U.S. Government Printing Office.

Needle, R. H., Su, S. S., & Doherty, W. J. (1990). Divorce, remarriage, and adolescent substance use: A prospective longitudinal study. *Journal of Marriage and the Family, 152,* 157–159.

Negative pulmonary effects of marijuana. (1987). *British Medical Journal, 295,* 1516–1518.

Nemeth, M. (1993, February 22). Life on the streets. *Maclean's,* pp. 48–49.

Nemeth, M. (1994, October 31). An alarming trend: Suicide among the youth has quadrupled. *Maclean's,* p. 15.

Neuspiel, D. R. (1992). Cocaine-associated abnormalities may not be causally related [Letter to the editor]. *American Journal of Diseases of Children, 146,* 278.

Neuspiel, D. R. (1993). Cocaine and the fetus: Mythology of severe risk. *Neurotoxicology and Teratology, 15,* 305–306.

Newcomb, M. D., & Bentler, P. M. (1988). *Consequences of adolescent drug use: Impact on the lives of young adults.* Newbury Park, CA: Sage.

Newcomb, M. D., & Bentler, P. M. (1989, February). Substance use and abuse among children and teenagers. *American Psychologist,* 242–248.

Newcomb, M. D., Maddahian, E., & Bentler, P. M. (1986). Risk factors for drug use among adolescents: Concurrent and longitudinal analyses. *American Journal of Public Health, 76,* 525–531.

Newcomb, M. D., & McGee, L. (1989). Adolescent alcohol use and other delinquent behaviors: A one-year longitudinal analysis controlling for sensation seeking. *Criminal Justice and Behavior, 16,* 345–369.

Newlin, D. B., & Thomson, J. B. (1990). Alcohol challenge with sons of alcoholics: A critical review and analysis. *Psychological Bulletin, 108,* 383–402.

Newman, L. F., & Buka, S. L. (1991). Preventing the risk factors in childhood learning impairment. *Rhode Island Medical Journal, 74,* 251–262.

Newton, B. (1985). Tough love: Help for parents with troubled teenagers—reorganizing the heirarchy in disorganized families. *Pediatrics, 76,* 691–694.

Newton, M. (1981). *Gone way down: Teenage drug use is a disease.* Chicago: American Studies.

Ney, P. G., Fung, T., & Wickett, A. R. (1992). Causes of child abuse and neglect. *Canadian Journal of Psychiatry, 37,* 401–405.

Nicotine patches. (1992). *Medical Letter on Drugs and Therapeutics, 34,* 37–38.

Nora, J. J., Vargo, T. A., Nora, A. H., Love, K. E., & McNamara, D. G. (1970). Dexamphetamine: A possible environmental trigger in cardiovascular malformations [Letter]. *Lancet, 1,* 1290.

Norem-Hebeisen, A. A., & Lucas, M. S. (1977). A developmental model for primary prevention of chemical abuse. *Journal of Drug Education, 7*(2), 141–148.

Norman, E., & Turner, S. (1993). Adolescent substance abuse prevention programs: Theories, models, and research in the encouraging 80s. *Journal of Primary Prevention, 14,* 3–20.

Norris, C. R., Jr., & Extein, I. L. (1991). Diagnosing dual diagnosis patients. In M. S. Gold & A. E. Slaby (Eds.), *Dual diagnosis in substance abuse* (pp. 159–184). New York: Dekker.

Norwood, G. R. (1985). A society that promotes drug abuse: The effects on pre-adolescence. *Childhood Education, 61,* 267–271.

Nucci, P., & Brancato, R. (1994). Ocular effects of prenatal cocaine exposure. *Ophthalmology, 101,* 1321.

Nurco, D. N., Cisin, I. H., & Ball, J. C. (1985). Crime as a source of income for narcotic addicts. *Journal of Substance Abuse Treatment, 2,* 113–115.

Nwanyanwu, O. C., Chu, S. Y., Green, T. A., Buehler, J. W., & Berkelman, R. L. (1993). Acquired immunodeficiency syndrome in the United States associated with injecting drug use, 1981–1991. *American Journal of Drug and Alcohol Abuse, 19,* 399–408.

O'Brien, W., & Biase, D. V. (1984). The therapeutic community: A current perspective. *Journal of Psychoactive Drugs, 16,* 9–21.

O'Connell, D. F. (Ed.). (1990). *Managing the dually diagnosed patient: Current issues and clinical approaches.* New York: Haworth.

O'Donnell, C. R. (1995). Firearm deaths among children and youth. *American Psychologist, 50,* 771–776.

Oei, T., & Jackson, P. (1980). Long-term effects of group and individual social skills training with alcoholics. *Addictive Behaviors, 5,* 129–136.

Oetting, E. R., & Beauvais, F. (1986). Peer cluster theory: Drugs and the adolescent. *Journal of Counseling and Development, 65,* 17–22.

Oetting, E. R., & Beauvais, F. (1987). Common elements in youth drug abuse: Peer clusters and other psychosocial factors. *Journal of Drug Issues, 17,* 133–151.

Oetting, E. R., & Beauvais, F. (1990–91). Orthogonal cultural identification theory: The cultural identification of minority adolescents. *International Journal of the Addictions, 25,* 655–685.

Oetting, E. R., & Beauvais, F. C. (1991). Critical incidents: Failure in prevention. *International Journal of the Addictions, 26,* 797–820.

O'Hagan, K. (1993). *Emotional and psychological abuse of children.* Toronto, ON: University of Toronto Press.

O'Keefe, N. K., Brockopp, K., & Chew, E. (1986). Teen dating violence. *Social Work, 31,* 465–468.

Okwumabua, J. O., Okwumabua, T. M., Winston, B. L., & Walker, H., Jr. (1989). Onset of drug use among rural black youth. *Journal of Adolescent Research, 4,* 238–246.

Olds, D. L., Henderson, C. R., Jr., & Tatelbaum, R. (1994). Intellectual impairment in children of women who smoke cigarettes during pregnancy. *Pediatrics, 93,* 221–226.

Olsen, J., Overvad, K., & Frische, G. (1991). Coffee consumption, birthweight, and reproductive failures. *Epidemiology, 2,* 370–374.

Olson, C. H. (1994). The effects of prenatal alcohol exposure on child development. *Infants and Young Children, 6*(3), 10–25.

Olson, D. H. (1980). *Clinical rating scales for the circumplex model of marital and family systems: Family social science.* St. Paul, MN: University of Minnesota.

Olson, D. H. (1986). Circumplex model VII: Validation studies and FACES III. *Family Process, 25*(3), 337–352.

Olson, D. H., McCubbin, H. I., Barnes, H., Larsen, A., Muxen, M., & Wilson, M. (1983). *Families: What makes them work.* Beverly Hills, CA: Sage.

Olson, D. H., Russell, C., & Sprenkle, D. (1979). Circumplex model of marital and family systems II: Empirical studies and clinical interventions. In J. Vincent (Ed.), *Advances in family intervention, assessment and theory* (pp. 128–179). Greenwich, CT: JAI.

Olson, D. H., Russell, C., & Sprenkle, D. (1980). Marital and family therapy: A decade review. *Journal of Marriage and the Family, 42,* 973–993.

Olson, D. H., Russell, C. S., & Sprenkle, D. H. (1983). Circumplex model of marital and family systems VI: Theoretical update. *Family Process, 22*(1), 69–83.

Olson, D. H., Sprenkle, D., & Russell, C. (1979). Circumplex model of marital and family systems I: Cohesion and adaptability dimensions, family types, and clinical applications. *Family Process, 18,* 3–28.

Olson, H. C., Sampson, P. D., Barr, H., Streissguth, A. P., & Bookstein, F. L. (1992). Prenatal exposure to alcohol and school problems in late childhood: A longitudinal prospective study. *Development and Psychopathology, 4,* 341–359.

O'Malley, P. M., & Bachman, J. G. (1987). Psychotherapeutic, licit, and illicit use of drugs among adolescents. *Journal of Adolescent Health Care, 8,* 36–51.

O'Malley, P. M., Bachman, J. G., & Johnston, L. D. (1988). Period, age, and cohort effects on substance use among young Americans: A decade of change, 1976–86. *American Journal of Public Health, 78,* 1315–1321.

O'Malley, P. M., Johnston, L. D., & Bachman, J. G. (1991). *Quantitative and qualitative changes in cocaine use among American high school seniors, college students, and young adults* (NIDA Research Monograph No. 110, pp. 19–43). Rockville, MD: U.S. Department of Health and Human Services, National Institute on Drug Abuse.

O'Malley, P. M., & Wagenaar, A. C. (1991). Effects of minimum drinking age laws on alcohol use, related behaviors and traffic crash involvement among American youth: 1976–1987. *Journal of Studies on Alcohol, 52,* 478–491.

O'Malley, S. S., Jaffe, A., Chang, G., Schottenfeld, M. D., Meyer, R. E., & Rounsaville, B. J. (1992). Naltrexone and coping skills therapy for alcohol dependence: A controlled study. *Archives of General Psychiatry, 49,* 881–887.

O'Mara, N. B., & Nahata, M. C. (1995). Drugs excreted in human breast milk. In L. A. Pagliaro & A. M. Pagliaro (Eds.), *Problems in pediatric drug therapy* (3rd ed., pp. 247–335). Hamilton, IL: Drug Intelligence.

Ord, R. A., & Benian, R. M. (1995). Baseball bat injuries to the maxillofacial region caused by assault. *Journal of Oral & Maxillofacial Surgery, 53,* 514–517.

Orford, J. (1985). *Excessive appetites: A psychological view of addictions.* New York: Wiley.

Osofsky, J. D. (1995). The effects of exposure to violence on young children. *American Psychologist, 50,* 782–788.

Osran, H. C., & Weinberger, L. E. (1994). Personality disorders and "restoration to sanity." *Bulletin of the American Academy of Psychiatry & the Law, 22,* 257–267.

Pagliaro, A. M. (1990a). Addiction as disease: The life and death of a theory of drug and substance abuse [Abstract]. *Proceedings of the Western Pharmacology Society, 33,* 286.

Pagliaro, A. M. (1990b). The relationship between coping with cancer and drug & substance abuse: Psychologic and related theories of explanation. *Alberta Psychology, 19*(4), 20–22.

Pagliaro, A. M. (1991). The contributions of psychologic theories to the understanding of substance abuse phenomenon [Abstract]. *Canadian Journal of Psychology, 32,* 334.

Pagliaro, A. M. (1995). *Theoretical Foundations of Substance Abusology.* Manuscript in preparation.

Pagliaro, A. M., & Pagliaro, L. A. (1994, March 8). What do 261 "hard-core" intravenous drug using women know and do in relation to HIV infection and AIDS? A report from the PIARG major study [Abstract]. In *Proceedings of the Eighth Annual Margaret Scott Wright Lectureship and Research Conference* (p. 27). Edmonton AB: University of Alberta.

Pagliaro, A. M., & Pagliaro, L. A. (1995). Abusable psychotropic use among children and adolescents. In L. A. Pagliaro & A. M. Pagliaro, (Eds.), *Problems in pediatric drug therapy* (3rd ed., pp. 507–540). Hamilton, IL: Drug Intelligence.

Pagliaro, A. M., Pagliaro, L. A., Thauberger, P. C., Hewitt, D. S., & Reddon, J. R. (1990). AIDS and injection drug use: Changing dimensions of the epidemic. *Alberta Psychology, 19*(5), 5–7.

Pagliaro, A. M., Pagliaro, L. A., Thauberger, P. C., Hewitt, D. S., & Reddon, J. R. (1992, May 28). *Knowledge, behaviours, and risk perceptions of intravenous drug users in relation to HIV infection and AIDS.* Poster session presented at the Second Annual Conference of the Canadian Association for HIV Research, Vancouver, BC.

Pagliaro, A. M., Pagliaro, L. A., Thauberger, P. C., Hewitt, D. S., & Reddon, J. R. (1993). Knowledge, behaviors, and risk perceptions of intravenous drug users in relation to HIV infection and AIDS: The PIARG projects. *Advances in Medical Psychotherapy, 6,* 1–28.

Pagliaro, L. A. (1979). Instructional interactions and the Mega Interactive Model of instruction. *Educational Technology, 19,* 35–39.

Pagliaro, L. A. (1983). Up in smoke? A brief overview of marijuana toxicity. *Kerygma, 41,* 1–4.

Pagliaro, L. A. (1985a, August). *The Mega Interactive Model of Drug Abuse (MIMDA).* Paper presented at the 34th International Congress on Alcoholism and Drug Dependence, Calgary, AB.

Pagliaro, L. A. (1985b, March). *Methadone maintenance: An appraisal.* Unpublished report prepared for the Department of the Alberta Solicitor General.

Pagliaro, L. A. (1986). The phenomenon of addiction. *Alberta Psychology, 15*(4), 3–6.

Pagliaro, L. A. (1988a, April). Hooked on drugs: Overview of a growing problem. *Let's Talk, 13,* 4–5.

Pagliaro, L. A. (1988b, June). Marijuana and hashish: What are the risks? *Let's Talk, 13,* 12–14.

Pagliaro, L. A. (1988c). The straight dope: "The 'Ice Man' cometh." *Alberta Psychology, 18*(6), 17.

Pagliaro, L. A. (1989a). The straight dope. *Alberta Psychology, 18*(2), 20.

Pagliaro, L. A. (1989b). The straight dope. *Alberta Psychology, 18*(3), 25.

Pagliaro, L. A. (1990a). Overview of the problem of drug abuse in Canada [Abstract]. *Alberta Psychology, 19*(3), 11.

Pagliaro, L. A. (1990b). The straight dope: Dual diagnosis. *Alberta Psychology, 19*(5), 23–24.

Pagliaro, L. A. (1991a). The straight dope. *Psynopis, 13*(2), 7.

Pagliaro, L. A. (1991b). The straight dope: Cannibalism, birth defects, homosexuality, and other myths associated with drug and substance abuse. *Psynopsis, 13*(4), 8.

Pagliaro, L. A. (1991c). The straight dope: Focus on prisons. *Psynopsis, 13*(3), 8.

Pagliaro, L. A. (1992a). Dr. Jekyll and Mr. Hyde . . . Drug-induced automatism. *Psynopsis, 14,* 11.

Pagliaro, L. A. (1992b). The straight dope: Focus on learning—Interpreting the interpretations. *Psynopsis, 14*(2), 8.

Pagliaro, L. A. (1992c). The straight dope: Predictions for 1992. *Psynopsis, 14*(1), 8.

Pagliaro, L. A. (1993a). Issues in substance abuse for Canadian teachers. In L. Stewin (Ed.), *Contemporary educational issues: The Canadian mosaic.* Toronto, ON: Stewart.

Pagliaro, L. A. (1993b). The straight dope: Drug-induced violent behaviour: Questions and answers. *Psynopsis, 15*(3), 14.

Pagliaro, L. A. (1994). Pharmacopsychology updates: Attention-deficit/hyperactivity disorder. *Psymposium, 4*(3), 14–15.

Pagliaro, L. A. (1995a). Drug induced automatism: Fact or fiction? *Psymposium, 4,* 16–17.

Pagliaro, L. A. (1995b). Marijuana reconsidered. *Psymposium, 5,* 12–13.

Pagliaro, L. A. (1995c). Pharmacopsychology updates: Drugs and sexual (dys)function. *Psymposium, 4*(6), 20–21.

Pagliaro, L. A. (1995d, Spring). The straight dope: A consideration of substance-induced disorders. *Psynopsis,* p. 14.

Pagliaro, L. A. (1995e). Adolescent depression and suicide: A review and analysis of the current literature. *Canadian Journal of School Psychology, 11,* 191–201.

Pagliaro, L. A., & Foster, R. (1990). Cancer chemotherapy and extortion. *Medical Psychotherapist, 6,* 6–7.

Pagliaro, L. A., Jaglalsingh, L., & Pagliaro, A. M. (1992). Cocaine use and depression. *Canadian Medical Association Journal, 147,* 1636.

Pagliaro, L. A., & Pagliaro, A. M. (1991). Drug induced automatism: Psychological aspects [Abstract]. *Canadian Psychology, 32,* 204.

Pagliaro, L. A., & Pagliaro, A. M. (1992a). Drug induced aggression. *Medical Psychotherapist, 8*(2/3), 9.

Pagliaro, L. A., & Pagliaro, A. M. (1992b). The phenomenon of substance abuse among the elderly. *Journal of Pharmacy Technology, 8,* 65–73.

Pagliaro, L. A., & Pagliaro, A. M. (1993). The phenomenon of abusable psychotropic use among North American youth. *Journal of Clinical Pharmacology, 33,* 676–690.

Pagliaro, L. A., & Pagliaro, A. M. (1995a). Abuse potential of antidepressants: Does it exist? *CNS Drugs, 4,* 247–252.

Pagliaro, L. A., & Pagliaro, A. M. (1995b). Alcoholic cognitive impairment and reliability of eyewitness testimony: A forensic case report. *Medical Psychotherapist, 11*(1), 9–10.

Pagliaro, L. A., & Pagliaro, A. M. (1995c). Drugs as human teratogens. In L. A. Pagliaro & A. M. Pagliaro (Eds.), *Problems in pediatric drug therapy* (3rd ed., pp. 103–243). Hamilton, IL: Drug Intelligence.

Palmer, J. H., & Paisley, P. O. (1991). Student assistance programs: A response to substance abuse. *School Counselor, 38,* 287–293.

Pandina, R. J., & Johnson, V. (1989). Familial drinking history as a predictor of alcohol and drug consumption among adolescent children. *Journal of Studies on Alcohol, 50*(3), 245–253.

Pandina, R. J., & Johnson, V. (1990). Serious alcohol and drug problems among adolescents with a family history of alcoholism. *Journal of Studies on Alcohol, 51*(3), 278–282.

Pandina, R. J., Labouvie, E. W., & Raskin White, H. (1984). Potential contributions of the life span developmental approach to the study of adolescent alcohol and drug use: The Rutgers Health and Human Development Project, a working model. *Journal of Drug Issues, 14*(2), 253–268.

Pandina, R. J., & Raskin White, H. (1981). Patterns of alcohol and drug use of adolescent students and adolescents in treatment. *Journal of Studies on Alcohol, 42*(5), 441–456.

Pandina, R. J., & Schuele, J. A. (1983). Psychosocial correlates of alcohol and drug use of adolescents in treatment. *Journal of Studies on Alcohol, 44*(6), 950–973.

Parkin, A. J., Dunn, J. C., Lee, C., O'Hara, P. F., & Nussbaum, L. (1993). Neuropsychological sequelae of Wernicke's encephalopathy in a 20-year-old woman: Selective impairment of a frontal memory system. *Brain and Cognition, 21,* 1–19.

Paulson, M. J., Coombs, R. H., & Richardson, M. A. (1990). School performance, academic aspirations, and drug use among children and adolescents. *Journal of Drug Education, 20,* 289–303.

Pearson, M. A., Hoyme, H. E., Seaver, L. H., & Rimsza, M. E. (1994). Toluene embryopathy: Delineation of the phenotype and comparison with fetal alcohol syndrome. *Pediatrics, 93,* 211–215.

Peele, S. (1989). What can we expect from treatment of adolescent drug and alcohol abuse? *Pediatrician, 14,* 62–69.

Peele, S., Brodsky, A., & Arnold, M. (1991). *The truth about addiction and recovery: The Life Process Program for outgrowing destructive habits.* New York: Simon and Schuster.

Pelletier, D., & Coutu, D. (1992). Substance abuse and family violence in adolescents. *Canadian Mental Health, 40*(2), 6–12.

Penick, E. C., Nickel, E. J., Cantrell, P. F., Powell, B. J., Read, M. R., & Thomas, M. M. (1990). The emerging concept of dual diagnosis: An overview and implications. In D. F. O'Connell (Ed.), *Managing the dually diagnosed patient: Current issues and clinical approaches* (pp. 1–54). New York: Haworth.

Penick, E. C., Powell, B. J., Othmer, E., Bingham, S. F., Rice, A. S., & Liese, B. S. (1984). Subtyping alcoholics by coexisting psychiatric syndromes: Course, family history, outcome. In D. W. Goodwin, K. T. Van Dusen, & S. A. Mednick (Eds.), *Longitudinal research in alcoholism* (pp. 167–196). Boston, MA: Kluwer-Nijhoff.

Pennbridge, J. N., Freese, T. E., & MacKenzie, R. G. (1992). High-risk behaviors among male street youth in Hollywood, California. AIDS *Education & Prevention,* Suppl., 24–33.

Pentz, M. A., Johnson, A., Dwyer, J. H., MacKinnon, D. M., Hansen, W. B., & Flay, B. R. (1989). A comprehensive community approach to adolescent drug abuse prevention: Effects on cardiovascular disease risk behaviors. *Annals of Medicine, 21,* 219–222.

Perez-Bouchard, L., Johnson, J. L., & Ahrens, A. H. (1993). Attributional style in children of substance abusers. *American Journal of Drug and Alcohol Abuse, 19,* 475–489.

Pernanen, K. (1981). Theoretical aspects of the relationship between alcohol use and crime. In J. J. Collins, Jr. (Ed.), *Drinking and crime* (pp. 1–61). New York: Guilford.

Perrone, J. (1993). Adolescents with cancer: Are they at risk for suicide? *Pediatric Nursing, 19,* 22–25.

Perry, C. L., Grant, M., Ernberg, G., Florenzano, R., Langdon, M. C., Myeni, A. D., Waahlberg, R., Berg, S., Andersson, K., & Fisher, K. J. (1989). WHO collaborative study on alcohol education and young people: Outcomes of a four-country pilot study. *International Journal of the Addictions, 24,* 1145–1171.

Petersen, R. C. (1987). *Drug abuse and drug abuse research. The second triennial report to Congress.* Rockville, MD: U.S. Department of Health and Human Services, National Institute on Drug Abuse.

Pickens, K. (1985). *The young and the volatile: Coping with solvent abuse.* Wellington, NZ: New Zealand Council for Educational Research.

Pieper, M. H., & Pieper, W. J. (1992). It's not tough, it's tender love: Problem teens need compassion that the "tough-love" approach to child-rearing doesn't offer them. *Child Welfare, 71,* 369–377.

Pierce, W. E., Broste, S. K., & Layde, P. M. (1991). Characteristics of alcohol use by school children in a north central Wisconsin county. *Wisconsin Medical Journal, 90,* 520–524.

Pietrantoni, M., & Knuppel, R. A. (1991). Alcohol use in pregnancy. *Clinics in Perinatology, 18,* 93–111.

Pihl, R. O., Peterson, J. B., & Lau, M. A. (1993). A biosocial model of the alcohol-aggression relationship. *Journal of Studies on Alcohol, 11,* 128–139.

Pincus, J. H., & Lewis, D. O. (1991). Episodic violence. *Seminars in Neurology, 11,* 146–154.

Plant, M. L. (1985). Fetal alcohol syndrome: An overview. *Midwifery, 1,* 225–231.

Plessinger, M. A., & Woods, J. R., Jr. (1991). The cardiovascular effects of cocaine use in pregnancy. *Reproductive Toxicology, 5,* 99–113.

Poklik, A. (1984). Decline in abuse of pentazocine/tripelennamine (Ts and blues) associated with the addiction of naloxone to pentazocine tablets. *Drug and Alcohol Dependence, 14,* 135–140.

Poklis, A., Maginn, D., & Barr, J. L. (1987). Drug findings in "driving under the influence of drugs" cases: A problem of illicit drug use. *Drug and Alcohol Dependence, 20,* 57–62.

Polster, M. R., McCarthy, R. A., O'Sullivan, G., Gray, P. A., & Park, G. R. (1993). Midazolam-induced amnesia: Implications for the implicit/explicit memory distinction. *Brain & Cognition, 22,* 244–265.

Ponce, D. E., & Jo, H. S. (1990). Substance abuse and psychiatric disorders: The dilemma of increasing incidence of dual diagnosis in residential treatment centers. *Residential Treatment for Children and Youth, 8*(2), 5–15.

Powers, J. L., Eckenrode, J., & Jaklitsch, B. (1990). Maltreatment among runaway and homeless youth. *Child Abuse & Neglect, 14*(1), 87–98.

Pradhan, S. N. (1984). Phencyclidine (PCP): Some human studies. *Neuroscience & Biobehavioral Reviews, 8,* 493–501.

Prange, M. E., Greenbaum, P. E., Silver, S. E., Friedman, R. M., Kutash, K., & Duchnowski, A. J. (1992). Family functioning and psychopathology among adolescents with severe emotional disturbances. *Journal of Abnormal Child Psychology, 20*(1), 83–102.

Prevention Plus II: Tools for creating and sustaining drug-free communities (1989). Rockville, MD: Department of Health and Human Services, Office for Substance Abuse Prevention (DHHS Publication No. ADM 89-1649).

Pribor, E. F., & Dinwiddie, S. H. (1992). Psychiatric correlates of incest in childhood. *American Journal of Psychiatry, 149,* 52–56.

Program strategies for preventing fetal alcohol syndrome and alcohol-related birth defects. (1987). Rockville, MD: National Institute on Alcohol Abuse and Alcoholism.

Project MATCH (Matching Alcoholism Treatment to Client Heterogeneity): Rationale and methods for a multisite clinical trial matching patients to alcoholism treatment. (1993). *Alcoholism, Clinical & Experimental Research, 17,* 1130–1145.

Pronovost, J., Côté, L., & Ross, C. (1990, March). Epidemiological study of suicidal behaviour among secondary-school students. *Canada's Mental Health,* 9–14.

Pruitt, A. W., Jacobs, E. A., Schydlower, M., Stands, B. O., & Sutton, J. M. (1990). Selection of substance abuse treatment programs. *Pediatrics, 86,* 139–140.

Query, W. T., & Megran, J. (1984). Influence of depression and alcoholism on learning, recall, and recognition. *Journal of Clinical Psychology, 40,* 1097–1100.

Quine, S., & Stephenson, J. A. (1990). Predicting smoking and drinking intentions and behavior of pre-adolescents: The influence of parents, siblings, and peers. *Family Systems Medicine, 8,* 191–200.

Racine, A., Joyce, T., & Anderson, R. (1993). The association between prenatal care and birth weight among women exposed to cocaine in New York City. *Journal of the American Medical Association, 270,* 1581–1586.

Radó, S. (1933). The psychoanalysis of pharmacothymia (drug addiction). *Psychoanalytic Quarterly, 2,* 1–23.

Randall, T. (1992a). Ecstasy-fueled "rave" parties become dances of death for English youths. *Journal of the American Medical Association, 268,* 1505–1506.

Randall, T. (1992b). "Rave" scene, ecstasy use, leap Atlantic. *Journal of the American Medical Association, 268,* 1506.

Ratner, M. S. (Ed.). (1993). *Crack pipe as pimp: An ethnographic investigation of sex-for-crack exchanges.* New York: Lexington.

Rebeta-Burditt, J. (1977). *The cracker factory.* New York: MacMillan.

Reece, R. M. (1990). Unusual manifestations of child abuse. *Pediatric Clinics of North America, 37,* 905–921.

Reid, L. (1992). Alcohol misconceptions. *Nursing Times, 88*(42), 40–42.

Reilly, D. M. (1978). Family factors in the etiology and treatment of youthful drug abuse. *Family Therapy, 2,* 149–171.

Remkes, T. (1993). Saying no—Completely. *Canadian Nurse, 89*(6), 25–28.

Resnick, H. S. (1978). *It starts with people: Experiences in drug abuse prevention* (NIDA Publication No. 79–590). Washington, DC: U.S. Department of Health, Education, and Welfare.

Reulbach, W. (1991). Counseling chemically dependent HIV positive adolescents. *Journal of Chemical Dependency Treatment, 4*(2), 31–43.

Reus, V. I., Weingartner, H., & Post, R. M. (1979). Clinical implications of state-dependent learning. *American Journal of Psychiatry, 136,* 927–931.

Rew, L. (1989). Long-term effects of childhood sexual exploitation. *Issues in Mental Health Nursing, 10,* 229–244.

Rhoades, E. R., Mason, R. D., Eddy, P., Smith, E. M., & Burns, T. R. (1988). The Indian health service approach to alcoholism among American Indians and Alaska Natives. *Public Health Reports, 103,* 621–627.

Rhodes, J. E., & Fischer, K. (1993). Spanning the gender gap: Gender differences in delinquency among inner-city adolescents. *Adolescence, 28,* 879–889.

Rich, A. R., Kirkpatrick-Smith, J., Bonner, R. L., & Jans, F. (1992). Gender differences in the psychosocial correlates of suicidal ideation among adolescents. *Suicide and Listening Behavior, 22,* 364–373.

Richardson, J. L., Dwyer, K., McGuigan, K., Hansen, W. B., Dent, C., Anderson Johnson, C., Sussman, S. Y., Brannon, B., & Flay, B. (1989). Substance use among eighth-grade students who take care of themselves after school. *Pediatrics, 84*(3), 556–566.

Ritter, B. (1989). Abuse of the adolescent. *New York State Journal of Medicine, 89,* 156–158.

Rivas, F., Hernandez, A., & Cantu, J. (1984). Acentric craniofacial cleft in a newborn female prenatally exposed to a high dosage of diazepam. *Teratology, 30,* 179–180.

Rivers, K. O., & Hedrick, D. L. (1992). Language and behavioral concerns for drug-exposed infants and toddlers. *Transdisciplinary Journal, 2*(1), 63–73.

Robbins, E., Frosch, W. A., & Stern, M. (1967). Further observations on untoward reactions to LSD. *American Journal of Psychiatry, 124*(3), 393–395.

Robbins, E., Robbins, L., Frosch, W. A., & Stern, M. (1967). Implications of untoward reactions to hallucinogens. *Bulletin of the New York Academy of Medicine, 43*(11), 985–999.

Robertson, M. J., (1991). Homeless women with children: The role of alcohol and other drug abuse. *American Psychologist, 46,* 1198–1204.

Robin, A. L., & Foster, S. L. (1988). *Negotiating parent adolescent conflict: A behavioral-family systems approach.* New York: Guilford.

Robins, L. N. (1966). *Deviant children grown up: A sociological and psychiatric study of sociopathic personality.* Baltimore, MD: Williams & Wilkins.

Robins, L. N. (1973). *A follow-up of Vietnam drug users* (Interim Final Report, Special Action Office Monograph, Series A, No. 2). Washington, DC: U.S. Government Printing Office.

Robins, L. N. (1974). *The Vietnam drug user returns* (Final Report, Special Action Office Monograph, Series A, No. 2). Washington, DC: U.S. Government Printing Office.

Robins, L. N. (1975). Alcoholism and labelling theory. In W. R. Gove (Ed.), *The labelling of deviance* (pp. 21–33). New York: Wiley.

Robins, L. N. (1977). Surveys of target populations. In L. G. Richards & L. B. Blevens (Eds.), *The epidemiology of drug abuse: Current issues* (NIDA Research Monograph No. 10, pp. 39–48). Rockville, MD: U.S. Department of Health and Human Services, National Institute on Drug Abuse.

Robins, L. N. (1978a). The interaction of setting and predisposition in explaining novel behavior: Drug initiations before, in, and after Vietnam. In D. B. Kandel (Ed.), *Longitudinal research on drug use: Empirical findings and methodological issues* (pp. 179–196). New York: Wiley.

Robins, L. N. (1978b). Sturdy childhood predictors of adult antisocial behavior: Replications from longitudinal studies. *Psychological Medicine, 8,* 611–622.

Robins, L. N., Davis, D. H., & Wish, E. (1977). Detecting predictors of rare events: Demographic, family, and personal deviance as predictors of stages in the progression toward narcotic addiction. In J. S. Strauss, H. M. Babigian, & M. Roff (Eds.), *The origins and course of psychopathology: Methods of longitudinal research* (pp. 379–406). New York: Plenum.

Robins, L. N., Helzer, J. E., & Davis, D. H. (1975). Narcotic use in Southeast Asia and afterward: An interview study of 898 Vietnam returnees. *Archives of General Psychiatry, 23,* 955–961.

Robins, L. N., Hesselbrock, M., Wish, E., & Helzer, J. E. (1978). Polydrug and alcohol use by veterans and nonveterans. In D. A. Smith, S. M. Anderson, M. Buxton, N. Gottlieb, W. Harvey, & T. Chung (Eds.), *A multicultural view of drug abuse: Proceedings of the National Drug Abuse Conference, 1977* (pp. 74–90). Cambridge, MA: Schenkman.

Robins, L. N., & Murphy, G. E. (1967). Drug use in a normal population of young Negro men. *American Journal of Public Health, 57*(9), 1580–1596.

Robins, L. N., & Price, R. K. (1991). Adult disorders predicted by childhood conduct problems: Results from the NIMH epidemiologic catchment area project. *Psychiatry, 54,* 116–132.

Robinson, G. C., Conry, J. L., & Conry, R. F. (1987). Clinical profile and prevalence of fetal alcohol syndrome in an isolated community in British Columbia. *Canadian Medical Association Journal, 137,* 203–207.

Roehrs, T., Merlotti, L., Zorick, F., & Roth, T. (1994). Sedative, memory, and performance effects of hypnotics. *Psychopharmacology, 116,* 130–134.

Rokeach, M. (1970). *Beliefs, attitudes and values: A theory of organization and change.* San Francisco: Jossey-Bass.

Rolf, J., Masten, A. S., Cicchetti, D., Nuechterlein, K. H., & Weintraub, S. (Eds.). (1990). *Risk and protective factors in the development of psychopathology.* New York: Cambridge University Press.

Rolfs, R. T., Goldberg, M., & Sharrar, R. G. (1990). Risk factors for syphilis: Cocaine use and prostitution. *American Journal of Public Health, 80,* 853–857.

Roman, P. M. (1981). Situational factors in the relationship between alcohol and crime. In J. J. Collins, Jr., & M. E. Wolfgang (Eds.), *Drinking and crime: Perspectives on the relationships between alcohol consumption and criminal behavior* (pp. 143–151). New York: Guilford.

Room, R., & Greenfield, T. (1993). Alcoholics Anonymous, other 12-step movements and psychotherapy in the U.S. population, 1990. *Addiction, 88,* 555–562.

Rose, S. M., Peabody, C. G., & Stratigeas, B. (1991a). Responding to hidden abuse: A role for social work in reforming mental health systems. *Social Work, 36,* 408–413.

Rose, S. M., Peabody, C. G., & Stratigeas, B. (1991b). Undetected abuse among intensive case management clients. *Hospital and Community Psychiatry, 42,* 499–503.

Rosenberg, L., Mitchell, A. A., Parsells, J. L., Pashayan, H., Louik, C., & Shapiro, S. (1983). Lack of relation of oral clefts to diazepam use during pregnancy. *New England Journal of Medicine, 309,* 1282–1285.

Rosenberg, N. M., Meert, K. L., Knazik, S. R., Yee, H., & Kauffman, R. E. (1991). Occult cocaine exposure in children. *American Journal of Diseases of Children, 145,* 1430–1432.

Rosenthal, M. S. (1984). Therapeutic communities: A treatment alternative for many but not all. *Journal of Substance Abuse Treatment, 1,* 55–58.

Rosett, H. L., Weiner, L., Lee, A., Zuckerman, B., Dooling, E., & Oppenheimer, E. (1983). Patterns of alcohol consumption and fetal development. *Journal of the American College of Obstetricians and Gynecologists, 61,* 539–546.

Ross, G. R. (1994). *Treating adolescent substance abuse: Understanding the fundamental elements.* Needham Heights, MA: Allyn and Bacon.

Ross, H. E., Glaser, F. B., & Germanson, T. (1988). The prevalence of psychiatric disorders in patients with alcohol and other drug problems. *Archives of General Psychiatry, 45,* 1023–1031.

Rotheram-Borus, M. J., Koopman, C., & Ehrhardt, A. A. (1991). Homeless youths and HIV infection. *American Psychologist, 46,* 1188–1197.

Rotter, J. B. (1954). *Social learning and clinical psychology.* Englewood Cliffs, NJ: Prentice-Hall.

Rotter, J. B. (1966). Generalized expectancies for internal versus external control of reinforcement. *Psychological Monographs: General and Applied, 80*(1), 1–28.

Rotter, J. B., Chance, J. E., & Phares, E. J. (1972). *Applications of a social learning theory of personality.* New York: Holt, Rinehart and Winston.

Rowe, J. (1989). Nursing assessment of children of alcoholics. *Journal of Pediatric Nursing, 4,* 248–254.

Royce, J. E. (1989). *Alcohol problems and alcoholism: A comprehensive survey.* New York: Free Press.

Rubio-Stipec, M., Bird, H., Canino, G., Bravo, M., & Alegria, M. (1991). Children of alcoholic parents in the community. *Journal of Studies on Alcohol, 52,* 78–88.

Rueger, D. B., & Liberman, R. P. (1984). Behavioral family therapy for delinquent and substance-abusing adolescents. *Journal of Drug Issues, 14,* 403–418.

Ruegg, R. (1991). The International Catholic Child Bureau and drug abuse: Contributions to drug abuse prevention by a non-governmental organization concerned with children. *Bulletin on Narcotics, 43,* 9–15.

Runeson, B. S., & Rich, C. L. (1992). Diagnostic comorbidity of mental disorders among young suicides. *International Review of Psychiatry, 4,* 197–203.

Rush, B., & Ekdahl, A. (1990). Recent trends in the development of alcohol and drug treatment services in Ontario. *Journal of Studies on Alcohol, 51,* 514–522.

Rush, C. R., Higgins, S. T., Bickel, W. K., & Hughes, J. R. (1993). Acute behavioral effects of lorazepam and caffeine, alone and in combination, in humans. *Behavioural Pharmacology, 5,* 245–254.

Russell, F. F., & Free, T. A. (1991). Early intervention for infants and toddlers with prenatal drug exposure. *Infants and Young Children, 3,* 78–85.

Russell, M., Czarnecki, D. M., Cowan, R., McPherson, E., & Mudar, P. J. (1991). Measures of maternal alcohol use as predictors of development in early childhood. *Alcoholism, Clinical & Experimental Research, 15,* 991–1000.

Russell, M. J. (1993). *Drug use forecasting quarterly report* (NCJ No. 142454). Washington, DC: U.S. Department of Justice.

Ryan, N. D., & Puig-Antich, J. (1987). Pharmacological treatment of adolescent psychiatric disorders. *Journal of Adolescent Health Care, 80,* 137–142.

Sack, F., & Streeter, A. (1992). *Romance to die for: The startling truth about women, sex and AIDS.* Deerfield Beach, FL: Health Communications.

Sadava, S. W. (1984). Concurrent multiple drug use: Review and implications. *Journal of Drug Issues, 4,* 623–636.

Sadava, S. W. (1987). Interactional theory. In H. T. Blane & K. E. Leonard (Eds.), *Psychological theories of drinking and alcoholism* (pp. 90–130). New York: Guilford.

Samy, M. (1993). Preventing adolescent suicide: The role of the family practitioner. *Canadian Journal of Continuing Medical Education, 5*(1), 59–66.

Sanchis, A., Rosique, D., & Catala, J. (1991). Adverse effects of maternal lorazepam on neonates. *DICP, Annals of Pharmacotherapy, 25,* 1137–1138.

Sarathi, P., Sharan, P., & Saxena, S. (1992). Kerosene abuse by inhalation and ingestion. *American Journal of Psychiatry, 149,* 710.

Sarvela, P. D., & Ford, T. D. (1992). Indicators of substance use among pregnant adolescents in the Mississippi delta. *Journal of School Health, 62,* 175–179.

Sarvela, P. D., Pape, D. J., Odulana, J., & Bajracharya, S. M. (1990). Drinking, drug use, and driving among rural midwestern youth. *Journal of School Health, 60,* 215–219.

Savin-Williams, R. C. (1994). Verbal and physical abuse as stressors in the lives of lesbian, gay male, and bisexual youths: Associations with school problems, running away, substance abuse, prostitution, and suicide. *Journal of Consulting & Clinical Psychology, 62,* 261–269.

Sayette, M. A., Wilson, G. T., & Elias, M. J. (1993). Alcohol and aggression: A social information processing analysis. *Journal of Studies on Alcohol, 54,* 399–407.

Scanlon, J. W. (1991). The neuroteratology of cocaine: Background, theory, and clinical implications. *Reproductive Toxicology, 5,* 89–98.

Schaps, E., & Battistich, V. (1991). Promoting health development through school-based prevention: New approaches. In E. N. Goplerud (Ed.), *Preventing adolescent drug use: From theory to practice* (pp. 127–181). Rockville, MD: U.S. Department of Health and Human Serivces, Office for Substance Abuse Prevention.

Schaps, E., DiBartalo, R. D., Moskowitz, J., Palley, C. S., & Churgin, S. (1981). A review of 127 drug abuse prevention program evaluations. *Journal of Drug Issues, 11,* 17–43.

Schaps, E., Moskowitz, J., Malvin, J. H., & Schaeffer, G. (1986). Evaluation of seven school-based prevention programs: A final report on the Napa Project. *International Journal of the Addictions, 21,* 1081–1112.

Schinke, S. P., Botvin, G. J., & Orlandi, M. A. (1991). Patterns of substance abuse among adolescents. In S. P. Schinke, G. J. Botvin, & M. A. Orlandi (Eds.), *Substance abuse in children and adolescents: Evaluation and intervention* (pp. 1–17). Newbury Park, CA: Sage.

Schinke, S. P., & Gilchrist, L. D. (1985). Preventing substance abuse with children and adolescents. *Journal of Consulting and Clinical Psychology, 53,* 596–602.

Schuckit, M. A., Goodwin, D. A., & Winokur, G. (1972). A study of alcoholism in half siblings. *American Journal of Psychiatry, 128,* 1132–1136.

Schwarcz, S. K., Bolan, G. A., Fullilove, M., McCright, J., Fullilove, R., Kohn, R., & Rolfs, R. T. (1992). Crack cocaine and the exchange of sex for money or drugs: Risk factors for gonorrhea among black adolescents in San Francisco. *Sexually Transmitted Diseases, 19,* 7–13.

Schwartz, C. E., Dorer, D. J., Beardslee, W. R., Lavori, P. W., & Keller, M. B. (1990). Maternal expressed emotion and parental affective disorder: Risk for childhood depressive disorder, substance abuse, or conduct disorder. *Journal of Psychiatric Research, 24,* 231–250.

Schwartz, I. M. (1989). Hospitalization of adolescents for psychiatric and substance abuse treatment. *Journal of Adolescent Health Care, 10,* 473–478.

Schwartz, R. H. (1987). Marijuana: An overview. *Pediatric Clinics of North America, 34,* 305–317.

Schwartz, R. H., Hoffmann, N. G., & Jones, R. (1987). Behavioral, psychosocial, and academic correlates of marijuana usage in adolescence. *Clinical Pediatrics, 26,* 264–270.

Schwartz, R. H., Peary, P., & Mistretta, D. (1986). Intoxication of young children with marijuana: A form of amusement for "pot"-smoking teenage girls. *American Journal of Diseases of Children, 140,* 326.

Schwartzberg, A. Z. (1992). The impact of divorce on adolescents. *Hospital and Community Psychiatry, 43,* 634–637.

Schydlower, M., & Perrin, J. (1993). Prevention of fetal alcohol syndrome [Letter to the editor]. *Pediatrics, 92,* 739.

Segal, B. (1974). Locus of control and drug and alcohol use in college students. *Journal of Alcohol and Drug Education, 19*(3), 1–5.

Segal, B. (1978). Sensation seeking and drug use. In D. J. Lettieri (Ed.), *Drugs and suicide: When other coping strategies fail* (pp. 149–166). Beverly Hills, CA: Sage.

Segal, B. (1983). Drugs and youth: A review of the problem. *International Journal of the Addictions, 18,* 429–433.

Segal, B. (1985–86). Conformatory analyses of reasons for experiencing psychoactive drugs during adolescence. *International Journal of the Addictions, 20,* 1649–1662.

Segal, B. (1990). Comparisons: Alaska and the lower-48 states. In *Drug-taking behavior among school-aged youth: The Alaska experience and comparisons with lower-48 states* (pp. 101–111). Binghamton, NY: Haworth.

Segal, B., Huba, G. J., & Singer, J. L. (1980). Reasons for drug and alcohol use by college students. *International Journal of the Addictions, 15,* 489–498.

Segal, R., & Sisson, B. V. (1985). Medical complications associated with alcohol use and the assessment of risk of physical damage. In T. E. Bratter & G. G. Forrest (Eds), *Alcoholism and substance abuse: Strategies for clinical intervention* (pp. 137–175). New York: Free Press.

Seidman, D. S., Ever-Hadani, P., & Gale, R. (1990). Effect of maternal smoking and age on congenital anomalies. *Obstetrics and Gynecology, 76,* 1046–1050.

Seixas, F. A. (1982a). The course of alcoholism. In N. J. Estes & M. E. Heinemann (Eds.), *Alcoholism: Development, consequences, and interventions* (2nd ed., pp. 68–76). St. Louis, MO: Mosby.

Seixas, F. A. (1982b). Criteria for the diagnosis of alcoholism. In N. J. Estes & M. E. Heinemann (Eds.), *Alcoholism: Development, consequences, and interventions* (2nd ed., pp. 49–67). St. Louis, MO: Mosby.

Selected tobacco-use behaviors and dietary patterns among high school students—United States, 1991. (1992). *Morbidity and Mortality Weekly Report, 41,* 417–421.

Seligman, M. E. P. (1975). *Helplessness: On depression, development and death.* San Francisco: Freeman.

Senay, E. C., Kozel, N. J., & Gonzalez, J. P. (1991). Drug abuse and public health: A global perspective. *Drugs Safety, 6*(Suppl. 1), 1–65.

Seng, M. J. (1989). Child sexual abuse and adolescent prostitution: A comparative analysis. *Adolescence, 24,* 665–675.

Sexter, J., Sullivan, A., Wapner, S., & Denmark, R. (1984). Substance abuse: Assessment of the outcome of activities clusters in school-based prevention. *International Journal of the Addictions, 19,* 79–92.

Shaffer, D., Gould, M., & Hicks, R. C. (1994). Worsening suicide rate in black teenagers. *American Journal of Psychiatry, 151,* 1810–1812.

Shaffer, H. J. (1987). The epistemology of "addictive disease": The Lincoln-Douglas debate. *Journal of Substance Abuse Treatment, 4,* 103–113.

Shanks, J. (1990). Alcohol and youth. *World Health Forum, 11,* 235–241.

Shaywitz, B. A., & Shaywitz, S. E. (1991). Comorbidity: A critical issue in attention deficit disorder. *Journal of Child Neurology, 6*(Suppl.), S13–S22.

Shedler, J., & Block, J. (1990). Adolescent drug use and psychological health: A longitudinal inquiry. *American Psychologist, 45,* 612–630.

Sheley, J. F., McGee, Z. T., & Wright, J. D. (1992). Gun-related violence in and around inner-city schools. *American Journal of Diseases of Children, 146,* 677–682.

Sher, K. J. (1987). Stress response dampening. In H. T. Blane & K. E. Leonard (Eds.), *Psychological theories of drinking and alcoholism* (pp. 227–271). New York: Guilford.

Sher, K. J., & Levenson, R. W. (1982). Risk for alcoholism and individual differences in the stress-response-dampening effect of alcohol. *Journal of Abnormal Psychology, 91*(5), 350–367.

Sherman, D. (1992). The neglected health care needs of street youth. *Public Health Reports, 107,* 433–440.

Shiono, P. H., Klebanoff, M. A., & Berendes, H. W. (1986). Congenital malformations and maternal smoking during pregnancy. *Teratology, 34,* 65–71.

Shiono, P. H., & Mills, J. L. (1984). Oral clefts and diazepam use during pregnancy. *New England Journal of Medicine, 311,* 919–920.

Shoemaker, F. W. (1993). Prevention of fetal alcohol syndrome [Letter to the editor]. *Pediatrics, 92,* 738–739.

Shontz, F. C. (1993). A personological integration of chemical dependence and physical disability. In A. W. Heinemann (Ed.), *Substance abuse and physical disability* (pp. 21–39). Binghamton, NY: Haworth.

Shontz, F. C., & Spotts, J. V. (1986). Who are the drug users? *Drugs & Society, 1*(1), 51–74.

Siegel, L. (Ed.). (1988) AIDS *and substance abuse.* New York: Harrington Park.

Silberstein, C., Galanter, M., Marmor, M., Lifshutz, H., Krasinski, K., & Franco, H. (1994). HIV-1 among inner city dually diagnosed inpatients. *American Journal of Drug & Alcohol Abuse, 20,* 101–113.

Simpson, H. M., Mayhew, D. R., & Warren, R. A. (1982). Epidemiology of road accidents involving young adults: Alcohol, drugs and other factors. *Drug & Alcohol Dependence, 10*(1), 35–63.

Singer, M. I., & White, W. J. (1991). Addressing substance abuse problems among psychiatrically hospitalized adolescents. *Journal of Adolescent Chemical Dependency, 2*(1), 13–27.

Single, E. W. (1988). The availability theory of alcohol-related problems. In C. D. Chaudron & D. A. Wilkinson (Eds.), *Theories on alcoholism* (pp. 325–351). Toronto, ON: Addiction Research Foundation.

Sipe, J. W. (1984). *Youth and* AA. Center City, MN: Hazelden.

Slaby, A. A. (1991). Dual diagnosis: Fact or fiction? In M. S. Gold, & A. E. Slaby (Eds.), *Dual diagnosis in substance abuse* (pp. 3–28). New York: Dekker.

Sloan, E. P., Zalenski, R. J., Smith, R. F., Sheaff, C. M., Chen, E. H., Keys, N. I., Crescenzo, M., Barrett, J. A., & Berman, E. (1989). Toxicology screening in urban trauma patients: Drug prevalence and its relationship to trauma severity and management. *Journal of Trauma, 29,* 1647–1653.

Slutsker, L. (1992). Risks associated with cocaine use during pregnancy. *Obstetrics & Gynecology, 79,* 778–789.

Smart, L. S., Chibucos, T. R., & Didier, L. A. (1990). Adolescent substance use and perceived family functioning. *Journal of Family Issues, 11*(2), 208–227.

Smart, R. G. (1986). Solvent use in North America: Aspects of epidemiology, prevention and treatment. *Journal of Psychoactive Drugs, 18,* 87–96.

Smart, R. G., & Adlaf, E. M. (1991). Substance use and problems among Toronto street youth. *British Journal of Addiction, 86,* 999–1010.

Smart, R. G., Adlaf, E. M., Porterfield, K. M., & Canale, M. D. (1990). *Drugs, youth and the street.* Toronto, ON: Addiction Research Foundation.

Smart, R. G., Adlaf, E. M., & Walsh, G. W. (1992). Adolescent drug sellers: Trends, characteristics and profiles. *British Journal of Addiction, 87,* 1561–1570.

Smart, R. G., & Murray, G. F. (1985). Narcotic drug abuse in 152 countries: Social and economic conditions as predictors. *International Journal of the Addictions, 20,* 737–749.

Smiley, A., Moskowitz, H. M., & Ziedman, K. (1985). Effects of drugs on driving: Driving simulator tests of secobarbital, diazepam, marijuana, and alcohol. In *Clinical and behavioral pharmacology research report* (DHHS Publication No. ADM 85-1386, pp. 1–21). Rockville, MD: Department of Health and Human Services.

Smith, G. H. (1993). Intervention strategies for children vulnerable for school failure due to exposure to drugs and alcohol. *International Journal of the Addictions, 28,* 1435–1470.

Smith, G. M. (1977). *Correlates of personality and drug use—1.* (RAUS Cluster Review No. 3). Rockville, MD: U.S. Department of Health and Human Services, National Institute on Drug Abuse.

Smith, G. M. (1980). Perceived effects of substance use: A general theory. In D. J. Lettieri, M. Sayers, & H. Wallenstein Pearson (Eds.), *Theories of drug abuse: Selected contemporary perspectives* (NIDA Research Monograph No. 30, pp. 50–58). Rockville, MD: U.S. Department of Health and Human Services, National Institute on Drug Abuse.

Smith, G. M., & Fogg, C. P. (1977). Psychological antecedents of teenage drug use. In R. G. Simmons (Ed.), *Research in community and mental health: An annual compilation of research* (Vol. 1, pp. 87–102). Greenwich, CT: JAI.

Smith, G. M., & Fogg, C. P. (1978). Psychological predictors of early use, late use, and nonuse of marihuana among teenage students. In D. B. Kandel (Ed.), *Longitudinal research on drug use: Empirical findings and methodological issues* (pp. 101–113). New York: Wiley.

Smith, G. M., & Fogg, C. P. (1979). Psychological antecedents of teen-age drug use. *Research in Community and Mental Health, 1,* 87–102.

Smith, J D., Tracy, J. I., & Murray, M. J. (1993). Depression and category learning. *Journal of Experimental Psychology, 122,* 331–346.

Smitherman, C. H. (1994). The lasting impact of fetal alcohol syndrome and fetal alcohol effect on children and adolescents. *Journal of Pediatric Health Care, 8,* 121–126.

Smoking-attributable mortality and years of potential life lost—United States, 1988. (1991). *Morbidity and Mortality Weekly Report, 40,* 62–63, 69–71.

Smoking control: Summary of the problem. (1983, September–October). *Public Health Reports,* Suppl., 107–116.

Snodgrass, S. R. (1994). Cocaine babies: A result of multiple teratogenic influences. *Journal of Child Neurology, 9,* 227–233.

Sobell, M. B., & Sobell, L. C. (1972). *Individualized behavior therapy for alcoholics: Rationale, procedures, preliminary results and appendix* (California Mental Health Research Monograph No. 13). Sacramento, CA: Bureau of Research, California Department of Mental Hygiene.

Sokol, R. J., & Clarren, S. K. (1989). Guidelines for use of terminology describing the impact of prenatal alcohol on the offspring. *Alcoholism, Clinical & Experimental Research, 13,* 597–598.

Solowij, N., Michie, P. T., & Fox, A. M. (1991). Effects of long-term cannabis use on selective attention: An event-related potential study. *Pharmacology, Biochemistry & Behavior, 40,* 683–688.

Soueif, M. I., Darweesh, Z. A., & Taha, H. S. (1985). The non-medical use of prescription psychotropic drugs by school boys in greater Cairo. *Drug and Alcohol Dependence, 15,* 193–201.

Spear, L. P. (1993). Missing pieces of the puzzle complicate conclusions about cocaine's neurobehavioral toxicity in clinical populations: Importance of animal models. *Neurotoxicology and Teratology, 15,* 307–309.

Speck, D. W., & Santo, Y. (1981). Prevalence of interactive multiple substance abuse among youth in drug treatment. In A. J. Schecter (Ed.), *Drug dependence and alcoholism: Social and behavioral issues* (pp. 747–756). New York: Plenum.

Spencer, C. (1985). Tradition, cultural patterns and drug availability as predictors of youthful drug abuse: A comparison of Malaysia with post-revolutionary Iran. *Journal of Psychoactive Drugs, 17,* 19–24.

Spiegler, D. L., & Harford, T. C. (1987). Addictive behaviors among youth. In T. D. Nirenberg & S. A. Maisto (Eds.), *Developments in the assessment and treatment of addictive behaviors* (pp. 305–318). Norwood, NJ: Ablex.

Spindler, G. (1952). Personality and peyotism in Menomini Indian occulturation. *Psychiatry, 15,* 151–159.

Spohr, H. L., & Steinhausen, H. C. (1984). The course of alcoholic embryopathy. *Monatsschrift für Kinderheilkunde, 132,* 844–849.

Spohr, H. L., Wilms, J., & Steinhausen, H. C. (1993). Prenatal alcohol exposure and long-term developmental consequences. *Lancet, 34,* 907–910.

Spotts, J. V., & Shontz, F. C. (1980a). *Cocaine users: A representative case approach.* New York: Free.

Spotts, J. V., & Shontz, F. C. (1980b). A life theme theory of chronic drug abuse. In D. J. Lettieri, M. Sayers, & H. Wallenstein Pearson (Eds.), *Theories of drug abuse: Selected contemporary perspectives* (NIDA Research Monograph No. 30, pp. 59–70). Rockville, MD: U.S. Department of Health and Human Services, National Institute on Drug Abuse.

Spotts, J. V., & Shontz, F. C. (1982). Ego development, dragon fights, and chronic drug abusers. *International Journal of the Addictions, 17,* 945–976.

Spotts, J. V., & Shontz, F. C. (1984a). Correlates of sensation seeking in heavy, chronic drug users. *Perceptual Motor Skills, 58,* 427–435.

Spotts, J. V., & Shontz, F. C. (1984b). Drugs and personality: Extroversion-introversion. *Journal of Clinical Psychology, 40,* 624–628.

Spotts, J. V., & Shontz, F. C. (1984c). Drug induced ego states: 1. Cocaine: Phenomenology and implications. *International Journal of the Addictions, 19,* 119–151.

Spotts, J. V., & Shontz, F. C. (1984d). The phenomenological structure of drug induced ego states: 2. Barbiturates and sedative-hypnotics: Phenomenology and implications. *International Journal of the Addictions, 19,* 295–326.

Spotts, J. V., & Shontz, F. C. (1985). A theory of adolescent substance abuse. In J. S. Brook, D. J. Lettieri, D. W. Brook, & B. Stimmel (Eds.), *Alcohol and substance abuse in adolescence* (pp. 117–138). New York: Haworth.

Spotts, J. V., & Shontz, F. C. (1986). Drugs and personality: Dependence of findings on method. *American Journal of Drug and Alcohol Abuse, 12*(4), 355–382.

Spunt, B., Goldstein, P., Brownstein, H., & Fendrich, M. (1994). The role of marijuana in homicide. *International Journal of the Addictions, 29,* 195–213.

Stafford, J. R., Jr., Rosen, T. S., Zaider, M., & Merriam, J. C. (1994). Prenatal cocaine exposure and the development of the human eye. *Ophthalmology, 101,* 301–308.

Stall, R. (1988). The prevention of HIV infection associated with drug and alcohol use during sexual activity. In L. Siegel (Ed.), *AIDS and substance abuse* (pp. 73–88). New York: Harrington Park.

Stanton, B., & Galbraith, J. (1994). Drug trafficking among African-American early adolescents: Prevalence, consequences, and associated behaviors and beliefs. *Pediatrics, 93,* 1039–1043.

Stanton, M. D. (1977). The addict as savior: Heroin, death, and the family. *Family Process, 16*(2), 191–197.

Stanton, M. D. (1978a). Forum: Family therapy for the drug user: Conceptual and practical considerations. *Drug Forum, 6,* 203–205.

Stanton, M. D. (1978b). Some outcome results and aspects of structural family therapy with drug addicts. In D. A. Smith, S. M. Anderson, M. Buxton, N. Gottlieb, W. Harvey, & T. Chung (Eds.), *A multicultural view of drug abuse: Proceedings of the National Drug Abuse Conference, 1977* (pp. 378–388). Cambridge, MA: Schenkman.

Stanton, M. D. (1978c). The family and drug misuse: A bibliography. *American Journal of Drug and Alcohol Abuse, 5*(2), 151–170.

Stanton, M. D. (1979a). Drugs and the family. *Marriage and Family Review, 2*(1), 1–10.

Stanton, M. D. (1979b). Family treatment approaches to drug abuse problems: A review. *Family Process, 18*(3), 251–280.

Stanton, M. D. (1979c). The client as family member: Aspects of continuing treatment. In B. S. Brown (Ed.), *Addicts and aftercare: Community integration of the former drug user* (pp. 81–102). Beverly Hills, CA: Sage.

Stanton, M. D. (1980a). Aspects of the family and drug abuse. In B. G. Ellis (Ed.), *Drug abuse from the family perspective: Coping is a family affair.* Rockville, MD: U.S. Department of Health and Human Services, National Institute on Drug Abuse.

Stanton, M. D. (1980b). Some overlooked aspects of the family and drug abuse. In B. G. Ellis (Ed.), *Drug abuse from the family perspective.* Rockville, MD: U.S. Department of Health and Human Services, National Institute on Drug Abuse.

Stanton, M. D. (1981). An integrated structural/strategic approach to family therapy. *Journal of Marital and Family Therapy, 7,* 427–438.

Stanton, M. D. (1985). The family and drug abuse: Concepts and rationale. In T. E. Bratter & G. G. Forrest (Eds.), *Alcoholism and substance abuse: Strategies for clinical intervention* (pp. 398–430). New York: Free Press.

Stanton, M. D. (1988). Coursework and self-study in the family treatment of alcohol and drug abuse: Expanding Heath and Atkinson's curriculum. *Journal of Marital and Family Therapy, 14,* 419–427.

Stanton, M. D., & Coleman, S. B. (1980). The participatory aspects of indirect self-destructive behavior: The addict family as a model. In N. L. Farberow (Ed.), *The many faces of suicide: Indirect self-destructive behavior* (pp. 187–203). New York: McGraw-Hill.

Stanton, M. D., & Todd, T. C. (1982a). *The family therapy of drug abuse and addiction.* New York: Guilford.

Stanton, M. D., & Todd, T. C. (1982b). The therapy model. In M. D. Stanton & T. C. Todd (Eds.), *The family therapy of drug abuse and addiction* (pp. 109–153). New York: Guilford.

Stanton, M. D., Todd, T. C., Heard, D. B., Kirschner, S., Kleiman, J. I., Mowatt, D. T., Riley, P., Scott, S. M., & van Deusen, J. M. (1978). Heroin addiction as a family phenomenon: A new conceptual model. *American Journal of Drug and Alcohol Abuse, 5*(2), 125–150.

Stanton, M. P. (1990). *Our children are dying: Recognizing the dangers and knowing what to do.* Buffalo, NY: Prometheus Books.

Steinglass, P. (1975). The simulated drinking gang: An experimental model for the study of a systems approach to alcoholism. I. Description of the model. *Journal of Nervous and Mental Diseases, 161,* 100–109.

Steinglass, P. (1979). Family therapy with alcoholics: A review. In E. Kaufman & P. Kaufmann (Eds.), *Family therapy of drug and alcohol abuse* (pp. 147–186). New York: Gardner.

Steinglass, P. (1980). A life history model of the alcoholic family. *Family Process, 19,* 211–225.

Steinglass, P., Bennett, L. A., Wolin, S. J., & Reiss, D. (1987). *The alcoholic family.* New York: Basic Books.

Steinglass, P., Davis, D. I., & Berenson, D. (1977). Observations of conjointly hospitalized "alcoholic couples" during sobriety and intoxication: Implications for theory and therapy. *Family Process, 16,* 1–16.

Steinglass, P., Weiner, S., & Mendelson, J. H. (1971a). Interactional issues as determinants of alcoholism. *American Journal of Psychiatry, 128*(3), 275–280.

Steinglass, P., Weiner, S., & Mendelson, J. H. (1971b). A system approach to alcoholism: A model and its clinical application. *Archives of General Psychiatry, 24*(5), 401–408.

Steinhausen, H.-C., Willms, J., & Spohr, H.-L. (1993). Long-term psychopathological and cognitive outcome of children with fetal alcohol syndrome. *Journal of the American Academy of Child and Adolescent Psychiatry, 32,* 990–994.

Stevens, J. J., Freeman, D. H., Mott, L. A., Youells, F. E., & Linsey, S. C. (1993). Smokeless tobacco use among children: The New Hampshire study. *American Journal of Preventive Medicine, 9,* 160–167.

Stiffman, A. R. (1989). Physical and sexual abuse in runaway youths. *Child Abuse & Neglect, 13,* 417–426.

Stone, R. (1992). Bad news on "second hand" smoke. *Science, 257,* 607.

Stowell, R. J. A. (1991). Dual diagnosis issues. *Psychiatric Annals, 21,* 98–104.

Stowell, R. J. A., & Estroff, T. W. (1992). Psychiatric disorders in substance-abusing adolescent inpatients: A pilot study. *Journal of the American Academy of Child and Adolescent Psychiatry, 31,* 1036–1040.

Straus, M. A., & Kantor, G. K. (1994). Corporal punishment of adolescents by parents: A risk factor in the epidemiology of depression, suicide, alcohol abuse, child abuse, and wife beating. *Adolescence, 29,* 543–561.

Straus, M. B. (1994). *Violence in the lives of adolescents.* New York: Norton.

Streissguth, A. P., Aase, J. M., Clarren, S. K., Randels, S. P., LaDue, R. H., & Smith, R. A. (1991). Fetal alcohol syndrome in adolescents and adults. *Journal of the American Medical Association, 265,* 1961–1967.

Streissguth, A. P., Barr, H. M., Olson, H. C., Sampson, P. D., Bookstein, F. L., & Burgess, D. M. (1994). Drinking during pregnancy decreases word attack and arithmetic scores on standardized tests: Adolescent data from a population-based prospective study. *Alcoholism, Clinical & Experimental Research, 18,* 248–254.

Streissguth, A. P., Barr, H. M., & Sampson, P. D. (1990). Moderate prenatal alcohol exposure: Effects on child IQ and learning problems at age $7^{1}/_{2}$ years. *Alcoholism, Clinical and Experimental Research, 14,* 662–669.

Streissguth, A. P., Barr, H. M., Sampson, P. D., & Bookstein, F. L. (1994). Prenatal alcohol and offspring development: The first fourteen years. *Drug & Alcohol Dependence, 36*(2), 89–99.

Streissguth, A. P., Barr, H. M., Sampson, P. D., Parrish-Johnson, J. C., Kirchner, G. L., & Martin, D. C. (1986). Attention, distraction and reaction time at age 7 years and prenatal alcohol exposure. *Neurobehavioral Toxicology and Teratology, 8,* 717–725.

Streissguth, A. P., Clarren, S. K., & Jones, K. L. (1985). Natural history of the fetal alcohol syndrome: A 10-year followup of eleven patients. *Lancet, 2* (8446), 85–91.

Streissguth, A. P., Randels, S. P., & Smith, D. F. (1992). Fetal alcohol syndrome [Reply to letter to the editor]. *Journal of the American Academy of Child and Adolescent Psychiatry, 31,* 563–564.

Streissguth, A. P., Sampson, P. D., Barr, H. M., Bookstein, F. L., & Olson, H. C. (1994). The effects of prenatal exposure to alcohol and tobacco: Contributions from the Seattle longitudinal prospective study and implications for public policy. In H. L. Needleman & D. Bellinger (Eds.), *Prenatal exposure to toxicants: Developmental consequences* (pp. 148–183). Baltimore, MD: John Hopkins University Press.

Streissguth, A. P., Sampson, P. D., Olson, H. C., Bookstein, F. L., Barr, H. M., Scott, M., Feldman, J., & Mirsky, A. F. (1994). Maternal drinking during pregnancy: Attention and short-term memory in 14-year-old offspring: A longitudinal prospective study. *Alcoholism, Clinical & Experimental Research, 18,* 202–218.

Substance abuse: Frequent alcohol consumption among women of childbearing age. (1994). *Weekly Epidemiological Record, 69,* 180–182.

Suchman, E. A. (1968). The "hang-loose" ethic and the spirit of drug use. *Journal of Health and Social Behavior, 9,* 146–155.

Suh, E. K., & Abel, E. M. (1990). The impact of spousal violence on the children of the abused. *Journal of Independent Social Work, 4,* 27–34.

Sullivan, A. P. L. (1986). Measuring and interpreting school-based prevention outcomes: The New York City model. *Journal of Drug Education, 16,* 181–190.

Survey finds increased adolescent drug use. (1995, Winter). NIDA *Invest,* pp. 1–8.

Swadi, H. (1992). Drug abuse in children and adolescents: An update. *Archives of Disease in Childhood, 67,* 1245–1246.

Swan, N. (1995a). Marijuana, other drug use among teens continues to rise. *National Institute on Drug Abuse Notes, 10*(2), 8–9.

Swan, N. (1995b). NIDA *refocuses its research on drug-related violence* (NIH Publication No. 95-3478). Rockville, MD: U.S. Department of Health and Human Services.

Swanson, J., Cantwell, D., Lerner, M., McBurnett, K., & Hanna, G. (1991). Effects of stimulant medication on learning in children with ADHD. *Journal of Learning Disabilities, 24,* 219–230.

Swartz, J. (1991a). *Implications of drug use forecasting data for TASC programs: Female arrestees* (NCJ No. 129671, pp. 1–32). Washington, DC: U.S. Department of Justice, Bureau of Justice Assistance.

Swartz, J. (1991b). *Report III: Implications of the drug use forecasting data for TASC programs.* Washington, DC: U.S. Department of Justice, Bureau of Justice Assistance.

Sweet, R. W., Jr. (1991). OJJDP *and boys and girls clubs of America: Public housing and high-risk youth* (NCJ No. 128412). Washington, DC: U.S. Department of Justice.

Swerhun, P., & LeBreton, S. (1983). Chronic solvent abuse: Can you help? *Canadian Nurse, 79*(1), 40–50.

Swofford, A. (1991). A risk profile comparison of homeless youth involved in prostitution and homeless youth not involved. *Journal of Adolescent Health, 12,* 545–548.

Szapocznik, J., Kurtines, W., Santisteban, D. A., & Rio, A. T. (1990). Interplay of advances between theory, research, and application in treatment interventions aimed at behavior problem children and adolescents. *Journal of Consulting and Clinical Psychology, 58,* 696–703.

Tabor, B. L., Smith-Wallace, T., & Yonekura, M. L. (1990). Perinatal outcome associated with PCP versus cocaine use. *American Journal of Drug and Alcohol Abuse, 16,* 337–348.

Tardiff, K., Marzuk, P. M., Leon, A. C., Hirsch, C. S., Stajic, M., Portera, L., & Hartwell, N. (1994). Homicide in New York City: Cocaine use and firearms. *Journal of the American Medical Association, 272,* 43–46.

Tarr, J. E., & Macklin, M. (1987). Cocaine. *Pediatric Clinics of North America, 34,* 319–331.

Tarter, R. E. (1982). Psychosocial history, minimal brain dysfunction and differential drinking patterns of male alcoholics. *Journal of Clinical Psychology, 38,* 867–873.

Tarter, R. E. (1983). The causes of alcoholism: A biopsychological analysis. In E. Gottheil, K. A. Druley, T. E. Skoloda, & H. M. Waxman (Eds.), *Etiologic aspects of alcohol and drug abuse* (pp. 173–201). Springfield, IL: Thomas.

Tarter, R. E. (1988). Are there inherited behavioral traits which predispose to substance abuse? [Review]. *Journal of Consulting and Clinical Psychology, 56,* 189–196.

Tarter, R. E. (1990). Evaluation and treatment of adolescent substance abuse: A decision tree method. *American Journal of Drug & Alcohol Abuse, 16*(1–2), 1–46.

Tarter, R. E., Alterman, A. I., & Edwards, K. L. (1985). Vulnerability to alcoholism in men: A behavior-genetic perspective. *Journal of Studies on Alcohol, 46*(4), 329–356.

Tarter, R. E., Alterman, A. I., & Edwards, K. L. (1988). Neurobehavioral theory of alcoholism etiology. In C. D. Chaudron & D. A. Wilkinson (Eds.), *Theories on alcoholism* (pp. 73–102). Toronto, ON: Addiction Research Foundation.

Tarter, R. E., & Edwards, K. L. (1988). Psychological factors associated with the risk for alcoholism. *Alcoholism, Clinical & Experimental Research, 12,* 471–480.

Tarter, R. E., Hegedus, A. M., & Gavaler, J. S. (1985). Hyperactivity in sons of alcoholics. *Journal of Studies on Alcohol, 46,* 259–261.

Tarter, R. E., Kabene, M., Escallier, E. A., Laird, S. B., & Jacob, T. (1990). Temperament deviation and risk for alcoholism. *Alcoholism, Clinical & Experimental Research, 14,* 380–382.

Tarter, R. E., Laird, S. B., Kabene, M., Bukstein, O., & Kaminer, Y. (1990). Drug abuse severity in adolescents is associated with magnitude of deviation in temperament traits. *British Journal of Addiction, 85,* 1501–1504.

Tarter, R. E., McBride, H., Buonpane, N., & Schneider, D. U. (1977). Differentiation of alcoholics. Childhood history of minimal brain dysfunction, family history, and drinking pattern. *Archives of General Psychiatry, 34,* 761–768.

Tarter, R. E., & Mezzich, A. C. (1992). Ontogeny of substance abuse: Perspectives and findings. In M. Glantz & R. Pickens (Eds.), *Vulnerability to drug abuse* (pp. 149–177). Washington, DC: American Psychological Association.

Tata, P. R., Rollings, J., Collins, M., Pickering, A., & Jacobson, R. R. (1994). Lack of cognitive recovery following withdrawal from long-term benzodiazepine use. *Psychological Medicine, 24,* 203–213.

Taylor, P. L., & Albright, W. J., Jr. (1981). Nondrug criminal behavior and heroin use. *International Journal of the Addictions, 16,* 683–696.

Taylor, W. A., & Slaby, A. E. (1992). Acute treatment of alcohol and cocaine emergencies. In M. Galanter (Ed.), *Recent developments in alcoholism: Vol. 10. Alcohol and cocaine: Similarities and differences* (pp. 179–191). New York: Plenum.

Tennes, K., Avitable, N., Blackard, C., Boyles, C., Hassoun, B., Holmes, L., & Kreye, M. (1985). *Marijuana: Prenatal and postnatal exposure in the human* (NIDA Research Monograph No. 59). Rockville, MD: U.S. Department of Health and Human Services, National Institute on Drug Abuse.

Thibault, C. (1992). Preventing suicide in young people: Above all it's a matter of life. *Canada's Mental Health, 40*(3), 2–7.

Thomas, C. L. (Ed.). (1993). *Taber's cyclopedic medical dictionary.* Philadelphia: Davis.

Thompson, H. A. (1989). Consent requirements for treatment of minors. *Texas Medicine, 85,* 56–58.

Tobacco, alcohol, and other drug use among high school students—United States, 1991. (1992). *Morbidity and Mortality Weekly Report, 41,* 698–703.

Tobler, N. S. (1986). Meta-analysis of 143 adolescent drug prevention programs: Quantitative outcome results of program participants compared to a control or comparison group. *Journal of Drug Issues, 16,* 537–567.

Tobler, N. S. (1992). Drug prevention programs can work: Research findings. *Journal of Addictive Diseases, 11,* 1–28.

Tomori, M. (1994). Personality characteristics of adolescents with alcoholic parents. *Adolescence, 29,* 949–959.

Tonkin. R. S. (1987). Adolescent risk-taking behavior. *Journal of Adolescent Health Care, 8,* 213–220.

Tonnesen, P., Norregaard, J., Simonsen, K., & Sawe, U. (1991). A double-blind trial of a 16-hour transdermal nicotine patch in smoking cessation. *New England Journal of Medicine, 325,* 311–315.

Torabi, M. R., Bailey, W. J., & Majd-Jabbari, M. (1993). Cigarette smoking as a predictor of alcohol and other drug use by children and adolescents: Evidence of the "gateway drug effect." *Journal of School Health, 63,* 302–306.

Tranmer, J. E. (1985). Disposition of ethanol in maternal venous blood and the amniotic fluid. *Journal of Obstetric, Gynecologic, and Neonatal Nursing, 14,* 484–490.

Treiman, D. M. (1986). Epilepsy and violence: Medical and legal issues. *Epilepsia, 27*(Suppl. 2), S77–S104.

Trends in drug and alcohol use by youth in the U.S.A. (1993). *Statistical Bulletin, 74*(3), 19–27.

Trice, H. (1983). Alcoholics Anonymous. In D. A. Ward (Ed.), *Alcoholism: Introduction to theory and treatment* (2nd ed.). Dubuque, IA: Kendall/Hunt.

Triffleman, E. G., Marmar, C. R., Delucchi, K. L., & Ronfeldt, H. (1995). Childhood trauma and posttraumatic stress disorder in substance abuse inpatients. *Journal of Nervous & Mental Disease, 183,* 172–176.

Trimble, M. R., & Thompson, P. J. (1983). Anticonvulsant drugs, cognitive function, and behavior. *Epilepsia, 24*(Suppl. 1), S55–S63.

Tuakli, N., Smith, M. A., & Heaton, C. (1990). Smoking in adolescence: Methods for health education and smoking cessation. *Journal of Family Practice, 31,* 369–374.

Tueth, M. J. (1993). High incidence of psychosis in cocaine intoxication and preventing violence in the ED. *American Journal of Emergency Medicine, 11,* 676.

Tunving, K. (1987). Psychiatric aspects of cannabis use in adolescents and young adults. *Pediatrician, 14,* 1–2.

Turner, J. (1993). Incidental information processing: Effects of mood, sex and caffeine. *International Journal of Neuroscience, 72*(1/2), 1–14.

Tutton, C. S., & Crayton, J. W. (1993). Current pharmacotherapies for cocaine abuse: A review. *Journal of Addictive Diseases, 12,* 109–127.

U.S. Department of Education. (1986). *Schools without drugs.* Washington, DC: Author.

U.S. Department of Education. (1992). *Success stories from drug-free schools: A guide for educators, parents, and policymakers* (ED/OESE 92-47R). Washington, DC: Author.

U.S. Department of Justice. (1994a). *Fact sheet: Drug use trends.* Washington, DC: Author.

U.S. Department of Justice. (1994b). *Preventing interpersonal violence among youths.* Washington, DC: Author.

U.S. General Accounting Office. (1992). *Adolescent drug use prevention. Common features of promising community programs* (GAO/PEMD Publication No. 92-2). Washington, DC: Author.

Ugnat, A. M., Mao, Y., Miller, A. B., & Wigle, D. T. (1990). Effects of residential exposure to environmental tobacco smoke on Canadian children. *Canadian Journal of Public Health, 81,* 345–349.

Ulleland, C. N. (1972). The offspring of alcoholic mothers. *Annals of the New York Academy of Sciences, 197,* 167–169.

Unks, G. (Ed.). (1995). *The gay teen: Educational practice and theory for lesbian, gay, and bisexual adolescents.* New York: Routledge.

Unrug-Neervoort, A., van Luijtelaar, G., & Coenen, A. (1992). Cognition and vigilance: Differential effects of diazepam and buspirone on memory and psychomotor performance. *Neuropsychology, 26,* 146–150.

Vaillant, G. E. (1983a). *The natural history of alcoholism.* Cambridge, MA: Harvard University Press.

Vaillant, G. E. (1983b). Natural history of male alcoholism. *Archives of General Psychiatry, 39,* 127–133.

Vaillant, G. E. (1983c). Natural history of male alcoholism: 5. Is alcoholism the cart of the sociopathy? *British Journal of Addiction, 78,* 317–326.

Vaillant, G. E. (1989–92). Prospective evidence for the effects of environment upon alcoholism. In S. Saitoh, P. Steinglass, & M. A. Schuckit (Eds.), *Alcoholism and the family: The Fourth International Symposium of the Psychiatric Research Institute of Tokyo* (pp. 71–83). New York: Brunner/Mazel.

Vaillant, G. E. (1995). *The natural history of alcoholism revisited.* Cambridge, MA: Harvard University Press.

Valois, R. F., Vincent, M. L., McKeown, R. E., Garrison, C. Z., & Kirby, S. D. (1993). Adolescent risk behaviors and the potential for violence: A look at what's coming to campus. *Journal of American College Health, 41,* 141–147.

Van Aalst, J. A., Shotts, S. D., Vitsky, J. L., Bass, S. M., Miller, R. S., Meador, K. G., & Morris, J. A., Jr. (1992). Long-term follow-up of unsuccessful violent suicide attempts: Risk factors for subsequent attempts. *Journal of Trauma, 33,* 457–464.

Van Allen, M. I. (1992). Structural anomalies resulting from vascular disruption. *Pediatric Clinics of North America, 39,* 255–277.

Vanderburg, S. A., Weekes, J. R., & Millson, W. A. (1995). Early substance use and its impact on adult offender alcohol and drug problems. *Forum on Corrections Research, 7,* 14–16.

Vanderschmidt, H. F., Lang, J. M., Knight-Williams, V., & Vanderschmidt, G. F. (1993). Risks among inner-city young teens: The prevalence of sexual activity, violence, drugs, and smoking. *Journal of Adolescent Health, 14,* 282–288.

Van Dyke, D. C., & Fox, A. A. (1990). Fetal drug exposure and its possible implications for learning in the preschool and school-age population. *Journal of Learning Disabilities, 23,* 160–163.

Van Dyke, R. B. (1991). Pediatric human immunodeficiency virus infection and the acquired immunodeficiency syndrome. *American Journal of Diseases of Children, 145,* 529–532.

Van Hasselt, V. B., Ammerman, R. T., Glancy, L. J., & Bukstein, O. G. (1992). Maltreatment in psychiatrically hospitalized dually diagnosed adolescent substance abusers. *Journal of the American Academy of Child and Adolescent Psychiatry, 31,* 868–874.

Van Hasselt, V. B., Hersen, M., & Milliones, J. (1978). Social skills training for alcoholics and drug addicts: A review. *Addictive Behaviors, 3,* 221–233.

Van Hasselt, V. B., Hersen, M., Null, J. A., Ammerman, R. T., Bukstein, O. G., McGillivray, J., & Hunter, A. (1993). Drug abuse prevention for high-risk African American children and their families: A review and model program. *Addictive Behaviors, 18,* 213–234.

Van Hasselt, V. B., Null, J. A., Kempton, T., & Bukstein, O. G. (1993). Social skills and depression in adolescent substance abusers. *Addictive Behaviors, 18,* 9–18.

Van Kammen, W. B., Loeber, R., & Stouthamer-Loeber, M. (1991). Substance use and its relationship to conduct problems and delinquency in young boys. *Journal of Youth and Adolescence, 20,* 399–413.

Van Natta, P., Malin, H., Bertolucci, D., & Kaelber, C. (1985). The influence of alcohol abuse as a contributor to mortality. *Alcohol, 2,* 535–539.

van Rensburg, P. H. J. J., Gagiano, C. A., & Verschoor, T. (1994). Possible reasons why certain epileptics commit unlawful acts during or directly after seizures. *Medicine & Law, 13,* 373–379.

Varenhorst, B. (1983). The adolescent society. In *Adolescent peer pressure: Theory, correlates and program implications for drug abuse prevention* (pp. 1–20). Rockville, MD: U.S. Department of Health and Human Services, National Institute on Drug Abuse. (Original work published 1981).

Vega, W. A. (1992). *Profile of alcohol and drug abuse during pregnancy in California, 1992.* Berkeley, CA: University of California, School of Public Health.

Vidailhet, P., Danion, J. M., Kauffmann-Muller, F., Grange, D., Giersche, A., van der Linden, M., & Imbs, J. L. (1994). Lorazepam and diazepam effects on memory acquisition in priming tasks. *Psychopharmacology, 115,* 397–406.

Vinogradov, S., Dishotsky, N. I., Doty, A. K., & Tinklenberg, J. R. (1988). Patterns of behavior in adolescent rape. *American Journal of Orthopsychiatry, 58,* 179–187.

Virkkunen, M., & Linnoila, M. (1993). Brain serotonin, type II alcoholism and impulsive violence. *Journal of Studies on Alcohol, 11,* 163–169.

Vitaro, F., Dobkin, P., Janosz, M., & Pelletier, D. (1992). Children and adolescents at risk for substance abuse. *Apprentissage et Socialisation, 15,* 109–120.

Volavka, J., Martell, D., & Convit, A. (1992). Psychobiology of the violent offender. *Journal of Forensic Sciences, 37*(1), 237–251.

Volkan, K. (1994). *Dancing among the Maenads: The psychology of compulsive drug use.* San Francisco: Lang.

Volpicelli, J. R., Clay, K. L., Watson, N. T., & Volpicelli, L. A. (1994). Naltrexone and the treatment of alcohol dependence. *Alcohol, Health & Research World, 18,* 272–278.

Volpicelli, J. R., Watson, N. T., King, A. C., Sherman, C. E., & O'Brien, C. P. (1995). Effect of naltrexone on alcohol "high" in alcoholics. *American Journal of Psychiatry, 152,* 613–615.

Wagner, J., Melragon, B., & Menke, E. M. (1993). Homeless children: Interdisciplinary drug prevention intervention. *Journal of Child & Adolescent Psychiatric & Mental Health Nursing, 6*(1), 22–30.

Wallace, J. (1982). Alcoholism from the inside out: A phenomenological analysis. In N. J. Estes & M. E. Heinemann (Eds.), *Alcoholism: Development, consequences, and interventions* (2nd ed., pp. 3–15). St. Louis, MO: Mosby.

Wallace, L., Breed, W., & Cruz, J. (1987). Alcohol and prime time television. *Journal of Studies on Alcohol, 48,* 27–34.

Wallace, P. (1991). Prevalence of fetal alcohol syndrome largely unknown. *Iowa Medicine, 81*(9), 381.

Wallack, L., & Corbett, K. (1990). Illegal drug, tobacco, and alcohol use among youth: Trends and promising approaches in prevention. In *Youth and drugs: Society's mixed messages* (OSAP

Prevention Monograph No. 6, DHHS Publication No. ADM 90-1689, pp. 5–29). Washington, DC: U.S. Government Printing Office.

Wallerstein, J. S. (1987). Children of divorce: Report of a 10-year follow-up of early latency-age children. *American Journal of Orthopsychiatry, 57,* 199–211.

Walpole, I., Zubrick, S., Pontré, J., & Lawrence, C. (1991). Low to moderate maternal alcohol use before and during pregnancy, and neurobehavioural outcome in the newborn infant. *Developmental Medicine and Child Neurology, 33,* 875–883.

Ward, A. J. (1992). Adolescent suicide and other self-destructive behaviors: Adolescent attitude survey data and interpretation. *Residential Treatment for Children and Youth, 9*(3), 49–64.

Ward, R. E., Flynn, T. C., Miller, P. W., & Blaisdell, W. F. (1982). Effects of ethanol ingestion on the severity and outcome of trauma. *American Journal of Surgery, 144,* 153–157.

Warner, R. H., & Rosett, H. L. (1975). The effects of drinking on offspring: An historical survey of the American and British literature. *Journal of Studies on Alcohol, 36,* 1395–1420.

Warren, K. R., & Bast, R. J. (1988). Alcohol-related birth defects: An update. *Public Health Reports, 103,* 638–642.

Washburn, L. (1994, May). Why kids join gangs: What counselors can do to help them. *Adolescence, 24*–28.

Washton, A. M., Gold, M. S., & Pottash, A. C. (1985). Opiate and cocaine dependencies. Techniques to help counter the rising tide. *Postgraduate Medicine, 77,* 293–297.

Watkins, L. O., & Strong, W. B. (1984). The child: When to begin preventive cardiology. *Current Problems in Pediatrics, 14*(6), 1–36.

Watson, J. M. (1980). Solvent abuse by children and young adults: A review. *British Journal of Addiction, 75,* 27–36.

Watson, J. M. (1982). Solvent abuse: Presentation and clinical diagnosis. *Human Toxicology, 1,* 249–256.

Watts, W. D., & Wright, L. S. (1990a). The drug use–violent delinquency link among adolescent Mexican-Americans. In M. De La Rosa, E. Y. Lambert & B. Gropper (Eds.), *Drugs and violence: Causes, correlates, and consequences* (NIDA Research Monograph No. 103, pp. 136–159). Rockville, MD: U.S. Department of Health and Human Services, National Institute on Drug Abuse.

Watts, W. D., & Wright, L. S. (1990b). The relationship of alcohol, tobacco, marijuana, and other illegal drug use to delinquency among Mexican-American, black, and white adolescent males. *Adolescence, 25,* 171–181.

Webber, M. (1991). *Street kids: The tragedy of Canada's runaways.* Toronto, ON: University of Toronto Press.

Weil, A. (1983). No bad drugs. *Newservice, 1,* 22–35.

Weil, A. T. (1972). *The natural mind: A new way of looking at drugs and the higher consciousness.* Boston: Houghton Mifflin.

Weingartner, H. J., Hommer, D., Lister, R. G., Thompson, K., & Wolkowitz, O. (1992). Selective effects of triazolam on memory. *Psychopharmacology, 106,* 341–345.

Weisman, A. M., & Taylor, S. P. (1994). Effect of alcohol and risk of physical harm on human physical aggression. *Journal of General Psychology, 121,* 67–75.

Weisman, G. K. (1993). Adolescent PTSD and developmental consequences of crack dealing. *American Journal of Orthopsychiatry, 63,* 553–561.

Weisner, C., Greenfield, T., & Room, R. (1995). Trends in the treatment of alcohol problems in the U.S. general population, 1979 through 1990. *American Journal of Public Health, 85,* 55–60.

Weiss, G., & Hechtman, L. (1986). *Hyperactive children grown up.* New York: Guilford.

Weiss, G., Kruger, E., Danielson, U., & Ellman, M. (1975). Effect of long-term treatment of hyperactive children with methylphenidate. *Canadian Medical Association Journal, 112,* 159–165.

Weiss, R. D. (1992). The role of psychopathology in the transition from drug use to abuse and dependence. In M. Glantz and R. Pickens (Eds.), *Vulnerability to drug abuse* (pp. 137–148). Washington, DC: American Psychological Association.

Weiss, R. D., Griffin, M. L., & Mirin, S. M. (1992). Drug abuse as self-medication for depression: An empirical study. *American Journal of Drug & Alcohol Abuse, 18,* 121–129.

Weissberg, R. P., Caplan, M., & Harwood, R. L. (1991). Promoting competent young people in competence-enhancing environments: A systems-based perspective on primary prevention. *Journal of Consulting and Clinical Psychology, 59,* 830–841.

Weisz, J. R., Martin, S. L., Walter, B. R., & Fernandez, G. A. (1991). Differential prediction of young adult arrests for property and personal crimes: Findings of a cohort follow-up study of violent boys from North Carolina's Willie M Program. *Journal of Child Psychology and Psychiatry, 32,* 783–792.

Weitzman, M., Gortmaker, S., Walker, D. K., & Sobol, A. (1990). Maternal smoking and childhood asthma. *Pediatrics, 85,* 505–511.

Wells, K. C. (1988). Family therapy. In J. L. Matson (Ed.), *Handbook of treatment approaches in childhood psychopathology* (pp. 45–61). New York: Plenum.

Wells, K. C., & Forehand, R. (1981). Childhood behavior problems in the home. In S. M. Turner, K. S. Calhoun, & H. E. Adams (Eds), *Handbook of clinical behavior therapy.* New York: Wiley.

Werblin, J. M. (1995, March). Conference seeks solutions to teen violence. *Adolescence,* pp. 44–46.

Westermeyer, J. (1987). The psychiatrist and solvent-inhalant abuse: Recognition, assessment, and treatment. *American Journal of Psychiatry, 144,* 903–907.

Westermeyer, J. (1990). Methodological issues in the epidemiological study of alcohol-drug problems: Sources of confusion and misunderstanding. *American Journal of Drug and Alcohol Abuse, 16,* 47–55.

Westermeyer, J. (1992). Substance use disorders: Predictions for the 1990s. *American Journal on Drug and Alcohol Abuse, 18,* 1–11.

Wetzel, R. D. (1976). Hopelessness, depression and suicide intent. *Archives of General Psychiatry, 33,* 1069–1073.

What lessons did thalidomide teach us? (1983). *Pharmaceutical Journal, 233,* 438–439.

Wheeler, S. F. (1993). Substance abuse during pregnancy. *Primary Care, 20,* 191–207.

Whitaker, L. C. (1989). Myths and heroes: Visions of the future. *Journal of College Student Psychotherapy, 4*(2), 13.

White, H. R., Brick, J., & Hansell, S. (1993). A longitudinal investigation of alcohol use and agression in adolescence. *Journal of Studies on Alcohol, 11,* 62–77.

Wikler, A. (1953). *Opiate addiction.* Springfield, IL: Thomas.

Wilens, T. E., Biederman, J., Spencer, T. J., & Frances, R. J. (1994). Comorbidity of attention-deficit hyperactivity and psychoactive substance use disorders. *Hospital and Community Psychiatry, 45,* 421–435.

Wilkins-Haug, L., & Gabow, P. A. (1991). Toluene abuse during pregnancy: Obstetric complications and perinatal outcomes. *Obstetrics & Gynecology, 77,* 504–509.

Williams, A. F., Peat, M. A., Crouch, D. J., Wells, J. K., & Finkle, B. S. (1985). Drugs in fatally injured young male drivers. *Public Health Reports, 100*(1), 19–25.

Williams-Petersen, M. G., Myers, B. J., Degen, H. M., Knisely, J. S., Elswick, R. K., Jr., & Schnoll, S. S. (1994). Drug-using and nonusing women: Potential for child abuse, child-rearing attitudes, social support, and affection for expected baby. *International Journal of the Addictions, 29,* 1631–1643.

Wilsnack, S. C., & Wilsnack, R. W. (1979). Sex roles and adolescent drinking. In H. T. Blane & M. E. Chafetz (Eds.), *Youth, alcohol, and social policy* (pp. 183–224). New York: Plenum.

Wilson, G. T., O'Leary, K. D., & Nathan, P. E. (1992). *Abnormal psychology.* Englewood Cliffs, NJ: Prentice-Hall.

Windle, M. (1990). A longitudinal study of antisocial behaviors in early adolescence as predictors of late adolescent substance use: Gender and ethnic group differences. *Journal of Abnormal Psychology, 99*(1), 86–91.

Windle, M. (1994). Substance use, risky behaviors, and victimization among a U.S. national adolescent sample. *Addiction, 89,* 175–182.

Wingard, J. A., Huba, G.H., & Bentler, P. M. (1979a). *A longitudinal analysis of personality structure and adolescent substance use* [Technical report]. Los Angeles: UCLA/NIDA Center for Adolescent Drug Abuse Etiologies.

Wingard, J. A., Huba, G. H., & Bentler, P. M. (1979b). The relationship of personality structures to patterns of adolescent drug use. *Multivariate Behavioral Research, 14,* 131–143.

Winick, C. (1957). Narcotics addiction and its treatment. *Law and Contemporary Problems, 22,* 9–33.

Winick, C. (1959–60). The use of drugs by jazz musicians. *Social Problems, 7*(3), 240–253.

Winick, C. (1961a). How high the moon—Jazz and drugs. *Antioch Review, 21,* 53–68.

Winick, C. (1961b). Physician narcotic addicts. *Social Problems, 9*(2), 174–186.

Winick, C. (1962a). Maturing out of narcotic addiction. *U.S. Bulletin on Narcotics, 14,* 1–7.

Winick, C. (1962b). The taste of music. *Jazz Monthly, 9,* 8–11.

Winick, C. (1964). The life cycle of the narcotic addict and of addiction. *U.N. Bulletin on Narcotics, 16,* 1–11.

Winick, C. (1968). *The new people.* New York: Pegasus.

Winick, C. (1973). Some reasons for the increases in drug dependence among middle-class youths. In H. Silverstein (Ed.), *Sociology of youth* (pp. 433–440). New York: Macmillan.

Winick, C. (1974a). Drug dependence among nurses. In C. Winick (Ed.), *Sociological aspects of drug dependence* (pp. 155–165). Cleveland, OH: CRC.

Winick, C. (1974b). Note on a theory of the genesis of drug dependence among adolescents. *Addictive Diseases, 1,* 5–6.

Winick, C. (1974c). A sociological theory of the genesis of drug dependence. In C. Winick (Ed.), *Sociological aspects of drug dependence* (pp. 3–13). Cleveland, OH: CRC.

Winick, C. (1980). A theory of drug dependence based on role, access to, and attitudes toward drugs. In D. J. Lettieri, M. Sayers, & H. Wallenstein Pearson (Eds.), *Theories on drug abuse: Selected contemporary perspectives* (NIDA Research Monograph No. 30, pp. 225–235). Rockville, MD: U.S. Department of Health and Human Services, National Institute on Drug Abuse.

Wister, A. V., & Avison, W. R. (1982). "Friendly persuasion": A social network analysis of sex differences in marijuana use. *International Journal of Addiction, 17*(3), 523–541.

Wodarski, J. S. (1990). Adolescent substance abuse: Practice implications. *Adolescence, 25,* 667–668.

Wolfner, G. D., & Gelles, R. J. (1993). A profile of violence toward children: A national study. *Child Abuse & Neglect, 17,* 197–212.

Woodside, M., Coughey, K., & Cohen, R. (1993). Medical costs of children of alcoholics—Pay now or pay later. *Journal of Substance Abuse, 5,* 281–287.

Wozencraft, T., & Ellegrin, A. (1991). Depression and suicidal ideation in sexually abused children. *Child Abuse & Neglect, 15,* 505–511.

Wray, S. R., & Young, L. E. (1992). Consequences of substance abuse: Future generations at risk. *West Indian Medical Journal, 41*(2), 47–48.

Wright, J. D., & Pearl, L. (1995). Knowledge and experience of young people regarding drug misuse, 1969–1994. *British Medical Journal, 310*(6971), 20–24.

Wright, L. S. (1985). High school polydrug users and abusers. *Adolescence, 20,* 853–861.

Wright, L. S. (1985). Suicidal thoughts and their relationship to family stress and personal problems among high school seniors and college undergraduates. *Adolescence, 20,* 575–580.

Wurmser, L. (1994). Preface. In K. Volkan, *Dancing among the Maenads: The psychology of compulsive drug use* (pp. xiii–xxii). San Francisco: Lang.

Wyatt, G. E. (1985). The sexual abuse of Afro-American and white-American women in childhood. *Child Abuse & Neglect, 9,* 507–519.

Wyse, G. (1973). Deliberate inhalation of volatile hydrocarbons. A review. *Canadian Medical Association Journal, 108,* 71–74.

Yama, M. F., Tovey, S. L., Fogas, B. S., & Teegarden, L. A. (1992). Joint consequences of parental alcoholism and childhood sexual abuse, and their partial mediation by family environment. *Violence & Victims, 7,* 313–325.

Yamaguchi, K., & Kandel, D. B. (1984). Patterns of drug use from adolescence to young adulthood: III. Predictors of progression. *American Journal of Public Health, 74,* 673–681.

Yamaguchi, K., & Kandel, D. B. (1985a). Dynamic relationships between premarital cohabitation and illicit drug use: An event history analysis of role socialization. *American Sociological Review, 50,* 530–546.

Yamaguchi, K., & Kandel, D. B. (1985b). On the resolution of role incompatibility: A life event history analysis of family roles and marijuana use. *American Journal of Sociology, 90,* 1284–1325.

Yarvis, R. M. (1994). Patterns of substance abuse and intoxication among murderers. *Bulletin of the American Academy of Psychiatry & the Law, 22*(1), 133–144.

Yates, G. L., Mackenzie, R. G., Pennbridge, J., & Swofford, A. (1991). A risk profile comparison of homeless youth involved in prostitution and homeless youth not involved. *Journal of Adolescent Health, 12,* 545–548.

Yellowlees, P. M., & Kaushik, A. V. (1992). The Broken Hill psychopathology project. *Australian & New Zealand Journal of Psychiatry, 26,* 197–207.

Yinger, J. M. (1965). *Toward a field theory of behavior: Personality and social structure.* New York: McGraw-Hill.

Young, M., Werch, C. E., & Bakema, D. (1989). Area specific self-esteem scales and substance use among elementary and middle school children. *Journal of School Health, 59,* 251–254.

Young, P. (1992). Smoking and the young. *British Journal of Nursing, 1,* 648–651.

Youth and alcohol: Dangerous and deadly consequences. (1992). Washington, DC: U.S. Department of Health and Human Services.

Yudofsky, S. C., Stevens, L., Silver, J., Barsa, J., & Williams, D. (1984). Propranolol in the treatment of rage and violent behavior associated with Korsakoff's psychosis. *American Journal of Psychiatry, 141,* 114–115.

Zagar, R., Arbit, J., Sylvies, R., Busch, K. G., & Hughes, J. R. (1990). Homicidal adolescents: A replication. *Psychological Reports, 67,* 1235–1242.

Zarkovic, D. (1982). Drug abuse among secondary school population in Zagreb. *Alcoholism, 18,* 118–121.

Zastowny, T. R., Adams, E. H., Black, G. S., Lawton, K. B., & Wilder, A. L. (1993). Sociodemographic and attitudinal correlates of alcohol and other drug use among children and adolescents: Analysis of a large-scale attitude tracking study. *Journal of Psychoactive Drugs, 25,* 223–237.

Zeichner, A., Allen, J. D., Giancola, P. R., & Lating, J. M. (1994). Alcohol and aggression: Effects of personal threat on human aggression and affective arousal. *Alcoholism, Clinical & Experimental Research, 18,* 657–663.

Zinberg, N. E. (1971, December 5). GIs and OJs in Vietnam. *New York Times Magazine,* pp. 37, 112, 114, 116, 118, 120, 122–124.

Zinberg, N. E. (1972a). Heroin use in Vietnam and the United States: A contrast and a critique. *Archives of General Psychiatry, 26,* 486–488.

Zinberg, N. E. (1972b). Rehabilitation of heroin users in Vietnam. *Contemporary Drug Problems, 1,* 263–294.

Zinberg, N. E. (1974a). *"High" states: A beginning study* (Drug Abuse Council Publication No. SS-3). Washington, DC: Drug Abuse Council. (Also in H. Shaffer & M. E. Burglass [Eds.]. [1981]. *Classic contributions in the addictions* (pp. 241–276). New York: Brunner/Mazel.)

Zinberg, N. E. (1974b). The search for rational approaches to heroin use. In P. G. Bourne (Ed.), *Addiction: A comprehensive trustee* (pp. 149–174). New York: Academic.

Zinberg, N. E. (1975). Addiction and ego function. *Psychoanalytic Study of the Child, 30,* 567–588. (Also in H. Shaffer & M. E. Burglass [Eds.]. [1981]. *Classic contributions in the addictions* [pp. 173–190]. New York: Brunner/Mazel.)

Zinberg, N. E. (1979). Nonaddictive opiate use. In R. L. DuPont, A. Goldstein, & J. O'Donnell (Eds.), *Handbook on drug abuse* (pp. 303–313). Rockville, MD: U.S. Department of Health and Human Services, National Institute on Drug Abuse.

Zinberg, N. E. (1980). The social setting as a control mechanism in intoxicant use. In D. J. Lettieri, M. Sayers, & H. Wallenstein Pearson (Eds.), *Theories of drug abuse: Selected contemporary perspectives* (NIDA Research Monograph No. 30, pp. 236–244). Rockville, MD: U.S. Department of Health and Human Services, National Institute on Drug Abuse.

Zinberg, N. E., & DeLong, J. V. (1974). Research and the drug issue. *Contemporary Drug Problems, 3,* 71–100.

Zinberg, N. E., & Fraser, K. M. (1979). The role of the social setting in the prevention and treatment of alcoholism. In J. H. Mendelson & N. K. Mello (Eds.), *The diagnosis and treatment of alcoholism* (pp. 457–483). New York: McGraw-Hill.

Zinberg, N. E., & Harding, W. M. (1979). Control over intoxicant use: A theoretical and practical overview. *Journal of Drug Issues, 9,* 121–143.

Zinberg, N. E., Harding, W. M., Stelmack, S. M. & Marblestone, R. A. (1978). Patterns of heroin use. *Annals of the New York Academy of Sciences, 311,* 10–24.

Zinberg, N. E., Harding, W. M., & Winkeller, M. (1977). A study of social regulatory mechanisms in controlled illicit drug users. *Journal of Drug Issues, 7*(2), 117–133.

Zinberg, N. E., & Jacobson, R. C. (1976). The natural history of "chipping". *American Journal of Psychiatry, 133*(1), 37–40.

Zinberg, N. E., Jacobson, R. C., & Harding, W. M. (1975). Social sanctions and rituals as a basis of drug abuse prevention. *American Journal of Drug and Alcohol Abuse, 2*(2), 165–182.

Zinberg, N. E., & Robertson, J. A. (1972). *Drugs and the public* (pp. 58–86). New York: Simon and Schuster.

Zinberg, N. E., & Shaffer, H. J. (1985). The social psychology of intoxicant use: The interaction of personality and social setting. In H. B. Milkman & H. J. Shaffer (Eds.), *The addictions: Multidisciplinary perspectives and treatment* (pp. 57–74). Lexington, MA: Heath.

Zoja, L. (1989). *Drugs, addiction and initiation: The modern search for ritual* (Marc E. Romano & Robert Mercurio, Trans.). Boston: Sigo.

Zubek, J. P. (Ed.). (1969). *Sensory deprivation: Fifteen years of research.* New York: Meredith.

Zucker. R. A. (1976). Parental influences on the drinking patterns of their children. In M. Greenblatt & M. A. Schuckit (Eds.), *Alcoholism problems in women and children* (pp. 211–238). New York: Grune and Stratton.

Zucker, R. A. (1979). Developmental aspects of drinking through the young adult years. In H. T. Blane & M. E. Chafetz (Eds.), *Youth, alcohol, and social policy* (pp. 91–146). New York: Plenum.

Zucker, R. A., & Devoe, C. I. (1975). Life history characteristics associated with problem drinking and antisocial behavior in adolescent girls: A comparison with male findings. In R. D. Wirt, G. Winokur, & M. Roff (Eds.), *Life history research in psychopathology* (Vol. 4, pp. 109–134). Minneapolis, MN: University of Minnesota Press.

Zucker, R. A., & Lisansky Gomberg, E. S. (1986). Etiology of alcoholism reconsidered: The case for a biopsychosocial process. *American Psychologist, 41,* 783–793.

Zucker, R. A., Noll, R. B., Draznin, T. H., Baxter, J. A., Weil, C. M., Theado, D. P., Greenberg, G. S., Charlot, C., & Reider, E. (1984, April). *The ecology of alcoholic families: Conceptual framework for the Michigan State University longitudinal study.* Paper presented at the National Council on Alcoholism, National Alcoholism Forum, Detroit, MI.

Zuckerman, M. (1969). Theoretical formulations 1. In J. P. Zubek (Ed.), *Sensory deprivation: Fifteen years of research* (pp. 407–449). New York: Appleton-Century-Crofts.

Zuckerman, M. (1971). Dimensions of sensation seeking. *Journal of Consulting and Clinical Psychology, 36,* 45–52.

Zuckerman, M. (1979). *Sensation seeking: Beyond the optimal level of arousal.* Hillsdale, NJ: Erlbaum.

Zuckerman, M. (1983a). A biological theory of sensation seeking. In M. Zuckerman (Ed.), *Biological bases of sensation seeking, impulsivity, and anxiety* (pp. 37–76). Hillsdale, NJ: Erlbaum.

Zuckerman, M. (1983b). Sensation seeking: The initial motive for drug abuse. In E. Gottheil, K. A. Druley, T. E. Skoloda, & H. M. Waxman (Eds.), *Etiologic aspects of alcohol & drug abuse* (pp. 202–220). Springfield, IL: Thomas.

Zuckerman, M. (1983c). A summing up with special sensitivity to the signals of reward in future research. In M. Zuckerman (Ed.), *Biological bases of sensation seeking, impulsivity and anxiety* (pp. 249–260). Hillsdale, NJ: Erlbaum.

Zuckerman, M. (1984). Sensation seeking: A comparative approach to a human trait. *Behavioral and Brain Sciences, 7,* 413–471.

Zuckerman, M. (1987). Is sensation seeking a predisposing trait for alcoholism? In E. Gottheil, K. A. Druley, S. Pashko, & S. P. Weinstein (Eds.), *Stress and addiction* (pp. 283–301). New York: Brunner/Mazel.

Zuckerman, M., Kolin, E. A., Price, L., & Zoob, I. (1964). Development of a sensation-seeking scale. *Journal of Consulting Psychology, 28,* 477–482.

Zuckerman, M., & Link, K. (1968). Construct validity for the sensation-seeking scale. *Journal of Consulting and Clinical Psychology, 32*(4), 420–426.

Zuckerman, M., Persky, H., & Link, K. (1967). Relation of mood and hypnotizability: An illustration of the state versus trait distinction. *Journal of Consulting Psychology, 31,* 464–470.

Zuckerman, M., Schultz, D. P., & Hopkins, T. R. (1967). Sensation seeking and volunteering for sensory deprivation and hypnosis experiments. *Journal of Consulting Psychology, 31*(4), 358–363.

Author Index

Subject Index